Guide to Good Food

Velda L. Largen
*Author of Home Economics
Instructional Materials
Ballwin, Missouri*

Deborah L. Bence, CFCS
*Family and Consumer Sciences
Author and Editor
Homewood, Illinois*

Publisher
The Goodheart-Willcox Company, Inc.
Tinley Park, Illinois

Acknowledgments

We wish to thank the following foods and nutrition teachers for their input and recommendations:

Jane Crossley
Judy Dedic
Dorothy Gunter
Leona Johnson

Patty Kozlowski
Jan Kreichelt
Sue Schierholtz

To my parents, without whose love and support this edition could never have been completed.

—DLB

Copyright 1996
by

The Goodheart-Willcox Company, Inc.

Previous Editions Copyright 1992, 1988, 1984, 1979

Library of Congress Catalog Card Number 95-38376

International Standard Book Number 1-56637-244-5

2 3 4 5 6 7 8 9 0 -96- 99 98 97 96

Library of Congress Cataloging-in-Publication Data
Largen, Velda L.
  Guide to good food / Velda L. Largen, Deborah L. Bence.
    p. cm. --
  Includes index.
  ISBN 1-56637-244-5
  1. Food. 2. Nutrition. I. Bence, Deborah L. II. Title. III. Series.
  [DNLM: 1. Cookery, International.]
TX354.L37 1995
641.3--dc20
                                  95-38376
                                       CIP
                                       AC

About the cover: The photograph on the cover shows paella (pronounced PY AY uh), a popular Spanish entree. This colorful dish includes rice, chicken, lobster, shrimp, mussels, clams, artichoke hearts, and peas. See if you can identify these ingredients in the photo. You can read about the preparation of paella on page 528. A recipe for another version of paella appears on page 531.

—Recipe photography courtesy of All-Clad Metalcrafters, Inc.

Introduction

Guide to Good Food is designed to give you information about food and nutrition that you can use every day. This practical, up-to-date text focuses on the latest dietary advice to help you make healthy food choices. Guidelines for selecting appliances, setting up a food budget, and buying and storing foods will assist you with consumer decisions. Tips on using space, time, and energy efficiently will help you manage your resources while working in the kitchen. Information on basic cooking methods will give you the background you need to prepare a wide variety of foods.

Throughout the text, you will find health, business etiquette, safety, consumer, and environmental tips. Descriptions of food industry careers from the *Dictionary of Occupational Titles* are listed at the beginning of each chapter. *Guide to Good Food* also includes several chapters devoted to foods from around the world. These features are intended to show you that food is more than just something to eat. Food is at the heart of scientific research. It provides a source of income for millions of people. It is also a part of people's cultural identity.

You will find the language of the book easy to read and understand. Hundreds of full-color illustrations will help you envision the many foods and techniques that are discussed. Numerous recipes will give you the chance to practice food preparation methods covered in the book. Terms are listed at the beginning of each chapter to help acquaint you with vocabulary related to text material. Learning objectives will help you key in on important points as you read. Review questions at the end of each chapter will help you assess your understanding of the subjects presented. Learning activities are also suggested to give you a chance to further explore topics of interest.

Rhodes Bake-N-Serv

Contents

Part 2
The Management of Food

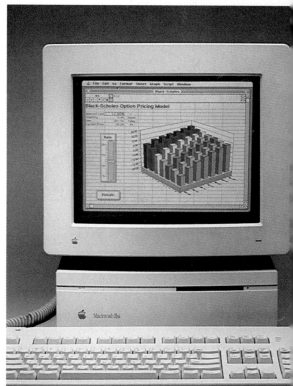

Part 4
Foods of the World

Part 1

The Importance of Food

In many homes, the kitchen is a center of activity, and much social interaction focuses on food.

Chapter **1**

How Food Affects Life

A "Taste" of the World of Work

Food Historian
Prepares in narrative, brief, or outline form chronological account or record of past or current events dealing with food habits of people within specific social, ethnic, political, or geographic groupings.

Demographer
Plans and conducts demographic research, surveys, and experiments to study human populations and affecting trends.

Advertising Production Manager
Coordinates activities of design, illustration, photography, paste-up, and typography personnel to prepare advertisements for publications and supervises workers engaged in pasting-up advertising layouts in art department or studio.

Terms to Know

culture
fasting
grazing

Objectives

After studying this chapter, you will be able to
    explain how the search for food led to the development of civilization.
    discuss factors that influence food habits.

©1995 Jenny Craig Weight Loss Centres, Inc.

Food has different meanings for different people. People who are starving see food as a means of survival. People who are proud of their culture consider traditional foods to be part of their heritage. Members of some faiths regard certain foods as religious symbols. People who are entertaining guests view food as a sign of hospitality.

Clearly, food does much more than meet a basic physical need. It meets emotional, social, and psychological needs, as well.

The search for food and the means to produce it began centuries ago. Efforts to improve food resources will continue as long as life exists.

The History of Food

Early peoples probably ate food raw. At some point, they accidentally discovered that cooked food tasted better and was easier to digest. By trial and error, they learned to control fire and use it to prepare food.

Eventually, these early peoples found they could protect themselves and secure food more easily by living in groups. They formed tribes and began to hunt for food together.

The hunters became herders when they discovered that they could capture and domesticate animals. They also discovered that they could plant seeds to produce large amounts of food. These two advances made the food supply much more dependable.

As food became easier to obtain, not all people had to spend their time hunting and farming. Some were able to learn a craft. Others became merchants. Trading in its simplest form began, and with it came the development of civilization.

The Migration of Food

As civilizations grew and developed, people began searching for food in distant places. Spanish, Portuguese, English, and Dutch sailors traveled across the oceans in search of tea, spices, and other foods. Even Christopher Columbus was searching for food (a new route to the Spice Islands) when he accidentally discovered America.

The explorers introduced foods they carried with them in the new lands to which they traveled. In the United States, Spanish explorers introduced cane sugar, wheat, oranges, and sheep. English explorers brought apples, pears, and walnuts. The explorers also carried foods from the lands they explored back to their homelands. Therefore, foods that were once native to one place are now found in many places. This type of exchange led to an increased variety of foods throughout the world.

Cultural Influences

What do you choose to eat when you are hungry? Where do you usually eat? Who is with you when you eat? When do you eat? How does food make you feel?

Your answers to all these questions reflect your food habits. Chances are, each of your friends would answer these questions a bit differently. That is because the factors that affect food habits are a little different for everyone.

One factor that affects food habits is culture. *Culture* is the customs and beliefs of a racial, religious, or social group. People of a certain race form a cultural group. Citizens of a given country and followers of a specific religion are also examples of cultural groups. Many people are part of more than one cultural group. See 1-1.

Cultural influences in the United States are many and varied. They began with the first explorers and the Native Americans. Later, as immigrants from Europe and Asia and slaves from Africa arrived, these influences grew. Today, people often refer to culture in the United States as a "melting pot." In other words, the United States is a *multicultural society.*

In Chapters 27 through 31, you will read more about the native countries of U.S. immigrants. You will also read about the foods of these countries. As you read, evaluate the variety of foods in the diet of each culture. Also think about how the foods contributed by immigrants have added to the U.S. diet.

Good Manners Are Good Business

More and more, business is transacted internationally. Even within the United States, dealing with people from different cultures is common. Make a point of learning about the culture of your business associates. This will allow you to be sensitive to their cultural differences. Your consideration will have a positive impact on your success in the marketplace.

Del Monte Corporation

1-1 Many of the foods you eat reflect cultural influences. For instance, many pasta dishes come from the Italian culture.

National Origin

The people who colonized various lands brought with them foods that were native to their homelands. The French who settled in the United States introduced chowders. The Germans brought sausages of every shape and size. The Dutch contributed cookies, coleslaw, and waffles. The Italians brought their pastas and rich tomato sauces. The Hungarians brought their goulash spiced with paprika. The Poles prepared pierogi (filled dumplings) and poppy seed cakes. The Chinese introduced stir-fried dishes.

When the immigrants could not obtain traditional ingredients, they had to adapt their recipes. They incorporated foods that were available locally into their diets.

In the United States, immigrants tended to settle together based on nationality. As a result, many foods are typical of particular regions of the country. For instance, foods of Mexican and Spanish origin are found in the West and Southwest. Asian influence is seen in foods of the Pacific Coast. New England, the mid-Atlantic, the Midwest, the South, and Hawaii all claim regional dishes, too.

Religion

Religion has influenced the food habits of many groups of people. Some religions have certain customs regarding food and how people should eat it. For instance, Hindus will not use cattle for food because they consider cattle to be sacred. The foods that Hindus can eat depend on social class. Moslems and Orthodox Jews cannot eat pork because they consider swine to be unclean. Moslems can eat only with the right hand. Jews must follow the dietary laws of their faith. Foods must be processed and prepared in a prescribed manner. Jewish dietary laws state that Jews cannot eat meat and dairy foods together. They also specify that Jews can eat only fish with scales and fins.

Some foods have special symbolic meanings for members of certain religions. The bread and wine used in Christian churches during communion symbolize Christ's body and blood. The eggs that people color and decorate for Easter symbolize rebirth. Unleavened bread is an important symbol for Jewish people during Passover, the eight-day festival that commemorates their flight from Egypt. Because the Jews had to leave their homes so quickly, their bread had no chance to rise.

Fasting, or denying oneself food, has long been a religious custom. Some Christians fast during Lent. Jews fast on Yom Kippur, the Day of Atonement. At one time, Catholics would not eat meat on Friday. Some Catholics still follow this practice.

Through the ages, people have used food for sacrifices and religious offerings. They would place special foods on an altar and offer prayers of thanks for a bountiful harvest. Many cultures still hold harvest festivals. The annual celebration of Thanksgiving Day in the United States began as a harvest festival.

Early peoples also used food as part of their burial ceremonies. The Egyptians, for example, buried food with their dead. The ancient Egyptians believed that the deceased needed food for their journey into the next world. Some Shintos, Taoists, and Buddhists still offer food and coins at shrines honoring deceased relatives and friends.

Social Influences

For many people, preparing and eating food are social activities, 1-2. Food can bring people together. It brings family members together at the dinner table. It brings friends together at parties and picnics. When guests come to visit, the host usually offers them something to eat or drink. People often transact business over lunch. In each of these situations, food is part of the social interaction.

Just as food plays a part in social life, social life plays a part in eating habits and food choices. For instance, your family and friends can affect your meal patterns and food preferences. Mass media and current trends may affect your grocery purchases. Are you aware of how these social influences affect the foods you eat?

Family

Family has a great impact on the foods people eat and how they eat them. For many people, favorite foods are those they grew up eating at home. They may associate certain foods with family traditions or happy memories. Perhaps a special menu was chosen to celebrate family birthdays. Maybe a blanket was spread on the living room floor and foods were served picnic-style. These types of customs help form a person's preferences and attitudes toward food.

A recent trend affecting family food habits is a decrease in the number of meals family members eat together. This is often the result of busy schedules. In some households, everyone seems to be going in a different direction. Working family members often have business meetings. Children are involved in after-school activities.

1-2 For most people, getting together with friends involves sharing food.

Some sociologists feel this trend away from family meals is unfortunate. Mealtime was traditionally a chance for family members to share the day's events and discuss problems. Some families also used this time for spiritual growth. When family members do not eat together, they miss an important opportunity to communicate.

A second trend that has affected family food habits is a change in who prepares the meals. In many homes, women were once the primary meal managers. However, more women are now working outside the home and have less time for meal management tasks. Therefore, family members may share the tasks of menu planning, grocery shopping, and food preparation.

Sharp Compact Microwave Oven

1-3 Friends can influence food choices and eating habits.

Modern technology and rising incomes have also affected family food habits. Technology has created labor-saving equipment and convenience foods. Rising incomes have made it easier for people to buy these items. Families can also afford to eat more meals away from home.

Friends

Your friends have an affect on the foods you choose. You may feel a small amount of peer pressure to eat the same foods your friends are eating. For instance, suppose you are in a restaurant with friends. If they all order pizza, you are likely to order pizza, too. See 1-3.

Friends may also encourage you to try new foods or preparation techniques. A friend might persuade you to sample a food such as squid, which might have little appeal to you. A friend might convince someone used to eating buttered vegetables to try a vegetable casserole instead.

Mass Media

Mass media, such as television, radio, and magazines, can affect your food selections. The media introduces you to, reminds you of, and informs you about food products.

Advertisements use a number of techniques to encourage you to try new food products. They may appeal to your curiosity by asking you to try something because it's different. They may appeal to your desire to belong by saying that everyone is trying the product. They may appeal to your pride by implying that the most worthwhile people are those that eat this food. Coupons, rebates, and special introductory offers may also prompt you to try new food products.

Advertisers also use the techniques described above to encourage you to continue buying products that have been available for years. Although media influences your grocery purchases, you are the one who decides which foods you buy. When you buy a food product, perhaps it is because you enjoy the flavor. The product may include ingredients that you know are good for you. Maybe you just like the way the product is packaged.

News reports and articles in the media can inform you about new health findings related to various food products. Sometimes food products are found to be unsafe. The media can warn you to avoid these products. On the other hand, researchers may make a new discovery about special health properties of a food. For instance, research has found that some foods may reduce your risk of certain types of cancer. Learning this information through the media can help you make wise food purchase decisions.

Current Trends

A number of current trends affect what foods you eat and when and how you eat them. One such trend is that people today live in smaller living units than people in the past. The size of the average family has decreased through the years. There are also more people living alone today than in the past. This is because many people marry later, and many marriages end in divorce. People are also living longer today, many living alone in their later years. As a result, food manufacturers are offering smaller portions of food to meet single people's food needs.

Another trend is the way in which people spend their leisure time. The cost of movies and other entertainment keeps rising. This prompts many families to stay home and rent videos or watch television. They often eat snack foods while enjoying these activities. They frequently choose to have foods, such as pizzas and sandwiches, delivered directly to their homes, 1-4.

Many people are enjoying cooking as a leisure activity. This is seen in the success of stores and catalogs that specialize in cooking and baking utensils. Many magazines also focus on cooking and eating. Meals during the week may center on quick-and-easy convenience foods and carry-out items. On weekends, however, many families are spending time in the kitchen. Many people find cooking gives them a creative outlet. They have fun trying their hand at gourmet cooking. They like to experiment with new ingredients, recipes, and cooking methods. They also welcome the chance to spend some quality time with family members.

Be a Clever Consumer

Use advertisements as a resource to help you learn about products. However, be aware of the words advertisers use to persuade you to buy. Words like *delicious, fun,* and *wholesome* are subjective—they have different meanings to different people. You need to evaluate products for yourself to know if they will meet your needs.

1-4 Home delivery of food is an increasingly popular trend in today's busy lifestyle.

An increase in the number of dual-income families is another current trend. These families often have more disposable income but less time for food shopping and preparation. This has led to the growing popularity of carry-out foods. An increase in the number of meals eaten away from home is also linked to this trend.

Another trend is an increased emphasis on fitness. People are interested in taking care of their bodies. They are walking more, jogging, joining health clubs, and becoming involved in sports to stay in shape. This trend has caused many people to start eating lighter meals. They seek foods that are lower in calories to help them maintain a healthy body weight. They may also try to promote good health by reducing the amounts of fats, salt, and sugar in their diets. Restaurants are fea-turing more salad bars and lower calorie menus. Menus may even include special items, such as fat-free and low-cholesterol foods.

Eating ethnic foods is also a current trend. People are preparing ethnic foods at home or are trying these foods at various ethnic restaurants. Mexican, Italian, Middle Eastern, Chinese, Thai, and Ethiopian foods are popular.

Current trends even influence the way in which people eat foods. For instance, grazing is a serving and eating style that is popular at parties. *Grazing* involves sampling small portions of a variety of appetizer-type foods. A buffet may include such foods as pasta salad, quiche, cheeses, kabobs, and vegetables and dips. Grazers can eat light, yet still try a number of food items.

Psychological Influences

People prepare food and eat meals for many psychological reasons. Food can satisfy certain emotional needs. Babies learn to connect food with the warmth and security provided by the person who feeds them. Children associate foods with pleasurable experiences, such as cake with birthday parties and popcorn with movies. Adults associate food with times of happiness and security, such as turkey with a family Thanksgiving gathering. Pleasant experiences may cause you to like certain foods. Unhappy experiences may cause you to dislike certain foods.

Children may eat in a certain way because of examples set by family members or friends. If a parent dislikes a food, a child may also claim to dislike it without even trying it. Younger brothers nd sisters often follow the examples of older siblings. Have you ever thought that you may be influencing others by the way you eat?

Emotions may also cause undereating and overeating. Some underweight people may not eat because of sadness, loneliness, or a deep emotional shock. Some overweight people may find comfort in foods they like. Food psychologically makes up for anger, frustration, or feelings of inadequacy in certain people.

Most people find eating psychologically satisfying. See 1-5. Food appeals to the senses of sight, taste, and smell. It also appeals to people's need for social contact. Enjoying the appearance, flavors, and aromas of a meal in the company of others is a psychologically pleasing experience.

Preparing food can be as satisfying as eating it. Cooking a meal that tastes good and looks attractive can give a person a psychological lift. It also can serve as a creative outlet. Perhaps you have made cookies or baked bread just for a change of pace from your daily activities. Praise for creative cooking can give a boost to the ego. The cook who receives praise for a beautifully prepared dish feels a sense of pride and self-esteem.

Evenflo Products Company, Inc.

1-5 From the time they are born, most people find eating to be a psychologically pleasing experience.

Healthy Living

Good nutrition is important to the healing process when you have been sick. However, if you have been vomiting, do not eat your favorite foods until you are feeling better. This will help you avoid associating these foods with illness. Such an association can make the food less appealing to you.

This guideline is especially important for people who have chronic illnesses. Cancer patients undergoing chemotherapy and people with AIDS often lose their appetite. However, these people need to maintain a healthy weight to help them fight their disease. Keeping up the appeal of favorite foods can make this task easier.

Summary

In prehistoric ages, people viewed food solely as a means of survival. Early peoples spent most of their time and energy hunting and gathering food. As time passed, people learned to herd and farm. Food resources became more plentiful, and people became able to spend their time in other pursuits. With the development of a more stable food supply came the development of civilization.

Today, people view food as more than a basic physical need. Many factors influence the foods people eat and how they eat them. Cultural factors like national origin and religion affect people's food choices. Social factors such as family, friends, mass media, and current trends have an impact, too. Even psychological factors like experiences and emotions play a role in people's food habits.

Review What You Have Read

Write your answers on a separate sheet of paper.
1. What two discoveries made the food supply much more dependable for early peoples?
2. How did apples, pears, and walnuts come to be among the foods available in the United States?
3. Give a general example of a cultural group.
4. True or false. Foods of Mexican and Spanish origin are found in the West and Southwest regions of the United States.
5. Name two religious groups that cannot eat pork and explain why.
6. Why do sociologists feel that a decrease in the number of meals family members eat together is an unfortunate trend?
7. True or false. Friends can encourage people to try new foods and preparation techniques.
8. Give an example of how mass media can affect food selections.
9. List two current trends that are influencing food choices and eating habits in the United States.
10. How can food satisfy some emotional needs of a baby?

Build Your Basic Skills

1. Investigate one of the stages in the development of civilization illustrated in Chart 1-1. Write a report explaining the role food played in bringing about the stage you investigated.
2. Talk with your grandparents or senior citizens in your community about family food customs they followed as children. Discuss how their family's food customs differed from those of your family.

Build Your Thinking Skills

1. Work in a small group to prepare an oral report on one of the cultural influences that can be seen in foods of the United States. Your report should include the use of visual aids. Each member of the group should be responsible for a different aspect of the report.
2. Invite faculty members to join your class for a grazing party. Plan a menu of foods that are easy to eat with your fingers. Your menu should include both hot and cold foods with a variety of flavors, textures, and colors. Prepare the foods in lab.

Chapter 2

Nutritional Needs

A "Taste" of the World of Work

Research Dietitian
Conducts nutrition research to expand knowledge in one or more phases of dietetics.

Dietetic Technician
Provides services in assigned areas of food service management, teaches principles of food and nutrition, and provides dietary consultation under direction of a clinical dietitian.

Teaching Dietitian
Plans, organizes, and conducts educational programs in dietetics, nutrition, and institution management for dietetic interns, nursing students, and other medical personnel.

Terms to Know

nutrition
malnutrition
nutrient
carbohydrate
simple carbohydrate
complex carbohydrate
fiber
fat
fatty acid
saturated fatty acid
unsaturated fatty acid
monounsaturated
  fatty acid
polyunsaturated
  fatty acid

hydrogenation
cholesterol
protein
amino acid
complete protein
incomplete protein
vitamin
mineral
trace element
peristalsis
metabolism
basal metabolism
calorie

Objectives

After studying this chapter, you will be able to
  define good nutrition.
  name the key nutrients, describe their functions, and list important sources of each.
  explain the processes of digestion, absorption, and metabolism.

National Live Stock and Meat Board

The variety of foods available in the marketplace is virtually unlimited. Even so, many people do not choose foods wisely. Children and teenagers often eat too many sweets and fats and not enough breads, cereals, vegetables, fruits, and milk. The elderly often skip meals or fail to eat the foods that supply the nutrients they need. Many people do not eat balanced meals because they do not know the amounts of foods they need to eat for good nutrition.

Food is what you eat. **Nutrition** is the study of how your body uses the food you eat. If you do not eat the foods your body needs, you may suffer from malnutrition. **Malnutrition,** in its simplest form, is poor nutrition over an extended period of time. The body does not receive the nutrients it needs for energy, growth, repair, and the regulation of various body processes.

Eating enough food does not necessarily mean you are eating all of the foods you need. The amount of food eaten is not as important as the right variety and mixture of foods. A person who is malnourished may be overweight or underweight.

Some of the effects of malnutrition may be long-lasting. The foods a teenage girl eats today may affect her pregnancy in later years. The foods a pregnant woman eats may affect her unborn child's growth and development. The foods a child eats may affect his or her growth, development, and resistance to disease. The foods people eat may affect their health and the length of their lives.

The Nutrients

A **nutrient** is a chemical substance in food that helps maintain the body. Some of the nutrients supply energy for the body. All of the nutrients help build cells and tissues. They also regulate bodily processes, such as breathing. No single food supplies all of the nutrients the body needs to function.

You need over 50 nutrients for good health. You can divide all of these nutrients into the following six groups:

- carbohydrates
- fats or lipids
- proteins
- vitamins
- minerals
- water

A diet that meets all of the body's needs contains nutrients from all six groups in the right proportions.

Carbohydrates

Carbohydrates are the body's chief source of energy. Carbohydrates include starches, sugars, and cellulose. Most carbohydrates are plant materials produced by a process called *photosynthesis.*

Carbohydrates are classified into three groups based on their molecular structure. *Monosaccharides* are the simplest form of sugar molecules. They cannot be broken down into a simpler sugar form. *Disaccharides* can be broken down into two monosaccharide molecules. The monosaccharides and disaccharides are often called **simple carbohydrates.** *Polysaccharides* can be broken down into more than two monosaccharide molecules. The polysaccharides are known as **complex carbohydrates.**

Glucose is an important monosaccharide. *Glucose* occurs naturally in fruits, vegetables, honey, corn syrup, and molasses. In addition, the body forms glucose during digestion when it breaks down more complex carbohydrates. The bloodstream carries glucose throughout the body. It provides constant and immediate energy for all body cells and tissues.

Fruits, vegetables, honey, and molasses also contain *fructose,* another monosaccharide. It is the sweetest of all sugars, and the body absorbs it easily. See 2-1.

Sucrose, lactose, and maltose are disaccharides. *Sucrose* is ordinary table sugar. Sugar beets, sugarcane, maple syrup, molasses, sorghum, and corn syrup contain sucrose. The milk of mammals contains *lactose,* or milk sugar. Sprouting cereal grains, malted milk, and malted cereals contain *maltose,* or malt sugar. During digestion, the body breaks down disaccharides into the simpler monosaccharides. Then the body can absorb them and use them for energy.

Cellulose, starch, dextrin, and glycogen are polysaccharides. *Cellulose* is the fibrous material found in plants. Fresh fruits and vegetables, nuts, whole grain cereals, and dried fruits are the best sources of cellulose. Humans cannot digest cellulose. However, it is a main source of **fiber,** which provides bulk in the diet.

Starch is the most abundant carbohydrate in the body. Roots, seeds, and tubers are important sources of starch. Before the body can absorb starch, it must break the starch down into glucose.

Dextrin is a by-product of the breakdown of starch. It also is present in the preparation of foods

2-1 Honey is a good source of fructose, the sweetest of all sugars.

such as toasted bread. Corn syrup, wheat flour, peanuts, corn, beans, rice, and honey are sources of dextrin.

Glycogen is the storage form of carbohydrates in animals. Liver and muscle meats are good sources of glycogen. The body must also convert glycogen to glucose before absorbing it.

Functions of Carbohydrates

Carbohydrates have many important functions. They furnish the body with energy. They help the body digest fats efficiently. Carbohydrates make foods more palatable (agreeable to your sense of taste). They also allow the body to use proteins for growth and maintenance instead of energy.

Another function of carbohydrates that are rich in fiber may be as a cancer preventative. Research indicates that a high-fiber diet may reduce the risk of colorectal cancer. *Colorectal cancer* is cancer of the colon or rectum—the lowest part of the digestive tract. Fiber stimulates the action of the muscles in the digestive tract, helping to speed food through the body. Some experts believe this reduces the time *carcinogens* (cancer-causing agents) in food are in contact with the colon and rectum. The bulk created by the fiber may also help dilute compounds believed to cause cancer. For these reasons, experts recommend that adults include 20 to 35 grams of fiber in their daily diet.

Sources of Carbohydrates

Many foods are rich sources of carbohydrates. Foods high in simple carbohydrates are sugars, syrups, candies, jams, jellies, pastries, and dried fruits. Sources of complex carbohydrates are cereal grains, legumes, pasta products, breads, and crackers. Whole grain cereal products and fresh fruits and vegetables are good sources of fiber.

Carbohydrate Deficiencies and Excesses

A diet low in carbohydrates may cause you to lack energy. If fiber is lacking in the diet, constipation may occur. Because foods high in carbohydrates are abundant and inexpensive, deficiencies are usually the result of self-prescribed limitations.

Excess complex carbohydrates are not a health concern. In fact, many nutrition experts recommend increased intakes of complex carbohydrate foods, especially those high in fiber. They also recommend limiting the number of calories consumed from fat. Eating a diet high in whole grain breads and cereals will accomplish both goals. These foods are fiber-rich sources of complex carbohydrates. By consuming more calories from these foods, you may consume fewer calories from foods high in fat.

On the other hand, too many simple carbohydrates, particularly sucrose, can be a concern. Foods high in sugar, such as candy and soft drinks, tend to be low in other nutrients. These foods also produce a medium upon which bacteria in the mouth thrive. Tooth decay and gum disease may result. To help avoid these problems, dentists suggest that people limit their intake of sweets.

Fats

Like carbohydrates, *fats* are important energy sources. Fats belong to a larger group of compounds called *lipids*, which include both fats and oils.

Types of Fats

All lipids contain fatty acids. **Fatty acids** are chemical chains containing carbon, hydrogen, and oxygen. Different types of fatty acids contain different amounts of hydrogen. **Saturated fatty acids** are fatty acids that have as many hydrogen atoms as they can hold. **Unsaturated fatty acids** are fatty acids that have fewer hydrogen atoms than they can hold. Unsaturated fatty acids may be monounsaturated or polyunsaturated. **Monounsaturated fatty acids** are missing one hydrogen atom. **Polyunsaturated fatty acids** are missing two or more hydrogen atoms.

A fat is saturated, monounsaturated, or polyunsaturated depending on the kind of fatty acid it contains. For instance, a polyunsaturated fat is a fat containing polyunsaturated fatty acids.

Foods contain combinations of the three types of fats. However, most foods contain a majority of one type. Meat and dairy products are high in saturated fats, 2-2. Palm, palm kernel, and coconut oils are also high in saturated fats. Peanut and olive oils are good sources of monounsaturated fats. Corn, soybean, sunflower, and some fish oils are rich in polyunsaturated fats.

Saturated fats are usually solid at room temperature. Unsaturated fats usually are liquid at room temperature. A process called **hydrogenation** can make unsaturated fats solid. In this process, hydrogen atoms are added to an unsaturated fat. Solid vegetable shortening and margarine are hydrogenated fats.

The body can produce some fatty acids from the chemicals found in fats. However, there are a

National Pork Producers Council

2-2 Many cuts of meat tend to be high in saturated fats.

few fatty acids that the body cannot produce. These are called *essential fatty acids.* You must obtain these fatty acids from the foods you eat. *Linoleic acid* is one of the essential fatty acids.

Cholesterol

Cholesterol is a fatlike substance found in every cell in the body. Cholesterol serves several important functions. It is part of skin tissue. It aids in the transport of essential fatty acids in the body. The body also needs it to produce hormones.

Your body makes the cholesterol it needs. Therefore, you do not need to include cholesterol in your diet.

Cholesterol occurs only in foods of animal origin. Liver and egg yolks are especially high in cholesterol. Plant foods do not contain cholesterol.

Functions of Fats

Fats have many important functions in the body. The body stores energy as fat. Fats protect internal organs from injury and insulate the body from shock and temperature changes. They also carry the fat-soluble vitamins and serve as a source of the essential fatty acids.

Healthy Living

Choose canola, corn, olive, peanut, safflower, sesame, or soybean oil for cooking, baking, and pouring on salads. Some studies have suggested that these polyunsaturated or monounsaturated oils might help reduce cholesterol levels in the blood. However, you should limit your use of even these "good oils" to no more than 8 teaspoons (40 mL) per day.

Avoid coconut, palm, and palm kernel oils (sometimes called *tropical oils*). These oils are highly saturated. They are often used in snack foods, so read ingredient labels carefully.

Sources of Fats

Fats can be visible or invisible. You can see butter, margarine, and marbling (flecks of fat found throughout lean muscles of meat) in meat cuts. These are *visible fats.* You cannot see fat in foods like eggs, whipped cream, and baked products. These are *invisible fats.* See 2-3.

Many foods contain some fat. Foods that are high in fat include butter, margarine, most salad dressings, oils, vegetable shortenings, egg yolks, many dairy products, meats, and avocados.

Fat Deficiencies

Fat deficiencies are rare in the United States. However, a diet too low in fat may result in a loss of weight and energy. Also, too little fat may cause deficiencies of the fatty acids and fat-soluble vitamins carried by fats.

Brooks Tropicals

2-3 With heavy cream as a main ingredient, this rich mousse is high in fat, even though it cannot be seen.

Limiting Excess Fats and Cholesterol

The typical diet in the United States is high in fat. A high-fat diet can contribute to weight problems. This is because fat is a concentrated source of food energy. It provides more than twice as many calories per gram as carbohydrates and proteins. Therefore, a diet that is high in fat may also be high in calories. If your diet contains too much fat, your body will store the excess as *adipose tissue,* or body fat.

Experts recommend that no more than 30 percent of the total calories in your daily diet come from fat. No more than 10 percent of total calories should come from saturated fat. You should limit your daily cholesterol intake to 300 mg.

These recommendations are based on more than possible weight problems. Saturated fats and dietary cholesterol can increase the blood cholesterol level in some people. High blood cholesterol is one of several risk factors for heart disease. (Your doctor can check your blood cholesterol level.) High-fat diets have also been linked to increased risk of several types of cancer.

Reducing your fat intake means limiting fried foods, baked goods, cheeses, creamy salads, and luncheon meats. You should use salad dressings and oils, butter, margarine, and cream sparingly, too. Limiting high-fat meat and dairy products will help you cut back on saturated fats. Using margarine instead of butter and vegetable shortening instead of animal fat will help you decrease dietary cholesterol.

Proteins

Proteins are chemical compounds that are found in every body cell. They are made up of small units called **amino acids.** Scientists have isolated 20 amino acids. All 20 amino acids are important to the human body. Nine of these amino acids are called *essential amino acids.* The body cannot synthesize (produce) some essential amino acids. It can synthesize others, but not at a rate fast enough to meet nutritional needs. You must get the essential amino acids from the foods you eat. The other amino acids are called *nonessential amino acids.* Your body can synthesize them fast enough to meet its needs.

Complete proteins contain all nine essential amino acids in sufficient amounts. Complete proteins will support growth and normal maintenance of body tissues. *Partially complete proteins* contain all nine essential amino acids. However, they have only a limited amount of one or more of these amino acids. Partially complete proteins will provide for normal maintenance, but they will not support growth. **Incomplete proteins** are missing one or more of the essential amino acids. Incomplete proteins will neither support growth nor provide for normal maintenance of body tissues.

Animal foods (meat, poultry, fish, milk, cheese, and eggs) have complete proteins, 2-4. Most plant foods have incomplete proteins. However, soybeans provide complete proteins and other legumes provide partially complete proteins.

Incomplete proteins can complement one another. In other words, you can supplement a protein food lacking an amino acid with a protein food containing that amino acid. When combined, the two foods provide a higher quality protein than either would have provided alone. The proteins in legumes and grains generally complement each other in this way. Beans and rice is an example of this combination. Combining incomplete protein sources with complete sources can also improve protein values. Serving cereal with milk is an example. The complete proteins in the milk improve the protein value of the cereal.

Functions of Proteins

Proteins provide amino acids, which your body needs for growth (the formation of new tissue), maintenance, and repair of tissues. They aid in the formation of enzymes, some hormones, and antibodies. Proteins also provide energy. (Your diet needs to supply enough carbohydrates and fats to meet your energy needs. Otherwise, your body will use proteins for energy before using them to support growth and maintenance.) Regulation of bodily processes, such as fluid balance in the cells, is also a function of proteins.

Several factors affect a person's need for protein. Age, body size, quality of the proteins, and physical state are four important factors. Children need more protein per pound of body weight than adults because they are growing so rapidly. A larger, heavier person needs more protein than a smaller, lighter person. An injured person needs extra protein for the repair of body tissues.

Sources of Protein

Many animal and plant foods provide proteins. Important protein sources are lean red meats, poultry, fish, milk and milk products, and eggs. Dried beans, peas, and nuts are also protein sources.

2-4 Meats are a source of complete protein.

Protein Deficiencies and Excesses

If the diet does not contain enough protein, tiredness, loss of weight, and lack of energy may occur. Lack of protein in a child's diet may stunt growth. In advanced cases, kwashiorkor may result. *Kwashiorkor* is a serious protein deficiency disease found in many underdeveloped areas of the world. Symptoms of kwashiorkor include discolored skin, stunted growth, body sores, bulging abdomen, listlessness, and lack of energy. If kwashiorkor goes untreated, it can eventually cause mental retardation and death.

If the diet contains too much protein, the body converts the extra protein to fat and stores it in the adipose tissue. The body cannot covert stored protein back into amino acids for use in building tissues. You must continuously replenish your body's supply of amino acids. You should include sources of protein in the meals you eat throughout the day. You especially need a supply of proteins in the morning. A good breakfast will replenish the amino acids used by the body during the night.

Vitamins

Vitamins are complex organic substances. You need them in small amounts for normal growth, maintenance, and reproduction. Your body cannot produce vitamins, at least not in large enough amounts to meet your nutritional needs. Therefore, you must get the vitamins you need from food. Normally, a well-balanced diet provides all of the needed vitamins. If a diet is not well balanced, serious vitamin deficiencies may result.

Vitamins are either fat-soluble or water-soluble. The body can store *fat-soluble vitamins.* Over a period of time, fat-soluble vitamins can build up in the body and may reach dangerous levels. The body cannot store *water-soluble vitamins.* You excrete excess water-soluble vitamins. Scientists, however, now believe that too much of some water-soluble vitamins may be harmful. This is why it is important never to diagnose your own vitamin requirements.

Vitamins A, D, E, and K are the fat-soluble vitamins. Vitamin C and the B-complex vitamins are water-soluble.

Vitamin A

Scientists discovered vitamin A in the early part of the twentieth century. They found that test animals fed olive oil developed eye diseases and showed signs of stunted growth. Animals fed butter instead of olive oil did not develop these ill effects. This was because the fat in the butter contained vitamin A.

Functions of Vitamin A

Vitamin A has many important functions in the body. These include the formation and maintenance of a chemical compound the eyes need to adapt to darkness. Vitamin A promotes normal growth (especially of bones and teeth). Healthy skin tissue and other epithelial tissues, such as mucous membranes, also depend on the presence of vitamin A.

Sources of Vitamin A

Your body obtains vitamin A in two forms. The first form is as the vitamin itself. Vitamin A is in foods like liver, egg yolk, whole milk or fortified dairy products, butter, and fish oils.

The second form is as the provitamin *carotene,* which the body can convert to vitamin A. Carotene is in foods like spinach and squash. See 2-5.

Vitamin A Deficiencies and Excesses

If the diet contains too little vitamin A, the eyes will become sensitive to light. The skin will become rough, and susceptibility to disease may increase. In severe cases, night blindness and stunted growth may result.

People seldom get too much vitamin A from food. However, if they take too many vitamin A supplements, fatigue, headaches, nausea, and vomiting may eventually occur.

Vitamin D

Before the discovery of vitamin D, many children (especially poor children), suffered from a disease called *rickets.* These children showed symptoms such as crooked legs and misshapen breast bones.

Two scientists took the first steps to find a cure for rickets. One scientist found that fish liver oil cured rickets in both dogs and people. The other scientist noted that in southern, sunny climates people did not develop rickets. He tried using sunlamps on some of his young patients who were suffering from rickets. The children soon became healthy.

Later, a third scientist discovered a relationship between rickets and calcium and phosphorus. Today, nutrition experts know that vitamin D works with calcium and phosphorus to produce strong bones and teeth.

Be a Clever Consumer

When buying fruits and vegetables, note their color. The color of fruits and vegetables is a good indication of their vitamin A value. Deeper color indicates the presence of more carotene. Therefore, deep yellow and dark green fruits and vegetables normally have a higher vitamin A value than lighter colored produce.

2-5 The deep green color of broccoli shows that it contains a lot of carotene. Fruits and vegetables rich in carotene are good sources of vitamin A.

Functions of Vitamin D

The major function of vitamin D is to promote the growth and proper mineralization of bones and teeth. Vitamin D performs this function by helping the body use calcium and phosphorus.

Sources of Vitamin D

Vitamin D occurs naturally in a few foods. These include egg yolk, liver, sardines, tuna, and fish liver oils. In addition, several commonly eaten foods are fortified with vitamin D. Milk, butter, and margarine are frequently fortified with this important nutrient.

The body can also make vitamin D with exposure to sunlight. Thus, people sometimes call vitamin D the "sunshine vitamin." Sunlight helps convert a substance found in the skin to vitamin D. However, heavy clothing, smog, and irregular exposure to the sun keep sunlight from being a reliable source of vitamin D. In addition, sun exposure is responsible for about 30 percent of all cancers.

Therefore, experts recommend that you get vitamin D from your diet, *not* from the sun.

Vitamin D Deficiencies and Excesses

If the diet does not contain enough vitamin D, the body will not be able to use calcium and phosphorus as it should. In severe cases, children with vitamin D deficiencies can develop rickets. Adults may develop other bone abnormalities.

If the diet contains too much vitamin D, the body will store the excess. Over an extended period of time, excesses of vitamin D may result in nausea, diarrhea, and loss of weight. In severe cases, kidneys and lungs may be damaged, and bones may become deformed.

Vitamin E

Scientists are familiar with the effects of vitamin E on animals. Rats with a vitamin E deficiency, for example, are unable to reproduce. Monkeys develop anemia, and rabbits develop muscular dystrophy. However, these symptoms of vitamin E deficiency have not been found in human beings.

Functions of Vitamin E

Vitamin E's main function is that of an *antioxidant*. Vitamin E is easily *oxidized*—it readily combines with oxygen. By doing so, it reduces the amount of oxygen available to react with other substances that oxygen could harm. This antioxidant effect is especially important in membranes of red and white blood cells and cells in the lungs. These cell membranes are constantly exposed to high levels of oxygen, which can destroy them. Vitamin E also inhibits the oxidation of fatty acids, carotene, and vitamin A.

Sources of Vitamin E

Vitamin E is widely distributed throughout the food supply in foods that are not highly processed. Sources include fats and oils, whole grain breads and cereals, liver, eggs, whole milk dairy foods, and leafy green vegetables. See 2-6.

Vitamin E Deficiencies and Excesses

The average diet in the United States supplies sufficient amounts of vitamin E. Therefore, deficiencies are rare. However, premature infants may have deficiencies. Babies that do not reach full term fail to receive enough vitamin E from their mothers before birth. Toxicity from excess dietary vitamin E also seems to be rare.

Vitamin K

Scientists in Denmark discovered vitamin K as a result of experimentation with chickens. Chickens raised on a purified diet developed hemorrhages under the skin. The chickens were suffering from a blood-clotting disorder. Adding whole grain cereals to their diets cured the chickens. Further study found that a fat-soluble substance in the cereal promoted blood coagulation. The scientists named this substance vitamin K.

Functions of Vitamin K

Vitamin K is known as the "blood clotting" vitamin. Vitamin K performs this function by helping the liver make a substance called *prothrombin*. Prothrombin is a protein blood needs to clot. If vitamin K is not available, the liver cannot form prothrombin and other similar substances. As a result, the blood cannot clot properly.

Sources of Vitamin K

Bacteria in the intestinal tract can synthesize vitamin K. Leafy green vegetables and cauliflower are good sources of vitamin K. Additional sources include other vegetables, organ meats, and egg yolk.

Vitamin K Deficiencies and Excesses

Because vitamin K is in many well-liked foods, most people receive enough vitamin K from the foods they eat. In cases where vitamin K deficiency is severe, however, hemorrhaging can occur due to lack of blood clotting.

The amount of vitamin K consumed in a normal diet is not harmful. However, toxicity can develop through the use of vitamin K supplements.

Vitamin C (Ascorbic Acid)

During Vasco da Gama's voyage around the Cape of Good Hope, nearly two thirds of his crew died. The cause of these deaths was *scurvy,* a feared disease. Those who became ill suffered from bleeding gums, loss of teeth, internal bleeding, and anemia. People at that time thought scurvy was contagious and incurable.

As early as the sixteenth century, a British admiral recognized the value of oranges and lemons in curing scurvy. Many years later, the British navy began feeding sailors a diet that included citrus fruits and leafy green vegetables. Later, when researchers isolated vitamin C, they found these foods to be rich sources of the vitamin.

2-6 Whole wheat bread is a source of vitamin E.

When sailors ate the diet rich in vitamin C, scurvy did not occur.

Functions of Vitamin C

Vitamin C performs many important functions in the body. It helps in the formation and maintenance of *collagen,* a protein that is part of connective tissue. Collagen is the cementing material that holds body cells together. Vitamin C helps make the walls of blood vessels firm, and it helps wounds heal and broken bones mend. It also aids in the formation of hemoglobin (a substance in red blood cells) and helps the body fight infections.

Sources of Vitamin C

Almost all vitamin C in the diet comes from eating fruits and vegetables. Fresh fruits and vegetables are the best sources. Citrus fruits, strawberries, and cantaloupe are good fruit sources of vitamin C. Leafy green vegetables, green peppers, broccoli, and cabbage are good vegetable sources. See 2-7.

Air, water, and heat easily destroy vitamin C. Therefore, always keep juices and cut fruits and vegetables tightly covered during storage. When cooking fruits and vegetables, use only a small amount of water. Also, keep the cooking time as short as possible. This will help prevent the loss of large amounts of vitamin C. You can preserve the vitamin C lost in cooking liquid by using the cooking liquid in gravies, sauces, and soups.

Vitamin C Deficiencies and Excesses

Because vitamin C is a water-soluble vitamin, the body cannot store it. Therefore, you need a daily supply. Too little vitamin C in the diet can cause poor appetite, weight loss, and soreness in the joints. A prolonged deficiency may result in bleeding gums, bruising, loss of teeth, anemia, and more severe symptoms of scurvy.

Although vitamin C does help the body fight infection, scientists do not agree that it will prevent or cure the common cold. You should take supplementary vitamin C only if prescribed by a physician. Excess vitamin C increases the risk of urinary stones and may cause diarrhea.

2-7 People often think of citrus fruits when they think of vitamin C, but strawberries are also a good source.

Thiamin

Thiamin, or vitamin B-1, is part of a larger group of vitamins called the *B-complex vitamins.* All of the B-complex vitamins are water-soluble. Although each has distinct properties, the B-vitamins work together in the body.

The disease *beriberi* led to the discovery of thiamin. Beriberi, a disease of the nervous system, was most widespread in the Far East. Japanese sailors who ate a diet of polished rice developed beriberi and died by the thousands. Severe cramping and subsequent paralysis followed numbness in the ankles and legs. Heart disturbances in many cases led to death.

In the late 1800s, one Japanese physician discovered that beriberi disappeared when the sailors ate meat and evaporated milk in addition to the rice. A few years later, a Dutch scientist observed similar symptoms in chickens fed a diet of polished rice. When the outer layers and embryo of the rice were added to the diet, the chickens recovered.

These experiments identified a thiamin deficiency as the cause of beriberi. Whole grain cereals and meats contain sufficient amounts of thiamin. However, polished rice does not contain sufficient amounts.

Functions of Thiamin

Thiamin has several important functions in the body. It helps the body release energy from food. It forms part of the *coenzymes* (chemical substances that work with enzymes to promote enzyme activity) needed for the breakdown of carbohydrates. Thiamin also helps promote normal appetite and digestion.

Another function of thiamin is keeping the nervous system healthy and preventing irritability. Some people call thiamin the "morale vitamin." This is because one of the first signs of a thiamin deficiency is depression and nervousness.

Sources of Thiamin

Nearly all foods except fats, oils, and refined sugars contain some thiamin. However, no single food is particularly high. Wheat germ, pork products, legumes, and whole grain and enriched cereals are good sources of thiamin.

Like all water-soluble vitamins, cooking causes the loss of some thiamin. To prevent severe losses, use a small amount of water and a short cooking time.

Thiamin Deficiencies

Too little thiamin in the diet will first cause nausea, apathy, and loss of appetite. Numbness in the feet and ankles and cramping pains in the legs may follow. If the deficiency is severe or prolonged, leg stiffness; paralysis of the arms, legs, and other body parts; and heart disturbances may result.

Riboflavin

Riboflavin, or vitamin B-2, is the second member of the B-complex group. Scientists discovered riboflavin after noting that removing thiamin from a food did not keep it from promoting growth in animals. This experiment proved that "vitamin B" was not a single vitamin. Instead, "vitamin B" was a vitamin complex—a group of vitamins.

Functions of Riboflavin

Riboflavin has several important functions in the body. It forms part of the coenzymes needed for the breakdown of carbohydrates. Riboflavin helps cells use oxygen and helps keep skin, tongue, and lips normal. Helping to prevent scaly, greasy areas around the mouth and nose is also a function of riboflavin.

Sources of Riboflavin

Organ meats, milk and milk products, eggs, and oysters are good sources of riboflavin. Leafy green vegetables and whole grain and enriched cereal products are good sources, too. See 2-8.

Water and light destroy riboflavin. To keep cooking losses to a minimum, use a small amount of water and cook for the shortest time possible. The paper and opaque plastic cartons used to package milk prevent the destruction of riboflavin by light.

Riboflavin Deficiencies

Too little riboflavin in the diet can cause swollen and cracked lips and skin lesions. Later symptoms include inflammation of the eyes and twilight blindness.

Niacin

Some people call niacin the "pellagra-preventing" vitamin. *Pellagra* is a disease caused by a deficiency of niacin. It affects the skin, the gastrointestinal tract, and the nervous system. Severe symptoms include a raw and inflamed skin rash, abdominal pain, diarrhea, dementia, and paralysis. If not treated, pellagra can cause death.

2-8 Like other milk products, cottage cheese is a good source of riboflavin.

Functions of Niacin

Niacin has several important functions. Niacin forms part of two coenzymes involved in complex chemical reactions in the body. It helps keep the nervous system, mouth, skin, tongue, and digestive tract healthy. Niacin also helps the cells use other nutrients.

Sources of Niacin

The best sources of niacin are liver and kidney. Other sources include muscle meats, poultry, peanuts, and peanut butter. The bodies of animals and human beings can convert *tryptophan,* one of the essential amino acids, into niacin. Milk contains large amounts of tryptophan.

Niacin is the most stable of the B-complex vitamins. Light, heat, and temperature do not affect niacin, but it is water-soluble. To preserve the niacin value of foods, use a small amount of water and short cooking times when possible.

Niacin Deficiencies

Too little niacin in the diet can cause pellagra. Skin lesions and digestive problems are the first symptoms. Mental disorders and death may follow if the disease goes untreated. Pellagra normally occurs only when the diet is limited to just a few foods that are not good sources of niacin.

Vitamin B-6 (Pyridoxine)

Diet experimentation with rats resulted in the discovery of vitamin B-6 (pyridoxine). Three closely related compounds make up vitamin B-6. All have potential vitamin B-6 activity.

Functions of Vitamin B-6

Vitamin B-6 has several important functions in the body. It helps nerve tissues function normally and plays a role in the regeneration of red blood cells. It takes part in the breakdown of proteins, carbohydrates, and fats. Vitamin B-6 also plays a role in the reaction that changes tryptophan into niacin.

Sources of Vitamin B-6

Vitamin B-6 is in many plant and animal foods. The best sources of this vitamin are muscle meats, liver, vegetables, and whole grain cereals.

Vitamin B-6 Deficiencies

Vitamin B-6 is in so many foods that a deficiency rarely occurs naturally. In cases of prolonged fasting, however, a B-6 deficiency can occur. Skin lesions, soreness of the mouth, and a smooth red tongue can develop. In advanced cases, nausea, vomiting, weight loss, irritability, anemia, and convulsive seizures may result.

Folic Acid

Folic acid is another B-complex vitamin. Folic acid is essential for all vertebrates, including human beings.

Functions of Folic Acid

Folic acid has several functions in the body. It helps the body produce normal blood cells. It plays a role in biochemical reactions in cells that convert food into energy.

Folic acid is especially important in the diets of pregnant women. It has been shown to help prevent severe birth defects affecting the brain and spinal cord. Experts recommend that all women of childbearing age consume 0.4 mg of folic acid every day. The need for folic acid is most critical during the weeks before becoming pregnant and in the early part of a pregnancy. See 2-9.

Sources of Folic Acid

Food sources of folic acid include broccoli, asparagus, leafy green vegetables, and legumes. Liver, yogurt, strawberries, bananas, oranges, and whole grain cereals are good sources, too. However, getting enough folic acid from your diet can be difficult. Young women should consult a dietitian about taking a multivitamin supplement to make sure they get an adequate supply.

Folic Acid Deficiencies

A poor diet, impaired absorption, or an unusual need by body tissues may cause folic acid deficiencies. Some scientists believe that combined deficiencies of folic acid, vitamin B-12, and vitamin C are more common than deficiencies of any one of these vitamins by itself. Folic acid deficiencies can occur in human beings under normal conditions. For example, women sometimes develop folic acid deficiencies during the latter stages of pregnancy and lactation.

Evenflo Products Company, Inc.

2-9 Getting enough folic acid before and during pregnancy can help a mother protect her baby against serious birth defects.

Symptoms of folic acid deficiency include inflammation of the tongue, diarrhea, other digestive disturbances, and two types of anemia.

Vitamin B-12

Pernicious anemia is a chronic disease characterized by abnormally large red blood cells and neurological disturbances, such as depression and drowsiness. By 1926, scientists knew they could control pernicious anemia by giving patients liver. However, they were not able to isolate the factor in liver that controlled pernicious anemia until 1948. They called this factor vitamin B-12.

Functions of Vitamin B-12

Vitamin B-12 has several important functions in the body. Vitamin B-12 promotes normal growth and protects against the development of pernicious anemia. (For this reason, some people call it the *antipernicious anemia factor*.) It also plays a role in the normal functioning of cells, especially those in the bone marrow, nervous system, and intestines.

Sources of Vitamin B-12

Vitamin B-12 is in animal protein foods and brewer's yeast. Cereals, vegetables, fruits, and legumes have little or no vitamin B-12. A well-balanced diet that includes animal foods should supply sufficient vitamin B-12. Vegetarians who eat no animal foods, however, may have a vitamin B-12 deficiency.

Vitamin B-12 Deficiencies

Because vitamin B-12 is in so many well-liked animal foods, a deficiency of vitamin B-12 is unusual in the United States. In simple dietary deficiency cases, a sore tongue, weakness, loss of weight, apathy, and nervous disorders may result. In extreme cases, pernicious anemia can develop. Pernicious anemia can be fatal unless treated.

Pantothenic Acid

Scientists first thought pantothenic acid was a growth factor for yeast. Later, they discovered it was a B-complex vitamin needed by human beings and many animals.

Functions of Pantothenic Acid

Pantothenic acid's main function is that of a constituent of coenzyme A. Coenzyme A is one of the most important substances in metabolism (the chemical changes that nutrients undergo after digestion). The body needs it to metabolize the energy nutrients and to produce cholesterol. The body also needs pantothenic acid to produce antibodies.

Sources of Pantothenic Acid

Pantothenic acid is in all plant and animal tissues. Organ meats, yeast, egg yolk, bran, wheat and rice germ, and legumes are the best sources of pantothenic acid. Milk is also a good source.

Pantothenic Acid Deficiencies

Pantothenic acid is in so many foods that a natural, well-defined deficiency is rare in humans. In cases where a deficiency does exist, symptoms include irritability, restlessness, alternate periods of insomnia and sleepiness, and a staggering walk.

Biotin

Of all the B-complex vitamins, biotin is one of the least well known. However, it is as essential in the diet as the other B-vitamins.

Functions of Biotin

The body needs biotin for the breakdown of fats, carbohydrates, and proteins. It also is an essential part of several enzymes.

Sources of Biotin

Biotin is in both plant and animal foods. Kidney and liver are the richest sources of biotin. Chicken, eggs, milk, most fresh vegetables, and some fruits are also good sources, 2-10.

Biotin Deficiencies

Because biotin is in most foods and the body produces it in the intestinal tract, deficiencies are rare. Symptoms of a biotin deficiency are scaly skin, mild depression, fatigue, sleeplessness, muscular pain, and nausea.

Minerals

Carbohydrates, fats, proteins, and water make up about 96 percent of your body weight. *Minerals* are inorganic substances that make up the other four percent. They become part of the bones, tissues, and body fluids. Scientists have found that the body needs at least 21 minerals for good health. However, they do not yet completely understand the roles of some of these minerals.

The body needs minerals to build bones, soft tissues, and other compounds. Minerals also help regulate body processes. The body contains large amounts of some minerals. These are called *macrominerals*. Calcium, phosphorus, magnesium, sodium, potassium, and chlorine are macrominerals. The body contains very small amounts of other minerals. These are called *microminerals* or **trace elements.** Iron, iodine, zinc, and fluorine are trace elements. They are just as important for good health as macrominerals.

Calcium

The body contains more calcium than any other mineral. Most of the calcium is in the bones and teeth. The fluids and soft tissues contain the rest. The body stores a reserve of excess calcium inside long bones.

Functions of Calcium

Calcium has several important functions in the body. It combines with phosphorus to build and strengthen bones and teeth. Calcium helps blood clot and keeps heart muscles and nerves working properly. It also helps regulate the use of other minerals in the body.

Sources of Calcium

Calcium supplements are available. However, most experts agree that food sources supply the most beneficial balance of calcium with other nutrients (like phosphorus and vitamin D).

2-10 Eggs supply biotin in the diet.

Milk and milk products like yogurt and cheese are the best food sources of calcium. Whole fish, leafy green vegetables, and broccoli are also good sources of this mineral.

Calcium Deficiencies

Because the body needs calcium for proper bone growth and development, children with severe deficiencies may develop poor (or malformed) bones. Usually, however, these bone disorders are the result of a vitamin D deficiency. This is because vitamin D affects the body's ability to use calcium.

Few adults in the United States get the recommended dietary allowance of 800 milligrams of calcium per day. If the diet does not supply enough calcium, the body will take the calcium it needs from the bones. This becomes an increasing problem in old age, when bone mass naturally decreases. Bones weakened further by the draw on their calcium supply become porous and brittle. This is a condition known as *osteoporosis*.

Osteoporosis afflicts up to 20 million people in the United States. Hip fractures and resulting complications caused by osteoporosis make it a leading cause of crippling and death among older women. Women are most often afflicted because they have less bone mass than men. Osteoporosis is also related to hormone changes that take place in older women. Therefore, postmenopausal women are at the greatest risk of developing this disease.

Doctors cannot correct osteoporosis. However, obtaining enough calcium (and phosphorus) can help to prevent it. This is especially important during the formative years when bones are developing. Research has shown that maintaining a lifelong program of exercise can also help reduce the risk of osteoporosis. This is because weight-bearing exercise, such as walking, helps to increase bone mass.

Phosphorus

Phosphorus is second only to calcium in the amount found in the body. Phosphorus works with calcium to give strength to bones and teeth. Like calcium, the body stores a reserve of excess phosphorus in the bones.

Functions of Phosphorus

Phosphorus has several important functions in the body. Phosphorus helps build bones and teeth and aids the body in storing and releasing energy. It helps balance the alkalies and acids in the blood. Phosphorus also helps the body use other nutrients.

Sources of Phosphorus

Meat, poultry, fish, eggs, and milk and other dairy products are good sources of phosphorus. If you eat enough foods that are high in protein and calcium, you should receive enough phosphorus. See 2-11.

Phosphorus Deficiencies

Because calcium and phosphorus work together, phosphorus deficiencies are similar to those of calcium.

Magnesium

About half of the body's magnesium is in the skeleton. The other half is in the soft tissues and body fluids.

Functions of Magnesium

Magnesium has several important functions in the body. Magnesium helps cells use proteins, fats, and carbohydrates to produce energy. It helps regulate the body's temperature and keeps the nervous system working properly. Magnesium also helps muscles contract and improves the balance between alkalies and acids.

Sources of Magnesium

Whole grains and grain products, nuts, beans, meat, and dark green leafy vegetables are good sources of magnesium.

Magnesium Deficiencies

Healthy people who eat a well-balanced diet receive enough magnesium. A deficiency, however, can occur in alcoholics. People suffering from malfunctioning kidneys, severe diarrhea, or malnutrition can also experience deficiencies. Symptoms include twitching, muscle tremors, an irregular pulse, insomnia, and muscle weakness.

Sodium, Chlorine, and Potassium

Like calcium and phosphorus, sodium, chlorine, and potassium work as a nutrient team. Blood

2-11 Milk is an excellent source of both calcium and phosphorus.

plasma and other fluids outside the cells contain most of the body's sodium and chlorine. In addition, some sodium is in bones, and some chlorine is in gastric juices. Most of the body's potassium is within the cells.

Functions of Sodium, Chlorine, and Potassium

Sodium, chlorine, and potassium work together to control osmosis. *Osmosis* is the process whereby fluids flow in and out of the cells through the cell walls. These minerals also help maintain the acid-alkali balance in the body. They help the nervous system and muscles function properly. They also help the cells absorb nutrients.

Sources of Sodium, Chlorine, and Potassium

Sodium, chlorine, and potassium are in many plant and animal foods. Sodium is in many processed foods. Table salt provides additional amounts of sodium and chlorine. Meat, milk, bananas, citrus fruits, and dark green leafy vegetables are especially good sources of potassium, 2-12.

Dole Food Company

2-12 Bananas are a rich source of potassium.

Sodium, Chlorine, and Potassium Deficiencies and Excesses

Deficiencies of sodium, chlorine, and potassium are rare in healthy individuals with balanced diets. Cases of severe diarrhea, vomiting, and burns may require increased amounts of these minerals to replace losses. Persons taking diuretics (medication taken to relieve water retention) may need to take additional potassium. Persons who perspire a great deal during heavy work or exercise may lose some sodium. However, normal eating usually replaces these losses.

Normally, you excrete excess sodium through urine. In some cases, however, the body cannot get rid of the sodium, and fluids build up. The resulting swelling is called *edema.* Thus, people with medical problems in which the body retains fluid may have to restrict their sodium intake.

Research has shown there is a link between sodium and high blood pressure. Therefore, doctors also prescribe low-sodium diets for people suffering from hypertension and congestive heart failure.

People wishing to reduce their sodium intake can begin by limiting their use of salt in cooking and at the table. Sodium is also in many processed foods. Many cured meats, canned soups, frozen entrees, snack foods, and condiments like mustard and catsup are high in sodium. Reading nutrition labels will help make you more aware of foods containing sodium. Limiting your use of these foods as well as salt can help lower the amount of sodium in your diet.

Trace Elements

The body contains very small amounts of trace elements. Experts have determined that some of these minerals are essential for good health. However, they do not yet completely understand the functions of some trace elements.

Iron

The human body contains about four grams of iron. Over half of this iron is in the blood, where it combines with a protein to form hemoglobin. *Hemoglobin* is a protein pigment found in red blood cells. It takes oxygen from the lungs and carries it to cells throughout the body.

Iron is one mineral that the body does not excrete in any quantity. The body stores iron and uses it over and over again. When the body does not have enough iron reserves, anemia can result. *Anemia* is a condition in which the blood lacks red blood cells, hemoglobin, or total volume. Infants, children, and women suffer from anemia more often than men. Loss of appetite, pale skin, and tiredness are general symptoms of anemia.

Women lose varying amounts of iron each month during menstruation. Frequently eating foods rich in iron can maintain iron reserves. If the diet does not supply enough iron, however, a physician may prescribe an iron supplement.

Infants have some iron reserves when they are born. When these reserves are depleted, however, the infant must receive iron from foods. Milk is not a source of iron. Infants kept on a milk-only diet may develop anemia.

Liver is one of the best sources of iron. Other meats, egg yolks, legumes, leafy green vegetables, and enriched breads and cereals are also good sources of this mineral.

Iodine

The thyroid gland stores a third of the body's iodine. This small gland is located at the base of the neck. Iodine is an essential part of *thyroxine,* a hormone produced by the thyroid gland. Thyroxine increases oxidation rates in body cells.

If the diet does not contain enough iodine, the thyroid gland has to work very hard to produce enough thyroxine. As a result, it enlarges. This condition is called *endemic goiter.*

Insufficient iodine during the prenatal period and early childhood may cause severe mental retardation. Combined with a retarded growth rate, this deficiency can cause swollen facial features and enlarged lips and tongue. Early treatment can reverse some of these characteristics. Seafood, seaweed, and iodized salt are good sources of iodine.

Manganese

Certain enzymes must have manganese in order to function properly. Although doctors have not found deficiencies in human beings, they have seen toxic conditions. Miners loading manganese-rich ores have developed manganese poisoning. As a result, they have masklike faces and spastic movements. Instant coffee, bran flakes, and shredded wheat are good sources of manganese.

Copper

Copper plays a role in the formation of hemoglobin. When the body does not obtain enough copper, the number of red blood cells decreases. Copper also helps the body protect nerve cells and make collagen, the protein in connective tissue. Copper-deficient anemia can occur in children who are severely malnourished, but it is not common in adults. Cocoa powder, beef and pork liver, and bran flakes are good sources of copper.

Zinc

Zinc helps certain enzymes release oxygen from the lungs. It also aids in the digestion of protein. Doctors do not completely understand zinc deficiency. Meat, poultry, seafood, eggs, and milk are good sources of zinc.

Fluorine

The greatest quantities of fluorine are in the teeth and bones. The teeth need fluorine for maximum resistance to dental caries. Fluorine is most helpful during the development of teeth, but it serves a protective function for the life of the tooth. Studies have also shown that fluorine may be effective in maintaining the health of bones.

Commonly eaten foods contain little fluorine. In some areas, drinking water contains fluorine naturally. In areas where the natural fluorine level is low, the Food and Nutrition Board recommends adding fluorine to the public drinking water. Some toothpastes also contain fluorine.

Water

The body must have water to function. People can live more than a month without food. However, they can live only a few days without water. See 2-13.

BRITA®

2-13 *Great-tasting water is more than just a thirst quencher—it is your body's most essential nutrient.*

Play It Safe

You never know when a disaster, such as an earthquake or flood, might occur. Being prepared can help you cope with an emergency situation.

One way to prepare is to gather supplies that you would need in the event of a disaster. Water is one of the basic supplies you should stock. Store three gallons of water for each family member in sealed, unbreakable containers. This is enough water to allow for food preparation and sanitation as well as drinking for a three-day period. Date the containers and replace the water every six months so it stays fresh.

Functions of Water

Between 50 and 75 percent of your body weight is water. Water is found both inside and outside all of your cells. Water aids proper digestion and cell growth and maintenance. All chemical reactions within the body rely upon water. Water also lubricates the joints and body cells and helps regulate body temperature.

Water Intake and Excretion

Your body takes the water it needs from the liquids you drink and the foods you eat. About 54 percent of your water intake comes from liquids. These liquids include water, milk, clear soups, coffee, tea, fruit juices, and other beverages. About 37 percent of your water intake comes from the food you eat. Different foods contain different amounts of water. For instance, lettuce contains more water than a slice of bread.

Your body also obtains about nine percent of the water it needs as a by-product of metabolism. Because the body continuously metabolizes carbohydrates, fats, and proteins for energy, this is a constant source of water. The amount of water produced, however, varies.

The body excretes most of the water it uses through the kidneys as urine. It excretes the remaining water through the skin and lungs and in the feces.

Water Requirements

Eight glasses of fluids a day supply enough water for most people. Some people need more water. People who are in a coma or suffering from fever or diarrhea have increased water needs. People on a high-protein diet and those living in a hot climate must also increase their water intake.

Diarrhea, vomiting, excessive sweating, or the unavailability of drinking water can deplete body fluids. Thirst is the first symptom of water loss. If water is not replaced, dryness of the mouth, weakness, increased pulse rate, flushed skin, and fever can result.

To review the functions of the major nutrients, see 2-14.

Digestion and Absorption

Suppose you ate a hamburger for lunch. Your body can absorb a few nutrients, like sodium and glucose, as soon as you ingest them. However, most of the nutrients in that hamburger must undergo many changes before your body can use them. These changes occur during the process called *digestion.*

The Digestive Tract

The digestive or gastrointestinal tract is a tube about 30 feet (9 m) long. It extends from the mouth to the anus. It contains the esophagus, the stomach, the small intestine, and the large intestine (colon). These parts of the digestive tract work together both mechanically and chemically to help the body use food.

The Digestion Process

During digestion, the body breaks down complex molecules obtained from food into simple, soluble materials. These simple materials can pass through the digestive tract into the blood and lymph systems. Vitamins and minerals undergo very little chemical change during digestion. However, fats, proteins, and carbohydrates undergo many changes.

The Mechanical Phase

The digestion process involves two phases. The mechanical phase of digestion begins in the mouth and continues throughout the digestive tract. In the mouth, the teeth chew the food and break it down into smaller pieces.

Key Nutrients

Nutrient	Functions	Sources
Carbohydrates	Supply energy Provide bulk in the form of cellulose (needed for digestion) Help the body digest fats efficiently Spare proteins so they can be used for growth and regulation	Sugar: Honey, jam, jelly, sugar, and molasses Fiber: Fresh fruits and vegetables and whole grain cereals and breads Starch: Breads, cereals, corn, peas, beans, potatoes, and macaroni products
Fats	Supply energy Carry fat-soluble vitamins Insulate the body from shock and temperature changes Protect vital organs Add flavor and satisfying quality to foods Serve as a source of essential fatty acids	Butter, margarine, cream, cheese, marbling in meat, nuts, whole milk, olives, chocolate, egg yolks, bacon, salad oils, and dressings
Proteins	Build and repair tissues Help make antibodies, enzymes, hormones, and some vitamins Regulate fluid balance in the cells and other body processes Supply energy, when needed	Complete proteins: Meat, poultry, fish, eggs, and milk and other dairy products Incomplete proteins: Cereals, grains, peanuts, peanut butter, and lentils and legumes
Vitamins **Vitamin A**	Helps keep skin clear and smooth and mucus membranes healthy Helps prevent night blindness Helps promote growth	Liver, egg yolk, dark green and yellow fruits and vegetables, butter, whole and fortified milk, fortified margarine, and Cheddar-type cheese
Vitamin D	Fortified milk, butter, and margarine; fish liver oils; liver; sardines; tuna; egg yolk; and the sun	Helps build strong bones and teeth in children Helps maintain bones in adults
Vitamin E	Acts as an antioxidant that protects cell membranes of cells exposed to high concentration of oxygen	Liver and other variety meats, eggs, leafy green vegetables, whole grain cereals, salad oils, shortenings, and other fats and oils
Vitamin K	Helps blood clot	Organ meats, leafy green vegetables, cauliflower, other vegetables, and egg yolk
Vitamin C	Promotes healthy gums and tissues Helps wounds heal and broken bones mend Helps body fight infection Helps make cementing materials that hold body cells together	Citrus fruits, strawberries, cantaloupe, broccoli, green peppers, raw cabbage, tomatoes, leafy green vegetables, and potatoes and sweet potatoes cooked in the skin
Thiamin (Vitamin B-1)	Helps promote normal appetite and digestion Forms parts of the coenzymes needed for the breakdown of carbohydrates Helps keep nervous system healthy and prevent irritability Helps body release energy from food	Pork, other meats, poultry, fish, eggs, enriched or whole grain breads and cereals, and dried beans
Riboflavin	Helps cells use oxygen Helps keep skin, tongue, and lips normal Helps prevent scaly, greasy areas around the mouth and nose Forms part of the coenzymes needed for the breakdown of carbohydrates	Milk, all kinds of cheese, ice cream, liver, other meats, fish, poultry, eggs, and dark green leafy vegetables

2-14 Being aware of nutrient functions and sources can help you choose foods that give you the nutritional balance you need.

Nutrient	Functions	Sources
Niacin	Helps keep nervous system healthy Helps keep skin, mouth, tongue, and digestive tract healthy Helps cells use other nutrients Forms part of two coenzymes involved in complex chemical reactions in the body	Meat, fish, poultry, milk, enriched or whole grain breads and cereals, peanuts, peanut butter, and dried beans and peas
Vitamin B-6	Helps nervous tissue function normally Plays a role in the breakdown of proteins, fats, and carbohydrates Plays a role in the reaction in which tryptophan is converted to niacin Plays a role in the regeneration of red blood cells	Liver, muscle meats, vegetables, and whole grain cereals
Folic Acid	Helps produce normal blood cells Helps convert food into energy Helps prevent birth defects of the brain and spinal cord	Broccoli, asparagus, leafy green vegetables, legumes, liver, yogurt, strawberries, bananas, oranges, and whole grain cereals
Vitamin B-12	Protects against pernicious anemia Plays a role in the normal functioning of cells	Eggs, fish, liver, and other meats, milk, and cheese
Minerals **Calcium**	Helps build bones and teeth Helps blood clot Helps muscles and nerves work Helps regulate the use of other minerals in the body	Milk, cheese, other dairy products, leafy green vegetables, and fish eaten with the bones
Phosphorus	Helps build strong bones and teeth Helps regulate many internal bodily activities	Protein and calcium food sources
Iodine	Promotes normal functioning of the thyroid gland	Iodized table salt and saltwater fish and shellfish
Iron	Combines with protein to make hemoglobin Helps cells use oxygen	Liver, lean meats, egg yolk, dried beans and peas, leafy green vegetables, dried fruits, and enriched and whole grain breads and cereals
Water	Aids in proper digestion Plays a role in cell growth and maintenance Plays a role in all chemical reactions in the body lubricates the joints and body cells Helps regulate body temperature	Liquids such as water, milk, clear soups, coffee, tea, fruit juices, and other beverages Most foods, especially fruits and vegetables Metabolism to carbohydrates, fats, and proteins

2-14 (continued)

In the rest of the digestive tract, muscle fibers carry out the mechanical action. Circular muscle fibers contract and squeeze the food particles, causing them to mix and break apart into smaller pieces. The longitudinal fibers contract and push the food through the digestive tract. The longitudinal and circular fibers work together to produce a wavelike movement called *peristalsis*. **Peristalsis** is the process that pushes food through the digestive tract.

Emotions affect peristalsis. Sadness, depression, and fear can inhibit gastric movement. Anger and aggression can increase gastric movement.

The Chemical Phase

Like the mechanical phase, the chemical phase of digestion begins in the mouth. As you chew, food is mixed with enzyme-containing saliva. Mucus produced by the mouth enables you to swallow the food. It also helps the food particles move down the esophagus into the stomach.

In the stomach, *gastric juices* break down the food further. Gastric juices contain hydrochloric acid and several enzymes. As you eat, your stomach expands. This expansion, as well as the sight, smell, and taste of food, stimulates the secretion of gastric juices. The type of food eaten also affects the production of gastric juices.

The length of time food remains in the stomach depends on the individual and the combination of foods eaten. An ordinary meal usually leaves the stomach in about three to five hours. Carbohydrates leave the stomach first. Proteins are second to leave the stomach, followed by fats. As a result, you will feel hungry sooner after a meal high in carbohydrates than a meal high in proteins and fats.

As digestion continues, the semiliquid food mass leaves the stomach and enters the small intestine. Here, intestinal juices, pancreatic juices, and bile act upon the food. These secretions contain the enzymes needed to complete the digestion of the proteins, fats, and carbohydrates. Once digestion is complete, absorption can take place.

Indigestible residues, unabsorbed digestive end products, bile pigments, other wastes, and water travel from the small intestine to the large intestine. The large intestine acts as a reservoir, or storage area. Eventually the body will excrete these materials in the feces.

The glands and organs of the gastrointestinal system produce digestive enzymes. These enzymes break down the chemical components of the food you eat. They help break down carbohydrates, proteins, and fats into simple substances that the body can absorb and use. Each type of enzyme has a specific function. An enzyme that breaks down proteins, for example, will not break down fats.

The Absorption Process

The body can absorb water, ethyl alcohol, and simple sugars directly from the stomach. They pass through the stomach walls into the bloodstream. Most absorption, however, takes place in the small intestine.

Millions of hairlike fingers called *villi* line the small intestine. The villi increase the absorptive surface of the small intestine by more than 600 percent. Each villus contains a lymph vessel surrounded by a network of capillaries. Nutrients absorbed by the capillaries pass into the portal vein and travel directly to the liver.

The body absorbs nearly all carbohydrates as monosaccharides. The body absorbs fats and other lipids in two forms: as fatty acids and glycerol and as mono- and diglycerides. (*Glycerol* is an alcohol obtained from the breakdown of fat. *Diglycerides* are compounds formed by the combination of glycerol and fatty acids.) The body absorbs nearly all proteins as amino acids.

Metabolism

Metabolism refers to the chemical processes that take place in the cells after nutrients have been absorbed by the body. Enzymes catalyze nearly all of the changes that take place after absorption. As a result of metabolic reactions, some nutrients replace substances that the body uses for growth or to carry out bodily processes. Other nutrients release energy as they break down into even simpler substances. The body uses part of this energy to carry out metabolic reactions. It converts the rest into heat.

Each nutrient follows a specific metabolic pathway. Carbohydrates, for example, can be used for energy, converted to glycogen, or stored as fat. Their use depends upon the body's need. During fat metabolism, oxidation occurs. This shortens the fatty acid chains. The body uses most fat for fuel. It can use amino acids for cell maintenance; cell growth; or the synthesis of enzymes, antibodies, and nonessential amino acids. The body can also use amino acids as an energy source.

Energy Needs

Energy, in the physical sense, is the power to do work. The human body needs energy to perform physical activity. It also needs energy to carry on its internal work. During certain periods of life, the body also needs energy for growth, repair, milk production, and heat generation. The body produces energy by *oxidizing* (using oxygen to burn up) the foods you eat. See 2-15.

Basal Metabolism

Basal metabolism is the amount of heat a person gives off when the body is at physical, digestive, and emotional rest. It refers to the amount of energy the human body needs just to stay alive and carry on vital life processes.

2-15 Physical activity is just one of several factors that affect the body's energy needs.

A person's basal metabolism varies depending upon body size and composition, age, health, and secretions of the endocrine glands. Two people who are the same weight and age, for example, may have different basal metabolic rates (BMR). This is because their body shapes are different. The tall person has a larger body surface area than the short person. Therefore, the tall person has a higher basal metabolism per unit of body weight.

The kinds of tissues that make up the body also affect basal metabolism. Men usually have a larger amount of lean tissue than women. This causes them to require more energy per unit of body weight than women.

Age can affect basal metabolism. Children and adolescents have a higher basal metabolism than adults. This is because basal metabolism is greater during periods of rapid growth. After about age 20, basal metabolism gradually declines.

A person's general health can affect basal metabolism. The basal metabolism of a well-nourished person is higher than that of a malnourished person. An increase in body temperature also increases basal metabolism. For this reason, the basal metabolism of a person with a fever is higher than that of a person with a normal body temperature.

Gland secretions can affect basal metabolism. The thyroid gland affects metabolism more than any other gland. Undersecretion of the thyroid gland may depress basal metabolism. Oversecretion can elevate it. Adrenaline, which the adrenal glands secrete during times of stress, also increases metabolism.

Physical Activity

When you engage in any physical activity, your energy needs become greater than your basal metabolism. Different activities require different amounts of energy. For instance, it takes more energy to wash dishes than it takes to read a book. It takes still more energy to rake leaves or swim.

Several factors can influence the amount of energy a person needs to perform a physical task. The intensity with which you perform a task can affect energy needs. A person who walks briskly, for example, needs more energy than a person who walks slowly. Body size can affect energy needs. A 220 pound (81 kg) student, for example, requires more energy to take notes in class than a 120 pound (20 kg) student. The temperature of the environment also can affect energy needs. It takes more energy to wash windows when the temperature is 90°F (32°C) than when the temperature is 70°F (21°C).

Total Energy Value of Food

Each food you eat has a particular energy value. A *calorie* is a unit used to measure the energy value of food when it is burned in the body. It equals the amount of heat needed to raise one gram of water one degree Celsius. The *kilojoule* (kJ) is also used to measure energy.

The total energy value of a food depends on that food's chemical composition. Placing a food sample inside a device called a *bomb calorimeter* is one way to determine the food's energy value. The food is surrounded by water and ignited. As the food burns, it releases energy as heat. You can then determine the energy value of the food by measuring the heat of the water.

When researchers burn pure carbohydrates in a laboratory, the carbohydrates produce 4.10 calories per gram (17.2 kJ/g). Fats produce 9.45 calories per gram (39.5 kJ/g), and proteins produce 5.65 calories per gram (23.6 kJ/g). Carbohydrates, fats, and proteins burn completely in a calorimeter. The human body is not as efficient as a calorimeter. Therefore, the physiological value of both carbohydrates and proteins is only 4 calories per gram (17 kJ/g). The physiological value of fats is 9 calories per gram (38 kJ/g).

Because few of the foods you eat are pure carbohydrates, pure proteins, or pure fats, foods vary widely in their energy value. Foods that are normally high in fat and low in water are called *high fuel value foods*. Some examples are nuts, mayonnaise, cheese, and fatty meats. Foods that are high in water and cellulose and low in fat are called *low fuel value foods*. Most fresh fruits and vegetables are low fuel value foods. Lean meats, cereal foods, and starchy vegetables are *intermediate fuel value foods*. See 2-16.

Total Energy Needs

An adult's total energy needs depend on basal metabolism, physical activity, and the heat produced by ingesting food. A child's total energy needs also depend on growth.

When the energy (calories or kilojoules) you obtain from food equals the energy you expend, your body weight remains the same. When the energy you obtain from foods is less than the energy you expend, your body weight decreases. When the energy you obtain from food is greater than the energy you expend, your body weight increases. It takes about 3,500 calories (15,062 kJ) to make up 1 pound (.45 kg) of body weight. (Chapter 4, "Nutrition in the Life Cycle," includes a discussion of how to estimate your energy needs.)

2-16 With their high water and low fat contents, most fruits and vegetables have a low fuel value.

Summary

Food provides the body with six basic types of nutrients. These are carbohydrates, fats, proteins, vitamins, minerals, and water. Individual nutrients within these groups each serve specific functions. No one food supplies all of the nutrients the body needs. Health problems arise when there are deficiencies or excesses of various nutrients. Eating a variety of foods is the best way to get appropriate amounts of all of the nutrients.

Your body must break down the foods you eat into components it can use. This happens during the digestion process. The digestion process involves both a mechanical and a chemical phase. After foods have been broken down in the digestive tract, the body absorbs them. Then they are metabolized in the cells.

Your energy needs are based on your basal metabolic requirements and your activity level. The energy value of the foods you eat depends on the amount of carbohydrate, fat, and protein in the food. The way the energy provided by the foods you eat compares with your energy needs affects your body weight.

Review What You Have Read

Write your answers on a separate sheet of paper.
1. True or false. The foods a child eats can affect his or her health as an adult.
2. List the six basic groups of nutrients.
3. Match the following carbohydrates with their descriptions:
   ___ Table sugar.
   ___ Sweetest of all sugars.
   ___ Immediate source of energy for cells.
   ___ Found in mammal's milk.
   ___ Important source of bulk in the diet.
   A. cellulose
   B. fructose
   C. glucose
   D. lactose
   E. sucrose
4. Fatty acids that have as many hydrogen atoms as they can hold are called _____.
5. List three functions of each: carbohydrates, fats, and proteins.
6. What type of protein will support growth and normal maintenance?
7. List the fat-soluble vitamins and explain the basic way in which they differ from water-soluble vitamins.
8. Give three functions of vitamin C and four important food sources.
9. Which vitamin was discovered because of the disease beriberi?
10. What is the process controlled by sodium, potassium, and chlorine, whereby fluids flow in and out of cells through the cell walls?
11. What is the process by which food is pushed along the digestive tract?
12. True or false. Basal metabolism refers to the amount of energy the human body needs just to stay alive and carry on vital life processes.

Build Your Basic Skills

1. Make a set of nutrient flash cards. On one side of each card, write the name of a nutrient. On the other side, list functions of that nutrient. Divide into pairs. Using the flash cards, take turns quizzing your partner. First show the side of the card with the nutrient's name and ask your partner to list its functions. The second time around, show the side of the card with the functions and ask your partner to name the nutrient.
2. Using poster board and magazine pictures, make a poster or mobile for one of the nutrients. Show foods that are good sources of that nutrient.
3. Make a crossword puzzle using words that are important in the study of nutrition.

Build Your Thinking Skills

1. Read the label of a multivitamin supplement. Note the percent Daily Value provided for each of the vitamins in the supplement. Summarize your findings in a report on the effects of excess fat-soluble and water-soluble vitamins in the body.
2. Plan a basic nutrition lesson for a primary school child. Use visual aids that appeal to children like magazine pictures, colorful posters, or puppets.

Chapter 3

Making Healthy Food Choices

A "Taste" of the World of Work

Nutrition Consultant
Develops, tests, and promotes various types of food products.

Food Columnist
Analyzes news and writes column commentary for publication, based on personal knowledge and experience with foods and nutrition.

Family and Consumer Science Professional
Organizes and conducts consumer education service or research programs for food companies, utilizing principles of family and consumer sciences.

Terms to Know

Recommended Dietary Allowances (RDA)
Dietary Guidelines for Americans
Food Guide Pyramid
processed foods

Objectives

After studying this chapter, you will be able to
  explain how you can use the Recommended Dietary Allowances.
  list the Dietary Guidelines for Americans.
  identify how many daily servings you need from each group in the Food Guide Pyramid.
  explain how you can use the Dietary Guidelines when shopping for food, preparing food, and eating out.

American Iron & Steel Institute

Knowing about nutrients gives you an idea of the important role food can play in your health. However, you need to know a bit more to choose foods that will supply adequate amounts of those nutrients. Some general guidelines can help you select a balanced diet. You can use these guidelines when shopping for food, preparing food at home, and eating out.

Making wise food choices can help you maintain good health and may improve your health. However, you should note that eating wholesome foods will not guarantee that you have good health. Your heredity and environment have an effect on your physical well-being. Your personal habits affect your state of health, too. You need to get adequate rest and exercise. You also need to avoid smoking and abusing alcohol and other drugs. These factors all play a role in how you look and feel. They have an impact on your susceptibility to various diseases, as well.

The Recommended Dietary Allowances

The *Recommended Dietary Allowances (RDA)* is a list of the nutrient requirements for various groups of people. The Food and Nutrition Board of the National Research Council originally published the RDA in 1943. Since the first publication, they have revised the RDA a number of times to reflect the latest nutrition research.

The RDA includes recommendations for energy needs, protein, and several vitamins and minerals. There are allowances for each sex and for several age groups. (See Appendix A.) The RDA goes beyond the minimum nutrient requirements to provide a margin of safety. The allowances permit full growth and productivity for nearly all healthy people in the United States.

The RDA is not a useful guide for people with abnormal nutrient requirements. People who are sick or convalescing have special nutrient needs. They should heed the advice of their physician and follow a diet prescribed by a dietitian.

How the RDA Is Used

The RDA is used to calculate the approximate nutritional needs of a large group of people. It is used to evaluate the diets of individuals. It is also used to formulate regulations for the composition of foods, dietary supplements, and drugs.

You can use the RDA to evaluate your diet. Begin by keeping track of all the foods you eat.

Your intake of each nutrient will vary from one day to the next. Therefore, you should list foods eaten over a three-day period to get an average. Be sure to include snacks as well as foods eaten at meals.

After your list is complete, you can analyze the nutrient content of the foods. You can do this using dietary charts (like those found in Appendix B) or a computer program. Compare your analysis with the RDA for your sex and age group. This comparison will show you whether or not you are getting enough of the various nutrients. You may discover that your diet is low in some nutrients. If so, you can select more foods that are good sources of those nutrients.

Dietary Guidelines for Americans

The U.S. departments of Agriculture and Health and Human Services have published a set of seven *Dietary Guidelines for Americans.* The guidelines encourage healthy people over age two to form healthful diet habits. Following the guidelines involves considering the components in food choices. The guidelines recommend including adequate amounts of some components, while limiting intakes of others.

The Dietary Guidelines for Americans are general enough to fit with many lifestyles and food preferences. Following them can help you get needed nutrients while avoiding excess calories, fat, cholesterol, sugar, sodium, and alcohol. See 3-1. The seven Dietary Guidelines are as follows:

- **Eat a variety of foods.** Different foods provide different nutrients, and no single food provides every nutrient. Eating a variety of foods is the best way to get all the nutrients you need.

- **Balance the food you eat with physical activity. Maintain or improve your weight.** The guidelines also recommend that you eat the right amounts of foods to meet your energy needs. Eating more calories than you need can cause you to be overweight. Being overweight is a risk factor for high blood pressure, heart disease, stroke, certain types of cancer, and diabetes.

    Physical activity, such as exercise or participation in sports, helps you use energy. This will help you burn off excess calories. It will also improve your muscle tone, strengthen your heart and lungs, and give you an overall sense of well-being.

Dietary Guidelines for Americans

Makes one healthy diet

Eat a variety of foods.

Balance the food you eat with physical activity. Maintain or improve your weight.

Choose a diet with plenty of grain products, vegetables, and fruits.

Choose a diet low in fat, saturated fat, and cholesterol.

Choose a diet moderate in sugars.

Choose a diet moderate in salt and sodium.

If you drink alcoholic beverages, do so in moderation.

M/G

1. Follow the above guidelines at all stages of life.
2. Enjoy feeling your best while reducing major risk factors for several chronic diseases.

3-1 The seven Dietary Guidelines for Americans are a "recipe" for good health.

- **Choose a diet with plenty of grain products, vegetables, and fruits.** These foods provide complex carbohydrates needed for energy and fiber needed for bulk. They are rich sources of vitamins and minerals. They also tend to be low in fats, sugars, and sodium.

- **Choose a diet low in fat, saturated fat, and cholesterol.** The amount of fat you consume should not equal more than 30 percent of your total daily calorie intake. No more than one third of this fat, or 10 percent of your total calories, should be saturated. You should consume no more than 300 mg of cholesterol per day. Research has linked obesity, heart disease, stroke, and some forms of cancer to diets high in these components.

- **Choose a diet moderate in sugars.** Sugars include white sugar, brown sugar, honey, molasses, and table syrups. These simple carbohydrates contribute only calories to your diet. They supply very little in terms of other nutrients. Consuming too many foods high in sugars may limit your intake of foods containing other needed nutrients. Sugars also contribute to dental caries.

- **Choose a diet moderate in salt and sodium.** Experts recommend that you consume no more than 2400 mg of sodium per day. Much of the sodium in your diet comes from salt. (A teaspoon of salt provides roughly 2000 mg of sodium.) Many food additives also provide sodium. Limiting your use of salt and sodium-containing foods may reduce your risk of high blood pressure.

- **If you drink alcoholic beverages, do so in moderation.** This is a general guideline written for the population at large. However, many people, including children, teens, people who will be driving, and pregnant women, should avoid alcohol completely. Alcohol supplies little more than calories to the diet. Drinking alcohol has been linked with many health problems, including liver disease and some cancers. Alcohol consumption causes many accidents, and alcohol can be addictive.

Following the Dietary Guidelines does not mean you have to give up all the foods you love. In fact, you do not have to give up any foods at all. You must simply make an effort to balance your food choices. For instance, suppose you have a high-fat lunch of fried shrimp, French fries, and coleslaw. You could balance this with homemade vegetable soup, a fresh fruit cup, and a whole wheat roll for your evening meal. Your total diet is what matters. No single food, or even a whole day's worth of meals, will ruin your health forever.

Be aware that balancing your food choices does not mean splurging one day and then starving the next. An occasional splurge is not harmful when balanced with moderation. However, getting into a pattern of splurging and fasting is not healthful. In addition to balance, variety and self-control are keys to a healthy diet. Eating a wide range of foods will help keep you from going overboard with any one food.

The Food Guide Pyramid

The *Food Guide Pyramid* is a visual representation of an eating plan designed to help people choose a well-balanced diet, 3-2. This plan corresponds to the Dietary Guidelines for Americans. It groups foods of similar nutritive values into categories and gives a recommended number of daily servings for each category.

The Food Guide Pyramid is a flexible plan. You can choose servings to form almost any combination of meals and snacks. People from any ethnic background and at any economic level can use it. It also allows for the seasonal availability of foods and personal likes and dislikes.

The Food Guide Pyramid categorizes foods into the following five groups:
- breads, cereals, rice, and pasta
- vegetables
- fruits
- meat, poultry, fish, dry beans, eggs, and nuts
- milk, yogurt, and cheese

Typical foods and serving sizes for foods in each of these groups are shown in 3-3.

The groups in the Food Guide Pyramid work together to form a balanced diet. Eating the suggested number of servings from each group daily will provide you with the nutrients you need.

Bread, Cereal, Rice, and Pasta Group

Foods from grain products make up the breads, cereals, rice, and pasta group. These foods are excellent, lowfat sources of complex carbohydrates, which supply energy. They are good sources of B-vitamins and iron, too.

Foods in this group are shown at the bottom of the Food Guide Pyramid. This illustrates that these foods should form the foundation of your diet. You should eat 6 to 11 servings from this group each day. Several of these servings should be from whole grain sources to provide you with fiber.

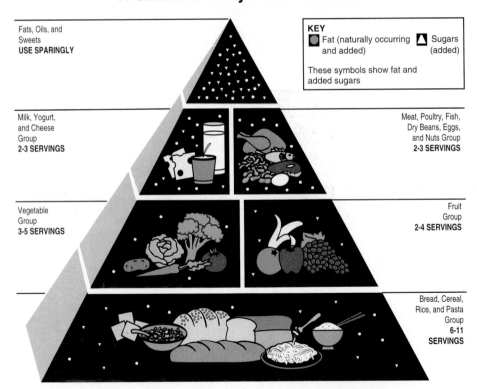

3-2 *The Food Guide Pyramid can help you visualize how the different food groups work together to form a balanced diet.*

Breads, Cereals, Rice, and Pasta

Count as one serving:
- 1 slice of bread
- 1 ounce of ready-to-eat cereal
- ½ cup of cooked cereal, rice, or pasta

whole-wheat bread, rolls, or
  cereals
bagels
english muffins
biscuits
pancakes
tortillas
grits
oatmeal
brown rice
popcorn
noodles
macaroni

Fruits

Count as one serving:
- 1 medium orange, apple, or banana
- ½ cup chopped, cooked, or canned fruit
- ¾ cup fruit juice

blueberries
honeydew melon
kiwifruit
lemon
strawberries
watermelon
apricot
cherries
figs
grapes
mango
peach
pineapple
raisins

Vegetables

Count as one serving:
- 1 cup raw leafy vegetables
- ½ cup vegetables, cooked or chopped raw
- ¾ cup vegetable juice

broccoli
spinach
carrots
pumpkin
sweet potatoes
potatoes
corn
squash
peas
kidney beans
split peas
beets
cabbage
lettuce
mushrooms
tomatoes

The Food Guide Pyramid

Meat, Poultry, Fish, and Alternates

Count as one serving:
- 2-3 ounces cooked lean meat, poultry, or fish
- ½ cup cooked dry beans, 1 egg, or 2 tablespoons peanut butter count as 1 ounce of meat

beef
ham
lamb
chicken
fish
pork
shellfish
turkey
luncheon meats
eggs
nuts and seeds
dry beans and peas
peanut butter
tofu

Fats, Oils, and Sweets

- Use in moderation–no specific number of servings recommended for these foods.

butter
margarine
cream
sour cream
mayonnaise
shortening
vegetable oil
candy
honey
jams and jellies
syrup
sherbets and ices
soft drinks
sugar (brown and white)

Milk, Yogurt, and Cheese

Count as one serving:
- 1 cup of milk or yogurt
- 1½ ounces natural cheese
- 2 ounces process cheese

lowfat milk (1%, 2%)
skim milk
buttermilk
whole milk
lowfat plain yogurt
flavored or fruit yogurt
cheddar cheese
American cheese
Swiss cheese
process cheeses

3-3 For a well-balanced diet, select a variety of foods from each group in the Food Guide Pyramid.

Vegetable Group

The vegetable group includes vegetable juices and all fresh (raw and cooked), canned, frozen, and dried vegetables. Different vegetables provide different nutrients. However, they all tend to be high in fiber and low in fat. Leafy, dark green vegetables are high in calcium, iron, vitamin A, vitamin C, and the B-vitamins. Deep yellow vegetables are good sources of vitamin A. Starchy vegetables provide complex carbohydrates. Dry beans and peas supply incomplete protein.

You should eat three to five servings of vegetables each day. To get the most from this food group, choose a variety of vegetables.

Fruit Group

The fruit group includes all forms of fruits and fruit juices. Like vegetables, fruits (except avocados) are lowfat, high-fiber sources of vitamins and minerals.

The Food Guide Pyramid recommends two to four servings from this group each day. At least one serving should be a citrus fruit, melon, or berries. These fruits are especially rich in vitamin C.

Milk, Yogurt, and Cheese Group

Milk, yogurt, and cheese are your best sources of calcium. They also provide riboflavin, phosphorus, and protein. Whole and fortified milk products provide vitamins A and D, too.

Teens, young adults, and pregnant or breast-feeding women need three servings from this group each day. Most other people need only two daily servings to meet their RDA for calcium.

Meat, Poultry, Fish, Dry Beans, Eggs, and Nuts Group

Meat, poultry, fish, and such alternates as dry beans, eggs, and nuts, are good sources of protein. They also supply vitamins and minerals, including B-vitamins and iron.

You should eat the equivalent of five to seven ounces (140 to 196 g) of lean, cooked meat each day. This usually means about two to three servings per day.

Fats, Oils, and Sweets

At the tip of the Pyramid are fats, oils, and sweets. These foods include butter, margarine, jams, jellies, syrups, candies, gravies, salad dressings, and many snack foods. They add flavor and variety to meals. However, they tend to be high in calories and low in nutrients. Therefore, you must use them sparingly.

You must remember that many foods in the five groups at the base of the Pyramid also include fats and sugars. For instance, a doughnut, which is in the breads group, contains about 11 grams of fat. Ice cream, which is in the milk group, contains about 3 teaspoons (15 mL) of added sugar. You must consider these contributions, as well as those from the tip of the Pyramid, when evaluating the fats and sugars in your diet.

Recommended Servings

Each of the groups in the Food Guide Pyramid has a suggested range of servings, 3-4. (Fats, oils, and sweets do not have a specific recommended number of servings.) The number of servings you need from each group depends on your calorie

Recommended Daily Servings for Various Groups of People

	Calories	Bread Group	Vegetable Group	Fruit Group	Milk Group	Meat Group	Total Fat (grams)	Total Added Sugars (teaspoons)
sedentary women, older adults	1600	6	3	2	2-3*	5 ounces (140 g)	53	6
children, teenage girls, active women	2200	9	4	3	2-3*	6 ounces (168 g)	73	12
teenage guys, active men, very active women	2800	11	5	4	2-3*	7 ounces (196 g)	93	18

*Pregnant or nursing women, teenagers, and young adults need 3 servings from the milk group.

3-4 The recommended number of food group servings and limits for fat and sugar intakes are based on a person's daily calorie needs.

needs. Your age, sex, body size, and activity level determine your calorie needs.

The shape of the Food Guide Pyramid illustrates the relationships between the groups. Note that fats, oils, and sweets form the smallest part of the Pyramid. The illustration indicates that these foods should make up the smallest part of your diet. This is because these foods tend to be high in fat and calories and low in vitamins, minerals, and protein.

When choosing foods, begin by selecting the recommended number of servings from the five groups at the bottom of the Food Guide Pyramid. Evaluate what portion of your calorie needs are met by these selections. Then you can add moderate amounts of fats, oils, and sweets without exceeding your calorie needs.

Choosing Wisely When Shopping for Food

The foods you choose at the grocery store become the foods you will later choose to eat at home, 3-5. Plan nutritious menus before you go to the store. Then make careful grocery purchases to ensure that you stock your shelves with healthful

3-5 Your ability to choose wisely when shopping for food affects the choices you will have available at home.

foods. Keeping the Dietary Guidelines for Americans in mind can help you choose wisely when shopping for food.

Fresh or Processed?

When shopping for food, you must consider the time and energy you will have available to prepare it. You must also consider nutrition and your family food budget. Many times, these factors become trade-offs. For instance, you might have to pay more for a frozen dinner in order to save preparation time. (You will find more shopping guidelines in Chapter 11, "The Smart Consumer.")

Processed foods are foods that have undergone some preparation procedure, such as canning, freezing, drying, cooking, or fortification. In most cases, processing decreases the nutritional value of foods. For instance, when potatoes are processed into potato chips, they lose nearly all of their nutrients. In addition, their fat and sodium content increase. There are, however, some exceptions to the processing rule. For instance, when skim milk is processed to remove the fat found in whole milk, it becomes more healthful.

Fresh foods, such as fresh meat, poultry, eggs, and produce, have not been processed. In general, the closer a food is to its fresh state, the more nutritious it is likely to be. Fresh foods are often more economical than processed foods, too.

Some fresh foods take longer to prepare than processed foods. For instance, making spaghetti sauce from fresh tomatoes takes longer than opening a jar of ready-made sauce. On the other hand, a fresh peach requires no more time than a canned peach to make it ready to eat.

Shopping Tips for Fresh Foods

You will need to evaluate whether or not fresh foods will fit into your food budget and preparation plans. Whenever you feel fresh foods will meet your needs, the following tips can help you buy them:

- Choose a variety of fresh vegetables. They are high in fiber, vitamins, and minerals and low in fat. They are also lower in sodium than most canned vegetables.
- Choose a variety of fresh fruits. They are higher in fiber than fruit juices and lower in sugar than many canned and frozen fruits.
- Stock up on extra fresh fruits to eat as snacks. They can take the place of other snack foods that are higher in sugars, sodium, and fat.
- Look for lean cuts of meats, such as beef round steak, pork tenderloin, and leg of lamb. (For more information on meat cuts, see Chapter 13, "Meats.")
- Choose meats with little marbling and visible fat. Choose select grade meats when available.
- Choose fresh chicken and turkey often. Light meat pieces are lower in fat than dark meat pieces.
- Choose fresh fish and shellfish often. Most varieties are low in fat.
- Choose nuts and seeds less often as meat alternates. They are high in fat.

Shopping Tips for Processed Foods

When fresh foods will not fit into your meal management plans, you may decide to buy processed foods. Be aware that some processed foods are more nutritious than others. For instance, applesauce and a fried apple pie are both processed foods. The applesauce has less fiber and more sugar than fresh apples. However, it is lower in fat than the pie, which is more highly processed.

Processed foods have nutrition information on their label. Reading and comparing package labels can help you get the most healthful products available. Nutrition labeling can help you evaluate how a food fits with the Dietary Guidelines for Americans. You can use calorie information to help you maintain a healthy weight. Look at the calories per serving listed on a label. Consider these calories along with those in your other food choices. Then decide if eating the product will exceed your daily energy needs.

Look at the amounts of fat, sodium, and sugars listed on nutrition labels, too. Remember that the Guidelines suggest choosing a diet low in fat. They also recommend using sodium and sugars only in moderation. Suppose a label shows 18 g of fat, 456 mg of sodium, and 13 g of sugars per serving. This information tells you the food is fairly high in fat, sodium, and sugars. This does not mean you should not purchase the food. However, you will have to choose accompanying foods carefully to stay within recommended limits.

Nutritional labeling can help you compare similar products and different brands of the same product. Suppose you are choosing between a macaroni and cheese or a beef and broccoli frozen entree. Comparing labels can show you which product is lower in calories, fat, sodium, and sugars. Comparing labels can also tell you which product is higher in protein and listed vitamins and minerals. Perhaps you know you want macaroni and cheese, but you cannot decide which brand. Again, comparing the nutrition labels can help you make a healthful choice.

The following tips can also help you choose wisely when buying processed foods:

- Choose whole grain bread and cereal products to help you get plenty of fiber.
- Choose bread, English muffins, rice, and pasta often for lowfat, complex carbohydrates.
- Choose cakes, cookies, and doughnuts less often. They are high in fat and sugar and low in other nutrients.
- Check the labels on breakfast cereals carefully. Many are good sources of fiber. However, some are high in added sugar

and sodium. Granola-type cereals also tend to supply fat.

- Select regular and quick-cooking hot cereals instead of instant products, which tend to be much higher in sodium.
- When buying canned vegetables, choose no-salt-added products, when available.
- Choose fruits canned in juice or water. They are lower in sugar than those canned in syrup.
- Read labels on fruit juices to be sure they are 100 percent juice. Fruit drinks and punches tend to be high in added sugar and may not contain much juice.
- Choose beans, peas, and lentils often as lowfat, high-fiber alternates to meats, 3-6.
- Buy processed meats, like luncheon meats

3-6 Dried beans and lentils are a lowfat alternative to plain meat entrees.

and hot dogs, less often. They are high in fat and sodium.

- Choose canned fish products that are packed in water. They are lower in fat than those canned in oil.
- Choose nonfat or lowfat milk and yogurt. They are lower in fat than whole milk products.
- Choose reduced-fat versions of dairy products like sour cream and cheese.
- Choose lowfat frozen desserts, such as nonfat ice cream and frozen yogurt, instead of regular ice cream.
- Consider buying lowfat forms of salad dressings and mayonnaise.
- Read labels on soups, sauce mixes, and packaged entrees carefully. Many are high in sodium.
- Look for lighter versions of snack foods that are high in calories, fat, sugars, and sodium.
- Choose cookies that include fruit and whole grains, such as raisin oatmeal cookies. Avoid those containing more highly saturated fats.
- Look for a margarine that lists a liquid vegetable oil as the first ingredient. It will be lower in saturated fats than one listing partially hydrogenated oil first.

Choosing Wisely When Preparing Food

Making wise food choices at the grocery store is a good beginning to a healthful diet. However, the way you choose to prepare these foods greatly affects their nutritional quality.

Try to prepare foods from fresh food ingredients whenever time allows. Preparing foods from scratch gives you more control over what goes into them. You can decide how much fat to use when sautéing vegetables. You can decide when to omit salt or reduce sugar listed in a recipe. The ability to make these decisions can help you prepare foods in keeping with the Dietary Guidelines.

Start with the Main Course

Most meal managers plan meals around a main course, which is often a meat, poultry, or fish dish. A few pointers can help you prepare main courses that will get your meals off to a healthy start.

Healthy Living

Fat-free and reduced-fat products can make it easier for you to fit some foods into a healthful diet. As you consider purchasing these foods, however, be sure to read labels carefully. Some of them are higher in sodium and sugars than their high-fat counterparts. Also remember that reduced-fat products are not dietary cure-alls. Only a fraction of all food products are available in reduced-fat versions. Many other foods will continue to supply dietary fat that you cannot ignore.

When cooking meat and poultry, start lean. Trim all visible fat from meat. Remove the skin from poultry. These simple steps will reduce fat and calories.

You can use lowfat cooking methods to prepare tasty, nutritious entrees. Broiling, roasting, grilling, braising, stewing, stir-frying, and microwaving are all lowfat cooking methods. Use a rack when broiling or roasting to allow fats to drain. Avoid using basting sauces that are high in sugar, fat, or sodium when grilling and roasting. Add herbs to braising and stewing liquids to season them without salt. Use a nonstick skillet or wok to reduce your need for added fat when stir-frying. Try microwaving to save time as well as fat. (You will find more information about these cooking methods in Chapters 13, 14, and 15.)

Keep serving sizes in mind when preparing meat, poultry, and fish. You do not need a platter-sized steak or half a chicken to meet your protein needs. Remember, 2 to 3 ounces (56 to 84 g) of lean, cooked meat, poultry, or fish is a serving. A 3-ounce (84 g) portion is about the size of the palm of a woman's hand. See 3-7.

Rounding Out the Meal

After you have planned the main course, you can concentrate on other menu items. Keep in mind that not every food you eat must be low in calories, fat, sodium, and sugar. You can balance your food choices to create a total diet that is healthful. For instance, you can balance a high-fat entree, such as spareribs, with lowfat side dishes.

3-7 Two thin slices of cooked turkey is a full-sized portion.

Be a Clever Consumer

When shopping for a main course, consider buying legumes once in a while. These meat alternates are not only inexpensive, they are also high in fiber and low in fat.

You can also stretch your food dollars by mixing meat, poultry, and fish with grain products and vegetables. Casseroles and soups provide more carbohydrates, vitamins, minerals, and fiber than plain meat entrees. Make enough to serve as leftovers. Leftovers save money and heat up quickly for homemade meals in a hurry.

Likewise, if you want to serve a rich dessert, you might choose a lighter entree.

When evaluating your menu, do not forget about the items you serve with entrees and side dishes. Toppings and spreads used at the table can affect the nutritional value of foods. Items like sour cream, cream cheese, and jam can add fat, sugar, and calories.

Healthful Preparation Tips

Preparation methods can be as important as food choices when it comes to healthful eating. The following tips can help you reduce, replace, or omit ingredients that add fat, sugars, or sodium to foods:

- Avoid adding oil or salt to cooking water when preparing pasta.
- Use only half the amount of butter or margarine suggested when preparing packaged pasta, rice, stuffing, and sauce mixes.
- Use salad dressings, mayonnaise, sour cream, and cream cheese with moderation. Try reduced fat versions, or use plain nonfat yogurt in place of these products. You can season yogurt with herbs for tasty dressings and dips.
- Flavor vegetables with herbs and lemon juice instead of salt and butter.
- Omit salt from recipes calling for other sodium-containing ingredients, such as cheese or condensed soup.
- Reduce the amount of sugar listed in recipes for baked goods. Add vanilla or

spices, such as cinnamon, ginger, and cloves, to make these recipes seem sweeter.
- Dust cakes with powdered sugar instead of spreading them with frosting.
- Use skim or lowfat milk in place of whole milk in recipes. Use evaporated milk in place of cream, except for whipping.
- Use a gravy separator to make it easy to prepare gravies from meat drippings without the fat. See 3-8.
- Chill meat drippings and stocks. Then skim the fat that forms on the top before making gravies and soups.
- Reduce the number of egg yolks used in recipes for baked goods. They are high in cholesterol. Use two egg whites to replace one whole egg. Stretch portions of omelets and scrambled eggs by adding extra egg whites.

Choosing Wisely When Eating Out

Many people choose to eat out when they do not have the time or energy to cook at home. Others eat out as a form of entertainment. In either case, choosing wisely will allow foods eaten away from home to fit into a healthful diet.

You may not want to worry about nutritional value when you are dining out with friends. That's fine. There is nothing wrong with occasionally eating a high-fat, high-sodium meal in a restaurant. Simply balance this meal with other meals throughout the day that are lower in fat and sodium. Remember, your *total diet* is what matters.

Although you cannot control how restaurants prepare food, you can control what you order. The more varied a menu is, the easier it is to find healthful food options. You can keep this in mind when choosing a restaurant. Choosing a family restaurant is likely to give you more selection than a fast-food restaurant.

In any type of restaurant, menu terms can give you clues about the food you order. Many menu items are high in fat, sugars, and sodium. Watch out for buttered vegetables, fish broiled in butter, and pasta with butter sauce. Also be aware of items served with cream sauces, gravy, or cheese. Notice items that are breaded, fried, or wrapped in pastry, too. These items are all likely to be high in fat. Smoked, pickled, and barbecued items are likely to be high in sodium. Many soups and sauces are also high-sodium items.

Progressive International Corp.

3-8 A gravy separator makes it easy to separate the fat from meat juices for preparing lowfat gravies.

Keep in mind what you have learned about shopping for and preparing food when ordering food in restaurants. For health-conscious menu selections, choose foods prepared with lowfat cooking methods. Ask to have foods prepared without salt or butter. Ask to have high-fat sauces and dressings served on the side. You can add just enough to flavor, rather than smother, your food. Choose whole grain rolls, when they are available. Load up on fresh vegetable salads, but go easy on dressing and toppings like bacon bits and cheese. Opt for fresh fruits in place of rich pastries or heavy ice creams for dessert.

Remember that the amount of food you eat affects your fat, sodium, and sugar intake. Do not feel you have to be a member of the "clean plate club." You can always ask to have a take-home bag for food you do not finish. Ask for a petite or half-size portion. Consider ordering an appetizer instead of an entree. Split an entree with a friend. These are all ways to help keep yourself from overeating.

Keep in mind that foods eaten away from home are not always eaten in restaurants. Use the guidelines given above when choosing foods from vending machines and in the school cafeteria. They apply at the snack bar at the mall and the conces-sion stand at ball games, too. See 3-9.

Eating out, like shopping for and preparing food, requires you to use the principles of variety, moderation, and balance. Follow the Dietary Guidelines for Americans and choose the right number of servings from the Food Guide Pyramid. Make healthful eating a lifetime habit.

Good Manners Are Good Business

Sharing an entree is an option for light eating when dining with family members or friends. However, it is generally not appropriate at an important business meal. Sharing may be acceptable for casual business dining, but be sure to do it with finesse. Transfer a portion of the food being shared to your dining companion's plate before you begin eating. Eating off the same plate is definitely beyond the bounds of good manners.

3-9 Follow guidelines for making healthy food choices when eating in the school cafeteria.

Summary

A number of resources can help you make healthy food choices. The RDA suggest appropriate amounts of calories, protein, vitamins, and minerals for someone of your age and gender. The Dietary Guidelines for Americans provide advice for forming good eating habits. The Food Guide Pyramid tells you how many servings you should have from various groups of foods to meet your daily nutritional needs.

Using these resources, you can make informed choices when shopping for fresh and processed foods. You can also make wise decisions about how you prepare those foods. You can make nutritious selections when eating away from home, too.

Review What You Have Read

Write your answers on a separate sheet of paper.
1. What are three factors besides food choices that can affect your health?
2. List the seven Dietary Guidelines for Americans.
3. What is the recommended limit of daily calories people should consume from fat?
4. True or false. Following the Dietary Guidelines means giving up foods that are high in calories, fat, sugars, and/or sodium.
5. Name the five food groups in the Food Guide Pyramid and give the number of servings you should obtain from each group each day.
6. True or false. Foods in all groups of the Food Guide Pyramid may contain fats and sugars.
7. How does processing affect the nutritional value of foods?
8. List five tips to follow when shopping for fresh foods.
9. What should a consumer look for when buying fruit juice?
10. Name four lowfat cooking methods for preparing entrees.
11. How can you reduce the fat in gravies made from meat drippings?

12. Which of the following items on a restaurant menu is likely to be your best bet for a lowfat side dish?
    A. Mashed potatoes with gravy.
    B. Steamed broccoli with cheese sauce.
    C. French fries.
    D. Sliced tomatoes sprinkled with fresh herbs.

Build Your Basic Skills

1. Conduct library research to find out when the most recent revision of the RDA took place. Investigate what changes were made in that revision and the reasons for the changes. Share your findings in a brief oral report.
2. Work in a small group to design a pamphlet listing and explaining the Dietary Guidelines for Americans. Vote to choose the most creative pamphlet design in your class. Then make copies of the winning pamphlet and distribute them in the school cafeteria.
3. Give a food preparation demonstration showing a technique for reducing the calories, cholesterol, fat, sodium, or sugar in a food product.

Build Your Thinking Skills

1. Record all the foods you have eaten in one 24-hour period. Using the Food Guide Pyramid, determine whether you have met nutritional requirements for that day. If you have not, make a list of foods could you add to supply the missing nutrients.
2. Bring in two nutrition labels from similar processed foods, such as frozen entrees or breakfast cereals. Prepare a written comparison identifying the nutritional strengths and weaknesses of each product. Summarize your comparison with a paragraph stating which product you would prefer to buy. Give reasons for your choice.
3. Contact a local fast-food restaurant to request nutrition information about its menu items. Use this information to select a healthful meal from the restaurant's menu.

Good nutrition is important at all stages of the life cycle.

Chapter 4

Nutrition Through the Life Cycle

School Cafeteria Head Cook

Supervises and coordinates activities of workers engaged in preparing, cooking, and serving food in one or more school cafeterias or a central school district kitchen.

Dietary Aide

Prepares and delivers food trays to hospital patients, performing any combination of duties on tray line.

Reducing-Salon Attendant

Measures, weighs, and records patrons' body statistics; refers information to supervisor for evaluation and planning of exercise program; and demonstrates exercises and use of equipment.

Terms to Know

diet
growth spurt
fitness
vegetarian diet
medical diet
weight management

overweight
obesity
underweight
anorexia nervosa
bulimia nervosa

Objectives

After studying this chapter, you will be able to
   plan a well-balanced diet for yourself and for other people in different stages of the life cycle.
   discuss the importance of exercise in maintaining a suitable level of fitness.
   identify factors that contribute to weight problems and eating disorders.
   explain the philosophy behind weight management.

Little Kids, Inc.

A person's *diet* is all the food and drink he or she regularly consumes. Each stage of a person's life cycle is affected by his or her diet. From the prenatal period to old age, each stage has different nutritional needs. Poor nutrition in any stage may create health problems, shorten the life span, or both.

Nutrition During Pregnancy and Lactation

Diet during pregnancy affects both the mother and the fetus. Good nutrition is especially important during pregnancy. This is because the mother nourishes the fetus through her body. The foods the mother eats must supply the nutrient needs of the fetus. Otherwise, nutrients for the fetus may be taken from the mother's tissues. This could cause the mother to suffer deficiencies. See 4-1.

Nutrient deficiencies can especially be a problem in the case of teenage pregnancies. Teen mothers need high levels of nutrients to support their own growth. Deficiencies could negatively affect a teenage mother's development as well as the development of her baby.

A woman should strive to be well nourished and form good food habits before becoming pregnant. If she reaches this goal, she probably will not need to make any major changes in her diet during pregnancy. In most cases, eating more of the foods she is accustomed to eating will meet her added nutrient needs. However, the woman who is not well nourished before becoming pregnant may have borderline deficiencies. With the strain of pregnancy, these deficiencies can become apparent.

Special Needs During Pregnancy

During the first three months of pregnancy, the daily nutrient needs of the fetus are small. A normal, well-balanced diet should meet the needs of a well-nourished woman.

By the beginning of the second trimester, needs for almost all of the essential nutrients increase. Some of the extra nutrients are needed to build the child's tissues. Others are needed to protect the mother.

Evenflo Products Company, Inc.

4-1 Eating a good diet during pregnancy will help a woman give her baby a healthy start in life.

Protein, calcium, and iron are especially important during pregnancy. The mother needs increased amounts of protein to support the growth of the fetus. When the diet does not supply enough protein, the protein needed by the fetus is taken from the mother's tissues. The fetus needs calcium for well-formed bones and strong teeth. Iron needs are especially large during the last six months of pregnancy. Milk, the baby's main source of nourishment after birth, is not a good source of iron. Thus, the baby must build up iron reserves before birth. If the mother already has low iron reserves, she may become anemic toward the end of her pregnancy.

Diet During Pregnancy

A pregnant woman should follow a well-balanced diet consisting of a variety of foods. She should build the diet around the Food Guide Pyramid. If the woman's diet was adequate before pregnancy, a simple modification is all she should need. She should add one glass of milk and one extra serving of leafy green vegetables. She would be wise to choose fruits instead of rich desserts. She should also substitute organ meats for other meats, poultry, and fish once in a while.

Depending on the health of the woman, the obstetrician may prescribe vitamin and mineral supplements. For instance, a woman may take iron during pregnancy. This is because a woman's iron reserves often are low. She may also take folic acid to help prevent certain birth defects. A pregnant woman should never take vitamin and mineral supplements without consulting her doctor. Too many vitamins and minerals can be harmful to the developing fetus.

During pregnancy, the average woman gains about 25 to 35 pounds. However, weight gain and energy needs vary from woman to woman. A pregnant woman should be neither overweight nor underweight. An obstetrician will suggest a suitable weight gain. The obstetrician will also specify the number of calories (kilojoules) required daily to meet increased energy needs.

Drugs and Other Medications During Pregnancy

Drugs and over-the-counter medications like aspirin taken by a pregnant woman can pass through the placenta. (The *placenta* is an organ that nourishes the developing child in the mother's womb.) Many drugs can have an adverse effect on a developing fetus. A pregnant woman should never take *any* medication except under the advice of her obstetrician.

Special Needs During Lactation

During *lactation* (the production of breast milk), a woman has increased energy, protein, mineral, and vitamin needs. The woman needs these extra nutrients to replace the nutrients secreted in the milk. She also needs them to cover the energy cost of producing the milk and to protect her body.

Diet During Lactation

The diets of a lactating woman and a pregnant woman are similar. However, the lactating woman's needs for some nutrients are greater.

Nutritionists recommend a diet that is high in energy. Lactating women should be sure to get an adequate number of servings from each of the food groups each day. They should increase fluid intake to 2 to 3 quarts (2 to 3 L) each day. Lactating women need fluids to provide water in the milk and to meet their own needs.

Drugs and Other Medications During Lactation

More than nutrients pass into a mother's milk. Alcohol and other drugs can pass to a baby through breast milk. For this reason, lactating mothers should not drink alcohol. They should also avoid taking medications, except under a doctor's advice. See 4-2.

Nutrition in Infancy and Early Childhood

Infants and preschool children need good nutrition to grow and develop normally. Food is more important during the first year of life than at any other time in the life cycle.

Nutrient Needs of the Infant

At birth, a baby has no reserves of needed nutrients (except for iron). However, his or her nutrient requirements per unit of body weight are higher than the needs of an adult.

Growth patterns vary, but an infant's rate of growth is fastest during the first few months of life. During the first three months, a normal, healthy infant will gain about 1 ounce (28 g) a day. This is about 2 pounds (910 g) a month. The growth rate then slows to about 1 pound (454 g) a month. By the end of the first year, the infant's weight has almost tripled. His or her length is one and one-half times the birth length.

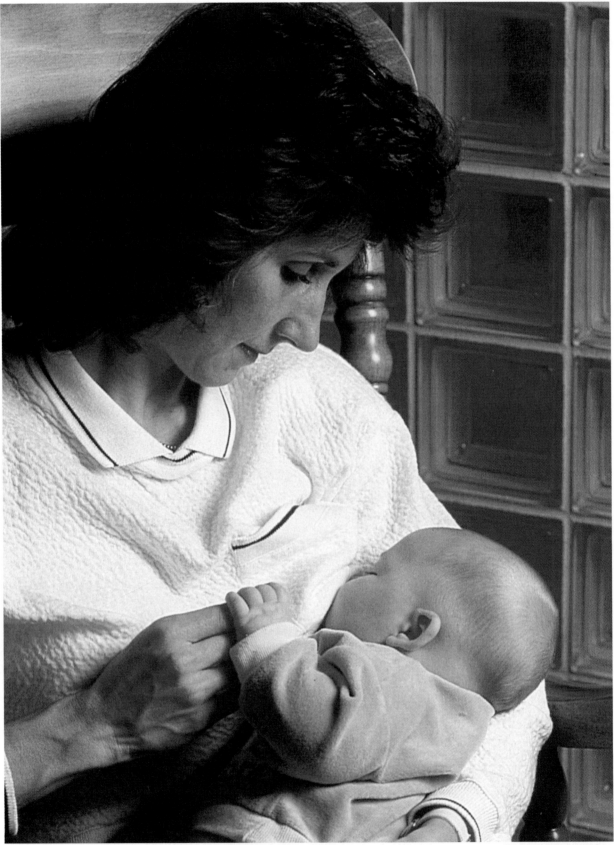

4-2 A woman must avoid using alcohol and other drugs while she is breast-feeding because she can pass these substances to her baby.

Energy needs vary somewhat, depending on the baby. The RDA for energy for the first six months of life is 108 calories (450 kJ) per kilogram of body weight. A 7 pound (3.2 kg) baby would require about 350 calories (1,500 kJ) per day. Energy needs decrease slightly at six months of age.

Sufficient fat, carbohydrates, protein, calcium, sodium, iodine, and vitamin A are found in human milk and cow's milk formulas. Both are low in iron. However, a full-term baby should have enough reserve iron to last for the first three months of life. This is especially true when the baby's mother has had good iron reserves.

Both infants and young children often receive a supplemental source of vitamin D because of their rapid growth. Infants usually need vitamin C soon after birth. They often obtain it by drinking apple juice.

Feeding Infants

Milk is an infant's most important food. A baby may be breast-fed or formula-fed. See 4-3.

Many experts recommend that mothers breast-feed their infants. Breast milk is easy for a baby to digest. It contains immune substances that help a baby resist infection. It also helps protect the baby from allergies. Human milk contains more lactose (milk sugar), iron, vitamin C, and vitamin A per unit of volume than cow's milk.

Commercial formulas are available for mothers who choose not to breast-feed their infants. Some of these are made with cow's milk, which contains more protein, calcium, phosphorus, riboflavin, and thiamin than breast milk. When cow's milk is used for infant formulas, it usually is diluted. Lactose, cane sugar, or corn syrup is added. These modifications make cow's milk more like human milk.

Commercial formulas vary somewhat in composition. Pediatricians can recommend formulas suited to a particular infant.

Parents usually feed newborns seven or eight times a day. Gradually, they decrease feedings to five times a day by the time the infant is two months old. The total amount of milk varies from infant to infant. Most infants will drink about 1 quart (1 L) of milk each day.

Nutritionally, babies do not need more than milk until they are five or six months old. In the United States, however, parents often introduce their babies to solid foods much earlier. Many babies begin eating cereals when they are about three months old.

The transition from milk to solid foods is gradual. Parents may introduce pureed fruits and vegetables into their babies' diets after cereals. They often follow these with strained meats, poultry, and simple desserts. Parents can purchase strained foods or prepare them at home with a blender.

Most pediatricians tell parents to start with a small amount of just one new food at a time. Parents should feed the baby the same food several times in a row. This will enable the parent to see if the food agrees with the infant. See 4-3.

As infants begin to eat solid foods, their need and desire for milk will decrease. Sometime between the ages of eight months and one year, infants can begin to drink milk out of a cup. Parents can add chopped foods to a child's diet by his or her first birthday. As their teeth appear, babies will enjoy chewing on crackers and zwieback.

Nutrient Needs of the Preschool Child

Growth is slower between the ages of two and six than it is during the first year of life. However, growth is still quite rapid. As toddlers and preschoolers grow, they become taller and thinner.

Nutrient needs vary from child to child, depending on growth and activity. The diet should supply enough calories (kilojoules) for a continuous weight gain. The amount of weight a child gains should fit his or her normal rate of development.

A diet consisting of foods from the Food Guide Pyramid should supply sufficient nutrients. The child's pediatrician will determine if he or she needs additional vitamins and minerals.

Meals for Preschoolers

Preschool children often have unpredictable eating habits. They have definite likes and dislikes. The likes and dislikes of family members can influence them, too.

Parents can encourage eating by keeping the preschooler's likes and dislikes in mind at mealtime. Most preschool children tend to like foods that are mild flavored, soft, and lukewarm. Finger foods, bright colors, and small portions also appeal to them. A pleasant eating atmosphere with a chair, table, and eating utensils that are the right size can encourage good eating. Most pediatricians agree that parents should not force children to eat. Often if children will not eat at one meal, they will make up for it at another.

When planning meals for a preschooler, follow the Food Guide Pyramid. Some children will not drink the recommended 2 cups (500 mL) of milk. In these cases, parents can feed children more foods prepared with milk. Some toddlers would

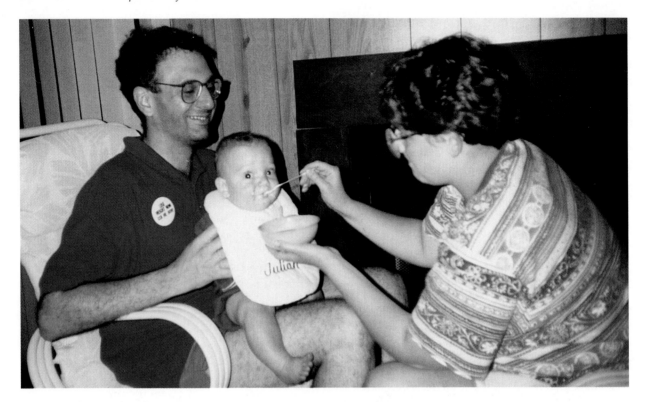

4-3 Most parents introduce their child to solid foods gradually to be sure the food agrees with the child.

rather eat five or six small meals than three large meals. Begin with small portions and add more as needed. How and when children consume food is not important. What is important is that each day's diet include all the necessary nutrients.

Nutrition in the Elementary School Years

During the elementary school years, children grow at a fairly steady rate. Between the ages of 6 and 12, children develop many of the food habits they will carry with them throughout life. Parents can promote healthy attitudes about good nutrition by setting good examples. They should encourage their children to try new foods. However, parents should refrain from using food as a punishment or a reward.

Nutritional Needs of School-Age Children

A six-year-old child does not need as much food as a 12-year-old child. However, both children need the same kinds of food. The amount of food a child needs depends on his or her growth rate and physical activity. Normally, a child's appetite is a fairly reliable indication of energy needs.

The school-age child should eat foods from all of the food groups. The foods selected should contain high proportions of proteins, vitamins, and minerals to promote growth and development. Many young school-age children prefer simple, familiar foods that are mild in flavor and easy to handle. As children grow older, their food tastes gradually change. They will eat larger servings and enjoy a greater variety of foods.

Planning Meals for School-Age Children

A school-age child's nutritional needs begin with breakfast. Breakfast should supply about one-fourth of the day's total nutrients. Children who skip breakfast do not obtain nutrients when the body needs them most—after a night without food. Studies have shown that children who eat breakfast do better in school than children who skip breakfast.

Children can eat any nutritious food for breakfast. Breakfast does not have to include traditional breakfast foods. A bowl of tomato soup, a grilled cheese sandwich, or a hamburger is just as nutritious at breakfast as it is at lunch or dinner.

A school-age child's lunch should supply about one-third of the total nutritional needs each day. It should contain foods from each of the food groups. Children can often purchase milk at school, or they can carry it in a thermos. See 4-4.

Dinner should supply about one-third of the day's total nutritional needs. The basic meal pattern for a school-age child's dinner is similar to the lunch pattern. A simple dessert, such as pudding or fruit, often is added.

Many school-age children have trouble eating enough at meals to meet their nutritional needs. Snacks can provide added nutrients. Most children like fresh fruit, fruit-flavored yogurt, raw vegetables, cheese cubes, custard, raisins, and crackers with peanut butter.

Childhood Obesity

An *obese* child has more than the normal amount of body fat. Obesity is common among children. Children do not have the decision-making skills to make wise lifestyle choices. Therefore, parents have to help obese children manage their weight. Otherwise, obese children are likely to become obese adults.

Parents may begin to address a child's weight problem by encouraging the child to be more active. They can provide healthy snacks, such as fresh fruit and pretzels, to help the child avoid empty calories. These steps will help slow a child's weight gain. In time, his or her growth will catch up to the excess weight.

Parents should consult a dietitian before making major changes in a child's diet. Children need a well-balanced diet to support growth. Restricting foods may result in a lack of important nutrients.

GE Plastics

4-4 School-age children need a healthy lunch to give them energy in the middle of the day.

Nutrition in the Teen Years

All teenagers undergo a *growth spurt.* This is a period of rapid growth that varies in intensity and length from person to person. Boys usually experience it between the ages of 12 and 17. Girls experience it somewhat earlier, usually between the ages of 10 and 14.

During the growth spurt, teens of both sexes need more energy. Teenage girls need about 2,200 calories (9,200 kJ) per day. Teenage boys need about 2,800 calories (11,750 kJ) per day. Teens need more of other nutrients, too. They need the same amount of protein, minerals, and vitamins as adults. However, U.S. dietary studies show that many teens do not get enough calcium, iron, vitamin A, and vitamin C. Busy schedules, skipped meals, reducing diets, and junk foods make it difficult for teens to meet their daily nutrient needs.

Teenage boys often have fewer nutritional deficiencies than teenage girls. They have good appetites, and their energy needs are larger. As a result, they eat more. Teenage girls are generally more weight conscious. When eating smaller amounts of food, it is even more important to choose nutritious foods. However, the smaller amounts of food eaten by teenage girls often are low in nutritive value.

Planning Meals for Teens

The family meal pattern should be satisfactory for teenagers. Teens can increase portion sizes where needed to supply additional energy, protein, and iron.

The busy lifestyles of many teens make snacks an important part of the total meal plan. Snacks often count for one-fourth of a teen's total daily calorie intake. Thus, nutritious snacks are especially important.

Fresh fruit, juices, cheese, yogurt, fresh vegetables, and sandwiches make nutritious snacks, 4-5. Cookies made with whole wheat flour and oatmeal, raisins, or nuts add nutrients and satisfy the desire for sweets.

Acne

Acne often appears during the teen years. In the past, some people thought greasy foods, chocolate, and cola drinks caused acne. Studies have not shown a link between these foods and acne. However, other foods are connected to this

4-5 Yogurt, fresh fruit, and cereal bars make nutritious snacks for teens.

troubling disorder. Foods rich in iodine, including beef liver, broccoli, asparagus, and white onions, can contribute to acne. Nutritional supplements containing iodine may promote acne, too.

Keeping your skin and hair clean is one of your best defenses against acne. Also avoid touching your face, limit sun exposure, and avoid oil-based creams and lotions. Of course, eating a balanced diet can help you have healthy skin, too. If you have problems with acne, over-the-counter cleansers and medications may provide relief. Consult a dermatologist if you have a severe or persistent problem.

Adolescent Obesity

Obesity is common among adolescents, just as it is among children. Unlike children, however, teens have the decision-making skills needed to manage their weight. They can learn to make healthy food choices. They can include exercise in their weekly activities. They can also learn how to handle situations that might prompt them to overeat.

The information on weight management found later in this chapter applies to teens as well as adults. Teens who are striving to apply this information to their lives should ask family members for support. Family support will increase a teen's success in following a weight management plan. Family members may also be encouraged to adopt weight management principles in their lives.

Nutrition for Athletes

Many teens are actively involved in sports, dance, and other physically demanding activities. Nutrition plays an important role in the performance of these teens.

Gone are the days when knowledgeable trainers and coaches encourage athletes to eat a big steak dinner before a game. A plate of spaghetti might be more likely on today's training tables. Why the switch? One reason is that trainers once thought athletes needed the protein from the steak for energy. Although athletes do need protein, they need it for growth and repair of muscle tissue—not for energy! That's why the spaghetti makes a better pre-game meal. It is an excellent source of complex carbohydrates—an athlete's main energy source. Another reason to avoid the steak is that it is high in fat. Fat stays in the stomach longer, so energy needed to compete ends up being used for digestion.

One nutrient about which athletes need to be concerned is water. Athletes lose a lot of water through sweat when they are training and competing. They need to drink water before, during, and after events to replace these losses. Without enough water, athletes can become dehydrated, causing their performance and their health to suffer.

Some athletes choose sports drinks to replace their fluid losses. Sports drinks contain sodium to replace sodium lost through sweat. Sports drinks also contain sugars to give athletes a boost of energy. The truth is, a normal diet can easily meet sodium needs. Excess sodium in sports drinks just makes the kidneys work harder to eliminate it. Sugars seem to help only endurance athletes, such as marathon runners. Sugars in sports drinks are just a source of empty calories for people engaged in less strenuous exercise. Some sports drinks actually pull fluids from body tissues to dilute the salts and sugars they contain. Therefore, many exercise physiologists feel that plain water is a better choice for active teens.

Athletes have some other special nutrient needs besides water. Their high level of activity increases the need for calories. Most of these calories, 60 to 65 percent, should come from complex carbohydrates. Breads, cereals, pasta, rice, and starchy vegetables are all excellent sources of complex carbohydrates. Choosing lean meats, poultry, and fish will supply an athlete's slightly increased need for protein. Lowfat dairy products provide needed calcium. Fresh fruits and vegetables furnish vitamins, minerals, and fiber.

If the above diet sounds familiar, it's not a coincidence. Like less active teens, athletes can meet their nutrient needs by following the Food Guide Pyramid. Athletes should avoid nutrient supplements unless they are being taken on the advice of a dietitian. These costly supplements are not always what they claim to be. Tests have shown some products to be ineffective, or even harmful.

Healthy Living

If you are an athlete, there is an easy way to determine your water needs. Weigh yourself before and after workouts. You should drink 2 cups (500 mL) of water for each pound of weight you lose.

bone tissue weigh more than fat tissue. These factors explain why two people may be the same height, but have different weights. The person with greater muscle mass and heavier bones will have the higher weight. However, what concerns health experts most is the amount of weight attributed to fat tissue.

You can use a *height-weight table* to see if your weight falls within the appropriate range for your height. However, falling within the right range is no guarantee that your weight is healthy. The weight ranges in such a table are wide to account for varying body composition. The high end of the range is for people who have more muscle mass and heavier bones. Most men meet this description. Someone who has low muscle mass, but falls at the high end of the range may have excess body fat. See 4-10.

One way to evaluate whether you have too much body fat is the pinch test. The *pinch test* measures the amount of fat stored below the skin. The back of the upper arm is the best spot for taking this test. Simply grasp a fold of skin between your thumb and forefinger. A fold that measures more than an inch (2.5 cm) thick is often a sign of excess fat.

Healthy Weight Ranges[1]

Height[2]	Weight in Pounds[3]
5'0"	97-128
5'1"	101-132
5'2"	104-137
5'3"	107-141
5'4"	111-146
5'5"	114-150
5'6"	118-155
5'7"	121-160
5'8"	125-164
5'9"	129-169
5'10"	132-174
5'11"	136-179
6'0"	140-184
6'1"	144-189
6'2"	148-195
6'3"	152-200
6'4"	156-205
6'5"	160-211
6'6"	164-216

[1] For people ages 19 to 34 years.
[2] Without shoes.
[3] Without clothes.

Derived from National Research Council, 1989

4-10 Height-weight tables can help you determine whether your weight is healthy.

Appearance is another indication of weight problems. A roll around the midsection or heavy hips and thighs are signs of overweight.

The degree to which a person exceeds the healthy weight for his or her height and body composition identifies weight problems. A person who exceeds the healthy weight by 10 percent has a condition called **overweight.** A person who exceeds the healthy weight by 20 percent or more has a condition called **obesity.**

Hazards of Being Obese

Obesity is a danger to health. *Hypertension* (abnormally high blood pressure), diabetes, heart disease, cancer, and other diseases are more common among obese people. Records of life insurance companies show that obese people die at an earlier age than nonobese people. Some insurance companies view obese people as "high risk" and charge them higher rates.

Too much weight puts a strain on the body's bones, muscles, heart, and other organs. A thick layer of fat interferes with the body's natural cooling system. Overweight people use more effort to walk and breathe.

Obese people also face social pressures. The fashion industry focuses little attention on designs for larger sizes. Television and magazines promote the image that being attractive means being thin. Some employers hesitate to hire obese people for certain jobs.

Factors That Contribute to Overeating

People can be overweight for several reasons. Some people are overweight because of medical problems. However, most people are overweight because they eat more than their bodies need and they do not get enough exercise.

People overeat for both social and emotional reasons. People associate food with social occasions. Many people keep snacks on hand to serve guests. They go out to dinner with friends. They plan large meals for holidays.

Food marketing encourages people to eat. Advertisements on billboards, television, and radio and in newspapers and magazines all encourage eating. Restaurants, supermarkets, vending machines, and refreshment stands at movie theaters and sports arenas are other temptations. See 4-11.

Courtesy of Service America Corporation

4-11 Vending machines make food readily available in schools, businesses, and shopping and entertainment centers.

People eat to fill emotional needs. Strong emotions, such as anger, frustration, depression, and even extreme happiness, cause overeating. Some people eat because they are happy. Other people eat because they are sad. Some people reward themselves with food. Others find security in food.

Some people eat because of habit. They may be used to having a snack before bed. Even though they are not hungry, habit will cause them to have a snack.

Deciding to Lose Weight

If height-weight tables and the pinch test indicate that you are overweight, you may decide you want to lose weight. Losing weight will bring you a number of benefits. You will be able to buy clothes in smaller sizes. Other people may praise your will power. You are also likely to have more energy and a more positive self-concept.

Although all of these benefits are worthwhile, try to focus on the impact of weight loss on your overall health. To successfully lose weight, you must want to lose weight. You should base this desire on more than wanting to fit into a new outfit. Efforts to

lose weight are most successful when they are part of a lifelong commitment to maintain good health.

Once you have decided to lose weight, you might want to see a dietitian. A dietitian can help you design a weight management plan suited to your individual needs. The dietitian might also recommend a vitamin-mineral supplement.

Most successful weight-loss plans involve three main components: changing poor eating habits, controlling energy intake, and increasing physical activity.

Identifying Eating Habits

One of the first steps in losing weight is to keep a *food log*. This is a list of all the foods you eat. You should also note where you ate, who you were with, and how you felt when eating. Keep this list for at least a week. Studying it will help you discover some of your eating habits. For instance, you may find that you snack only in front of the television. You may also learn that you eat when feeling sad, frustrated, or nervous.

Once you identify some of your eating habits, you can take steps to change them. If you idly snack while watching television, try keeping your hands busy with an activity instead of with food. If you eat when nervous, try taking a brisk walk instead of eating. If you eat when feeling lonely, call a friend when the urge to nibble strikes.

Controlling Energy Intake

Weight management involves being aware of the energy value of the foods you eat. The amount of energy the body receives from food is measured in calories. The body needs the energy obtained from the foods you eat to function. However, if you eat more calories than your body uses, you will gain weight.

The number of calories your body needs each day to maintain your present weight is called your *daily calorie need*. This need depends on your sex, age, size, body composition, and level of activity. Men usually need more calories than women. (This is partly because they are larger.) Teens need more calories than adults, and young adults need more calories than older adults. A large person needs more calories each day than a small person. An active person needs more calories than an inactive person.

Your daily calorie need must account for your basal metabolism and your activity level. Your body needs about 10 calories per pound (.45 kg) to support basal metabolism. You need additional calories to give you energy for activities. Figure about 5 calories per pound (.45 kg) if you are sedentary; 10 calories per pound (.45 kg) if you are moderately active. Therefore, a moderately active 120 pound (54 kg) woman would need about 2400 calories per day (120 pounds × 20 calories/pound = 2400 calories). A 160 pound (72 kg) sedentary man would also need about 2400 calories per day (160 pounds × 15 calories/pound = 2400 calories).

To lose weight, you must consume fewer calories than your daily calorie need. You will want to remember that 1 pound (.45 kg) of fat equals about 3,500 calories. To lose 1 pound (.45 kg) a week, you would need to increase the difference between your energy intake and expenditure by 3,500 calories. This is roughly 500 calories a day. You should make this adjustment through a combination of reduced calories and increased physical activity.

Losing a pound (.45 kg) a week may not bring you to your goal weight as soon as you had hoped. However, losing weight too quickly can strain your body systems. You may deprive yourself of needed nutrients if you eat too little food. You will also be more successful in maintaining your weight goal if you lose weight slowly. Most experts recommend a steady weight loss at the rate of fi to 1 pound (.23 to .45 kg) per week. After all, you did not gain your excess weight in a week. Therefore, you should not expect to lose it in a week.

Food labels and recipes can help you keep track of the calories you eat. Packaged food products and many recipes list the number of calories per serving. Be aware of the stated serving size. Many people cannot understand why they do not lose weight when they are following a weight management plan. Often, the problem is that they misjudge portion sizes. When you begin following your weight-loss plan, you may find it helpful to measure portions. Soon you will become familiar with what a cup (250 mL), half cup (125 mL), or tablespoon (15 mL) portion looks like.

You should also be aware of the amount of fat in the foods you eat. Again, food labels and recipes can help you keep track. A gram of fat contains more than twice as many calories as a gram of carbohydrate or protein. Therefore, calories can add up quickly when you are eating high-fat foods. See 4-12.

Health experts recommend that no more than 30 percent of your daily calories come from fat. An easy way to figure your daily limit for fat grams is to divide your weight in half. In other words, a 150 pound person would have a daily limit of about 75 grams of fat (150 ÷ 2 = 75). If you are moderately active, you can add a few extra grams of fat. If you are trying to lose weight, you should decrease your daily limit of fat by at least 10 grams.

Increasing Physical Activity

Watching your food intake is only part of a weight management plan. You also need to get plenty of exercise. Regular exercise speeds up metabolism, promotes good muscle tone, and burns calories.

Check with your doctor to be sure there are no restrictions to the type of activity you might pursue. Then choose an activity that you enjoy. You may want to participate in a sport. Perhaps you would prefer to join an aerobics class. The kind of exercise is not as important as its regularity.

Chart 4-13 can help you see the effect physical activity can have on weight management. Just four or five hours of moderate activity each week would burn half of your 3,500 calorie weekly reduction goal.

Along with planned exercise, try to build extra movement into your daily routine. Take the stairs instead of riding the elevator. Play ball with a friend instead of watching TV.

4-12 Once you adopt weight management as a lifestyle, you will quickly learn how to prepare delicious, lowfat foods.

Tips for Success

If you have a goal to lose weight, your weight management plan should meet several criteria. It should include as many of your favorite foods as possible. It should provide a variety of choices. It should be nutritious and fit into your food budget.

Do not avoid all of your favorite high-calorie foods when you are working to lose weight. If you feel as if you are being deprived, you may give up on your weight management plan. Simply learn to enjoy your favorites less often and in smaller portions. Go out for pizza once a week instead of twice a week. Try settling for 5 French fries instead of 10.

Avoid fad diets that focus on just a few foods or omit certain groups of foods. These plans lack variety and are not nutritionally balanced. You are likely to become bored with these diets and stop following them. If you do stick with them, you may be missing important nutrients. In addition,

Calories and Activity

Activity	Calories Burned in 1 Hour for Person Weighing	
	120 Pounds	150 Pounds
basketball, half-court	255	300
bicycling	178	210
bowling	176	208
calisthenics	263	310
dance, exercise	289	340
golf	212	250
hiking	255	300
horseback riding	204	240
jogging, 5½ mph	552	650
racquetball	510	600
running, 10 mph	765	900
skating	297	350
skiing, cross-country	595	700
skiing, downhill	510	600
softball, slow	246	290
swimming, fast	530	630
swimming, slow	272	320
tennis	357	420
walking	178	210
weight training	399	470

Data from Corbin C, Lindsey R. *The Ultimate Fitness Book.* Champaign, Ill: Leisure Press; 1984.

4-13 An activity chart tells you the number of calories your body uses each hour when doing different activities.

Protect the Planet

Whenever possible, walk or ride a bicycle to get where you need to go. These activities help you stay in shape and burn calories (roughly 400 calories per hour). They also save energy over taking a car.

these diets do not help you form good eating habits. Therefore, when you go off these diets you are likely to regain the weight you lost.

A weight-loss plan should include at least the minimum number of servings from each group in the Food Guide Pyramid. This will ensure that you obtain needed nutrients. You can choose foods from each group that are lower in fat and sugar. For example, skim milk can replace whole milk. You can select canned fruits packed in juice instead of fruits packed in syrup. You can substitute toast for doughnuts. Plain vegetables can replace creamed vegetables. Lean meats can replace heavily marbled meats.

When working to reduce weight, try using a smaller plate to make portions look larger. Eat slowly and chew food thoroughly to extend the length of the meal. Use herbs and spices to add variety to foods.

Avoid weighing yourself more than once a week. Your goal is a gradual weight loss. Checking your weight too often may cause you to feel discouraged.

When you are trying to lose weight, the first few pounds may come off rather quickly. (This initial loss is usually due to water loss.) However, weight loss is seldom steady. Plateaus during which you may seem to make little or no progress are normal. Do not be discouraged—be patient!

When working toward a lower weight goal, you should not skip any meal. In fact, you may want to eat extra meals. Eating six small meals each day rather than three large meals will increase your metabolic rate. It will also reduce your chances of overeating.

Do not allow your weight management plan to turn you into a hermit. Skipping holiday meals or trips to the ice cream shop may help you resist the temptation to eat high-calorie foods. However, you may also start to resent your weight-loss plan and give up completely. When a special occasion arises, feel free to attend. Simply eat moderate portions of the foods that are offered, just as you would at any other meal.

You do not have to avoid eating in restaurants as long as you make sensible food choices. Choose fruit or vegetable juice for an appetizer. Pass up salad dressings, gravies, and rich sauces. Avoid fried menu items and ask to have vegetables served unbuttered. Select fresh fruit for dessert, 4-14.

You are not a failure if you stuff yourself at the class picnic or eat five candy bars for lunch. Everyone makes unwise choices now and then. Turn your mistake into a learning experience. Continuing to keep the food log you used to identify your eating habits can help you avoid repeating your mistake. Think about what might have caused you to overeat. Then try to avoid that situation in the future.

Reward yourself when you reach intermediate goals in your weight management plan. Set realistic intermediate goals that present a challenge. Choose nonfood rewards that are meaningful to you. For instance, if you stick to your exercise plan all week, you might reward yourself with a trip to the movies. If you avoid unplanned snacking, you might reward yourself with a new CD.

4-14 Colorful and refreshing fresh fruits can replace high calorie foods in a weight management plan.

Maintaining Healthy Weight

Once you have reached your goal weight, you can begin eating at, rather than below, your daily calorie need. This does not mean you can abandon your weight management plan. Remember, weight management is part of your lifestyle. Maintaining this lifestyle will help you continue to enjoy food in a whole new way.

Keep practicing moderation and balance as you make food choices. You can slightly increase portion sizes or choose an extra food now and then. Follow the Food Guide Pyramid to make nutritious selections. Maintain the limit of 30 percent of calories from fat. Continue your program of physical activity, too.

Underweight

People in some jobs may want to be slightly below healthy weight. Jockeys and fashion models, for instance, often weight slightly less than their healthy weight. They exercise and watch their calorie intake to maintain their weight.

Unlike jockeys and fashion models, people who are underweight may have a health problem. *Underweight* is a condition whereby a person weighs 10 percent less than the healthy weight for his or her height and body composition. Not eating enough food to meet the body's needs can cause a person to be underweight. An inability to use food properly or a stressful environment can also cause underweight.

People who are chronically underweight often suffer from more infections. They tire easily and feel cold even when the temperature is moderate. Wearing swimsuits and other figure-revealing clothes may embarrass them.

Following a Weight-Gain Plan

Before trying to gain weight, an underweight person should see a physician. The physician will find out if there are any medical reasons the person's body is not using the food it receives. If emotional problems are causing the weight problems, a physician may be able to recommend a therapist.

A weight management plan for gaining weight should provide more energy than the body needs. An extra 500 calories per day will lead to a weight gain of about a pound (.45 kg) a week. Someone trying to gain weight should select foods from the Food Guide Pyramid. He or she can select more foods from each food group and increase portion sizes.

People trying to gain weight should choose foods that will provide nutrients as well as calories. For instance, cheese, nuts, and dried fruits are nutritious as well as calorie dense. Therefore, they would work well in a weight-gain plan. Fats should still make up no more than 30 percent of total calories.

Underweight people may have trouble eating large quantities of food. Therefore, they need to consume calories in more concentrated forms. They can add nonfat dry milk to soups, baked goods, sauces, and cooked cereals. It adds nutrition and additional calories without adding bulk. Starchy vegetables, such as peas, potatoes, and corn, contain more calories per serving than non-starchy vegetables.

Sometimes drinking calories is easier than eating them. Some people use nutrient-loaded drinks in place of meals to lose weight. People trying to gain weight can use these drinks in addition to meals. They can use delicious shakes made with fruit and yogurt in the same way. See 4-15.

Underweight people can increase their calorie intake by eating small meals every few hours throughout the day. Nutritious snacks are also a good way to add calories.

The goal of a weight-gain plan should not be a rapid weight gain. Rapid gains usually are the result of increased fat deposits. Instead, people trying to gain weight need to build up muscle tissue. High quality proteins, found in meat, fish, poultry, and eggs, help cause gradual weight gain and muscle development. Regular exercise helps build muscle tissues further.

California Apricot Advisory Board

4-15 Delicious frozen desserts and beverages made with yogurt and fresh fruit are easy to eat and drink. They may help people who are trying get extra calories and nutrients in their diet.

Eating Disorders

An *eating disorder* is not a weight problem. It is a type of mental illness that affects a person's food habits. Eating disorders can result in malnutrition, a life-threatening illness, or even death.

Doctors do not know what causes eating disorders. However, some type of personal stress often triggers them. The disorders become sources of more stress. They tend to progress until the victims feel unable to handle their problems.

Eating disorders most often affect women and teenage girls. Two common eating disorders are anorexia nervosa and bulimia nervosa.

Anorexia nervosa is an eating disorder characterized by self-starvation. People with anorexia have a distorted body image. They may look like skin and bones, yet they complain that they are fat.

Starvation causes some body processes to slow down or stop. Blood pressure drops and respiration slows. Hormone secretions become abnormal. The body cannot absorb nutrients properly. Body temperature drops and sensitivity to cold increases. Anorexic women stop menstruating. The heart cannot function correctly, and in some cases it may stop entirely.

Bulimia nervosa is an eating disorder characterized by repeated eating binges. These binges are followed by purging via vomiting or taking laxatives or diuretics. Bulimia is often called the *binge-purge syndrome.*

Bingeing and purging just once would not be healthy. However, it would not result in a health problem. The problem occurs when people become hooked on the binge-purge pattern. Bulimics feel a lack of control over their eating behavior. They may eat thousands of calories in just over an hour. Bulimics have at least two binge-eating episodes a week. This behavior continues for at least three months.

Frequent purging upsets the body's chemical balance. This can cause fatigue and heart abnormalities. Repeated vomiting can harm the teeth, gums, esophagus, and stomach.

Early detection of anorexia and bulimia improves the chance of recovery with no severe medical problems. See 4-16. These disorders require professional care. Treatment may begin with hospitalization to combat malnutrition. Once the victim's body is renourished, he or she must begin psychological counseling. Therapists often urge family members to take part in therapy. They can help anorexics and bulimics learn how to change their behavior. Group therapy is also used to provide anorexics and bulimics with peer support.

Symptoms of Eating Disorders

abnormal weight loss
binge eating
vomiting
refusal to eat
excessive exercise
absent or irregular menstruation in women
depression

4-16 You should suspect a person has an eating disorder when one or more of these symptoms is present. Early detection leads to a better chance of recovery.

Summary

Good nutrition is important at all stages of the life cycle. During pregnancy, a woman must eat a range of foods to supply her developing baby with the nutrients it needs. For the first few months after birth, infants obtain needed nutrients from breast milk or formula. Preschoolers and school-age children may need help to choose foods that will meet their needs. Teens need more nutrients and calories to support their rapid growth. Adults must select foods carefully to meet their nutrient needs without getting too many calories. Older adults may need to choose foods that will help them counter problems with digestion and mobility. Throughout life, the Food Guide Pyramid can help people choose foods to meet their nutrient needs.

Exercise is nearly as important as nutrition to your body's state of fitness. Choosing a variety of activities will meet all your fitness needs. Finding activities that you enjoy will allow you to reap the benefits of exercise for a lifetime.

People at any life stage may have special dietary needs. Vegetarians must choose plant foods carefully to meet their needs for protein and other nutrients. People on medical diets must follow a doctor's or dietitian's advice to address a specific health problem.

Weight management is a lifestyle that will help people maintain a healthy weight throughout life. A height-weight table and the pinch test can help you judge whether your weight is healthy. Being overweight or obese may lead to a number of health problems. People overeat for many reasons. Deciding to lose weight and identifying eating habits are the first steps to reaching healthy weight goals. Weight management involves watching energy intake and increasing physical activity. Weight management principles apply to people who are underweight, too.

Anorexia nervosa and bulimia nervosa are two common eating disorders. Treatment requires nutrition therapy and psychological counseling.

Review What You Have Read

Write your answers on a separate sheet of paper.
1. What can happen if the nutrient needs of a fetus are not provided by the foods eaten by the mother?
2. Why should lactating mothers avoid drinking alcohol and taking medications?
3. True or false. Full-term babies usually need a supplemental source of iron shortly after birth because they have no iron reserves.
4. List three things a parent can do to encourage a preschooler to eat.
5. How can school-age children who have trouble eating large meals meet their nutritional needs?
6. An athlete's main source of energy should be ____.
   A. complex carbohydrates
   B. fats
   C. protein
   D. sugar
7. True or false. The need for vitamins and minerals drops dramatically when people reach adulthood.
8. What are two problems that might affect the diets of older adults?
9. Give examples of exercises that target each of the areas of fitness.
10. True or false. Lacto-ovo vegetarians include dairy products and eggs in their diets.
11. List four ways drinking liquids can help treat common illnesses.
12. Explain why falling within the appropriate range on a height-weight table does not guarantee that weight is healthy.
13. Briefly describe a weight management plan for losing 1 pound (.45 kg) a week.
14. True or false. In a weight-gain plan, fats should make up no more than 30 percent of total calories.
15. What usually triggers an eating disorder?

Build Your Basic Skills

1. Choose one medical condition that requires a special diet. Find out as much as you can about that diet and report to the class.
2. Calculate your daily calorie need for a sedentary lifestyle and a moderately active lifestyle. Also, calculate your daily limit for fat grams.

Build Your Thinking Skills

1. Divide a sheet of paper into four sections. Label the sections "Busy Schedules," "Skipped Meals," "Reducing Diets," and "Junk Food." In each section, write suggestions that teens could use to avoid or make up for that particular cause of nutrient deficiencies.
2. Evaluate a reducing diet suggested in a popular magazine. Give an oral report comparing the diet with the weight management principles discussed in this chapter.

Chapter 5

Safeguarding the Family's Health

A "Taste" of the World of Work

Scullion
Performs any combination of tasks involved in cleaning a ship's galleys, bakery, and butcher shop.

Sanitarian
Supervises and coordinates activities of workers engaged in duties concerned with sanitation programs in food processing establishments.

Safety Inspector
Inspects machinery, equipment, and working conditions in industrial or other settings, such as food processing plants, to ensure compliance with occupational safety and health regulations.

Terms to Know

food-borne illness
toxin
Heimlich maneuver

Objectives

After studying this chapter, you will be able to
discuss causes, symptoms, and treatment of common food-borne illnesses.
describe important standards of personal and kitchen cleanliness.
give examples of how following good safety practices can help you prevent kitchen accidents.
apply basic first aid measures in the home.

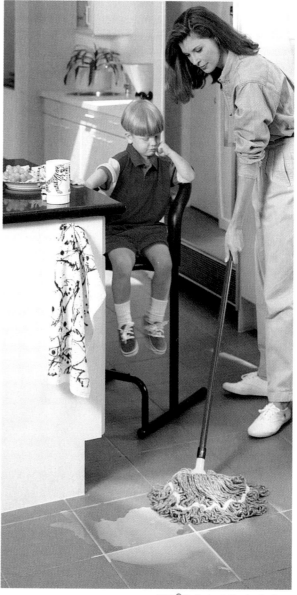

HMP® Professional Cleaning Products

Sanitation and safety in the kitchen are keys to good health. Improper food handling can make you ill. Kitchen accidents can cause severe injuries. You can prevent both illness and accidents by following sanitation and safety principles.

Food-Borne Illnesses

Perhaps you have heard news reports about people getting sick from *salmonella* or *E. coli.* These are both bacteria that cause food-borne illnesses. Millions of cases of food-borne illness occur in the United States each year. A *food-borne illness* is a disease transmitted by food.

Bacterial Illnesses

Common food-borne illnesses include *botulism, campylobacteriosis, E. coli infection,* and *listeriosis. Perfringens poisoning, salmonellosis, shigellosis, staphylococcal poisoning,* and *vibrio infection* are also on the list. All of these diseases are caused by bacteria or *toxins* (poisons) produced by bacteria.

Harmful bacteria are in many foods, including eggs, poultry, ground beef, dairy products, canned foods, and seafood. Thorough cooking will kill many harmful bacteria. Refrigeration will hinder their growth. However, food that is not cooked completely can harbor unsafe levels of bacteria. Food left at room temperature can provide a breeding ground for bacteria. Improper handling can introduce harmful bacteria into previously unaffected food.

The bodies of healthy people can usually handle limited amounts of harmful bacteria. However, when the bacteria count becomes too great, illness can occur. Food-borne illnesses pose a greater risk to infants, pregnant women, the elderly, and people with impaired immunity.

Symptoms vary depending on the type of bacteria. They may appear between 30 minutes and 30 days after eating tainted food. Common symptoms include abdominal cramping, diarrhea, fatigue, headache, fever, and vomiting. These symptoms usually last only a day or two. In some cases, however, they can last a week or more.

The symptoms of botulism differ from those of most other food-borne illnesses. This disease affects the nervous system. Symptoms include double vision, inability to swallow, speech difficulty, and gradual respiratory paralysis. The death rate for botulism is high. However, a doctor can treat botulism with an antitoxin if he or she diagnoses it in time. See 5-1.

Treating Bacterial Food-Borne Illnesses

Infants, pregnant women, the elderly, and those with chronic illnesses should see a doctor about symptoms of food-borne illness. If you are not in these high-risk groups, you may not require professional treatment for food-borne illness. Resting will help you get your strength back. Drinking plenty of liquids will help replace body fluids lost through diarrhea and vomiting. If you suspect that you have botulism, or if your symptoms are severe, you should call your doctor immediately.

Other Food-Related Illnesses

Food can transmit some illness-causing parasites. *Trichinosis* is a parasitic disease associated with eating undercooked pork. This disease is now quite rare in the United States. Hogs are no longer raised in conditions in which they are likely to acquire the parasite. Thorough cooking will kill any parasites that might be present in pork. Health experts recommend cooking all pork to an internal temperature of at least 160°F (71°C).

A couple of food-borne illnesses are caused by *protozoa* (tiny, one-celled animals). *Amebiasis* is caused by drinking polluted water or eating vegetables grown in polluted soil. *Giardiasis* can also be caused by drinking impure water.

Food can also transmit some viral diseases. Raw shellfish, such as oysters and clams, can transmit *hepatitis A virus.* This virus is highly heat-resistant, and people eat many types of shellfish raw or just slightly cooked. Therefore, prevention can be difficult. Contaminated water and sewage are the major sources of this virus. The best way to avoid contamination is to buy shellfish that come only from commercial sources. People who gather fresh shellfish should be sure to stay safely away from any source of pollution.

A few foods have *natural poisons.* Certain varieties of mushrooms and leaves of the rhubarb plant are two such foods. Unless you are a mushroom expert, do not go mushroom picking on your own. Buy varieties available in grocery stores. When preparing rhubarb, carefully remove leaves and dispose of them in an area away from children and pets. Avoid picking wild fruits, roots, and berries unless you are knowledgeable about them. Some varieties can be poisonous.

Food-Borne Illnesses

Illness	Food Sources	Symptoms
Staphylococcal poisoning	Salami; ham; cheese; custard; cream pies; egg, chicken, potato, and macaroni salads	Abdominal cramping, nausea, vomiting, diarrhea Appear: 8 to 20 hours after eating infected food Last: 1 to 2 days
Salmonellosis	Poultry, red meats, eggs, dried foods, dairy products	Severe headache, nausea, vomiting, abdominal pain, diarrhea, fever Appear: 3 to 8 hours after eating contaminated food Last: 2 to 3 days
Perfringens poisoning	Stews, soups, gravies	Nausea without vomiting, diarrhea, acute inflammation of the stomach and intestines Appear: 8 to 20 hours after eating the infected food Last: 24 hours
E. coli infection	Undercooked ground beef, raw milk, contaminated water, vegetables grown in cow manure	Bloody stools, stomachache, nausea, vomiting Appear: 12 to 72 hours after eating contaminated food Last: 4 to 10 days
Listeriosis	Soft cheese, unpasteurized milk, imported seafood products, frozen cooked crab meat, cooked shrimp, cooked imitation shellfish	Fever, headache, nausea, vomiting Appear: 48 to 72 hours after eating contaminated food
Botulism	Improperly processed home-canned foods	Double vision, inability to swallow, speech difficulty, progressive respiratory paralysis that can lead to death Appear: 12 to 36 hours after toxin enters the body

5-1 These are among the many food-borne illnesses that can be caused by improper handling of food.

Kitchen Sanitation

Most food-borne illnesses are spread through improper food handling. You can help prevent these illnesses by using good personal hygiene and keeping your kitchen sanitary. Preparing, serving, and storing food properly will also help keep it safe.

Personal Cleanliness

State and county health officials have established strict personal hygiene standards for food service workers. You can prevent food-borne illness by following these standards in your kitchen.

- Wash hands thoroughly with soap and water before beginning work. Also wash your hands after sneezing, coughing, using the toilet, or touching your face, hair, or any unsanitary object. Use soap and hot water. Keep fingernails clean and well groomed.
- Keep your hair away from your face and avoid touching it while you work.
- Wear clean clothes and a clean apron when working around food. Bacteria can accumulate on dirty clothes. Avoid loose sleeves, which can dip into foods.
- If you have an open sore or cut on your hand, put on plastic gloves before handling food. Open sores are a major source of staphylococcal bacteria.
- Do not smoke while working around food. Ashes can fall into food.
- Cover coughs and sneezes with a disposable tissue. Wash hands immediately.
- Do not taste and cook with the same spoon. Use one spoon for tasting and one for stirring. To taste, pour a little of the food from the stirring spoon onto the tasting spoon. Do not lick your fingers.

- After handling raw meat, fish, poultry, or eggs, wash your hands thoroughly before touching cooked foods. This will prevent the transfer of bacteria.

Kitchen Cleanliness

Kitchen cleanliness is as important as personal cleanliness. You can easily transfer bacteria from dirty cutting boards, counters, and utensils to food. To keep your kitchen sanitary, observe the following guidelines:

- Keep your work area clean. Wipe up spills as you work, and remove dirty utensils from your work area before proceeding to the next task. Bacteria grow quickly in spills and on dirty utensils, 5-2.
- Use clean utensils and containers. Never use the same utensil or cutting board for both raw and cooked meat, poultry, fish, or eggs. Utensils can transfer bacteria from raw foods to cooked foods.
- Never use a dish towel to wipe hands or spills. Dirty towels can transfer bacteria.

- Wash the tops of cans before opening them. Otherwise, dust and dirt could fall into food when you open the can.
- Periodically wash counters and cutting boards with a chlorine bleach solution to kill bacteria.
- Keep pets and insects out of the kitchen. Do not feed pets in the kitchen or wash their dishes with the family dishes. Remove leftover pet food and dispose of it promptly.
- Wash dishes and utensils promptly. Use hot water and detergent. Wash glasses first, then flatware, dishes, pots and pans, and greasy utensils. Rinse with scalding water. Air dry or use a clean dish towel.
- Dispose of garbage properly and promptly. Frequent washing and air drying of garbage pails prevent odors and bacterial growth.
- Never store sacks of onions or potatoes, canned goods, or any other foods under the kitchen sink. Drain pipes can leak and damage the food.

3M Home & Commercial Care Division

5-2 Wipe up spills immediately with a germ-resistant sponge. Ordinary dishcloths can spread bacteria.

Protect the Planet

Many commercial cleaning products contain harsh chemicals that damage the environment. Try doing many of your common cleaning tasks with a less toxic cleaner. A low-cost one that you probably already have on hand is baking soda! Sprinkle a little on a sponge dampened with vinegar. Use this vinegar and baking soda mixture for wiping sinks, countertops, and appliances.

• Rinse and air dry sponges and dishcloths between uses.

Sanitation in Food Preparation and Storage

Proper food preparation and storage are essential to prevent bacteria from multiplying. The following tips will help you maintain sanitary conditions:

• Always keep hot foods hot—above 140°F (60°C). Keep cold foods cold—below 40°F (5°C). Bacteria multiply rapidly between these temperatures. They multiply fastest at temperatures between 60° and 126°F (16° and 52°C), 5-3. This danger zone includes room temperature, so it is important not to leave food sitting out of the refrigerator.

• Use a refrigerator thermometer to check the temperature of your refrigerator and freezer regularly. Refrigerator temperatures should be 40°F (5°C) or just slightly below. Freezer temperatures should be 0°F (-18°C) or below. Also, check the gaskets around the doors to be sure they are tight.

• Keep refrigerator and freezer clean.

• Package refrigerated and frozen foods properly. Use moistureproof and vaporproof wraps for the freezer. For the refrigerator, cover fresh meats loosely and store leftovers in tightly covered containers. Use foods within recommended storage time.

• Thaw foods properly. Do not thaw on the kitchen counter or table. Refrigerator thawing is safer.

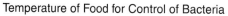

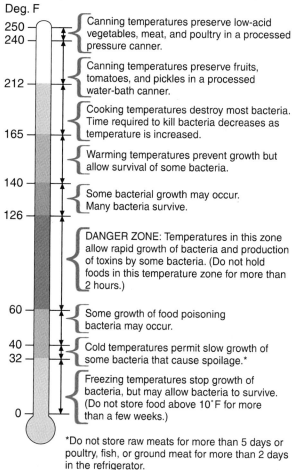

5-3 Bacteria multiply rapidly at moderate temperatures. To prevent this, keep hot foods hot and cold foods cold.

• Do not allow food to sit out for more than two hours. Refrigerate leftovers promptly. Divide large amounts of leftovers into small portions for faster cooling. Eat or freeze refrigerated leftovers within three days. Reheat leftovers to 165°F (74°C).

• Refrigerate custards, meringue, cream pies, and foods filled with custard mixtures when they have cooled slightly.

• Hasten cooling by placing containers of food in an ice water bath.

• Stuff raw poultry, meat, and fish just before baking. Stuffing should reach an internal temperature of at least 165°F (74°C). Remove stuffing promptly and refrigerate it separately. Refrigerate gravy, stuffing, and meat immediately after the meal.

- Do not partially cook foods and then set aside or refrigerate to complete the cooking later.
- Boil low-acid, home-canned foods for 10 to 20 minutes before tasting. Dispose of any bulging, leaking, or otherwise damaged container of food.
- Never taste any food that looks or smells questionable. Dispose of it promptly.
- Store nonperishables in tightly sealed containers to keep them fresh and free from insects and rodents.
- Do not refreeze foods unless they still contain ice crystals. Do not refreeze ice cream that has thawed. Use defrosted foods promptly.
- Use only clean, fresh, unbroken eggs for eggnog, custard, and other egg dishes. Modify recipes calling for uncooked or partially cooked eggs. Cook eggs until they are firm, not runny.
- Do not eat raw cookie dough or taste partially cooked dishes containing meat, poultry, fish, or eggs.

Cooking for Special Occasions

Cooking for large crowds or cooking outdoor meals requires additional precautions to keep food safe to eat. Before planning any large gathering, be sure the equipment you have can handle large quantities of food. Refrigerators must be large enough to chill increased quantities of warm foods without raising the temperature above the safety level. Heating appliances must be able to keep hot foods above 140°F (60°C) until serving.

If using buffet service, put the food in small serving dishes, which you can refill or replace as needed. Another way to keep hot foods hot and cold foods cold is to use heated serving appliances and ice.

Large amounts of food take longer to heat and chill than do small or average amounts. Divide food in small, shallow containers for quicker heating and cooling.

Be sure to thoroughly cook all foods. Then serve them promptly. Refrigerate leftovers immediately after the meal.

If time is limited, prepare some foods several weeks in advance and freeze. Freezing foods ahead will prevent overloading your refrigerator the day before the party.

Picnic and barbecue foods present other problems. You may carry these foods some distance before serving them. Use insulated containers to

Play It Safe

Pack moist towelettes in your picnic basket. Use them to wipe your hands before and after handling raw meat.

keep these foods at the proper temperature to prevent the growth of bacteria, 5-4. Wrap raw meat, poultry, and fish carefully to keep them from leaking onto other foods. You may want to use a separate cooler for beverages. This will help you avoid repeatedly opening the cooler containing the perishable foods. Do not take perishables from the cooler until you are ready to serve.

Use sanitary procedures when preparing picnic foods. Be sure utensils are clean. Do not let hamburgers, hot dogs, or other meats sit next to the grill while the charcoal heats. Keep them in the ice chest. Do not put cooked meat on the same plate that held raw meat.

Eating Safely When Eating Out

Most of the food-borne illness cases reported each year occur in food service establishments. Restaurants have strict sanitation guidelines they must follow when preparing food for the public. State health departments inspect food service facilities regularly to ensure that guidelines are being met. However, occasional problems still occur.

You can do several things when eating out to protect yourself from food-borne illness. First, look at the surroundings on your way into a restaurant. The parking lot should be free from litter. The way the outside of a restaurant is maintained can give you a clue about how the inside is maintained.

When you enter the restaurant, you should see a concern for cleanliness throughout the establishment. Tables should be wiped. Walls and floors should be clean. Restrooms should be tidy.

Observe the employees as they wait on you. They should appear to be in good health. Their clothes should be clean. If they have long hair, they should have it tied back. When they serve you, they should not touch the eating surfaces of your tableware.

When your food is served, it should look and smell wholesome. Hot foods should be hot. Cold foods should be cold.

If you have a concern about your food, do not be afraid to speak to your server. If your server

5-4 Picnic and barbecue foods are often carried some distance before serving. They must be kept at the proper temperatures to be safe.

cannot answer your questions or correct the problem, ask to speak to the manager.

Most servers will wrap leftovers for you if you wish to take them home. However, be sure you are going directly home and promptly put leftovers in the refrigerator. If you cannot refrigerate food within two hours from the time it was *served*, discard it.

If you choose restaurants with care, you may never have a problem with food-borne illness. However, if you get ill from something you ate at a restaurant, call local health authorities. Others should be warned that they may have been exposed to the infected food also.

Safety in the Kitchen

Hospital emergency personnel see the results of thousands of kitchen accidents each year. Some kitchen accidents are due to ignorance. Many result from carelessness. Chemical poisonings, cuts, burns, and falls are the most common of these accidents. You can prevent many accidents by properly using and caring for equipment. Following good safety practices and keeping the kitchen clean will also help you avoid accidents.

When someone becomes injured in the kitchen, a knowledge of basic first aid is important. A simple first aid kit kept in the kitchen will also come in handy if someone is injured.

Preventing Chemical Poisonings

Children are especially susceptible to chemical poisonings. To many children, poisonous household products, such as furniture polishes, cleaners, and bleach, look like food. The following guidelines will help you prevent chemical poisonings:
- Do not rely on containers with safety closures. Some children can open safety caps.
- Read all warning labels, and keep a poison chart handy. This will help you know what first aid to give if someone is accidentally poisoned. It will also help you know what to tell the doctor.
- Keep all hazardous products in their original, clearly labeled containers. Do not put them in soda bottles or other food containers. Keep all containers tightly closed.
- Keep medication out of the kitchen and out of a child's reach. Never refer to medicine as candy. Dispose of unused medication promptly where a child cannot reach it.
- If the phone or doorbell interrupts you while you are using a hazardous product, take the product with you.

- Pesticides and insecticides used on food can be poisonous. To protect family members, wash all fresh fruits and vegetables thoroughly before use. Cover all food and cooking and eating utensils before using a pesticide in your home.
- Keep all hazardous products in a location where children cannot reach them. In a home with young children, do not store household cleaners under the sink. See 5-5.

Treating Poisonings

In a case of accidental poisoning, call a physician immediately. If the label on the poison lists an antidote, give it to the victim. If there is no label, call the nearest poison control center and describe the poison taken. Do not induce vomiting if the victim has swallowed a petroleum product, strong acid, strong alkali, strychnine, or kerosene. Keep victim comfortable and calm until help arrives.

Preventing Cuts

Knives, sharp appliances, and broken glass cause most kitchen cuts. The following guidelines will help you prevent cuts:
- Never pick up broken glass with your bare hands. Wear rubber gloves to pick up the large pieces. Sweep the smaller pieces into a throwaway dustpan and wipe up fragments with a damp paper towel. Dispose of broken glass immediately.
- Keep knives sharp. Dull blades can slip and cause cuts. Wash and store knives separately from other utensils.
- Use knives properly. Move the blade away from your body as you cut. Never point a sharp object at another person.
- Do not try to catch a falling knife in midair. You can cut yourself badly. Let the knife fall to the floor, then carefully pick it up.
- Use a knife only for its intended purpose. Do not use it to pry open cans or other containers. Do not use it as a screwdriver or hammer. To do so can cause serious injuries.
- Never put fingers near beaters, blender blades, food processor blades, or food waste disposers to dislodge foods or objects. Instead, disconnect the appliance and use a nonmetal utensil. If you cannot dislodge the object, call a repair person.
- When opening a can, dispose of the lid immediately.

5-5 Household chemicals should not be stored under the sink in a home with young children.

Treating Cuts

To treat a cut, cover the wound with a sterile cloth or clean handkerchief. Apply firm pressure to the wound to stop bleeding. If a cut is minor, wash it with soap and water. Apply an antiseptic solution and bandage it with a sterile dressing. If a cut is severe, continue to apply pressure to the wound. Take the victim to the hospital emergency room or family doctor.

Preventing Burns and Fires

Scalding liquids, spattering grease, malfunctioning electric appliances, and hot cooking utensils cause most kitchen burns. The following guidelines will help you prevent burns:

- Be sure to ground all electric appliances. (See Chapter 7.) Avoid using extension cords and multiple plugs.
- Follow manufacturer's directions for use and care of all electric and gas appliances.
- Keep a fire extinguisher handy. Be sure all family members know how to use it. Have it checked periodically. Do not store the extinguisher over the range.
- When working near the range, wear tight-fitting clothing. Do not hang towels, curtains, or other flammable materials near the range.
- Use pot holders to handle hot utensils. Turn all pan handles inward to prevent accidental tipping.
- Never leave a pan of grease unattended; it could burst into flames. If grease should ignite, *do not* pour water on the flames. Use salt, baking soda, or your fire extinguisher.
- If you must light a gas range manually, do not turn on the gas first. Light the match and then turn on the gas to prevent an accidental explosion. If you smell gas, turn off the controls, open a window, and call the gas company.
- Do not let children play near the range or cook without help. Teach them proper safety procedures.
- If your clothes should catch on fire, do not panic and run. Drop on the floor and roll over to smother the flames.
- To avoid a steam burn, open pan lids away from you so the steam will escape safely.
- Use fondue pots and chafing dishes carefully. Be sure they are sturdy and well constructed. Do not fill liquid alcohol burners more than half full because the liquid will expand. Never try to refill a hot alcohol burner; it could burst into flames. Watch oil in a fondue pot closely, and do not allow it to smoke.
- Turn off range and oven controls and disconnect small appliances when not in use.
- Clean grease from exhaust hoods frequently to prevent grease fires.
- Install a smoke alarm in the kitchen. Check it monthly to be sure batteries are operating. See 5-6.

Treating Burns

When someone becomes burned, place the burned area immediately under cold running water or in a cold water bath. Do not apply ointments or grease of any kind. Do not break blisters that may form. Call a physician immediately if burn is severe or if pain and redness persist.

First Alert®

5-6 The batteries in a smoke detector should be tested regularly to be sure they are functioning.

Preventing Falls

Most kitchen falls result from unsteady step stools and spilled foods. The following guidelines will help you prevent falls:

- Wait until a freshly washed floor dries before walking across the room. Apply nonskid wax thinly and evenly.
- Do not stand on a chair or box to reach high places. Use a sturdy step stool or ladder.
- Wipe up spills from floors immediately. Be sure no sticky or greasy residue remains.
- Avoid throw rugs. If you must use them, find rugs with nonskid backings.
- Do not let children leave their toys on the kitchen floor. Remove shoes, boots, sports equipment, and other objects from kitchen walkways.

Treating Falls

When someone is injured in a fall, stop bleeding if necessary. Loosen clothing around the victim's neck. If you suspect a broken bone, do not move the victim unless absolutely necessary. Make the victim as comfortable as possible. Do not give the victim anything to eat or drink. Call a physician.

Preventing Electric Shock

Faulty wiring, overloaded electrical outlets, and damaged appliances are common causes of electric shock. Electrical hazards can also be fire hazards. The following guidelines will help you prevent electric shock:

- When you disconnect appliances, hold onto the plug, not the cord. Replace all cords and plugs when they become worn.
- Never stand on a wet floor or work near a wet counter when using electric appliances.
- Do not overload electrical outlets by plugging several appliances into the same outlet.
- Do not touch any electrical plugs, switches, or appliances when your hands are wet.

- Unplug the toaster before trying to pry loose food that has become stuck.
- Place safety covers over unused electrical outlets to prevent children from sticking fingers or objects into them.
- Do not use damaged appliances.
- Do not run electrical cords under rugs or carpeting.
- Do not use lightweight extension cords with small appliances. If possible, plug appliances directly into electrical outlets. If you must use an extension cord, choose a heavy-gauge one that is designed to carry a heavier electrical load.

Treating Electric Shock

If someone receives an electric shock, immediately disconnect the appliance or turn off the power causing the shock. Do not touch the victim if he or she is connected to the power source. If you do, you will receive a shock, too. Use some nonconducting material to pull the victim away from the electrical source. A rope, a long piece of dry cloth, or a wooden pole would be suitable choices. Call for help. Begin rescue breathing.

Preventing Choking

Choking occurs when a piece of food becomes stuck in the throat. The trapped food blocks the airway, making it impossible for the victim to speak or breathe. Someone choking on food quickly turns blue and collapses. The choking victim can die of strangulation in four minutes if the airway is not cleared. The following guidelines will help you prevent choking:

- Chew food thoroughly before swallowing.
- Avoid talking and laughing when you have food in your mouth.
- Do not give children small, round pieces of food, such as slices of hot dogs or carrots. Cut slices in halves or quarters.

Treating Choking

The *Heimlich maneuver* is a procedure used to save choking victims, 5-7. Through the Heimlich maneuver, you exert pressure on the victim's abdomen, forcing the diaphragm upward. This compresses the air in the lungs, causing the food that is blocking the breathing passage to be expelled.

Being familiar with the following steps for performing the Heimlich maneuver may help you save someone's life:

1. If the victim is standing, stand behind him or her. If the victim is sitting, stand behind his or

5-7 The Heimlich maneuver can save the life of a choking victim.

her chair. Wrap your arms around the victim's waist.

2. With your thumb toward the victim, place your fist against the victim's abdomen. Your fist should be above the navel and just below the rib cage.
3. Grasping your fist with your other hand, use a quick thrust to press upward into the victim's abdomen. Repeat the thrust several times, if needed.

You can also perform the Heimlich maneuver on a victim who has fallen to the floor. If necessary, move the victim so he or she is lying face up. Face the victim and kneel astride his or her hips. Place one of your hands on top of the other. Place the heel of your bottom hand against the victim's abdomen, above the navel and just below the rib cage. Use a quick thrust to press upward into the victim's abdomen, repeating several times, if needed.

If no help is available, a victim can perform the Heimlich maneuver on himself or herself before losing consciousness.

Although the Heimlich maneuver can keep someone from choking to death, it can injure the victim. The victim should see a physician immediately after the rescue.

Avoiding Other Dangers

Kitchen drawers and pressure cookers may seem harmless. However, these and other items can be dangerous if you do not take safety precautions.

Cabinets and Drawers

People can injure themselves by bumping into open cabinet doors and drawers. Keep all kitchen cabinets and drawers closed. Keep latches or magnetic locks in good repair. See 5-8.

Aerosol Cans

Use products in aerosol cans carefully. Do not use them near a heat source or anyone who is smoking. Make sure that the area where you spray is well ventilated. Store cans in a cool place. Dispose of them properly; do not puncture or burn them. Cans that seem empty may still contain aerosol propellant and can explode.

Pressure Cookers

Pressure cookers cook foods more quickly than conventional surface cooking pans. However, they can be dangerous if used improperly. Always follow the manufacturer's directions carefully. Never open a pressure cooker before the pressure has gone down to zero. The pressurized steam within the cooker can rush out and cause a severe burn.

5-8 This kitchen appears safe. All cabinet doors and drawers are closed.

Summary

Food-borne illnesses are extremely common in the United States. Bacteria cause many of them. However, people are often responsible for spreading the bacteria. Most symptoms of food-borne illnesses affect the digestive system and last only a few days. However, food-borne illnesses can be deadly.

Maintaining high standards of personal and kitchen cleanliness while preparing foods is your key defense against food-borne illnesses. You need to handle food carefully and store it properly. You need to take special precautions when cooking for a large group or transporting food. You also need to be wary when you are eating in restaurants to avoid the risk of illness.

Exercising safety is another concern when you are working in the kitchen. Many kitchen injuries are the result of poisonings, cuts, burns, falls, shock, and choking. Even common items like cabinet doors and aerosol cans can present dangers if you are not careful.

Review What You Have Read

Write your answers on a separate sheet of paper.

1. For what groups of people do food-borne illnesses pose a greater risk?
2. What is the recommended internal temperature for cooked pork?
3. List six standards for personal hygiene that should be followed in the kitchen.
4. List five standards for kitchen cleanliness.
5. What are the proper temperatures for serving hot and cold foods?
6. How can large amounts of food be heated or chilled quickly?
7. Where do most of the food-borne illness cases reported each year occur?
8. True or false. The elderly are especially susceptible to chemical poisonings.
9. List five safety precautions that can prevent burns.
10. Describe the correct way to pick up and dispose of broken glass.
11. Describe how to extinguish a grease fire.
12. List three guidelines for preventing falls.
13. What should be used to pull a shock victim away from an electrical source?
14. Briefly describe the steps for performing the Heimlich maneuver.
15. How can kitchen cabinets and drawers be dangerous?

Build Your Basic Skills

1. Conduct a safety check of your kitchen. Report the results to your classmates.
2. Prepare a pamphlet listing simple first aid procedures for poisonings, cuts, burns, falls, and electric shock.

Build Your Thinking Skills

1. Work in a group of four to research one type of food-borne illness. Each group member should focus on a different one of the following aspects: cause, food sources, symptoms, prevention. Prepare a poster to use in giving a presentation to the rest of the class.
2. Make puppets and write a puppet show to present information about kitchen safety to young children. If possible, perform your show at a local preschool or kindergarten.

Chapter 6

Career Opportunities

A "Taste" of the World of Work

Employment Agency Manager
Manages employment services and business operations of private employment agency.

Personnel Psychologist
Specializes in development and application of such techniques as job analysis and classification, personnel interviewing, ratings, and vocational tests for use in selection, placement, promotion, and training of workers.

Career Placement Services Counselor
Collects, organizes, and analyzes information about individuals through records, tests, interviews, and professional sources, to appraise their interests, aptitudes, abilities, and personality characteristics, for vocational and educational planning.

Terms to Know

career ladder
leader
catering
extension agent
dietitian
nutritionist
reference
interview
entrepreneur

Objectives

After studying this chapter, you will be able to
describe three general career areas in the field of foods.
list the qualifications needed to work in each career area.
explain the steps involved in finding a job.

Wendy's International, Inc., George Anderson, photographer

How will I know which career is right for me? Where will I find a job that I will enjoy and that will pay well? What are my interests? What are my capabilities? Where can I find information to help me make career decisions? These questions are only a few of those you may ask yourself as you consider your immediate and future goals. Choosing a career is exciting, but it is not always easy.

Choosing a Career

Before choosing a career, you need to do some self-analysis. You can begin by thinking about your likes and dislikes, your interests, and your abilities.

Do you like working with people, or would you rather work on your own? Are you artistic? Do you like to write? Do you have a special interest, such as creative cooking, music, or acting? Are you a leader, or would you rather have others make the decisions? Do you want to stay in one place, or are you willing to travel? Do you want to continue your education, or are you ready to begin working right after graduation from high school?

The answers to these and other similar questions can help you find a career in which you can be both happy and successful. Once you have a particular career in mind, find out as much as you can about that career.

You can obtain career information from many sources. Talk to your school counselor, your teachers, and your parents. Find people in your community involved in various careers and ask them questions. If you know the career of your choice requires further education, research colleges that have the curriculum you will need. Many high school libraries have college catalogs and career manuals.

Preparing for a Career

The classes you take in high school can help you prepare for a career. If you think you would like a career in a particular field, try to take courses related to that field. For instance, foods classes offered by the family and consumer science department would help you prepare for a career in the food industry.

Many careers require education beyond high school. The classes you take now can help prepare you for further education. English, math, communications, social studies, computer training, and science can prepare you for vocational school, community college, or a university.

Another way to prepare for a career is to work part-time while you are still in school. Working during summers and after school can give you valuable experience that can help you later.

Preparing for a career also involves learning about career ladders. A *career ladder* is a series of related jobs that form a career. See 6-1. Each job in a career ladder builds on the skills learned in the job below. A career ladder shows you positions into which you can advance. It also gives you an idea of skills you need to do so.

Choosing a Career in Foods

Do you think a career in the food industry might interest you? When choosing a career, you need to remember that work is only one part of your life. The time you spend alone and with family and friends is also a part of your life. These two areas of your life can affect each other. If you enjoy your work, you are more likely to be content when you are not at work. Likewise, if you are happy in your home life, you are more likely to perform well on the job.

Some careers in the food industry can be very demanding. They involve long hours, often at night and on weekends. Some people find this schedule difficult to manage. It prevents them from spending time with family and friends.

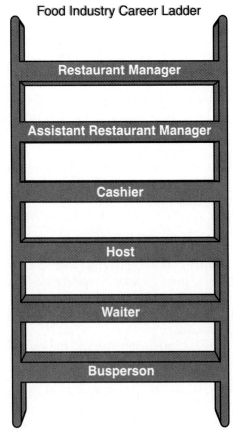

6-1 *Looking at this career ladder, a young person knows he or she needs to be a busperson and a waiter before becoming a host. From there, the person can advance to the positions of cashier, assistant manager, and manager.*

Careers in the food industry can also be quite rewarding. They often offer chances for advancement into managerial positions. Many people find the opportunities in this industry well worth the challenges.

If you are thinking about a career in the food industry, find out what specific demands it entails. Also find out what rewards it may offer. Finally, think about how this career would affect your personal and family life. If the job still sounds appealing after you have completed your evaluation, then it may be right for you.

Food-related careers can be divided into three main groups

- careers in the food service industry
- careers in the food handling industry
- food-related careers in business and education

Careers in all three areas would utilize the same basic set of skills.

Skills for Success

One important job skill is the ability to maintain a professional appearance. Like anywhere else, first impressions can often be lasting ones in the food industry. Your personal grooming habits influence the impressions you make. They also affect the comfort and safety of the people who will eat the food with which you work. You need to be sure that you dress appropriately for the work you are doing. You should practice good hygiene by having clean skin and hair, trimmed nails, and freshly washed clothing.

Another work skill is the ability to communicate effectively. Through communication, you can share opinions, facts, work, and ideas. You need to be able to speak, write, and listen well to be an effective communicator.

You need to have the ability to get along with others. You may be dealing with customers, employers, and coworkers. Keeping a positive outlook and a pleasant, enthusiastic attitude will help you maintain good working relationships with these people.

You need to develop dedication to your job. This means getting to work on time. It means doing your share of the work. It also means being willing to do a little extra work when special needs arise.

Knowledge of nutrition is more important in some food industry jobs than others. However, some nutrition knowledge can be helpful in almost any position. For instance, food preparation workers should know how to plan nutritious, well-balanced meals. Food handlers should know how their work can affect the nutritional value of food. Dietitians should be able to share their knowledge of nutrition with others.

Artistic skill is also helpful in some food industry positions. For instance, chefs need to know how to arrange food attractively. They use color, texture, and garnishes to increase food's appeal to customers. Food stylists need to know how to make food look appetizing in photographs.

Leadership Skills

Employers in the food industry often seek leadership skills in their employees. A *leader* is a person who commands authority and takes a principal role in a group. A leader has to assume responsibility for making decisions. He or she has to establish priorities, organize procedures, and delegate work. Leaders need to set goals and see that the group reaches them.

You need a thorough knowledge of your area of the food industry. This means knowing the terms that people in the workplace frequently use. It also involves becoming familiar with how to use any tools or equipment that relate to your job. As a leader, you will use this knowledge to direct others.

Leadership experiences teach you to use your own initiative. You are able to decide what needs doing and you take action without being told. You also become more capable of meeting the needs of the moment.

Make an effort to gain leadership experience while you are in school. One good way to do this is by joining Future Homemakers of America (FHA). FHA is a student vocational organization that promotes families, career exploration, and community involvement. It prepares students to balance family and work life. It also allows students to explore various occupations related to family and consumer sciences. See 6-2.

The Food Service Industry

If you are ambitious, willing to work hard, and able to get along well with people, a career in the food service industry could be for you.

Job forecasters predict that job prospects in food service will remain bright. Government and food service industry figures show a growing need for food service personnel. The industry will need many people to fill positions for chefs and cooks and for restaurant managers. As more people eat more meals away from home, the need for eating establishments and skilled personnel to staff them increases.

6-2 FHA teaches consumer, home management, leadership, and career skills to students in family and consumer science classes.

Types of Jobs in the Food Service Industry

Jobs are available in four areas of food service: food preparation, customer service, sanitation, and management. Your educational background, your goals, and your abilities will help determine which of these areas might be right for you.

Food Preparation

Food preparation jobs are available in coffee shops, snack bars, fast-food chains, restaurants, private clubs, school cafeterias, hotels, hospitals, and other large institutions. Entry-level positions require little, if any, previous experience.

Usually, you begin working as an assistant to an experienced employee. In small establishments, workers learn how to do many different food preparation tasks. For instance, one day you might prepare soups. The next day you might prepare salads or sandwiches or help with breakfast orders. In large establishments, workers specialize in one area. For example, you might become the baker's assistant or the grill cook's assistant.

In many food service careers, you can work your way up the career ladder as you gain experience. After learning to be a salad maker, for example, you might advance to the position of assistant cook. With additional experience, you might later become a cook.

Customer Service

Customer service involves working with the people the food establishment serves—its customers. You might work as a waiter and serve food to customers. You might work as a busperson and set and clear the tables. As you gain experience, you could advance to the positions of host, head waiter, cashier, assistant manager, or manager.

Sanitation

Sanitation involves cleaning and maintenance. Jobs in this area of food service are for dishwashers, pan scrubbers, and maintenance people. Their responsibility is to be sure the kitchen, cooking equipment, serving utensils, and tableware remain clean, safe, and sanitary. They must pay special attention to cleanliness in order to protect the health and safety of both customers and staff. With experience, dishwashers and maintenance people can advance to supervisory positions.

Management

Management positions involve working with both employees and customers. Management positions include owner, manager, assistant manager, dietitian, and executive chef. Some of these positions require additional education. A dietitian, for example, must have a college degree and have served an internship in a hospital or other institution. Workers may obtain other management positions through management training programs, experience, and hard work. See 6-3.

Job Requirements for the Food Service Industry

Some positions in the food service industry are entry-level positions. Other positions require special training. Employees can obtain this training in several different ways.

Many high schools offer work-study programs. In these programs, you can gain on-the-job training while you finish school.

Vocational schools offer courses in food preparation and management. If you have graduated from a vocational school, you probably will be able to begin your food service career at a higher level.

Many food service operations have management training programs. These programs vary. Not all of them require a college degree. However, most have their own specific requirements, which you must meet before being admitted into the program.

Community colleges and universities offer programs that can prepare you for management positions. Many community colleges have programs in quantity food preparation and hotel and restaurant management. At a university, you can obtain a bachelor's degree in family and consumer sciences, dietetics, institution management, or hotel-restaurant management.

Catering

Once you have gained experience in food service, you might want to start your own restaurant or food service business. One such business is *catering.* Catering combines all four areas of food service—food preparation, customer service, sanitation, and management.

Caterers prepare food for parties and other business and social functions. They plan small parties in private homes as well as banquets and wedding receptions for large groups. Some caterers specialize in baking wedding cakes or preparing fancy hors d'oeuvres. Others prepare complete dinners and supply serving equipment and personnel as well.

Caterers may operate out of their own homes or from a separate business location. Some caterers work on a large scale and employ other trained people to help them. Other caterers work alone.

6-3 An executive chef is responsible for planning menus, ordering ingredients, and supervising kitchen staff.

The Food Handling Industry

Food production is primarily the job of farmers. However, many people handle the food farmers produce before it reaches consumers.

After harvesting, most food products go to processing plants. Here, skilled workers perform many jobs. Sorting, washing, peeling, slicing, grinding, roasting, and packing are just a few of the many processes that food products may undergo.

After processing, food products follow a transportation chain. This chain involves truck, air freight, and train personnel; food brokers; distributors; food wholesalers; and finally food retailers.

At the grocery store, stock personnel help price products and put them on the shelves. They also help customers carry their groceries to their cars and keep the carts orderly. The dairy, produce, meat, and bakery managers supervise their particular departments. Meat cutters and butchers cut large wholesale cuts of meat into the smaller retail cuts you buy. Customer service personnel answer your questions, cash checks, and perform other service-related functions. Checkers record the prices of the groceries you buy and put those groceries into bags. In addition to all of these people, someone must take care of store advertising and displays. Stores also need several people to work in managerial positions.

Job Requirements for the Food Handling Industry

Many people in the food handling industry, such as workers in canning plants and checkers in food stores, have entry-level positions. In these positions, you would receive on-the-job training. As you become more experienced, your employer might promote you to a supervisory position.

Some workers, such as government inspectors and butchers, require special skills. Acquiring these skills may or may not involve vocational school training or a college degree.

Some managerial positions require a college education. You can achieve others through hard work and experience.

If you think a career in the food handling industry might interest you, try working part-time as a supermarket checker or stock person. This experience could be helpful when you are ready to apply for a full-time job. See 6-4.

Photo courtesy of Northwest Cherry Growers

California Artichoke Advisory Board

The Kroger Co.

6-4 Careers in the food handling industry involve harvesting, processing, and selling food products.

Food-Related Careers in Education and Business

Many people work in food-related careers to educate and communicate with others about food. These people include teachers, extension agents, dietitians, consumer specialists, and researchers. Most of these careers require a bachelor's degree. Some require advanced degrees and many years of experience.

The departments that offer food-related degrees have different names at different colleges and universities. Departments of family and consumer sciences often offer these programs. Comparable departments have such names as home economics and human ecology. Degrees from any of these departments would prepare students for food-related careers in education and business.

Teaching

One career that involves teaching people about foods is that of family and consumer science teacher. These teachers work at all educational levels—elementary, junior high, high school, college, and adult education. These teachers are knowledgeable about all areas of family and consumer sciences. However, most choose to specialize in one particular area, such as foods and nutrition. Foods classes emphasize nutrition, family health, safety and sanitation, consumer economics, household equipment, food preparation, and meal management.

To teach at any level, you must have a bachelor's degree in family and consumer sciences or a similar discipline. To teach at the college level, you must have at least a master's degree. Many teachers expand their careers and become administrators. Others become consultants or authors. They write educational materials for use by teachers and students.

Extension Work

The Cooperative Extension Service employs *extension agents.* Extension is a part of the United States Department of Agriculture. It falls under the supervision of land grant universities.

Extension agents work with adults and with young people involved in 4-H programs. They offer classes in many areas including nutrition, consumer education, food safety, and home management. They also train assistants to help them with their programs.

Some extension agents write educational materials published by the Department of Agriculture.

These publications are available to consumers free of charge or for a small cost. You may have seen home canning or freezing directions written by your county extension agent.

To be an extension agent, you must have a bachelor's degree in family and consumer sciences. Some positions require a master's degree.

Dietetics and Nutrition

Dietitians are members of the health care team. They have special knowledge and training in food and nutrition, the health sciences, and institution management. Dietitians work in nutritional care, administration, education, research, and business and industry.

Nutritional Care

Dietitians in nutritional care work for hospitals, clinics, and nursing homes. These dietitians work with physicians and other medical personnel to plan diets for patients with special needs. They also supervise the purchase and preparation of food to ensure that meals are healthy and nutritious.

Administration

Some dietitians work as administrators in the food service industry. They plan meals and supervise and train personnel. They also oversee the purchase and preparation of food and the purchase of equipment. Hospitals, schools, and other large institutions with food services employ administrative dietitians.

Education

Dietitians who work in the area of education may teach nutrition, diet therapy, and other related courses at the college level. They also might teach nutrition to students studying to be doctors and nurses. Other dietitians conduct community nutrition workshops.

A *nutritionist* is a registered dietitian or a family and consumer science professional with a degree in foods and nutrition. Nutritionists work directly in nutrition education. Through classes, clinics, and community programs, they help people form good food habits. Hospitals, medical schools, clinics, community health organizations, and public health agencies hire nutritionists. Nutritionists usually have advanced degrees. See 6-5.

Research

Dietitians involved in research study the relationships between good health and diet. They also help conduct nutritional studies for the government, private industry, hospitals, and medical schools.

6-5 A nutritionist might work in a weight management center to help educate clients about good eating habits.

Job Requirements for Dietitians

To become a dietitian, you must graduate from an accredited college or university with a degree in dietetics or foods and nutrition. In addition, you must complete an internship or a similar professional experience. Depending on your area of interest, you might intern in a hospital or in a school or business with a food service program. To become a registered dietitian (RD), you must also pass a national test. Most dietitians become registered because most hospitals and businesses prefer to hire only registered dietitians.

Communications

Food professionals in communications usually work with the mass media. Many are newspaper or magazine food editors and writers. Others work with television and radio stations, public relations agencies, advertising agencies, and food companies. They inform the public about new food products, food-related appliances, consumer issues, and legislation that affects consumers.

A food-related career in communications usually requires at least a bachelor's degree in family and consumer sciences. A background in journalism and a specialization in foods and nutrition are helpful. Food professionals in communications need to be able to work well with people and to express themselves orally and in writing.

Business

Private companies, associations like the American Egg Board, and utility companies hire food professionals in business. These professionals explain how to select, use, and care for a particular product. They serve as the link between the consumer and the manufacturer.

Some food professionals in business work in test kitchens where they test new food products or develop recipes. Others are food stylists who work with photographers to prepare food for photographing. Some prepare advertisements, consumer literature, and product directions. Others demonstrate food preparation techniques or the use and care of cooking appliances in department stores, supermarkets, and schools.

To be a food professional in business, you need a bachelor's degree in family and consumer sciences. Some positions require an advanced degree. Most food professionals in business have a broad background in family and consumer sciences. In addition, they have an area of specialization, such as foods or household equipment. Their college education usually includes courses in consumer education, management, marketing, sales, accounting, and business law.

Consumer Affairs

Food professionals in consumer affairs work for private industries. Many supermarkets hire food professionals to answer consumer questions and help promote services and products. They act as a link between the consumer and the store manager.

Government agencies like the Federal Trade Commission also hire food professionals in consumer affairs. They investigate consumer complaints and conduct follow-up studies. Some write consumer information published by the government. Others work as lobbyists involved in consumer legislation.

To be a food professional in consumer affairs, you usually need a bachelor's degree in family and consumer sciences. You may or may not have to specialize in one area, such as foods and nutrition. Courses in communication, business, and consumer affairs are helpful.

Research

Food professionals in research work in many areas of family and consumer sciences. Some researchers conduct nutritional studies. For instance, they might study the relationship between obesity and eating habits. Some food professionals in research work with engineers to develop new equipment like microwave ovens. They also develop new foods, such as grains with higher levels of protein and fruits that ripen more slowly, 6-6. Others test new products to see if they perform correctly and are suitable for consumer use. Still other researchers find new ways for consumers to use products like cake mixes.

Universities, the government, and private industries employ researchers. Most have advanced degrees.

Finding a Job

If a career in the food industry interests you, you can start getting job experience now. Many entry-level positions are available in restaurants, grocery stores, and other food-related businesses. Getting experience while you are still in high school will prepare you for higher level positions in the future.

Look for Job Openings

How can you find job openings? The want ads in your local newspaper are a good place to start. Many businesses post signs in their windows when

Protect the Planet

Regardless of what type of career you choose, take steps to care for the earth's environment in your work environment. Carpool to your job. Use a reusable lunch bag to carry your lunch to work. Keep a ceramic mug in your workplace so you will not have to use disposable cups. Recycle office paper and cardboard cartons and reuse manila envelopes. Small efforts made by you and your coworkers can make a big difference!

The Consulate General of Israel to the Midwest
Richard T. Nowitz, photographer

6-6 Genetic engineers work to develop better food products.

they want to hire someone. Family members, friends, and neighbors may know of businesses that are hiring. Your guidance counselor or school placement office is another source of job information.

Apply for a Position

When you hear of a position that interests you, you need to contact the employer to express your interest. Depending on the position and how you heard about it, you may make this contact by letter, by telephone, or in person.

If the position is still available, the employer is likely to ask you to fill out an application form. Job applications commonly request certain types of information. If you are ready to relate this information, you will be able to fill out the form quickly and accurately.

You will need to know your Social Security number when filling out an application form. All workers need a Social Security number for tax and identification purposes. You will also need to write your name, address, and telephone number on an application form. You may need to specify the position for which you are applying, your expected wages, and when you can start working. You will need to list the name and location of the schools you have attended. You will have to provide information about any other jobs that you have had. You may also have to give the names of references. (**References** are people other than friends and relatives that employers can call to ask about your capabilities as a worker.)

Interview for the Position

If your application form impresses an employer, he or she may ask you to come in for an interview. An *interview* is an opportunity for an employer and a job applicant to discuss the applicant's qualifications.

In order to make a good impression at an interview, you should be well groomed and neatly dressed. You should speak in a clear voice and have a positive attitude. Be prepared to answer a variety of questions about your skills, interests, and previous work experiences. See 6-7.

If the interview goes well, the employer may decide to offer you a job. However, the employer is probably interviewing other applicants for the same job. It may take a week or more for the employer to make a hiring decision. You can ask the employer at the interview when you can expect to hear his or her decision.

Receive an Offer or a Rejection

When you receive an offer, let the employer know as soon as possible if you will accept the job. Ask when you should report to work. Find out any necessary information regarding items such as uniforms and training sessions.

If the employer does not offer you the job, ask yourself the following questions:

- Was my application form filled out neatly?
- Did I arrive for my interview on time and appropriately dressed?
- Did I display interest in the job and willingness to work?
- Did I appear friendly and cooperative?
- Did I answer all questions accurately?

If you answer yes to these questions, it may not be your fault that you did not get the job. Perhaps the employer merely felt that another applicant was more qualified. If you answer no to

Be a Clever Consumer

One way you might learn about job openings is through an employment agency. Agencies charge a fee to match people with job openings. Sometimes the employer pays this fee. Sometimes the person looking for the job pays it. Carefully read employment agency contracts before signing them. Be sure you understand how much, if anything, you will have to pay.

Common Interview Questions

In what position are you interested?

Woud you be interested in any other positions?

What other jobs have you had?

How many hours a week can you work?

Are you involved in other activities that could cause time conflicts with your work schedule?

What kinds of classes do you take in school?

What class do you like best?

In what activities do you participate at school?

Would you have transportation to and from work?

How much do you expect to earn?

How well do you work with others?

Why should we hire you?

6-7 Employers ask questions like these to help them evaluate the qualifications of a job applicant.

Good Manners Are Good Business

Arriving late for an interview keeps a busy employer waiting. This is not only bad manners, it is likely to cost you a chance for the job. An employer may assume you will not arrive on time for work if you cannot arrive on time for an interview.

Try to arrive about 10 or 15 minutes before the scheduled time of your interview. This will show the prospective employer that you are punctual. It will also give you time to collect your thoughts before the interview begins.

a question, however, you may have a clue about why the employer did not offer you the job. This will help you improve for your next interview.

Entrepreneurship

Some people do not want to work for an employer. They prefer to find opportunities, make decisions, and set schedules on their own. In other words, they prefer to be self-employed. These people are often called *entrepreneurs.* Entrepreneurs are people who set up and run their own businesses.

Many people in food-related businesses are entrepreneurs. Farmers are frequently self-employed. Grocers, butchers, and bakers often own their own stores. Many restaurateurs and caterers operate their own businesses. Dietitians may go into business as freelance consultants. Food stylists often set up their own contracts with clients and hire their own photographers. See 6-8.

Entrepreneurship holds great appeal for some people. Being their own boss makes them feel independent. They achieve a sense of satisfaction from setting and reaching their own business goals. However, entrepreneurship also involves some risks.

Starting a business takes money. The amount depends on the type of business. However, every business involves some operating expenses and requires the purchase of some equipment and supplies.

Starting a business requires responsibility and organization. If a customer is dissatisfied, an entrepreneur must be responsible for correcting the situation. Entrepreneurs must be organized to keep accurate records of their income, expenses, and money owed for taxes. They must also keep track of appointments, equipment orders, and employee files.

If entrepreneurship interests you, you should first consider several factors. Think about what kind of business you would like to start. Find out how much need there is for a business of this nature. Be sure it is something you can manage.

Consider working for someone else before starting your own business. This will give you work experience and show you some of the points involved in operating a business.

Once you have thought through your business plan, the sky is your limit. Teen entrepreneurs have been successful starting such food-related businesses as party planning, pizza delivering, and cookie baking. If you are ambitious, you too can be successful in starting a business.

6-8 Many farmers are entrepreneurs.

Summary

Thinking about your interests and abilities can help you choose a career. Getting part-time job experience and taking related classes can help you begin preparing for a career.

There are many different food-related careers. However, they all require some common skills. You need to look professional, communicate well, and get along with others. Nutrition knowledge, artistic skill, and leadership abilities would also be helpful.

Careers in the food service industry may involve preparing, serving, or cleaning up food. They may also involve managing other people. Many entry-level positions are open to people with little or no food service background. Upper-level positions may require training and/or previous experience. Catering involves a variety of food service tasks. It may appeal to people interested in running their own business.

Food handling jobs involve growing, processing, transporting, and selling food. Positions in this field are also available at a range of levels.

Most food-related careers in education and business require at least a four-year degree. These careers include teaching, extension work, dietetics and nutrition, communications, business, consumer affairs, and research.

Finding a job begins with looking for job openings. When you find an opening that interests you, you must apply for it. The impression you make in an interview with the employer will help determine whether he or she offers you the job.

If you decide working for someone else is not for you, you may want to become an entrepreneur. Starting your own business can be risky. However, many people feel the rewards are worth it.

Review What You Have Read

Write your answers on a separate sheet of paper.

1. List five questions you should ask yourself before choosing a career.
2. List four sources of information on career planning.
3. List five skills needed for success in a food-related career.
4. A person who commands authority and takes a principal role in a group is a _____.
5. Name the four types of jobs available in the food service industry. Give an example of each.
6. A career that combines all four areas of food service is _____.
7. After harvesting, foods must be processed, transported, and prepared for retail sale. Give an example of a job in each of these areas of the food handling industry.
8. True or false. A person must have a bachelor's degree to teach family and consumer sciences at any level.
9. What type of professional in a food-related career works in areas such as recipe development, food styling, and demonstration?
10. Who might employ a food professional in consumer affairs? Give two examples.
11. List three sources of information about job openings.
12. An opportunity for an employer and a job applicant to discuss the applicant's qualifications is called a(n) _____.
13. People who set up and run their own businesses are called _____.

Build Your Basic Skills

1. Check the job advertisements in your local newspaper. What types of job openings are available in the areas of food service, food handling, and business and education?
2. Interview people employed in the food industry. What are their responsibilities? What qualifications did they need to enter their career area? What are the chances for advancement? Report your findings in class.
3. Talk with your school's dietitian or cafeteria manager to learn about quantity food preparation, food purchasing, and food service management.
4. Write a one-page paper describing a food-related career that interests you. Explain what qualifications the position demands.

Build Your Thinking Skills

1. Form a research team with two of your classmates. As a team, pick a food-related career. Investigate the educational and experience requirements, responsibilities, and salary range. Prepare a report to the class. Each team member should speak on a different aspect of the career you investigated.
2. Role-play interview situations between an employer and a job applicant for a food service position. If possible, videotape the mock interviews. Play the tape and offer constructive criticism of the applicant.

Part 2
The Management of Food

The design of kitchen and dining areas should meet the needs of all family members.

Chapter 7

Kitchen and Dining Areas

A "Taste" of the World of Work

Interior Designer
Plans, designs, and furnishes interior environments of residential, commercial, and industrial buildings.

Tableware Salesperson
Displays and sells china, glassware, silver flatware, and holloware.

Formal Waiter
Serves meals to patrons according to established rules of etiquette, working in formal setting.

Terms to Know

work center
work triangle
natural light
artificial light
grounding
pigtail
dinnerware
flatware
sterling silver
silver plate
stainless steel
beverageware
lead glass
lime glass
tumbler
stemware
holloware
table linens
American (family) service
Russian (continental) service
English service
compromise service
blue plate service
buffet service
cover

Objectives

After studying this chapter, you will be able to
❑ describe the three major work centers in a kitchen and the six basic kitchen floor plans.
❑ discuss considerations in kitchen and dining area design.
❑ identify different kinds of tableware and list selection factors applicable to each.
❑ set a table attractively.
❑ wait on a table correctly.

Courtesy of Marvin Windows & Doors

The kitchen and dining areas are often the busiest areas of the home. Family members spend a lot of time in these areas planning, preparing, and eating meals. Therefore, consider the likes, dislikes, and needs of all family members when designing these areas.

When planning the design of kitchen and dining areas, family members should discuss several questions. Do you want to eat your meals in the kitchen, or do you want a separate dining room? How much storage and work space do you need in these areas? How much time will each family member spend in the kitchen and dining areas? What kinds of flooring, lighting, wall coverings, and furnishings do you like? What kind of atmosphere do you want these areas to have?

Planning the Kitchen

The entire family uses the kitchen in today's homes. Children like to make their own snacks. Teens enjoy serving food at parties. Adults share in meal preparation. Because all these people share the kitchen, it needs to be a comfortable, convenient, and efficient place to work.

Major Work Centers

When designing a kitchen, you need to think in terms of **work centers.** Kitchens have three main work centers. Each center focuses on one of the three basic groups of kitchen activities—food preparation and storage, cooking and serving, and cleanup.

The focal point of the *food preparation and storage center* is the refrigerator-freezer. This center requires cabinets for food storage. Cabinets also hold containers and tools used to store and serve frozen and refrigerated foods. Sometimes baking and mixing are done in this center. If so, the electric mixer, blender, baking utensils, and staple foods are stored here.

The *cooking and serving center* focuses on the range and oven. One side of the range should have at least 24 inches (60 cm) of counter space. This counter will hold the ingredients when you cook. Cabinets and drawers in this center store utensils, cookware, and serving pieces.

The *cleanup center* always contains the sink. It may also include a dishwasher and food waste disposer. Work done in this center includes dishwashing, cleaning vegetables and fruits, cleaning fresh fish, and soaking pots and pans. Plenty of counter space and storage space are necessities in this work center. Keep coffee and teapots, dishwashing detergent, dishcloths, towels, and a wastebasket here. You might also store canned goods and vegetables that require no refrigeration in this center. However, never store food under the sink. See 7-1.

Additional Work Centers

If the kitchen is large, it may include additional work centers. A counter between the range and refrigerator can serve as a *mixing center.* It needs to be at least 36 inches (90 cm) wide. An electric mixer, a blender, mixing bowls, measuring tools, and baking utensils need storage space. Baking ingredients, such as flour and sugar, need to be stored, too.

An *eating center* can have a variety of shapes. A separate table in the kitchen, a built-in breakfast nook, or a counter can serve as an eating area. When planning a counter eating area, provide 18 to 24 inches (45 to 60 cm) of space per person. The counter should be at least 15 inches (38 cm) deep. If the eating area is to be separate, plan to leave at least 30 inches (75 cm) clearance around the table. Add 6 inches (15 cm) more if you place the table in an area where people often walk past it.

Consider tucking a *planning center* into a corner where it can double as a communications center. Use shelves to store cookbooks, recipe cards, and phone books. Provide a desk for meal planning. Hang a bulletin board to serve as a family message center.

Some kitchens have a *laundry center.* A laundry facility within the kitchen can save steps. However, be sure to locate it away from food preparation areas.

Work Triangle

To make a kitchen as efficient as possible, place the focal points of the major work centers at the corners of an imaginary triangle. This triangle is called a **work triangle.**

Ideally, the work triangle follows the normal flow of food preparation. You remove food from the refrigerator or freezer and take it to the sink for cleaning. From the sink, you take the food to the oven or range for cooking. After cooking and eating, you return leftovers to the refrigerator.

The total distance from the range to the refrigerator to the sink should not exceed 21 feet (6.3 m). If the work triangle is large, performing tasks will require more energy.

Kitchen Floor Plans

Work centers fit into a variety of kitchen floor plans. U-shaped, L-shaped, corridor, peninsula, island, and one-wall kitchens represent the six most common floor plans. The shape of the kitchen depends largely on the size of the room.

KitchenAid

7-1 All phases of food preparation center around one of three major work centers in the kitchen.

The *U-shaped kitchen* represents the most desirable kitchen floor plan because of its compact work triangle. All the appliances and cabinets are arranged in a continuous line along three adjoining walls.

The *L-shaped kitchen* is popular because it easily adapts to a variety of room arrangements. Appliances and cabinets form a continuous line along two adjoining walls. In a large room, you might use the open area beyond the work triangle as an eating area.

Appliances and cabinets in a *corridor kitchen* are arranged on two nonadjoining walls. This can be an efficient kitchen if the room is not too long and is closed at one end. However, a long room can create a long work triangle that requires many steps.

A room that is open at both ends allows traffic through the kitchen, which can interfere with the work triangle.

The *peninsula kitchen* is most often found in large rooms. In this kitchen, a counter extends into the room, forming a peninsula. The peninsula can serve as storage space or an eating area. It can also hold a cooktop or other built-in appliance.

The *island kitchen* is also found in large rooms. In this kitchen, a counter stands alone in the center of the room. An island and a peninsula serve similar functions. In some kitchens, the island also serves as a mixing center.

The *one-wall kitchen* is found most often in apartments. All of the appliances and cabinets are along one wall. This arrangement generally does not give adequate storage or counter space. It also creates a long, narrow work triangle. Often, a folding or sliding door sets off the one-wall kitchen from other rooms. See 7-2.

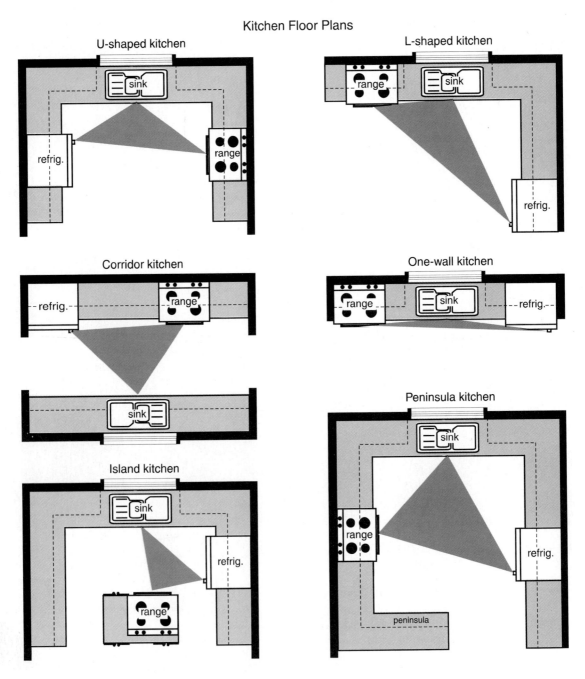

7-2 The size and shape of the work triangle depends on the kitchen floor plan.

Meeting Design Needs of People with Physical Disabilities

People with physical disabilities have special needs that must be addressed when planning kitchens for their use. A homemaker who uses a wheelchair, for instance, needs a kitchen design that allows for his or her limited mobility. Peninsula, U-shaped, and L-shaped floor plans provide the fewest restrictions to movement. A floor plan with a compact work triangle prevents a homemaker in a wheelchair from expending excess energy.

Work surfaces in a barrier-free kitchen need to be at a comfortable level. Lowering countertops, including the sink and cooktop areas, will make them easier to reach when seated in a wheelchair.

Installing a narrow shelf above the counter will provide a convenient place for items the homemaker uses often. Removing lower cabinets will allow a wheelchair to roll up to counters. A shallow sink with a rear drain also allows room underneath to accommodate a wheelchair. Undercoating the sink and insulating the hot water pipes will protect the homemaker's legs. Mounting a single-control faucet on the side of the sink will make it easy to reach. See 7-3.

Planning the Dining Area

As mentioned, you may serve meals at an eating center in the kitchen. A kitchen eating area saves steps when serving and clearing meals.

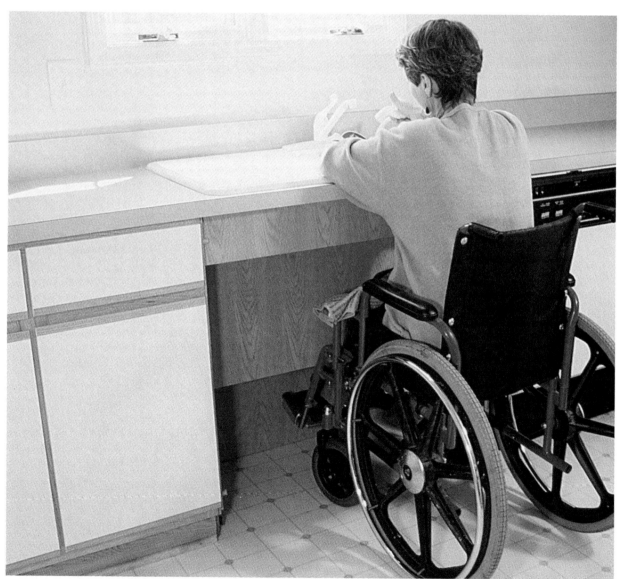

The Center for Universal Design

7-3 Removing lower cabinets increases this woman's access to the kitchen sink.

However, it may create traffic problems if the kitchen is small or poorly designed.

Many homes have a kitchen eating area for informal dining. They also have a separate dining room or attached dining area for formal meals. The location of the dining area depends on the layout of the home, the size of the family, and the preferences of family members.

Separate Dining Rooms

Some homes have space for a separate dining room. Dining rooms vary greatly in size. Some may seat just 4 people, while others seat more than 20 people.

A separate dining room encourages more gracious dining. It also provides storage for tableware and linens. However, a separate dining room may require extra steps to serve and clear meals.

Attached Dining Areas

Some homes do not have the space needed for a separate dining room. This creates a problem for family members who do not feel comfortable serving guests in a kitchen eating area. A dining area attached to the living room can be a practical solution to this problem. An attached dining area, sometimes called a *dinette,* provides the attractive decor of a dining room without the space requirements.

An attached dining area creates an excellent atmosphere for entertaining. Guests can enjoy appetizers in the comfort of the living room. Then they can move easily to the dining area for dinner. After dinner, guests can return to the comfortable seating of the living room for dessert and conversation.

You may use decorative screens to divide one area from the other, if desired. When entertaining larger groups, you can take the screens down and set up additional tables in the living room.

Other Eating Areas

Patios, porches, and decks may be used as eating areas when weather permits, 7-4. In many homes, these areas are located near the kitchen. If they are not, trays and carts with wheels can help save steps.

Meals may be eaten in the family room, living room, or den. You can carry food from the kitchen and serve it on lap trays, tray tables, or a card table.

Kitchen and Dining Area Design

At one time, kitchens were considered to be strictly utilitarian. As a result, all kitchens tended to look much alike.

Today, design has moved into the kitchen. Kitchen decoration often complements the other rooms in a home. Wall coverings, flooring, counters, cabinets, and lighting are all chosen to create a desired effect.

Like today's kitchens, dining areas require careful design consideration. Guests frequently come into these areas. Therefore, you want to select design features that will create a comfortable atmosphere.

Wall Coverings

Kitchen wall coverings should be smooth and easy to clean. Wall coverings in the dining area should enhance the mood you are trying to create. Many wall covering materials are available.

Paint gives a smooth finish and is available in many colors. Flat finish paints are suitable for dining rooms, but semigloss paints are best for kitchens. Semigloss paints are durable and their finish makes them easy to wash.

Tile is used primarily in kitchens. It is available in ceramic and metal. Tile is easy to keep clean. It can be washed with a soapy cloth, rinsed, and dried. However, tile is expensive. Some kitchen designers install tile over the sink and range areas and use paint or wallpaper for the rest of the room.

Wallpaper can add to the cheer of a kitchen or the elegance of a dining room. It is available in many colors and patterns. It is relatively inexpensive. Choose only washable wallpaper for use in kitchens.

Like wallpaper, *vinyl wall coverings* come in many patterns. They are easy to maintain and can be wiped clean with a damp cloth. This makes them an excellent choice for use in the kitchen.

Paneling can vary widely in price and appearance. It can be used to cover rough, unattractive walls in kitchen and dining areas. If used near the range or sink, it must be grease- and water-resistant.

Floor Coverings

Like wall coverings, kitchen and dining area floor coverings must be easy to clean. Floors should also provide walking comfort and durability. You can choose from several materials.

Vinyl sheets or *tiles* are popular in kitchens. They are durable and easy to maintain. All are grease- and water-resistant. Many do not need waxing. Vinyl sheets and tiles are fairly expensive.

Carpeting is available in many patterns and colors. It provides good walking comfort and reduces noise. For the kitchen, choose carpeting especially designed for use in the kitchen. For

7-4 An outdoor eating area, such as this redwood deck, provides an appealing setting for casual, warm-weather dining.

dining areas, stain-resistant carpeting is a good choice. Carpeting is fairly expensive. It requires frequent vacuuming, and spills must be wiped up immediately.

Area rugs can add to the elegance of a formal dining room. However, avoid rugs in the kitchen. The danger of tripping on rugs causes them to be a safety hazard.

Some people choose to use no floor covering in their kitchens and dining areas. Instead, they prefer the beauty of natural wood flooring. *Wood* can be expensive, but its durability makes it economical. Some wood floors require cleaning and waxing. However, newer floors are often treated with a protective coating. This coating requires only damp mopping, but it needs renewing every year or two. See 7-5.

Countertops

In the kitchen, countertops provide work space. In dining areas, counter space is used for serving food and clearing dirty dishes.

7-5 Wood flooring lends natural warmth and beauty to a dining room.

Most kitchen countertops are made of laminated plastic or ceramic tiles. *Laminated plastic* comes in many colors and patterns. It is easy to clean, moisture-resistant, and durable. Cost varies depending on quality. Heat can damage laminated plastics.

Unlike laminated plastic, *ceramic tiles* are heatproof. They are available in many colors and patterns, and they are durable. Special design effects can be achieved with ceramic tiles. Tiles can be costly, however, and the grouting between the tiles can be difficult to clean.

Counter surfaces in dining areas are often made of *wood*. The tops of wooden buffets or sideboards are frequently used for counter space. Use hot pads or trivets to protect wooden surfaces from the heat of hot dishes. Wooden surfaces also need protection from spills and the moisture created by condensation on cold dishes.

Cabinets

Cabinets are needed in kitchen and dining areas to store food, appliances, cleaning supplies, cooking utensils, dinnerware, and table decorations. Like other kitchen fixtures, kitchen cabinets need to be easy to clean. Cabinets in dining areas should complement other furnishings.

Cabinets may support countertops or be mounted on walls or ceilings above countertops and appliances. Tall, freestanding cabinets and specialty cabinets, such as corner cabinets with a lazy Susan, are also common in kitchens. In dining areas, china cabinets may be used to display china, crystal, and other items.

Cabinets are made from a number of materials. *Wood* and *wood veneer* are popular. They add warmth and natural beauty to a room. Wood cabinets should be protected with a moisture-resistant finish.

Plastic laminates are popular for kitchen cabinets. They come in a variety of colors and are easy to clean.

Glass insets are popular on the doors of some kitchen and dining room cabinets. They allow people to see china, crystal, and other items displayed inside the cabinet. Glass cabinets are somewhat fragile and must be cleaned often to look their best.

Lighting

In the kitchen, you need adequate lighting to prevent eyestrain and accidents while performing food preparation tasks. In the dining room, you might use dimmer lighting to create a cozy or romantic atmosphere. However, lighting must be sufficient to allow diners to see what they are eating.

The amount of light needed depends on the size of the room. The color of the walls and ceiling and the arrangement of furnishings and equipment also affect lighting needs.

Lighting can be classified as natural or artificial. *Natural light* comes from the sun. The amount of natural light available during daylight hours depends on the size and placement of windows, doors, and skylights. If natural light is not adequate for performing kitchen and dining tasks, it must be supplemented with artificial light.

Artificial light most often comes from electrical fixtures. Ceiling fixtures provide general lighting for a room. However, they may not provide enough light for detailed kitchen tasks. On the other hand, light from ceiling fixtures may be too bright in dining areas. Therefore, additional light fixtures are often installed over the range and under cabinets to provide task lighting in the kitchen. Accent lamps and candles may be used to achieve softer lighting in dining areas. See 7-6.

Ventilation

You need ventilation in the kitchen to remove steam, heat, and cooking odors. Proper ventilation also helps maintain a comfortable dining atmosphere. Room size and the number and placement of windows and outside doors determine the

ComEd

7-6 This kitchen receives natural light through the window as well as artificial light from the overhead fixture.

Protect the Planet

Try using compact fluorescent light bulbs in kitchen and dining areas. They use less energy and last much longer than standard incandescent bulbs.

amount of natural ventilation available. Velocity and direction of the wind also affect ventilation.

If natural ventilation is not adequate, a fan is necessary. In the kitchen, you can put an exhaust fan in a hood over a cooking surface. You can also install a fan in the ceiling or wall over the range. In the dining area, you might install a ceiling fan to circulate air. Some ceiling fans are combined with light fixtures to provide lighting as well as ventilation.

Electrical Wiring

Kitchens need a large supply of electricity to safely operate food preparation and cleanup appliances. In dining areas, electricity is needed primarily for lighting. You also need electricity to operate serving appliances, such as coffeemakers and warming trays.

When wiring is inadequate, circuits often become overloaded. Be aware of the warning signs of overloaded circuits. Circuit breakers may trip or fuses may blow frequently. Motor-driven appliances, such as mixers, may slow down during operation. Lights may dim when an appliance is being used. Appliances that heat, such as toasters, may take a long time to become hot. If any of these signals occurs, call a qualified electrician to check the wiring in your home.

For safety, appliances should be **grounded.** If an appliance with a damaged wire is grounded, the electric current will flow to the ground instead of through your body. Thus you will not receive a severe or fatal shock.

The National Electrical Code requires all new homes to have an equipment grounding wire installed as part of the wiring system. Appliances are grounded to this wire. If the outlets in your home have three holes, an equipment grounding wire has been installed. Many appliances have a three-pronged plug that fits into the three holes, thereby grounding the appliance. See 7-7.

If the outlets in your home have just two holes, you will need a two-pronged adapter for your grounded appliances. Insert one end of the adapter into the outlet. Insert the appliance plug into the

ComEd

7-7 Electrical outlets with three holes indicate that an equipment grounding wire has been installed in the home. Appliances that plug into these outlets are automatically grounded.

other end. The adapter has a small wire called a *pigtail* attached to it. Attach the pigtail to the screw on the electrical outlet plate. This grounds the appliance.

Low-Cost Redecorating

Most kitchens and dining rooms do not require major remodeling to be efficient and attractive. In many cases, a little redecorating is all you need to update the look of these rooms.

Before beginning any redecorating, analyze the room to decide what you want to improve. Then establish a budget that you feel will allow you to affordably reach your goals.

A fresh coat of paint or some new wallpaper can perk up the dullest kitchen or dining area. Hardware and department stores have frequent sales on both paint and wallpaper.

Worn cabinets may not require replacement. Painting or refinishing the doors and adding new hardware can do wonders.

Stained or marred countertops do not always have to be removed. You may be able to refinish a marred surface or replace a stained section with a new piece of laminated plastic.

If storage space is a problem, try hanging inexpensive shelves. Put a freestanding storage cabinet in an unused corner. Use pegboard to hang pots, pans, and other utensils.

Play It Safe

Extension cords can increase your flexibility when you have a limited number of electrical outlets. However, ordinary extension cords are not suitable for use with many appliances. They become too hot and can be fire hazards. Use a heavy-duty extension cord designed for appliance use. A heavy-duty cord uses a heavier wire than a normal cord, and thus can carry a heavier electrical load.

When decorating a kitchen or dining area, consider cleanliness. Food must be prepared and served in sanitary surroundings, so decorative objects should be washable. Items used in the kitchen should also be resistant to moisture and heat. Live plants can add color to a room. However, be sure they are nonpoisonous, and keep them away from food preparation areas.

Look through magazines for low-cost redecorating suggestions. Visit decorating stores to investigate your options. Ask family members for their ideas. With a little effort and creativity, you can make your kitchen and dining areas more attractive and efficient.

Table Appointments

In the dining area, the table becomes the center of attention. The dinnerware, flatware, beverageware, linens, and other table appointments help make the table an attractive setting for food.

Dinnerware

Dinnerware includes plates, cups, saucers, and bowls. Many qualities and patterns are available. The material used to make dinnerware helps determine its durability and cost.

China, stoneware, earthenware, and pottery are all *ceramic* materials used to make dinnerware. Ceramic dinnerware is made from clay that is shaped and fired in a kiln (heated to high temperatures in a special oven). The dinnerware then is glazed with a protective coating and fired again. Variations in clays, firing temperatures, and firing processes make each type of dinnerware different in strength, appearance, and cost.

China is the most expensive type of dinnerware, but it is elegant and durable. Most china is white, off-white, or pastel, but many patterns are available. *Stoneware* is heavier and more casual than china, but it is less expensive. Like stoneware, *earthenware* is moderately priced. However, it is less durable than stoneware. *Pottery* is the least expensive type of ceramic dinnerware. It is thick and heavy and tends to chip and break easily. Stoneware, earthenware, and pottery are all available in a variety of colors and patterns.

Glass-ceramic and plastic are other materials used to make dinnerware. *Glass-ceramic* is strong and durable, and is available in plain white as well as a number of patterns. *Plastic* is lightweight, break-resistant, and colorful, although it may stain and scratch over time. It is most suitable for very casual meals. Dinnerware made from both of these materials is relatively inexpensive.

Flatware

Flatware, often called "silverware," includes knives, forks, spoons, serving utensils (such as serving spoons), and specialty utensils (such as seafood forks). Most flatware is made of sterling silver, silver plate, or stainless steel. As with dinnerware, the material helps determine appearance and cost.

Sterling silver contains 92.5 percent silver, with copper added for strength. It is heavy and durable. It is also the most expensive type of flatware.

Silver-plated flatware is made by coating a base metal with silver. Silver plate will last many years, but eventually the silver will begin to wear off. It is less expensive than sterling silver, but is still costly.

Stainless steel is an alloy composed of steel, nickel, and chromium. It is not impervious to stains; it just stains less than ordinary steel.

Be a Clever Consumer

When selecting dinnerware, consider how the color and design will look with food. Pick up a cup to see if it is comfortable to hold. Check the finish of the dinnerware. There should be no chips, cracks, or unglazed spots. China should be translucent, and the glaze should not be wavy or bumpy.

Stainless steel is durable and generally less expensive than silver plate.

Sterling silver and silver plate require polishing to remove tarnish caused by exposure to air and certain foods. Stainless steel does not tarnish, but like silver, it can be affected by eggs, vinegar, salt, tea, and coffee. To prevent staining, avoid prolonged contact with these foods and carefully rinse flatware as soon as possible.

When selecting flatware, consider the general shape of each piece, its weight, and the way it feels in your hand. A well-designed piece should feel sturdy and well balanced. Look at the finish. All edges should be smooth. Silver plate should be evenly plated.

Beverageware

Beverageware includes glasses of many shapes and sizes, 7-8. Beverageware adds both beauty and height to a table setting. It may be clear or colored, transparent or opaque. It may be plain or decorated by cutting, etching, or frosting.

Beverageware is often called *glassware.* Glassware can be made of lead glass or lime glass. *Lead glass* is used to make higher quality, more expensive glassware. *Lime glass* is lighter and more brittle than lead glass, but it is ideal for many kinds of glassware.

Plastic beverageware is the most casual and least costly of all beverageware. Because it is unbreakable, plastic beverageware is a good choice for serving young children.

Beverageware comes in two basic shapes—tumblers and stemware. *Tumblers* do not have stems. Juice, highball, and cooler are popular tumbler sizes. *Stemware* has three parts—a bowl, a stem, and a foot. Water goblets, wine glasses, and champagne glasses are popular stemware pieces.

When choosing beverageware, consider the look and feel. Think about how it will look with your dinnerware and flatware. Look to see that the joints between the different parts of stemware are invisible. Examine the edges of beverageware to be sure they are smooth and free from nicks. Check the shape and design of the glasses. They should

Libbey

7-8 Different shapes of glasses are designed to hold different types of beverages.

feel comfortable to hold and be well balanced so they will not tip over when filled or empty.

If selecting lead glassware, look at how the glass catches light. Brilliance is an indication of quality. Gently tap the glass with your finger. It should produce a lingering, bell-like ring. Choose pieces that are multipurpose. For instance, you can use some stemware for serving shrimp cocktails, fruit cups, and ice cream sundaes as well as beverages.

Holloware

Holloware includes bowls and tureens, which are used to serve food, and pitchers and pots, which are used to serve liquids. Holloware may be made of metal, glass, wood, or ceramic. Some holloware pieces have heating elements.

Holloware tends to be expensive, fragile, and difficult to store. You may purchase holloware pieces to match your dinnerware. However, unmatched holloware that complements other table appointments is less expensive and more popular.

Purchasing Tableware

Dinnerware, flatware, beverageware, and holloware are all referred to as *tableware*. All three types of tableware are available in many patterns and at a variety of prices. When purchasing tableware, you will want to choose items that go well together. You also will want to consider your personal taste, your lifestyle, and the amount of money you have to spend. If you enjoy formal entertaining and can afford the expense, you might select china, sterling silver, and lead glass to grace your table. If you prefer more casual, less expensive tableware, you might choose stoneware, stainless steel, and lime glass for your table.

You can purchase tableware in several ways. You can buy some tableware as *open stock*. This means you can purchase each piece individually. Purchasing open stock tableware has several advantages. You can add serving pieces as you need them and are able to afford them. You can also replace pieces that have broken. Before choosing tableware that is open stock, however, be sure to ask how long your particular pattern will be produced. Some patterns are produced for just a few years.

Dinnerware and flatware are often sold in *place settings*. A place setting includes all the pieces used by one person. For instance, a place setting of dinnerware usually includes a dinner plate, salad plate, sauce dish or bread and butter plate, cup, and saucer. A place setting of flatware usually includes a knife, dinner fork, salad fork, teaspoon, and soup spoon.

You can also buy some tableware *by the set*. A box of four water glasses and a set of dinnerware for eight are examples of sets. You can often save money by purchasing by the set. However, it may be difficult to replace broken pieces.

Caring for Tableware

Proper handling and storage will extend the life and beauty of your tableware. Rinse tableware as soon as possible after use. Dried food particles are difficult to remove.

Most tableware is dishwasher-safe. However, flatware and beverageware may water spot if allowed to dry in a dishwasher.

Some delicate china and stemware may require hand washing. Use warm, soapy water, and handle items carefully to avoid chipping and breaking. Avoid plunging cold tableware into hot water. Severe temperature changes can cause cracking.

Store tableware carefully. Careless handling of dinnerware and beverageware may result in chipped, cracked, or broken pieces. Tossing flatware carelessly into a drawer can cause scratching and bending. Store china with protective pads between individual pieces. Avoid stacking bowls, cups, and glasses. Cover sterling silver and silver-plated flatware and store it in a dry place. Taking these precautions will keep your tableware looking lovely for years.

Table Linens

The term **table linens** includes both table coverings and napkins. Table linens are used to protect the surface of the table. They also deaden sounds of serving and clearing and add beauty to the table setting.

Tablecloths provide a background for your table setting. The *drop* is the part of the tablecloth that hangs over the edge of the table. The drop should be 6 to 8 inches (15 to 20 cm) on all sides of the table for a casual table setting. The drop should be 8 to 10 inches (20 to 25 cm) for a formal table setting. A greater drop is needed on buffet tables.

Place mats and table runners are also popular table coverings. *Place mats* usually measure about 11 by 17 inches (28 to 43 cm). They come in several shapes and can be used for all but the most formal occasions. *Table runners* usually are 13 to 17 inches (33 to 43 cm) wide and slightly longer than the length of the table. They are often used with tablecloths or place mats. See 7-9.

Napkins can match the other table linens or provide a contrast. Common napkin sizes are as follows: cocktail—10 inches (25 cm), luncheon—13 inches (33 cm), and dinner—17 inches (43 cm) or more.

At one time, all table linens were made from linen fabrics. Today, many materials are used to make table linens, including linen, lace, plastic, and paper. Table linens are available in a rainbow of solid colors as well as a variety of prints.

If your dinnerware has a definite pattern, it probably will look best against a plain background. If your dinnerware is very plain, patterned table linens can add interest to the table setting. Table linens with rough textures and bright colors look best in casual settings. Table linens with smooth textures and plain white or pastel colors complement formal settings.

The amount of care table linens need depends on the materials used in their construction. Paper tablecloths, place mats, and napkins are inexpensive and save cleanup time. However, paper linens are generally appropriate only for casual dining. Vinyl-coated tablecloths and place mats can be wiped clean with a damp cloth, but they too are considered casual. Most fabric cloths can be machine washed and dried. Linen cloths and napkins must be laundered carefully and then ironed while still damp.

The table linens you choose will depend on your other table appointments and your lifestyle. Before purchasing table linens, you should consider

Product and photo from Domestications catalog

7-9 This table runner looks attractive used in conjunction with the matching place mat and napkin.

durability, ease of laundering, colorfastness, and shrinkage.

Centerpieces

Centerpieces add interest to the dining table. They may be simple or elaborate, depending on your other table appointments and the mood you are trying to create.

You can buy centerpieces or make them. When making a centerpiece, be creative in your choice of materials and the arrangement you use. However, avoid using potted plants. Soil and food do not mix.

A centerpiece should be in proportion to the size of the table. Check to see that the centerpiece is not so large that guests cannot see over it while seated.

Candles should not be used on the table during the day. However, they can create a special mood at evening meals. If you put candles on your table, light them and be sure they burn above or below eye level.

Meal Service

You can serve meals in several ways. The style of service you select will depend on the formality of the meal, the menu, and the availability of help.

The six major styles of meal service are American or family, Russian or continental, English, compromise, blue plate, and buffet. They differ in three ways

- the manner in which the guests are served
- the number of courses served
- the person who serves the food

American or *family service* is the style most often used in homes in the United States. In this style of service, the host fills serving dishes in the kitchen and takes them to the table, 7-10. Diners

Whirlpool Corp.

7-10 American service requires table space for serving dishes.

serve themselves as they pass the serving dishes around the table. After clearing the table, the host may serve dessert at the table or from the kitchen.

Russian or *continental service* is the most formal style of meal service. In Russian service, serving dishes are never placed on the table. Instead, servants serve guests filled plates of food, one course at a time. Plate replaces plate as one course is removed and another is served. This type of service often is used in fine restaurants and at state dinners.

In *English service,* one of the hosts fills plates at the table and passes them from guest to guest until everyone is served. Because English service requires a lot of passing, it is best for use with small groups.

Compromise service is a compromise between Russian service and English service. The salad or dessert course is often served from the kitchen. For the other courses, one of the hosts fills the plates and passes them around the table. One person acts as waiter to clear one course and bring in the next.

Blue plate service is used at home when serving small groups of people. It is also used at banquets where waiters are able to serve a crowd quickly. In blue plate service, the host fills plates in the kitchen and carries them to the dining room. The host may offer second helpings at the table or refill plates in the kitchen. One person clears the main course and then brings in the dessert course.

Buffet service is often used for serving large numbers of people. A dining table, a buffet, or another surface may hold the serving dishes and utensils, dinnerware, flatware, and napkins. The guests serve themselves from the buffet.

Depending on the amount of space available, guests may eat at one large table, at several smaller tables, or from lap trays. If space is limited, they may eat from a plate held in the hand while sitting or standing. If guests will be seated at a table, the host may place napkins, flatware, and beverageware on the table ahead of time.

Buffet service requires careful menu planning. Meats will need to be precarved unless someone will carve at the buffet table. Equipment may be needed to keep hot foods hot and cold foods cold. Precutting foods into individual pieces and pouring beverages ahead of time will make serving easier.

Setting the Table

You should set a table for convenience as well as beauty. However, there is no "right" way to set a table. The occasion, the style of service, the size of the table, and the menu help determine how you set the table.

When setting the table, it is helpful to think in terms of individual covers. A *cover* is the amount of space needed by each person. The cover contains the linen, dinnerware, flatware, and beverageware needed by one person. Each cover should be at least 24 inches (61 cm) wide. Each guest should know which appointments are his or hers.

Begin setting the table with the table linens. A tablecloth should extend evenly on each side of the table. You may lay place mats flush with the edge of the table or 1 to 1½ inches (2.5 to 4 cm) from the table edge. Place runners down the center of the table, along both sides of the table, or around the perimeter of the table.

You can fold napkins in several ways. Traditionally, the rectangle has been the preferred shape. Place the napkin to the left of the forks or on the service plate or dinner plate.

You do not have to place the centerpiece in the middle of the table. You might place small arrangements diagonally at two corners of the table. You might place a large centerpiece along the back edge of a buffet table that is against a wall.

The pieces of dinnerware placed on the table depend on the menu and style of service. Place the dinner plate or service plate in the center of each cover, 1 inch (2.5 cm) from the edge of the table. (A *service plate* is larger than a dinner plate. In formal service, a waiter places the pieces of dinnerware containing courses preceding the main course on the service plate. The waiter removes the service plate just before placing the dinner plate for the main course.) Handle dinnerware without touching the eating surfaces.

Place flatware on the table with the forks on the left and the knives and spoons on the right. The bottom of each piece should be in line with the bottom of the dinner plate. Be sure to turn all knife blades toward the plate. Place forks and spoons with tines and bowls turned upward.

Place flatware in the order in which it will be used. For instance, suppose you are serving the salad course before the main course. In this case, place the salad fork to the left of the dinner fork. However, if you are serving the salad after the main course, place the salad fork to the right of the dinner fork. Salad forks are not necessary if you are serving the salad with the main course. Place a soup spoon to the right of the teaspoon if you are serving soup before the entrée. You can place dessert spoons or forks above the dinner plate.

The placement of beverageware revolves around the water glass. Place the water glass just above the tip of the knife. Place other glasses below and to the right of the water glass. Place the cup and saucer to the right of the knife and spoon.

Diners will need additional pieces of dinnerware at more formal meals. Place the salad plate to the left of the dinner plate above the napkin. Place the bread and butter plate just above the salad plate, between the salad plate and the dinner plate. See 7-11.

Serving utensils include carving forks and knives and serving spoons and forks. If using only one utensil, place it to the right of the serving dish. If using two utensils, place the utensil that will assist to the left of the dish. Place the utensil that will pick up to the right of the dish. For instance, place a carving fork on the left of a meat platter. Place the knife on the right.

Place salt to the right of the pepper when setting the table. Place rolls, butter, and other foods that will be self-served to the right or left of the host's cover. Place serving utensils needed for any of these foods to the right of the dish unless using an underliner.

Waiting on the Table

Rules for waiting on the table are as flexible as rules for setting the table. The style of service and the menu help determine the way in which you clear the table and serve new courses.

Establishing the Order

Clear the table in a counterclockwise direction. The person who is waiting on the table usually begins with the cohost. However, if a female guest is present, she is seated to the host's left and her cover is cleared first. If an elderly guest is present, his or her cover is cleared first.

Serve a new course in the same manner. Serve the cohost first, followed by the person seated to his or her right, and so forth around the table.

Clearing and Serving

You will use both hands when serving and clearing, but usually at different times. When serving or clearing plates, you should stand at the guest's left and place or remove the plate with your left hand. This avoids a possible collision with the water glass on the right.

Remove beverageware and unused knives and spoons from the guest's right side with your right hand. Place dessert flatware in the same manner, and pour water from the right with the right hand.

When clearing or serving, a cart or large tray can save time and steps. The order for the removal of a course is as follows:

1. All serving dishes and utensils are removed from the table or side table and taken to the kitchen.

2. Beginning with the appropriate person, clear each cover. Remove the dinner plate with the left hand and transfer it to the right hand. If removing a second plate, remove it with your left hand. If removing a third plate, place the second plate on top of the first plate. Then remove the third

Oneida Silversmiths

7-11 A properly set table provides each diner with the tableware pieces he or she will need for the meal being served.

plate with the left hand. Take cleared plates to a serving cart or the kitchen. Continue this process around the table in a counterclockwise direction until all covers have been cleared.

3. Use a small tray to remove flatware and other items not needed for the next course.

4. If necessary, refill the water glasses from each guest's right, using the right hand. Avoid picking up glasses. Instead, carefully slide them by the base toward the edge of the table. Use a clean napkin to catch drips.

The order for serving a new course is the opposite of the order for removing a course.

1. Place needed flatware, such as cake forks or dessert spoons, at each cover.

2. Place cream, sugar, and other needed items on the table.

3. Place needed dinnerware at each cover.

4. Place food and/or beverages, 7-12

7-12 After clearing the dishes from the main course, the table can be reset to serve dessert.

Summary

Kitchen and dining areas are heavily used spaces in the home. With careful planning, their design will meet the needs of all family members. Three major kitchen work centers focus on the tasks of preparing and storing food, cooking and serving, and cleanup. If space allows, a home may include additional work centers for such tasks as mixing, eating, planning, and doing laundry. An imaginary line connects the three major work centers to form a work triangle. This triangle takes on different dimensions in different kitchen floor plans. Peninsula, U-shaped, and L-shaped plans can most easily be adapted to meet the needs of family members with physical disabilities.

Dining space in the home may be in a separate dining room or in a dining area attached to the living room. You can also serve food in other areas of the home, depending on family preferences.

The design of kitchen and dining areas should be both attractive and functional. Choose wall coverings, floor coverings, countertops, and cabinets to suit a family's decorating tastes. Plan adequate lighting, ventilation, and electrical wiring to safely handle necessary tasks. With a little planning and creativity, updating the appearance of kitchen and dining areas will not cost a lot of money.

Table appointments can be chosen to suit any taste, lifestyle, and budget. Plates, cups, saucers, and bowls are called dinnerware. Various knives, forks, spoons, and serving utensils are referred to as flatware. Tumblers and stemware are the two basic shapes of beverageware. Items used to serve food and liquids, such as bowls and pitchers, are known as holloware. Table linens protect the table and provide a background for other table appointments. A centerpiece adds beauty to the dining table. The materials used to make table appointments affects their cost, durability, and care requirements.

You can serve meals in a variety of ways, depending on the menu and the occasion. The style of meal service will help determine the way you should set the table. Style of service will also affect the way you serve and clear courses.

Review What You Have Read

Write your answers on a separate sheet of paper.
1. List the three major kitchen work centers.
2. What is the most desirable kitchen floor plan?
3. Briefly describe three different dining areas.
4. What qualities do floor coverings used in kitchen and dining areas require?
5. Name the two classifications of lighting and give sources of each.
6. What factors determine the amount of natural ventilation available in a room?
7. What are the four ceramic materials used to make dinnerware?
8. What are the two basic shapes of beverageware?
9. Describe the three ways tableware may be purchased.
10. List three types of table linens.
11. What type of meal service is used most often in homes in the United States?
12. Make a drawing that shows how you would set the table for a family meal in which the salad is eaten with the main dish and water is the only beverage.

Build Your Basic Skills

1. Go to a home improvement store that sells flooring and carpeting. Choose kitchen carpeting and a vinyl sheet design that appeal to you. Figure the cost of covering a 10- by 14-foot (3.0- by 4.3-meter) kitchen floor with each of these products.
2. Investigate where and when one of the styles of meal service developed. Share your findings in a brief oral report.

Build Your Thinking Skills

1. Pretend to make a cake in your foods lab, following the directions on a packaged mix. While you are doing this, have a partner count the number of times you walk along each side of the work triangle. When you have finished, brainstorm with your partner to come up with ideas for reducing the distance you walked. Share your suggestions with the rest of the class.
2. Develop a checklist of desirable characteristics for kitchen and dining area wall coverings, floor coverings, countertops, cabinets, lighting, ventilation, and electrical wiring. Use the checklist to determine how many of these positive characteristics are found in the kitchen and dining area in your home.
3. Compare flatware made of sterling silver, silver plate, and stainless steel. List the advantages and disadvantages of each material.

Today's appliances make food preparation and cleanup easier. Major appliances are available in a range of styles and offer a wide variety of features. Portable appliances perform a multitude of kitchen tasks. Keep in mind that kitchen appliances are an investment. You can spend a lot of money for appliances. You will probably be using the appliances you choose for many years. Therefore, you will want to plan your appliance purchases carefully.

Safety and Service

Information is available when you buy an appliance to help you know what you can expect from your purchase. Using this information can help you buy safe, efficient products. Safety seals, warranties, and EnergyGuide labels can help you get your money's worth when you shop for appliances.

Safety Seals

Check to see that an electrical appliance has the *Underwriters Laboratories* (UL) seal, 8-1. If the seal is on the body of the appliance, the entire appliance has met safety standards.

Gas appliances should have the blue star seal given by the *American Gas Association* (AGA), 8-2. The blue star certification indicates that the appliance meets safety, durability, and performance standards.

Warranties

A *warranty* is the seller's promise that a product will be free of defects and will perform as specified. A warranty can be full or limited. A *full warranty* states that the issuer will repair or replace a faulty product free of charge. The warrantor may also opt to give you a refund for the product. A *limited warranty* states conditions under which the

8-1 Electrical appliances carrying the Underwriters Laboratories seal have been carefully tested for safety.

8-2 Gas appliances carrying the blue star certification of the American Gas Association have met safety standards.

issuer will service, repair, or replace an appliance. For instance, you may have to pay labor costs, or you might have to take the appliance back to the warrantor.

Carefully check the warranty and be sure you understand the terms before you buy an appliance. Both limited and full warranties must state how and where you can fulfill them. They must also give other details about coverage. Review the warranty to see if it covers the entire item, or just parts. Find out if it includes labor costs. Note how long the warranty is in effect.

Terms of a warranty should be stated clearly so you can understand them. If you have any questions, call or write the manufacturer.

Service Contracts

A *service contract* is like an insurance policy for major appliances that you can buy from an appliance dealer. Service contracts cover the cost of needed repairs for a period of time after the warranty has expired. However, if your appliance does not need repairs, you receive no service for the money you spent on the contract.

Most warranties cover the time period during which you are likely to need service. If you are thinking about buying a service contract, be sure you know what you are getting. Read the terms of the contract carefully. Find out if it covers both parts and labor. Ask if the coverage will be good if you sell the appliance or move out of the service area. Check to see if there is a limit to the amount of service you may receive. Be sure you understand all the terms fully before you buy the contract.

EnergyGuide Labels

EnergyGuide labels show an estimated yearly energy usage for major appliances. This estimate is expressed on a scale in kilowatt-hours. The end points of the scale show the highest and lowest energy usage of similar models. An estimated yearly operating cost is also given for the model on which the label appears. This cost is based on national average energy costs.

The Federal Trade Commission (FTC) requires EnergyGuide labels on refrigerators, refrigerator-freezers, freezers, and dishwashers as well as several nonkitchen appliances. You can use these labels when you shop. Compare EnergyGuide labels on appliances of similar style and size. This will tell you which model is the most energy efficient and least costly to operate. See 8-3.

Major Kitchen Appliances

Every part of kitchen activity involves major appliances. You use them to cook and store food and to clean up after preparing food. Today's appliances have many convenience features that reduce the time and effort needed to do these tasks.

When shopping for an appliance, you should consider your need for it and your family's requirements. You should also think about your space limitations and your budget.

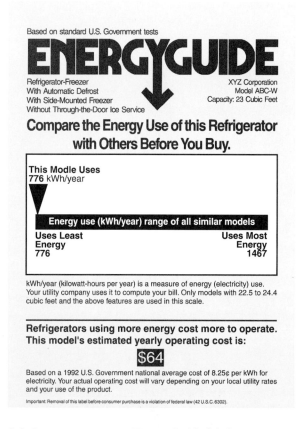

8-3 Consumers can use EnergyGuide labels to compare the energy efficiency of various models of an appliance.

The size and capacity of appliance you need depends on the size of your family. For instance, a family of eight might find a dishwasher a necessity, but a single person might not.

The style and features you desire in an appliance will also depend on family members' needs. For instance, appliances are available to help meet the needs of people with disabilities. Appliances with Braille touch pad controls assist homemakers who are blind. A built-in oven would be a good choice for a homemaker who uses a wheelchair. It can be installed in the wall at a level that is comfortable to reach while seated. Oven and cooktop controls can be mounted on the front of appliances to make them easy to reach. A side-by-side refrigerator-freezer is also a good choice. It gives the disabled homemaker easy access to both refrigerated and frozen foods. Some manufacturers are working on voice-activated appliances to meet the needs of people with disabilities. See 8-4.

Size is an important factor to consider when buying an appliance. Measure the appliance to find out if it will fit in the area where you want to put it. There must be adequate space for servicing and ventilation. Also measure the doors in your home. They must be wide enough to move the appliance into the room where you plan to install it.

Major appliances require a large financial investment. You must plan their purchase just like any other major household purchase. However, do not buy strictly on the basis of price. Service is also an important consideration. A bargain appliance may not seem to be such a good buy if no one in your area will service it.

Some consumers choose to purchase major appliances through *rent-to-own* plans. A customer makes small weekly or monthly payments. At the end of a contract term (usually one to two years), the customer owns the appliance. These plans may seem attractive because they require no down payment and no customer credit check. However, consumers should be aware that appliances

Be a Clever Consumer

When appliance hunting, visit several dealers to compare prices. Inquire about installation and delivery costs and any other costs not included in the purchase price. These items vary from dealer to dealer. They can significantly add to the price of an appliance.

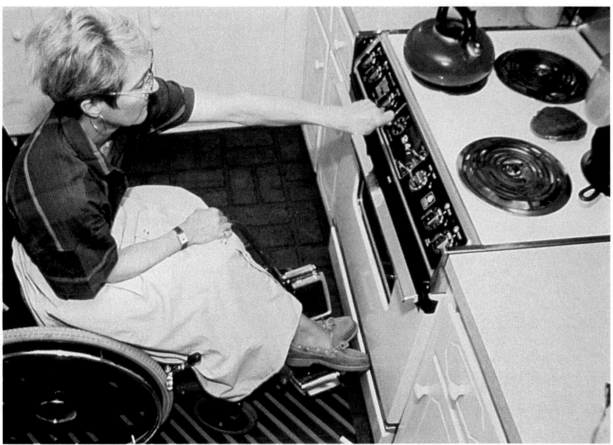

8-4 A range with front-mounted controls installed in an area with adequate clearance space would help meet the needs of a homemaker who uses a wheelchair.

purchased in this way often cost two to three times the retail price.

Trends in Major Kitchen Appliances

Consumers today are looking for appliances that perform a variety of functions but require little effort from the user. They want compact models to conserve space in smaller homes and apartments. They also want energy efficient features to help reduce utility bills. Current appliance designs reflect all of these needs.

Today's appliances do more tasks in less space and with less energy. Appliances have more convenience features than ever before. Appliances are easy to use and may be self-monitoring. Space-saving appliances are available as an alternative to standard models. Some are smaller than full-size appliances. Others just make better use of existing space. Many new appliances do a better job than appliances of the past while using less energy. Heavier insulation and temperature sensors help

appliances operate efficiently. Redesigned appliances also run more quietly than appliances built in the past.

Another trend in the appliance industry is the use of high-tech electronics. Electronics allow consumers to use touch pad controls to program their appliances for specific tasks. Electronics also monitor the systems in the appliance and provide feedback for the consumer.

Many appliances now have digital displays and some even have voice modules. These features tell the user what settings he or she has selected on the appliance. They can show how a programmed cycle is progressing. They can also indicate when something is not working properly.

Today's consumers want appliances that look modern. This has led manufacturers to design sleek, European-styled appliances. Smooth surfaces, stainless steel finishes, and gourmet features give appliances a European look. White and almond are popular appliance colors because they fit into almost any decor.

Ranges

Ranges are available in several types and styles with a variety of features. Before purchasing one, carefully analyze your own cooking and baking needs. Then study the many models available.

Fuel

You first need to choose the type of fuel you wish to use—gas or electricity. One fuel might be more plentiful in your area or be less expensive to use. Fuel hookups in your home may determine your choice. Many times, you may decide based on your personal preferences.

Electric ranges require a 240 volt electrical circuit for operation. Electric current flows through coils of wire called heating elements. The current produces heat. Coils can be visible; hidden under a smooth, glass-ceramic top; or concealed under cast iron solid elements.

Some electric ranges now feature high speed *radiant* elements and *quartz halogen* elements under glass-ceramic cooktops. These elements heat much faster than traditional electric coils.

Gas ranges require both a gas line and a 120 volt electrical circuit. Range accessories, such as timers, clocks, and lights, require electricity. Gas ranges can use bottled manufactured gas (liquefied petroleum or LP gas) or natural gas, 8-5.

In the burners, heat results from the combustion of the gas with oxygen from the air. Controlling the amount of gas that comes through the valve regulates the heat. As more gas flows through the valve, the flame becomes higher and the temperature becomes hotter. In the oven, a thermostat controls the opening and closing of the gas valve. This, in turn, maintains the flame for the appropriate temperature.

Many gas ranges have **pilotless ignition.** Electric igniters replace pilot lights on the range surface and in the oven. Since pilot lights can use as much as 30 percent of the total gas used by a range, this feature saves energy. The pilotless ignition system requires electricity to work. However, you can use a match to light the burners when the electricity is off.

KitchenAid

8-5 A gas range burns bottled or natural gas to cook food.

In most gas ranges, the broiler is a separate unit located under the oven. In electric ranges and in some gas ranges, the broiler is in the oven.

A few appliance manufacturers are now making ranges and cooktops that allow consumers to cook with both gas and electricity. These mixed-fuel ranges are designed for consumers with specific cooking needs and preferences. One model has a gas cooktop with an electric oven. Another features a modular cooktop. It allows a consumer to place modules with gas burners and electric elements side by side.

Range Styles

Ranges are available with several different oven arrangements. Some have a single gas or electric oven. Some have two ovens, one of which may be a convection or microwave oven. Some have an oven that does both conventional and convection cooking. These models add the speed and even cooking of a convection oven to the capacity of a conventional oven.

Ranges come in four basic styles: freestanding, built-in, slide-in, and drop-in. *Freestanding ranges* can have an oven below the surface unit or both above and below. Freestanding ranges have finished sides so you can place them at the end of a counter. They can appear to be built-in when placed between two counters. Freestanding ranges are the most popular style today. They offer the widest selection of colors and features.

Built-in ranges often have an oven that is separated from the cooktop. The oven is built into a wall or a specially designed cabinet. The cooktop generally is installed in a countertop. This arrangement provides great flexibility in kitchen design.

Both slide-in and drop-in ranges have unfinished sides and fit snugly between two cabinets. *Slide-in ranges* sit on the floor. *Drop-in ranges* sit on a cabinet base. Both styles have the oven below the cooktop.

Special Range Features

Ranges offer many special features. *Griddle, grill,* and *rotisserie units* are available on some ranges. These usually snap in place over a portion of the cooking surface. *Thermostatically controlled cooking units* keep food at a constant temperature, which you select.

Consumers often want some kind of ventilation system to remove steam, heat, and odors in the range area. Many ranges are available with a *hood* mounted over the cooktop. The hood contains an exhaust fan to draw away heat and odors as they rise from the food. A system available on some newer ranges that eliminates the need for an overhead hood is **downdraft ventilation.** This

system has a fan mounted under the cooktop. It draws cooking fumes away from food before they have a chance to rise through the room. See 8-6.

Automatic cleaning features allow consumers to avoid the chore of cleaning the oven. *Self-cleaning* ovens use very high temperatures (750° to 1000°F or 400° to 540°C) to burn away oven spills. The consumer must wipe away a small amount of ash after cleaning.

Self-cleaning ovens have extra insulation. This extra insulation keeps the exterior cool during cleaning. It reduces heat loss, allowing the oven to reach the high temperatures needed for cleaning. It also saves energy during normal oven use.

Self-cleaning ovens cost more than conventional ovens. However, the cost of cleaning is less than that of commercial oven cleaners.

Continuous cleaning ovens have specially coated walls. Food spills oxidize over a period of time during normal operation. Continuous cleaning ovens cost less than self-cleaning ovens. However, some people find them less effective.

Using and Caring for Ranges

Read the instruction manual that comes with a range before using the range. It provides information about how to properly operate and care for the range. Using this information will help you get the best service from your appliance.

Always practice good safety habits. Place pans on surface units before turning on the units. This

8-6 The downdraft vent installed beside the modular grill cooktop in this island unit eliminates the need for an overhead hood.

will prevent accidents and also save energy. Turn all pan handles inward to prevent accidental tipping. Avoid wearing loose-fitting clothes when working around the range. They are a fire hazard.

Be careful not to drop heavy objects on top of the range. Most ranges have a porcelain-enamel coating, which can crack or chip if struck. Wipe up spills immediately with a damp cloth. Do not use cold water when the range is hot. Porcelain can crack from severe temperature changes.

To keep your oven clean, wipe up spills when they occur. In addition, clean the oven regularly, using a commercial oven cleaner or the self-cleaning feature.

Wash the surface of the range regularly. Wash removable parts in warm, soapy water. Then rinse and dry them carefully.

Microwave Ovens

Over twenty-five companies manufacture microwave ovens. The models they manufacture vary widely in terms of price, size, and features. When buying a microwave oven, you need to consider what best fits your lifestyle. Analyze your needs. Start by considering what you expect from a microwave oven. Do you want to use it for full cooking procedures, or will you mainly use it to defrost frozen foods and heat prepared foods? Do you need several levels of power, or will a simple model with one power level meet your needs?

Microwave ovens can defrost, cook, or reheat food in a fraction of the time required by conventional ovens. Microwave cooking can also save up to 75 percent of the energy used by conventional ovens.

Microwave cooking is done by high frequency energy waves called **microwaves.** In a microwave oven, a *magnetron tube* generates microwaves. A *stirrer fan* in the oven then distributes the microwaves throughout the oven cavity. The oven walls, floor, and door liner are made of metal. The metal confines the microwaves and reflects the energy to cook the food. This allows the microwaves to penetrate the food from the top and all sides. The energy from the microwaves vibrates the molecules of the food. The resulting friction creates heat, which cooks the food.

Safety of Microwave Ovens

Some people are concerned that microwave ovens may be hazardous. Exposure to certain levels of microwave energy can be dangerous. However, research has shown no evidence that microwave ovens pose a health risk to consumers. This is because manufacturers have built consumer

protection features into microwave ovens. For instance, a metal screen backs the window found in the door on most microwave ovens. This screen prevents microwaves from going through the glass. In addition, you cannot operate a microwave oven when the door is open.

As with all electrical appliances, follow safety measures when installing and using a microwave oven. Do not plug a microwave oven into an extension cord. Plug it into a 120-volt grounded electrical outlet. The microwave oven should be the only appliance on the electrical circuit. Sharing the circuit with another appliance can reduce the amount of electrical power to the microwave oven. This can affect the cooking time and may harm the oven itself.

The microwave oven is actually one of the safest appliances in the kitchen. It does not use an open flame or a hot burner. Therefore, you can even teach children how to safely operate this appliance.

Microwave Oven Styles

Four styles of microwave ovens are available. *Countertop microwave ovens* are the most popular and offer the greatest choice of features. You can place them on a countertop, table, or cart. You can use a manufacturer's kit to convert some models to other styles.

Two types of *over-the-range microwave ovens* are available. One type has a light and exhaust vent located underneath it. This type hangs over the range in place of a standard range hood. The other type is the upper oven on a two-oven range. These are available with both gas and electric ranges. Both types of over-the-range microwaves are similar to countertop models. However, they often have less capacity and offer fewer options.

Built-in microwave ovens are installed into a wall or cabinet. They are often seen in combination with built-in conventional ovens, 8-7. Fewer of these models are available, so consumers may have fewer options.

Under-the-cabinet microwave ovens are a good choice in kitchens with limited counter space. You can place these microwaves on a countertop, but they have a smaller capacity than many countertop models.

All four styles are available as combination microwave/convection ovens. This type of oven allows you to cook with microwaves only, convection heat only, or both methods simultaneously.

Special Microwave Oven Features

Basic model microwave ovens may have only one to three power levels and a dial timer. More sophisticated models have 10 power levels. These

Whirlpool Corp.

8-7 This built-in double oven has a microwave oven on top and a self-cleaning conventional oven on the bottom.

microwaves generally have electronic touch pad controls and a digital display. This display shows a precise time and power setting and may also include a clock and a kitchen timer.

You will need to evaluate how simple or complex a microwave oven should be to meet your needs. This will help you decide what special features you want when you shop for a microwave. Such features include temperature probes, child locks, automatic programming, automatic settings, and turntables.

A *temperature probe* senses the internal temperature of food. Some probes work by turning off the oven when food reaches a specific temperature. Others work by holding the food at a preset temperature once it is reached. Temperature probes are helpful when cooking roasts, casseroles, soups, and stews.

A *child lock* allows an adult to program in a code so that a child cannot operate the microwave oven. This safety feature reduces the risk of accidental injury to the child or damage to the appliance.

Automatic programming automatically shifts power levels at preset times. For example, this feature can allow you to program the oven to start food on high, then simmer.

Automatic settings determine cooking times and correct power levels for you. You just set the controls for the type and sometimes the amount of food, and the oven does the rest. Many microwave ovens have automatic settings for defrosting foods and making popcorn.

Turntables slowly revolve food throughout the cooking period. This eliminates the need to periodically interrupt the cooking cycle and turn food by hand.

Using and Caring for Microwave Ovens

Take care not to turn on the microwave oven when it is empty. This could damage the interior.

One of the most important rules to follow when caring for your microwave is to keep the door seal clean. The door seal on a microwave prevents radiation leakage. Do not let anything become caught between the sealing surfaces. Immediately clean up any food spills to keep the seal intact. If the door or hinges should become damaged, do not use the oven until you have it repaired.

To clean the interior and exterior of the oven, use a damp cloth and mild detergent. Never use an oven cleaner or abrasive cleansers.

Convection Ovens

Convection ovens have been available in gas ranges for many years, but they were mainly used in commercial bakeries and restaurants. Now, convection ovens are available in electric ranges as well and are being used more and more in home kitchens.

Convection cooking uses a stream of heated air to bake and roast foods. This system of cooking has many advantages. Convection ovens use less energy than conventional ovens. They can reduce cooking times by as much as 30 percent. You can cook many foods at lower temperatures. Foods cook more evenly than in either conventional or microwave ovens. In addition, you can use the same cooking utensils in a convection oven that you use in a conventional oven.

Although convection ovens are available by themselves, they are usually combined with conventional or microwave ovens, 8-8. The combination models allow you to use two different cooking methods. Convection ovens are available in countertop models, electric or gas range models, and wall models.

Induction Cooktops

Induction cooktops are rather new on the kitchen appliance market. They cook foods just like a conventional cooktop, but without the use of gas flames or electric coils.

Induction cooking is done with *electromagnetic energy.* This is energy that is generated when a magnetic attraction is formed by an electric current. When you turn on an induction unit, a coil below the surface sends a current into the cookware on top. A magnetic attraction must exist between the induction coil and the cookware. The current meets resistance in the cookware and creates heat directly in the pan.

Pans must be made of magnetic metals such as iron or steel to be used for induction cooking. Any pan that will attract a household magnet will work on an induction cooktop.

The induction cooktop will not generate heat unless you place cookware on the surface of the appliance. Cookware must be a certain size. This prevents the appliance from heating when you inadvertently place a small metal object, such as a spoon, on the unit.

Because heat is generated in the pan itself, the cooktop stays cooler during cooking. It also cools down instantly when you turn off the unit. This reduces the hazard of burns and prevents spills from baking onto the surface.

Sharp Convection Microwave Oven

8-8 This built-in appliance combines the speed of a microwave oven with the browning of a convection oven.

Induction cooktops have a modern design. They are smooth surfaced units, which often have touch pad controls. These cooktops drop into a counter. They are not currently available as ranges with ovens below. See 8-9.

Refrigerators

A refrigerator's main job is to keep foods cold and retard food spoilage. A **refrigerant,** or cooling agent, performs this job by going through four basic steps.

1. In the *compressor,* a refrigerant is compressed, becoming a super hot vapor.
2. This vapor moves to the *condenser* where it cools and turns into a liquid.
3. The liquid is pumped into a *capillary tube,* which restricts the flow and causes the pressure to rise.
4. This high pressure liquid moves to the *evaporator* where it expands and cools as it vaporizes. As the vapor circulates through the evaporator, it absorbs heat from food. The compressor then sucks in the vapor, and the cycle begins again.

Several sizes and styles of refrigerators are available. When shopping for a refrigerator, consider the size of your family. Also consider how often you buy groceries and whether or not you need a separate freezer section. Then choose a refrigerator that is well insulated and stain-resistant. It should have the features you want and need.

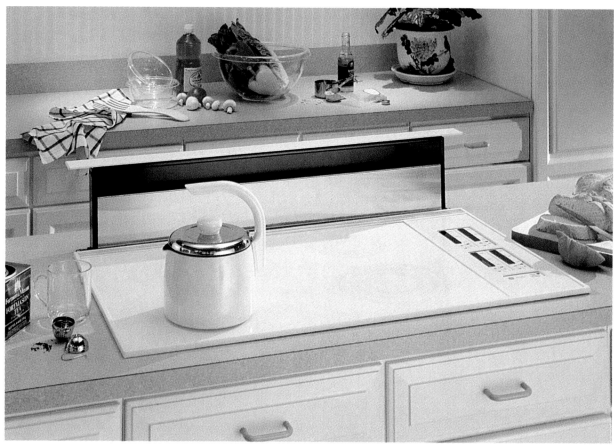

8-9 This smooth-surfaced induction cooktop is paired with a telescopic downdraft ventilation system, which retracts when not in use.

Refrigerator space is measured in cubic feet (or liters). Fresh food storage compartments should provide about 3.5 cubic feet (.1 cubic meters) of space for each adult family member. Freezers should provide about 1.5 cubic feet (.04 cubic meters) of space per person. If you shop less often than once a week, you may need additional storage space.

Refrigerator Styles

Refrigerators are available in three basic styles. These styles are single-door refrigerators, refrigerator-freezers, and compact and portable refrigerators.

Single-door refrigerators are the least expensive style. They contain a small compartment sealed by an inner door. This compartment holds a temperature of 10° to 15°F (-12° to -9°C), which keeps foods colder than the rest of the unit. This temperature is satisfactory for making ice cubes. It is also adequate for storing commercially frozen foods for up to a week. However, it is not satisfactory for freezing fresh foods.

Refrigerator-freezers are the most common style manufactured today. They usually have two doors but some models have three. The freezer may be above, below, or beside the refrigerator. Temperatures in the freezer range from -5° to 5°F (-21° to -15°C). Therefore, you can use the freezer to freeze foods as well as to store foods that are already frozen.

Compact and *portable refrigerators* generally are variations of the single-door refrigerator. They are popular in college dorm rooms and recreation rooms. They contain a small compartment for ice cubes, but you cannot use them to store frozen foods.

Defrosting a Refrigerator

The amount of defrosting a refrigerator needs depends on the model. You must regularly defrost some refrigerators *manually*. Frost should never accumulate to a depth of more than ½ inch (1.3 cm). A thick layer of frost increases operating costs because the unit must work harder. It also can cause the unit to break down entirely. Manually defrosted refrigerators are the least expensive to purchase and operate.

Some refrigerators *defrost automatically*. The refrigerator will not require defrosting but the freezer will. This feature adds to the purchase and operating costs.

Other refrigerators are *frostless*. Frost does not accumulate in either the refrigerator or the freezer. Refrigerators with this feature usually have the greatest purchase and operating costs.

Special Refrigerator Features

Refrigerators can have many special features. The features you choose should depend on your needs.

Refrigerators can have an automatic ice maker in the freezer section. They can have an ice and water dispenser in the door, too. See 8-10. Many refrigerators have adjustable shelves to make storage space more flexible. Temperature controlled compartments for meat and other foods are also available in some models. Wheels make moving the refrigerator easier.

Check to see if the door swings open to the left or right. Ideally, the opening should be next to a countertop near the sink. Some models have reversible doors.

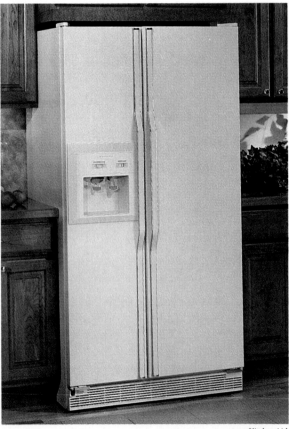

KitchenAid

8-10 This side-by-side refrigerator-freezer features an ice and cold water dispenser in the door.

Using and Caring for Refrigerators

Tightly wrap foods to prevent unpleasant odors in the refrigerator. Try to take out all of the items you need from the refrigerator at one time. Each time you open the refrigerator door, warm air enters. The refrigerator then has to use more energy to lower the temperature again.

To ensure food safety, keep both the inside and the outside of the refrigerator clean. Regularly clean the interior with a baking soda and water solution. Combine 2 tablespoons (30 mL) baking soda with 1 quart (1 L) warm water. Wash all the inside surfaces, rinse, and dry with a clean towel. Clean the exterior of the refrigerator with warm, soapy water, rinse, and dry.

Refrigerator parts and accessories also need regular cleaning. Wash ice cube trays, door gaskets, crisper drawers, and shelves with warm, soapy water. Rinse and dry carefully.

Freezers

If the frozen food storage in a refrigerator-freezer is not adequate for your needs, you may want a separate freezer. A separate freezer can save you time and money. It allows you to take advantage of supermarket specials and seasonal food buys by making quantity purchases.

Freezer Styles

Freezers are available in two styles: chest and upright. Both work equally well.

The *chest freezer*, 8-11, is less expensive to operate than the upright model. Less cold air escapes when you open the door. You can store large, bulky packages more easily than in an upright freezer. However, a chest freezer requires more floor space.

The *upright freezer* takes up less floor space than the chest model. It is easier to organize for quick storage and removal of frozen foods. It also

Protect the Planet

The condenser is the long, folded tube on the back of the refrigerator. You need to keep the condenser clean for the refrigerator to operate efficiently. To clean the condenser, use the crevice tool or long brush attachment of your vacuum cleaner. (Refer to your vacuum cleaner's instruction manual.)

Whirlpool Corp.

8-11 Although chest freezers require more floor space than upright models, they are less costly to operate.

has in-door storage. Upright freezers cost more to operate.

Both chest and upright freezers are available in different sizes. Most families find they need 2 to 4 cubic feet (.06 to .11 cubic meters) of freezer space per adult family member. This is in addition to the freezer space already provided by a refrigerator-freezer.

Regardless of which style you choose, your freezer should have a lock and a safety alarm or light. The lock prevents curious children and pets from accidentally becoming trapped inside the freezer. The safety alarm or light tells you when the temperature has become too high or if the freezer is not operating.

Defrosting a Freezer

Like refrigerators, the amount of defrosting a freezer requires depends on the model. Some freezers require manual defrosting. Others have automatic, frostless systems. Frostless models are more expensive to buy and to operate.

Using and Caring for Freezers

Place your freezer in a cool, dry, well-ventilated area to reduce operating costs. Wrap foods in moistureproof and vaporproof materials and date them for freezer storage. Be sure the freezer temperature remains at 0°F (-18°C) or below. You can use a special freezer thermometer to check the temperature.

If your freezer shuts down during a power failure, there are steps you can take to preserve the food inside. Find out the source of the problem. If there has been an electrical failure, call the electric company. If it is a mechanical failure, call your service representative.

Find out how long the power company expects the power to be off. Normally, food in a fully loaded freezer will remain frozen for two days. If the freezer is only half full, food should stay frozen for one day. During this time, keep the freezer door closed. Each time you open it, warm air enters.

Clean the exterior of the freezer when needed. Use a damp, soapy cloth. Rinse and dry well. Do not use abrasive cleansers. They can scratch the finish.

Dishwashers

Family size and the amount of time available to do dishes help determine a family's need for a dishwasher. A dishwasher could save considerable time and energy for a large family. However, a single person could find a dishwasher to be a costly luxury.

Dishwashers have a number of advantages. They can save time and personal energy. Dishes washed in a dishwasher are more sanitary. This is

Run the cold water before activating the disposer and for a short time after turning off the disposer. This ensures that all of the particles go down the drain. Running water also prevents the motor from burning out.

Never pour lye or chemical drain cleaners down the sink. These will damage a food waste disposer.

Use your disposer only to grind food. It will grind small bones, but large bones can damage the blades.

Always keep your fingers away from the disposer. Use a rubber spatula or wooden spoon to push food into the disposer opening.

Trash Compactors

A trash compactor provides a convenient way to dispose of food scraps and nonfood waste, such as cereal boxes, 8-14. Trash compactors operate electrically to compact waste to about one fourth its original size. A special bag stores food within the unit. When you lock the door, the compactor puts pressure on the waste, forming a compact bundle.

Before purchasing a trash compactor, consider your needs. Compare other means of trash disposal available versus the cost of the appliance.

Trash Compactor Styles

Compactors can be built-in or freestanding. They are available in several different sizes.

All kinds of compactors have safety locks. The safety lock prevents the unit from being opened accidentally during operation. Most compactors are available with a deodorizing spray. Some also have a sanitizing spray.

Using and Caring for Trash Compactors

Operate your trash compactor according to the manufacturer's instructions. Remove the bag after compacting and insert a new, clean bag. Do not try to compact aerosol cans or flammable materials. Dispose of these separately.

Portable Kitchen Appliances

Major appliances are needed for basic kitchen functions. However, they cannot do many of the individual preparation tasks meal managers must perform. For these tasks, meal managers often rely on the time and energy savings provided by portable appliances.

Portable kitchen appliances offer many advantages. You can move them easily from one place to another. Sometimes you can use them instead of

KitchenAid

8-14 A trash compactor compresses food scraps, large bones, milk cartons, tin cans, and other non-food items into a small bundle. Disposable bags are placed in the compactor and removed when full.

major appliances. They can do many tasks faster and better than you could do them by hand.

Trends in Portable Kitchen Appliances

Consumers want portable appliances that simplify their work in the kitchen. However, today's appliances are used far beyond the kitchen. Coffeemakers, for instance, may be found anywhere from the office to the garage. Several models are available that will even plug into the cigarette lighter in a car. They allow consumers to brew fresh coffee on the road!

To meet consumer needs, appliances should perform quickly and safely. They should be easy to clean and take up a minimum of space. They should also be conveniently sized and look attractive. These needs have set the pace for today's portable appliances.

One current trend in the portable appliance market is an increased number of cordless appliances. These appliances are easy to operate because you can use them anywhere. When you are not using them, you can attach them to a power source to recharge.

Many portable appliances today are designed with safety features. Monitors may sense when an appliance is not in use and turn it off. Heat resistant materials may protect the user from burns. Safety guards may keep consumers from getting

cut by sharp blades. These features not only protect the consumer, they also prevent damage to the appliance.

Another trend is appliances that are easy to clean. Easy cleaning means appliances with few pieces to take apart. Many appliances have parts that are dishwasher safe for added ease in cleanup.

Under-the-cabinet and wall-mount appliances have remained popular. These portables save counter space by using space that might otherwise be wasted. See 8-15.

Many appliances are now available in compact sizes. These are designed to meet the needs of single people and smaller families. Small-quantity food processors, for instance, are convenient for people who do not need full-size models.

The appearance of portable appliances is changing to reflect current trends. Modern appliances are designed with smooth, sleek shapes in trim sizes. Bright white is a popular color for these portables. It gives them a contemporary look that fits into almost any kitchen decor. Jewel tones, such as cobalt blue and hunter green, are also popular appliance colors.

Purchase Considerations for Portable Appliances

When purchasing small appliances, select those that give the most satisfaction for the money spent. Consider what the appliance does, its

Black & Decker

8-15 Under-the-cabinet appliances free counter space for food preparation tasks.

limitations, and its special features. Then decide what to buy.

The following are some points to consider:

- Does the appliance come with a warranty?
- Is it brand-name merchandise from a reputable dealer?
- Who provides servicing when the appliance needs repairs?
- Will you use the appliance frequently?
- Does another appliance you already have do the same job?
- Do you have adequate, convenient storage space for it?
- Does the appliance have adequate power to perform its intended tasks?
- Does it have a convenient size and shape for your needs?
- Are the materials durable enough to suit your needs?
- Is it sturdy and well balanced? (Motor-driven appliances should not tip or "walk" during use.)
- Is there a sufficient number of heat or power settings to suit your needs?
- Are the controls distinctly marked for easy reading and conveniently located for easy operation?
- Are handles easy and comfortable to hold?
- Are the legs, handles, and controls heat-resistant?
- Are parts easy to assemble for operation and easy to disassemble for cleaning?

- Is it easy to clean?
- Are the legs or table rests constructed to prevent damage to the work surface?
- Does the appliance have built-in safety features?
- Does it have the Underwriters Laboratories (UL) seal of approval to guarantee that it meets electrical safety standards?

General Use and Care for Portable Appliances

Before using any portable appliance, you should carefully read the manufacturer's instruction booklet. The booklet will give directions for proper use that will help your appliance last for years. The booklet will also tell you how to clean your appliance.

Clean most portable appliances after each use. Allow hot appliances to cool before cleaning. Wash most removable parts in warm, soapy water. Some may be safely cleaned in the dishwasher. You should not immerse most appliance motor bases and heating elements. You can wipe them clean with a damp cloth.

Toasters

Toasters are one of the most common kitchen appliances, 8-16. They brown bread quickly on both sides at once. Most toasters have an adjustable knob to control the darkness of the

T-Fal Corporation

8-16 Toasters are the most commonly owned portable kitchen appliance in the United States.

toast. Both two-slice and four-slice toasters are available. Some have extra wide openings to accommodate thick slices of bread, English muffins, and bagels.

Toaster-ovens are also available. These appliances bake and broil small food items in addition to toasting bread. This type of toaster can be a convenient choice when preparing small portions. It uses less energy and creates less heat in the kitchen than a full-size oven.

When purchasing a toaster, choose a model that fits your needs. A four-slice toaster would be more practical for a large family than for a single person. A toaster-oven would be a good choice for someone who wishes to bake or broil small portions as well as toast. Look for openings wide enough to accommodate thick bread slices.

Using and Caring for Toasters

Allow toast to rise automatically. Do not push up the lever yourself.

Clean crumbs out of the toaster regularly. Many models have a snap-out crumb tray to make this easier.

Electric Mixers

The electric mixer is one of the most frequently used appliances in the kitchen. Mixers are available in two styles: standard and hand. Both can do many jobs. They can mix, beat, whip, stir, and blend.

Standard mixers are larger and heavier than hand mixers. They are better for heavy-duty mixing jobs. Many have attachments such as choppers and juicers. Standard mixers leave your hands free to do other tasks. See 8-17.

When purchasing a standard electric mixer, be sure it has provisions for mixing small and large amounts of food. It should also have a motor unit that provides even, constant mixing at every speed. The motor should be strong enough to beat

KitchenAid

8-17 This sturdy standard mixer comes with a dough hook as well as a beater.

stiff mixtures without overheating. The beaters should be easy to insert and remove. They should cover the full bowl diameter for thorough mixing.

Hand mixers are smaller and lighter than standard mixers. You must hold them during the entire mixing operation. They should have stable heel rests or other means of support for standing on the counter when not in use.

Hand mixers are less expensive than standard mixers. However, they are not as versatile. You can remove some standard mixer heads from the stand and use them as hand mixers.

Using and Caring for Mixers

For safety, turn the mixer off before inserting or removing beaters. If the cord is detachable, remove it from the wall outlet before removing it from the appliance.

Electric Blenders

A blender has surgical steel blades that cut foods, 8-18. This differs from a mixer, which incorporates air into food. A blender can shred, chop, puree, liquefy, and blend food. You can use it to

Play It Safe

Never use a fork, knife, or other metal object to dislodge a piece of food while the toaster is plugged in. You could receive an electrical shock or damage the heating elements. Instead, unplug the toaster before trying to dislodge stuck food.

Sanyo

8-18 Electric blenders shred, chop, puree, grind, and liquefy foods quickly and easily.

quickly prepare baby foods for an infant, milk shakes for an older child, and soft meals for a senior citizen. You can use it to make dips, beverages, and desserts for people of all ages. It also can help complete other food preparation tasks such as grinding nuts for cookies. Blenders are not satisfactory for whipping cream, beating egg whites, mashing potatoes, grinding raw meat, extracting juices, or kneading stiff doughs.

A blender should have a removable container, molded of heat-resistant glass or plastic. The container should have a wide opening, a convenient handle, and a pouring spout. Also look for a self-sealing vinyl cover that resists odors and stains. A removable center cap makes adding ingredients easy.

Using and Caring for Blenders

Do not overload the blender. For thick mixtures, fill the container to one half of its capacity. For lighter loads, fill to two-thirds capacity. When blending liquids, always fill the container with at least enough food to cover the blades. This is less critical when pulverizing dry ingredients such as nuts or crackers.

Check to see that the blender container and lid are firmly in place before starting the appliance. Blenders work quickly. Follow recipe instructions to prevent overblending. Always stop the motor before scraping the sides of the container. Use a rubber scraper rather than a metal one. Do not remove the container until the motor has stopped completely.

Coffeemakers

Automatic coffeemakers can take the guesswork out of making good coffee. Thermostatic controls in the coffeemaker brew coffee without boiling it and keep it at drinking temperature. Special types of coffeemakers are available for brewing espresso and cappuccino.

The two types of automatic coffeemakers are the percolator and the drip coffeemaker. In an *electric percolator*, hot water is repeatedly forced up from the bottom of the pot. It goes through a pump stem into a basket where it spreads over ground coffee. In an *automatic drip coffeemaker*, hot water slowly drips down through ground coffee into a pot below. See 8-19.

Cuisinart®Coffee Bar™ Flavor System™ Coffeemaker Model DCC-100

8-19 This automatic drip coffeemaker brews 2 to 10 cups of delicious, hot coffee in just minutes.

A number of features are available that add to a coffeemaker's convenience. Some models have a signal light that indicates when the coffee is ready to serve. A strength control dial allows you to brew coffee to your taste. An automatic timer allows the coffeemaker to begin brewing at a preset time.

Using and Caring for Coffeemakers

Always start with a clean coffeemaker, cold water, and fresh coffee. Use a filter to keep fine grounds and sediment from going into the coffee. Measure the coffee accurately according to the manufacturer's directions. Never let an empty coffeemaker remain plugged in since this could ruin the appliance.

Carefully clean the coffeemaker after each use. Oils and sediment that accumulate in the coffee pot can affect the flavor of future pots.

Electric Can Openers

An electric can opener quickly and easily cuts lids off metal cans, 8-20. A magnet holds the lid for easy removal. Some models adjust to accommodate cans of different heights. Most have removable cutting assemblies for easy cleaning. Many can openers also sharpen knives.

Using and Caring for Can Openers

Always wash off can lids before opening cans. This prevents dust on the top of the can from getting into the food. Clean the cutting assembly with hot, soapy water after each use. Food residue left on the cutting blade can serve as a breeding ground for bacteria. If the blade is not cleaned, these bacteria could contaminate other foods the next time you use the appliance.

Food Processors

The food processor has become a very popular small appliance because it performs many time-consuming jobs quickly and easily. It kneads dough, mixes dressings and batters, slices meats and vegetables, shreds cabbage, grates cheese and onions, and chops nuts. See 8-21. A food processor also beats, blends, and purees. The few things a food processor cannot do are beat egg whites, whip

Sanyo

8-20 An electric can opener saves time and effort during meal preparation.

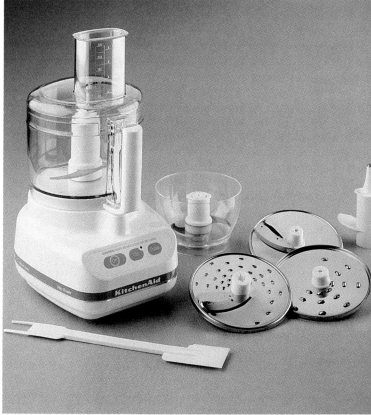

KitchenAid

8-21 Food processors handle many time-consuming kitchen tasks quickly and efficiently. Processors grind meats, shred vegetables, mix dough, and perform many other preparation jobs.

cream, mash potatoes, grind coffee beans, and crush ice (unless it has a special blade or attachment).

When buying a food processor, look for one that meets your needs for features. A safety interlock switch ensures that you have locked the cover in place before starting the processor. A dishwasher-safe container and cutting disks or blades will ease cleanup. You may want a food pusher that adapts to processing small or slender foods. Also make sure the control panel is easy to operate.

Using and Caring for Food Processors

For best results, do not overload a food processor. Medium-sized loads process more evenly than large ones. Also, small pieces of food, about one inch in size, chop more evenly than large pieces.

Another factor that affects food processing is the amount of pressure applied when processing foods through the feed tube. Most foods need steady, even pressure. However, hard foods, such as lemons, need firm pressure. Soft foods, such as strawberries, need lighter pressure.

Before processing, make sure you lock the cover into place and put the food pusher (if chopping, slicing, or shredding) in the feed tube. When processing is complete, turn the control switch to off. Wait until the blade or disc comes to a complete stop before removing the cover.

Electric Skillets

A portable electric skillet eliminates excess oven heat and the need for "pot-watching." A thermostat controls the temperature throughout the entire cooking process. The electric skillet can take the place of the oven in some instances, thus saving energy. You can use it to fry, roast, panbroil, stew, or simmer foods. You can also use it to bake casserole dishes, quick breads, cakes, custards, and desserts. See 8-22.

National Presto Industries, Inc.

8-22 Electric skillets can be used to roast, fry, panbroil, stew, simmer, and bake foods.

An electric skillet should have a high dome cover to provide maximum capacity and versatility. The cover should have a vent. Also look for a clearly visible heat indicator light and a cooking surface that suits your needs. Aluminum is least expensive, stainless steel is durable, and a nonstick coating provides easy cleaning.

Using and Caring for Electric Skillets

You may need to *condition* an electric skillet before you use it. To condition the skillet, wash it in warm soapy water. Rinse it and dry it. Then brush its inner surfaces with salad oil.

Be sure the heat control is off before connecting or disconnecting the skillet. Do not overcrowd foods when browning. Open the steam vent to brown foods, close the vent to bake or moist cook. Remove acidic foods immediately after cooking to prevent discoloration of the pan.

Do not immerse a hot skillet in water. Cool it to room temperature first. Avoid extreme temperature changes. Running cold water into a hot pan can cause warping.

Automatic Bread Machines

One of the most popular items to hit the portable appliance market in recent years is the automatic bread machine. Bread makers mix and knead bread dough. They allow the dough to rise, and then they bake the bread. See 8-23.

Many models feature a timer. This allows you to preset the machine at bedtime so family members can awake to freshly baked bread. You can also preset the timer before going to work so fresh bread will be ready in time for dinner.

Bread makers can make a variety of kinds of bread. They can also prepare the dough for pizza, rolls, and other yeast products. (You must then shape these products by hand and bake them in a conventional oven.) The time needed to make bread in a bread maker varies according to the

Welbilt

8-23 An automatic bread machine does everything needed to prepare homemade bread except measure the ingredients!

bread in a bread maker varies according to the model and the recipe being used.

Automatic bread makers are at the high end of the portable appliance price range. However, homemakers who enjoy fresh bread, but do not have time to make it, may feel the investment is worthwhile.

Using and Caring for Bread Machines

As with conventional baking, measuring ingredients accurately will give you the best results when making bread in a bread machine. Do not use the delay timer if you are preparing a recipe that includes perishable ingredients like milk and eggs.

Some parts of the bread machine may have nonstick surfaces that can be scratched by metal utensils. One of these parts may be the kneading paddle that mixes the ingredients and kneads the dough. This paddle may stick in the loaf of baked bread. You should remove it gently to avoid damaging it. Read the use and care information that accompanies the machine to find out which parts are dishwasher safe.

Some parts of the appliance may become hot during baking. Therefore, you should wear oven mitts when removing the baked bread. Wait for the appliance to cool down before touching or cleaning

it. Do not allow children to use the bread machine without supervision.

Do not open the lid or unplug the appliance during kneading or baking. This may cause the bread to bake improperly.

Other Portable Kitchen Appliances

In addition to the small appliances discussed, there are many others available on the market. These include pasta makers, cappuccino makers, electric tea kettles, and iced tea makers. Electric woks, knives, coffee grinders, ice cream makers, waffle bakers, grills, and slow cookers are also among the variety of portable appliances offered. See 8-24.

Many portable appliances are versatile, performing several functions. Others do just one task. These single-function appliances are often fad items that appear on the market one year and disappear the next. Others meet real consumer needs and become lasting options for appliance buyers.

When choosing a more specialized appliance, consider your storage space. Think about how often you will use the appliance. Also check to see if you have another appliance that will perform the same task. As with all appliances, make your selections based on need, available features, quality construction, and ease of use and care.

Model 3000 Deni/Keystone Manufacturing Company, Inc.

National Presto Industries, Inc.

8-24 From making tender, fresh pasta to crisp, hot French fries, portable appliances are available to perform a broad range of kitchen tasks.

Summary

You can do nearly every kitchen task more easily with the help of appliances. Use available information to help you make wise consumer choices. Safety seals on appliances assure you that the appliances have been tested to work safely. Warranties state what you can expect from a manufacturer if an appliance does not perform as intended. EnergyGuide labels tell you the energy cost of running many major appliances.

Major kitchen appliances handle the basic tasks of cooking, storage, and cleanup. Cooking appliances include gas and electric ranges, microwave ovens, convection ovens, and induction cooktops. Refrigerators and freezers store perishable foods. Dishwashers, food waste disposers, and trash compactors ease cleanup.

All major appliances come in several sizes and styles. Different models offer different features. Major appliances are expensive. You must weigh your options carefully to choose the appliances that best meet your family's needs. Following manufacturers' recommendations for use and care will help your appliances work properly and last for a long time.

There are many portable appliances available to help do food preparation tasks. These include toasters, mixers, blenders, coffeemakers, can openers, food processors, electric skillets, and bread machines. When choosing portable appliances, choose those that are convenient to use and store. Look for well-built models that provide the features you desire.

Review What You Have Read

Write your answers on a separate sheet of paper.
1. Which of the following is *not* a safety seal of approval?
   A. UL seal of approval.
   B. AGA blue star seal.
   C. Good Housekeeping seal of approval.
2. Explain the difference between a full warranty and a limited warranty.
3. List three trends in major appliances.
4. An energy-saving feature found on some gas ranges is _____.
5. Explain the difference between self-cleaning ovens and continuous cleaning ovens.
6. List four special features that are available on microwave ovens.
7. Which type of oven uses a stream of heated air to bake and roast foods?
   A. Convection oven.
   B. Conventional oven.
   C. Induction oven.
   D. Microwave oven.
8. List three basic styles of refrigerators.
9. True or false. Detergents made for washing dishes by hand can also be used in automatic dishwashers.
10. What are the two models of food waste disposers?
11. List five points to consider when purchasing portable appliances.
12. True or false. Unplug a toaster before trying to dislodge stuck food.
13. True or false. Blenders can be used to whip cream.
14. True or false. When making coffee, start with a clean coffeemaker, hot water, and fresh coffee.
15. True or false. When browning foods in an electric skillet, the steam vent should be open.

Build Your Basic Skills

1. Investigate appliance testing at Underwriters Laboratories or the American Gas Association. Find out what kinds of tests appliances must pass in order to meet safety standards. Write a brief report of your findings.
2. Look through a catalog and make a list of all the different types of portable appliances that are available. Place a check beside appliances that perform a variety of functions. Place a star beside appliances that perform a function that another appliance can do. Use your list as the basis for a discussion of how portable appliances meet consumer needs.

Build Your Thinking Skills

1. Visit an appliance or department store. Compare the prices and features of several models of the major or portable appliance of your choice. Ask about the warranties that come with each model. Find out if service contracts are available. Check safety features and energy ratings. Use your findings to give an oral report in class.
2. Bake equal portions of a casserole dish, such as macaroni and cheese, in a conventional oven and a microwave oven. Compare the cooking times and the quality of the dishes. If possible, also compare the results using a convection oven.

Quality knives are among the many utensils required in a well-equipped kitchen.

A baster is a long tub
bulb. A baster uses suction
meat and poultry for bastir
liquid). You can also use it
and gravies.

Colanders are perforat
fruits, vegetables, and pas
have heat-proof handles.

Strainers are available
them to separate liquid and
and other preparation tools

Can openers have a r
tures the top of cans. M
handles that you squeeze t
proper position. Then you t
the can opener. This causes
cut around the edge of the

9-7 Small utensils are designe

Chapter 9

Kitchen Utensils

A "Taste" of the World of Work

Housewares Designer
Originates and develops
ideas to design the form
of manufactured house-
wares products.

**Wholesale Housewares
Demonstrator**
Demonstrates use, care,
and features of kitchen
utensils to encourage retail
business owners to carry
products in their stores.

Cutlery Grinder
Sharpens knives,
cleavers, and other fine-
edged cutting tools, using
whetstone and grinding
and polishing wheels.

Terms to Know

whisk	porcelain enamel
stockinette	nonstick finish
serrated blade	saucepan
tang	pot
French knife	double boiler
colander	pressure saucepan
pitting	springform pan
glass-ceramic	casserole

Objectives

After studying this chapter, you will be able to
❏ identify various small kitchen utensils and
discuss their functions.
❏ explain how to select, use, and care for
cooking and baking utensils.

Photograph by Paul Rocheleau, courtesy of OXO International

constructed for maxim
tang (prong of the bla
dle) should extend at
into the handle. At leas
blade and handle. Thr
knives.

Never soak knives.
dle to loosen.

The most popular
knives, slicing knives,
knives. A *French knife,*
is the most versatile of
cut, chop, and dice f
might choose a slicing l
try, bread, and soft veg
utility knife is a good a
it to cut tender vegeta
and to trim fat from r
smallest knife used in
fruits and vegetables.
kitchen knives are pictu

Other Preparatio

Tongs usually are
helpful for turning mea

1—Paring Knife
2—Trimmer
3—Turning Fork
4—Petite Carver

9-6 Choose different

Cookware and Bakeware Materials

Cooking and baking utensils are made from a number of materials. Metal, ceramic, and plastic materials are the most popular of these materials.

Metal Materials

Several different metals are used for conventional cookware and bakeware. Cast iron is a traditional cookware material. Iron distributes and holds heat well. Its porous surface holds oils that help prevent sticking. Iron is heavy, however. It can also rust, retain food flavors, and lose its nonstick qualities unless you care for it properly.

Aluminum is a lightweight, corrosion-resistant cookware and bakeware material. It conducts heat rapidly and is reasonably priced. It comes in several thicknesses. Cast aluminum is used for heavier utensils, such as skillets. Sheet aluminum is used for lighter utensils, such as cookie sheets. Aluminum is susceptible to scratches, dents, and detergent damage. Food and minerals can cause *pitting* (marking with tiny indentations). Hard water, eggs, and alkalis, such as baking soda, can cause darkening.

Copper is a good heat conductor. However, you cannot use pure copper utensils for cooking. When heated, copper reacts with food and forms poisonous compounds. Copper cooking utensils must be lined with another material to make them safe for cooking. You must clean copper with a special cleaner to keep it from discoloring.

Stainless steel is an alloy of steel, nickel, and chromium. It resists stains, does not discolor, and is strong and durable. However, it does not distribute heat evenly, so hot spots can occur. Stainless steel may darken if overheated. It is relatively expensive.

Some stainless steel pieces have a copper or aluminum bottom to improve heat distribution. Other pieces may have a core of copper, carbon steel, or other heat conducting metal. These materials help conduct heat across the pan bottom and up the sides. A heat conducting core prevents scorching, conserves fuel, and allows low temperature cooking.

Ceramic Materials

Ceramic materials are made from nonmetallic minerals that are fired at very high temperatures. Ceramic materials include glass, porcelain, earthenware, and terra-cotta.

Glass is attractive and does not react to food flavors or colors. Glass is a poor heat conductor, however, and can chip, crack, and break.

Glass-ceramic is attractive and durable. However, it may develop hot spots and heat unevenly. Unlike glass, you can take glass-ceramic from the freezer and put it directly in the oven.

Porcelain enamel is a glasslike surface fused to a base metal at very high temperatures. Porcelain enamelware is easy to clean and attractive. It requires careful handling to prevent cracking and chipping.

Earthenware and terra-cotta are not suitable for rangetop cooking. However, their ability to retain heat makes them a good choice for many bakeware pieces. These materials will break and chip easily if you do not care for them properly.

Plastic Materials

Plastic utensils have recently gained popularity. They are dishwasher safe, stain-resistant, break-resistant, and easy to clean. However, plastic utensils cannot withstand oven temperatures above 350° to 400°F (180° to 200°C), depending on the type of plastic. They cannot withstand direct heat, either. This makes plastics impractical for broiling or rangetop cooking. Plastic bakeware, however, is excellent for use in microwave ovens.

Nonstick Finishes

Nonstick finishes prevent food from sticking to utensils. They may be applied to both the inside and outside of cookware and bakeware for easier cooking and cleanup. See 9-8. The effectiveness of a nonstick finish depends on the type of finish and how it is applied. Take care to avoid damaging these finishes. Metal utensils and scouring pads can scratch them.

Microwavable Materials

The main requirement for a microwave cookware material is that microwaves must be able to pass through it. Otherwise, the microwaves will not be able to reach the food. Microwaves can pass through materials such as ceramic, plastics, glass, wood, and paper. These materials can all be used for cooking in a microwave oven.

Healthy Living

Choose skillets with a nonstick finish for frying. Because foods won't stick to the surface, you can reduce or eliminate added fat when you cook. This will help you reduce fat and calories in your diet.

Nordic Ware

9-8 The nonstick finish in this baking pan will make cleanup quick and easy.

Metal cookware reflects microwaves and prevents them from cooking food in a microwave oven. Therefore, metal cookware is generally not recommended for microwave cooking. However, some cookware containing metal is specially designed for microwave use. Some microwave griddles and browning dishes use metal cooking surfaces to achieve the desired browning of foods. When considering these and other metal items for use in a microwave oven, refer to the manufacturer's directions.

Most people own conventional cookware pieces that they can also use for microwave cooking. However, many people still choose to buy a few special pieces for their microwave ovens. A wide variety of microwave cookware is on the market. Some of the most popular items are molded plastic pieces for cooking specific foods like bacon, muffins, and popcorn. Such pieces are designed to suit the special cooking characteristics of a microwave oven.

Not all containers made from microwavable materials are microwave safe. For instance, you should not use cookware made from microwavable material if it has bands of metal trim. The trim can cause arcing. Disposable plastic containers from margarine and whipped toppings are not recommended for microwave cooking. They are made of soft plastics that may melt when they come in contact with hot food. You should not use containers that absorb liquid, such as wooden bowls, when microwaving liquids. The moisture absorbed by such a container will attract microwave energy away from the food.

Cooking Utensils

You probably use saucepans and pots for cooking foods in water or other liquids over direct surface heat. *Saucepans* generally have one handle. *Pots* have two handles. Sizes range from a 1 pint (0.5 L) saucepan to a 12 quart (12 L) pot. For maximum cooking efficiency, the bottoms of pots and pans should be about the same diameter as the surface unit. Handles should be heat-resistant and

Play It Safe

Because microwaves pass through microwavable cookware, the cookware itself does not become hot. However, heat transferred from the food can warm cookware. Therefore, you should use pot holders when removing food containers from a microwave oven.

comfortable to hold. You can buy some pots and pans with matching lids.

A *double boiler* is a small pan that fits into a larger pan. You put the food into the smaller pan. Then you put a small amount of water in the larger pan. As the water simmers, the heat produced by the steam gently cooks the food.

Pressure saucepans cook foods more quickly than conventional saucepans. This is because as pressure increases, temperature increases. Pressure saucepans come in several sizes. Choose a pressure saucepan that carries an Underwriters Laboratories

seal of approval. Be sure to read manufacturer's directions carefully before using a pressure saucepan.

Skillets are available in a variety of sizes with and without lids. Skillets have wide bottoms and low sides. They are generally heavier than saucepans. Use skillets for panbroiling foods or for cooking foods in a small amount of fat. See 9-9.

Griddles and omelet pans are variations of skillets. A griddle is a skillet without sides. Use it for grilling sandwiches and making foods like

CHANTAL Cookware

9-9 The wide bottom and low sides of a skillet make it easy to stir foods that need a lot of contact with the cooking surface.

French toast and pancakes. It often is coated with a nonstick finish. An omelet or crepe pan is an uncovered skillet with a narrow bottom and sloping sides. Use it to make omelets and delicate French pancakes.

Baking Utensils

When selecting baking utensils, it is especially important to consider whether the utensil's surface is shiny or dull. The outer surface of a pan affects the amount of heat it absorbs. A shiny or bright surface reflects part of the heat away from the food. A dull or dark surface absorbs heat. Products baked in bright, shiny pans will have softer, lighter crusts. Products baked in dull, dark pans will have darker and crisper crusts.

Cookie sheets are often made of aluminum. They are flat sheets of metal with a low rim on one or more sides for strength. Use them for baking cookies, toasting bread, and supporting small utensils, such as custard cups.

Cake, loaf, angel food, springform, and muffin pans are usually made of aluminum. Cake and loaf pans also are available in glass and glass-ceramic. See 9-10.

Cake pans can be round, square, or oblong. They come in several sizes. You can make angel food, sponge, and chiffon cakes in an angel food

ClayBakers a division of The Hibiscus Group

9-10 These unusual clay pots can be used to bake uniquely-shaped loaves of bread.

cake pan. It is a deep, round pan, narrower at the bottom than at the top. It has a tube in the center, and the bottom may be removable. A ***springform pan*** also is round and has a removable bottom. Its sides hook together with a latch or spring. Use springform pans for making cheesecakes, tortes, and other desserts that are delicate and difficult to remove from the pan. Muffin pans are oblong pans with round depressions. Muffin pans are available in several sizes. Use them for baking muffins and cupcakes. Loaf pans are deep, narrow, oblong pans. They are available in several sizes. You will use them most often for breads and loaf cakes.

Pie plates are generally made of glass or aluminum. Popular sizes are 8 inches (20 cm), 9 inches (22.5 cm), 10 inches (25 cm), and deep dish.

Casseroles are baking dishes with high sides. They can be made of glass, glass-ceramic, or earthenware. Standard sizes are 1 quart (1 L), 1½ quart (1.5 L), 2 quart (2 L), and 3 quart (3 L). Some casseroles are designed for freezer-to-oven use.

Soufflé dishes are a variation of a casserole. They have high, steep sides and are available in several sizes.

Roasting pans can be oval or oblong. They are larger and heavier than pots, pans, and skillets. Several sizes are available. Most have high, dome lids, and many have racks or trivets.

Microwave Cookware

The type of cookware you use in a microwave oven can affect the outcome of the food you cook. You need to evaluate the cookware material when deciding if you can use a utensil in a microwave oven. The size and shape of pieces are also factors to consider when choosing microwave cookware.

Shape and Size of Microwave Cookware

The shape of cookware can affect how evenly foods cook in a microwave oven. Cookware shapes can also affect cooking time.

Round-shaped containers allow microwaves to hit food evenly. Microwaves can overlap in the corners of square cookware pieces. This causes the corners to overcook.

Ring-shaped pans give great results when microwaving cakes, meat loaves, and other foods. This shape accounts for the fact that foods tend to cook slower in the center of a microwave oven. The circular arrangement allows foods to cook more evenly. Ring shapes also allow microwaves to hit foods from the center as well as the top, bottom, and sides. This increased microwave penetration speeds cooking time. (You can improvise a ring-shaped pan by placing a microwavable glass in the center of a round container.)

Cookware pieces should correspond to the amount and kind of food you are microwaving. Choose single-serving size pieces when cooking for one. They work well for quickly reheating leftovers. Try custard cups for poaching eggs one at a time. Use a rack with a slotted or raised surface when cooking meats so fats and juices can drain. Select deeper containers when cooking foods like milk that may boil over.

Select microwavable cookware in a variety of sizes and shapes to meet all your cooking needs. Pieces that nest together provide easy storage. Pieces with lids allow you to cover foods in the refrigerator and hold in steam in the microwave oven.

Choosing Cooking and Baking Utensils

Consider the following features when buying cooking and baking utensils:

- Utensils should be sturdy and well balanced to prevent tipping. All edges should be smooth. Pan bottoms should be flat for good heat conduction. Beware of crevices where food particles can collect.
- Handles should be heat-resistant, sturdy, and securely attached.
- Lids should be well constructed and should fit tightly. Handles on lids should be heat-resistant and easy to grasp with a pot holder.
- Utensils should be light enough for you to handle comfortably and safely. They should be heavy enough to be durable and to withstand warping.
- Utensils should be able to stack or hang from a wall rack if you have limited storage space.

Use and Care of Cooking and Baking Utensils

To maintain your cooking and baking utensils, proper use and care are essential. Some materials only tolerate certain temperatures. You must condition some utensils before you use them. You must use special cleaning compounds to clean some utensils. Always read the use and care information that accompanies cooking and baking utensils. Follow manufacturer's directions for use and cleaning, 9-11.

Also check use and care information to see if cookware is designed for use in a microwave oven. You can do a simple test to determine whether you can use a piece of cookware in a microwave oven. Put the utensil you are testing inside the microwave oven. Place a glass of water in or near the cookware piece. Turn the microwave oven on high power for one minute. If the cookware stays cool, it is microwavable. If the cookware becomes warm, that means it is absorbing microwaves and you should not use it for microwave cooking.

Betty Crocker Metallic Bakeware

9-11 Following the manufacturer's directions for use and care can help utensils last for years.

Summary

Small kitchen equipment includes measuring, mixing, baking, and cutting tools as well as thermometers and other preparation tools. When selecting these items, think about the types of tasks you perform. Also consider the quality and cost of the tools.

Cookware refers to items used on top of the range. Bakeware includes items used in the oven. You can use many conventional cookware and bakeware pieces in the microwave oven. Cookware and bakeware are commonly made from metal, ceramic, and plastic materials. In addition to the material, the shape and size of microwave cookware can affect its performance. When buying cookware and bakeware, look for pieces that are well made and that are easy to handle and store. Follow manufacturers' use and care directions.

Review What You Have Read

Write your answers on a separate sheet of paper.
1. True or false. Most chefs prefer a rotary beater to a whisk.
2. Which type of spatula would be used to level ingredients in dry measures?
   A. Bent-edged spatula.
   B. Rubber spatula.
   C. Straight-edged spatula.
   D. None of the above.
3. True or false. One thermometer can be used for all kitchen tasks.
4. List three uses for kitchen shears.
5. What is the smallest knife used in the kitchen?
   A. French knife.
   B. Paring knife.
   C. Slicing knife.
   D. Utility knife.
6. A perforated bowl used to drain fruits, vegetables, and pasta is a _____.
7. What are the three most common types of materials for cooking and baking utensils?
8. True or false. Pure copper cannot be used for cooking because it reacts with food and forms poisonous compounds.
9. What is the difference between a saucepan and a pot?
10. Which of the following cookware materials is not recommended for use in a microwave oven?
    A. Ceramic.
    B. Metal.
    C. Paper.
    D. Plastic.
11. True or false. Round containers cook foods more evenly than square containers in a microwave oven.
12. List three features to consider when buying cooking and baking utensils.

Build Your Basic Skills

1. Make a display of small kitchen tools for a showcase in your school. Write a brief description of each tool and explain its use in the kitchen.
2. Make a list of cooking and baking utensils a single person would need in his or her first apartment. Then visit the cooking and baking utensil section of a department store. Figure how much it would cost to equip this hypothetical kitchen.

Build Your Thinking Skills

1. Make a poster chart about the different materials used for cooking and baking utensils. List the characteristics, uses, care requirements, advantages, and disadvantages of each material.
2. Bake some cookies on a cookie sheet with a shiny finish and on one with a dull finish. Compare results and explain any differences.
3. Make a list of the small equipment, cookware, and bakeware found in the kitchen labs in your classroom. Investigate the functions of any utensils that you did not read about in the chapter.

Chapter 10

Planning Meals

A "Taste" of the World of Work

Domestic Cook
Plans menus, orders ingredients, prepares food, and cleans kitchen and cooking utensils in private home. May also serve meals and perform seasonal cooking duties, such as canning.

Caterer
Prepares and serves food and refreshments at social affairs.

Head Banquet Waiter
Plans details for banquets, receptions, and other social functions. Hires extra help, directs setting up of tables and decorations, supervises wait staff.

Terms to Know

meal manager
meal pattern
budget
income
fixed expense
flexible expense

garnish
convenience food
finished food
semiprepared food
work simplification

Objectives

After studying this chapter, you will be able to
- plan nutritious menus using the Food Guide Pyramid and basic meal patterns.
- prepare a family food budget.
- plan menus with an appealing variety of flavors, colors, textures, shapes, sizes, and temperatures.
- discuss resources a meal manager can use as alternatives to time and energy.

National Pork Producers Council

A *meal manager* is someone who uses resources to reach goals related to preparing and serving food. A meal manager's resources include money, time, energy, knowledge, and skills. Food and equipment are resources, too. Meal managers must make many decisions based on these resources. They must decide how much time and money they are willing to spend planning and preparing meals. This will affect their decisions about what foods to serve and how to prepare them.

A meal manager will use available resources to reach the following four goals:

- Provide good nutrition to meet the needs of each family member.
- Use planned spending to make meals fit into the family food budget.
- Prepare satisfying meals that look and taste appealing.
- Control the use of time and energy involved in meal preparation.

The meal manager is responsible for seeing that these goals are reached. However, he or she may not be the only one working to reach them. The meal manager may assign various tasks to other family members.

Provide Good Nutrition

People tend to eat foods they like. However, foods people like may not always be the foods they need to stay healthy. For good health, the foods people eat must supply their bodies with certain essential nutrients. These nutrients include proteins, carbohydrates, fats, vitamins, minerals, and water. Everyone needs the same nutrients, but not in the same amounts. For instance, pregnant women need more of some nutrients than other adults. Active people need more of some nutrients than inactive people.

A diet that follows the Food Guide Pyramid can provide all of the essential nutrients. (Refer to Chapter 3, "Making Healthy Food Choices," for a review of the food groups in the Food Guide Pyramid.) Meal managers can use the Food Guide Pyramid when planning nutritious meals. It helps them determine the number of servings each family member needs from each food group. It also provides information about how to select foods within each group.

Meal Patterns

Meal patterns are outlines used for meal planning. They center on the basic foods that meal managers normally serve at each meal. They can also include other foods to meet the needs of individual family members. When used together, the Food Guide Pyramid and meal patterns can serve as a framework for planning nutritious meals. The meal pattern for breakfast, for example, tells meal managers to include bread or cereal in the breakfast menu. The Food Guide Pyramid tells them that the bread or cereal should be whole grain or enriched. It also tells them that the average person should have six or more servings each day. Examples of basic meal patterns are given in 10-1.

Careful planning allows the meal manager to make sure that foods served throughout the day will meet each family member's nutritional needs. Together, breakfast, lunch, dinner, and snacks provide the day's total nutrient intake. Breakfast generally supplies one-fourth of the day's total needs. Lunch and dinner each supply one-third, and snacks supply the remaining needs. See 10-2.

Breakfast

Eating breakfast provides you with energy and helps prevent a midmorning slump. A good breakfast contains a food rich in vitamin C—usually fruit or fruit juice. Enriched or whole grain bread and/or cereal and milk are also part of a good breakfast. Children, teens, and active adults might want to add a protein food, such as eggs or meat, to the basic breakfast plan.

Lunch

Lunch should supply one-third of the day's total nutrients. A serving from each group in the Food Guide Pyramid provides the nutrients needed by most people.

Basic Meal Patterns

Breakfast	Fruit or fruit juice Main dish Bread Milk or other beverage
Lunch	Main dish Vegetable and/or fruit Milk or other beverage Occasional dessert
Dinner	Main dish Potatoes or one or two alternate vegetables Salad Bread Dessert Milk or other beverage

10-1 Meal patterns are outlines of the basic foods that are served at breakfast, lunch, and dinner.

National Live Stock and Meat Board

10-2 Foods served at breakfast, lunch, and dinner generally supply the majority of nutrient needs.

Many meal managers make good use of leftovers at lunchtime. They use leftovers to prepare nutritious salads, casseroles, and sandwiches. For instance, you could use leftover roast beef in two ways. Family members who carry their lunches to work or school could take hearty roast beef sandwiches. Those who eat their lunches at home could add strips of roast beef to a chef's salad.

Healthy Living

Research has shown that going to work or school without breakfast has a negative impact on work and studies. If you never seem to have time for breakfast, set your alarm 15 minutes earlier. If getting up earlier does not appeal to you, try starting breakfast preparations before you go to bed. Peel an orange, wrap it tightly in plastic, and put it in the refrigerator. Prepare a hard-cooked egg or place a bowl and spoon next to the cereal box. In the morning, you can eat your fruit and cereal (or egg) while making toast.

If traditional breakfast foods do not appeal to you, try eating nonbreakfast foods that you like. Hamburgers, soup, pizza, or yogurt provide many important nutrients and may appeal to you more than cereal and milk.

In cold weather, hot foods are popular for lunch. Those who must take their lunches can carry soups, stews, and casseroles in wide-mouthed vacuum containers. In warmer weather, you can use the same containers to carry fruit juice, milk, or cold main dish salads.

Dinner

Dinner is the one meal of the day that many people can eat leisurely and share with family members. Like lunch, dinner should provide one-third of the day's total nutrients. Dinner is a heavier meal than lunch, and it usually is the richest meal in terms of protein. Many times meal managers serve a light appetizer, such as tomato juice, as a first course. The main course is usually a protein entree. It often includes meat, poultry, or fish. Meal managers often serve potatoes, one or more vegetables, and a salad as part of the main course. Bread or rolls are optional. In some menus, bread takes the place of potato, noodles, or rice. Meal managers may also serve a dessert to complement the rest of the meal.

The meal manager can add variety to dinners in many ways. Instead of serving chicken, peas, and hot biscuits separately, you can combine these foods and serve them as chicken and dumplings. A tossed salad, dessert, and beverage would complete the meal. Other popular one-dish meals are New England boiled dinner, tuna noodle casserole, and pizza.

Some families enjoy trying new and unusual foods. The meal manager can add variety by serving just one unusual dish, such as chicken chow mein, or by planning an entire meal with an international theme.

In hot weather, appetites often become sluggish. You might replace the usual meat, potatoes, and vegetable with a cool, refreshing salad made with meat, cheese, and crisp vegetables. Hot rolls and a fresh fruit dessert would complete the meal.

Varying preparation methods is another way to add variety to meals. For instance, you can use ground beef to make meat loaf, sloppy joes, or Swedish meatballs. You can bake, boil, mash, oven-brown, fry, or cream potatoes.

Snacks

If the meal manager plans ahead, between-meal snacks can satisfy nutritional needs as well as hunger. Fresh fruits and vegetables, cheese and crackers, milk shakes, and hard-cooked eggs are good snacks. They supplement other foods eaten during the day by adding important nutrients to the diet. Family members who need to watch their weight can select snacks that are nutritious and low in calories (kilojoules).

Use Planned Spending

The second goal of meal management is planned spending. Nearly all families find they need to establish a food spending plan. Families in the United States spend, on the average, about 20 percent of their income for food. This figure varies with income level. Families with low incomes may spend as much as 50 percent of their total income for food. High-income families may spend 12 percent or less.

Many factors affect a family's food needs, and household income is not the only influence on food purchases. A family must consider a variety of information when determining the amount of money they can spend for food.

Factors Affecting Food Needs

The activity, size, sex, and age of each member affect a family's food needs. It costs more to feed some people than it does to feed others because people's nutrient needs differ. It costs more to feed an athlete, for example, than it does to feed an office worker. It costs more to feed a person who weighs 250 pounds (112 kg) than a person who weighs 110 pounds (49 kg). After the age of 12, it costs more to feed boys than it does to feed girls. It also costs more to feed a teenager than it does to feed a senior citizen. See 10-3.

Special health problems also influence food needs. A family member who is allergic to wheat or milk, for example, would need special foods. These special foods are often expensive.

Factors Affecting Food Purchases

You might think that all families with similar food needs would spend the same amount of money for food. However, this is not always true. You can acquire similar quantities of nutrients at very different costs depending on the foods purchased.

Think of two baskets of food. One basket contains a beef rib roast, fresh asparagus, fresh oranges, bakery bread, and a frozen cake. The other basket contains ground beef, canned green beans, frozen orange juice concentrate, a house brand loaf of bread, and a cake mix. Both baskets provide similar nutrients. However, the second basket will cost quite a bit less.

The following factors determine the amount of money a meal manager spends for food:

- family income
- meal manager's ability to choose foods that are within the family food budget
- meal manager's shopping skills and knowledge of the marketplace
- amount of time the meal manager has to plan and prepare meals
- food preferences of family members
- family values

Income is a major factor in determining the amount of money a family spends for food. Generally, as income increases, a meal manager spends more money for food. As income increases, the use of milk and milk products, better cuts of meat, bakery goods, and convenience products tends to increase. Meanwhile, the use of less expensive staple foods, such as beans and rice, tends to decrease.

Knowing how to choose the tastiest, most nutritious foods for the money spent is an important meal management skill. A meal manager needs to know how similar products differ in quality and nutrition. He or she needs to know when buying a brand name is important. He or she should be able to identify products that contain hidden service costs. A meal manager also needs to know how to compare prices on a per serving basis. Recognizing seasonal food values and choosing quality meats and produce are other meal management skills.

The meal manager's available time and energy affect the family food budget. If time and energy are limited, the meal manager will have to spend more money on convenience foods. For instance, a meal manager who has ample time and energy could buy ingredients to make homemade lasagna. However, a meal manager who has little time and

10-3 Physically active people need more food energy than less active people.

energy might purchase a frozen entree instead. The frozen entree costs more, but it cooks quickly and requires no preparation.

Food likes and dislikes affect spending on food purchases. A family that eats steaks and fresh produce will spend more than a family that eats casseroles and canned goods.

A family's value system affects spending. Some families view food as merely a basic need. They would rather spend their money on other goals. Other families value meals as a source of entertainment. These families are likely to spend more money for food.

Preparing a Food Budget

Most families have a set amount of money that must cover many expenses. To keep from overspending in one area, such as food, they establish a household spending plan. It is up to the meal manager to stay within this plan.

The first step in evaluating what you can afford to spend for food is to prepare a household budget. A *budget* is a plan for managing how you spend the money you receive, 10-4. The following steps will help you prepare a budget:

1. On a piece of paper, record your average monthly income. *Income* is money received. You will probably receive most

income as wages earned by working. Income also includes money you receive as tips, gifts, and interest on bank accounts. Unless you can count on receiving a set amount from these sources, however, do not include them in your budget. Also, be sure to list only your take-home pay. Money deducted from your paycheck for taxes and other payments is not available for you to use for household expenses.

2. List your monthly fixed expenses and the cost of each. A *fixed expense* is a regularly recurring cost in a set amount. Fixed expenses include rent or mortgage payments, car payments, insurance premiums, and installment loan payments. You should also list savings as a fixed expense. Otherwise, you might end up spending money that you intended to save.

3. List your flexible expenses and their estimated monthly costs. *Flexible expenses* are regularly recurring costs that vary in amount. Flexible expenses include food, clothing, utility bills, transportation, and entertainment.

4. Figure the total of your fixed and estimated flexible expenses. Compare this amount with your income. If your income equals your expenses, you will be able to provide for your needs and meet your financial obligations. If your income is greater than your expenses, you can put the extra money toward future goals. If your expenses are greater than your income, however, you will need to make some adjustments.

Reducing Food Expenses

You can handle a budget shortage in two ways: increasing income and decreasing expenses. Working overtime or getting another job would provide you with extra income. Looking at your current spending patterns will help you see how you can reduce expenses.

Although you cannot do much to change your fixed expenses, you can adjust your flexible expenses, including food. Save your grocery store receipts for a few weeks to see what kinds of foods you are buying.

You already know that the cost of food has little or no bearing on its nutritional value. Each group of the Food Guide Pyramid includes both expensive and inexpensive foods. Protein foods are the most costly, but prices of foods in this group

Monthly Budget	
Income	$ *1200*
Fixed expenses	
Rent	$ *395*
Car payment	*240*
Insurance premium	*55*
Savings	*60*
Flexible expenses	
Food	*120*
Other grocery items	*25*
Clothing	*65*
Utility bills	*80*
Gasoline/oil	*45*
Entertainment	*80*
Gifts and contributions	*35*
Total expenses	$ *1200*

10-4 Figuring your monthly budget will help you decide how much you can afford to spend for various items, including food.

vary widely. T-bone steak, for example, costs more than ground beef. Both, however, provide similar nutrients. See 10-5. Milk, eggs, and cheese also are protein foods. Dried milk costs less than fluid fresh milk. Medium eggs usually cost less than large eggs. Domestic cheeses cost less than imported cheeses. Dried legumes are an inexpensive source of protein that can help stretch food dollars.

The fruit and vegetable groups are the next most costly food groups. However, foods in these groups vary widely in price, too. Before you buy, compare prices of fresh produce with frozen and canned products. Fresh fruits and vegetables are usually economical when they are in season. However, during off seasons, canned and frozen products usually are cheaper. Grocers often price small pieces of fresh produce lower than larger pieces. House brand and generic canned and frozen fruits and vegetables cost less than national brands.

The skillful meal manager also knows that margarine usually costs less than butter. Unsweetened ready-to-eat breakfast cereals usually cost less than presweetened cereals. Cereals you cook yourself cost even less. House brand bread usually costs less than brand name bread or bakery bread. Large packages usually are better buys than small packages. However, wise shoppers compare prices on a per serving basis before buying one size over another.

Convenience products and snack foods are often costly. You may be able to save money by preparing more foods from scratch and buying fewer snack foods. Using coupons and taking advantage of store specials will also help you cut costs.

Remember that the grocery store is not the only place you buy food. Restaurants, concession stands, and vending machines also take a portion of your food dollar. You will need to evaluate these purchases in relation to your overall budget.

After identifying ways you can reduce food costs, determine a realistic figure for your monthly food budget. If you do your shopping weekly, divide this amount by four. Then keep careful track

National Pork Producers Council

10-5 Skilled meal managers check the meat counter. They look for the kind and cut of meat that will provide the most protein for the money.

of your food purchases for a few weeks to see whether you are overspending. Sometimes your records may show that you have spent more than your weekly budget. For instance, stocking up on sale items one week may cause you to spend more than your estimated amount. However, this may enable you to spend less money the following week.

Food is only one of the flexible expenses in your budget. You can take similar steps to reduce other spending areas, such as clothing, transportation, and entertainment.

Prepare Satisfying Meals

The third goal of meal management is to prepare satisfying meals. All family members should find a meal appealing. The meal manager must work within time and money limits and around food preferences of family members. Therefore, this goal can be one of the most difficult to accomplish.

Food Preferences

People eat the foods they like. People like some groups of foods better than others. Studies have shown that people find vegetables, salads, and soups least appealing. They like breads, meats, and desserts best. Studies also show wide ranges of preferences within a liked class of foods. In the meat class, for instance, respondents listed grilled steak, fried chicken, and roast turkey as their three favorites. The least-liked foods in the same group were lamb, liver, fish, and creamed and combination dishes.

The foods you prefer to eat usually are familiar foods that taste good to you. Many factors affect food preferences. Ethnic origin, religious beliefs, socioeconomic status, and family background can affect a person's food preferences. Education, standard of living, and goals and ambitions also impact likes and dislikes.

Sight, smell, and touch influence food preferences, too. As a result, the flavor, color, texture, size, shape, and temperature of foods help determine how they are received.

Flavor

Flavor is a mixture of taste, aroma, and texture. The four basic tastes recognized by human beings are sweet, sour, salty, and bitter. Some foods have one distinct flavor. Sugar, for example, is sweet. Other foods have a blend of flavors. Sweet and sour pork has the sweetness of sugar. It also has the sourness of vinegar and the saltiness of pork.

Odor is closely associated with flavor. Foods that smell good taste better. The smell of coffee perking or steak broiling, for example, stimulates your appetite and taste buds.

Flavor should be an important consideration when planning meals. Some flavors seem to go together. Turkey and cranberry sauce, peanut butter and jelly, and apples and cinnamon are popular flavor combinations. Other flavors seem to fight one another. For instance, you should not serve rutabagas and Brussels sprouts together. Their strong flavors do not complement each other.

When planning meals, do not repeat similar flavors. For instance, avoid serving tomatoes on a salad that will accompany pasta with tomato sauce. Your menus should not include all spicy foods or all mild foods. Plan to serve foods with different flavors. See 10-6.

Color

When used correctly, color not only appeals to the eyes, but also stimulates the appetite. The colors of a meal should provide a pleasing contrast, but they should not clash. If you serve tomatoes and red cabbage together, for instance, the result would not be pleasing. The colors of carrots and red cabbage also are unattractive when served together. See 10-7.

Garnishes can add color to a meal. A sprinkling of nutmeg on custard or paprika on cheese sauce adds a touch of color. Meal managers can use lemon wedges, green pepper strips, and parsley sprigs to add color to a plate. Spiced peach halves, orange twists, cucumber slices, and radish roses are also simple garnishes. They can add eye appeal to many foods.

Be a Clever Consumer

If you are like most people, your grocery purchases include more than just food. It may be convenient to pick up items like shampoo, lightbulbs, and 35 mm film when you are at the grocery store. However, these items generally cost less at discount stores. Therefore, unless they are on sale, you might be smart to leave these items off your grocery list.

Flavor

This meal repeats the flavor of cheese in the cottage cheese salad, the au gratin potatoes, and the cheese sauce. It also repeats the flavor of pineapple in the salad and the garnish.

By changing the salad to lettuce with dressing and topping the broccoli with pimento, important flavor contrasts are made.

Dianne Debnam

10-6 Think about the flavors of foods that will be served together. Avoid repeating flavors when planning meals.

Color

Everything in this meal is pale in color.

Add color by garnishing the fish and replacing the macaroni salad with a colorful slaw. Then switch the steamed cabbage for a baked tomato.

Dianne Debnam

10-7 A little garnishing and some simple substitutions make a color transformation that greatly improves the appeal of this meal.

Texture

Texture is the feel of food in the mouth. Familiar food textures are hard, chewy, soft, crisp, smooth, sticky, dry, gritty, and tough. A meal made up of foods that are all soft or all crisp lacks interest. A meal made up of a variety of textures is much more appealing. See 10-8.

Serve foods in combinations that have texture contrasts. Crisp cookies and soft, smooth pudding is one example. You can add a small amount of one food to another food to introduce a texture contrast. For instance, tossing toasted, slivered almonds into a pan of green beans adds a nice difference in texture.

When planning meals, work for a balance between soft and solid foods. Be sure to consider chewy versus crunchy, dry versus moist, and smooth versus crisp. Avoid serving two or more chopped, creamed, or mashed dishes together.

Texture

All the foods in this meal have soft textures.

The soft yams have been replaced with crisp-tender green beans. Almonds in the green beans and water chestnuts in the wild rice add crunch. Seeds on the roll and fruit in the gelatin also add texture variation.

Dianne Debnam

10-8 Texture contrasts can be seen by the eyes and felt in the mouth.

Shape and Size

The size and shape of food items affect how appetizing they look. Avoid serving several foods made up of small pieces. For instance, a chicken and rice casserole would be better accompanied by spears of broccoli than peas. When choosing a salad to serve with the casserole, a lettuce wedge would be more appealing than coleslaw. Choose foods with various shapes and sizes when planning meals. See 10-9.

Temperature

The temperature of foods can also affect appetite appeal. A cold salad, for example, provides a pleasing temperature contrast to a piping hot entree. Icy cold sherbet cools the sensation created by spicy chili.

Hot foods should be hot and cold foods should be cold. Imagine a steaming bowl of soup and the same soup barely warm. Picture a cold, crisp tossed salad next to a salad bowl filled with wilted

Shape and Size

The use of so many round shapes makes this meal look boring.

Substituting noodles for the potatoes and changing the shapes of other foods make this meal look much more appealing.

Dianne Debnam

10-9 Meals look much more interesting when they include foods in a variety of shapes and sizes.

Play It Safe

Lukewarm foods are not only unappetizing, they may be unsafe. Keep foods above 140°F (60°C) or below 40°F (5°C). Foods kept between these temperatures provide an excellent medium for the growth of microorganisms that can cause food-borne illness.

greens. Foods served lukewarm do not stimulate the senses of taste and sight.

Planning a Meal

Generally, the best menus center on one food. In most cases, that one food is the main dish. The meal manager then chooses other foods to complement the main dish.

When planning a meal, you probably will find it easiest to make your menu selections in the following order:

1. Choose the main dish of the main course.
2. Select the staple food (potatoes, rice, noodles, or stuffing) that will accompany the main dish.
3. Select one or two vegetables, considering flavor, color, texture, and shape.
4. Choose the salad.
5. Select the dessert and/or first course.

As you choose individual menu items, be sure to include foods from each group of the Food Guide Pyramid. This will help you make sure the meal is nutritionally well balanced.

Control the Use of Time

The fourth goal of successful meal management is controlled use of time. Many meal managers think of this goal before any of the others. A meal manager's lack of time for planning and preparing meals can affect decisions involving the other management goals. For example, the meal manager with little time may have to choose convenience foods. This will cause him or her to spend extra money.

Several factors help determine the amount of time the meal manager needs to plan and prepare meals. These include family size, food preferences, meal standards, budget, and the efficiency of equipment. The meal manager's knowledge and skills will affect his or her use of time, too.

Alternatives to the Use of Time and Energy

The meal manager uses time and energy to plan menus, buy and store food, and prepare and serve meals. He or she also needs time and energy to care for the kitchen and dining area.

A meal manager can use several alternatives to time and energy. These include eating out, money, knowledge, skills, abilities, and time itself.

Eating out helps many busy meal managers meet their goal to control the use of time. With a little thought, eating out can meet the other three meal management goals, too. Meal managers can help family members choose items from the menu that meet the goal of good nutrition. They can limit the frequency of dining out to meet the goal of planned spending. They can choose restaurants with varied menus to meet the goal of satisfying meals.

Money is a good alternative to time and energy for some families. However, many families find money too limited to use often as a time alternative. When money is available, the meal manager can buy time by purchasing ready-made foods. Buying efficient kitchen appliances and hiring help are other ways a meal manager can use money as an alternative.

A meal manager's *knowledge* and *skills* can be alternatives for both time and money. A meal manager's assets include knowing when, where, or how to shop to gain the most value for each dollar spent, 10-10. Knowing how to creatively prepare a variety of foods and efficiently organize the kitchen are also assets. A meal manager obtains many of his or her skills through experience. He or she gains other skills by studying and asking questions.

A meal manager can use *time* itself to save time. Successful meal managers are aware of how they use time, and they look for ways to save it. Using time to organize the kitchen for efficiency can save time later when preparing meals. Using time to plan menus can save time later by helping you shop more efficiently. You can make the most of the time you spend cooking by preparing extra food to freeze for later use.

Meal managers can save time in other ways. Many meal managers keep records of good menus, recipes, and products that they use when planning meals. Others keep a bulletin board in the kitchen and use it to jot down menu ideas and shopping needs.

Using Convenience Foods

Some meal managers use convenience foods to reduce or eliminate food preparation and cooking

10-10 Knowing how to shop for the best food values is one of a meal manager's most valuable assets.

time at home. *Convenience foods* are foods that have had some amount of service added to them. Some convenience foods, such as canned soups, have been available so long that people do not think of them as convenience products. Other convenience foods, such as ready-to-eat puddings, are newer.

You can group convenience foods according to the amount of service they contain. *Finished foods* are convenience foods that are ready for eating either immediately or after simply heating or thawing. Packaged cookies, canned spaghetti, and frozen fruits are examples of finished foods. *Semiprepared foods* are convenience foods that still need to have some service performed. Cake mixes are semiprepared foods. The meal manager beats in eggs and liquid, pours the batter into pans, and bakes it for a specified time.

The cost of convenience depends on the amount of service a product contains. Generally, the more built-in service a product contains, the more the product costs. A product that contains more service reduces the amount of time the meal manager spends measuring, mixing, and cooking. Most convenience foods cost more than their homemade counterparts. However, there are some exceptions. Frozen orange juice concentrate and some commercial cake mixes cost less than their homemade counterparts.

Convenience foods have both advantages and disadvantages as explained in 10-11. Before buying a convenience product, ask yourself the following questions:

- How do the appearance and flavor of the convenience product compare with those of its homemade counterpart?
- How does the cost of the convenience product compare with the cost of the homemade product?
- Does buying convenience foods fit into my food budget? (Is the time I save worth the extra cost?)
- How costly are any additional ingredients that I must add? (Some convenience mixes require the addition of foods like meat, eggs, or sour cream.)
- How much do I need to feed my family? (The cost of a convenience product may seem reasonable if you are feeding one or two people. However, it may seem costly if you are feeding three or more.)

Work Simplification

Work simplification is the performance of tasks in the simplest way possible in order to

Convenience Foods

Advantages	Disadvantages
Time and energy are saved because the meal manager does not have to measure, mix, peel, and slice. The inexperienced cook can prepare meals confidently. The meal manager who does not like to cook can prepare nutritious meals for the family without spending hours in the kitchen.	Many mass-produced foods do not taste as good as home-prepared foods. Frequent use of convenience foods is expensive. Some convenience foods are high in fat and sodium.

10-11 Before buying a convenience food, a meal manager should consider both the advantages and disadvantages.

conserve both time and energy. Work simplification techniques can help meal managers reach their goal for controlling the use of time. The meal manager can simplify tasks by minimizing hand and body motions. He or she can organize work space and tools. Changing the product or the method used to prepare the product can also simplify some tasks.

You can minimize hand and body motions in many ways. Performing a task again and again can eventually result in reduced preparation time. This is because the person performing the task develops a skill. A professional cook who chops celery every day eventually learns an efficient method for chopping celery.

Another way to minimize motions is to rinse and soak dishes. This simplifies the task of washing dishes.

Saving yourself steps in the kitchen is a method of work simplification, too. Try not to walk back and forth across the kitchen while preparing a meal. Instead, get all your equipment ready first. Then go to the cabinets and then to the refrigerator to get the foods you need.

An organized kitchen simplifies work, 10-12. Store tools in the area where you most often use them. For instance, you can store pots and pans in a cabinet close to the range. Many experienced meal managers buy duplicates of inexpensive tools like rubber spatulas, wooden spoons, and measuring utensils. They store these tools in different parts of the kitchen where the tools will be easy to reach. By using the correct tool for each task, the meal manager can also simplify work. Measuring flour in a dry measure is much more efficient than measuring it in a liquid measure.

You can simplify work by changing the food product or changing the method used to prepare the product. For instance, if the meal plan calls for rolled biscuits but time is short, you can make dropped biscuits instead. Making a cake from a cake mix takes less time and effort than making one from scratch. However, the end results are similar.

Aristokraft, Inc.

10-12 Keeping cupboards neatly organized and well stocked with frequently used ingredients makes the kitchen more efficient and simplifies work.

Summary

Meal managers have four main goals in planning meals for their families. The first goal is to provide good nutrition. They can use the Food Guide Pyramid and basic meal patterns as resources to help them meet this goal.

The second goal is to use planned spending. A family must consider factors that affect food needs and food purchases when preparing a household budget. A meal manager can use his or her consumer skills to reduce food expenses and stay within the established budget.

The third goal of meal management is to prepare satisfying meals. Meal managers must be mindful of family food preferences in order to achieve this goal. They must also consider flavors, colors, textures, shapes, sizes, and temperatures of foods to plan menus that are varied and appealing.

The fourth meal management goal is to control the use of time. Meal managers can use a number of resources as alternatives to time and energy. They can also use convenience foods and work simplification techniques to reduce the time they spend planning and preparing meals.

Review What You Have Read

Write your answers on a separate sheet of paper.

1. Name the four goals of meal management.
2. What percent of a day's total nutrient intake do breakfast, lunch, dinner, and snacks generally supply?
3. True or false. All families with similar food needs spend the same amount of money for food.
4. List four factors that help determine the amount of money a meal manager spends for food.
5. Describe the steps you would take to estimate the amount of money you could spend for food each week.
6. Which of the following statements about food costs is not true?
   A. Dried milk costs less than fresh milk.
   B. During off-seasons, canned fruits and vegetables cost less than fresh.
   C. House brands cost less than national brands.
   D. Presweetened cereals cost less than unsweetened cereals.
7. List the six elements that affect the sensory appeal of a meal. Give examples of foods that show contrast for each element.
8. List four resources a meal manager can use as alternatives to time and energy.
9. Convenience foods that are ready for eating either immediately or after simply heating or thawing are called _____.
10. Describe three ways a meal manager can simplify tasks.

Build Your Basic Skills

1. Compare the costs of foods with built-in convenience with their less convenient counterparts. Examples might include shredded cheese and bulk cheese, instant rice and long grain rice, and ready-made juice and frozen concentrate.
2. Visit the school cafeteria or a nearby food service operation and observe employees involved in food preparation. How are work simplification techniques being used? How could employees use them? Report your findings to the other class members.

Build Your Thinking Skills

1. Keep track of all the meals you have eaten for one week. Evaluate the meals according to the Food Guide Pyramid. If each day's meals were not nutritionally balanced, add or subtract menu items until the meals would meet each day's total nutrient needs.
2. Write menus for your family's meals for a week. Attach the menus to a report analyzing how they meet the four goals of meal management.

The Kroger Co.

Many supermarkets have a deli department that sells party trays, freshly sliced meats and cheeses, and ready-to-eat salads and entrees.

Chapter **11**

The Smart Consumer

A "Taste" of the World of Work

Comparison Shopper
Compares prices, packaging, physical characteristics, and styles of merchandise in competing stores.

Retail Food Demonstrator
Prepares samples of food products for grocery store customers in order to promote sales; answers customer questions.

Nutrition Aide
Advises low-income family members about how to plan, budget, shop, prepare balanced meals, and handle and store food following prescribed standards.

©1995 Jenny Craig Weight Loss Centres, Inc.

Terms to Know

comparison shopping
impulse buying
house brand
national brand
organic food
organically processed
    food
additive

GRAS list
Daily Value
universal product
    code (UPC)
open dating
unit pricing
generic product

Objectives

After studying this chapter, you will be able to
- ❏ make wise decisions in the marketplace.
- ❏ organize a shopping list and comparison shop.
- ❏ explain how labeling, unit pricing, and generic products affect you as a consumer.

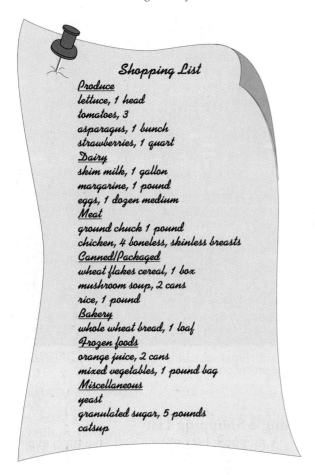

Shopping List

Produce
lettuce, 1 head
tomatoes, 3
asparagus, 1 bunch
strawberries, 1 quart
Dairy
skim milk, 1 gallon
margarine, 1 pound
eggs, 1 dozen medium
Meat
ground chuck 1 pound
chicken, 4 boneless, skinless breasts
Canned/Packaged
wheat flakes cereal, 1 box
mushroom soup, 2 cans
rice, 1 pound
Bakery
whole wheat bread, 1 loaf
Frozen foods
orange juice, 2 cans
mixed vegetables, 1 pound bag
Miscellaneous
yeast
granulated sugar, 5 pounds
catsup

11-2 Organizing your shopping list by areas of the store will make shopping quicker and easier.

substitutions, wise shoppers choose the less expensive items.

Stores may sell some items in multiples, such as three boxes of macaroni and cheese for $5.00. In a case such as this, determine what you would pay for one box. This will help you decide if the multiple price is a good value.

The smart consumer also determines the cost per serving when comparing costs of different foods. Several factors enter into this calculation. The form of the food affects cost per serving. In the summer months, fresh peas may cost less than frozen peas.

Brands also affect cost per serving. A *house brand* is a brand sold only by a store or chain of stores. A *national brand* is a brand that is advertised and sold throughout the country. Manufacturers of national brands often package some of their products with house brand labels. However, because the house brands are not promoted with big advertising budgets, they often cost less than national brands.

To determine the cost per serving, you need to know the size of an average serving of that food.

You also need to know the number of servings a container or package of that food will provide. Food labels will tell you the size of an average serving and the number of servings the package contains. With this information, you can determine the cost per serving. For example, the label on a can of nationally advertised peaches tells you the can contains seven ½ cup (125 mL) servings. The price of the can is $1.49. The cost per serving is about $.21. The same size can of house brand peaches costs $1.29. The cost per serving is about $.18. You would save $.03 a serving if you bought the house brand.

Shopping Tips

You can save money in the grocery store without sacrificing nutrition, quality, or taste. Consider the following points when shopping for food:

- Read labels to be sure you know what you are buying.
- Compare brands and then select the brand that best meets your needs.
- Compare prices on a cost per serving basis.
- Buy foods that are in season when possible. Foods that are in season are generally low in price and high in quality.
- Take advantage of advertised specials, but be sure the advertised price is a sale price. Some stores feature regular prices in their advertisements.
- Compare the costs of different forms of the same food. For instance, find out which costs less—fresh peaches or canned peaches. If either form will fit your intended use, buy the less costly form.
- If you have the time, prepare foods from scratch. Most convenience foods cost more than homemade ones.
- Use nonfat dry milk and margarine in cooking to stretch dairy dollars.

Protect the Planet

Avoid buying individually packaged products, such as one-serving juice containers and single-portion entrees. These smaller packages not only tend to cost more per serving, they also require more packaging material. Choose larger packages instead. You can use small, reusable containers to divide large items into single servings at home.

11-3 The meat case is one place where consumers can easily compare costs. They can use the price per pound as a basis for comparing different cuts to help them save money.

- Buy large pieces of meat and cut them into smaller pieces at home, 11-4. Likewise, buy large pieces of cheese and slice, cube, and grate them at home.
- Try planning some meatless meals, substituting dried legumes, eggs, and cheese for meat.
- Resist the temptation to make impulse purchases encouraged by store displays. Such displays include gum in the checkout area, shortcakes beside the fresh strawberries, and toys next to the baby foods.
- Do not take a grocery cart if you plan to buy just one or two items. You will be less tempted to buy items you do not need if you have to carry them through the store.

Other Factors to Consider

What are the facts about organic foods and additives? Are organic foods really better for your health? Are all additives dangerous, and should you avoid them?

Organic Foods

Organic foods are foods that have been grown in soil enriched with organic fertilizers (rather than chemical fertilizers) and without the use of pesticides. People also call them "natural foods" and "health foods." *Organically processed foods* are organically grown foods that have not been treated with preservatives, hormones, antibiotics, or synthetic additives.

The organic materials used to fertilize organic foods include animal manures, plant composts, peat moss, and aged sawdust. Inorganic or commercial fertilizers contain the same chemical nutrients. However, the nutrients in commercial fertilizers are in simpler form, and they are not always combined with carbon. Plants cannot distinguish between organic and inorganic fertilizers. However, plants can use only nutrients that are in inorganic form. This means that organic fertilizers must be broken down into simpler forms before plants can use them for growth.

No scientific evidence has shown that organic foods have greater nutritive value than foods

National Live Stock and Meat Board

11-4 You can save money by buying a large chuck blade steak and dividing it into smaller portions at home.

Play It Safe

Organisms that cause food-borne illnesses multiply quickly at temperatures above 40°F (5°C). Put refrigerated and frozen foods in your grocery cart last to prevent the growth of these organisms. Store all food properly when you arrive home. If you will not be going directly home after grocery shopping, take an insulated cooler to the store with you. Use it to keep perishable foods cool until you can store them properly.

produced by standard agricultural methods. However, some people are willing to pay considerably more for "health foods." Prices in health food stores usually are four to 10 times greater than prices in conventional food stores. There are several reasons for the higher prices. One is that crop yields are often lower, so the cost of growing the food is greater. Another is that you cannot store organically processed foods as long as ordinary foods. A third reason for the high prices in health food stores is that the volume of business may be lower. Therefore, the seller has to charge higher prices to make a profit. Finally, the seller may be making a higher margin of profit than conventional stores typically make.

If you choose to eat organic foods, you should consider the following:

- Shop in stores where you can be sure the selling practices are ethical. The stores should sell foods as advertised.
- Be willing to pay more for the foods you are buying.
- Do not expect the higher cost to buy greater nutritional value.
- Be aware that the variety of organic foods may be limited. Therefore, you will have to shop carefully to meet all your nutritional needs.

Food Additives

Additives are substances that are added to food for a specific purpose, such as preserving the food. The use of additives is not new. People have been preserving food by smoking and salting for centuries. Although over 1,800 additives are in use today, they all fill four basic purposes.

- **Additives add nutrients.** Cereals are often enriched with thiamin, niacin, riboflavin, and iron.
- **Additives preserve quality.** Adding calcium propionate to bread prolongs its shelf life by preventing the growth of mold. BHA and BHT are *antioxidants* that are added to foods to prevent changes in quality caused by exposure to air.
- **Additives aid processing or preparation.** Additives in this group may serve one of several functions. Lecithin and monoglycerides act as *emulsifiers* to keep foods like peanut butter and mayonnaise from separating. Gelatin and gum arabic are *texturizers* and *stabilizers* used in foods like ice cream. Sodium bicarbonate serves as a *leavening agent* to affect the texture and volume of baked goods. Some additives control acidity or alkalinity, also known as *pH level,* in certain foods. Citric acid, for example, gives tartness to some carbonated drinks and gelatin desserts. *Humectants,* such as glycerin and propylene glycol, help foods like shredded coconut retain moisture. Potassium bromate acts as a *maturing agent* that speeds up the necessary aging of foods like cheese. Acetone peroxide is a *bleaching agent* used to whiten flour. Calcium silicate and silicon dioxide act as *anticaking agents* to prevent lumping in powdered mixes.
- **Additives enhance flavors or colors.** Spices and vanilla are flavor additives. MSG (monosodium glutamate) is a flavor enhancer. It magnifies the taste of foods without adding a flavor of its own. Sweeteners, such as aspartame and fructose, are also considered to be flavor additives. Carotene and ultramarine blue are coloring agents. They give color to foods that lose some of their natural color during processing.

The Food and Drug Administration (FDA) and the United States Department of Agriculture (USDA) rigidly control the kinds and amounts of additives manufacturers can use in foods. Federal laws ensure that all foods sold across state lines are safe. This means they are processed under sanitary conditions and are honestly prepared, labeled, and packaged. Government safety experts inspect processing plants. Scientists continually test foods, colors, and chemicals under government supervision to ensure their safety. See 11-5.

Before the government passed more rigid food additive laws in the 1950s, about 600 different

11-5 Federal laws ensure that food is processed under sanitary conditions.

additives were in use. The FDA placed these additives on the "Generally Recognized as Safe" or **GRAS list.** The FDA has retested the additives that appear on this list to make sure they are safe according to today's standards.

Food manufacturers can use any additive that appears on the GRAS list without permission. However, they must obtain permission from the FDA for use of additives that are not on the GRAS list.

Help for the Consumer

The food industry, federal and state governments, and private agencies help consumers receive the most value for their food dollars. They do this through labeling guidelines, unit pricing, and generic products. Learn to take advantage of such items and information when you shop for food.

Food Labeling

Food labels provide a wealth of information that can be helpful to consumers. This includes nutrition information, which the FDA requires on almost all food packages. Nutrition information appears under the heading "Nutrition Facts." See 11-6. The first item under this heading is the *serving size* in both household and metric measures. This is followed by the number of *servings per container.* Serving sizes are the same for similar

Nutrition Label

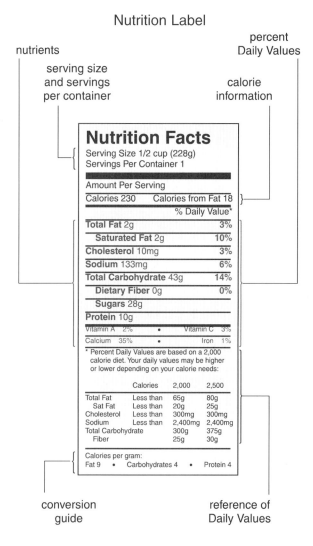

nutrients

serving size
and servings
per container

percent
Daily Values

calorie
information

conversion
guide

reference of
Daily Values

*11-6 Some food products may carry a simpler version
of the nutrition label. However, all nutrition labels
provide consumers with valuable information.*

food products to help consumers make comparisons between products.

Calorie information includes the number of calories per serving along with the number of calories from fat. This can help you limit fat to no more than 30 percent of your total calories.

Nutrients found in each serving of food products also appear on nutrition labels. The nutrients listed are those that are most directly linked to the health concerns of today's consumers. The list must include the total number of calories and the number of calories from fat. It must list the amount of total fat, saturated fat, cholesterol, sodium, total carbohydrate, dietary fiber, sugars, and protein. Vitamin A, vitamin C, calcium, and iron are listed, as well. Information about other nutrients, such as thiamin and monounsaturated fat, is optional.

However, foods about which manufacturers make nutritional claims and foods with added nutrients must include additional information on the label.

At the bottom of larger nutrition labels, a reference set of Daily Values is shown for 2,000 and 2,500 calorie diets. *Daily Values* are dietary references that appear on food labels. They are designed to help consumers use label information to plan healthy diets. The reference of Daily Values includes maximums for fat, saturated fat, cholesterol, and sodium for both calorie levels. Daily minimums for total carbohydrate and fiber are also given. This reference information is the same on all nutrition labels that include it.

Percent Daily Values based on a 2,000 calorie diet are given for each of the nutrients listed on the label. Your daily calorie needs may be higher or lower than 2,000 calories. Therefore, your Daily Values may also be higher or lower. You will need to keep this in mind when reading the percent Daily Values on food labels. For instance, the Daily Value for dietary fiber for a 2,000 calorie diet is 25 grams. If you need only 1,600 calories per day, your Daily Value for dietary fiber would be 20 grams. A food that supplies 5 grams of fiber per serving would list 20 percent of the Daily Value for fiber on the label. However, a serving of this food would actually provide 25 percent of *your* Daily Value.

Many manufacturers make nutritional claims about their food products. In the past, nutritional claims, such as "lowfat," "high fiber," and "reduced calories," sometimes misled consumers. To reduce confusion, the FDA has now established standard definitions for these terms. See 11-7.

In addition to nutrition information, federal law requires that the following items appear on food labels:

- the common name and form of the food
- the weight of the contents, including any liquid in which foods are packed
- the name and address of the manufacturer, packer, or distributor
- a list of ingredients, in descending order according to weight. For instance, suppose a label lists "chicken, noodles, and carrots." The product would need to contain, by weight, more chicken than noodles, and more noodles than carrots.

Universal Product Code

The *universal product code*, or *UPC*, is a series of lines, bars, and numbers that appears on packages of food and nonfood items. The first five numbers of the code identify the manufacturer. The next five numbers identify the product and its size,

Nutrient Content Claims

cholesterol free	Less than 2 milligrams of cholesterol and 2 grams or less of saturated fat per serving.
fat free	Less than 0.5 grams of fat per serving.
fresh	Food is raw, has never been frozen or heated, and contains no preservatives.
high fiber	5 grams or more fiber per serving. (Foods making high-fiber claims must also meet the definition for low fat, or the level of total fat must appear next to the high-fiber claim.)
light/lite	A nutritionally altered food product contains one-third fewer calories or half the fat of the "regular" version of the food. This term can also be used to indicate that the sodium of a low-calorie, lowfat food has been reduced by 50 percent. In addition, labels may state that foods are light (lite) in color or texture.
*low calorie	40 calories or less per serving.
*low cholesterol	20 milligrams or less of cholesterol and 2 grams or less of saturated fat per serving.
*low fat	3 grams or less fat per serving.
*low sodium	140 milligrams or less sodium per serving.
reduced calories	At least 25 percent fewer calories per serving than the "full-calorie" version of the food.
sodium free	Less than 5 milligrams of sodium per serving.
sugar free	Less than 0.5 grams of sugar per serving.

*Foods with a serving size of 30 grams or less or 2 tablespoons or less must meet the specified requirement for portions of 50 grams of the food.

11-7 Manufacturers must adhere to these definitions when making nutrient content claims about food products.

style, or form. If a "0" appears on the bar to the left of the code, the product is a regular grocery item.

Food manufacturers and food store chains developed the UPC to save time and labor. Grocery checkers pass the, UPC on items, over a laser beam scanner. As the items pass over the scanner, the store's computer reads the codes. The correct prices are then rung up on the computer terminal at the clerk's counter. The computer prints a description of the items and their prices on the customer's receipt. See 11-8.

The computer system also functions as an automatic inventory system. It can tell the store management how much of each product is in stock. It also records how fast products are selling and indicates when and how much to order. Store managers use this information to analyze the buying patterns of their customers.

Open Dating

Open dating is a system of putting dates on perishable and semiperishable foods to help consumers obtain products that are fresh and wholesome. The date also helps you know which product to use first. Manufacturers use four different types of dates.

The *pack date* is the day the food was manufactured or processed and packaged. It tells you how old the food is at the time you buy it. Canned foods often have this type of date.

The *pull* or *sell date* is the last day a store should sell a product. The pull date allows for some storage time in your refrigerator. Milk, ice cream, and cold cuts often have pull dates stamped on their containers or packages.

The *expiration date* is the last day a consumer should use or eat a food. Yeast and baby food have expiration dates.

The *freshness date* is often found on bakery products like bread and rolls. A product with an expired freshness date has passed its quality peak. However, you can still use it.

Unit Pricing

Many, but not all, grocery stores use unit pricing. *Unit pricing* is a system of listing a cost per standard unit, weight, or measure of a product. Examples are the cost per pound (.45 kg), the cost per quart (L), and the cost per dozen. Unit prices generally appear with selling prices on shelf tags underneath the products to which the prices refer, 11-9.

With unit pricing, you can compare the cost of different forms of products quickly and easily. For example, you can purchase green beans fresh, canned, and frozen. Suppose the unit price labels

11-9 *Unit price shelf tags help consumers compare costs of different sizes and brands of products.*

X canned pears costs $.05 per ounce (28 g), while Brand Y canned pears costs $.06 per ounce (28 g).

Generic Products

In many grocery stores across the country, consumers are choosing between national brand products, house brand products, and generic products. A *generic product* is a plain-labeled, no-brand grocery product.

Generic products include canned products, pet food, staple items like flour and sugar, cleaning agents, and a variety of paper products. Although the packaging is plain, it does state the name of the product and a list of ingredients. The net weight or contents and the name and address of the manufacturer, packer, or distributor are also given.

Generic products generally cost consumers about 30 percent less than national brands. They cost about 15 to 19 percent less than house brands. The prices are lower because manufacturers spend less money on packaging and advertising. In addition, a generic product may be of lower quality.

Generic food products usually are nutritionally equivalent to brand name items. However, they may not be of the same quality as brand name products. For instance, generic fruits and vegetables may have uneven sizes and shapes. Their colors and textures may vary. Generic paper products may be lighter in weight. Detergents may be less concentrated than brand name products.

You can avoid possible disappointment with the quality of generic products by first considering how you intend to use them. For instance, the appearance of peaches in a cobbler is not as important as in a fruit cup. Therefore, generic brand sliced peaches might be a good choice when making cobbler. However, you may prefer the more uniform appearance of a higher quality brand when making a fruit cup. See 11-10.

U.S. Department of Agriculture

11-8 *A scanner at the grocery checkout counter reads the UPC on food product labels.*

told you the canned green beans cost $.04 per ounce (28 g). Frozen green beans cost $.07 per ounce (28 g), and the fresh green beans cost $.08 per ounce (28 g). Obviously, the canned green beans would be the most economical.

Unit pricing can also help you compare different package sizes and different brands. For example, unit pricing may tell you that 1 ounce (28 g) of ready-to-eat breakfast cereal from a small box costs $.27 while the same amount of cereal from a large box costs $.22. Unit pricing may also tell you that Brand

Be a Clever Consumer

Consider the impact of coupons on unit cost. Small packages often have a higher unit cost than large packages of the same product. When using a coupon, however, the small package often becomes the better buy. For instance, suppose a 10-ounce (284 g) box of cereal costs $2.49 and a 20-ounce (568 g) box costs $4.39. The small box would have a unit cost of $.25 per ounce (28 g). The large box would have a unit cost of $.22 per ounce (28 g). With a $.75 coupon, the small box would cost $1.74; the large box would cost $3.64. With the coupon, the unit cost of the small box would be $.17; the unit cost of the large box would be $.18.

Sources of Consumer Information

Many times you can solve problems you encounter in the marketplace yourself. Suppose you purchase a loaf of bread, bring it home, and find that it is moldy. If you return the bread to the store, most managers will be happy to give you another loaf.

Sometimes you may need help to solve consumer problems. Many sources of consumer help are available. Federal, state, and local governments can help. Business organizations and organized consumer groups can also help. These sources provide consumer information; answer questions; handle product complaints; and do testing, grading, and inspecting.

Consumers Union is a nonprofit organization that provides information and assistance in the area of consumer purchasing. The Consumers Union buys products and tests them in their laboratories. They rate the products and report their results to the public in a monthly publication called *Consumer Reports*.

American Iron & Steel Institute

11-10 Although generic products usually cost less, there may be times when you prefer to buy national or house brand products.

Consumer's Research Inc. is a nonprofit corporation that provides consulting and advisory services. It presents information to the public in monthly and yearly reports.

Underwriters Laboratories tests electrical products for safety. Products carrying the UL seal have been tested and are safe for consumer use.

Better Business Bureaus protect consumers and businesses from misrepresentation, fraud, and trickery in business transactions. They also promote and maintain advertising and selling practices that are fair to both consumers and businesses. Better Business Bureaus investigate and publicize cases of fraud and unfair treatment of consumers. They issue warnings when they establish that fraud has occurred.

The *United States Department of Agriculture (USDA)* serves as a regulatory agency for food products sold across state lines. The USDA establishes grades for many products and provides an inspection service for foods such as meat and canned goods.

The *Food and Drug Administration (FDA)* protects consumers against economic fraud and health hazards. The FDA prevents any food that might be harmful from being sold across state lines. It controls the use of additives and pesticides. The FDA also enforces fair packaging and labeling of products and establishes standards for food products.

The *Office of Consumer Affairs* works as a clearinghouse to process consumer complaints. This office refers complaints that it does not handle to the appropriate federal, state, or local office.

The *Federal Trade Commission (FTC)* has many functions and enforces numerous laws. Two functions that directly help consumers are the administration of the false advertising law and jurisdiction over fraudulent sales promotion.

Other sources of consumer information include magazines, newspapers, and trade journals. Family and consumer science professionals are also sources. See 11-11.

11-11 Family and consumer science professionals may evaluate recipes, answer telephone inquiries, and publish information to help consumers.

Summary

Smart consumers must shop carefully to get the most from their food dollars. Evaluating store features can help them decide where to shop. Knowing when to shop can help them avoid crowds. Using a shopping list and comparing costs can help them know what to buy. Knowing about organic foods and food additives can help consumers make purchase decisions, too.

A number of resources can assist consumers at the grocery store. Food labeling provides information about the nutritional value of food products. The UPC speeds checkout. Open dating helps consumers select foods that are fresh and wholesome. Unit pricing makes it easy to compare costs of different brands, forms, and sizes. Generic products provide a cost-saving alternative to national and house brands. Various organizations and government agencies serve as sources of consumer information.

Review What You Have Read

Write your answers on a separate sheet of paper.
1. True or false. Twenty-four hour convenience stores often charge higher prices to cover the cost of long business hours.
2. Why is a shopping list important?
3. A 16 ounce (473 mL) can of green beans usually costs $.69. This week, a large supermarket chain is advertising 2 cans for $1.29. Is this a bargain? Explain why or why not.
4. List four tips to help consumers save money when shopping for food.
5. What are the four basic purposes of food additives?
6. Why might food products provide people with different percents of their Daily Values than those listed on labels?
7. True or false. The net weight shown on canned foods includes the liquids in which the foods are canned.

8. Describe how the UPC works at the checkout stand in a grocery store.
9. The last day a product should be sold is called the _____.
   A. expiration date
   B. freshness date
   C. pack date
   D. pull or sell date
10. Consumers can easily compare the cost of different brands, sizes, and forms of the same or similar products with _____.
11. Why do generic products cost less than national and house brands?
12. Name four sources of consumer information.

Build Your Basic Skills

1. Visit a farmers' market. Compare prices with those of a local supermarket.
2. Do a price comparison study of the cost of different forms of a food product. For example, compare the cost per serving of a chocolate cake made from scratch, a chocolate cake made from a mix, a frozen chocolate cake, and a bakery chocolate cake. (All of these cakes should be two-layer, 8-inch (20-cm) cakes with chocolate frosting.)
3. Visit a health food store. What kinds of products are available? How do prices compare with those of foods produced by standard agricultural methods?

Build Your Thinking Skills

1. Visit several supermarkets of comparable size. Using the criteria for choosing a food store given in the chapter, evaluate each store. At which store would you most like to shop?
2. Ask to do your family's grocery shopping for the week. Organize your shopping list to match the order of the food aisles in the store. If the store where you shop has unit pricing, take advantage of it. Otherwise, try to compare prices yourself.

Chapter 12

Getting Started in the Kitchen

A "Taste" of the World of Work

Sandwich Maker
Prepares sandwiches to individual order of customers.

Time-Study Engineer
Develops work measurement procedures and directs time-and-motion studies to promote efficient and economical utilization of personnel and facilities.

Food Technologist
Develops and tests new food products in test kitchen and develops specific processing methods in laboratory pilot plant. Also confers with process engineers, flavor experts, and packaging and marketing specialists to resolve problems.

Terms to Know

recipe
yield
watt
dehydration
standing time
venting

rotating
shielding
arcing
elevating
time-work schedule
dovetail

Objectives

After studying this chapter, you will be able to
- ❏ identify abbreviations and define cooking terms used in recipes.
- ❏ measure liquid and dry ingredients and fats for use in recipes.
- ❏ change the yield of a recipe.
- ❏ plan time-work schedules.
- ❏ follow a recipe to prepare a sandwich.

Photograph by Paul Rochaleau, courtesy of OXO International

You do not have to have cooking skills to satisfy hunger. You can eat convenience foods that require little or no preparation. However, you can add unlimited variety and interest to meals when you know how to prepare foods from scratch.

Before you can begin working in the kitchen, you need to have some basic knowledge and food preparation skills. You need to know how to read a recipe and measure ingredients. You also need to be able to plan your use of time in the kitchen.

Choosing a Recipe

A *recipe* is a set of instructions for preparing a specific food. Some cooks start with a selection of recipes and then decide how they can work them into a menu. Other cooks start with a menu and then select recipes for the different items.

Cookbooks are sources of recipes used by both experienced and beginning cooks. Many basic cookbooks provide menu ideas as well as recipes. The meal manager can use these resources to help plan and prepare daily meals. Specialty cookbooks contain many ideas and recipes for international foods and unusual dishes. Bookstores and libraries carry a variety of cookbooks, 12-1.

Magazines, newspapers, and appliance manuals can also be good sources of recipes. Many newspapers feature weekly food sections. A few magazines focus entirely on food; others carry one or two food features in each issue. Many food articles are seasonal. For instance, during summer months locally grown produce is available. At this time of year, many articles feature fresh fruit and vegetable recipes.

Good recipes are written in a clear, concise manner. A recipe should list ingredients in the

Photograph used with permission from Company's Coming Publishing Limited, Edmonton, Alberta, Canada

12-1 Many kinds of cookbooks are available for both beginning and experienced cooks.

order in which you will be combining them. Amounts should be easy to measure. Directions for mixing and/or handling procedures must be complete. Baking or cooking times and temperatures and pan sizes need to be accurate. The recipe should state the *yield,* which is the number of average servings the recipe makes. Many recipes also include a nutritional analysis to help you evaluate how the food will fit into a healthy diet. Information provided often begins with the number of calories. The amount of protein, carbohydrate, fat, cholesterol, fiber, and sodium per serving may also be given. See 12-2.

A recipe is your work plan for the food you are going to prepare. You will want to read through the recipe before you begin to prepare it. This will allow you to be sure you understand the directions and have all the ingredients you will need. When you are ready to begin, reread the recipe. Follow the directions carefully as you prepare the product.

For review, ask yourself the following questions each time you use a recipe:

- Have I read the recipe carefully?
- Do I understand all the terms and directions?
- Do I have the necessary ingredients?
- Do I have the correct tools for the job?
- What do I need to do to the ingredients to get them ready to use? For instance, do I need to chop vegetables or melt chocolate?
- Do I need to preheat the oven?

Abbreviations

The amounts of ingredients listed in recipes are often given as abbreviations. You need to be able to interpret these abbreviations. This will help you make sure you include ingredients in the right proportions. See 12-3.

Cooking Terms

Recipes use a variety of terms to describe exactly how you are to handle the ingredients. For instance, a recipe that includes carrots is not likely to tell you to *cut* the carrots. This term is too general to let you know how the carrots should look in the finished product. Instead, the recipe might tell you to *slice, dice, shred,* or *julienne* the carrots. Becoming familiar with specific cooking terms will help your food products turn out as expected. See 12-4.

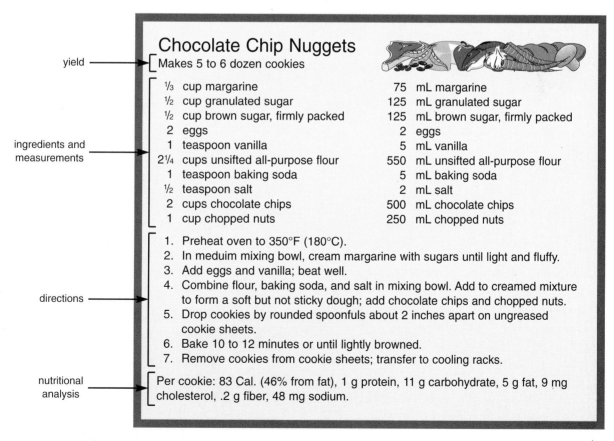

yield

Chocolate Chip Nuggets
Makes 5 to 6 dozen cookies

ingredients and measurements

⅓ cup margarine	75 mL margarine
½ cup granulated sugar	125 mL granulated sugar
½ cup brown sugar, firmly packed	125 mL brown sugar, firmly packed
2 eggs	2 eggs
1 teaspoon vanilla	5 mL vanilla
2¼ cups unsifted all-purpose flour	550 mL unsifted all-purpose flour
1 teaspoon baking soda	5 mL baking soda
½ teaspoon salt	2 mL salt
2 cups chocolate chips	500 mL chocolate chips
1 cup chopped nuts	250 mL chopped nuts

directions

1. Preheat oven to 350°F (180°C).
2. In meduim mixing bowl, cream margarine with sugars until light and fluffy.
3. Add eggs and vanilla; beat well.
4. Combine flour, baking soda, and salt in mixing bowl. Add to creamed mixture to form a soft but not sticky dough; add chocolate chips and chopped nuts.
5. Drop cookies by rounded spoonfuls about 2 inches apart on ungreased cookie sheets.
6. Bake 10 to 12 minutes or until lightly browned.
7. Remove cookies from cookie sheets; transfer to cooling racks.

nutritional analysis

Per cookie: 83 Cal. (46% from fat), 1 g protein, 11 g carbohydrate, 5 g fat, 9 mg cholesterol, .2 g fiber, 48 mg sodium.

12-2 A well-written recipe should include all the information you need to prepare a particular food.

Abbreviations Used in Recipes

Conventional	
tsp. or t.	teaspoon
tbsp. or T.	tablespoon
c. or C.	cup
pt.	pint
qt.	quart
oz.	ounce
lb. or #	pound
Metric	
mL	milliliter
L	liter
g	gram
kg	kilogram

12-3 Recipes often include these abbreviations.

Using Microwave Recipes

Cooking foods in a microwave oven is not hard. However, microwave cooking does differ from conventional cooking. Therefore, using microwave recipes requires some specific knowledge.

Cooking Time

Cooking power for a microwave oven is measured in *watts.* You should know the maximum wattage of your model. This will help you anticipate how fast it will cook. Microwave recipes are generally designed for ovens with a maximum of 500 to 700 watts. Therefore, if you are using a microwave oven with a lower wattage, you may need to add cooking time. However, it is always wise to start with the smallest amount of time stated in a recipe. Then check the food to see if it needs more time.

Just a few minutes of overcooking can cause *dehydration,* or drying out. Dehydration may occur when microwave cooking continues until foods are fully cooked. This is because many foods will continue cooking after the allotted time in the oven. To account for this tendency, many microwave recipes specify *standing time.* This is the time during which foods finish cooking by internal heat after being removed from a microwave oven. For instance, a recipe for baked potatoes may specify four minutes of cooking time and five minutes of standing time. Wrapping foods in aluminum foil will help hold in heat during standing time.

Covering Foods

Many microwave recipes state that you should cover foods during cooking. Covering foods in a microwave oven serves several purposes. Covering distributes heat more evenly and helps foods retain moisture so they will not dry out. The steam held in by the cover can help speed cooking time and tenderize foods. Covers are also useful for preventing spatters inside the microwave oven.

You can use a number of materials to cover foods in a microwave oven. Tight fitting casserole lids are excellent for foods that require steam for cooking. Waxed paper works well as a loose covering. Covering foods with paper towels will help absorb spatters. (Choose paper towels designed for microwave use as they are free of ingredients not approved for food contact.)

Covering food with plastic wrap or placing it in a plastic cooking bag will help retain moisture. (Plastic wraps designed for the microwave oven work best because they will not melt during cooking.) However, pressure from steam can build up inside containers that are tightly covered with plastic. Therefore, recipes often recommend *venting* the plastic wrap. This means turning back a corner of the wrap to form a steam vent, 12-5.

Not all foods require a cover in the microwave oven. You may leave some foods uncovered to allow excess moisture to evaporate. You may need to cover other foods for only part of the cooking time. For best results, follow the directions in your recipe.

Evenness of Cooking

Microwaves are not always distributed evenly throughout the microwave oven cavity. This tends to be more of a problem in older models. Uneven distribution of microwaves can cause foods to cook unevenly. The shape of food pieces can also affect how evenly they cook. Microwave recipes use a number of techniques to combat this problem.

Many microwave recipes recommend *rotating* food at one or more intervals in the cooking period. Rotate food one-quarter to one-half turn to allow microwaves to hit it in a more even pattern. (*Turntables* included in some microwave ovens or bought as a separate accessory rotate food automatically during the entire cooking cycle.)

Foods tend to cook more slowly in the center of a microwave oven. Therefore, recipes often suggest arranging individual foods in a circular pattern. They recommend placing large or dense foods

Play It Safe

Take care when removing plastic and all coverings from microwaved foods. Lift covers away from you to avoid the danger of steam burns.

Glossary of Food Preparation Terms

bake. To cook in the oven with dry heat.

baste. To spoon pan juices, melted fat, or another liquid over the surface of food during cooking in order to keep the food moist and add flavor.

beat. To mix ingredients together with a circular up and down motion using a spoon, whisk, or rotary or electric beater.

bind. To thicken or smooth out the consistency of a liquid.

blend. To stir ingredients until they are thoroughly combined.

boil. To cook in liquid over 212°F (100°C).

bone. To remove bones from fowl or meat.

braise. To cook in a small amount of liquid in a tightly covered pan over low heat.

bread. To coat with dry bread crumbs or cracker crumbs.

broil. To cook uncovered under a direct source of heat.

brown. To turn the surface of a food brown by placing it under a broiler or quickly cooking it in hot fat.

caramelize. To heat sugar until a brown color and characteristic flavor develop.

chill. To make a food cold by placing it in a refrigerator or in a bowl over crushed ice.

chop. To cut into small pieces.

clarify. To make a substance clear or pure.

coat. To thoroughly cover a food with a liquid or dry mixture.

combine. To mix or blend two or more ingredients together.

cool. To let a food stand until it no longer feels warm to the touch.

cream. To soften solid fats, often by adding a second ingredient, such as sugar, and working with a wooden spoon or an electric mixer until fat is creamy.

crush. To pulverize.

cube. To cut into small squares of equal size.

cut in. To combine solid fat with flours using a pastry blender, two forks, or the fingers.

deep-fry. To cook in a large amount of hot fat.

devein. To remove the large black or white vein along a shrimp's back.

dice. To cut into very small cubes of even size.

dot. To place small pieces of butter or another food over the surface of a food.

drain. To remove liquid from a food product.

dust. To lightly sprinkle the surface of a food with sugar, flour, or crumbs.

flake. To break fish into small pieces with a fork.

fold. To incorporate a delicate mixture into a thicker, heavier mixture with a whisk or rubber spatula so that the finished product remains light.

fricassee. To cook pieces of meat or poultry in butter and then in seasoned liquid until tender.

fry. To cook in a small amount of hot fat.

garnish. To decorate foods by adding other attractive and complementary foodstuffs to the food or serving dish.

grate. To reduce a food into small bits by rubbing it on the sharp teeth of a grating tool.

grease. To rub fat on the surface of a cooking utensil or on a food itself.

julienne. To cut food into thin, stick-sized strips.

knead. To work a dough by pressing it with the heels of the hand, folding it, turning it, and repeating each motion until the dough is smooth and elastic.

marinate. To soak meat in a solution containing an acid, such as vinegar or tomato juice, that helps tenderize the connective tissue.

mash. To break a food by pressing it with the back of a spoon, a masher, or forcing it through a ricer.

mince. To cut or chop into very fine pieces.

panbroil. To cook in a skillet uncovered and without fat.

parboil. To boil in liquid until partially cooked.

pare. To remove the stem and outer covering of a vegetable or fruit with a paring knife or peeler.

poach. To cook a food immersed in simmering liquid.

preheat. To heat an oven, broiler, or toaster oven to a desired temperature about 5 to 8 minutes before the appliance is to be used.

punch down. To push a fist firmly into the top of yeast dough that has completed the first rising.

puree. To put food through a fine sieve or a food mill to form a thick and smooth liquid.

refresh. To quickly plunge blanched vegetables in cold water to stop the cooking process.

roast. To cook uncovered in the oven with dry heat.

rotate. To turn food in a microwave oven one-quarter to one-half turn at one or more intervals in the cooking period to allow microwaves to hit it in a more even pattern.

sauté. To cook food in a small amount of hot fat.

scald. To heat liquid to just below the boiling point; to dip food into boiling water or pour boiling water over the food.

score. To make small, shallow cuts on the surface of a food.

sear. To brown the surface of a food very quickly with high heat.

season. To add herbs, spices, or other ingredients to a food to increase the flavor of the food; to prepare a cooking utensil, such as a cast iron skillet, for cooking.

separate. To remove the yolk from the white of an egg.

shred. To cut or break into thin pieces.

simmer. To cook in liquid that is barely at the boiling point.

skim. To remove a substance from the surface of a liquid.

steam. To cook with vapor produced by a boiling liquid.

steep. To soak in a hot liquid.

stew. To cook one food or several foods together in a seasoned liquid for a long period of time.

stir-fry. To cook foods quickly in a small amount of fat over high heat just until crisp-tender.

strain. To separate solid from liquid materials.

thicken. To make a liquid more dense by adding a food like flour, cornstarch, egg yolks, rice, or potatoes.

vent. To leave an opening through which steam can escape in the covering of a food to be cooked in a microwave oven.

whip. To beat quickly and steadily by hand with a whisk or rotary beater.

12-4 Being able to interpret these terms will help you prepare recipes successfully.

The Reynolds Wrap Kitchens

12-5 When covering foods with plastic wrap for microwave cooking, turn back one edge to allow steam to escape.

around the edge of a dish. Arrange unevenly shaped foods with the thicker parts toward the outside of the container. Place quick-cooking foods in the center where they will receive less microwave energy.

Uneven distribution of microwaves may cause some foods cooked in a microwave oven to develop "hot spots." Although parts of the food may barely be warm, these spots are very hot. Stirring foods part way through the cooking will help them cook more evenly by redistributing the heat. Stir toward the center the heated outer portions that the microwaves have penetrated. In the middle of the cooking cycle, rearrange foods that you cannot stir. Switch pieces on the outside with those in the center.

Unevenly shaped foods can overcook in the areas that are most directly exposed to microwaves. For instance, the outer edge of a pie may finish cooking before the center. Some recipes recommend *shielding* areas that might overcook with small pieces of aluminum foil. You will often use shields only during the last part of the cooking time. The foil will reflect the microwaves so the covered areas will not continue to cook. However, microwaves will penetrate the uncovered areas, allowing them to finish cooking. Thus the food product as a whole will cook more evenly.

Take care to keep foil shields at least one inch from the oven walls. When metal meets oven walls, *arcing,* or sparking, can occur. The presence of narrow bands of metal, such as twist ties and metal trimmed china can also cause arcing. Arcing is not dangerous, but it can mar oven walls. Be sure to check manufacturer's directions before using any type of metal in a microwave oven.

Some microwave recipes recommend elevating foods to promote faster, more even cooking. *Elevating* means lifting a food off the floor of a microwave oven. This allows microwaves to penetrate foods from the bottom as well as the top and sides. Some microwave ovens have a glass tray on the oven floor that provides elevation. You can also place foods on a rack or an inverted glass dish to achieve the same results.

Browning Techniques

Many foods cook so quickly in a microwave oven that they do not have time to brown. Browning does not affect the quality and flavor of food. However, browning does affect appearance, which in turn affects appetite appeal.

Some microwave recipes suggest techniques to compensate for a lack of browning. Some meat recipes suggest using browning agents to give the appearance of browning. You can use gravies and sauces to cover many dishes. For baked goods, lack of browning is less noticeable on dark-colored items, such as chocolate or spice cakes. Use frostings and toppings to cover lighter items. See 12-6.

High-Altitude Cooking

Atmospheric pressure decreases at high altitudes. At an altitude of 3,000 feet (914 m), this decrease begins to affect the outcome of food products. As the altitude increases, so does the effect on food. If you are cooking at high altitudes, you may need to make some adjustments to your recipes.

Water boils at a lower temperature at high altitudes. Therefore, most foods cooked in liquid will require more cooking time. Liquids also evaporate faster at high altitudes. You may need to add extra liquid when preparing some foods. You may need to reduce the temperature of deep fat to keep foods from overbrowning before they are thoroughly cooked.

Breads and cakes tend to rise more during baking at high altitudes. To account for this, you may need to increase oven temperature. This will help set the batter before air cells formed by leavening gases have a chance to expand too much. You may need to decrease baking time to keep foods from overcooking at the higher oven temperatures. Reducing the amount of leavening agents used in recipes will help compensate for excess rising. Using larger baking pans will also keep baked goods from overflowing the pan as they rise.

For best results when cooking at high altitudes, choose recipes designed for high-altitude cooking. Many commercial mixes include high-altitude directions on the package.

Measuring Ingredients

Some experienced cooks can combine "a little of this and a little of that" and end up with something delicious. However, less experienced cooks will have greater success if they measure ingredients exactly. You will measure different types of ingredients in different ways. Knowing how to measure ingredients correctly will help your food products turn out right.

Measuring Dry Ingredients

Dry ingredients include sugar, flour, baking powder, baking soda, salt, and spices. Measure these ingredients in dry measuring cups. Spoon the ingredient into the correct measuring cup until it is overfilled. (If your recipe calls for *sifted flour,* you should sift the flour before spooning it into the dry measuring cup.) Do not shake or tap the

12-6 Shielding can help keep the corners of foods prepared in square containers from overcooking in a microwave oven. Frosting can help hide lack of browning.

measuring cup. Hold the measuring cup over the ingredient container or a sheet of waxed paper. Then use a straight-edged spatula to level off any excess. The ingredient should be even with the top edge of the measuring cup, 12-7.

Brown sugar is a dry ingredient, but you measure it a bit differently. As you spoon brown sugar into a dry measuring cup, press it down firmly with the back of the spoon. This is called *packing*. Overfill the measuring cup, then level it off with a straight-edged spatula. The brown sugar should hold the shape of the measuring cup when you turn it out into a mixing bowl.

Use measuring spoons to measure small amounts (less than ¼ cup [50 mL]) of dry ingredients. Dip the correct measuring spoon into the ingredient container and bring it up heaping full. Level off the top with a straight-edged spatula.

Measuring Liquid Ingredients

Liquid ingredients include milk, water, oil, juices, food colorings, and extracts. Measure these ingredients in liquid measuring cups. The handle and spout on liquid measuring cups make it easy to pour liquid ingredients. The extra room at the top of the cup will help you avoid spilling.

You cannot get an accurate measurement when you look through a measuring cup at an angle. Therefore, set the liquid measuring cup on a flat surface. Then bend down so the desired marking on the measuring cup is at eye level. Slowly pour the liquid ingredient into the measuring cup until it reaches the mark for the desired amount.

Use measuring spoons to measure small amounts (less than ¼ cup [50 mL]) of liquid ingredients. Carefully pour the ingredient into the correct spoon until it is filled to the edge.

Measuring Fats

Butter, margarine, shortening, and peanut butter are fats used in recipes. You can measure them in one of several ways. Markings on the wrapper of stick butter or margarine can help you measure the amount you need. A stick of butter or margarine equals 8 tablespoons or ½ cup (125 mL). Use a sharp knife to cut through the wrapper at the marking for the desired number of tablespoons.

12-7 Carefully spoon dry ingredients into a dry measuring cup and level off any excess with a straight-edged spatula.

You can measure shortening and peanut butter in dry measuring cups. Use a rubber spatula to press these ingredients into the measuring cup, making sure you eliminate any air pockets. Overfill the measuring cup, then level it with a straight-edged spatula.

You can also use the *water displacement method* to measure solid fats. Fill a 2-cup (500 mL) liquid measuring cup with 1 cup (250 mL) of cold water. Then carefully spoon in the solid fat until the water level rises by the amount you need. For instance, suppose you need ¹/₂ cup (125 mL) of shortening. You would spoon the shortening into the measuring cup until the water level reached 1¹/₂ cups (375 mL). Make sure the fat is not clinging to the side of the measuring cup. Drain off the water before using the fat.

Adjusting Recipes

You may need to adjust some recipes before you can use them. You may want to change the amount the recipe makes. You may want to adjust a conventional recipe for microwave cooking. Knowing some basic information can help you make these adjustments with success.

Changing Yield

Some recipes will make more or less of a food product than you want. For instance, a recipe might make four dozen chocolate chip cookies. When making them for a family reunion, you may

Healthy Living

Changing the amounts of some ingredients in recipes can allow you to make more healthful food products. For instance, you may be able to reduce the amount of fat, salt, sugar, and eggs in baked goods. Such reductions are in keeping with the Dietary Guidelines for Americans. Follow standards for basic ingredient proportions to produce quality food products.

want twice that many. A recipe for a chicken and rice casserole might make eight servings. When preparing dinner for four, you might want only half that amount.

Measuring Equivalents

Conventional units of measure used in recipes are teaspoons, tablespoons, and cups. Changing the yield of a conventional recipe can be tricky. You may have to convert from one unit to another. Being familiar with measuring equivalents will help you adjust the yield of a recipe. For instance, 3 teaspoons is the equivalent of 1 tablespoon. Suppose you are doubling a recipe that calls for 1½ teaspoons of baking soda. Two times 1½ teaspoons equals 3 teaspoons, or 1 tablespoon. Likewise, ¼ cup equals 4 tablespoons. Suppose you are halving a recipe that calls for ¼ cup sugar. You can easily figure that half of 4 tablespoons is 2 tablespoons.

Metric Measurements

The main metric unit of measure used in recipes is the milliliter. Changing the yield of a metric recipe is easy. You do not have to convert from one unit to another. Chart 12-8 gives common equivalents for conventional and metric measurements.

Tips for Easy Adjustment

When you are changing the yield of a recipe, you can choose the method that is easiest for you. For instance, suppose you are halving a recipe that calls for 1½ cups of sugar. You could use your math skills to convert the mixed number into a fraction. Then multiply that fraction by ½ ($\frac{3}{2} \times \frac{1}{2} = \frac{3}{4}$). On the other hand, you might find it easier to divide each part of the mixed number in half. In other words, half of 1 cup is ½ cup and half of ½ cup is ¼ cup. Therefore, you would use ½ cup of sugar and ¼ cup of sugar. This would give you the amount you need for half a recipe. Whatever method you choose, figure the adjusted amounts of each ingredient before you begin cooking. Write down the adjusted amounts so you will remember them as you work.

Converting Recipes for Microwave Use

You can convert most conventional recipes for use in a microwave oven by adjusting the proportions of some ingredients. Reduce the amount of liquid used in recipes by one third. This will account for the lack of evaporation inside a microwave oven. Eliminate cooking oils and fats from recipes unless they provide flavor or consistency. Halve the amount of seasonings, as their flavors intensify with microwave cooking. If needed, you can add more seasonings after cooking.

Choose the power setting according to the type of food you are preparing. Most foods are microwaved on high power. Cook delicate foods, such as cheese, eggs, and milk products, on medium-high power.

For guidelines on cooking times, look in a microwave cookbook for a recipe similar to the one you are preparing. As a rule, start with one fourth of the conventional cooking time. Check food and add time as needed. Remember that some foods will continue cooking after you remove them from the microwave oven. Remove these foods just before they finish cooking to allow for this standing time. (Chapters 13 through 23 include additional tips for microwaving various foods.)

Common Equivalent Measures

Conventional Measure	Conventional Equivalent	Approximate Metric Equivalent*
¼ teaspoon	— — —	1 milliliter
½ teaspoon	— — —	2 milliliters
1 teaspoon	— — —	5 milliliters
3 teaspoons	1 tablespoon	15 milliliters
2 tablespoons	⅛ cup	30 milliliters
4 tablespoons	¼ cup	50 milliliters
5⅓ tablespoons	⅓ cup	75 milliliters
8 tablespoons	½ cup	125 milliliters
10⅔ tablespoons	⅔ cup	150 milliliters
12 tablespoons	¾ cup	175 milliliters
16 tablespoons	1 cup, ½ pint	250 milliliters
2 cups	1 pint	500 milliliters
4 cups	1 quart	1 liter

* Based on measures seen on standard metric measuring equipment.

12-8 Knowing equivalent measures can help you change recipe yield and convert between conventional and metric measures.

Ingredient Substitutions

You should read through a recipe to be sure you have all the needed ingredients before you begin cooking. If you are out of a needed ingredient, you may be able to make a substitution. See 12-9.

Using a Time-Work Schedule

A meal manager is responsible for making sure all the parts of a meal are ready at the same time. How can you be sure the roast, mashed potatoes, and peas will be ready to serve at exactly 6 o'clock? The skilled meal manager prepares a *time-work schedule* before meal preparations begin.

A time plan should be specific enough to tell you what task you should be doing at any given moment. On the other hand, it should be flexible enough to allow you to make adjustments. If you underestimate your speed or you need to substitute an ingredient, you may need this flexibility.

Time schedules differ depending on the menu. Some menus, 30-minute dinner menus for example, have all the actual cooking time concentrated in one short period. Other menus, such as a menu for a pot roast dinner, have long cooking times, which result in broken schedules. The meal manager begins cooking the meat in the afternoon. He or she then has time for other activities before returning to the kitchen to complete meal preparations.

Time schedules also differ depending on the skills of the meal manager. Experienced meal

Substituting One Ingredient for Another

You may use these	For these
1 whole egg, for baking or thickening	2 egg yolks
1 cup (250 mL) fluid whole milk	½ cup (125 mL) evaporated milk plus ½ cup (125 mL) water
1 cup (250 mL) fluid skim milk	1 cup (250 mL) reconstituted nonfat dry milk
1 cup (250 mL) heavy cream	¾ cup (175) mL milk plus ⅓ cup (75 mL) butter
1 cup (250 mL) sour milk or buttermilk	1 tablespoon (15 mL) vinegar or lemon juice plus milk to make 1 cup (250 mL) (Allow this mixture to stand several minutes before using.)
1 cup (250 mL) butter	1 cup (250 mL) margarine
1 ounce (28 g) unsweetened chocolate	3 tablespoons (45 mL) unsweetened cocoa powder plus 1 tablespoon (15 mL) butter or margarine
1 cup (250 mL) corn syrup	1¼ cups (300 mL) sugar plus ¼ cup (50 mL) liquid used in recipe
1 tablespoon (15 mL) cornstarch	2 tablespoons (30 mL) flour
1 cup (250 mL) cake flour	⅞ cup (220 mL) all-purpose flour

12-9 You can sometimes make substitutions for ingredients you do not have on hand.

managers can work with less detailed schedules. They have developed the necessary knowledge and skills to order their tasks as they work. Beginners need more detailed schedules until they have gained experience in meal preparation and timing.

Making a Schedule

The meal manager needs the following four tools when making a time schedule:
1. A recipe, cookbook, or knowledge of the cooking times of different foods.
2. Some ability to estimate the time needed to accomplish different tasks, such as peeling potatoes.
3. A pad of paper and a pencil to make calculations.
4. A clock for timing individual tasks.

Once you have decided when to serve a meal, you are ready to plan a time-work schedule. The following four steps outline how to plan a time-work schedule for the meal shown in 12-10.
1. On a piece of paper, set up a chart as shown in 12-11. List the menu items in the left-hand column. Add table setting to this list because you need to reserve time for this task.

Reprinted with permission from Kellogg USA.

Menu

Corn Flakes
Bran Muffin
Fresh Cherries
Milk

12-10 You can prepare and serve this simple, nutritious breakfast in just 12 minutes.

Breakfast Time-Work Schedule
(Steps One and Two)

Menu Item	Prepare for Cooking	Allow for Cooking	Prepare for Serving	Time in Minutes
corn flakes*	—	—	2	2
bran muffins**	2	2	—	4
cherries	—	—	5	5
milk	—	—	2	2
table setting	—	—	5	5

*Diners will pour ready-to-eat cereal into bowls at the table.
**Prepared bran muffins will be heated in a microwave oven.

12-11 The preliminary time schedule includes menu items and preparation times.

2. List estimates for the time required for preparation, cooking, and serving in the second, third, and fourth columns, respectively. (Some recipes give estimated preparation and cooking times, which will help you with this task.) In the last column, list the total time for preparing each food item.
3. Rearrange the menu items in descending order of the estimated time needed to accomplish them, as shown in 12-12. (This information gives an idea of the amount of time needed to prepare the meal. It also helps you decide which menu items to prepare first.)
4. List all the tasks you need to do in the order you will do them. See 12-13. Beginning with the time you will serve the meal, work backward to clock the cooking times. Then list the time each item needs to start and stop cooking or baking. Also list the time for setting the table.

The final step forms the actual time-work schedule you would follow. Limit specific timings to the most critical preparation moments to avoid confusion. For instance, you will have to adjust the cooking period of the egg, depending on the desired degree of doneness.

You can use these steps to set up a time-work schedule for preparing and serving your meals. Your schedule can help you decide when you will have to enter the kitchen to begin preparations.

Even a complete schedule is no guarantee that plans will go smoothly from start to finish. This is why schedules need to be flexible. Sometimes one dish might cook in less time than you originally estimated. You could hold that dish or modify the rest of the menu. For example, the biscuits might be ready before the eggs and bacon. You could remove them from the baking sheet and put them in a napkin-lined breadbasket to keep warm. Sometimes, one dish might take longer to cook

Breakfast Time-Work Schedule
(Step Three)

Menu Item	Total Time in Minutes
setting the table	5
cherries	5
bran muffins	4
corn flakes	2
milk	2

12-12 By looking at this chart, a meal manager knows which tasks he or she needs to perform first.

Breakfast Time-Work Schedule
(Step Four)

Time	Tasks
7:40	Set table. Get out corn flakes.
7:45	Wash and dry cherries and place them in a serving bowl.
7:50	Place bran muffins in a lined basket, cover with a paper towel, and place basket in microwave oven. Pour milk into serving pitcher.
7:52	Pour milk. Serve muffins and cherries.

12-13 The final schedule lists actual times for doing specific preparation tasks.

than you originally estimated. You could hold all the other dishes and wait. For example, you can place the bacon and biscuits in a warm oven while the eggs finish cooking.

As you become more skilled in the kitchen, you will be able to use less detailed schedules. Until that time, however, a schedule that is both detailed and flexible will be helpful.

Remember to dovetail your meal preparation tasks as you plan your schedule. *Dovetail* means to overlap tasks to use your time more efficiently. For instance, you might begin to fry bacon while biscuits are in the oven. Once you get the bacon started, you can mix up the orange juice.

Cooperation in the Kitchen

You will not always work alone in the kitchen. At home, family members may help you prepare meals. At school, you will work with classmates to prepare food products. The kitchen can become crowded when several people are working together. Therefore, you will need to cooperate in order to make the best use of your time, space, and skills.

Consider each person's skills when assigning meal preparation tasks. If you are in a hurry, you may not want someone with little baking experience to make biscuits. If you have the time, however, you might want this person to help you with the biscuits. This will give him or her more baking practice.

Your time-work schedule should indicate who will do each task listed. Be sure to rotate tasks from one time to the next to give everyone a range of kitchen experience.

Preparing Simple Recipes

You can put your basic food preparation knowledge to work by making a simple recipe. While you are developing your cooking skills, choose recipes with just a few ingredients and a short list of directions. As you gain experience, you can move on to recipes that require more advanced preparation techniques.

Sandwiches

Many sandwich recipes are simple to prepare. Sandwiches are popular party and picnic foods. They travel well and are convenient to serve.

Ingredients for Sandwiches

All sandwiches are made with some type of bread and a filling. You can use many different kinds of breads and rolls to make sandwiches. Rye, whole wheat, pumpernickel, French, Italian, potato, and raisin are just a few of the many breads you might choose. Pita bread, kaiser rolls, bagels, and other ethnic breads and rolls add still more variety. The bread or roll chosen should be fresh and either whole grain or enriched.

Sandwich fillings usually are protein foods. Leftover meats and poultry are good choices. Cheese, hard-cooked eggs, peanut butter, and canned fish also make good fillings.

Lettuce, pickles, tomatoes, and other vegetables complement some sandwiches. Bacon curls, ripe olives, and spiced fruits complement others. First choose the filling; then choose the extras. See 12-14.

Preparing Sandwiches

The following guidelines will help you prepare nutritious, attractive, and flavorful sandwiches:

- Use a variety of breads and fillings.
- Spread soft butter, margarine, or mayonnaise to the edge of the bread. This will keep the filling from soaking into the sandwich.
- Cut sandwiches into halves or quarters to make them easier to eat. For party sandwiches that are extra interesting and attractive, cut bread into shapes, such as circles, diamonds, and hearts.
- Garnish sandwiches attractively. Garnishes can improve the appearance and food value of a sandwich. See 12-15.
- Keep sandwiches refrigerated until serving

Be a Clever Consumer

Take advantage of sale prices on sandwich ingredients. Then prepare sandwiches and freeze them. (Do not use mayonnaise, hard-cooked egg white, jelly, or lettuce or other raw vegetables. These foods do not freeze well, and you can add them to sandwiches later.) Wrap all sandwiches for the freezer in moistureproof and vaporproof wrapping and label them.

12-14 You can use a variety of breads, fillings, and extras to prepare an almost unlimited number of sandwich combinations.

Hero Sandwich
Serves 6

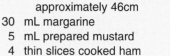

1	loaf Italian or French bread, approximately 18 inches	1	loaf Italian or French Bread, approximately 46cm
2	tablespoons margarine	30	mL margarine
1	teaspoon prepared mustard	5	mL prepared mustard
4	thin slices cooked ham	4	thin slices cooked ham
4	slices bologna	4	slices bologna
4	slices turkey or chicken	4	slices turkey or chicken
4	slices Swiss cheese	4	slices Swiss cheese
1	medium green pepper sliced into rings	1	medium green pepper sliced into rings
2	medium tomatoes, sliced	2	medium tomatoes, sliced
4 to 6	lettuce leaves	4 to 6	lettuce leaves

1. Slice bread in half lengthwise.
2. Combine margarine and prepared mustard; spread on both sides of bread.
3. Arrange meats, cheese, tomatoes, and green pepper on bottom half of bread; top with lettuce.
4. Put top half of bread in place and slice diagonally.

1/6 of sandwich loaf: 450 Cal. (37% from fat), 22 g protein, 47 g carbohydrate, 18 g fat, 48 mg cholesterol, 3.1 g fiber, 1105 mg sodium.

12-15 Lettuce, tomato, and green pepper rings can be attractively arranged to garnish this hero sandwich.

time. Bacteria grow quickly above 60°F (16°C). Therefore, pack sandwiches in a cooler when transporting them. Use ice, frozen gel packs, or chilled drinks to keep perishable ingredients safe. Wrap sandwiches well to prevent staling. Pack lettuce, pickles, tomatoes, and other relishes separately to keep sandwiches from getting soggy.

- Make hot sandwiches just before serving. Serve them hot, not lukewarm.
- Use freshly toasted bread for sandwiches served on toast.

Microwaving Sandwiches

Using a microwave oven is a fast way to heat sandwiches. Most sandwiches can be microwaved in under a minute. However, the size of most microwave ovens makes it hard to heat more than a few sandwiches at a time. Therefore, you may wish to use a conventional oven if you are serving hot sandwiches to a crowd.

Follow a few tips when microwaving sandwiches. Because the bread is porous, it will warm faster than the filling. Using frozen bread will keep the bread from drying out before the filling is warm. Using several thin slices of meat will allow sandwiches to heat faster and more evenly than using one thick slice. Wrapping sandwiches in paper toweling will help absorb excess moisture during heating.

Summary

To prepare meals, you need to know how to choose and read recipes. You need to be familiar with abbreviations and cooking terms used in recipes. If you live in a high-altitude area, you should be aware of how the atmospheric pressure can affect food products. You should also know the correct way to measure dry and liquid ingredients and fats.

Knowing how to adjust recipes is another basic food preparation skill. Being familiar with measuring equivalents will help you easily adjust the yield of a recipe. Following a few guidelines can help you adjust conventional recipes for microwave cooking. Knowing how to substitute one ingredient for another will come in handy when you run out of something you need.

As a meal manager, you will need to know how to make a time-work schedule. This will help you plan your use of time in the kitchen. It will also help you when working with others, such as in a school foods lab.

You can put basic cooking skills to use when preparing simple recipes. Sandwiches are a good food for beginning cooks to make. Using a variety of ingredients, you can easily prepare many different hot and cold sandwiches. Sandwich recipes also adapt easily to microwave preparation.

Review What You Have Read

Write your answers on a separate sheet of paper.
1. What are the components of a well-written recipe?
2. Give the unit of measure for which each of the following abbreviations stands:
   A. c.
   B. oz.
   C. t.
   D. tbsp.
3. Complete each of the following statements.
   A. To stir ingredients until they are thoroughly combined is to _____.
   B. To cut into very small cubes of even size is to _____.
   C. To rub fat on the surface of a cooking utensil or on a food itself is to _____.
   D. To heat an oven, broiler, or toaster oven to a desired temperature about 5 to 8 minutes before the appliance is to be used it to _____.

4. How can dehydration occur during microwave cooking?
5. Why should plastic wrap used to cover food in a microwave oven be vented?
6. What happens to the boiling point of water at high altitudes?
7. True or false. Dry ingredients should be spooned into a dry measuring cup until the cup is filled just to the edge.
8. Double and halve each of the following amounts:
   A. 2 tablespoons
   B. 1½ teaspoons
   C. ¾ cup
   D. 1⅔ cups
9. Explain why time-work schedules for preparing meals need to be flexible.
10. What sandwich ingredients should not be frozen?

Build Your Basic Skills

1. On a photocopy of a map of the United States, color in the areas where high-altitude cooking principles would apply.
2. Find a sandwich recipe with a yield of 8 servings or fewer. Copy the recipe and calculate how much of each ingredient would be needed to serve 40 party guests.

Build Your Thinking Skills

1. Select two types of cookbooks from your school or local library. Compare them and write a critique stating which one you prefer and why.
2. Select a breakfast or luncheon menu. Collect recipes for the foods you have selected. Plan a time-work schedule for the members of your group. Prepare the menu following your schedule.

Even inexperienced cooks find sandwiches easy to prepare.

Part 3
The Preparation of Food

A meat dish, such as this crown roast, often becomes the center of a meal.

Chapter 13

Meat

A "Taste" of the World of Work

Barbecue Cook
Prepares, seasons, and barbecues pork, beef, and other types of meat.

Meat Cutter
Cuts and trims meat to size for display or as ordered by customer, using hand tools and power equipment, such as grinder, cubing machine, and power saw.

Livestock Sales Representative
Sells cattle, hogs, and other livestock to farmers, packing houses, and other purchasers. Reviews market information and inspects livestock to determine value.

Terms to Know

meat
beef
wholesale cut
retail cut
veal
pork
lamb
variety meats

marbling
elastin
collagen
marinate
coagulation
cooking losses
braising

Objectives

After studying this chapter, you will be able to
❏ list factors affecting the selection of meats.
❏ describe how to properly store meats to maintain their quality.
❏ describe the principles and methods of cooking meat.
❏ prepare meats by moist and dry cooking methods.

National Live Stock and Meat Board

Many meal managers choose the meat course first when planning menus. The meat you prepare should be tender, flavorful, and attractive.

What Is Meat?

Meat is the edible portion of mammals. It contains muscle, fat, bone, connective tissue, and water. The major meat-producing animals are cattle, swine, and sheep. Beef and veal come from cattle. Pork comes from swine. Lamb and mutton come from sheep. See 13-1.

Nutritional Value of Meat

Meats are high in protein. All meat and meat products contain proteins essential for tissue building and repair. Meats also are good sources of iron, phosphorus, copper, thiamin, riboflavin, and niacin. (Liver is very high in iron.)

The amount of fat meat contributes to the diet depends on the kind and quality of the meat. Fat gives meat flavor and appeal. However, experts recommend that people in the United States lower the percentage of calories they get from fats in their diet. These experts especially stress limiting saturated fats, which occur in larger amounts in cuts that are less lean.

Following recommendations to limit fats does not mean you have to eliminate meat from your diet. However, it does mean keeping some guidelines in mind when selecting meat. Choose lean cuts of meat. This is easier than it was in days past. Breeders now use scientific breeding techniques and feed livestock monitored diets to produce leaner meats. Choose cuts from the round and loin sections of beef and the loin and leg sections of pork when buying meats. These cuts come from the leanest part of the animal. Also, limit portion sizes to three-ounce (85 g) cooked servings (four ounces, 113 g, of boneless raw meat). A three-ounce (85 g) serving is about the size of a deck of playing cards.

There are also some tips to follow when preparing meat as part of a healthful diet. Use cooking methods like broiling and grilling, which allow fat to drip away during cooking. Use nonstick pans when frying and browning meat to eliminate the need for added fat during cooking. Skim the fat from the surface of chilled meat soups and stocks.

Beef

Beef comes from mature cattle over 12 months of age. It has a distinctive flavor and firm texture.

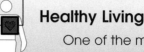

Healthy Living

One of the most significant ways you can reduce the fat content of meats is to trim all visible fat. This can reduce the total fat content by about 50 percent. Trimming meat before cooking results in the greatest fat reduction. This prevents fat from melting into the meat during cooking.

Beef is usually bright, cherry red in color with creamy white fat.

Beef carcasses are classified according to age and sex. Animals sold for meat are most often steers and heifers. *Steers* are young, castrated males. *Heifers* are young females who have never had a calf.

Of all animals used for food, the beef carcass is the largest. The carcass first is cut lengthwise through the backbone into halves. The two halves are called *sides*. The sides are cut into *quarters* and then into smaller pieces, called **wholesale cuts,** for easier handling. Meat cutters divide the wholesale cuts into still smaller pieces, called **retail cuts,** at the grocery store.

Ground Beef

Some people incorrectly call ground beef, hamburger. *Ground beef* contains only the fat originally attached to the meat before grinding. *Hamburger* can have extra fat added to it during grinding. The fat content of both ground beef and hamburger cannot be more than 30 percent of the total weight. However, you can buy ground beef that is leaner. The label lists the percentage lean.

Veal

Veal is very young beef. It comes from cattle that are less than three months of age. Because the animal is so young, little fat has developed. Thus, most veal is lean. Veal also has quite a bit of connective tissue, but it is still considered to be tender. Veal has a light pink color and a delicate flavor.

A veal carcass is next to beef in size, but still much smaller. It does not require splitting for shipment. Because the wholesale cuts are smaller than beef, retail cuts differ somewhat. For example, the loin and rib sections of beef are used for steaks. Those of veal are used for chops.

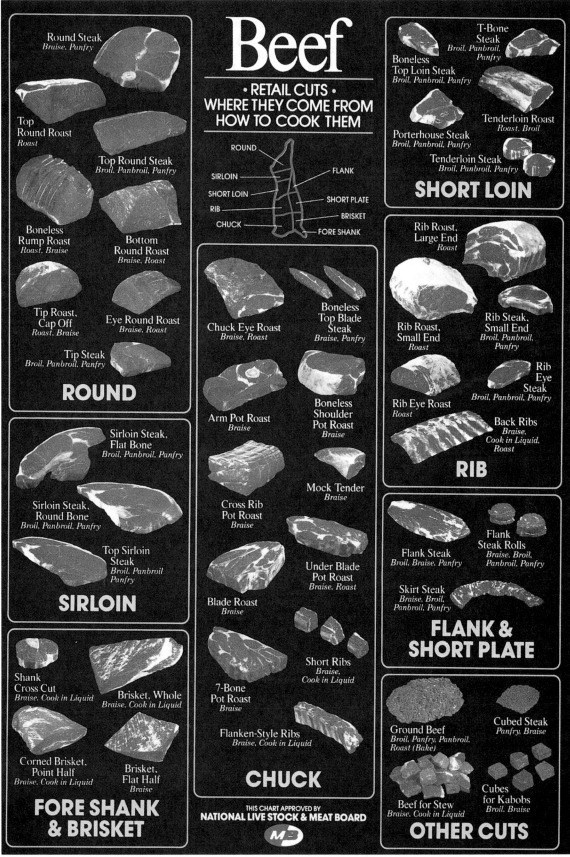

Beef

• RETAIL CUTS •
WHERE THEY COME FROM
HOW TO COOK THEM

Round Steak
Braise, Panfry

Top Round Roast
Roast

Top Round Steak
Broil, Panbroil, Panfry

Boneless Rump Roast
Roast, Braise

Bottom Round Roast
Braise, Roast

Tip Roast, Cap Off
Roast, Braise

Eye Round Roast
Braise, Roast

Tip Steak
Broil, Panbroil, Panfry

ROUND

Sirloin Steak, Flat Bone
Broil, Panbroil, Panfry

Sirloin Steak, Round Bone
Broil, Panbroil, Panfry

Top Sirloin Steak
Broil, Panbroil Panfry

SIRLOIN

Shank Cross Cut
Braise, Cook in Liquid

Brisket, Whole
Braise, Cook in Liquid

Corned Brisket, Point Half
Braise, Cook in Liquid

Brisket, Flat Half
Braise

FORE SHANK & BRISKET

ROUND
SIRLOIN
SHORT LOIN
RIB
CHUCK
FLANK
SHORT PLATE
BRISKET
FORE SHANK

Chuck Eye Roast
Braise, Roast

Boneless Top Blade Steak
Braise, Panfry

Arm Pot Roast
Braise

Boneless Shoulder Pot Roast
Braise

Mock Tender
Braise

Cross Rib Pot Roast
Braise

Under Blade Pot Roast
Braise, Roast

Blade Roast
Braise

7-Bone Pot Roast
Braise

Short Ribs
Braise, Cook in Liquid

Flanken-Style Ribs
Braise, Cook in Liquid

CHUCK

THIS CHART APPROVED BY
NATIONAL LIVE STOCK & MEAT BOARD

T-Bone Steak
Broil, Panbroil, Panfry

Boneless Top Loin Steak
Broil, Panbroil, Panfry

Tenderloin Roast
Roast, Broil

Porterhouse Steak
Broil, Panbroil, Panfry

Tenderloin Steak
Broil, Panbroil, Panfry

SHORT LOIN

Rib Roast, Large End
Roast

Rib Roast, Small End
Roast

Rib Steak, Small End
Broil, Panbroil, Panfry

Rib Eye Steak
Broil, Panbroil, Panfry

Rib Eye Roast
Roast

Back Ribs
Braise, Cook in Liquid, Roast

RIB

Flank Steak
Broil, Braise, Panfry

Flank Steak Rolls
Braise, Broil, Panbroil, Panfry

Skirt Steak
Braise, Broil, Panbroil, Panfry

FLANK & SHORT PLATE

Ground Beef
Broil, Panfry, Panbroil, Roast (Bake)

Cubed Steak
Panfry, Braise

Beef for Stew
Braise, Cook in Liquid

Cubes for Kabobs
Broil, Braise

OTHER CUTS

13-1 Beef is the most popular type of meat in the United States.

13-6 Cooking improves the flavor and tenderness of meat.

Meat cooked at high temperatures shrinks more and develops a hard crust. This crust can make carving and eating difficult. If you use a high temperature and a long cooking time, the meat will also be tough and dry.

Meat cooked at low temperatures will shrink less. It also will be juicier, more flavorful, and easier to carve. Cleanup will be easier because less fat will have spattered on the oven walls or burned onto the pan. Although low cooking temperatures have these advantages, you should not cook meat below 325°F (165°C). Temperatures lower than this may allow bacteria to grow before meat has finished cooking.

The internal temperature of the meat or *degree of doneness* also affects shrinkage. Higher internal temperatures cause greater shrinkage. Overcooked meat (cooked to an internal temperature that is too high) is tough and dry.

The most accurate way to determine the internal temperature of meat is to use a meat thermometer. Insert the meat thermometer into the thickest part of the muscle. Make sure the tip is not touching bone or resting in fat. Cook meat only to the recommended temperature. See 13-7.

Preventing food-borne illness is another reason to be aware of temperatures when cooking meat. Thorough cooking kills harmful bacteria. You should cook roasts and steaks at least to the medium rare stage (internal temperature of 145°F, 65°C). You should cook ground meats to an internal temperature of 160°F (70°C). Reheat leftover meats to an internal temperature of 165°F (75°C).

Controlling Time When Cooking Meat

The total time you cook a cut of meat affects its appearance and eating quality just as temperature does. The cooking temperature, the size and shape of the cut, and the degree of doneness desired all affect cooking time.

Cooking temperature affects cooking time. Higher temperatures result in shorter cooking times. Lower temperatures result in longer cooking times. Changing the cooking temperature by just a few degrees can affect cooking time. If you are broiling a steak and open the broiler door every few minutes to check the steak, the steak will take longer to cook. This is because cool air enters the broiler compartment when you open the door, reducing the temperature.

The size and shape of the cut affect cooking time. Large cuts of meat need longer cooking times than small cuts. However, large cuts take fewer minutes *per pound* to cook than small cuts. A rolled rib roast will take longer to cook than a standing rib roast because the meat is more compact.

The degree of doneness desired affects cooking time. The cooking time for rare beef is less than for well-done beef. The more well done the meat is to be, the longer it will take to cook.

Methods of Cooking Meat

You can use variations of six different methods for cooking meat: roasting, broiling, panbroiling, frying, braising, and cooking in liquid. The method used depends on the tenderness of the meat and its size and thickness. Roasting, broiling, panbroiling, and frying are *dry cooking methods.* Use them for tender cuts of meat, such as steaks and rib roasts. Braising and cooking in liquid are *moist cooking methods.* Use them for less tender cuts of meat, such as chuck roasts and corned beef brisket.

Cooking Meat Safely

Most cases of food-borne illness result from improper food handling. Using care when buying, storing, cooking, serving, and reheating foods will help you avoid illness. Review the precautions outlined in Chapter 5, "Safeguarding the Family's Health." In addition, be aware of the following guidelines when cooking meat:

- Store meats at or below 40°F (5°C).
- Cook or freeze refrigerated meats within recommended time frames (1 to 2 days for ground meats, 3 to 4 days for nonground products, 3 days for leftovers).
- Wash your hands with hot, soapy water before you begin cooking.
- Thoroughly wash cutting boards and utensils used for raw meat before using them to prepare raw vegetables or cooked meat.
- Marinate meat in the refrigerator, *not* at room temperature.
- Discard marinade used for raw meat, or bring it to a rolling boil for 1 minute before using it on cooked meat.
- Brush sauces only on cooked surfaces of meat.
- Do not set the oven below 325°F (165°C) when cooking meats.
- Cook ground meats to an internal temperature of 160°F (70°C) and nonground products to at least 145°F (65°C).
- Reheat leftover meats to 165°F (75°C).

Roasting Meat

Roasting is recommended for large, tender cuts of beef, veal, pork, and lamb, 13-8. For best results when roasting, place meat with the fat side up on a rack in a large, shallow pan. The fat bastes

Recommended Internal Temperatures for Meat

Medium rare	145°F (65°C)
Medium	160°F (70°C)
Well done	170°F (75°C)

13-7 Meat is moist and flavorful when it has been cooked to the recommended temperature.

14-2 A serving of chicken is 3 ounces (85 g) of cooked meat. This is about the amount of meat on a medium breast half.

Play It Safe

Some fresh poultry carries bacteria that can cause food-borne illness. Therefore, you should put poultry in a separate plastic bag at the store when you take it from the refrigerated poultry case. This will keep poultry drippings from getting on other items in your grocery cart and possibly contaminating them.

Storing Poultry

All poultry, except canned, is very perishable. Poultry parts are more perishable than whole birds. Poultry needs proper storage to retard spoilage. Proper storage is also important to inhibit the growth of salmonellae, an illness-causing bacteria often found in poultry.

For refrigerator storage, remove store wrapping. Rewrap the bird loosely in waxed paper. Wrap and store giblets separately. Place poultry in the coldest part of the refrigerator and use within two to three days.

For longer storage, rewrap the bird in moistureproof and vaporproof wrapping and store it in the freezer. You should place poultry that you buy frozen in the freezer immediately after purchase. You can store poultry in the freezer for six to eight months. Once you thaw poultry, however, you should not refreeze it.

Store all canned poultry products in a cool, dry place. Store all unused portions and cooked poultry in tightly covered containers in the refrigerator. Remove stuffing from cooked poultry and store it separately. Use leftovers within two or three days. See 14-3.

National Turkey Federation

14-3 Promptly store leftover turkey and stuffing in the refrigerator in separate covered containers.

Food Science Principles of Cooking Poultry

Like meat, poultry is a protein food. Cooking principles for poultry are similar to those used for other high-protein foods. Low temperatures and careful timing are important. Cooking poultry for too long or at too high a temperature can make it tough, dry, and flavorless.

A meat thermometer is the most accurate way to test poultry for doneness. Insert the bulb of the thermometer ½ to 1 inch (1.5 to 2.5 cm) deep in the thickest part of the breast or in the center of the thigh. It should not touch bone. When the thermometer reaches 185°F (85°C), the bird is cooked.

If you do not have a meat thermometer, grasp a drumstick on a whole bird gently with a clean cloth. On a cooked bird, the drumstick will twist easily at the thigh joint. The breast meat will pierce easily with a fork, and juices will be clear.

You must cook poultry to the well-done stage, but you should not overcook it. Pink flesh does not always mean a bird is undercooked. A chemical reaction causes a pink color in cooked poultry. Gases in the oven combine with substances in the poultry and turn the flesh pink. The pink color is not harmful.

Poultry bones sometimes will turn a dark color during cooking. Blood cells in the bone that have broken down during freezing cause this discoloration. When heated, they turn a dark brown. The color has no effect on flavor, and the bird is safe to eat.

Methods of Cooking Poultry

You can roast, broil, fry, braise, or stew poultry. The method you choose will depend mainly on your taste preferences. Regardless of the cooking method, your first step in preparing poultry will be to wash the bird. Wash poultry under cold running water and pat it dry with paper towels.

Roasting Poultry

You can roast turkeys, chickens, ducks, and geese. To roast poultry, you should place the bird breast side up in a shallow pan. Season the cavity with salt and pepper unless you will be stuffing the bird. Roast the bird in a 325°F (160°C) oven until a meat thermometer reaches 185°F (85°C) or it tests done. (For faster roasting, you can wrap poultry in aluminum foil and cook it in a 450°F [230°C] oven.)

Healthy Living

Save fried chicken for an occasional treat. For lower fat eating, choose roasted, baked, and broiled chicken most often. Also, be sure to remove the skin, which is high in fat. When making chicken soup, chill the broth and skim off the fat before serving the soup.

If you allow poultry to stand 10 to 15 minutes after you take it from the oven, it will be easier to carve.

Be sure to remove the neck and the packet of giblets found inside the cavity of whole birds before roasting. *Giblets* are the edible internal organs, such as the heart and liver. People often use them in appetizers and to flavor soups and gravies.

You should truss large birds before roasting. A *trussed* bird has its wing tips turned back onto the shoulder and the drumsticks tied to the tail. Trussing prevents the wing and leg tips from overbrowning. It also makes the bird easier to handle and more attractive to serve.

If you will be stuffing the bird, do not add the stuffing until you are ready to put the bird in the oven. This will prevent the growth of harmful bacteria, which can cause food-borne illness. Pack the stuffing loosely into the cavity. You can bake any extra stuffing in a greased casserole. The temperature of the stuffing should reach at least 165°F (75°C). Be sure to remove the stuffing from the cooked bird promptly and refrigerate it in a separate container as soon as possible.

Sometimes the breast of a large bird will brown too quickly. To prevent overbrowning, you can make a tent out of aluminum foil. Cover the breast with the foil when the bird is about half cooked.

Some people prefer to roast poultry in oven cooking bags. Cooking bags shorten cooking time because they use steam to help cook the bird. Since steam is a form of moist heat, this method is not true roasting.

Broiling Poultry

You can broil turkeys and chickens. To broil poultry, split the bird into halves or quarters. Place pieces on broiler pan and brush lightly with melted margarine, if desired. Broil 4 to 5 inches (10 to 12 cm) from the heat source until done. Cooking time depends on the size of the bird. Chicken usually will take about 40 minutes. Turkey will take about 80 to 90 minutes. Thinner pieces will cook faster than thicker pieces. Remove pieces from broiler when they are cooked and keep them warm until ready to serve.

Frying Poultry

You can cut chickens and turkeys into pieces and fry them, 14-4. To fry poultry, first roll the pieces in flour, egg, and bread crumbs or dip them in a batter. Then brown the pieces in about ½ inch (1.5 cm) of hot fat. (The fat should not be so hot that it smokes.) Turn poultry pieces with tongs as they brown. After browning, the bird can finish cooking in the skillet over low heat. You can also complete the cooking in a moderate oven.

Oven-Frying Poultry

Oven-frying is sometimes called baking. You can oven-fry chicken pieces by coating them with

14-4 Fried chicken has a crispy texture and a delicious-looking brown color.

seasoned flour. Place them on a baking sheet. Cook in a moderate oven until done. Brushing chicken lightly with melted margarine will produce a crisp golden crust.

Braising Poultry

To braise turkey or chicken, brown individual pieces in a small amount of fat. Add a small amount of water to the skillet and cover tightly. Cook the poultry over low heat until tender, about 45 minutes to 1 hour. You can braise poultry on a surface unit or in the oven. For a crisp crust, uncover the pan for the last 10 minutes of cooking.

Stewing Poultry

To stew poultry, put the bird in a big kettle and cover it completely with water. You can add carrots, celery, and seasonings for flavor. Cover the kettle tightly and simmer over low heat until the bird is tender. (You should never allow the liquid to boil.) If desired, you can easily remove the stewed meat from the bone for use in soups and casseroles.

Microwaving Poultry

Poultry prepared in a microwave oven comes out tender and juicy. It generally cooks in much less time than poultry cooked in a conventional oven. However, when roasting large birds, you may save little or no time. In addition, most microwave ovens are not big enough to hold birds over a certain size.

You can use a microwave oven to defrost or partially cook poultry that you are preparing by another method. For instance, partial cooking speeds grilling time and ensures that grilled poultry is thoroughly cooked.

To ensure even cooking in a microwave oven, arrange poultry pieces with the bony portions to the center. Arrange drumsticks like the spokes of a wheel. Place the meaty ends toward the outside of the dish. On whole birds, the breast area and wing and leg tips may cook faster than the rest of the bird. To prevent overcooking, you can cover these areas with foil shields.

Frozen Poultry

You should thaw frozen poultry before cooking. (If the bird is commercially stuffed, you should cook it without thawing.) To thaw, leave the bird in its original wrapping and let it thaw in the refrigerator.

For quicker thawing, wrap frozen poultry in a tightly closed plastic bag. Place it in a sink full of cold water. Change the water about every 30 minutes to keep it cold until the bird defrosts.

Boning Chicken

Many recipes call for boneless chicken breasts and thighs, 14-5. Purchasing boneless chicken pieces is expensive. You can save money by boning chicken at home. Be sure to thoroughly wash cutting boards, knives, and other utensils after preparing raw poultry. This helps avoid the possibility of transferring harmful bacteria that may be in the poultry to other foods.

14-5 Use boned chicken to make dishes like this colorful stir-fry.

Summary

Poultry is a good source of protein and B vitamins. Most poultry is marketed young. When buying poultry, look for meaty birds with well-distributed fat and blemish-free skin.

All poultry is perishable. Store it in the coldest part of the refrigerator and use it within two to three days. You can carefully wrap poultry and place it in the freezer for longer storage.

You should always be sure poultry is thoroughly cooked before you serve it. However, use moderate cooking temperatures and careful timing to avoid overcooking. Overcooking can result in meat that is tough and dry.

Because most poultry is tender, it is suitable for any cooking method. You might choose roasting, broiling, frying, braising, stewing, or microwaving.

Review What You Have Read

Write your answers on a separate sheet of paper.
1. Name the four most common kinds of poultry.
2. True or false. All poultry is tender and can be cooked by dry heat methods.
3. Why do you need to allow more weight per serving when buying poultry than when buying red meat?
4. Within what time period should refrigerated poultry be used?
5. True or false. Stuffing should be left inside a poultry carcass for refrigerator storage.
6. True or false. Poultry should be cooked to the well-done stage.
7. What is the first step in every method of poultry cookery?
8. Turning back the wing tips and tying the drumsticks to the tail of the bird before roasting is known as _____.
9. How should poultry pieces be arranged in a microwave oven to assure even cooking?
10. Why is it important to thoroughly wash cutting boards and utensils after preparing raw poultry?

Build Your Basic Skills

1. Write three questions about poultry selection, storage, and preparation. Then contact the U.S. Department of Agriculture's Meat and Poultry Hotline for answers to your questions.
2. Compare the price per pound of boneless, skinless chicken breasts with the price per pound of bone-in, skin-on chicken breasts. Calculate the price per ounce of each chicken product. Remove the bone and skin from the bone-in, skin-on breasts. Weight the bone and skin on a scale. Determine the percentage of waste in the bone-in, skin-on product. Then calculate the cost per ounce of the meat portion of this product. How does this cost compare with the cost of the product sold without bone and skin?

Build Your Thinking Skills

1. Roast chicken, turkey, duck, and goose. Compare the appearance, flavor, and texture of the various meats.
2. Find at least three different recipes for stuffing. Note what ingredients the recipes have in common and which ingredients are unique to each recipe. Also note the ingredient proportions. Use this analysis to create your own recipe for stuffing. Prepare and sample the recipe. Explain why you would or would not choose to serve it with poultry.

Chapter 15

Fish and Shellfish

A "Taste" of the World of Work

Raw Shellfish Preparer
Cleans and prepares shellfish for serving to customers.

Fish Hatchery Attendant
Performs a combination of tasks to trap and spawn game fish, incubate eggs, and rear fry in fish hatchery.

Net Fisher
Catches finfish, shellfish, and other marine life alone or as a crewmember on shore or aboard fishing vessels, using a variety of equipment.

Terms to Know

finfish
shellfish
lean fish
fat fish
mollusk

crustacean
drawn fish
dressed fish
fish steak
fish fillet

Objectives

After studying this chapter, you will be able to
- ❏ list factors affecting the selection of fish and shellfish.
- ❏ describe how to properly store fish to maintain its quality.
- ❏ describe the principles and methods for cooking fish and shellfish.
- ❏ prepare fish by moist and dry cooking methods.

USA Rice Council

Commercial fishers in the United States catch several billion fish each year for food, 15-1. However, the U.S. is a small consumer of fish and fish products compared to other countries.

Classification of Fish and Shellfish

Two kinds of water animals are eaten as food: finfish (often called fish) and shellfish. *Finfish* have fins and backbones. *Shellfish* have shells instead of backbones. Both finfish and shellfish can be divided into further classes.

Finfish can be lean or fatty. *Lean fish* have very little fat in their flesh. Because their flesh is white, they are often called *white fish*. Swordfish, haddock, and cod are lean fish. *Fat fish* have flesh that is fattier than that of lean fish. They usually are pink, yellow, or gray in color. Mackerel, catfish, and salmon are fat fish.

You can divide shellfish into two groups: mollusks and crustaceans. *Mollusks* have soft bodies that are partially or fully covered by hard shells. Oysters, clams, and scallops are mollusks. *Crustaceans* are covered by crustlike shells and have segmented (divided into sections) bodies. Shrimp, lobster, and crabs are crustaceans.

Nutritional Value of Fish and Shellfish

Both fish and shellfish are excellent sources of complete protein. In some parts of the world, people use fish flour (concentrated fish protein) to increase the protein level of the diet.

Fat content varies with the kind of fish. Lean fish have fewer calories (kilojoules) than fat fish. Most fish have fewer calories (kilojoules) and less saturated fat and cholesterol than moderately fat red meat. This makes most varieties suitable for reduced-fat diets.

New England Fisheries Development Association, Inc.

15-1 Much of the commercial fishing in the United States is done off the New England coast.

Mineral content also varies, but the edible portion of all fish is slightly higher in minerals than red meat. Shellfish have even more minerals than finfish. Fish provide important amounts of phosphorus and fair amounts of iron and calcium. Saltwater fish are one of the most important sources of iodine.

Fish and shellfish contribute the same vitamins as red meat. Fat fish have higher amounts of vitamins A and D.

Selecting and Purchasing Fish and Shellfish

When selecting fish and shellfish, use inspection seals and grade shields to help you determine quality. The appearance and form of fish and shellfish can also guide your purchases.

Inspection and Grading of Fish and Shellfish

The National Marine Fisheries Service provides a voluntary inspection program for the fish industry. All fish products that have passed inspection carry a round inspection seal.

A grade shield appears on fish that have been voluntarily graded. Appearance, odor, flavor, and lack of defects determine quality grades. Grades include U.S. Grade A, U.S. Grade B, and U.S. Grade C. *Grade A* products are top quality. They are uniform in size and have good flavor and few defects. *Grade B* products are good, but not as uniform in size or free from defects as Grade A. *Grade C* products are nutritious, but less attractive.

Forms of Finfish

A fresh fish should have a stiff body, tight scales, and firm flesh. The gills should be red, and

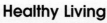

Healthy Living

Some nutritionists suggest including fish in your diet three or more times a week. They believe the omega-3 fatty acids in fish may reduce your risk of heart attack or stroke. Although many experts favor eating fish, most caution against the use of fish oil supplements. These supplements do not contain the other nutrients found in fish. In addition, their use may have some negative side effects.

the eyes bright and bulging. A finger pushed into the flesh should leave no indentation. The outside should have little or no slime, and the fish should smell fresh.

You can purchase fresh fish whole, drawn, dressed, or as steaks or fillets. A *whole (round) fish* is marketed as it comes from the water. You must clean it before cooking. A **drawn fish** has the entrails (insides) removed. A **dressed fish** has the entrails, head, fins, and scales removed. It is ready for cooking. **Steaks** are cross-sectional slices taken from a dressed fish. **Fillets** are the sides of the fish cut lengthwise away from the backbone. Fillets have few, if any, bones. See 15-2.

Drawn and dressed fish, as well as fish steaks and fillets, can be purchased frozen. Frozen fish should be solidly frozen in moistureproof and vaporproof wrapping. There should be no discoloration and little or no odor.

Types of Shellfish

Shellfish available in most markets include shrimp, oysters, crabs, lobsters, clams, and scallops.

Forms of Finfish

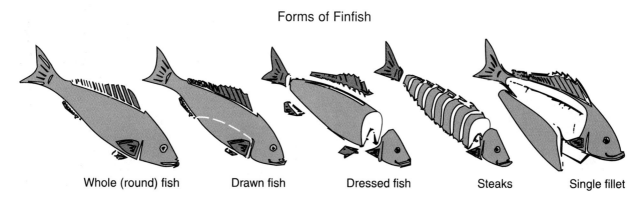

| Whole (round) fish | Drawn fish | Dressed fish | Steaks | Single fillet |

15-2 Fresh fish can be purchased in several forms.

15-5 These fish cakes are made with precooked fish and then panfried until golden.

will cause the proteins to overcoagulate and make the fish tough.

You can simmer, bake, broil, panfry (sauté), deep-fry, or microwave shellfish. The cooking method used depends on the kind of shellfish and whether you purchased it live, frozen, or canned.

If you live in an area where fresh shellfish is available, you may purchase your shellfish live. Shellfish purchased in the shell must be alive when cooked. (Fresh, uncooked shellfish deteriorates very rapidly.)

Parboil live lobster, shrimp, and crab by plunging the shellfish into boiling, salted water until it is partially cooked. (Plunge lobster into the water head first.) Shellfish then should be simmered, not boiled. After parboiling, you can broil, bake, panfry, or deep-fry shrimp. You may bake or broil lobster and crab. You may combine all three with other ingredients to make such seafood specialties as Lobster Thermidor, Shrimp Scampi, and Crab Newburg.

The shells of live oysters and clams should be tightly closed. If they are open, you should discard the oysters or clams. When you drop the live oysters or clams into simmering water, the shells will open. You can then remove the edible part of the shellfish. After removal from the shell, you can simmer, deep-fry, or sauté oysters and clams. See 15-6.

Shellfish cooked in a microwave oven require the same timing whether cooked in or out of the shell. Refer to a microwave cookbook for exact cooking times and methods. Remember to place thicker portions of shellfish toward the outside of the dish. This will promote more even microwave cooking.

In inland areas, most of the available shellfish is frozen or canned. Cook uncooked frozen shrimp in salted simmering water until pink. Frozen lobster tails are partially cooked. You may thaw and broil them, or you may cook them in simmering liquid like uncooked frozen shrimp. You may bake, broil, or fry cooked frozen shrimp, crab, or scallops.

You may serve canned shellfish without further cooking. You may also combine them with other foods in salads and main dishes.

Good Manners Are Good Business

Being served shellfish at a business dinner may make you rather nervous if you are unfamiliar with how to eat them. Clams and oysters often are served in open shells. Use one hand to hold the shell in place on your plate. With your other hand, use a seafood fork to lift the oyster or clam out of the shell. If you wish, dip the shellfish in the accompanying cocktail sauce before eating it in one bite.

Egg dishes are tasty, nutritious, and easy to prepare.

Chapter 16

Eggs

A "Taste" of the World of Work

Egg Candler
Inspects eggs to ascertain quality and fitness for consumption or incubation, according to prescribed standards.

Egg Breaker
Separates yolk and white of eggs for use in food products.

Egg-Producing Farm Farmworker
Collects eggs from trap nests, releases hens from nests, records number of eggs laid by each hen, and packs eggs in cases or cartons.

Terms to Know

candling	soufflé
emulsion	meringue
folding	weeping
coagulum	beading
omelet	custard

Objectives

After studying this chapter, you will be able to
❑ list factors affecting the selection of eggs.
❑ describe the principles and methods for cooking eggs.
❑ cook eggs properly for breakfast menus and use eggs as ingredients in other foods.

American Egg Board

Eggs are one of the most versatile and nutritious food sources. You can prepare them in many different ways. Since eggs are easy to digest, you can serve them to people at all stages of the life cycle.

Selecting and Storing Eggs

Egg prices vary according to grade and size. Large eggs are the size most shoppers buy, regardless of price.

Nutritional Value of Eggs

Eggs are one of the best protein foods. They contain all of the essential amino acids as well as thiamin, riboflavin, iron, phosphorous, and vitamins A and D. However, egg yolks are high in cholesterol. Therefore, many experts urge people to limit the number of egg yolks they eat.

Egg Grades

Eggs for retail sale are graded. Four quality factors determine grades. These are condition of the shell, size of the air cell, clearness and thickness of the egg white, and condition of the yolk. Eggs are graded for quality by a system called *candling.* The eggs move along rollers over bright lights. The lights illuminate the eggs' structure. Skilled people can then look at the eggs carefully and remove any that do not meet standards.

The two grades of eggs available in most supermarkets are U.S. Grade AA and U.S. Grade A. Look for the grade shield on the egg carton or on the tape that seals the carton.

A *Grade AA egg* has a clean, unbroken shell and a small air cell. When broken into a dish, it has a thick, clear white that covers a small area. The yolk is thick and stands high above the white. Grade AA is the best quality you can buy. Use it when appearance is important, as in poaching or frying.

A *Grade A egg* has a clean, unbroken shell with a slightly larger air cell. When broken into a dish, it covers a wider area than a Grade AA egg. The white is fairly thick, and the yolk is firm and high.

Some eggs are rated *Grade B.* A Grade B egg has an unbroken shell that is clean or slightly stained. The air cell is larger than that of a Grade A egg. It may be bubbly. When broken into a dish, a Grade B egg has a thin white and yolk. It covers a much wider area than a Grade A or AA egg. You will rarely see Grade B eggs in food stores. They are usually used in other food products.

Egg Size and Color

Eggs are sized on the basis of a medium weight per dozen. Extra large, large, and medium eggs are the most common sizes sold. Most recipes are formulated to use medium or large eggs.

Within each grade, egg prices vary according to size. Extra large eggs cost more than large eggs, and large eggs cost more than medium eggs.

Size has no relation to quality. Eggs of any size can be Grade AA, A, or B.

Both white-shelled and brown-shelled eggs are available in some areas. The breed of chicken determines egg color. The color of the shell does not affect quality, flavor, or nutritional value, 16-1.

Storing Eggs

You may safely store fresh eggs in the refrigerator for four to five weeks. For maximum quality and flavor, however, use eggs within a week.

Always handle eggs carefully to prevent cracking. Cracked eggs can contain harmful bacteria, which can cause food poisoning. Use cracked eggs as soon as possible, but only in thoroughly cooked foods.

Some recipes call only for egg yolks or egg whites. To store leftover yolks, cover them with cold water and refrigerate in a tightly covered container. To store egg whites, refrigerate them in a tightly covered container. Use both yolks and whites within one or two days.

Play It Safe

Some eggs contain illness-causing bacteria. These bacteria can multiply rapidly at warm temperatures. Neither smell, taste, nor appearance will help you identify a contaminated egg. However, proper storage of eggs can help you control any bacteria that may be present. Store eggs, large end up, in their original carton. Keep them in the main compartment of the refrigerator, not on the refrigerator door, which does not stay as cold.

16-1 Brown-shelled and white-shelled eggs have the same quality, flavor, and nutritional value.

Eggs as Ingredients

Eggs are used as emulsifiers, a means of incorporating air, thickeners, binding agents, and interfering agents. They also add structure, nutrients, flavor, and color to foods.

Emulsifiers

An *emulsion* is the mixture that forms when you combine liquids that ordinarily do not mix. (Oil and water or a water-based liquid, such as lemon juice, are commonly combined to form an emulsion.) An emulsion can be either temporary or permanent.

A true French dressing is a *temporary emulsion* made with oil, vinegar, water, and seasonings. When you agitate (shake) the dressing, an emulsion forms. When you stop the agitation and allow the dressing to rest, however, the oil and water-based liquid separate, and the emulsion breaks.

You form a *permanent emulsion* when you add a third ingredient to the oil and water-based liquid. This ingredient is called an *emulsifying agent*. Egg yolk is an excellent emulsifying agent. The yolk surrounds the oil droplets and keeps them suspended in the water-based liquid. Mayonnaise and hollandaise sauce are permanent emulsions.

Foams

Egg foams are used to add air to foods. When you beat air into egg whites, many air cells form. A thin film of egg white protein surrounds each cell. As beating continues, the cells become smaller and more numerous. The protein film also becomes thinner. As a result, the foam thickens.

Factors Affecting Egg Foams

Temperature, beating time, fat, acid, and sugar affect the formation of an egg white foam. When preparing egg foams, two temperatures are needed. Eggs separate most easily when they are cold.

However, egg whites reach maximum volume when you beat them at room temperature. This is why it is best to separate the whites from the yolks when you take the eggs from the refrigerator. Then let the egg whites stand until they reach room temperature before beating them.

The amount of time you should beat an egg white depends somewhat on the product. You must avoid both too little and too much beating time. Too little beating time produces underbeaten egg whites, which lose volume quickly and do not hold their shape. Too much beating time produces overbeaten egg whites, which also lose volume quickly. In addition, overbeaten egg whites have little elasticity and will break down into curds.

Fat and fat-containing ingredients, such as egg yolk, inhibit the formation of an egg white foam. This is why you must be careful that no fat is present on the beaters or in the bowl when beating egg whites.

Acid makes egg white foams more stable. It also adds whiteness. This is why many recipes that use egg white foams call for a small amount of cream of tartar.

Sugar increases the stability of an egg white foam. It also increases beating time. You will usually add sugar to the foam after it has reached most of the volume.

Stages of Egg Foams

Recipes will direct you to beat egg whites to one of three stages: foamy, soft peak, or stiff peak. Each stage requires increased beating time.

Egg whites at the *foamy stage* are fairly transparent. They have bubbles and foam on the surface. The mixture will begin to flow out of the bowl if you tilt it.

Egg whites beaten to the *soft peak stage* have reached full volume. They are white and shiny. When you lift the beater, the foam stands in peaks that bend at the tips.

Egg whites beaten to the *stiff peak stage* also have reached full volume and are white and shiny. When you lift the beater, the peaks stand up straight. If you beat egg whites past the stiff peak stage, you have overbeaten them.

Using Egg Foams

You will use foams to make soft and hard meringues. You will also use them to give structure to angel food and sponge cakes, soufflés, and puffy omelets.

To avoid a loss of air, you must quickly but gently blend egg white foams into other ingredients.

This blending process is called *folding.* Wire whisks and rubber spatulas are the best tools for folding. Using either tool, cut down into the mixture, across the bottom, up the opposite side, and across the top. The whisk or spatula should remain in the mixture the entire time you are folding.

Thickeners

Heat causes egg proteins to coagulate (thicken). Because of this property, whole eggs and egg yolks are used as thickening agents in such foods as sauces, custards, and puddings.

Eggs are the only thickening agent in some food products, such as custards. In other food products, such as sauces and puddings, both eggs and starch are used as thickening agents.

In egg-starch mixtures, you can add eggs in two ways. You can mix the eggs with the other ingredients and cook the mixture over low to moderate heat until thickened. You can also add the eggs to the mixture after the starch paste has cooked and thickened. Once you add the eggs, return the mixture to the heat and cook it for a short time longer.

When you must add eggs to a hot mixture, you should quickly fold a small amount of the hot mixture into the beaten eggs. Then, you can add the warmed eggs to the remainder of the hot mixture. Warming the eggs slightly keeps them from coagulating into lumps.

Binding and Interfering Agents

You can use eggs as binding and interfering agents. Eggs act as binding agents that hold together the ingredients in foods such as meat loaf and croquettes, 16-2. Frozen desserts like ice cream and sherbet stay creamy because the eggs in them act as interfering agents. The eggs inhibit the formation of large ice crystals, which would ruin the texture of frozen desserts.

Healthy Living

Pregnant women, young children, older people, and people who are sick are at greater risk if they contract food poisoning. Therefore, you should not serve foods containing raw or lightly cooked eggs to these people.

16-2 Eggs bind together the other ingredients in this vegetarian rice-nut loaf.

Structure

Eggs add structure to baked products, such as muffins and cakes. People limiting cholesterol in their diets can still use eggs as ingredients in recipes for baked goods. You can substitute two egg whites for each whole egg. Add 1 teaspoon (5 mL) of oil and decrease liquid in the recipe by 1⅓ table-spoons (20 mL) for each egg being replaced.

Nutrition, Flavor, and Color

Eggs contribute important nutrients to food products. Eggs add flavor and color to foods such as custards and puddings. Eggs also give an appealing color to the interior of baked goods like cakes.

Using Raw Eggs

A small percentage of raw eggs may be contaminated with salmonellae bacteria, which can cause food poisoning. You can destroy these bacteria by cooking. However, you do not cook some recipes calling for eggs, such as eggnog. To guard against food poisoning when preparing these recipes, use only clean, fresh, uncracked eggs that you have properly refrigerated. Also plan to consume the food containing the raw eggs immediately.

Egg Substitutes

Nutrition experts recommend that people limit their intake of dietary cholesterol to 300 mg daily. Whole eggs and egg yolks contain 213 mg of cholesterol each. As with all foods, with balance and moderation, most people can easily include eggs as part of a healthy diet. However, some people are still reluctant to eat eggs due to a concern about cholesterol. In response to this concern, several manufacturers have begun marketing egg substitutes.

Egg substitutes are made largely from real egg whites. However, they contain no egg yolks. Therefore, these products are cholesterol-free, fat-free, and lower in calories than whole eggs. They compare closely to whole eggs in most other nutrient values.

Egg substitutes are nearly as versatile as whole eggs. You can scramble them or use them to prepare omelets or quiches. You can also use them in most recipes calling for eggs. Typically, you will use ¼ cup (50 mL) of egg substitute in place of each whole egg or egg yolk. You can even use egg substitutes in recipes calling for hard-cooked eggs.

Consumers who choose to use egg substitutes must remember that eggs are only one source of dietary fat and cholesterol. Using egg substitutes alone will not lead to a lowfat, low-cholesterol diet. Lowering cholesterol and fat in the diet must become part of a total eating plan. Consumers should also know that egg substitutes can cost over three times as much as whole eggs.

Food Science Principles of Cooking Eggs

Eggs coagulate when heated during cooking. Temperature, time, and the addition of other ingredients affect coagulation.

The egg white coagulates at a slightly lower temperature than the egg yolk. The coagulation temperature of both egg white and egg yolk is below boiling. Temperatures that are too high can cause egg proteins to lose moisture, shrink, and toughen. This is why you should use low to moderate temperatures for cooking eggs.

Cooking time also affects coagulation. Cooking egg proteins too long can cause them to lose moisture and shrink. When both high temperatures and long cooking times are used, moisture loss and shrinkage become even greater.

The addition of other ingredients changes the coagulation temperature of eggs. This is because extra ingredients dilute the proteins found in eggs. As the concentration of egg proteins decreases, the coagulation temperature increases. As the concentration of egg proteins increases, the coagulation temperature decreases. For instance, eggs scrambled without added milk will coagulate at a lower temperature than eggs scrambled with milk. Eggs with sugar added will coagulate at a higher temperature than eggs without sugar. On the other hand, acid and salt both lower the coagulation temperature of eggs.

Good Manners Are Good Business

Some people like to eat their scrambled eggs with catsup. If you are one of those people, you might want to order something besides scrambled eggs at a business breakfast. Putting anything on any food that was not prepared and served with the food is considered an insult to the chef.

Methods of Cooking Eggs

Eggs can be scrambled, fried, poached, baked, cooked in the shell, or microwaved. You can use them to make omelets, soufflés, meringues, and custards. In all methods of cooking eggs, low to moderate temperatures and accurate cooking times are important.

Scrambling Eggs

To scramble an egg, break the egg into a bowl. Beat the egg with a fork or whisk until blended. You can add milk, tomato juice, or other liquid. However, the amount of liquid cannot exceed the amount of protein available to thicken the mixture. Use about 1 tablespoon (15 mL) of liquid per egg. Pour the egg mixture into a lightly greased or non-stick heated skillet. Occasionally give the eggs a gentle stir until a fluffy, soft *coagulum* (smooth mass) forms. For variety, bits of bacon or finely chopped chives can be added to the eggs before scrambling.

When scrambling eggs, adding too much liquid will cause the eggs to be watery and the coagulum small and firm. Too high a temperature will cause the egg proteins to toughen and shrink. Too much stirring will cause the coagulum to be small.

Poaching Eggs

To poach an egg, break the egg into a custard cup. Slip the egg into a saucepan filled with 2 to 3 inches of boiling water. You may add a small amount of salt or acid (such as vinegar) to the water. This will cause the proteins to coagulate faster and help keep the egg white from spreading. Reduce the temperature to keep the water below boiling. Cook the egg until the white is firm, and the yolk is semiliquid. This will take about three to five minutes, 16-3.

You can also use an egg poacher to poach eggs. Break an egg into a small cup in the poacher. You may also place a small amount of butter or margarine in the cup. Place the cup on a rack over simmering water, and cover the poacher. The egg cooks from the heat of the steam.

16-3 Poached eggs should have smooth, not ragged edges.

Frying Eggs

When frying eggs, temperatures that are too high quickly toughen egg proteins. Temperatures that are too low can cause the egg white to spread too far before it sets. Low temperatures can also toughen egg proteins because they increase cooking time.

To fry an egg, add the egg to a moderately hot skillet containing vegetable oil spray or a small amount of fat (1 teaspoon, or 5 mL, per egg). You may add a little water to the skillet, too. Cover the skillet and cook the egg for three to five minutes. The steam that forms in the covered skillet will cook the upper surface of the egg. You can also cook the upper surface by gently turning the egg.

Baking Eggs

To bake an egg, break the egg into an individual, greased baking dish. Then put the baking dish in a shallow casserole filled with 1 inch (2.5 cm) of warm water. Bake in a moderate oven for 12 to 18 minutes, depending on the firmness desired. You can add variety to baked eggs. Try lining the dish with a strip of bacon or grating cheese on top of the egg to add flavor.

Cooking Eggs in the Shell

Eggs cooked in the shell can be soft-cooked or hard-cooked. Time determines the degree of doneness. You can use the cold water method or the hot water method.

To prepare soft-cooked eggs by the cold water method, place the eggs in a deep pan. Add enough cold water to come 1 inch above the eggs. Cover the pan and quickly bring the water to a boil. Let the eggs remain in the water for four to five minutes, depending on the desired degree of doneness. For the hot water method, add the eggs to simmering water. Keep the water simmering for one to four minutes. Never let the water boil. Boiling can cause overcoagulation of the egg proteins and discoloration of the egg yolk.

To prepare hard-cooked eggs, use either of the methods used for soft-cooked eggs, but increase the cooking times. For the cold water method, keep the eggs in the water 15 to 17 minutes. For the hot water method, keep the eggs in the simmering water for 13 to 15 minutes. See 16-4.

Cool hard-cooked eggs immediately under cold running water. Rapid cooling stops the egg from cooking and prevents the formation of a greenish-colored ring around the yolk. A chemical reaction between iron in the egg yolk and hydrogen sulfide in the egg white causes this discoloration. It takes place when you overcook eggs. The discoloration is harmless, but it looks unappetizing.

After cooling, store hard-cooked eggs in the refrigerator. You can keep them for up to one week. You should not eat hard-cooked eggs, or any other perishable food, kept at room temperature for over two hours.

Microwaving Eggs

You can scramble, poach, and shirr (bake) eggs in a microwave oven. You can also make them into plain omelets or use them in tasty egg dishes such as quiche. However, conventional cooking methods are best for airy egg dishes, such as puffy omelets and soufflés.

Eggs cook rapidly in a microwave oven and they continue to cook during standing time. Overcooking toughens the protein and produces a rubbery egg. Therefore, start cooking eggs with the minimum time stated in microwave recipes. Remove them from the microwave oven just before they are done.

In a microwave oven, steam builds up in foods covered by a tight skin or shell. This buildup could cause these foods to explode. For this reason, you should remove eggs from the shell before cooking them in a microwave oven. In addition, gently puncture egg yolks with a fork or toothpick before microwaving to prevent them from bursting.

Omelets

Omelets are beaten egg mixtures that are cooked without stirring and served folded in half. Omelets can be plain (also called French) or puffy. You make both types of omelets from eggs, a small amount of liquid (usually milk or water), and seasonings. You may serve an omelet with or without a filling.

To make a plain omelet, gently beat together the eggs, liquid, and seasonings. Pour the mixture into a lightly greased or nonstick skillet or omelet pan. The pan should be hot enough to sizzle a drop of water. The edges of the egg mixture should set immediately. With a wide spatula, gently lift the cooked edges to allow the uncooked egg to run underneath. Gently tilting the skillet will help. Gently slide the pan over the heat to keep the eggs in motion. The omelet is ready to fill and serve when the eggs have set but the top is still creamy and moist.

To make a puffy omelet, beat the egg whites with salt, pepper, cream of tartar, and water until stiff (but not dry) peaks form. Beat the egg yolks

16-4 This molded tuna salad includes hard-cooked eggs as both an ingredient and a garnish.

until they are thick and lemon-colored. Gently fold the beaten whites into the beaten yolks. Pour the mixture into a lightly greased skillet that is hot enough to sizzle a drop of water. Cook the omelet slowly over medium heat until puffy, about 5 minutes. (The bottom should be lightly brown.) Place the omelet in a preheated 350°F (180°C) oven. Bake it 10 to 12 minutes, or until a knife inserted in the center comes out clean.

Soufflés

Soufflés are fluffy baked preparations made with a starch-thickened sauce into which stiffly beaten egg whites are folded. They are similar to puffy omelets. Both use beaten egg whites for structure. You can serve soufflés for dessert or as a main dish.

To prepare a soufflé, add beaten egg yolks to a basic white sauce. The white sauce may contain chocolate, fruit, cheese, pureed vegetables, or pureed seafood. Gently fold beaten egg whites into the white sauce mixture. Bake the soufflé in a moderate oven until puffy and golden. Serve the soufflé immediately. See 16-5.

Meringues

Meringues are a fluffy white mixture of beaten egg whites and sugar, which may be soft or hard. Use soft meringues in fruit whips and as toppings on pies and other baked goods like Baked Alaska. Use hard meringues to make meringue shells, which you can fill and serve as desserts. You can also use hard meringues to make confections, such as meringue cookies.

Make soft meringues from egg whites, cream of tartar, sugar, and flavoring. Beat the egg whites and cream of tartar to the foamy stage. Add the sugar gradually, followed by the flavoring. Beating continues until the egg whites reach the upper limit of the soft peak stage. See 16-6.

When using a soft meringue on a pie, spread it over hot pie filling. Carefully seal the meringue to the edge of the pastry. These important steps will help minimize both weeping and beading. *Weeping* is the layer of moisture that sometimes forms between a meringue topping and a pie filling. *Beading* appears as golden droplets on the surface of a meringue. Bake the meringue-topped pie at 350° to 400°F (180° to 200°C), until lightly browned.

You make hard meringues from the same ingredients as soft meringues. However, they contain a higher proportion of sugar and you bake them at a lower temperature for a longer time. You will usually shape hard meringues with a spoon and bake them on an oiled or paper-covered baking sheet. When you break a hard meringue with a fork, the interior should be dry and crisp, not soft and sticky.

Custards

Custards are a mixture of milk (or cream), eggs, sugar, and a flavoring that is cooked until thickened. Custards can be soft (sometimes called stirred) or baked. You must cook both types with low heat.

Soft custards usually contain slightly less egg than baked custards. Cook them over low heat. Constant stirring breaks up the coagulum as it forms, giving soft custard a creamy texture. Overheating causes curdling (the formation of lumps), which you can prevent by using low heat. A soft custard will coat the back of a metal spoon when properly thickened.

Baked custards usually use a greater proportion of eggs to milk than soft custards. Bake them in the oven in a pan of warm water. The extra eggs and lack of stirring result in a product that will hold its shape when removed from the baking dish. The pan of warm water helps prevent the custard from overheating, which can result in *syneresis* (the leakage of liquid from a gel). Overbaked custard will have visible bubbles and leakage. To test a baked custard for doneness, insert the tip of a knife into the center. If the knife is clean, the custard is baked. See 16-7.

You might serve a soft custard as a dessert sauce. You can also use it as the base for desserts like English trifle. Serve a baked custard plain or with a topping of caramel, fruit, or toasted coconut. You can make bread pudding by pouring custard over bread cubes before baking. See 16-8.

American Egg Board

16-5 A cheese soufflé served with a green vegetable and a fruit salad makes a special luncheon or light supper.

Fruit Whip
Serves 2

2 egg whites	2 egg whites
¼ teaspoon cream of tartar	1 mL cream of tartar
5 tablespoons sugar	75 mL sugar
1 small jar strained plum or apricot baby food	1 small jar strained plum or apricot baby food

1. In a small, deep bowl, sift cream of tartar over egg whites; beat to foamy stage.
2. Continue beating and gradually add sugar. Beat whites to the upper limit of the soft peak stage.
3. Fold baby food into beaten egg white.
4. Spoon mixture into a small, shallow baking dish. Place the baking dish in a larger dish containing 1 inch (2.5 cm) of warm water.
5. Bake fruit whip at 350°F (180°C) until a knife inserted in the center comes out clean, about 20 to 30 minutes.

Per serving: 153 Cal. (1% from fat), 4 g protein, 36 g carbohydrate, 0 g fat, 0 mg cholesterol, 1.1 g fiber, 51 mg sodium.

16-6 A soft meringue forms the base of fruit whip, a light and nourishing dessert.

Baked Custard
Serves 6

2 cups skim milk	500 mL skim milk
3 large eggs	3 large eggs
⅓ cup sugar	75 mL sugar
½ teaspoon vanilla	2 mL vanilla
nutmeg	nutmeg

1. Scald milk.
2. Beat eggs until blended; add sugar, salt, and vanilla.
3. Slowly add milk to egg mixture, stirring constantly.
4. Pour custard into baking dish or custard cups; sprinkle with nutmeg.
5. Place the baking dish or custard cups in a shallow pan; fill the pan with warm water to about 1 inch (2.5 cm) from the top of the cups.
6. Bake at 350°F (180°C) until a knife inserted in the center comes out clean, about 40 to 50 minutes.

Per serving: 111 Cal. (25% from fat), 6 g protein, 16 g carbohydrate, 3 g fat, 138 mg cholesterol, 0 g fiber, 77 mg sodium.

16-7 Extra eggs and a lack of stirring give baked custard a firm texture that holds its shape when removed from the baking dish.

16-8 Custard layered with fresh fruit makes an attractive, healthful dessert.

Summary

Eggs are a nutritious, inexpensive, and versatile food. Grade AA and A are the grades of eggs most commonly sold at retail stores. Extra large, large, and medium are the most common sizes. Fresh eggs keep well in the refrigerator, but require careful handling to prevent cracking.

Eggs serve a number of functions in recipes. They are used as emulsifiers to keep oil suspended in water-based liquids. They are used as foams to add air and give structure to foods like meringues and sponge cakes. They are used to thicken puddings and sauces and to hold ingredients together in foods like meat loaf. They interfere with the formation of ice crystals in frozen desserts. Eggs also add structure, nutrition, flavor, and color to many foods.

You can scramble, fry, poach, bake, soft-cook, hard-cook, or microwave eggs. You can also use them to prepare plain and puffy omelets, soufflés, soft and hard meringues, and stirred and baked custards. No matter how you prepare them, eggs require moderate cooking temperatures. They also need carefully monitored cooking times to prevent egg proteins from shrinking and becoming tough.

Review What You Have Read

Write your answers on a separate sheet of paper.
1. How is candling used in the egg industry?
2. What are the three most commonly used egg sizes?
3. How should eggs be stored in the refrigerator?
4. List five ways eggs are used as ingredients.
5. What four factors can affect the formation of an egg white foam?
6. Name three products that use an egg white foam.
7. True or false. Egg yolk coagulates at a slightly lower temperature than egg white.
8. Describe two basic egg preparation methods.
9. What is poaching?
10. What precautions should be taken to keep eggs from exploding in a microwave oven?
11. Golden droplets of moisture that sometimes appear on the surface of a meringue are called _____.
12. How do hard meringues differ from soft meringues?
13. How do soft custards differ from baked custards?
14. The leakage of liquid from baked custard is called _____.
    A. coagulum
    B. emulsion
    C. syneresis
    D. weeping

Build Your Basic Skills

1. Break a Grade AA egg into a saucer. Break a Grade A egg into a separate saucer. Discuss possible uses of each grade based on its appearance.
2. Beat the egg white of a small egg in one bowl. Beat the egg white of an extra large egg in a second bowl. Measure and compare the volume of the two egg white foams.

Build Your Thinking Skills

1. Beat four egg whites to the stiff peak stage. Add nothing to the first egg white. Add $\frac{1}{8}$ teaspoon (0.5 mL) oil to the second egg white. Add $\frac{1}{8}$ teaspoon (0.5 mL) cream of tartar to the third egg white. Add $\frac{1}{4}$ cup (50 mL) sugar to the fourth egg white. Compare volume, appearance, and required beating time of the four samples. Summarize your observations in a brief written report.
2. Beat an egg with milk and seasonings. Divide the mixture into three equal portions. Scramble one portion over high heat. Scramble a second portion over low heat, stirring occasionally just until cooked. Scramble the third portion over low heat stirring constantly. Evaluate each product on the basis of appearance, tenderness of the coagulum, and flavor.

Chapter 17

Dairy Products

1 A "Taste" of the World of Work

Cheese Blender
Prepares charts of quantities, grades, and types of cheese required for blending to make cheese products.

Ice Cream Chef
Mixes, cooks, and freezes ingredients to make frozen desserts, such as sherbets, ice cream, and custards.

Dairy Farm Supervisor
Supervises and coordinates activities of workers engaged in milking, breeding, and caring for cows, and performs lay-veterinary duties on dairy farm.

Terms to Know

pasteurization
UHT processed milk
homogenization
fortified
milkfat
milk solids
curd
whey
unripened cheese
ripened cheese
process cheese
scum

scorching
caramelize
curdling
white sauce
roux
bisque
chowder
puree
gelatin
gelatin cream
hydrate

Objectives

After studying this chapter, you will be able to
❏ list factors affecting the selection of dairy products.
❏ describe guidelines for preventing adverse reactions when cooking with milk.
❏ prepare many different dishes using milk, cream, cheese, and other dairy products.

Dairy Sweet

Dairy products make up the milk, yogurt, and cheese group of the Food Guide Pyramid. These dairy foods are essential for good health, and you should include them in your diet each day. They are your major source of calcium. They also contain high quality protein, riboflavin, phosphorous, vitamin A, and other important vitamins and minerals.

Cream, butter, sour cream, ice cream, and sherbet are also dairy products. However, calorie for calorie, they are higher in fat and lower in other nutrients than milk, cheese, and yogurt.

You can enjoy dairy products fresh or use them as ingredients in cooking and baking. Chocolate pudding, pizza, and scalloped potatoes are just a few of the many popular foods that contain dairy ingredients. In addition to contributing important nutrients, dairy products contribute flavor, texture, and richness to many foods. Milk products also help baked goods brown.

Selecting and Storing Dairy Products

A variety of dairy products are available. Your choice of products will depend on personal preference as well as your drinking and cooking needs. Most dairy products are highly perishable. They require careful storage to maintain their flavor and nutrient qualities.

Milk

A number of different animals provide milk for people throughout the world. People in some countries consume milk from camels and water buffalo. People often use goat's milk in areas where grazing land is scarce. However, since cow's milk is the most widely consumed, it will be the focus of this chapter. See 17-1.

Agricultural Research Service, USDA

17-1 Most of the milk consumed in the United States comes from cows.

Healthy Living

Getting enough calcium in your diet during the teen years is important. You need calcium to support the rapid bone growth that occurs at this stage in your life. A calcium-rich diet during the teen years can also help reduce your risk of osteoporosis (excessive bone tissue loss) later in life.

While all dairy products provide calcium, they do not all provide it in the same amounts. Cottage cheese and ice cream provide about half as much calcium as equal portions of milk or yogurt. Choose three servings of calcium-rich foods daily and exercise several times a week to build strong, healthy bones.

Milk is one of the most well-liked foods. You can purchase it in fresh fluid, canned, and dried forms. When used as a beverage, most people like milk served icy cold. You can flavor milk with chocolate, strawberry, or malted milk powder. You can combine it with eggs and nutmeg and serve it as eggnog. You might mix it with ice cream and flavorings and serve it as a milkshake. You could blend it with cocoa, heat it, and serve it as hot chocolate. Milk drinks, hot or cold, are nutritious and enjoyed by people of all ages.

Milk Processing

Milk may go through several processes between the dairy farm and the retail store. Milk and milk products sold in the United States are pasteurized. During *pasteurization,* milk is heated to destroy harmful bacteria. Pasteurization improves the keeping quality of the milk. It does not change the nutritional value or the flavor.

UHT processed milk is heated to a higher temperature than regular pasteurized milk to further increase its shelf life. After heating, the milk is sealed in presterilized containers. You can use UHT milk just like other milk products for drinking and recipes. It provides the same flavor and nutrition. The main advantage is that you can store unopened UHT milk products for up to six months without refrigeration, 17-2.

Fresh whole milk is usually homogenized. *Homogenization* is a mechanical process that prevents cream from rising to the surface of milk. This process breaks globules of milkfat into tiny particles and spreads them throughout the milk. Homogenized milk has a richer body and flavor than nonhomogenized milk.

Milk and milk products can be *fortified.* This mean nutrients have been added in amounts greater than what would naturally occur. Whole milk is often fortified with vitamin D. Skim milk may contain added vitamins A and D. Milk fortified with calcium is available for people who are concerned about getting enough calcium in their diet.

Milk is graded. Grading is based on the bacterial count of the finished product and the conditions under which the milk was produced. Only pasteurized, Grade A milk can be shipped across state lines for retail sale in the United States.

Types of Milk

The U.S. Public Health Service sets and enforces standards for milk products. Under these standards, *whole milk* must contain at least 3.25 percent milkfat and 8.25 percent milk solids.

17-2 UHT processed milk is found in presterilized boxes on the grocer's shelf—not in the dairy case.

Milkfat is the fat portion of milk. **Milk solids** contain most of the vitamins, minerals, protein, and sugar found in milk.

Whole milk, lowfat milk, and skim milk all begin as pasteurized whole milk. *Lowfat milk* has some of the fat removed. *Skim* or *nonfat milk* has more fat removed. The less fat the milk has, the fewer calories (kilojoules) it contains. This is why many people on reducing diets use skim milk.

Many people experience gas, cramps, bloating, and diarrhea after drinking and eating regular milk products. They have a condition called *lactose intolerance,* which means their body cannot produce enough lactase. Lactase is the enzyme needed to digest lactose—the natural sugar in milk. People with lactose intolerance may choose to buy *lactose-reduced milk,* which has been treated with lactase to break down milk sugar.

Doctors prescribe antibiotics for people who have bacterial infections. In addition to killing the bacteria that cause the infection, however, these drugs can kill helpful organisms in the digestive tract. Therefore, some doctors may recommend acidophilus milk for patients taking antibiotics. *Acidophilus milk* contains an added bacterial culture that helps restore a proper intestinal environment.

Many popular milk products are made from whole, lowfat, and skim milk. These include flavored milks, cultured buttermilk, and yogurt. Milk with added flavoring becomes flavored milk, such as chocolate milk. A bacterium that produces lactic acid turns milk into *cultured buttermilk.* It has a characteristic thickness and sour flavor. *Yogurt* also is a cultured milk product. It may contain added nonfat milk solids and flavorings or fruits.

Filled milk is a dairy product containing milk solids. However, the milkfat in filled milk has been replaced with other types of fats or oils. *Imitation milk* is not a dairy product. It contains neither milkfat nor milk solids.

Cream

Types of cream are defined according to the amount of milkfat they contain. *Heavy whipping cream* has the most fat, followed by *light whipping cream.* Both hold air when whipped, and they are often used in desserts. *Light cream,* or *coffee cream,* has less fat than light whipping cream. You can use it as a table cream and in cooking. *Half-and-half* is made from half milk and half cream. It has the least amount of fat, so it is the lowest in calories (kilojoules).

Sour cream is made from light cream. Special organisms are added to the cream to give it a thick, creamy body and sour flavor. *Sour half-and-half* has

fewer calories (kilojoules) than sour cream because it has less fat. You can use sour half-and-half and sour cream interchangeably, except in baking where fat content can change the final product.

Nondairy coffee whiteners, whipped toppings, and *imitation sour cream products* do not contain real cream. These products contain vegetable fats, soy protein, emulsifiers, vegetable gums, and other substances to give them the body and appearance of dairy products.

Concentrated Milk Products

Removing water from fluid milk produces concentrated milk products. These products can be canned or dried.

Evaporated milk is sterilized, homogenized whole or skimmed milk that has had some of the water removed. When diluted with an equal amount of water, it matches fresh milk in nutritional value. You can then use it in place of fluid, fresh milk for drinking and in recipes. Evaporated milk costs more than fluid whole milk.

Sweetened condensed milk is whole or skimmed milk with some of the water removed and a sweetener added. It is used most often in cooking and baking. Sugar affects the flavor and texture of cooked and baked products. Therefore, you should use condensed milk only in recipes that call for it. Sweetened condensed milk cannot be used interchangeably with evaporated milk. You cannot dilute it and use it in place of fluid, fresh milk, either.

Removing most of the water from whole milk produces dried whole milk. Removing most of the water and fat from whole milk produces nonfat dry milk. Dried whole milk is used most often in baby formulas. Nonfat dry milk can be used in home baking. You can also reconstitute it and use it like fluid milk. When you add water, it costs one-half to two-thirds less than fluid milk.

Frozen Dairy Desserts

Ice cream, frozen yogurt, and sherbet all are frozen dairy desserts. Ice cream is made from a pasteurized mixture of milk, cream, sugar, stabilizers, flavorings, and sometimes eggs. Frozen yogurt contains active yogurt cultures, sugar, stabilizer, nonfat solids, and flavorings. Sherbet is a pasteurized mixture of sugar, milk solids, stabilizer, fruit juice, and water.

The names of frozen dairy dessert products used on labels indicate fat content. Product names may include one of the following adjectives: reduced fat, light, lowfat, or fat-free. If the label does not include one of these adjectives, you may assume that the product is a "regular" product. Regular products contain the most fat. *Reduced fat products* must show at least a 25 percent reduction in fat over regular products. *Light products* must show at least a 50 percent reduction in fat over regular products. *Lowfat products* must not contain more than 3 grams of fat per serving. *Fat-free products* must contain less than 0.5 grams of fat per serving. See 17-3.

Butter

Churning pasteurized and specially cultured sweet or sour cream produces butter. The churned product is usually salted and artificially colored.

Sweet butter is butter made without salt. Salt acts as a preservative, so sweet butter is more perishable than salted butter. It may also cost more.

Whipped butter is butter that has air whipped into it. It is more perishable and more costly than regular butter.

Margarine

Margarine is not a dairy product. It is included in this discussion because many people use it as a butter substitute. Some people use margarine in place of butter because it is less expensive. However, some people choose margarine for health reasons.

Butter is high in cholesterol. Most margarines, on the other hand, are cholesterol free. It is important to note, however, that full margarine contains the same amount of fat and calories as butter. Butter contains milkfat, but margarine contains vegetable oil, animal fat, or some of each. For a margarine lower in saturated fats, choose one that lists a liquid vegetable oil as the first ingredient on the label.

Be a Clever Consumer

Be sure to check the date stamped on dairy product containers when choosing items at the store. Look for products stamped with the furthest date. Keep in mind that the date on dairy products is a pull date. This is the last day a store should sell the product. If stored properly, dairy products remain wholesome and can be consumed for a few days past the pull date.

The ingredients in margarine are emulsified with cultured milk, sweet milk, nonfat dry milk solids, water, or a mixture of these. Salt and color are added for flavor and appearance. Many margarines are fortified with vitamin A.

Cost of Dairy Products

Milk and milk products differ in cost depending on fat content, form, and size of container. Whole milk usually costs more than skim milk. Fluid skim milk usually costs more than nonfat dry milk. Ounce for ounce (milliliter for milliliter), milk sold in small containers usually costs more than milk sold in large containers. Thus, fluid milk usually is a better buy in large containers.

Place of purchase and brand also affect milk costs. Home-delivered milk costs more than milk you buy at a store. The cost of all milk and milk products also varies according to the region of the country where purchased and the brand.

The cost of frozen desserts depends on the amount of fat. The kind and amount of extra ingredients, flavorings, container size, and brand also affect cost. Rich ice cream with many added ingredients costs the most.

The cost of butter depends on packaging, grade, and brand. Bulk butter often costs less than butter packaged in small amounts. Lower grades and house brands often cost less than higher grades and national brands.

Margarines differ in cost according to kind of oil used, packaging, and brand. Generally, margarines made with a combination of fats cost less than those made with pure vegetable oil. Margarine packaged in quarters costs less than margarine that is whipped and packaged in tubs. House brands cost less than national brands.

Fat Content of Ice Cream Products

Type of Ice Cream	Typical Percent Milkfat	Fat per ½ Cup (125 mL) Serving
Regular ice cream	10.0% or more	6-8 g
Reduced fat ice cream	7.0%	4-5 g
Light ice cream	5.0%	3 g
Lowfat ice cream	3.0%	3 g or less
Fat-free ice cream	0.5%	0 g

17-3 Reading labels can help you determine the fat content of ice cream products.

Storing Dairy Products

All dairy products are highly perishable. Cover them and store them in the coldest part of the refrigerator. Pour out just the amount of milk and cream you intend to use and return the rest to the refrigerator. Keep containers tightly closed to prevent contamination and off flavors.

You can store sealed UHT milk products unrefrigerated for up to six months. Once opened, you should refrigerate them and use them like other milk products.

Cover ice cream and other frozen desserts tightly and store them in the coldest part of the freezer. If frozen desserts become soft, large ice crystals will form when they are refrozen. This damages their texture. For best quality, use these products within a month.

Store dried and canned milk products in a cool, dry place. Reseal opened packages of dried milk carefully. Store reconstituted dry milk like fresh milk. Cover the unused portions of canned milk products and store them in the refrigerator. Use them within a few days.

Refrigerate all butter and margarine. Do not let either product stand at room temperature longer than necessary. Freezing will extend the life of both butter and margarine. Sweet butter and whipped butter benefit most from freezing as they spoil most quickly.

Cheese

Few foods are as versatile as cheese. Its many flavors, textures, and nutrients make it suitable for any meal or snack. See 17-4.

Cheese is a concentrated form of milk, so it is an excellent source of complete protein. A 1 pound (450 g) package of cheese contains the protein and fat of about 1 gallon (4 L) of whole milk. Cheeses are important sources of calcium and phosphorus. They are fair sources of thiamin and niacin. Whole milk cheeses are excellent sources of vitamin A.

Kinds of Cheese

All cheese is made from milk. The milk used can be from cows, goats, sheep, reindeer, or other animals. In simple terms, the milk is coagulated, and the *curd* (solid part) is separated from the *whey* (liquid part).

Using different kinds of milk and changing the basic steps of production can produce hundreds of different cheeses, 17-5

Cheeses may be classified in two main groups: unripened and ripened. *Unripened cheeses* are ready for marketing as soon as the whey has been removed. They are not allowed to ripen or age. Cottage cheese, cream cheese, farmer's cheese, and ricotta cheese are examples of unripened cheeses. They are mild in flavor. All are highly perishable. You must refrigerate them and use them within a short time.

U.S. Department of Agriculture

17-4 Cheeses are eaten alone and used as ingredients in appetizers, salads, sandwiches, snacks, and desserts.

Cheese Guide

Kind	Color	Texture	Flavor	Use
Roquefort	White marbled with a blue-green mold	Semisoft	Sharp, tangy	Appetizers, snacks, salads, desserts
Blue cheese	Visible veins of blue-green mold	Semisoft to crumbly	Spicy, tangy	Appetizers, snacks, salads, desserts
Gorgonzola	Tan surface with creamy interior marbled with blue-green mold	Less moist than blue cheese	Tangy, spicy	Snacks, salads, desserts
Cheddar	Light yellow to orange	Hard, smooth	Mild to very sharp	Desserts, snacks, sandwiches, cooking
Colby	Orange	Hard with numerous small holes	Mild	Snacks, sandwiches, cooking
Monterey Jack	Creamy white	Semisoft, smooth	Mild	Snacks, sandwiches
Gouda	Creamy yellow, may have waxy red coating	Hard, open, mealy	Nutlike	Desserts, snacks
Edam	Creamy yellow	Hard, open, mealy	Nutlike	Desserts, snacks
Romano	Yellowish-white interior, greenish-black surface	Hard, granular	Sharp, tangy	Cooking, seasoning
Parmesan	Light yellow with brown or black coating	Granular, brittle	Sharp, spicy	Cooking, seasoning
Mozzarella	Creamy white	Semisoft, plastic	Mild, delicate	Pizza, sandwiches, cooking
Provolone	Yellowish-white	Hard	Mild to sharp or smoky	Salads, cooking
Muenster	Yellow, tan, or white surface with creamy white interior	Semisoft, smooth	Mild to mellow	Sandwiches, snacks
Brick	Light yellow to orange	Semisoft, smooth	Mild	Snacks, sandwiches
Gruyère	Light yellow	Hard with tiny holes	Sweet, nutlike	Snacks, desserts, cooking
Swiss	Light yellow	Hard with large holes	Sweet, nutlike	Sandwiches, snacks, desserts, cooking
Cream cheese	Creamy white	Soft, smooth	Mild	Desserts, snacks, dips
Cottage cheese	White	Soft large or small curds	Delicate	Salads, dips, cooking

17-5 With a broad range of textures and flavors, cheese is a versatile food.

Controlled amounts of bacteria, mold, yeast, or enzymes are used to make **ripened cheeses.** During ripening, the cheese is stored at a specific temperature to develop texture and flavor. Some cheeses become softer and more tender. Others become hard or crumbly. Over 400 varieties of ripened cheeses are produced. Each has a distinctive flavor, ranging from mild to strong.

Some ripened cheeses require further storage to develop flavor. This process is called *aging.* Cheese is aged anywhere from two weeks to two years, depending on the kind.

17-8 Pureed vegetables are used to thicken this rich cream soup.

Tapioca pudding contains milk, tapioca, sugar, salt, eggs, and flavoring. The eggs are separated, and the beaten egg whites are folded into the cooked pudding. Tapioca puddings usually are served chilled.

Bread and *rice puddings* both contain milk, sugar, salt, eggs, and flavoring. You blend these ingredients together. Then you add the rice or bread cubes and bake the puddings until a knife inserted in the center comes out clean. The eggs and milk form a custard around the bread or rice. You may serve bread and rice puddings warm or chilled, with or without cream.

Indian pudding contains milk, cornmeal, eggs, salt, and molasses. You cook the milk, cornmeal, and molasses together until thickened. Then add the remaining ingredients, pour the pudding into a casserole dish, and bake it.

Food Science Principles of Cooking Puddings

All puddings require the use of moderate cooking temperatures to prevent scorching and overcoagulation of the egg and milk proteins. You must separate the starch grains before cooking to prevent lumping. You will usually place rice, bread, and Indian puddings in a dish of hot water during baking. This provides further protection against the overcoagulation of proteins.

Some old-fashioned pudding recipes call for *scalded* milk. Scalding means heating to just below the boiling point. In the past, this step was necessary to kill bacteria in unpasteurized milk. As long as you are using pasteurized milk, however, you can skip this step whenever you see it in a recipe.

When you use eggs in pudding, you should first add a small amount of the hot pudding to the beaten eggs. You can then add the diluted egg mixture to the rest of the hot pudding. (Eggs added directly to a hot mixture can coagulate into lumps.) You should cook the pudding a few minutes longer after adding the eggs to completely cook the egg proteins.

Preparing Cornstarch Pudding

Of all the puddings, cornstarch pudding is the most versatile. You can serve it alone or use it to make fillings for other desserts.

To prepare a basic cornstarch pudding, combine the sugar, salt, and cornstarch in a heavy saucepan and mix well. Add a small amount of the

Used by permission of Dean Foods

17-9 Creamy chocolate pudding is a nutritious dessert.

Fresh fruit is colorful, delicious, low in calories, and high in nutrients.

Fruits

A "Taste" of the World of Work

Extractor-Machine Operator
Tends machines that extract juice from citrus fruit.

Produce Broker
Sells bulk shipments of produce to wholesalers and other buyers for growers and shippers on a commission basis.

Grove Supervisor
Supervises and coordinates activities of workers engaged in cultivating, pruning, spraying, thinning, propping, and harvesting tree crops, such as apples, lemons, oranges, and peaches.

Terms to Know

berries	underripe fruit
drupes	immature fruit
pomes	enzymatic browning
citrus fruits	sauté
melons	fritters
tropical fruits	

Objectives

After studying this chapter, you will be able to
❑ describe how to properly select and store fruits.
❑ discuss the principles and methods of fruit cookery.
❑ prepare fruits, preserving their color, texture, flavor, and nutrients.

Photo Courtesy of Borden, Inc.

18-3 A fresh fruit salad adds color and texture variety to a meal.

removes any soil, sand, or pesticide residues that may be present. Never let fruits soak, as this may cause them to lose some of their water-soluble nutrients.

Serve raw fruits whole or sliced. Some fruits, such as bananas and peaches, darken when exposed to the air. This is called *enzymatic browning.* Dipping these fruits in lemon, orange, grapefruit, or pineapple juice will prevent enzymatic browning and make them look more appealing.

Use a sharp, thin-bladed knife when peeling raw fruit. Peel as thinly as possible to preserve nutrients found just under the skin.

If you are sectioning citrus fruits, cut a small slice from the top of the fruit. Pare deeply enough to remove the rind and membrane, but do not cut into the fruit itself. Use a sawing motion as you cut. This technique will prevent bruising and keep juice losses to a minimum. Cut toward the center of the fruit along the membrane, removing one section at a time. Hold the fruit over a bowl to catch the juices as you cut.

Food Science Principles of Cooking Fruit

People cook some fruits, like rhubarb, to make them more palatable and easier to digest. They cook other fruits, like pears, to give variety to a menu. Cooking allows you to use overripe fruits that are past prime eating quality. For instance, you

can use apples that are becoming overripe to make applesauce.

During cooking, several changes take place within fruit. Cellulose softens and makes fruit easier to digest. Colors change. Heat-sensitive and water-soluble nutrients may be lost. Flavors become less acidic and more mellow.

Overcooked fruits become mushy. They lose color, nutrients, natural flavor, and shape. Correctly cooked fruits can retain these characteristics.

Fruits that undergo enzymatic browning will retain their colors if cooked with a small amount of lemon or orange juice. Water-soluble nutrients will be retained if you cook the fruit in a small amount of water just until tender. Natural flavors will be retained if you do not overcook the fruit. Shape will be retained if you cook the fruit in a sugar syrup instead of plain water.

Sometimes you will want a fruit to retain its shape; other times you will not. For instance, if you are making applesauce, you will want the apples to lose their shape and form a smooth pulp. If you are poaching apple slices for a garnish, however, you will want the slices to retain their shape.

Methods of Cooking Fruit

You can prepare fruits by cooking them in liquid. You might also choose to bake, broil, fry, or microwave fruits.

Cooking Fruit in Liquid

You can use water or a sugar syrup when cooking fruits in liquid. Fruits cooked in a sugar syrup will retain their shape. Those cooked in water will not. How you intend to use the fruit will determine the cooking method. See 18-4

When you cook fruits in syrup, use a two to one ratio of water to sugar. (Too much sugar will cause the fruit to harden.) Use a low temperature and cook the fruit just until it is tender and translucent. Serve cooked fruit warm or chilled.

When you cook fruits in water, use as little water as possible. Cook the fruit over low heat until tender, then add sugar as your recipe directs. When you add sugar at the end of cooking, it will thin a fruit sauce. Thus, the amount of cooking water used must be small so the sauce will not be too thin. For a smoother sauce, force the cooked fruit through a sieve or run it through a food mill. Serve cooked fruit pulp warm or chilled.

Baking Fruit

You can bake apples, pears, and bananas. Baked fruits should be tender, but they should keep their shape. If you bake a fruit in its skin, the

Good Manners Are Good Business

Business travelers often find themselves entertaining clients in hotel restaurants, where fresh fruits frequently appear on breakfast and lunch buffets. Knowing the proper way to eat fresh fruits will help you make a good impression in business settings. Peel a banana and set the skin aside on your plate. Break off pieces of the banana with your fingers to eat it. You also can cut bananas with a knife and fork. Use your fingers to pick up fresh strawberries by the hulls. Peel and quarter kiwifruit with a knife. Then cut them into bite-size pieces with a fork. Discreetly remove fruit seeds from your mouth with your fingers and place them on your plate.

18-4 The pear and apple chunks in this fruit sauce kept their shape because they were cooked in a sugar syrup.

skin will hold in the steam that forms during baking. This steam cooks the interior of the fruit. If you skin the fruit before baking, a covered casserole dish will serve the same purpose as the skin. Bake fruits in a small amount of liquid just until they are tender.

Broiling Fruit

Bananas, grapefruit halves, and pineapple slices often are broiled. Sprinkle these fruits with brown sugar or drizzle them with honey before broiling. Fruits broil quickly, so watch them carefully to prevent overcooking.

Frying

You can fry some fruits in a small amount of fat in a skillet. This is called *sautéing.* You can also dip fruits into a batter and deep-fat fry them. These deep-fat fried fruits are called *fritters.* All fried fruits should be tender, but they should retain their shape.

Microwaving Fruit

Fruits cooked in a microwave oven maintain their flavors and nutrients because they cook quickly using little or no water. When microwaving several pieces of fruit, choose pieces of similar size to ensure even cooking. Pierce fruits covered with a tight skin if you are microwaving them whole.

When microwaving fruit, the type of fruit, its size, and its ripeness will affect cooking time. Fruits with a higher moisture content, such as strawberries, will cook more quickly than dense fruits, like rhubarb. Berries and other small pieces of fruit will cook more quickly than larger pieces like apples. Ripe fruit requires less cooking time than firmer, underripe fruit.

Preparing Preserved Fruits

You can serve canned fruits right from the can. You may drain them or serve them in the syrup or juice in which they were packed. You can use canned fruits like fresh or frozen fruits. Unless a recipe tells you otherwise, drain canned fruits well before using them in baked products.

Use frozen fruits in the same ways you use fresh and canned fruits. Completely thawing frozen fruits causes them to become soft and mushy. Therefore, serve frozen fruits with a few ice crystals remaining in them.

You can use dried fruits for cooking or baking or eat them right from the box. Before cooking, soak dried fruits in hot water for about an hour. Soaking helps restore the moisture removed during the drying process. Cooking softens the fruit tissues. Because dried fruits vary in moisture content, follow package directions. See 18-5.

California Prune Board

18-5 Prunes add sweetness and a moist, chewy texture to baked goods.

Summary

You can classify fruits as berries, drupes, pomes, citrus fruits, melons, or tropical fruits. No matter what class they are in, however, fruits are high in nutrition. Choose fresh fruits that are mature, ripe, and high in quality. You should wash all fruits except berries before storing them in the refrigerator.

You might choose canned, frozen, and dried fruits when their fresh counterparts are not available. Look for undented cans and solidly frozen packages. Store canned and dried fruits in a cool, dry place. Store frozen fruits in the freezer until you are ready to serve them.

Wash fresh fruits and cut them as desired for serving raw. If necessary, treat cut fruits to prevent enzymatic browning.

Cooking fruits affects their texture, color, flavor, and nutrients. You can cook fruit in liquid. You can also bake, broil, or microwave it.

You can serve canned fruits right from the can or drain them to use in recipes. Serve frozen fruits with a few ice crystals on them. Eat dried fruits straight from the package, or soak them and cook them.

Review What You Have Read

Write your answers on a separate sheet of paper.
1. List the six fruit families and give one example of each.
2. The citrus fruits are the best dietary sources of _____.
    A. vitamin A
    B. the B vitamins
    C. vitamin C
    D. calcium
3. Explain the difference between underripe and immature fruit.
4. Give three guidelines for buying fresh fruit.
5. True or false. Unlike most fruits, berries should not be washed before they are stored in a refrigerator.
6. When are fresh fruits usually least expensive?
7. What types of liquids are canned fruits packed in?
8. Some fruits darken when they are exposed to air. This is called _____.
9. Describe three changes that take place in fruit during cooking.
10. True or false. Fruits will retain their shape if they are cooked in syrup instead of water.
11. What is the suggested ratio of water to sugar when making a syrup for cooking fruit?
12. Fruits that are dipped in a batter and deep-fried are called _____.
13. List three factors that will affect the microwave cooking time of fruit.
14. What is usually done to dried fruits before they are cooked?

Build Your Basic Skills

1. Visit the produce section of a grocery store. Compare different varieties of the same fruit in terms of shape, size, and color. Report your findings in class.
2. Slice a banana. Place half of the slices on a plate and set aside. Dip the remaining slices in lemon juice, place on a plate and set aside. Compare slices 30 minutes later.

Build Your Thinking Skills

1. Sample and compare one type of fruit in all its available forms. For instance, compare fresh peaches with canned peaches, frozen peaches, and dried peaches. Note differences in flavor, texture, and color. Make a chart suggesting ways to serve each form.
2. Slice an apple into rings. Cook half of the slices in a sugar syrup and the other half in plain water until tender. Evaluate appearance, texture, and flavor.

Vegetables

Terms to Know

succulents
crisp-tender
chlorophyll
carotene
flavones
anthocyanin
new potatoes

Objectives

After studying this chapter, you will be able to
- ❏ explain how to properly select and store vegetables.
- ❏ discuss food science principles of cooking vegetables.
- ❏ describe methods for cooking vegetables.
- ❏ prepare vegetables, preserving their color, texture, flavor, and nutrients.

Photo courtesy of Mann Packing Co., Inc., Salinas, CA

How to Buy Fresh Vegetables

Vegetables	Choose	Avoid
Asparagus	Rich, green color; tender stalk; closed, compact tips; round spears	Open, moldy, or decayed tips; ribbed spears, excessive sand
Beans (snap)	Bright color, tender bean, crisp pods	Thick, tough, or wilted pods; serious blemishes
Beets	Slender root; rich red color; smooth, round bulb	Wilted, elongated beets; brown, scaly patches
Broccoli	Stems not too thick or tough; firm, compact cluster of small flower buds; dark, deep green color	Open buds; wilted, soft condition; yellow color
Brussels sprouts	Bright green color, tight outer leaves, no blemishes	Yellow or wilted leaves, holes or ragged edges
Cabbage	Firm heads, heavy for size; bright red or green color; fresh; no blemishes	Wilted, decayed, yellow outer leaves; worm holes
Carrots	Bright color; well-rounded, smooth, firm roots	Flabby, decaying roots; patches of green
Cauliflower	Creamy white to white head; comp`ct, clean, solid florets	Discolored spots, wilting
Celery	Bright color; smooth, rigid stalks; fresh leaves	Discoloration; flabby or pithy stalks; wilting
Corn	Ears with plump, not overly mature kernels; fresh, green husks; silk ends free from damage	Yellow, wilted, or dried husks; kernels that are very small, very large, or dark yellow
Cucumbers	Well-shaped, rounded body; bright green color; firm	Signs of wilting, large diameter, yellowing
Lettuce	Bright color, crisp leaves for iceberg and romaine, soft texture for leaf lettuce, no blemishes	Very hard heads of iceberg lettuce, poor color, brown or soft spots, irregular heads
Mushrooms	White, creamycolor; small to medium size; caps closed or slightly open around stem; pink or light tan gills	Badly pitted or discolored caps, wide open caps, dark gills
Onions Yellow, white, and red Green	Hard, smooth, and firm with small necks; papery outer covering Fresh, green tops; well-formed, white bulbs	Wet or soft necks, woody or sprouting areas Yellow, wilted, or decayed tops
Peppers (bell)	Bright color, glossy sheen, firm walls, heavy for size	Thin, wilted; cut or punctured walls; decayed spots
Potatoes	Firm, well-shaped, free from blemishes and sunburn	Large cuts, bruises, or green spots; soft and decaying areas; signs of sprouting or shriveling
Radishes	Plump, round, and firm; medium size; bright red color	Large or flabby radishes, decaying tops
Squash Summer Winter	Tender, well-developed, firm body glossy skin Hard, tough rind; heavy for size	Dull appearance; hard, tough skin Tender rind; cuts; soft, sunken, or moldy spots
Tomatoes	Well-formed, smooth, free from blemishes, bright red for fully ripe, pink to light red and slightly firmer for ripening	Soft spots, moldy areas, growth cracks. bruises

19-2 Choose vegetables that are brightly colored, firm, and at their peak of ripeness.

Cost of Fresh Vegetables

The cost of fresh vegetables depends a great deal on the time of year. Vegetables cost less when purchased during their peak growing season. During other seasons, costs vary due to storage, handling, and shipping charges.

Choosing Canned, Frozen, and Dried Vegetables

Most people prefer fresh vegetables for salads and relish trays. For use in recipes or as hot side dishes, however, canned, frozen, and dried vegetables often work just as well.

Canned Vegetables

Canned vegetables can be whole, sliced, or in pieces. Most are canned in water. A few, like Harvard beets, are canned in sauces.

Most canned vegetables are packed in cans. A few are available in jars. Choose a container size to meet your needs.

Buying and Storing Canned Vegetables

Canned vegetables usually cost less than either frozen or fresh produce. Cost per serving depends on brand, can size, quality, and packing liquid. Choose house brands to save money. Use generic products when making soups and other recipes where appearance is not vital.

Choose cans that are free from dents, bulges, and leaks. Choose the quality that meets your needs and intended use. Store all cans in a cool, dry place. After opening, store unused portions in the refrigerator.

Frozen Vegetables

Frozen vegetables retain the appearance and flavor of fresh vegetables better than canned and dried vegetables. However, freezing may alter their texture somewhat. They are available in paper cartons and plastic bags. Some vegetables are frozen in combinations or in sauces.

Buying and Storing Frozen Vegetables

Frozen vegetables usually cost less than fresh. Green beans are one example. During winter months, frozen green beans are less expensive than fresh green beans. (During the summer months when green beans are in season, fresh beans may cost less than frozen.) Prices will vary according to brand, packaging, size of container, and added ingredients such as butter and sauces.

Choose packages that are clean and solidly frozen. A heavy layer of ice on the package may indicate that the food thawed and refroze. Store packages in the coldest part of the freezer.

Dried Vegetables

A few vegetables are dried. The dried legumes—peas, beans, and lentils—are the most commonly purchased dried vegetables. Most dried vegetables are not graded.

Legumes are high in protein and often used as meat substitutes. Many people use dried navy beans, lima beans, split peas, and lentils in soups. They use pinto and red beans in chili and many Mexican foods. Black-eyed peas are a popular side dish in the South. Garbanzo beans and kidney beans are tasty in salads. Soybeans are the most nutritious of all beans and are most often used in combination with other foods. See 19-3.

Buying and Storing Dried Vegetables

Choose legumes that are uniform in size, free of visible defects, and brightly colored. Store them in covered containers in a cool, dry place.

Courtesy of W. Atlee Burpee & Co.

19-3 Dried beans are an excellent source of incomplete protein and an inexpensive meat extender.

Preparing Vegetables

Vegetables come in a spectrum of colors and a range of flavors. These characteristics, combined with various cooking methods, allow you to use vegetables in countless ways to add interest to meals.

Preparing Raw Vegetables

You can eat many vegetables raw. You probably have eaten raw celery, salad greens, cucumbers, radishes, tomatoes, green peppers, and carrots. You also may have eaten raw cabbage, cauliflower, and broccoli. Raw vegetables are attractive to serve because they are colorful, and their crunchiness adds texture to meals and snacks.

If you have seen a vegetable garden, you know that the edible part of most vegetables grows in or near the soil. Soil can carry harmful bacteria, so it is important to wash all vegetables. Careful washing removes dirt, bacteria, and pesticide residues.

Whether you are preparing fresh vegetables to eat raw or cooked, the first step is to wash and trim them. To wash vegetables, use cool running water or several changes of cool water. A vegetable brush will remove stubborn dirt from crevices. Wash vegetables carefully, but do not let them soak. Water-

soluble nutrients can be lost during soaking. Trim any bruised areas, wilted leaves, and thick stems. When peeling vegetables, use a vegetable scraper or floating edge peeler rather than a paring knife. This will help protect as many nutrients as possible.

You can eat raw vegetables out-of-hand. You can also use them on relish trays and in salads. Cut raw vegetables into pieces that are easy to handle. Sticks, wedges, slices, rings, and florets are good choices.

Raw vegetables taste best when served cold. You can place a relish tray on a bed of ice or arrange vegetables in a bowl lined with ice. Store washed and thoroughly drained vegetables in covered containers in the refrigerator. You can add a few ice cubes or a small amount of cold water to the containers, if desired.

Food Science Principles of Cooking Vegetables

When you cook vegetables, several changes take place. The cellulose (fiber) in vegetables softens to make chewing easier. Starch absorbs water, swells, and becomes easier to digest. Flavors and colors undergo changes, and some of the nutrients may be lost.

Properly cooked vegetables are colorful and flavorful. They also have a *crisp-tender* texture. This means they are tender, but still slightly firm. You can pierce them with a fork, but not too easily.

Overcooked or incorrectly cooked vegetables may suffer undesirable changes in color, texture, and flavor. They also may lose many of their nutrients. The amount of cooking liquid and the cooking time greatly affect nutrient retention and degree of doneness.

Amount of Cooking Liquid

Some nutrients in vegetables, including minerals, vitamin C, and the B vitamins, are water-soluble. They will dissolve in cooking liquid. Vegetables cooked with no added water or in a small amount of water retain more of these water-soluble nutrients.

Cooking Time

Cooking vegetables too long causes several undesirable changes to take place. Heat-sensitive nutrients, such as thiamin, are lost. Unpleasant flavor, texture, and color changes also occur. Vegetables cooked for a short time retain more heat-sensitive nutrients, flavor, texture, and color.

In most cases, you should cook vegetables for a short time in a small amount of water. Serve them when they are crisp-tender.

Protect the Planet

Although vegetable scraps are biodegradable, they will not break down rapidly in a landfill. Therefore, do not throw scraps like potato peelings and carrot tops into the garbage when preparing fresh vegetables. Instead, compost your vegetable trimmings.

Find a small area in your yard where you can start a compost pile. A corner of a garden or a spot behind some bushes will work fine. Collect all your organic kitchen waste in a small covered container. Every day or two, empty the scrap container onto your compost pile. Soon, your scraps will decompose into compost.

You can mix your compost into the soil in your garden. This will condition the soil and create a rich medium for planting new vegetables.

Effect of Cooking on Vegetable Color

Cooking can affect the color of vegetables. For this reason, cooking times and methods may need adjustment to suit the vegetables you are cooking. See 19-4.

Vegetables can be green, yellow, white, or red. *Green vegetables* contain the green pigment **chlorophyll.** Heat affects chlorophyll. Overcooked green vegetables lose their bright green color and look grayish-green.

Some cooks add a pinch of baking soda to the cooking water of a green vegetable. Baking soda is a weak alkali, which will turn chlorophyll a bright green. However, it can also cause a loss of important nutrients. Therefore, you should not use it.

To keep vegetables green, cook them in a small amount of water. Use a short cooking time and keep the pan lid off for the first few minutes of cooking. Then cover the pan for the remainder of the cooking period.

Yellow vegetables contain **carotene,** a source of vitamin A. Carotene gives vegetables a yellow or orange color. Heat does not destroy it. However, it will escape into the cooking liquid if you overcook a yellow vegetable. (Overcooking causes the cellular structure to break down, releasing the carotene.) You should cook most yellow vegetables in a small amount of water with the pan covered.

White vegetables contain pigments called **flavones.** Flavones are soluble in water. If you overcook white vegetables, they turn yellow or dark gray. Take care when cooking to avoid these undesirable color changes.

Red vegetables contain a pigment called **anthocyanin.** An alkali present in some water can affect this pigment. If the cooking water is alkaline, the red pigment will turn purple. A small amount of vinegar or lemon juice (an acid) added to the water will neutralize the alkali and keep red vegetables red. Cook most red vegetables in a small amount of water, with the pan lid on, just until tender. (If you cook beets in the skins, cover them with water.)

Effect of Cooking on Vegetable Flavor

Vegetables can have mild, strong, or very strong flavors. Cooking can affect these flavors. Therefore, you must consider flavors, as well as colors, when deciding how to prepare a vegetable.

Mildly flavored vegetables include green vegetables, such as peas, green beans, and spinach. Yellow vegetables, such as corn; red vegetables, such as beets; and white vegetables, such as parsnips, also have mild flavors. Cook most mildly flavored vegetables in a small amount of water, with the pan covered for a short time.

Strongly flavored vegetables, such as cabbage, broccoli, Brussels sprouts, yellow turnips, and rutabagas, are exceptions to general cooking rules. Cover these vegetables with water. Cook them in an uncovered pan for a short time. Following these guidelines will allow some of the strong flavor substances to escape into the water and air.

Very strongly flavored vegetables, such as onions and leeks, should also be covered with water. You should cook them in an uncovered pan for a longer time. As they cook, these vegetables will release strong flavor substances and develop a milder flavor.

Methods of Cooking Vegetables

You can cook vegetables by boiling, steaming, pressure cooking, baking, frying, stir-frying, broiling, and microwaving. Regardless of the cooking method, vegetables cooked in their skins retain more nutrients. Consider your taste preferences and the other items in your menu when choosing a cooking method.

Cooking Vegetables in Water

Use a pan with a tight-fitting lid when cooking vegetables in water. Add salt to a small amount of water and bring the water to a boil. Add the vegetables, cover, and quickly bring to a boil again. Then reduce the heat and cook the vegetables at a

Photo courtesy of Mann Packing Co., Inc., Salinas, CA

19-4 The color of vegetables can help you determine the method you should use to cook them.

simmering temperature until they are crisp-tender. Drain and serve the vegetables immediately.

After vegetables have cooked, do not throw away the cooking liquid. It contains many valuable nutrients. You can serve a small amount of the cooking liquid with the vegetables in a separate dish. If you do not want to use the liquid right away, freeze it in small amounts. (Ice cube trays work well.) Later, you can add the frozen liquid to sauces, soups, and gravies.

Steaming Vegetables

You can steam young tender vegetables that cook quickly. To steam vegetables, place them in a steaming basket over simmering water. Tightly cover the pan and steam the vegetables until they are tender. You can successfully steam shredded cabbage, broccoli, diced root vegetables, celery, sweet corn, and French-style (thinly sliced) green beans.

Pressure Cooking Vegetables

To pressure cook vegetables, follow the directions that accompany the pressure cooker. The pressure in a pressure cooker produces high temperatures, so foods cook quickly. Time vegetables carefully to prevent overcooking.

Baking Vegetables

You can bake some vegetables in their skins. You can also peel them. Wrap peeled vegetables in foil or place them in a covered casserole with a small amount of liquid before baking. Potatoes, tomatoes, and onions are popular vegetables for baking. Baking takes longer than other cooking methods.

Frying Vegetables

You can dip vegetables in batter and deep-fry them. You can sauté them in a small amount of fat. They also can be stir-fried in very little fat. See 19-5.

19-5 This colorful vegetable stir-fry takes just minutes to cook.

Stir-frying works well with succulent vegetables. To stir-fry vegetables, shred them or cut them into small pieces. Place the vegetables in a heavy pan or wok containing a small amount of melted fat. (The fat helps prevent sticking.) Cover the pan tightly and cook the vegetables just until tender. (The lid holds in steam, which cooks the vegetables.)

Broiling Vegetables

Tomato halves and eggplant slices often are broiled. To broil vegetables, brush the cut surfaces with oil or melted fat. Place the vegetables under the broiling unit and broil until tender. Because vegetables cook quickly under the broiler, you must watch them carefully.

Microwaving Vegetables

Vegetables cooked in a microwave oven retain their shapes, colors, flavors, and nutrients. This is due to the short cooking time and the use of little or no cooking liquid.

Use high power to cook vegetables in a microwave oven. Remember to allow standing time for vegetables to finish cooking. Stir vegetable dishes during the cooking period to redistribute heat. Rearrange whole vegetables during the cooking period to ensure even cooking. Vegetables that have tight skins can explode when cooked in a microwave oven. To prevent this, you should pierce their skins in several places.

You can prepare frozen vegetables in a microwave oven as easily as fresh vegetables. Slit pouches of vegetables to allow steam to escape. Place vegetables that do not come in pouches in a microwavable casserole for cooking.

Potatoes

Although potatoes are a vegetable, they are treated somewhat differently from other vegetables. The cooking method followed to prepare potatoes depends on the type of potato being used.

Potatoes are classified on the basis of appearance and use. They can be long or round with white skins or round with red skins. They can be all-purpose potatoes, baking potatoes, or new potatoes. (*New potatoes* are not a variety. They are potatoes that are sent to market immediately after harvesting.)

New potatoes and round red varieties are best for boiling, oven-browning, frying, and making potato salad. This is because these varieties hold their shape when cooked. Baking or russet potatoes are best for baking and mashing because they have a mealy texture. (They break apart easily.) You can use all-purpose potatoes for both baking and boiling.

Preparing Potatoes

Four popular potato preparations are boiling, mashing, frying, and baking. To prepare boiled potatoes, wash, peel, and halve potatoes. Cover the potatoes with lightly salted water and simmer until tender. (You can also cook potatoes in one inch (2.5 cm) of simmering, salted water. Check them during cooking to be sure the water has not boiled away. Add more water, if needed.) Drain potatoes and season with butter or margarine, salt, and pepper.

Prepare potatoes for mashing the same as boiled potatoes. Then add butter, milk, and salt and beat the potatoes with an electric mixer or mash them by hand, 19-6.

People enjoy fried potatoes as home fries, hash browns, potato pancakes, and French fries. To prepare French fried potatoes, cut washed, peeled potatoes into strips about ¼ inch thick. Place the strips in ice water to keep them from browning until you have finished cutting all the potatoes. (Do not allow potatoes to soak as they will absorb water, causing the French fries to be soggy.) Dry potatoes thoroughly before frying to prevent the fat from spattering. Fry potatoes in 375°F (190°C) fat until they are golden brown. Drain the potatoes on paper towels.

To prepare baked potatoes, scrub potatoes under cool running water. Oil potato skins lightly and pierce potatoes in several places with a fork. This prevents steam from building up inside the skin, which could cause the potato to explode. Bake potatoes in a 400°F (200°C) oven until they are tender, about 40 to 60 minutes. (You can adjust baking time and temperature so potatoes can bake with other foods.)

Good Manners Are Good Business

Eating catsup with French fries is acceptable during informal business meals. However, you should not pour catsup over the French fries. Instead, pour a small amount on the side of your plate. Then dip your French fries as you eat them.

This guideline applies to all bottled condiment sauces being used on any food. The exception is that you can pour condiments directly on sandwiches.

19-6 Light, fluffy mashed potatoes are a traditional accompaniment to turkey and dressing.

Preparing Canned, Frozen, and Dried Vegetables

Canned vegetables have already been cooked. Many vegetables suffer changes in color and texture during canning. Therefore, they will look and taste better if you heat them no more than necessary before serving.

To prepare canned vegetables, place the vegetables and the liquid from the can in a saucepan. Cook over low heat until the vegetables are heated through. Add seasonings to taste.

Frozen vegetables have already been blanched (preheated in boiling water or steam for a short time). Blanching reduces the cooking time needed to about half that needed for fresh vegetables.

To prepare frozen vegetables, bring a small amount of salted water to a boil. Add the vegetables and cover the saucepan. Quickly bring the water back to a boil. Then reduce the heat and simmer the vegetables until tender. Add seasonings to taste.

You must soak dried peas and beans before cooking unless you are using them in soup. You may soak them overnight in cold water or for about an hour in boiling water. You should use the soaking water for cooking to retain the water-soluble nutrients. Lentils need no soaking. Reconstitute other dried vegetables according to package directions.

Serving Vegetables

You can serve vegetables in many creative and delicious ways. Some people prefer their vegetables served simply, with just butter and salt. Others enjoy vegetables topped with crisp onion rings, chopped nuts, grated lemon rind, crumbled bacon bits, or sliced hard-cooked eggs. With just a little extra effort, you can cover a vegetable with a creamy white sauce or a tasty cheese sauce. Glazes of brown sugar or honey are also popular. See 19-7.

Cottage cheese is a tasty, lowfat alternative to sour cream for topping baked potatoes. Try sprinkling boiled potatoes with chopped parsley. Shape mashed potatoes into patties and brown them in shortening. You can also make them into colcannon by combining them with melted margarine and shredded, cooked cabbage. Brown small whole potatoes around a roast. French-fried potato nests will hold creamed chicken or diced carrots.

Dole Food Company

19-7 A creamy garlic sauce adds texture and flavor interest to a fresh vegetable side dish.

Summary

You can group vegetables according to flavor, color, or the part of the plant from which they come. Vegetables are low in fat, high in fiber, and rich in vitamins and minerals. When buying fresh vegetables, choose items that are in their peak growing season to get the best buy. Select medium-sized pieces that have good color and are free from bruises and decay. Store most vegetables in the refrigerator.

Canned, frozen, and dried vegetables can be a good buy when fresh vegetables are not in season. Choose packages that are intact. Store frozen vegetables in the freezer. Keep canned and dried vegetables in a cool, dry place.

To prepare fresh vegetables, begin by washing and trimming them. Cooking affects the pigments in green, yellow, white, and red vegetables. Cook most vegetables for a short time in a small amount of liquid. This will help preserve flavor, texture, color, and nutrients.

Aside from cooking in liquid, you can also steam, pressure cook, bake, fry, broil, and microwave vegetables. The method you choose will depend on your taste preferences. Canned and frozen vegetables cook more quickly than fresh vegetables. Dried vegetables often require soaking before you can cook them.

Review What You Have Read

Write your answers on a separate sheet of paper.
1. List the eight parts of plants used as vegetable classifications. Give an example of a vegetable from each group.
2. Vegetables with a high moisture content are called _____.
3. List three guidelines to follow when shopping for fresh vegetables.
4. Why is it important to wash fresh vegetables? How should you wash them?
5. List three changes that take place in vegetables when you cook them.
6. True or false. Baking soda should be added to the cooking water of green vegetables to help them retain their color.
7. The pigments in white vegetables are called _____.
   A. anthocyanin
   B. carotene
   C. chlorophyll
   D. flavones
8. List the three flavor categories of vegetables and give cooking guidelines for each.
9. List four methods for cooking vegetables. Describe two.
10. How can vegetable cooking liquid be used?
11. What type of potato should you use when making mashed potatoes?
12. True or false. Canned vegetables have already been cooked.

Build Your Basic Skills

1. Compare the unit cost of a vegetable in fresh, frozen, and canned form.
2. Cook red cabbage in water made alkaline with baking soda and in water made acidic with vinegar. Compare color.

Build Your Thinking Skills

1. Evaluate the flavor, color, and texture of equal amounts of green beans prepared in each of the following ways:
   A. in a small amount of water, with the pan covered, for a short time.
   B. in a small amount of water, with the pan uncovered for the first few minutes of cooking, for a short time.
   C. in a large amount of water, with the pan covered, for a long time.
   D. in a small amount of water, with baking soda added, with the pan covered, for a short time.
2. Prepare two portions of small, whole onions. Use a small amount of water and a covered pan for one portion. Use a large amount of water and an uncovered pan for the other portion. Compare flavor and aroma.

Chapter 20

Salads, Casseroles, and Soups

A "Taste" of the World of Work

Salad Maker
Prepares salads, fruits, melons, and gelatin desserts.

Soup Cook
Prepares, seasons, and cooks soups and other foodstuffs for consumption in eating establishments.

Spice Sales Representative
Sells spices to retail food stores, wholesale grocers, restaurants, hotels, or institutions.

Terms to Know

salad
temporary emulsion
permanent emulsion
casserole
stock soup
strain
bouillon

consommé
clarify
herb
spice
blend
bouquet garni
gourmet

Objectives

After studying this chapter, you will be able to
❑ prepare attractive and nutritious salads and three basic dressings.
❑ prepare casseroles and stock-based soups.

National Live Stock and Meat Board

Salads, casseroles, and soups add versatility to menus. You may serve them as the main course or as an accompaniment to a meal. These combination dishes are nutritious as well as economical. They include a variety of ingredients, and preparing them can be a way to use leftovers.

Salads

The salad was not invented in the United States. However, the United States does receive credit for making salad an important part of meal planning.

What is a salad? A *salad* is a combination of raw and/or cooked ingredients, usually served cold with a dressing. All salads are nutritious. The vegetables, fruits, and protein foods they contain contribute important nutrients to the diet.

Kinds of Salads

Most salads fit into one of five groups: protein, pasta, vegetable, fruit, or gelatin. Most people serve *protein salads* as a main dish. When served with crisp crackers or warm rolls, they are a complete meal.

There are two common types of protein salads. One type has the protein foods cut into small pieces and combined with a dressing. Chicken, ham, crab, and egg salads are examples of this type. The second type of protein salad has the protein food cut into strips or slices. Then the pieces are attractively arranged on a plate with cold vegetables or fruits. A chef salad is an example of this type.

People often serve *pasta salads* as accompaniments. You may serve pasta salads that include protein foods as main dish salads. Pasta salads are a combination of cooked pasta, vegetables, and a dressing. They may also include meat, poultry, seafood, or cheese. You may or may not choose to serve pasta salads with salad greens. When making most pasta salads, you will toss the ingredients with the dressing several hours before serving. This gives the flavors a chance to blend.

Serve *vegetable salads* as accompaniments or appetizers. They are meant to stimulate the appetite, so they are small and light. You can make them from salad greens; raw vegetables; or cold, cooked vegetables. Tossed salad, coleslaw, and three bean salad are examples of vegetable salads.

Serve *fruit salads* as accompaniments or desserts. You can also arrange fruit on a plate with cottage cheese and serve it as a main dish salad. You may use canned, frozen, or fresh fruits. Serve

them on a bed of greens or in a hollowed fruit shell. Serve them alone or combined with whipped cream, gelatin, or a sweet dressing. See 20-1.

Gelatin salads may contain fruits, vegetables, protein foods, or a combination of all three. The salad ingredients are suspended in a flavored liquid thickened with gelatin. (You cannot use fresh pineapple in a gelatin salad. It contains enzymes that will prevent the gelatin from setting.)

You can use commercial fruit flavored gelatin, or you can mix fruit and vegetable juices with unflavored gelatin.

Parts of a Salad

Most salads have three parts: a base, a body, and a dressing. A salad also may have a garnish.

20-1 A bed of spinach provides an attractive color contrast for bright red apple wedges.

The *base* is the foundation upon which you place the main salad ingredients. It provides a contrast in color with the body of the salad. It also keeps the serving dish from looking bare. You will often use salad greens to make the salad base.

The *body* is the main part of the salad. The type of salad determines the body. You can use vegetables, fruits, pasta, protein foods, or a combination of several foods to make the salad body.

The *dressing* is a sauce served on or with a salad. It adds flavor to the salad and sometimes serves as a garnish. Avoid using too much dressing. The dressing should not mask the flavors of the other salad ingredients. Instead, it should complement them.

If you use a *garnish,* its main purpose is to add eye appeal. It should be simple and should complement the other salad ingredients. Grated hard-cooked egg yolk, pimiento strips, and vegetable curls are popular salad garnishes.

Preparing Salad Greens

Many people think of iceberg lettuce when they think of a salad. However, many other types of greens can add flavor, color, and texture variety to salads. Romaine, Boston bibb, watercress, spinach, escarole, endive, and leaf lettuce are some of the many salad greens available. A combination of three or four different greens will add eye appeal to a salad.

You must treat all salad greens carefully to preserve both texture and nutrients. Trim all bruised and inedible portions from greens. To remove the core from iceberg lettuce, strike the bottom of the head sharply against a counter. Remove the core with your fingers. See 20-2.

Cleaning Iceberg Lettuce

A – Grasp the head firmly. Strike the core end sharply against the counter or wooden cutting board.

B – Pull the core from the head with a twisting motion.

C – Run cold water into the hole to thoroughly wash the head.

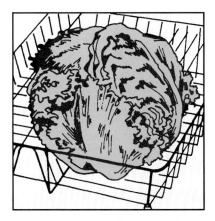

D – Drain lettuce well. Use a colander or dish rack.

E – Place cleaned and drained lettuce in a plastic bag. Store it in the refrigerator.

Adapted from Western Iceberg Lettuce

20-2 When cleaning iceberg lettuce, follow these step-by-step directions.

Wash greens carefully to remove all soil and pesticide residues that may be present. Drain them well. The small amount of water that clings to leaves and stems will help crisp the greens during refrigeration. Wrap greens loosely in plastic film or a damp cloth, or store them in a vegetable keeper.

To prevent nutrient losses, it is best not to clean salad greens too far in advance. You can store carefully prepared greens for a few hours in the refrigerator. They will be crisp when ready to serve and will still retain important vitamins and minerals.

You will usually serve salad greens in bite-sized pieces. Never cut greens; tear them instead. Cutting salad greens with a knife can cause bruising.

Preparing Other Salad Ingredients

You must carefully wash all fresh fruits and vegetables for use in salads. However, you should not allow them to soak during cleaning. Soaking may result in the loss of water-soluble nutrients.

After washing, drain excess water from fresh fruits and vegetables. Also drain liquid from canned fruits and vegetables. Extra liquid will make salads look and taste watery.

Most fruits and vegetables used in salads are very perishable. Preserving their freshness is important because freshness affects color, texture, and flavor. If fruits and vegetables are fresh, they will look bright and be crisp and full of flavor. If they lose their freshness, they will look dull and have little taste.

To preserve freshness, store fruits and vegetables in covered containers in the refrigerator. Use them as soon as possible after purchase. Storing ingredients too long may cause them to lose nutrients.

Salad Dressings

There are three basic types of salad dressings: French, mayonnaise, and cooked. You make a true *French dressing* by combining oil, vinegar, and seasonings. Oil does not mix with vinegar, so the dressing will separate on standing. This is called a **temporary emulsion.** You must shake or stir French dressing to mix it each time you use it.

You make *mayonnaise* from vinegar (or lemon juice), oil, seasonings, and egg yolk. It is uncooked. Mayonnaise does not separate because the egg yolk (the emulsifying agent) surrounds the droplets of oil and keeps them suspended in the liquid (vinegar or lemon juice). This is called a **permanent emulsion.** See 20-3.

Mayonnaise
(Makes 1¼ cups)

1	egg yolk	1	egg yolk
	dash pepper		dash pepper
½	teaspoon salt	2	mL salt
2	tablespoons lemon juice or vinegar*	30	mL lemon juice or vinegar*
½	teaspoon sugar	2	mL sugar
1	cup salad oil	250	mL salad oil
½	teaspoon dry mustard	2	mL dry mustard

1. Place egg yolk, salt, sugar, mustard, and pepper in a small, deep mixing bowl.
2. Beat at low speed until all ingredients are mixed.
3. Add lemon juice or vinegar, blending well.
4. Add oil, a few drops at a time, beating constantly until ⅓ of the oil has been used.
5. Continue to add the oil one tablespoon (15 mL) at a time. Beat vigorously after each addition until all of the oil is blended and the mixture is thick.
6. Pour into a jar, cover, and store in the refrigerator.

*You can use 1 tablespoon (15 mL) lemon juice and 1 tablespoon (15 mL) vinegar.

Per tablespoon (15 mL): 100 Cal. (98% from fat), 0 g protein, 0 g carbohydrate, 11 g fat, 14 mg cholesterol, 0 g fiber, 55 mg sodium.

20-3 The egg yolk in mayonnaise causes a permanent emulsion to form.

Good Manners Are Good Business

Some salad makers do not tear their greens into bite-sized pieces. Do not be unnerved if someone serves you such a salad at a business meal. You should not try to stuff a large piece of lettuce into your mouth. Most salad greens are tender enough to cut with your salad fork. However, if you have trouble, feel free to use your knife to help you cut one bite at a time.

A *cooked salad dressing* looks like mayonnaise. However, you thicken it with a food starch, such as cornstarch or flour. It also contains milk or water, an acid ingredient, such as lemon juice, and a small amount of oil. Egg and butter are optional ingredients. Cooked salad dressings are permanent emulsions.

You can add other ingredients to a basic cooked dressing. For a fruit salad, you might add whipped cream and crushed pineapple. For Thousand Island dressing, add catsup, pickle relish, and chopped hard-cooked egg.

You will usually pour the dressing over the salad just before serving. For some salads, you will combine the salad ingredients with the dressing several hours before serving. This gives the flavors a chance to blend.

Assembling the Salad

Consider flavor, texture, and color when you choose salad ingredients. Avoid too many strongly flavored foods and foods that are all crisp or all soft. Colors should complement each other.

The size of pieces of food in a salad should be easy to manage. However, you should never mince pieces. Foods cut too finely may form a paste when mixed with the dressing. You may serve canned peaches and pears in large pieces because they are easy to cut with a fork. You should cut other fruits and vegetables into bite-sized pieces.

Treat fruits such as apples, peaches, bananas, and pears with lemon juice after you cut them. This will prevent enzymatic browning, making your salad look fresher and more attractive.

Varying the shape of pieces will add interest to the appearance of the salad. You will usually section citrus fruits. You might cut tomatoes and hard-cooked eggs into wedges. You could slice or shred carrots. You will usually dice meats and poultry. Flake fish with a fork. You might crumble cheese or cut it into strips.

Prepare salads as close to serving time as possible. Have all ingredients chilled and ready. Then begin assembling the salad with the base. The base should not extend over the edge of the plate or serving dish. Arrange the salad body on top of the base. Be artistic but natural. Add the dressing just before serving to prevent wilting. (Salads that must be dressed early to blend flavors are an exception.) Serve salads well chilled.

If you are serving a molded gelatin salad, the salad must be unmolded before serving. Quickly dip the mold into warm water or cover it with a warm, damp cloth for a few seconds. (Be sure not to keep the mold in the water too long, or the gelatin will lose its shape.) Invert the loosened salad onto a serving plate. See 20-4.

Wilton Industries

20-4 This carefully unmolded gelatin salad makes an attractive presentation.

Healthy Living

The dressing can add a lot of fat and calories to a salad. To avoid this, serve dressings separately from salads. This allows diners to add just enough dressing to flavor salad ingredients without smothering them. You might also try some of the lowfat or fat-free dressings that are available. You can even make your own lowfat dressing. Yogurt can substitute for dressing on many salads. Its texture is similar to mayonnaise, but it is much lower in fat. You can flavor plain yogurt with herbs and use it on vegetable salads. Vanilla and fruit-flavored yogurts make creamy toppings for fruit salads.

If you are serving a frozen fruit salad, let the salad soften slightly before serving. This will give the individual flavors a chance to mellow.

Casseroles

A *casserole* is a combination of foods prepared in a single dish. Casseroles are quick and easy to prepare. Some people call them "one-dish meals." A simple salad and dessert are all you need to accompany them. Most casseroles freeze well, so you can prepare them ahead of time for emergency meals.

Casserole Ingredients

Most casseroles are a combination of a protein food, a vegetable, a starch, and a sauce. Many have a topping made of crumbs, cheese, or chopped nuts.

One or several foods high in protein can form the basis of a casserole. Turkey, chicken, ground beef, ham, luncheon meat, cheese, hard-cooked eggs, and seafood make good casserole bases.

You can use any canned, frozen, or cooked fresh vegetable in a casserole. Try peas, green beans, carrots, spinach, or a combination of vegetables.

You can combine starchy foods, such as potatoes, rice, and pasta, with a variety of protein foods and vegetables. Starchy ingredients help make casseroles filling.

A casserole sauce can be as simple as a can of condensed soup or as fancy as a homemade cheese sauce. Experiment with cream of tomato, shrimp, mushroom, or asparagus soups. As an alternative, try adding grated Swiss cheese and a sprinkle of nutmeg to a basic white sauce.

Extras can add crunch, color, and flavor to a casserole. Bean sprouts, Chinese noodles, celery, almonds, and French-fried onion rings add crunch. Tomato wedges, green pepper rings, chopped parsley, and pimiento add color. Horseradish, chili sauce, and chopped onions add flavor.

Toppings help keep a casserole from becoming dry. They also add color, flavor, and texture. Buttered bread crumbs are one popular topping. You might want to try crushed cereals, potato chips, or corn chips mixed with a little melted margarine. Dumplings, biscuits, and cornbread squares also make good toppings.

Putting It Together

The key to putting a casserole together is combining ingredients that complement each other. Personal likes and dislikes will guide you. Experience will also help.

Until you have become experienced in making casseroles, you probably will want to choose just one item out of each group. Use seasonings sparingly at first. Also avoid using too many highly seasoned foods at one time.

Cleanup of baked casseroles will be easier if you put the casserole in a greased dish. You can bake most casseroles in a moderate oven until they are brown and bubbly. Cooking time will depend on the size of the dish and the starting temperature of the casserole. The topping may begin to brown

Be a Clever Consumer

Making casseroles can help you stretch your food dollars. Starchy foods and vegetables help to extend more costly protein ingredients. Since you need to precook casserole ingredients, casseroles can also help you make use of leftovers. Most casseroles are easy to prepare, so they save time as well as money. They are an economical choice when serving a crowd, too.

before the casserole heats through. A piece of aluminum foil placed loosely over the top will keep it from getting too dark. See 20-5.

You can prepare some casseroles on top of the range. They are just as quick and easy as oven casseroles. However, they may require some stirring and a bit more attention during the cooking period.

Unlike soufflés and rare roast beef, most casseroles can wait for latecomers. Some casseroles even improve when they are held for a while. This is because their flavors have a chance to blend. When you will not be serving a casserole right away, cover it tightly and keep it warm in a low oven.

USA Rice Council

20-5 This turkey and rice casserole bakes in just 20 minutes in a moderate oven.

Microwaving Casseroles

Dinners can be ready in minutes when you assemble casseroles from leftovers and heat them in a microwave oven. The microwave oven is also excellent for reheating and defrosting casseroles.

Make casseroles for the microwave with precooked ingredients. You can prepare and serve most of them in the same dish. This saves time and effort in cleanup.

Stock Soups

People throughout the world serve soup in many forms. It can be hot or cold, hearty or light. It can be an appetizer or a main dish. You can eat it alone or serve it with other foods. Soup is most popular in the United States as an appetizer or luncheon dish.

You can make soup in two different ways. Make **stock soups** from meat, poultry, or fish. Make *cream soups* with milk. This chapter discusses stock-based soups. Chapter 17, "Dairy Products," discusses milk-based or cream soups.

Make stocks from less tender meat cuts, poultry, and fish. You might want to add vegetables such as celery and carrots for flavor.

Preparing Stocks

Stocks obtain their flavor from the flavors of their ingredients. Meats, poultry, fish, and vegetables release their flavors slowly. To make stocks rich and flavorful, cook them over low heat for a long time.

To make a stock more flavorful, you will want to increase the amount of surface area exposed to the cooking liquid. To do this, cut the meat, poultry, fish, and vegetables for a stock into small pieces. Also, crack any large bones that you put into a stock pot.

If you are making a *brown stock,* begin by browning the meat. If you are making a *light stock,* use poultry, fish, or unbrowned meat.

To prepare a stock, place all the ingredients in a large pan with a tightly fitted lid. Cover them with cold water, and cook them slowly for several hours at a simmering temperature. The liquid should never boil.

During the first stage of cooking, a foam will rise to the surface. Skim it from the stock. You can use a wooden spoon or paddle for skimming.

During the final stages of cooking, fat will rise to the surface of the stock if you have used fatty meats. You can remove the fat with a baster while the stock is hot. You can also remove fat after it congeals on chilled stock.

After cooking, strain the stock. *Straining* separates the broth from the solid materials. You can serve the meat, poultry, or fish separately or add it back to the stock to make soup. You can also add vegetables, rice, noodles or other pasta, and seasonings, if desired. See 20-6.

Preparing Bouillon and Consommé

Clear broth made from stock is called **bouillon.** Bouillon is most often made from beef stock. Clear, rich-flavored soup made from stock is called **consommé.** Both bouillon and consommé are low in calories (kilojoules). They make excellent appetizers and snacks for all age groups.

For both bouillon and consommé, you must first **clarify** the stock. You can clarify strained stock by adding a slightly beaten egg white and a few pieces of egg shell to the boiling broth. As the egg protein coagulates, it traps any solid materials. Strain the clarified stock to remove the egg, solid materials, and egg shell.

To prepare bouillon, reduce the strained and clarified stock in volume by further cooking. This additional cooking concentrates the stock, making it richer and more flavorful.

Prepare consommé by simmering the strained and clarified stock still longer. It has a richer flavor than bouillon.

Microwaving Soups

Stocks are best when prepared on a conventional rangetop. Long, slow cooking allows flavors to blend. Once you have made stocks into soups, however, you can heat them in a microwave oven in a matter of minutes. You can also prepare convenience soups in a microwave oven.

Microwave most stock soups on high power. Refer to a microwave cookbook for specific instructions. You may want to heat some soups on a lower power to allow ingredients to simmer.

Choose containers of ample size when microwaving soups to avoid boilovers. Cover soups and stir them during the microwaving period to promote more even cooking.

Herbs and Spices

Herbs, spices, and blends can greatly enhance the flavors of salads, casseroles, soups, and all other foods. *Herbs* are the leaves of plants usually grown in temperate climates. You may have seen an herb garden growing on a windowsill or in a

20-6 Vegetables, barley, and veal are used to make this nutritious stock soup.

corner of someone's backyard. Basil, bay leaf, and mint are examples of herbs. You can purchase some herbs fresh, but most are sold dried.

Spices are the dried roots, stems, and seeds of plants grown mainly in the tropics. Cinnamon, allspice, pepper, and ginger are examples of spices. Sometimes people use the word spice to mean "hot" or pungent. Not all spices are hot, however. Most just give flavor. Spices are sold in whole or ground forms.

Blends are combinations of ground herbs and spices. Poultry seasoning and pumpkin pie spice are examples of blends.

Using Herbs and Spices

You can use herbs fresh or dried. Fresh herbs are not as concentrated as dried herbs, so you need to use more of them to get the same flavor. Unless the recipe tells you otherwise, use dried herbs when you cook.

You can use a microwave oven to dry fresh herbs for use in recipes. Simply microwave fi cup (125 mL) fresh herbs on high power for two minutes.

Ground spices release their flavor immediately when added to food. Add them toward the end of cooking. Whole spices release their flavor more slowly, so you can add them at the beginning of cooking.

You might want to place whole spices and herbs in a cheesecloth bag before adding them to food. This is called a *bouquet garni.* After the herbs and spices have released their flavors, you can easily remove them from the food.

Gourmet Cooking

Gourmets are people who enjoy being able to distinguish the complex combinations of flavors that make up foods. Some people think gourmet cooking requires hours of work and ingredients that are hard to find. However, this is not necessarily the case. Gourmet food is simply food that is expertly seasoned. Creative use of herbs and spices can make gourmet dishes out of some of the simplest foods.

Becoming familiar with a range of herbs and spices can help you prepare foods with a gourmet touch. As you work with seasonings, you will learn that some herbs and spices go especially well with certain foods. For instance, many recipes for custard call for nutmeg. Rosemary and mint complement the flavor of lamb. People often add cinnamon to apple dishes.

Using herbs and spices well requires practice and skill. When learning to use seasonings, start with small amounts. Ideally, herbs and spices should enhance food, not overpower it.

Storing Herbs and Spices

Always store herbs and spices in a cool, dry place away from light. Keep the containers tightly closed, 20-7.

Buy herbs and spices in small amounts for ordinary cooking. All spices and herbs should keep their flavor and aroma for at least several months when properly stored. However, they lose their strength as they age, so date all containers. Whole spices will last longer than ground spices. You can tell if a spice or herb has lost its strength. Simply rub a little of it between your hands and smell it. If it has little or no odor, you have stored it too long.

Lillian Vernon Corporation

20-7 The tight-fitting stoppers on these spice bottles will help keep the spices fresh. For best keeping quality, the spice rack should be hung away from direct light.

Summary

You can serve a salad as almost any part of a meal, from appetizer to dessert. There are five main types of salads—protein, pasta, vegetable, fruit, and gelatin. To prepare most salads, you will begin with a base of washed and trimmed salad greens. Cut ingredients for the body of the salad into bite-sized pieces. Salad dressings may be temporary or permanent emulsions. When assembling a salad, keep flavor, texture, and color in mind.

Casseroles are both easy and economical to prepare. They generally contain a protein food, a vegetable, a starch, a sauce, and a topping. Although you cook some casseroles on the range-top, you cook most casseroles in a conventional or microwave oven.

You make stocks by covering meat, poultry, or fish with water and simmering it for a long time. You may also add vegetables for extra flavor. After cooking, you can strain a stock and add ingredients to make a hearty soup. You can also clarify stock and then reduce it through further cooking to prepare bouillon or consommé.

Herbs, spices, and seasoning blends are important ingredients in many foods. With practice, you will learn to use them to enhance the flavor of almost any dish.

Review What You Have Read

Write your answers on a separate sheet of paper.
1. Name the five main types of salads.
2. Which of the following fruits should not be used in a gelatin salad? Explain why.
   A. Fresh peach slices.
   B. Canned blueberries.
   C. Frozen cherries.
   D. Fresh pineapple.
3. What are the three main parts of a salad?
4. Name four different kinds of salad greens.
5. Why should salad greens be torn instead of cut?
6. What are the three basic types of dressings?
7. Give four guidelines you can follow when preparing salads.
8. List five components of a casserole and give an example of each.
9. What is a soup stock and how is one made?
10. How does bouillon differ from consommé?
11. List three common herbs and three common spices.
12. When should ground spices be added to food? When should whole spices be added?

Build Your Basic Skills

1. Compare the unit cost of instant bouillon, canned bouillon, and homemade bouillon. Taste samples of each and discuss when you might choose to use each product in cooking.
2. Smell samples of three herbs and three spices. Find recipes that include each of these herbs and spices. Make a list of foods that each herb or spice would enhance.

Build Your Thinking Skills

1. Plan and prepare a salad buffet. Choose a variety of vegetable, fruit, protein, pasta, and gelatin salads.
2. Write three dinner menus featuring meat, fish, or poultry entrees. Then write three more menus featuring casseroles that you could make with the leftovers from the first three menus.

Cereal products, such as rice, are an economical source of food energy.

Chapter 21

Cereal Products

A "Taste" of the World of Work

Cash Grain Farmer
Plants, cultivates, and harvests one or more grain crops, such as barley, corn, rice, and wheat, for cash sale.

Cereal Popper
Controls pressure cylinders to expand or puff whole grain to produce breakfast cereal.

Miller
Supervises and coordinates activities of workers engaged in cleaning and grinding grain and in bolting flour to ensure milling, according to specifications.

Terms to Know

cereal	refined
kernel	pasta
bran	enriched
endosperm	starch
germ	gelatinization
whole grain	syneresis

Objectives

After studying this chapter, you will be able to
❏ list a variety of cereal products.
❏ describe how heat and liquids affect starches.
❏ prepare cooked breakfast cereals, rice, and pasta.

Summary

Corn, wheat, rye, oats, rice, and barley are important crops throughout the world. These grains are made into a variety of staple food products, including breakfast foods, flours, and pasta. These products are generally nutritious, inexpensive, and easy to store.

Starches obtained from cereals are used chiefly as thickening agents in gravies, puddings, and sauces. When mixed with liquid and heated, starches absorb water and swell, causing the mixture to thicken. As they cool, most starch mixtures form a gel. Temperature, time, agitation, and mixing method used affect the cooking of starch mixtures.

Cooked breakfast cereals, rice, and pasta all contain a large amount of starch. Therefore, you need to keep the principles of cooking starches in mind when preparing these foods. During cooking, cereal products absorb water and increase in volume. The amount of water needed to make the starch granules in cereal products swell varies depending on the product. Cooked breakfast cereals require moderate temperatures and gentle stirring. The water for pasta should boil constantly throughout cooking. Properly cooked cereal products are tender, but they hold their shape and have no raw starch flavor. Microwaving cereal products does not save time, but it may reduce cleanup tasks.

Review What You Have Read

Write your answers on a separate sheet of paper.
1. List four cereals used for food.
2. Describe the three parts of a kernel of grain.
3. How do whole grain cereals differ from refined cereals?
4. List three products, other than breakfast food and flour, that come from grain.
5. True or false. Wild rice is not really a rice.
6. Pasta is made from _____.
   A. all-purpose flour
   B. cake flour
   C. self-rising flour
   D. semolina
7. The swelling and thickening of starch granules when heated in water is called _____.
8. Describe three ways to separate starch granules to prevent lumping.
9. Name three products that are thickened by starch.
10. True or false. Rice should absorb all of its cooking liquid.
11. True or false. Cereals should be stirred vigorously throughout the entire cooking time.
12. How can a raw starch flavor be prevented when cooking cereals?
13. How can you prevent pasta from sticking together during cooking?
14. True or false. Cereal products can be microwaved in about one-fourth of the time needed for conventional cooking.

Build Your Basic Skills

1. Research the types of grains that people in different parts of the world use as staple foods. (Use the international foods chapters in this textbook as one of your sources of information.) Summarize your findings in a two-page report.
2. Choose one of the following types of cereal products: breakfast foods, flours, pastas, or rice products. Visit a grocery store and make a list of as many products as you can find in the group you chose. Don't forget to list canned and frozen products as well as dried products. Make a poster showing a price graph of all the products you listed.

Build Your Thinking Skills

1. Prepare two white sauces. To prepare the first sauce, make a roux with the fat and flour. Add the milk slowly, stirring constantly, and cook the sauce until thickened. To prepare the second sauce, warm the milk with the fat. Add the flour all at once. Cook until thickened, stirring constantly. Compare the two sauces. Which would you rather serve? Why?
2. Prepare two recipes of cherry sauce. Thicken one with cornstarch. Thicken the other with flour. Compare the appearance, texture, and flavor of the two sauces. Which one would you rather serve? Why?
3. Prepare old-fashioned oatmeal, quick-cooking oatmeal, and instant oatmeal. Taste and compare the flavor, texture, and appearance of each product. Which do you prefer? Why?

Chapter 22

Breads

A "Taste" of the World of Work

Oven Tender
Tends stationary or rotary hearth oven that bakes bread, pastries, and other bakery products.

Baker
Mixes and bakes ingredients according to recipes to produce breads, pastries, and other baked goods.

Dividing-Machine Operator
Tends machines that automatically divide, round, proof, and shape dough into units of specified size and weight, according to work order, preparatory to baking.

Terms to Know

gluten
yeast
fermentation
baking soda
baking powder
batter

dough
tunnel
sponge
knead
oven spring

Objectives

After studying this chapter, you will be able to
❑ describe how to select and store baked goods.
❑ explain the function of ingredients in baked products.
❑ prepare quick breads and yeast breads.

Photo courtesy of The Quaker Oats Company

351

You can prepare *quick breads* in a short amount of time. Quick breads include biscuits, muffins, popovers, cream puffs, griddle cakes, and waffles. They also include coffee cakes and breads leavened with baking powder.

Yeast breads are bread products that are leavened with gases formed from chemical reactions with yeast. They require more time to prepare than quick breads. Yeast breads include breads, rolls, English muffins, raised doughnuts, crullers, and many other yeast-raised products.

Selecting and Storing Baked Products

Quick breads and yeast breads are *baked products*. Cakes, cookies, and pies are baked products, too. Some of the following information applies to *all* baked products. However, preparation of cakes, cookies, and pies differs from preparation of breads. Therefore, cakes, cookies, and pies will be discussed further in the next chapter.

You can purchase baked products freshly baked, partially baked, refrigerated, and frozen. *Freshly baked items* are sold in bakeries, in bakery sections of supermarkets, and on supermarket shelves. They are ready to serve. *Brown-and-serve baked goods* are partially baked. They need a final browning in the oven before serving. *Refrigerated doughs* are ready to bake. They are handy for quickly preparing items like biscuits, turnovers, cookies, and rolls. *Frozen doughs and baked goods* require thawing and/or baking. Yeast doughs and cookie doughs are available frozen. You can buy frozen pies, cakes, coffee cakes, and doughnuts, too.

Healthy Living

Breads are an excellent source of complex carbohydrates. You should be eating 6 to 11 servings of bread and cereal products every day to meet your body's energy needs. When buying bread products, choose whole grain items often. They are low in fat and rich in vitamins and minerals. They are also higher in fiber than refined bread products. Limit the amount of butter or margarine you spread on breads when eating them.

Cost of Baked Products

Cost factors vary considerably among baked products. The cost of rolls, cakes, and other bakery products depends a lot on the amount of convenience. Ready-to-serve items usually cost more than items that require some preparation. Bakery yeast rolls, for instance, usually cost more than frozen yeast rolls.

Sometimes, convenience products can be worth the extra cost. A cherry pie from the bakery might cost more than a homemade pie. If you are in a hurry, however, the time saved might be worth the extra cost.

Breads are popular sale items in many supermarkets. Bread costs depend on size of loaf, extra ingredients, and brand. Large loaves usually cost less per serving than small loaves. Breads with fruit and nuts cost more than plain white or wheat bread. Store brands generally cost less than national brands.

Storing Baked Products

You can store freshly baked items at room temperature or in the freezer, tightly wrapped, 22-1. Freezing bread in hot, humid weather prevents mold growth. You can take slices of bread from the freezer as needed to thaw and eat. Refrigerate any baked products with cream, custard, or other perishable fillings or frosting.

Keep refrigerated doughs refrigerated until you plan to bake them. Likewise, store frozen doughs and baked products in the freezer until you are ready to use them.

Ingredients for Baked Products

Nearly all baked products are made with flour. However, the kinds of ingredients added to the flour distinguish one product from another.

The principal ingredients used in baked products are flour, leavening agents, liquid, fat, eggs, sugar, and salt. Some baked products, like shortened cakes, contain all of these ingredients. Other baked products, like cream puffs, contain just a few. Each ingredient serves a specific purpose.

Flours

Flours are produced from cereal grains. (See Chapter 21, "Cereals.") White wheat flours are most often used for baking. They are classified as bread flour, all-purpose flour, and cake flour. Each of these flours contains protein and starch.

Coffee dessert photography, courtesy of KRUPS North America, Inc.

22-1 This freshly baked coffee cake can be wrapped and stored at room temperature.

Flour gives structure to baked products. This structure is created by two proteins found in wheat flour. These proteins are called *gliadin* and *glutenin.* When you combine wheat flour with liquid and mix it thoroughly, the glutenin and gliadin form gluten. *Gluten* gives strength and elasticity to batters and doughs.

To understand gluten, think of a piece of bubble gum. When you first put the gum into your mouth, it is soft and easy to chew. As you chew the gum, it becomes more elastic, and you can blow bubbles. As you continue to chew the gum for a long time, it becomes so elastic it makes your jaws hurt. Gluten behaves in a similar way.

The different kinds of white wheat flour contain different amounts of the proteins gliadin and glutenin. Therefore, the strength of the gluten produced by each of the flours differs.

Bread flour contains the largest amounts of gliadin and glutenin. It produces the strongest and most elastic gluten. Bread flour is used in home and commercial production of yeast breads and rolls.

Most home baking is done with *all-purpose flour.* The gluten formed by all-purpose flour is not as strong as the gluten formed by bread flour. However, it is satisfactory for homemade yeast breads.

Cake flour contains the smallest amounts of gliadin and glutenin. It forms the weakest gluten of all the white wheat flours. Use cake flour to make cakes and other baked products in which you desire a light and delicate texture.

In baking, you must use the correct type of flour. You cannot use bread flour for cakes, and you cannot use cake flour for breads. Breads made with cake flour would not have strong enough gluten to support the structure of the bread. Cakes made from bread flour would be tough and elastic because the gluten would be too strong.

Be a Clever Consumer

Compare carefully when shopping for baked products. Although added convenience usually means added cost, there are exceptions. For instance, a devil's food cake made from a mix often is less expensive than one made from scratch.

Leavening Agents

Leavening agents produce gases in batters and doughs that make baked products rise and become light and porous. The three leavening gases are air, steam (water vapor), and carbon dioxide. In some baked products, like popovers and cream puffs, one leavening gas predominates. In other baked products, like cakes, all three gases work together.

Beating eggs, creaming fat and sugar together, sifting flour, folding doughs, and beating batters incorporate *air* into baked products. All baked products contain some air.

Steam is produced in most baked products. High temperatures used in baking heat liquid ingredients enough to form steam. Popovers and cream puffs are leavened almost entirely by steam.

Carbon dioxide is a result of chemical reactions that occur between ingredients in baked products. Three ingredients may be used to produce carbon dioxide: yeast, baking soda, and baking powder.

Yeast is a microscopic, single-celled plant. When you add sugar to yeast, the yeast and certain bacteria act upon the sugar. As a result, carbon dioxide and ethyl alcohol are produced. This process is called **fermentation.** (Fermentation will be covered in more detail when yeast breads are discussed later in this chapter.)

Yeast is available in three forms: compressed, active dry, and fast rising. *Compressed yeast* is made from fresh, moist yeast cells. The yeast cells are pressed together in cake form. You must refrigerate compressed yeast because it is very perishable. See 22-2.

Active dry yeast is made from an active yeast strain that has been dried and made into granules. You can buy it in small foil packets and glass jars. Active dry yeast in packets will keep at room temperature. You must refrigerate jars after opening.

Fast rising yeast products are highly active yeast strains. The granules of these products are smaller than those of active dry yeast. Fast rising yeast is sold in small foil packets. It will stay fresh on the shelf for up to a year.

Baking soda (sodium bicarbonate) is an alkali. When added to a flour mixture and heated, baking soda releases carbon dioxide. However, when baking soda is mixed in this way, it often produces a disagreeable flavor and color in baked products. To avoid this, recipes calling for soda often contain a food acid ingredient. Such ingredients include buttermilk, molasses, brown sugar, vinegar, honey, applesauce (or other fruit), and citrus juices.

Baking powders contain a dry acid or acid salt, baking soda, and starch or flour. Most baking

22-2 Yeast is the leavening agent used to make this bread rise and become light and porous.

powders are *double-acting baking powders*. They release some of their carbon dioxide when they are moistened. However, they release most of their carbon dioxide when they are heated.

Be sure to use exactly the amount of baking powder a recipe recommends. Too much baking powder will produce too much carbon dioxide, and the baked product will collapse. Too little baking powder will not produce enough carbon dioxide, and the product will be small and compact.

Liquids

Water, milk, and fruit juices are liquids commonly used in baked products. Eggs and fats are also considered to be liquid ingredients.

Liquids serve several functions. They hydrate (cause to absorb water) the protein and starch in flour. Proteins must absorb water to later form gluten. Starches must absorb water to gelatinize during baking. Another function of liquids is to moisten or dissolve ingredients such as baking powder, salt, and sugar. Liquids also serve as leavening agents when they are converted to steam during baking.

Fat

Fat serves primarily as a tenderizing agent in baked products. The fat coats the flour particles and causes the dough structure to separate into layers. Fat also aids leavening. When you beat fat, air bubbles form. The fat traps these air bubbles and holds them.

Eggs

Eggs help incorporate air into baked products when you beat them. They also add color and flavor and contribute to structure. During baking, the egg proteins coagulate. The coagulated proteins give the batter or dough elasticity and structure.

Sugar

Sugar gives sweetness to baked products. It also has a tenderizing effect and helps crusts brown. In yeast breads, sugar serves as food for the yeast. Brown sugar gives a distinctive flavor to baked products. It also produces baked products that are moister than products made with granulated sugar.

Salt

Salt adds flavor to many baked products. In yeast breads, salt also regulates the action of the yeast and inhibits the action of certain enzymes. If a yeast dough contains no salt, the yeast will produce carbon dioxide too quickly. The bread dough will be difficult to handle, and the baked product will have a poor appearance.

Adjusting Ingredients

As you have read, baking powder, fat, eggs, sugar, and salt each perform certain functions in baked goods. However, some recipes call for more of these ingredients than is really necessary. You can follow some simple guidelines to adjust quick bread and yeast bread recipes to reduce excess ingredients. Cutting down on unneeded ingredients will result in breads that are lower in calories, fat, and sodium. Such changes are in line with the Dietary Guidelines for Americans.

Chart 22-3 shows minimum proportions of fat, eggs, sugar, salt, and baking powder for basic bread recipes. Ingredients are listed in the amounts needed for each cup of flour in the recipe. Many bread recipes call for cornmeal, oatmeal, and bran in addition to flour to give structure to products. You should count these ingredients as flour when figuring proportions of ingredients. However, these ingredients are heavier and may require a little extra baking powder for proper leavening.

You can make another simple adjustment by substituting skim milk for whole milk in bread recipes. This change will reduce the fat in each serving of bread products. A recipe for corn muffins has been modified in 22-4.

Mixing Methods for Baked Products

The method used to mix baked products is another factor that distinguishes one product from another. Yeast breads, cream puffs, and sponge cakes must be mixed by special methods. However, you will mix most batters and doughs by either the biscuit, muffin, or conventional cake method.

Minimum Ingredient Proportions per 1 Cup (250 mL) of Flour

Product	Fat	Eggs	Sugar	Salt	Baking Powder
Biscuits	2 tablespoons (30 mL)	—	—	1/4 teaspoon (1 mL)	1 1/4 teaspoons (6 mL)
Muffins	2 tablespoons (30 mL)	1/2	1 tablespoon (15 mL)	1/4 teaspoon (1 mL)	1 1/4 teaspoons (6 mL)
Popovers	1 tablespoon (15 mL)	2	—	1/4 teaspoon (1 mL)	—
Cream puffs	1/2 cup (125 mL)	4	—	1/4 teaspoon (1 mL)	—
Yeast breads	*	*	1 teaspoon (5 mL)	1/4 teaspoon (1 mL)	—

* Although many yeast breads can be made without any fat or eggs, some richer breads call for them. Limiting these ingredients to 1 tablespoon of fat and 1/2 egg per cup of flour should produce a suitably rich dough.

22-3 Following these proportions will reduce the amount of sugar, fat, and sodium in many quick bread and yeast bread recipes.

Recipe Comparison

Traditional Corn Muffins (Makes 12 muffins)	Light Corn Muffins (Makes 12 muffins)
1 cup flour	1 cup flour
1 cup cornmeal	1 cup cornmeal
¼ cup sugar	2 tablespoons sugar
1 teaspoon salt	½ teaspoon salt
4 teaspoons baking powder	1 tablespoon baking powder
1 egg	1 egg
1 cup milk	1 cup skim milk
⅓ cup shortening	¼ cup shortening

22-4 Adjusting ingredient proportions in this traditional recipe can save 25 calories, 2 grams of fat, and 115 mg of sodium per muffin.

You will often use the *biscuit method* when making biscuits and pastry. For the biscuit method, sift the dry ingredients together into a mixing bowl. Use a pastry blender, two knives, or your fingers to cut the fat into the dry mixture. Continue cutting in until the particles are the size of coarse cornmeal. Add the liquid last.

Use the *muffin method* to prepare muffins, waffles, griddle cakes, popovers, and some coffee cakes. For the muffin method, sift the dry ingredients together into a mixing bowl. Combine beaten eggs with milk and melted fat (all at room temperature). Add the liquid mixture to the dry mixture all at once, and stir the batter. The amount of stirring depends on the product.

Use the *conventional cake method* for shortened cakes (cakes made with fat). You may also use this method for some coffee cakes and breads leavened with baking powder. For the conventional cake method, cream (beat until light and fluffy) the fat and sugar together. Add the beaten eggs to the creamed fat and sugar. Add the sifted dry ingredients alternately with the liquid ingredients, beginning and ending with the dry ingredients.

Quick Breads

Quick breads may be made from batters or doughs. Both batters and doughs are mixtures of flour and liquid. **Batters** range in consistency from thin liquids to stiff liquids. Thin batters are called *pour batters*. They have a large amount of liquid and a small amount of flour. You make a pour batter to prepare griddle cakes and popovers. Stiff batters are called *drop batters*. They have a high proportion of flour, and you can drop them from a spoon. You make a drop batter to prepare some muffin recipes. **Doughs** have an even higher proportion of flour.

They are stiff enough to shape by hand. You use a soft dough to prepare shortcake.

Food Science Principles of Preparing Quick Breads

All quick breads contain basically the same ingredients. The proportion of ingredients and the mixing method determine the end product. All quick breads contain gluten. It is formed when you combine the flour with liquid ingredients and stir or knead the mixture. Gluten gives strength and elasticity to quick breads. It also holds the leavening gases, which is what makes quick breads rise.

If you mix or handle a batter or dough too much, the gluten will overdevelop. This can cause a quick bread to be compact and tough. To keep quick breads light and tender, mix them for only a short time and handle them carefully.

Preparing Biscuits

Biscuits require the correct proportions of ingredients and gentle handling. Use the biscuit method when making either rolled or dropped biscuits. Both kinds of biscuits contain flour, baking powder, salt, fat, and milk. Cut *rolled biscuits* with a biscuit cutter from a soft dough. Bake them on an ungreased baking sheet. If you add more milk to the dough, you will make a stiff batter. You can drop the batter from a spoon to make *dropped biscuits*. Bake dropped biscuits on a greased baking sheet.

To make rolled biscuits, begin by sifting the dry ingredients into a bowl. Then cut in the fat. Add the liquid all at once and stir until the dough forms a ball. Turn the dough out onto a lightly floured surface and gently knead it 8 to 10 times. Roll or pat the dough into a circle and cut it with a biscuit cutter. Place the biscuits on a baking sheet and bake them in a hot oven until they are golden brown. See 22-5.

Characteristics of Biscuits

A high-quality rolled biscuit has an even shape with a smooth and level top and straight sides. The crust is an even brown. When you break it open, the interior is white to creamy white. The crumb is moist and fluffy and peels off in layers.

An undermixed biscuit has a low volume and a rounded top with a slightly rough crust. The crumb is tender. An overmixed biscuit also has a low volume and a rounded top, but the top is smooth. The crumb is tough and compact.

Preparing Muffins

Muffins can be prepared quickly with just a few pieces of equipment. They contain flour, baking powder, salt, sugar, eggs, milk, and melted shortening. You may add fruits, nuts, cheese, or other ingredients for variety.

Mix muffins by the muffin method. Start by sifting the dry ingredients into a bowl. Make a well in the center of the dry ingredients. Pour in the combined liquid ingredients. Stir the batter just until the dry ingredients are moistened. Then gently drop the batter into a greased muffin pan and bake.

Characteristics of Muffins

A high-quality muffin has a thin, evenly browned crust. The top is symmetrical, but it looks rough. When broken apart, the texture is uniform, and the crumb is tender and light.

An undermixed muffin has a low volume and a flat top. The crumb is coarse. An overmixed muffin has a peaked top and a pale, slick crust. When broken apart, *tunnels* (narrow, open areas) are visible.

Preparing Popovers

Popovers look like golden brown balloons. You can eat them with just butter and jam. You can fill their hollow centers with creamed meat, poultry, or seafood; vegetables; or meat and vegetable combinations. A variety of sweet fillings, such as ice cream, pudding, fruit, and custard, are also popular in popovers.

Popovers contain flour, salt, eggs, and milk. (Some popovers also contain a small amount of fat.) After mixing these ingredients, place popovers in a hot oven for the first part of the baking period. This allows steam to expand the walls

---

Biscuits
Makes 10 to 12 medium biscuits

2	cups all-purpose flour	500 mL all-purpose flour
2 ½	teaspoons baking powder	12 mL baking powder
½	teaspoon salt	2 mL salt
¼	cup shortening	50 mL shortening
⅔ to ¾	cup skim milk	150 to 200 mL skim milk

1. Preheat oven to 425°F (220°C).
2. Sift flour, baking powder, and salt into mixing bowl.
3. Cut in shortening with pastry blender, two knives, or fingers until particles are the size of coarse cornmeal.
4. Add milk; stir with a fork until dough forms a soft ball.
5. Turn dough out onto a lightly floured pastry cloth or board. Knead gently 8 to 10 times.
6. With palm of hand or rolling pin, flatten dough into a circle about ½ to ¾ inch (1.5 to 2 cm) thick.
7. With round biscuit cutter, cut out biscuits.
8. Place biscuits on an ungreased baking sheet, about 1 to 2 inches (2.5 to 5 cm) apart for crusty biscuits. (For softer biscuits, place them closer together.)
9. Bake until golden, about 12 to 15 minutes. Serve immediately.

Per biscuit: 143 Cal. (34% from fat), 3 g protein, 20 g carbohydrate, 5 g fat, 0 mg cholesterol, .7 g fiber, 188 mg sodium.

22-5 A baking powder biscuit should have a smooth top; an even brown crust; and a moist, fluffy crumb.

of the popovers. Following this expansion, lower the temperature to prevent overbrowning before the interior has set. Do not open the oven door to check popovers during baking. If you do and they have not set, the steam can condense and cause the popovers to collapse.

Characteristics of Popovers

A high quality popover has a good volume. The shell is golden brown and crisp, and the interior contains slightly moist (but not raw) strands of dough. See 22-6.

Insufficient baking is one of the biggest causes of popover failures. If you have not baked a popover long enough, it will collapse when you take it from the oven. The exterior will be soft instead of crisp, and the interior will be doughy.

Preparing Cream Puffs

A cream puff is a golden brown, hollow shell with crisp walls. You can fill cream puffs with pudding, custard, ice cream, fruit, or whipped cream and serve them as a dessert. You can fill them with creamed meat, poultry, or fish and serve them as a main dish. You can also fill small cream puffs with cream cheese, shrimp salad, or another light filling and serve them as an appetizer. Elongated cream puffs filled with custard are called *eclairs*.

Cream puffs are made from flour, water, fat, and eggs. The dough for cream puffs is called *puff paste*. Begin baking cream puffs in a hot oven so that the steam will cause them to puff (rise). Then reduce the temperature. This will prevent the exteriors of the cream puffs from overbrowning before the interiors have set. Do not open the oven door to check the cream puffs during baking. If you do and the cream puffs have not set, the steam can condense and cause them to collapse.

Characteristics of Cream Puffs

A properly prepared cream puff has a good volume and a brown, tender crust. When broken apart, the interior of the cream puff is hollow. A few strands of moist, tender dough may be visible.

Cream puff failures usually are the result of underbaking. When you take an underbaked cream puff from the oven it will collapse. The

American Egg Board

22-6 High quality popovers look like golden brown balloons on the outside.

interior is moist and filled with strands of dough. Occasionally, cream puffs will ooze fat during baking. The evaporation of too much liquid can cause this. Evaporation may take place when the water and fat are heated together or when the puff paste is cooked.

Microwaving Quick Breads

You can use the microwave oven to prepare a variety of tasty quick breads in a matter of minutes. Nut breads, muffins, coffee cakes, corn bread, and biscuits all microwave beautifully. You can reheat frozen waffles and griddle cakes in a microwave oven, too. However, popovers and cream puffs do not microwave well due to the lack of dry heat needed for crust formation.

Many microwave quick bread recipes use baking mixes and refrigerated biscuits for added speed and convenience. You can use a variety of tasty toppings to disguise the lack of browning on these products. See 22-7.

Quick breads will microwave more evenly in ring-shaped pans or muffin rings. A round casserole with a juice glass placed in the center will serve as a ring-shaped pan. Custard cups arranged in a circle can take the place of a muffin ring. You can also use loaf pans, but you should place foil shields on the ends to prevent overcooking in the corners.

Yeast Breads

Baking bread was once a weekly activity in many homes. It is again becoming popular. For many homemakers, this is largely due to the introduction of the automatic bread maker. These machines allow even the busiest homemaker to serve homemade bread whenever he or she wants. All the homemaker has to do is measure the ingredients into the machine, and the bread maker does the rest.

Even without the convenience of an automatic bread maker, you can serve homemade breads. Try recipes for brown-and-serve breads and cool-proofed and frozen doughs. These recipes allow you to take advantage of time you have available to prepare products that you can bake later.

Yeast Bread Ingredients

All yeast breads must contain flour, liquid, salt, and yeast. Many recipes also include sugar, fat, and eggs.

Good Manners Are Good Business

You can use a piece of bread to help you push a bite of food onto your fork at a business meal. However, avoid using your bread to wipe your plate clean.

You can use all-purpose flour for making yeast breads at home. When mixed with liquid and kneaded, all-purpose flour develops enough gluten to support the carbon dioxide produced by the yeast.

You can use plain water, potato water, or milk as the liquid in yeast breads. You must warm all liquids to activate the yeast.

Milk adds nutrients to bread and helps bread stay fresh longer. It also gives bread a softer crust than breads made with water.

Some yeast bread recipes state that you should scald the milk. This step is unnecessary if using pasteurized milk. Pasteurization destroys enzymes in milk that can cause doughs to soften during fermentation.

Salt regulates the action of the yeast and inhibits the action of certain enzymes in the flour. Without salt, a yeast dough is sticky and hard to handle. When baked, the bread may look moth-eaten.

Yeast leavens bread. For best results, use the amount of yeast specified in your recipe. Using too much yeast will cause the dough to rise too quickly. Excess yeast will also give the bread an undesirable flavor, texture, and appearance. Using too little yeast will lengthen the fermentation time.

The temperature of the liquids affects yeast cells. Temperatures that are too high kill the yeast cells. Temperatures that are too low can slow down or stop yeast activity.

Sugar provides extra food for the yeast so the dough will rise faster. If you use too much sugar, however, the yeast will work more slowly. Sugar also influences browning, flavor, and texture.

Fat increases tenderness. Most recipes call for solid fat, but some call for oil.

Eggs add flavor and richness to yeast breads. They also add color and improve the structure.

You may add other ingredients, such as raisins, nuts, cheese, herbs, and spices, to bread dough, 22-8. They add flavor and variety. However, these ingredients tend to lengthen the rising time.

22-7 The streusel topping on these muffins would help hide the lack of browning characteristic of quick breads prepared in a microwave oven.

22-8 By adding different ingredients to yeast dough, you can create a wide variety of bread products.

Mixing Methods for Yeast Breads

You will use one of the following methods to mix yeast doughs
- straight-dough method
- fast mixing method
- sponge method
- batter, or "no-mix," method

Straight-Dough Method

For the straight-dough method, soften the yeast in warm water. (If using compressed yeast, the water should be 80° to 85°F [27° to 29°C]. If using active dry or fast rising yeast, the water should be 110° to 115°F [43° to 46°C].) Add the sugar, fat, and salt to the milk. The milk should be room temperature to lukewarm. Cold ingredients will slow the rising action when added to activated yeast. Combine the yeast with the liquid mixture, and add some of the flour. Beat the mixture until smooth. Add the remaining flour gradually to form a dough.

You can also use the straight-dough method to prepare refrigerator yeast breads and rolls. Refrigerator dough recipes often call for extra yeast, sugar, and salt. Mix and knead the dough and place it in a covered bowl in the refrigerator. The dough retains enough heat to allow fermentation to continue during refrigeration. (Before it becomes chilled, the dough doubles in bulk.) Shape the dough into bread or rolls and bake it the next day. When used in this way, the method is sometimes called cool-proofed or cool-rise.

Fast Mixing Method

The fast mixing method works well with active dry or fast rising yeast. Mix the yeast with some of the flour and all of the other dry ingredients. Heat the liquid and fat together to a temperature of 120° to 130°F (45° to 54°C) and add it to the dry ingredients. Add eggs, if required, and then add the remaining flour to form a dough. This method allows ingredients to blend easily and eliminates the need to soften the yeast.

Sponge Method

For the sponge method, mix the liquid, sugar, yeast, and part of the flour together. This mixture is called a *sponge*. When the sponge becomes bubbly and light, add the cooled melted fat, the salt, and the rest of the flour to form a dough.

Batter Method

Some recipes are prepared by the batter, or "no-mix" method. These recipes use less flour, so the yeast mixture is thinner than a dough. This method is a modification of the straight-dough method that eliminates kneading. Stirring develops the gluten. The batter method is the quickest of the mixing methods.

Food Science Principles of Preparing Yeast Breads

Preparing yeast bread requires the development of gluten and the formation of carbon dioxide. During mixing and kneading, the gluten develops. The gluten will form the framework of the bread and hold the carbon dioxide produced by the yeast during fermentation. The yeast will produce the carbon dioxide, which will give volume to the bread. The preparation of a successful yeast bread depends on careful measuring, sufficient kneading, controlled fermentation temperatures, correct pan size, and correct baking temperature.

Kneading

After forming a yeast dough by the straight-dough, fast mixing, or sponge method, you must knead it. Although some of the gluten develops during the initial beating, kneading develops most of the gluten. To *knead* means to press the dough with the heels of the hands, fold it, and turn it. You must rhythmically repeat this motion until the dough is smooth and elastic. See 22-9.

It is important not to add too much extra flour when kneading the dough. Too much flour will make the dough stiff. It also is important not to be too rough with the dough. Too much pressure at the beginning of kneading can keep the dough sticky and hard to handle. Too much pressure toward the end of kneading can tear or mat the gluten strands that have already developed.

Fermentation

After kneading a yeast dough, you must allow it to rest in a warm place. During this resting time, the yeast acts upon the sugars in the bread dough to form alcohol and carbon dioxide. This process is called fermentation. The alcohol evaporates during baking. The carbon dioxide causes the bread to rise.

The dough should at least double in volume. To see if a dough has doubled in size, gently push two fingers into the dough. If an indentation remains, the dough has risen enough.

Fermentation time varies depending on the kind and amount of yeast, the temperature of the room, and the kind of flour. The smaller granules of fast rising yeast spread through dough faster than regular yeast. The highly active yeast strains allow fermentation to happen more quickly. Thus, breads made with fast rising yeast rise up to 50 percent faster than products made with regular yeast.

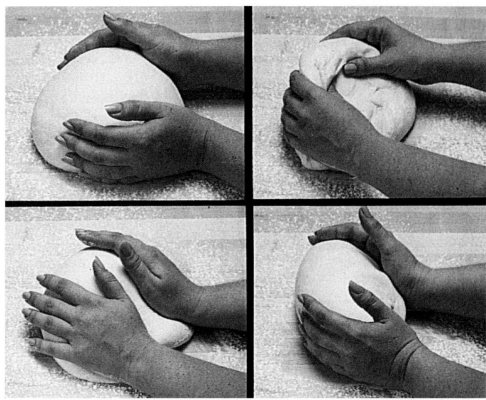

22-9 To knead dough, use your fingers to fold it in half toward your body. With the heels of your hands, push against the dough and turn it one-quarter turn.

The temperature of the room should be 80° to 85°F (27° to 29°C) for optimal fermentation. These temperatures are ideal for the production of carbon dioxide by the yeast. If the kitchen is not warm enough, you may place the dough on a rack over another bowl filled with warm (not hot) water. Too much warmth will cause the yeast to work too quickly, and the dough will rise too fast.

Punching the Dough

When the dough is light (has completed the first rising), you must punch it down to release some of the carbon dioxide. Punch dough down by firmly pushing a fist into the dough. Then fold the edges of the dough toward the center, and turn the dough over so that the smooth side is on top. At this point, some doughs require a second rising time. (Doughs made with bread flour need a second rising.)

Shaping

After punching the dough down, use a sharp knife to divide it into portions as the recipe directs. Allow the divided dough to rest about 10 minutes. After resting, the dough will be easier to handle and to shape as desired.

To shape yeast dough, first flatten the dough into a rectangle. The width of the dough should be about the length of the bread pan. Using a rolling pin will help you to work out any large air bubbles. Fold the ends of the rectangle to the center, overlapping them a little. This should give you a smaller rectangle. Use your rolling pin to flatten the rectangle into a square. Roll the dough into a cylinder. Pinch the edge of the dough into the roll to seal it. Seal each end of the roll by pressing down on it with the side of your hand. Fold the ends under. Place the shaped dough, seam side down, in a greased loaf pan. Brush the top with melted shortening, if desired. Cover the loaf with a clean towel, and shape the remaining dough. Let the loaves rise in a warm, draft-free place until they have doubled in bulk.

Baking

Baking times and temperatures vary somewhat depending on the kind of dough and size of the loaf. Place most yeast breads in a hot oven to begin baking. During baking, the gas cells (formed during fermentation) expand. The walls of dough around these cells set and become rigid. During the first few minutes of baking, the dough will rise dramatically. This rapid rising is called *oven spring.*

Shortly after oven spring has occurred, you may reduce the temperature so the bread finishes baking in a moderately hot oven. (The reduction in temperature helps prevent overbrowning of the crust.) After baking, immediately remove the bread from the pans and place it on cooling racks. Cool the bread thoroughly before you slice and store it.

You can use all four previously discussed mixing methods to prepare yeast breads. The steps shown in 22-10 illustrate how to make basic white bread using the straight-dough method. The recipe in 22-11 also describes the straight-dough method of mixing.

Characteristics of Yeast Bread

Homemade yeast bread is decidedly different from commercially prepared sandwich breads. It has a distinctively appealing sweet smell and delicious taste that cannot be matched.

A high-quality loaf of yeast bread has a large volume and a smooth, rounded top. The surface is golden brown. When sliced, the texture is fine and uniform. The crumb is tender and elastic, and it springs back when touched.

If a yeast dough has been under- or overworked, the finished product will have a low volume. This is because carbon dioxide has leaked out of the dough.

If you allow bread to rise for too long a time before baking, it may have large, overexpanded cells. The top of the loaf may be sunken with overhanging sides, much like a mushroom. The texture is coarse, and it may be crumbly.

If you have not allowed bread to rise long enough before baking, it may have large cracks on the sides of the loaf. Its texture is compact.

Microwaving Yeast Breads

You can defrost frozen bread dough in a microwave oven. You can also raise and bake yeast dough in a microwave oven. However, the resulting loaves will lack the crisp, brown crusts of conventionally baked breads.

Batter breads work especially well in a microwave oven because they do not have crusts. Raised coffee rings with toppings and dark breads also microwave well because they do not show the lack of browning.

To defrost frozen dough, start by microwaving 1 cup (250 mL) of water for 3 to 5 minutes on high

A—Combine ingredients and beat until smooth. Stir in enough additional flour to make a moderately stiff dough.

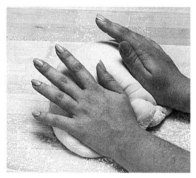
B—On a lightly floured pastry board or cloth, knead dough until smooth and elastic.

C—Place dough in a lightly greased bowl; turn once to grease top.

D—Let dough rise in a warm place until double in bulk. Test dough for lightness with two fingers.

E—When dough is light, punch down.

F—Shape dough into loaves or rolls and bake as directed.

Fleischmann's Yeast, Inc.

22-10 To prepare yeast bread by the straight-dough method, follow these easy steps.

White Bread
Makes 1 loaf

1	cup skim milk		250	mL skim milk
1	tablespoon sugar		15	mL sugar
½	teaspoon salt		2	mL salt
1	tablespoon shortening		15	mL shortening
1	package active dry yeast		1	package active dry yeast
¼	cup warm water		50	mL warm water
3 to 3 ½	cups all-purpose flour		750 to 875	mL all-purpose flour

1. In a small saucepan, warm milk to 80° to 85°F (27° to 29°C); add sugar, salt, and shortening. Pour mixture into a large mixing bowl.
2. Soften yeast in warm water, 110° to 115°F (43° to 46°C).
3. Add the softened yeast to the milk mixture. Then add half of the flour.
4. Beat with spoon until batter falls in sheets from the spoon. Stir in enough flour to make a soft dough which is easy to handle.
5. Turn dough out onto a lightly floured pastry cloth or bread board and let rest 5 minutes.
6. Knead until smooth and blistered, about 10 minutes.
7. Place dough in a greased bowl, turning to lightly grease top. Cover bowl and let dough rise in a warm place until double in bulk, about 1 to 1 ½ hours.
8. Punch down and let rest about 10 minutes.
9. Shape into a loaf. Place loaf, seam side down into a greased loaf pan; cover and let rise in a warm place until almost double in bulk, about 30 to 45 minutes.
10. Bake loaf at 425°F (220°C) for 25 minutes.
11. Remove immediately from pan and cool.

Per slice: 101 Cal. (9% from fat), 3 g protein, 19 g carbohydrate, 1 g fat, 0 mg cholesterol, .7 g fiber, 75 mg sodium.

22-11 Homemade bread, warm from the oven, is a mouth-watering delight.

power, until boiling. This creates a warm, moist atmosphere for the dough. Then place the frozen dough in a greased, microwavable loaf pan. Microwave on the defrost setting for 3 minutes. Turn dough over and rotate the pan. Microwave on defrost for another 3 minutes, until the dough is soft to the touch. Allow the dough to stand for 5 minutes to become pliable.

To raise dough in a microwave oven, place dough in a greased bowl, turning to grease all sides. Cover the bowl with waxed paper and place it in a dish of warm water. Microwave on low power for 1 minute. Let the dough stand in the oven for 15 minutes. Rotate the dish one-quarter turn. Repeat the microwaving, standing, and rotating process as needed until the dough is doubled in size.

Bread baked in a microwave oven is microwaved on medium power until it is almost done. Complete the last few minutes of microwaving on high power until bread is no longer doughy. You may place bread in a preheated conventional oven for a final few minutes to brown the crust.

Yeast Bread Variations

Add variety to yeast bread by combining white flour with whole wheat flour, rye flour, or cornmeal. Try adding dried fruits, nuts, herbs, or cheese to the basic dough. Brush the tops of the loaves with butter and sprinkle them with poppy, sesame, or caraway seeds. See 22-12.

You can shape basic bread dough into rolls. After punching the dough down, allow it to rest for a short time. Then divide it into portions and shape it into rolls. Crescent rolls, cloverleaf rolls, Parker House rolls, fan tans, and bows are popular roll shapes. You can find directions for shaping rolls in many cookbooks.

22-12 This yeast bread variation contains oatmeal in addition to flour.

For many people, a meal is not complete without something sweet. Restaurants are famous for the richness of their cheesecakes. Bakeries pride themselves on their pastries. Candy stores guard their recipes for fudge, peanut brittle, and English toffee.

Cakes, cookies, and pies are three of the most popular desserts. Candies are not really desserts, but because they are sweet, many people serve them at the end of a meal.

Most desserts are high in calories (kilojoules) because they contain large amounts of sugar and fat. Desserts should never replace breads and cereals, fruits and vegetables, dairy products, and protein foods in the diet. However, they can add variety to meals and provide extra energy for people who are active.

Cakes

Cakes are a favorite dessert of many people, especially children. Bakers can make cakes to look like carousels, clowns, and dancing dolls. When served at children's birthday parties, cakes are often as important as the presents. Cakes add festivity to many special occasions. They also add variety to lunch boxes and make a plain meal something special.

Kinds of Cakes

Cakes are classified into two groups: shortened and unshortened. *Shortened cakes* contain fat. The fat may be butter, margarine, or hydrogenated vegetable shortening. Some people call shortened cakes *butter cakes*. Most shortened cakes are leavened by baking powder or baking soda and sour milk. *Pound cakes* are a type of shortened cake that do not contain a chemical leavener. They are leavened by air and steam. Shortened cakes are tender, moist, and velvety, 23-1.

Unshortened cakes, sometimes called *foam cakes,* contain no fat. They are leavened by air, which is beaten into eggs, and by steam, which forms during baking. Angel food and sponge cakes are unshortened cakes. The main difference between these two cakes is the egg content. Angel food cakes contain just the egg white. Sponge cakes contain the whole egg. Unshortened cakes are light and fluffy.

Chiffon cakes are a cross between shortened and unshortened cakes. They contain fat like shortened cakes and beaten egg whites like unshortened cakes. They have a large volume, but are not as light as unshortened cakes.

Cake Ingredients

Cakes contain flour, sugar, eggs, liquid, and salt. All shortened cakes also contain fat, and most cakes contain a chemical leavener. Unshortened cakes contain cream of tartar, too.

Flour gives structure to a cake. The gluten that develops when flour is moistened and mixed holds the leavening gases (carbon dioxide, air, and steam). You can make cakes with cake flour or all-purpose flour. Cakes made with cake flour are more delicate and tender. This is because cake flour has a lower protein content (so it yields less gluten) and is more finely granulated than all-purpose flour.

Although it is best to use the kind of flour a recipe recommends, you can substitute all-purpose flour for cake flour, if necessary. For each 1 cup (250 mL) of cake flour, use 1 cup minus 2 tablespoons (220 mL) of all-purpose flour.

Sugar gives sweetness to cakes. It also tenderizes the gluten and improves the texture of cakes. Recipes may call for either granulated or brown sugar. Both should be free of lumps.

Eggs improve both the flavor and color of cakes. The coagulated egg proteins also give cakes additional structure. In angel food and sponge cakes, eggs are important for leavening. Eggs hold the air that is beaten into them, and the evaporation of liquid from the egg whites creates steam.

Liquid provides moisture and helps blend ingredients together. Most cake recipes call for fluid fresh milk. However, some call for buttermilk, sour milk, fruit juices, or water instead. In angel food cakes, egg whites are the only source of liquid needed.

Be a Clever Consumer

Many consumers who want to cut fat and calories in their diets are buying lowfat margarines. In order to achieve the reduction in fat and calories, manufacturers replace some of the fat in these products with water. These products may be fine for spreading on toast. However, they cannot perform the function of fat in cooking and baking. Read labels carefully. Margarines need to contain at least 80 percent oil in order to produce satisfactory results in cooking and baking.

23-1 Tender, moist shortened cakes are popular as desserts and snacks.

Salt provides flavoring. Cakes require a smaller amount of salt than quick breads and yeast breads.

Fat tenderizes the gluten. Shortened cakes may contain butter, margarine, or hydrogenated vegetable shortening. Chiffon cakes contain oil instead.

Leavening gases cause cakes to rise and become porous and light. Shortened cakes are leavened by baking powder or baking soda and sour milk. Angel food and sponge cakes are leavened entirely by air and steam.

Angel food and sponge cake recipes call for *cream of tartar*. Cream of tartar is an acid that improves the color of egg whites (makes them whiter) and makes the cake grain finer. Cream of tartar also stabilizes the egg white proteins, which increases the volume of the baked cake.

Flavorings are not essential ingredients in cakes, but they help make cakes special. You can add spices, extracts (concentrated flavors), fruits, nuts, poppy seeds, and coconut to cake batters for variety.

Like bread recipes, many dessert recipes call for more of some ingredients than are needed to perform their specific functions. Chart 23-2 shows minimum proportions of fat, eggs, sugar, salt, and baking powder for some desserts. Try using these proportions to adjust cake, cookie, and pastry recipes. Your results will be products that are lower in fat, sugar, and sodium.

Food Science Principles of Preparing Cakes

Successfully preparing a cake depends on measuring, mixing, and baking. You must measure ingredients accurately and mix them correctly. You must bake the cake batter in the correct pans at the correct temperature. Baking time must be exact.

Measuring Ingredients

Flour, fat, sugar, liquid, and eggs affect the development of gluten. The correct proportions of each ingredient will produce a cake that is light

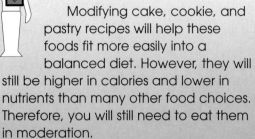

Healthy Living

Modifying cake, cookie, and pastry recipes will help these foods fit more easily into a balanced diet. However, they will still be higher in calories and lower in nutrients than many other food choices. Therefore, you will still need to eat them in moderation.

and tender. Too much or too little of one or more ingredients may affect the finished product.

The optimum amount of flour provides the correct amount of gluten needed for structure. A cake made with too much flour is compact and dry. A cake made with too little flour is coarse, and it may fall.

Optimum amounts of fat and sugar tenderize gluten. Too much fat or sugar overtenderizes the gluten and weakens it. A cake made with too much of either ingredient will be heavy and coarse, and it may fall. A cake made with too little of either ingredient will be tough.

The optimum amount of liquid provides the moisture needed for gluten to develop. Too much liquid will make a cake soggy and heavy. Too little liquid will make a cake dry and heavy.

The optimum number of eggs contributes proteins that strengthen the gluten framework. Too many eggs will make a cake rubbery and tough. See 23-3.

Mixing Cakes

You must mix the correct proportions of ingredients according to the method your recipe directs. Cake batters should be neither overmixed nor undermixed. Overmixing will cause the gluten to overdevelop. As a result, the cake will be tough. Overmixing angel food and sponge cakes will

Minimum Dessert Recipe Proportions per 1 Cup (250 mL) of Flour

Product	Fat	Eggs	Sugar	Salt	Baking Powder
Shortened cakes and dropped cookies	2 tablespoons (30 mL)	1/2	1/2 cup (125 mL)	1/8 teaspoon (.5 mL)	1 teaspoon (5 mL)
Pastry	1/4 cup (50 mL)	—	—	1/2 teaspoon (2 mL)	—

23-2 Using these proportions can help you cut the calories, fat, and sodium from some dessert recipes.

23-3 Measuring ingredients accurately is essential to successful baking.

cause air to be lost from the beaten egg whites. As a result, the volume of the cake will be smaller.

Baking Cakes

Bake cake batter in pans that are neither too large nor too small. If the pans are too small, the batter will overflow. If the pans are too large, the cake will be too flat and may be dry. The correct pan size will produce a cake with a gently rounded top.

You should grease the pans for most shortened cakes and flour them lightly. You may grease and flour both the bottoms and sides of the pans or just the bottoms. You should not grease the pans for unshortened cakes. This is because angel food and sponge cake batters must cling to the sides of the pan during baking.

Place cakes in a preheated oven set at the correct temperature and bake them just until they test done. Cakes baked at too high a temperature may burn. Cakes baked too long may be dry.

Mixing Methods for Cakes

You can mix shortened cakes by the conventional method or the quick mix method. For the *conventional method,* cream the fat and sugar together until light and fluffy. Beat the eggs into the creamed fat and sugar. Then add the sifted dry ingredients alternately with the liquid.

The *quick mix method,* also called the *one-bowl method,* takes less time than the conventional method. Sift the dry ingredients into the mixing bowl. Beat the fat and part of the liquid with the dry ingredients. Add the remaining liquid and unbeaten eggs last. See 23-4.

Shortened Cake
Quick Mix Method
Makes two 8-inch (20 cm) layers or one
13 by 9-inch (33 by 21 cm) cake

2¼ cups sifted cake flour	550 mL sifted cake flour
⅓ cup shortening	75 mL shortening
1¼ cups sugar	300 mL sugar
1½ teaspoons vanilla	7 mL vanilla
2¼ teaspoons baking powder	11 mL baking powder
1 cup skim milk	250 mL skim milk
¼ teaspoon salt	1 mL salt
2 eggs	2 eggs

1. Preheat oven to 350°F (180°C). Have all ingredients at room temperature.
2. Lightly grease and flour two 8-inch (20 cm) round layer pans or one 13 by 9-inch (33 by 21 cm) oblong pan.
3. Sift flour, sugar, baking powder, and salt together into mixing bowl.
4. Add shortening, vanilla, and about two-thirds of the milk.
5. Beat at medium speed with an electric mixer for 2 minutes or 200 strokes by hand.
6. Add remaining milk and eggs; beat an additional 2 minutes or 300 strokes by hand, scraping the bowl often.
7. Pour batter into prepared pans, spreading batter toward the edges, leaving a slight depression in the center.
8. Bake layers 30 to 35 minutes and oblong cake 35 to 40 minutes.

Per ¹⁄₁₂ of cake: 217 Cal. (28% from fat), 3 g protein, 36 g carbohydrate, 7 g fat, 46 mg cholesterol, .4 g fiber, 122 mg sodium.

23-4 A shortened cake can be prepared in one bowl when using the quick mix method.

Angel food and sponge cakes are mixed by a method that differs from either of those used for shortened cakes. For an angel food cake, beat the egg whites with some of the sugar until stiff. Carefully fold the flour and remaining sugar into the beaten egg whites. For a sponge cake, beat the dry ingredients into the egg yolks. Then fold the beaten egg whites into the egg yolk mixture.

Baking a Shortened Cake

When placing pans in the oven, you should arrange them so that the heat circulates freely around the cake. The pans should not touch each other or any part of the oven. If they do, hot spots may form, and the cake may bake unevenly.

To test a cake for doneness, lightly touch the center with your fingertip. If the cake springs back, it is baked. You also can insert a toothpick into the center of the cake. If the toothpick comes out clean, the cake is baked.

Most recipes will tell you to let cakes cool in the pans for about 10 minutes. This cooling period makes it easier to remove the cakes from the pans. To remove a cake from the pan, run the tip of a spatula around the sides of the cake to loosen it. Invert the cooling rack over the top of the pan and gently flip the cooling rack and the pan. The cake should slide out of the pan. Carefully remove the pan and place a second cooling rack on top of the cake. Turn the cake so that it is right side up. Let cake layers cool thoroughly before frosting them.

Characteristics of a Shortened Cake

A high-quality shortened cake is velvety and light. The interior has small, fine cells with thin walls. The crusts are thin and evenly browned. The top crust is smooth or slightly pebbly and gently rounded. The flavor is mild and pleasing.

Pound Cakes

Pound cakes contain no chemical leaveners. They rely on air and steam for leavening. You must thoroughly cream the fat and sugar. Beat the eggs into the creamed mixture until fluffy to incorporate enough air. Add the sifted dry ingredients and the liquid to the creamed mixture. Pound cakes are more compact than other shortened cakes, and they have a closer grain.

Microwaving Cakes

Shortened cakes prepared in a microwave oven come out moist and tasty. Unshortened cakes require a long cooking period and do not microwave well. For best results, prepare unshortened cakes in a conventional oven.

Microwaved cakes will not have the characteristic browning of conventionally prepared cakes. Lack of browning is less noticeable on chocolate, spice, and other dark cakes. Frosting will hide the lack of browning on white or yellow cakes.

Microwave cakes one layer at a time. Use microwavable round or ring-shaped pans for the most even cooking. Begin cooking at a medium power level. Then rotate the cake and complete the last few minutes of cooking on high power. Test cakes for doneness with a toothpick, as in conventional baking.

Preparing an Unshortened Cake

Angel food cake is the most frequently prepared unshortened cake. See 23-5. When preparing an angel food cake, the ingredients should be at

Wilton Industries

23-5 Angel food cake is leavened by air beaten into egg whites.

room temperature. Egg whites that are cold will not achieve maximum volume when beaten.

When you remove an angel food cake from the oven, immediately suspend the pan upside down over the neck of a bottle. Hanging the cake upside down prevents a loss of volume during cooling. Cool an angel food cake completely before removing it from the pan.

Characteristics of an Unshortened Cake

A high-quality angel food cake has a large volume. The interior is spongy and porous and has thin cell walls. The cake is tender and moist, but it is not gummy.

Sponge Cakes

Sponge cakes contain whole eggs rather than just egg whites. To make a sponge cake, you will use a variation of the mixing method used for angel food cakes. Beat the egg yolks until they are thick and lemon colored. Add the liquid, sugar, and salt to the yolks. Continue beating until the mixture is thick. Gently fold the flour into the yolk mixture. Then fold the stiffly beaten egg whites into the flour-yolk mixture.

Preparing a Chiffon Cake

Mix a chiffon cake by combining the egg yolks, oil, liquid, and flavoring with the sifted dry ingredients. Beat the mixture until smooth. Beat the egg whites with the sugar and cream of tartar. Then fold the egg white mixture into the other mixture.

Characteristics of a Chiffon Cake

A high-quality chiffon cake has a large volume, although not quite as large as that of an angel food cake. The interior is moist and has cells with thin walls. The cake is tender and has a pleasing flavor.

Filling and Frosting Cakes

The appeal of many cake recipes does not stop with tender, moist cake. Fillings and frostings can make a simple cake into a really special dessert. Fillings and frostings come in as wide a variety as the cakes they enhance.

Fluffy whipped cream, creamy puddings, and sweet fruits are among the popular fillings for cakes. You can spread fillings between layers of cake or roll them into the center of a jelly roll. You can also spoon them into a cavity dug into the middle of a cake.

Canned frostings and frosting mixes are available, but you can easily make frostings from scratch. Frostings may be cooked or uncooked. Cooked frostings use the principles of candy making. They include ingredients that interfere with the formation of crystals in a heated sugar syrup. Then you beat them until fluffy.

Uncooked frostings are popular for their creamy texture. You can easily make them by beating the ingredients together until they reach a smooth, spreadable consistency. Cream cheese frosting and butter cream are well-liked uncooked frostings.

Frostings not only enhance the flavor of cakes, they also enhance the appearance. You can cut cake layers into pieces and reassemble them to form the shapes of animals and objects. Use frosting as the "glue" to hold the pieces together.

Use decorators' frosting to personalize cakes and trim them with pretty flowers and fancy borders. Cake decorating takes time. With practice, however, you can create cakes that make any celebration extra special. A few simple tools are all you need to start. A *decorators' tube* is a cloth, plastic, or paper bag that you fill with frosting. A *coupler* holds various plastic or metal *decorating tips* onto the tube. Squeeze the frosting through these tips to create various designs. See 23-6.

Cookies

Children and adults find it hard to resist a cookie jar filled with fresh homemade cookies. People enjoy chocolate chip, peanut butter, oatmeal, and sugar cookies year round. At holiday time, many families make special cookies like Swedish pepparkakor, Norwegian krumkakke, German lebkuchen, and Scottish shortbread.

Cookies are easier to make than cakes, and baking cookies is a fun project for children on a rainy day. You can eat cookies alone as desserts or snacks. You can also serve them with ice cream, sherbet, puddings, fruits, and other light desserts.

Kinds of Cookies

All cookies belong to one of six basic groups: rolled, dropped, bar, refrigerator, pressed, or molded. The ingredients used to make different kinds of cookies are similar. However, the doughs differ in consistency, and you shape them differently.

You use a stiff dough to make *rolled cookies*. Roll the dough on a pastry cloth or board to a thickness of $1/8$ to $1/4$ inch (3 to 6 mm). Cut the cookies from the dough with a cookie cutter and transfer them to a cookie sheet. Cookie cutters are available in many shapes and sizes. Sugar cookies are popular rolled cookies.

You use a soft dough to make *dropped cookies*. Drop or push the dough from a spoon onto cookie

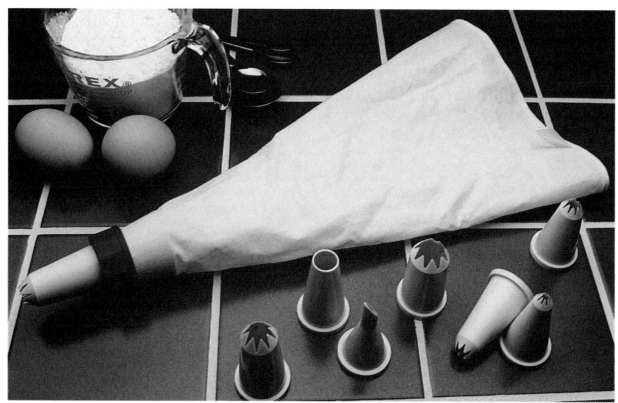

Progressive International Corp.

23-6 These accessories can be used to give any cake a festive trim. They are available at cake and candy supply stores.

sheets. Leave about 2 inches (5 cm) of space between cookies. Dropped cookies will spread more than rolled cookies. Chocolate chip cookies are popular dropped cookies.

You also use a soft dough to make *bar cookies.* Spread the dough evenly in a jelly roll pan or square cake pan and bake it. Depending on the thickness of the dough, bar cookies may be chewy or cakelike. You can cut bar cookies into different shapes after baking. Brownies are popular bar cookies.

Refrigerator cookies contain a high proportion of fat. Form the stiff dough into a long roll, about two inches (5 cm) in diameter. Wrap the roll in foil or plastic wrap and refrigerate it until firm. When the dough has hardened, cut it into thin slices. Place the cookies on lightly greased cookie sheets and bake them. Pinwheel cookies are popular refrigerated cookies.

You use a very rich, stiff dough to make *pressed cookies.* Pack the dough into a *cookie press.* This utensil has perforated disks through which you push the dough onto cookie sheets. The cookies vary in shape and size, depending on the disk used. Swedish spritz cookies are pressed cookies.

You also use a stiff dough to make *molded cookies.* Break off small pieces of dough and shape them with your fingers. Crescents and small balls are popular shapes, 23-7.

Cookie Ingredients

You use the same basic ingredients to make cookies that you use to make cakes. They contain flour, sugar, liquid, fat, salt, egg, and leavening. Most cookies contain more fat and sugar and less liquid than cakes. Rolled cookies often contain no liquid. The proportion of ingredients, as well as the way you shape the cookies, determines if cookies are soft or crisp.

Many cookie recipes call for ingredients such as spices, nuts, coconut, chocolate chips, and dried fruits. Some recipes tell you to add these ingredients to the dough during mixing. Other recipes say to sprinkle cookies or roll them in colored sugars, coconut, or nuts after baking.

Mixing Methods for Cookies

You will make many cookies using the conventional mixing method that you use for shortened cakes. Blend the sugar and fat until smooth. Add the eggs, liquid, and flavorings, followed by the dry ingredients. Cookies are crisp or chewy

Wilton Industries

23-7 Candied cherries add a festive touch of color to these molded thumbprint cookies.

rather than light and delicate. Therefore, you do not need to cream the fat and sugar as thoroughly as you do for a cake. Also, you can add the flour all at once rather than in parts.

Macaroons, meringues, and kisses contain beaten egg whites. You mix them like angel food and sponge cakes. You mix a few cookies, like Scottish shortbread, using the biscuit method. (Chapter 22, "Breads," describes the biscuit method.) Your recipe will tell you which method to use.

Pans for Baking Cookies

Bake dropped, rolled, refrigerator, pressed, and molded cookies on flat baking pans or cookie sheets. Cookie sheets should not have high sides, or cookies will bake unevenly. Bake bar cookies in pans with sides.

Baking pans made of bright, shiny aluminum reflect heat. Cookies baked on bright, shiny cookie sheets will have light, delicate brown crusts. Dark pans absorb heat. Cookies baked on dark cookie sheets will have dark bottoms.

Cookie sheets should be cool when you place cookies on them for baking. Warm sheets will cause cookies to spread and lose their shape.

If you bake two sheets of cookies at one time, you may have to rotate the pans during baking. This will help the cookies brown evenly. Baking pans should never touch each other or the sides of the oven.

Microwaving Cookies

Most microwave ovens are not large enough to efficiently cook dozens of individual cookies. However, bar cookies work well in a microwave oven because the whole pan cooks at once. If using a square or oblong pan, use foil shields to keep the corners from overcooking. Like cakes, bar cookies are often microwaved on medium power and tested with a toothpick for doneness.

Storing Cookies

Store crisp cookies in a container with a loose-fitting cover. To retain their crispness, crisp cookies need to remain dry. Store soft cookies in a container with a tight-fitting cover. Exposure to the air will dry out soft cookies. (Never store crisp and soft cookies together. The soft cookies will soften the crisp cookies.) You can store bar cookies in their baking pan if you cover them, and if you will be eating them in a short time.

For longer storage, you can freeze cookies. Many cookies freeze well both in dough form and after baking.

To freeze refrigerator cookie dough, wrap the shaped rolls tightly in plastic wrap and then in aluminum foil. Label the package and freeze. You can shape molded, rolled, and drop cookie doughs into a large ball. Then wrap and label them for freezer storage. You will need to thaw the dough before molding, rolling, or dropping it. You can freeze bar cookie dough in the baking pan. You can press pressed cookie dough or drop dropped cookie dough onto cookie sheets and quickly freeze it. You can then remove the frozen cookies from the cookie sheet with a spatula. Place them in airtight containers or plastic bags, 23-8. Before baking, thaw the cookies at room temperature on a cookie sheet. To freeze baked cookies, pack them in a sturdy container with a tight-fitting cover. Separate layers of cookies with waxed paper or plastic wrap. Cover the container tightly and label.

Freshening Stale Cookies

You can freshen cookies that have lost their characteristic texture. If crisp cookies have become soft or begun to stale, you can make them crisp again. Place cookies on a cookie sheet in a 300°F (150°C) oven for a few minutes. If soft cookies have become hard, you can make them soft again. Place a piece of bread, an apple slice, or an orange section in the cookie container. Replace bread or fruit every other day.

Pies

Apple pie is a favorite dessert in the United States. Who can resist the flavor, aroma, and eye appeal of golden flaky pastry filled with warm, spicy apples?

Apple pie begins with pastry. **Pastry** is the dough used to make pie crusts. You also use pastry to make tarts, turnovers, appetizers, and shells for main dishes.

Pastry making is not difficult. However, it does require practice and patience.

Uses for Pastry

You can use pastry in many ways. You may mainly use it when making dessert pies. However, you can use pastry when making main dish pies, such as meat pies and quiche. You can fill small pastry shells with foods, such as creamed tuna or chicken a la king, to make potpies. You can also use small pastry shells for individual desserts, such as tarts filled with pudding or ice cream. You can spread rounds of pastry with peanut butter and jelly. You can add cheese to the pastry dough to make cheese sticks.

Wilton Industries

23-8 Freezing scoops of dropped cookie dough in an airtight container allows you to have fresh-baked cookies in minutes anytime.

Kinds of Pies

The four basic kinds of pies are fruit, cream, custard, and chiffon. *Fruit pies* usually are two-crust pies. They may have a solid top crust, or they may have a lattice or other decorative top. You may make the fruit filling from canned, frozen, dried, or fresh fruit. It also may be a commercially prepared pie filling.

Cream pies usually are one-crust pies. Use a cornstarch-thickened pudding mixture to make a cream filling. The filling may or may not contain fruit, coconut, or nuts. Cream pies often have a meringue topping.

Custard pies are one-crust pies filled with a custard made from milk, eggs, and sugar. The custard may or may not contain other ingredients. You may bake the filling in the pie crust or in a separate pie plate the same size as the pie crust. You can then slip the cooled filling into the baked crust. Pumpkin pie is a popular custard pie. See 23-9.

Chiffon pies are light and airy. They are one-crust pies filled with a mixture containing gelatin and beaten egg whites. Some chiffon pie fillings

Wilton Industries

23-9 Sweet potato and pecan pies are especially popular during the autumn months.

also contain whipped cream. Chill all chiffon pies until the filling sets.

Ingredients for Pastry

You will use four basic ingredients to make pastry—flour, fat, salt, and water. When combined correctly, the four ingredients will produce pastry that is tender and flaky.

Flour gives structure to pastry. You may use either pastry or all-purpose flour. Pastry flour contains a lower percentage of protein than all-purpose flour. It requires a smaller amount of fat to produce a tender pastry. Commercial bakeries use pastry flour. Home bakers most often use all-purpose flour.

Fat makes pastry tender by inhibiting the development of gluten. It contributes to flakiness by separating the layers of gluten. Most bakers use lard or hydrogenated vegetable shortening. These fats produce tender and flaky pastry. Some pastry recipes call for oil. Oil-based pastry will be tender, but it will be mealy rather than flaky.

Water provides the moisture needed for the development of the gluten and the production of steam. You need only a small amount of water. For each 1 cup (250 mL) of flour, 2 tablespoons (30 mL) of water is ample.

Salt contributes flavor to pastry. If you eliminate the salt, it will not affect the pastry in any other way.

Food Science Principles of Preparing Pastry

To make pastry that is both tender and flaky, you must use the correct ingredients. You must measure them accurately. You must also handle the dough gently and as little as possible.

Measuring the Ingredients

Flour, fat, and liquid all affect the tenderness and flakiness of pastry. If you do not measure these ingredients accurately, a poor-quality pastry will result.

The gluten that develops when you moisten and stir the flour forms a framework. The gluten framework holds the air and steam that form during baking. Pastry needs the trapped air and steam for flakiness. The optimum amount of flour will produce enough gluten to hold the air and steam. The pastry will be tender and flaky. Too much flour will make the pastry tough.

The fat forms a waterproof coating around the flour particles. This prevents too much water from coming in contact with the proteins of the flour. It also prevents the subsequent development of too much gluten. Layers of fat physically separate the layers of gluten that do form. As a result, the pastry is both tender and flaky. If you use too little fat, the pastry will be tough. If you use too much fat, the pastry will be crumbly.

The liquid hydrates the flour so the gluten will develop. It also produces the steam needed for flakiness. An optimum amount of liquid will moisten the flour just enough to develop the optimum amount of gluten. Too much liquid will make the pastry tough. Too little liquid will make it crumbly and difficult to roll.

Handling the Dough

Too much flour, too much liquid, and too little fat can make pastry tough. Too much handling can also make pastry tough. Handling causes gluten to develop. The more the gluten develops, the tougher the pastry will be.

You should handle pastry gently at all times. You should also handle it as little as possible to prevent overdeveloping the gluten. It is especially important not to

- overmix the dough when adding the liquid.
- use the rolling pin too vigorously when rolling the pastry.
- stretch the pastry when fitting it into the pie plate.

Preparing Pastry

You can use several methods to mix pastry, but the biscuit method (sometimes called the pastry method) is most popular. This method produces pastry that is both tender and flaky. A recipe for pastry mixed by the biscuit method is shown in 23-10.

When making a one-crust pie that you will fill after baking, flute the edges. Prick the bottom and sides of the pie crust with a fork to prevent blistering during baking. Do not prick the bottom or sides of a crust that you will fill before baking.

Characteristics of Pastry

High-quality pastry is both tender and flaky. The amount and distribution of gluten determines tenderness. Flakiness is due to layers of gluten (with embedded starch grains) separated by layers of fat and expanded (puffed up) by steam.

If pastry is tender, it will cut easily with a fork and "melt in the mouth" when eaten. If pastry is flaky, you will be able to see thin layers of dough separated by empty spaces when you cut into the pastry with a fork.

Aside from having pastry that is tender, flaky, and crisp, a pie should be lightly and evenly browned. The filling should have a pleasing flavor and be neither too runny nor too firm.

Pastry

Makes enough pastry for one double-crust or two single-crust pies

2 cups sifted all-purpose flour	500 mL sifted all-purpose flour
½ cup shortening	125 mL shortening
1 teaspoon salt	5 mL salt
¼ to ⅓ cup cold water	50 to 80 mL cold water

1. Preheat oven to 425°F (220°C).
2. Sift flour and salt into a large mixing bowl.
3. Cut in shortening until particles are the size of coarse cornmeal.
4. Sprinkle mixture with cold water, 1 tablespoon (15 mL) at a time, while tossing it lightly with a fork. Push dough against sides of bowl a few times so it holds together; shape into a ball. (Dough may be allowed to rest at this point, if desired.)
5. Divide dough into two portions. On a lightly floured pastry cloth or board, roll one portion of dough into a circle 1 inch (2.5 cm) larger than the pie plate and 1/8 inch (3 mm) thick.
6. Carefully fit dough into pie plate without stretching. Trim excess dough, leaving a ½-inch (1.5 cm) overhang.
   a. If making a one-crust pie, roll under edge and flute. Prick bottom and sides of crust. Bake for 8 to 10 minutes or until golden brown.
   b. For a two-crust pie, roll out top crust and cut steam vents. Place filling in pie shell; moisten edge of bottom crust with water. Place top crust over filling and press gently around edge to seal. Fold top crust under bottom crust and flute. Bake as the recipe for the filling directs.

Per serving: 134 Cal. (59% from fat), 1 g protein, 13 g carbohydrate, 9 g fat, 0 mg cholesterol, .4 g fiber, 178 mg sodium.

23-10 Measuring the ingredients accurately and handling the dough carefully will produce tender, flaky pastry.

Microwaving Pie

You can prepare both pastry crusts and pies successfully in a microwave oven. You should prepare both in glass pie plates to allow the microwaves to penetrate.

Pastry crusts can be microwaved in six to seven minutes. As with many foods, however, pastry will not brown in a microwave oven. You can add cocoa or instant coffee to the flour when making pastry. You also could brush the pastry with a mixture of molasses and egg yolk before baking. Either technique will produce a crust that appears more traditionally brown.

Microwave times for pies vary according to the filling. Fruit pies are best when you place them in a preheated conventional oven for 10 to 15 minutes after microwaving.

Candy

People enjoy candy throughout the year. At holiday time, however, candy making becomes an important activity in many homes. Homemade fudge, divinity, peanut brittle, toffee, and caramels are fun to make and give as gifts.

To make good candy, you must follow directions exactly. You must mix candies correctly and cook them to the exact temperature specified in the recipe. Otherwise, they are likely to fail.

Kinds of Candy

You can make many different kinds of candy at home. A few kinds of candies do not require cooking, but these require special recipes. You will cook most candies. Cooked candies are either crystalline or noncrystalline candies.

Crystalline candies contain fine sugar crystals. They taste smooth and creamy. Fudge, fondant, and divinity are crystalline candies.

Noncrystalline candies do not contain sugar crystals. They can be chewy or brittle. Caramels, peanut brittle, and toffee are noncrystalline candies.

Food Science Principles of Candy Making

All cooked candies begin with a *sugar syrup*. To prepare a sugar syrup, mix sugar with a liquid and heat it. Successful candy making depends on how you treat this sugar syrup.

When making crystalline candies, you want the sugar syrup to form crystals. However, you want these crystals to be very small and fine. To produce small sugar crystals, you must heat the sugar syrup to a specific temperature. You must then cool it to a specific temperature and beat it vigorously.

Fudge is one of the most popular crystalline candies, 23-11. High-quality fudge tastes smooth and creamy because it contains small sugar crystals. It has a deep brown color and a satiny sheen. Poor-quality fudge tastes grainy because it contains large sugar crystals.

When making noncrystalline candies, you do not want the sugar syrup to form crystals. You can prevent crystal formation by heating the syrup to a very high temperature. You can add substances

Hershey Foods Corporation

23-11 A plate of creamy fudge is sure to tempt any sweet tooth.

like corn syrup, milk, cream, or butter, which interfere with crystallization. You can also use a combination of high temperatures and interfering substances to prevent crystals from forming.

Peanut brittle is a popular noncrystalline candy. High-quality peanut brittle has a golden color and looks foamy. Cooking the candy to a very high temperature and using interfering substances prevent crystal formation.

Whether you are making crystalline or noncrystalline candies, temperature is very important. A candy thermometer is the most accurate method of testing the temperature of sugar syrups. Each type of candy requires a specific temperature. The candy thermometer will accurately tell you when a sugar syrup reaches the correct temperature.

You will also want to use a heavy saucepan to cook candy. Mixtures that contain large amounts of sugar burn easily. A heavy saucepan will help prevent scorching.

Microwaving Candy

A microwave oven works well for melting chocolate, caramels, and marshmallows for use in

Play It Safe

Sugar syrups are extremely hot and can cause severe burns if they come in contact with the skin. Use caution when handling sugar syrups. Never leave children unattended while making candy.

recipes. These candies are less likely to stick and burn in a microwave oven than on a conventional range.

In addition to melting prepared candies, you can make fresh candy in a microwave oven. You can successfully prepare both crystalline and noncrystalline candies. Cooking procedures for candies vary. Refer to a microwave cookbook for specific directions. A recipe for peanut brittle prepared in a microwave oven is given in 23-12.

Micro Brittle
Makes 1 pound (450 g)

1	cup sugar	250 mL sugar
1	tablespoon margarine	15 mL margarine
½	cup light corn syrup	125 mL light corn syrup
1¼	teaspoons vanilla	6 mL vanilla
1¼	cups dry roasted peanuts	300 mL dry roasted peanuts
1	teaspoon baking soda	5 mL baking soda

1. Combine sugar and corn syrup in a 2-quart casserole. Microwave on high power for 5 minutes.
2. Blend in peanuts and microwave another 4 minutes, or until syrup and peanuts are lightly browned. Stir candy halfway through cooking.
3. Add margarine, vanilla, and baking soda and stir until light and foamy.
4. Pour brittle onto a margarine-coated baking sheet and spread to a thickness of ¼ inch (6 mm).

Per ounce: 151 Cal. (35% from fat), 3 g protein, 23 g carbohydrate, 6 g fat, 0 mg cholesterol, 1.0 g fiber, 67 mg sodium.

23-12 By using a microwave oven, this peanut brittle can be made in just 10 minutes!

Summary

The two basic types of cakes are shortened, which contain fat, and unshortened, which do not contain fat. Chiffon cakes are a cross between shortened and unshortened cakes. All cakes contain the same essential set of ingredients, each of which performs a specific function. You must measure ingredients carefully, then mix them by the conventional or quick mix method, according to your recipe. You also must use correct pan sizes, oven temperatures, and baking times to make sure that cakes bake properly. After baking, you can fill and/or frost a cake to enhance its flavor and appearance.

Rolled, dropped, bar, refrigerator, pressed, and molded cookies all contain ingredients similar to cakes. You will mix most cookies by the conventional mixing method and bake them on a cookie sheet. You should store crisp cookies in containers with loose-fitting lids and soft cookies in containers with tight-fitting lids.

Pastry is the primary component of fruit, cream, custard, and chiffon pies. Flour, fat, water, and salt are the basic ingredients in pastry. Carefully measuring these ingredients and gently handling the dough will help you produce a tender, flaky pastry.

You can make both crystalline and noncrystalline candies at home. Both types begin with a sugar syrup. You will heat, cool, and then beat sugar syrups for crystalline candies to produce fine sugar crystals. You will heat sugar syrups for noncrystalline candies to high temperatures and/or add interfering substances to keep crystals from forming.

Review What You Have Read

Write your answers on a separate sheet of paper.
1. What are the two groups into which cakes are classified? What type of cake has characteristics of both groups?
2. List the seven basic ingredients of a shortened cake (other than pound cake) and briefly describe the major function of each.
3. What are the functions of cream of tartar in angel food cake?
4. Name three different flavoring ingredients that might be used in a shortened cake.
5. What are the two most common mixing methods for making shortened cakes?
6. Why do baking pans need to be the correct size when baking a cake? How should you arrange them in the oven?
7. True or false. An angel food cake should be removed from the pan as soon as it comes out of the oven.
8. True or false. Both shortened and unshortened cakes can be microwaved successfully.
9. Name the six basic kinds of cookies. In which group do brownies belong?
10. Describe the appearance of cookies baked on a shiny aluminum cookie sheet and cookies baked on a dark cookie sheet.
11. What are the four basic ingredients used to make pastry?
12. What two characteristics are used to describe high-quality pastry?
13. List two reasons why pastry might be tough.
14. Describe two techniques that can be used to give a brown appearance to a pastry crust prepared in a microwave oven.
15. How does a crystalline candy differ in texture from a noncrystalline candy?

Build Your Basic Skills

1. Prepare two angel food cakes. In one cake, add cream of tartar to egg whites during beating. Do not add cream of tartar to the egg whites used in the other cake. Discuss the appearance, texture, and volume of the two cakes.
2. Choose a favorite cookie recipe. Write down the amount of each ingredient you would need to prepare a double batch. Also note the yield for the double batch.
3. Prepare enough pastry for a two-crust pie. Divide the dough in half. Roll half of the dough and cut it into 1 inch (2.5 cm) strips. Place the strips on a cookie sheet. Knead the other half of the dough for several minutes. Roll and cut the dough into 1 inch (2.5 cm) strips and place them on a second cookie sheet. Bake the pastry strips. After comparing the appearance and texture of the two samples, write a paragraph explaining why overhandling should be avoided.
4. Prepare two batches of fudge. Follow directions exactly for the first batch. For the second batch, stir fudge occasionally during cooling. After the fudge has set, compare texture, flavor, and appearance.

Build Your Thinking Skills

1. Prepare one shortened cake made with granulated sugar and another made with brown sugar. Store the cakes in covered containers for several days. Compare the flavor and texture.
2. Prepare one pie crust using hydrogenated vegetable shortening and another using oil. Compare the texture, flavor, and appearance of the two crusts. Which do you prefer? Why?

Chapter 24

Parties, Picnics, and Dining Out

A "Taste" of the World of Work

Social Director
Plans and organizes recreational activities and creates friendly atmosphere for guests in hotels and resorts or for passengers on board ships.

Coffee Roaster
Controls gas fired roasters to remove moisture from coffee beans.

Food and Beverage Analyst
Examines food samples and food service records to determine sales appeal and cost of preparing and serving foods in establishments, such as restaurants.

Terms to Know

RSVP
manners
etiquette
appetizer
blend
grind
decaffeinated

caffeine
tea
reservation
table d'hôte
a la carte
gratuity
tip

Objectives

After studying this chapter, you will be able to
- ❏ plan a party.
- ❏ prepare party foods and beverages.
- ❏ safely prepare and pack food for outdoor meals.
- ❏ follow etiquette rules when dining out.

Ashwood Basket Corp., Peterborough, New Hampshire

Try to participate in your party as much as possible. Circulate from guest to guest instead of spending the evening with just one or two close friends. It is up to you to make all of your guests feel welcome.

The Guest's Responsibilities

A good guest also has responsibilities. These begin with the invitation. Always answer an invitation as soon as possible. You may be able to give an immediate response to a telephoned invitation. If not, you should answer within a day or two. Formal events require a written response. When responding to an invitation, repeat the time and the date to avoid any misunderstandings. See 24-2.

Arrive at a party at the designated time. Guests who arrive too early can disrupt last minute preparations. Guests who arrive late can be the cause of a ruined meal.

Greet any members of your host's family who happen to be present. Follow house rules, and always be courteous.

Table Manners

When dining in a friend's home, you should use your best table manners. **Manners** refer to social behavior. Society sets rules of **etiquette,** which guide manners. Good manners help people feel comfortable in social situations. Knowing

proper etiquette will help you relax in unfamiliar settings because you will know how to behave. Those around you will also feel more at ease because your behavior will not be offensive to them.

The guidelines below will help you feel more comfortable and show your consideration for others at the dinner table. Some of these guidelines may be more casual than those taught to your parents and grandparents in years past. Although they are less strict, rules do still exist, and you still need to follow them.

- A man should help seat the woman who is nearest to him on his right. He sometimes also will help the woman on his left.
- Shortly after sitting down, open your napkin to a comfortable size and place it in your lap.
- When passing dishes at the table, always pass them in one direction.
- Wait for the host to begin eating.
- Try to eat at least a small portion of each food served. If you cannot eat something, leave it without comment.
- Use eating utensils in the order in which they have been placed on the table—from the outside toward the plate.
- Never set a used eating utensil on the table. Place a spoon used for coffee or tea on the edge of the saucer. Place your dessert spoon on the service plate. Place your knife across the upper rim of your dinner plate, with the sharp edge toward the center. Place your butter knife on your bread and butter plate.
- If you drop an eating utensil, do not use it anymore. Your host should give you another one.
- Do not place your elbows on the table while eating.
- Keep one hand in your lap while eating.
- Do not reach in front of another diner for food. Ask someone to pass the food to you. Take helpings of average size.
- Remove seeds, pits, or fish bones from your mouth with your fingers as inconspicuously as possible. Place them on the side of your plate.
- Tear a slice of bread into two parts and then in two again. Butter only one fourth of a slice at a time. Tear biscuits or rolls in half.
- If you cough or sneeze at the table, use your handkerchief and quietly excuse yourself. If you have a coughing or sneezing spell, quietly excuse yourself and leave the table.

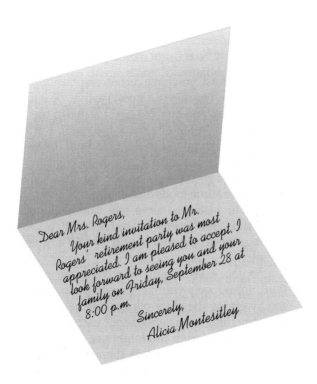

Dear Mrs. Rogers,
Your kind invitation to Mr.
Rogers' retirement party was most
appreciated. I am pleased to accept. I
look forward to seeing you and your
family on Friday, September 28 at
8:00 p.m.
Sincerely,
Alicia Montesitley

24-2 Acceptance of an invitation to a formal event should be made in writing.

- When you have finished eating, place your knife on the rim of the plate with the sharp edge pointing toward the center. Place the fork parallel to the knife. Lay your napkin casually to the left of the plate. Wait for your host to invite you to leave the table.

Offer to assist with last minute details or cleanup tasks if you see the host needs help. Most hosts will appreciate your help in picking up used glasses and food or napkins that are on the floor. If the host refuses help, do not insist.

Food for Parties

Party foods can be almost any foods. Try to plan foods you like to prepare and serve. Choose foods you think your guests will like.

Appetizers

Appetizers are small, light foods served to stimulate the appetite. They are often served at the beginning of a meal. Appetizers are also popular as party foods, 24-3.

National Pork Producers Council

24-3 Stuffed mushrooms, cheese spread and crackers, and meat-wrapped fruit slices make a nice variety of taste-tempting appetizers.

You can prepare many appetizers in advance, so they require little last minute attention. You can conveniently serve appetizers to a large group because guests can eat them while standing. You are also likely to spend less money for party food when serving appetizers than when serving a full meal.

Instead of serving chips and pretzels at your next party, be creative and try making your own appetizers. Choose appetizers that guests will find easy to nibble while they mingle. Remember to select both hot and cold appetizers, using ingredients with a variety of flavors, colors, and textures.

Microwaving Appetizers

You might use a microwave oven to save time when preparing hot appetizers. Mini pizzas, toasted nuts, cocktail sausages, chicken wings, and hot dips are just a few of the tasty appetizers that can be microwaved. You can prepare many of these foods ahead of time and then microwave them at the last minute.

You can adapt many conventional appetizer recipes for the microwave oven. Appetizers containing delicate ingredients, such as sour cream, cheese, eggs, milk, and mayonnaise, should be microwaved at lower settings. Stir dips and sauces halfway through the cooking period to promote even heating. Spread toppings on crackers or toast points just before microwaving to prevent them from getting soggy. Place egg rolls and foods with cracker bases on paper towels to help absorb excess moisture.

Beverages for Parties

Another concern of hosts is what to serve their guests to drink. The type of party you are giving may indicate the type of beverage that is appropriate. For instance, you might serve coffee and tea at a reception or dinner. However, guests are likely to expect cold drinks at a picnic.

Coffee

Coffee is a popular beverage at many social gatherings, especially when adults are present. You might serve coffee to accompany cookies or cakes at a reception. You can also serve it with a meal or with dessert at a luncheon or banquet. See 24-4.

You can serve coffee in mugs or disposable cups for informal occasions. However, cups and saucers are more appropriate at dinners and formal events. Offer cream and sugar with coffee and give guests spoons for stirring.

Coffee is made from the beans of the coffee plant. The beans are dried, roasted, and packaged for shipment. The flavor of coffee beans depends on the variety, growing conditions, and roasting technique.

You have many different choices when buying coffee. You can choose between individual varieties and coffee blends. Coffees that have added flavorings, such as hazelnut or French vanilla, are also quite popular.

Popular Coffee Beverages

Espresso	A strong coffee brewed by forcing very hot water under pressure through finely ground, darkly roasted coffee beans. Espresso is typically served as a 1½-ounce (42 g) portion in a small cup called a *demitasse*.
Cappuccino	A coffee beverage comprised of one part espresso, one part steamed milk, and one part frothed milk. It is often served with a sprinkling of cocoa or cinnamon.
Iced cappuccino	A chilled coffee beverage prepared by pouring 1½ ounces (42 g) of espresso over ice and adding 3 ounces (84 g) of cold milk. Frothed milk is spooned on top and the beverage is sweetened to taste.
Caffé latte	A coffee beverage of Italian origin prepared in a mug by adding 6½ to 8½ ounces (182 to 238 g) of steamed milk to 1½ ounces (42 g) of espresso. Italian syrups in flavors like hazelnut and almond are often added.
Café mocha	A coffee beverage prepared by mixing chocolate syrup or powder and 5 ounces (140 g) of steamed milk with 1½ ounces (42 g) of espresso. This beverage may be topped with whipped cream.

24-4 These are just a few of the many coffee beverages that are gaining popularity at coffee bars throughout the United States.

A coffee **blend** may contain as many as six different varieties of coffee beans. Blends vary from brand to brand. Many people try several brands before finding the blend they like best. Because the blend remains the same, one brand will always have the same flavor and aroma.

You can choose ground or whole bean coffee. Ground coffee comes in different **grinds.** Select the grind that fits the method of preparation you plan to use. Use *medium* or *drip grind* in a drip coffee maker. Use *coarse* or *regular grind* in a percolator. If you choose whole bean coffee, you can have it ground at the store. For freshness, however, you might prefer to grind it yourself just before brewing.

You may purchase coffee from bulk containers or in vacuum-sealed packages. You might choose bulk coffee so you can buy just as much as you want. However, coffee stales quickly when exposed to moisture and air. Therefore, you might choose vacuum packaging, which helps coffee stay fresh longer.

You can purchase coffee in instant form. *Instant coffee products* are dry, powdered, water-soluble solids made by removing the moisture from very strong, brewed coffee. Some brands are freeze-dried. Prepare instant coffee by adding simmering water to the coffee granules according to the manufacturer's directions.

Decaffeinated coffee is made by removing most of the caffeine from coffee beans before roasting. **Caffeine** is a compound that acts as a stimulant. Decaffeinated coffee is available in several grinds and in instant form.

Preparing Coffee

You can brew ground coffee by several methods. Regardless of the method you choose, be sure to start with fresh, *cold* water and a clean pot. Thoroughly wash the inside of your coffee pot with hot, soapy water and rinse it well after each use. Oily film that collects on the inside of a coffee pot can cause coffee to be bitter.

Coffee packers generally recommend 1 to 2 tablespoons (15 to 30 mL) ground coffee per 6-ounce (175 mL) serving. You may use more or less, depending on your taste preferences.

In most *electric percolators*, you place the ground coffee in a basket that fits over a slender tube or pump. The pump fits into a well in the bottom of the pot. This well contains the heating element. When a small amount of water under the pump becomes hot, the coffee begins to perk. The water is forced up the pump stem into the basket, where it spreads over the coffee grounds. The perking continues until the coffee reaches the correct strength.

Most homemakers use a *drip coffeemaker* to make coffee. This appliance has a water reservoir, a basket, and a serving pot. Measure water for the desired amount of coffee and pour it into the water reservoir. Place a filter in the basket and add the appropriate amount of coffee. Put the basket in place, with the serving pot below. When the water becomes hot, it filters through the coffee into the empty pot below.

Serve coffee as soon as possible after brewing it. Heating coffee for too long can cause it to become bitter. This is because bitter substances present in coffee become more soluble at high temperatures. Correctly prepared coffee is clear and flavorful. It is piping hot and has a pleasing aroma, 24-5.

Tea

An afternoon tea gives friends an opportunity to meet and enjoy conversation and light refreshments. Tea is often served with simple foods, such as finger sandwiches, nut breads, and cookies, at such gatherings. Hot tea may be served in place of or in addition to coffee at brunches, dinners, receptions, and other occasions. Iced tea is popular at picnics and other warm weather get-togethers.

You can serve tea at the dining table, from a buffet table, or from a tray. Use cups and saucers or serving sets (plates with wells to hold matching cups) so guests have a place to put food tidbits. Serve cream, sugar, and lemon with tea and offer spoons for stirring. Also provide cocktail napkins.

Tea is made from the leaves of a small tropical evergreen. India, Ceylon, China, Indonesia, and Japan are the major tea-producing countries.

Teas vary according to the age of the tea leaves and the way they are processed. The season of harvest, the altitude, the soil, and the climate also cause teas to vary. The three main types of tea are black, green, and oolong.

Black teas are made from tea leaves that are heated and dried (fermented). When brewed, black teas are amber in color and have a rich aroma and

Protect the Planet

Choose unbleached filters for brewing coffee in a drip coffeemaker. Bleaching does not improve the performance of a filter. However, it does involve a chemical process that contributes to water pollution.

24-5 Fresh, hot coffee is a delicious complement to rich desserts.

flavor. Broken orange pekoe is the best grade of black tea.

Green teas are made from tea leaves that are steamed and then rolled and dried. They are not fermented. When brewed, green teas are a greenish-yellow color. They are bitter and have little aroma. Gunpowder is one of the best grades of green tea.

Oolong teas are made from partially fermented tea leaves. The appearance and flavor of the beverage made from oolong teas falls between that of the black and green teas.

Other Forms of Tea

Tea is available in instant form. Instant teas may be flavored with sugar and lemon. You can dissolve them in cold or freshly boiled water.

Decaffeinated teas are available. People who drink tea but do not like its stimulating effects enjoy decaffeinated teas.

Tea can be flavored. Spices like cinnamon, herbs like mint, and floral fragrances like jasmine are popular flavorings.

Herbal teas are made from a variety of plants. These teas have become popular because they come in many interesting flavors and they do not contain caffeine. Fennel seeds, chamomile flowers, ginger root, and blackberry leaves are just a few of the ingredients commonly found in herbal teas.

Some people have allergic reactions to some of the plants used in herbal teas. When purchasing herbal teas, it is best to choose from among commercial brands. Avoid herbal mixtures that claim to have special health or medicinal properties.

Preparing Tea

A clean teapot and freshly boiled water are essential for good tea. When preparing tea, you must extract flavoring substances from the tea leaves without extracting substances that make tea bitter. If the tea leaves stay in contact with the water for too long, the tea can become bitter.

You can purchase tea in filter paper bags or in loose form. To prepare either form of tea, begin by rinsing a teapot with boiling water to preheat it. Place tea bags or loose tea in the preheated pot. (Place loose tea directly in the bottom of the pot, in a cheesecloth bag, or in a tea ball. A *tea ball* is a perforated ball made of silver or stainless steel.) Then pour freshly boiled water over the tea. Allow the tea to steep two to six minutes, until it reaches the desired strength. Remove the tea from the pot before serving.

Iced Tea

Iced tea is a refreshing cold drink, 24-6. Prepare it by first making hot tea. If desired, dissolve honey or sugar in the tea. Then pour it over

Anchor Glass Container Corp.

24-6 Tall, cool glasses of iced tea quickly satisfy thirst at summer gatherings.

Another factor that affects the speed of fast-food restaurants is self-service. Customers enter the restaurant and place their orders at a counter. They pay, receive their food, and leave or take a seat. When they have finished eating, they throw away their disposable food wrappers and containers. Customers do not have to wait to be seated or to place their orders. The dining area requires a minimum of cleanup. This allows a steady stream of people to keep moving in and out of the restaurant.

Food at fast-food restaurants is relatively inexpensive. The high sales volume and limited service help keep prices down. Because customers do not receive service from waiters, they do not have to leave tips in fast-food restaurants. This also saves customers money.

Cafeterias and Buffets

Cafeterias have a variety of prepared foods placed along a serving line. Customers carry a tray along the line and select the foods they want. Foods are served in individual portions and each item is priced separately. Customers pay for the items on their tray when they reach the end of the line.

Buffets are similar to cafeterias as far as the way the food is served. However, at buffets, customers generally pay a fixed price for the meal. They can serve themselves as much of each food on the buffet line as they like. They can also return to the serving line for more food as many times as they wish.

Neither cafeterias nor buffets have waiters to take customers' food orders at the table. However, servers may take beverage orders, refill coffee, and clear dirty dishes. For these services, leaving a tip of about 10 percent of the food bill is appropriate.

Family Restaurants

Family restaurants offer casual, comfortable dining. These restaurants appeal to people dining out with children. Prices are reasonable, so meals can fit into a family food budget. Family restaurants offer a variety of popular menu items. This allows each family member to order a different favorite food. See 24-11.

Formal Restaurants

Formal restaurants offer an elegant dining atmosphere. Customers dine on fine foods and receive excellent service. In keeping with the atmosphere, guests in formal restaurants should dress formally.

Skilled chefs usually prepare the foods served at formal restaurants. They use only the freshest ingredients. Menus may list daily specials created by the chef.

Some formal restaurants only seat guests at certain times. For instance, they may have a 6:00 P.M. seating and a 9:00 P.M. seating. All the guests for the first seating arrive at about the same time. After leisurely enjoying their meals, the guests depart. The restaurant staff then prepares the dining room for the guests who will be arriving for the second seating.

The high quality food and service at formal restaurants often cause them to be rather expensive. Some people also tend to tip a bit more in these restaurants than they would elsewhere. Be prepared for these expenses before you go to a formal restaurant.

Specialty Restaurants

Specialty restaurants focus on a specific type of food. Pizza parlors, steak houses, and ethnic restaurants are all specialty restaurants.

Specialty restaurants come in all price ranges. Some fast-food, family, and formal restaurants are also specialty restaurants.

24-11 Family restaurants offer a varied menu in a casual dining atmosphere.

Summary

Planning a party begins with choosing a theme. Then you need to make up a guest list and extend invitations. You need to choose a menu and determine how you will serve it. As a host, you have the responsibility of making your guests feel comfortable in your home. In return, your guests have the responsibility of using their best manners and respecting your property.

A party menu can include any foods and beverages that you enjoy making and that your guests will enjoy eating and drinking. Appetizers are a party favorite. You can make them ahead and microwave them at the last minute. Coffee, tea, chocolate and cocoa beverages, and cold drinks are all popular refreshments at social gatherings. Knowing how to prepare these beverages properly will make them welcome offerings when you are serving guests.

Almost everyone enjoys picnics and barbecues when the weather is nice. No matter what type of outdoor entertaining you do, you need to transport and serve food carefully to keep it safe. You also need to be sure the outdoor area is clean when your party leaves.

Dining out can be an everyday experience or a special treat. Knowing how to make reservations, order, and tip in a restaurant will help you feel more comfortable when dining out. Your choice of restaurants includes fast-food, cafeteria, buffet, family, formal, and specialty establishments. You should be able to find a menu and a price range to suit any taste.

Review What You Have Read

Write your answers on a separate sheet of paper.
1. What information should be included on all invitations?
2. List four factors that should be considered when planning a party menu.
3. Give three responsibilities of a host.
4. List five guidelines to follow when dining in a friend's home.
5. True or false. Appetizers containing sour cream, cheese, eggs, milk, and mayonnaise should be microwaved at lower settings.
6. Give one advantage of coffee sold in bulk containers and one advantage of coffee sold in vacuum-sealed packages.
7. Teas made from partially fermented tea leaves are called _____.
   A. black teas
   B. green teas
   C. oolong teas
   D. herbal teas
8. What cookery principles do you need to follow when preparing chocolate and cocoa beverages?
9. How can you prevent cold drinks from being diluted by ice cubes?
10. List four important safety precautions you should follow when cooking outdoors.
11. True or false. Picnic foods should sit out so picnickers can enjoy them all afternoon.
12. On what type of restaurant menu are food items priced individually?
13. What would be an appropriate tip for average service on a restaurant bill totaling $13.35?
14. What terms might be used on a menu to describe foods prepared in the following ways?
   A. Garnished with almonds.
   B. Sautéed with mushrooms, tomatoes, and olives.
   C. Served with ice cream.
   D. Prepared with spinach.

Build Your Basic Skills

1. Investigate food-borne illnesses that can result from improperly handling food. Write a two-page report about how to safely transport and serve picnic and barbecue food in order to avoid illness.
2. Obtain menus from several different restaurants ranging from casual to formal. Identify each menu as table d'hôte or a la carte. Find terms from Chart 24-9 used in the menus. In small groups, role-play making reservations and paying the bill at one of the restaurants.

Build Your Thinking Skills

1. Working in a small group, choose a theme, write an invitation, and plan a menu for a party.
2. Prepare several different coffee blends. Compare color, aroma, and flavor. Identify the blend you prefer and explain why you prefer it.

Chapter 25

Preserving Foods

A "Taste" of the World of Work

Pickler
Pickles prepared food products in preservative or flavoring solutions.

Dehydrator Tender
Tends sulfur and drying chambers to bleach and dehydrate fruit.

Freezer Tunnel Operator
Tends freeze tunnel to quick-freeze food products.

Terms to Know

microorganism	pectin
bacteria	marmalade
mold	jam
yeast	preserves
enzyme	conserves
blanch	quick-freezing
raw pack	freezer burn
hot pack	ascorbic acid
headspace	fruit leather
petcock	sulfuring
processing time	freeze-drying
flat-sour	aseptic packaging
botulism	retort packaging
jelly	irradiation

Objectives

After studying this chapter, you will be able to
- ❏ explain principles of food preservation.
- ❏ discuss techniques for home canning and making jellied products.
- ❏ describe procedures for freezing and drying foods.
- ❏ identify methods of commercial food preservation.

Alltrista Consumer Products Company, marketers of Ball® home canning products

Even primitive people realized that food is *perishable* (subject to spoilage). They understood that they needed some form of *preservation* to keep food from decaying. They learned to preserve food when it was bountiful for times of scarcity. The first preserved foods were probably dried seeds, seed pods, fruits, and vegetables. Later, meats were smoked and dried.

People in early times discovered that burying some foods in the earth kept the foods fresh longer. They built storage places called *cellars*. They dug several feet (meters) down into the ground and covered the space with a ceiling. They piled earth on top of the ceiling for insulation. They lined some cellars with concrete or brick. Nature kept the temperature between 50° and 60°F (10° and 16°C). In summer, it was a cool place to store food when there was no kind of refrigeration. In winter, food stayed cool without freezing. Cellars became a storage place for foods such as apples, potatoes, onions, carrots, turnips, and cured meats.

Today's homemakers can buy foods in all seasons, but many people still like to preserve food. This is especially true of people who have fruit and vegetable gardens. Three popular methods of food preservation are canning, freezing, and drying.

Food Spoilage

Microorganisms are microscopic living substances. Bacteria, mold, and yeast are all microorganisms related to food preservation. *Bacteria* are single-celled or noncellular microscopic plants. They live in soil, water, organic matter, and the bodies of plants and animals. They are important because they can produce chemical reactions in living organisms and cause disease. *Mold* is a growth produced on damp or decaying organic matter or on living organisms. *Yeast* is a microscopic fungus that can cause fermentation in preserved foods, resulting in spoilage.

These microorganisms, along with enzymes, have both good and bad effects on food. (*Enzymes* are complex proteins produced by living cells that cause specific chemical reactions.) Some bacteria are used to make buttermilk and sauerkraut. Certain molds are used in curing some cheeses such as Roquefort and Camembert. Yeast makes breads rise. Enzymes ripen foods and tenderize meats.

The bad effect of microorganisms is food spoilage. Enzymes can cause foods to deteriorate. They can soften the texture, change the color, and impair the flavor of foods. To preserve food, you must inactivate or destroy bacteria, mold, yeast, and enzymes.

Microorganisms need food, moisture, and favorable temperatures to grow. By removing one of these conditions, you can preserve food. Since you cannot eliminate food, you must remove moisture or favorable temperatures to stop the spoiling action of microorganisms. Enzyme action is controlled most often by extreme temperatures.

Freezing temperatures prevent microorganisms from growing and retard the action of enzymes. High temperatures, as those used in canning, destroy both microorganisms and enzymes.

Drying preserves food by removing moisture needed for the growth of microorganisms. To control enzyme activity, vegetables are blanched before drying. (**Blanch** means to scald or parboil in water or steam.) Some fruits are also blanched. Others are treated with sulfur dioxide or sulfates.

Canning Foods

People can foods at home for many reasons. Many home canners simply enjoy eating foods they can themselves. They often can their own special recipes of items like barbecue or spaghetti sauces. Some people can to avoid wasting an overabundance of seasonal fruits and vegetables. Others want to avoid the preservatives added to commercially canned foods.

Still another reason for home canning is the low cost, 25-1. Home canning can reduce food costs if you do it frequently. The equipment is expensive, so buy it only if you plan to can for several years. You can save more money if you grow the food yourself.

You must follow canning procedures carefully to ensure proper preservation of food. You can obtain step-by-step directions on home canning from manufacturers of canning products and county extension agents.

Foods for Canning

A wide variety of foods are suitable for home canning. Fruits, vegetables, juices, meats, pickles, and jellies are some of the most commonly home-canned items.

Thoroughly wash all fruits and vegetables before canning. Handle them gently as you wash a few at a time. Do not allow them to soak, as they may lose food value.

For best results, use only perfect fruits and vegetables. Choose young, tender vegetables and firm, fresh fruits. Sort them for size and ripeness so they will cook evenly. Can them while they are still fresh.

25-1 Canning food at home can be economical if foods are grown at home or purchased in season when prices are low.

jars. For raw-pack jars, heat water in the canner until it is hot. For hot-pack jars, heat the water to boiling. Set the filled jars on the rack in the canner so water surrounds each one. Add boiling water to bring the water level 1 to 2 inches (2.5 to 5 cm) above the tops of the jars. Cover the canner and allow the water to come to a rolling boil.

When the water comes to a rolling boil, the processing time begins. As with pressure canning, processing time varies with the type of food being canned. The water boils steadily throughout the processing time. Add more boiling water as needed to keep the jars covered. When processing time is up, quickly remove the jars from the canner and allow them to cool. See 25-4.

Other Canning Methods

In the past, people used several other canning methods, including open kettle canning, oven canning, and steam canning. However, food safety experts do not recommend these methods. New research has shown that these methods may not completely destroy all the microorganisms in food. Therefore, eating foods canned by these methods may be unsafe.

After Canning

Test the seals the day after canning. To do this, press the center of each lid. Make sure it is concave and does not flex up and down. Then remove the screw band and make sure you cannot lift the lid off with your fingertips. If the jars pass this inspection, they have formed a good vacuum seal.

If you find a leaky jar, use the food right away. You could also can the food again, treating it as if it were fresh. Check jars and lids carefully for defects before using them again.

When jars are completely cool, carefully remove screw bands. If a band sticks, a hot, damp cloth held against the band may help loosen it. Wash bands and store them in a dry place for future use.

Wipe jars clean with a soapy cloth, rinse them well, and dry them thoroughly. Label each jar, listing the type of food and the date. If you canned more than one lot on the same day, list the lot number, too.

Properly canned foods stored in a cool, dry, dark place will last as long as a year. A cool temperature helps foods maintain appearance, flavor, and nutrients. Do not allow canned foods to freeze. If this happens, the food becomes soft and loses much of its appeal. However, it is not spoiled unless the seal is broken. Dampness may corrode metal lids and cause leakage. This makes the foods spoil. Heat and light may cause food to lose some of its eating quality after only a few weeks.

Checking for Spoilage

Before eating home-canned foods, take certain safety precautions. Look for bulging lids and leaks. These are signs of broken seals and spoilage. When you open jars, look for other signs of spoilage. These include spurting liquid, an off odor, mold, gas bubbles on the surface, and unusually soft food. If you see any of these signs, do *not* taste the food. Dispose of it so that neither humans nor animals will eat it. Use a food waste disposer, or burn it.

Flat-sour is a type of spoilage caused by bacteria. Flat-sour bacteria cause canned food to become sour without creating gas. The food often looks normal, but it is lightly acidic. (A delay in processing or failure to cool jars quickly may cause flat-sour.) Although flat-sour spoilage may not make the food harmful, it is wise to discard such foods.

Botulism is a food-borne illness caused by eating foods containing the spore-forming bacteria *clostridium botulinum.* These bacteria can occur in home-canned foods that were improperly processed. Botulism is the most dangerous type of food poisoning. Even a taste of food containing the toxin produced by these bacteria can be fatal. This is why following only the latest, researched recommendations for canning methods and processing times is so important. Using proper canning methods is especially important for low-acid foods and unacidified tomatoes.

The texture of foods spoiled by botulism may be very soft and mushy. The foods may smell like rancid cheese. However, some spoiled foods look and smell normal. If you have any question about the safety of a home-canned food, you should not take any chances. Boil the food for 10 to 15 minutes in an uncovered saucepan before eating it. This will destroy any toxins and microorganisms. If the food looks spoiled, foams, or has an off odor during heating, *destroy it!*

Making Jellied Products

Jelly is made from fruit juice. It is clear and firm enough to hold its shape when removed from its container.

Canning principles are used in making jelly. You heat the ingredients to destroy microorganisms. Then you fill glass containers with jelly and seal them to prevent recontamination.

25-4 You can process high-acid foods, such as acidified tomatoes, in a boiling water bath.

Ingredients

You need four basic ingredients to make good jelly: fruit juice, pectin, acid, and sugar.

Fruit Juice

Fruit juice gives jelly its flavor and color. You can use the juice of almost any fruit. Flavorful fruits are best because the large amount of sugar in jelly dilutes the flavor of the fruit. Fruit also contributes some or all of two other ingredients—pectin and acid.

Use a *jelly bag* to extract juice from fruit. Make a jelly bag from several layers of closely-woven cheesecloth or a firm, unbleached muslin. A colander or sieve holds the jelly bag while juice is being extracted from the fruit. See 25-5.

Thoroughly wash fruit in cold water before preparing it for juice extraction. Follow the preparation method appropriate for the type of fruit you are using. Then place prepared fruit in a damp jelly bag. Letting the juice drip from the bag without squeezing it produces the clearest jelly. However, you can obtain more juice by squeezing the juice through the bag. You must place squeezed juice in a second jelly bag that is clean and damp. Allow the juice to drip through this bag without squeezing.

Pectin

Pectin is a carbohydrate found in all fruits. It makes fruit juices jell. Some fruits have more pectin than others. Unripe fruits have more pectin than mature, ripe fruits. Unripe figs, bananas, and pears, as well as sweet apples, are rich in pectin. However, these fruits are low in acid, another ingredient needed to make jelly.

If the fruit you are using is low in pectin, you can correct it. You can buy pectin in either powdered or liquid form. You can use either kind with any fruit. However, they are not interchangeable.

25-5 To collect juice for jelly making, place fruit inside a jelly bag. Put the bag in a colander over a bowl to catch the juices that drip through.

Follow your recipe. Use the form and amount of pectin it suggests.

Commercial pectin is an aid in making jelly. Using commercial pectin allows you to use fully ripe fruit and shorten the cooking time. It also allows you to make more jelly from the same amount of fruit.

Acid

Acid works along with pectin to make fruit juices jell. It also adds flavor to jelly. All fruits contain varying amounts of acids. Unripe fruits have more acid than ripe fruits. Apricots and strawberries are high in acid content, but have little pectin.

You can add lemon juice or citric acid to fruits that are low in acid. They are interchangeable. The equivalent of 1 tablespoon (15 mL) lemon juice is ⅛ teaspoon (0.5 mL) crystalline citric acid.

The ripeness of fruits affects pectin and acid content. The following fruits are rich in both pectin and acid: tart apples, blackberries, cranberries, sour plums, and grapes. Most peaches are low in both pectin and acid.

Sugar

Sugar helps jelly become firm. It also adds flavor and helps preserve the jelly. Leaving some of the sugar out of a jelly recipe will cause the jelly to be runny. However, recipes are available for making jellies with artificial sweeteners for people want to avoid sugar.

Making Jelly

To make jelly without added pectin, combine all ingredients in a kettle large enough to avoid boilovers. Bring the mixture to a full boil over a high heat. Carefully measure the temperature with a jelly, candy, or deep-fat thermometer. Allow the temperature to reach 8°F (4.5°C) above the boiling point of water. At this point, the concentration should be just right to form a good jell.

When the jelly is done cooking, remove the kettle from the heat. Skim off any foam that is present on the jelly. Then pour the jelly into jars.

Special decorator jars are available for canning jelly, or you can use regular canning jars. After being washed and sterilized, keep the jars in hot water until you are ready to use them. This prevents them from breaking when you pour the hot jelly into them. After filling and capping the jars, process them in a boiling water canner.

Jelly will jell as it stands overnight. (You can recook jelly that does not jell with added sugar, water, acid, and pectin to help it set.) Label containers with the type of jelly, the date, and the lot number.

Store jelly in a cool, dark, dry place. The sooner you eat it, the better it will taste.

You prepare jellies made with added commercial pectins a bit differently. If you are making jelly with powdered pectin, add the sugar after the mixture has reached a rolling boil. If you are using liquid pectin, bring the juice and sugar to a boil. Then add the pectin.

Other Jellied Products

Marmalade, jam, preserves, conserves, and fruit butters are all fruit spread products similar to jelly. You make them all from fruit, using sugar as a preservative.

Marmalade is a tender jelly containing small pieces of fruit and fruit rind. It is often made from citrus fruit and it may contain a mixture of fruits.

Make *jam* from crushed fruit. Cook it to a fairly even consistency. It tends to hold its shape, but it is less firm than jelly, 25-6.

Preserves are whole fruits or large pieces of fruit in a thick syrup. They are slightly jellied.

Conserves are jams made from a mixture of fruits, usually including citrus fruits. Raisins and nuts are sometimes added. Conserves are thicker with fruit than are marmalades and the fruit can be in slightly larger pieces.

Fruit butters are not a jellied product. They are made from cooked, pureed fruit.

Like jelly, you must process all of these products by the boiling water method. After you combine and boil the ingredients, pour the mixtures into hot, sterilized canning jars. Then seal and process the jars. After cooling, label the products and store them in a dark, dry, cool place.

Make *uncooked jams* by adding sugar and commercial pectin to crushed, fully-ripe fruit. Uncooked jams keep up to three weeks in the refrigerator or up to a year in the freezer. They spoil quickly at room temperature.

Alltrista Consumer Products Company, marketers of Ball® home canning products

25-6 Delicious homemade jam is a special treat on breads and rolls.

Good Manners Are Good Business

Homemade jam or preserves would be a special treat to offer your guests when hosting a business meal. However, you should not put the canning jar on your table. Instead, put the jellied product into a small dish with a spoon. If you wish to enjoy some of the jellied product on your food, spoon some onto your bread plate. Then use your knife to spread it on your food.

Freezing Foods

One of the best ways to preserve the fresh flavor of food is to freeze it. Frozen foods are popular because they offer consumers many advantages. A wide range of frozen foods are available, including fruits, juices, vegetables, meats, poultry, seafood, specialty items, and complete meals. Frozen foods have the appearance, taste, and nutritive value of fresh foods. They are available at any time of year, and they are easy to prepare. Frozen foods also can help you save money. You can buy them when prices are low and store them for later use.

Many frozen foods that you buy at the grocery store are preserved by *quick-freezing.* Quick-frozen foods are subjected to temperatures between -25° and -40°F (-32° and -40°C) for a short time. These extremely low temperatures produce very small ice crystals in foods. When foods are frozen more slowly, larger ice crystals may form. These large crystals damage the cell structure of foods and change their textures. After quick-freezing, foods are maintained at a normal freezing temperature of 0°F (-18°C).

Foods frozen at home have the same advantages as commercially frozen foods. Using the right equipment and following recommended procedures will ensure the highest quality in home-frozen foods.

Equipment

The right equipment is crucial to preserving the quality of frozen foods. You need to have a properly operating freezer and suitable containers.

Freezers

The freezer is the main piece of equipment required to freeze food. A freezer must be able to keep food at a temperature of 0°F (-18°C) or colder.

Many people have combination refrigerator-freezers. Separate freezers are available for those who need more freezer space. Many locker plants also rent freezer space.

Separate home freezers are very popular today. They are available in two styles—chest and upright. You can store large, bulky packages more easily in the chest model. Chest freezers use less electricity because less cold air escapes when you open them. They do require more floor space, however.

You can see and remove food more easily from upright freezers. They require a smaller amount of floor space, but they are more expensive to operate.

Containers

Containers used in freezing must be moisture- and vapor-resistant. This protects foods from exposure to air and loss of moisture during frozen storage. Foods that you have not wrapped securely may develop off flavors and lose nutrients, texture, and color. Some foods may develop *freezer burn,* or dry, tough areas. Freezer burn occurs where dry air from the freezer has come in contact with food surfaces, causing dehydration.

Properly sealed aluminum, glass, plastic-coated paper, and plastic containers are all suitable for freezer storage. You can also use aluminum foil and plastic-coated or transparent freezer wraps. These flat packaging materials work especially well when freezing bulky items, such as roasts and cakes.

The shape of containers affects how much food you can store in your freezer. Square containers are stackable and conserve freezer space. Plastic freezer bags do not stack as well. However, you can put bags in rigid containers before filling and freezing them. Then you can remove the bags and their frozen contents from the containers. The bags will have an even shape that is easy to store. You can then use the rigid containers for other foods.

Putting too many containers in the freezer at one time will prevent foods from freezing quickly. This will cause them to lose quality. Freeze food in batches, giving each batch a chance to freeze before adding the next batch. Leave a little space between items in the freezer to allow room for cold air to circulate. See 25-7.

ZIPLOC® brand freezer bags (®Trademark of DowBrands)
Phil Stein, photographer

25-7 Fill the freezer gradually, allowing a few food items to freeze before adding more items.

Freezing Fruits

When selecting fresh fruits for freezing, choose ripe, top quality pieces. Underripe fruit may develop a bitter or off flavor during freezing.

Work with small batches of fruit. Carefully sort and wash each piece. Do not soak. Depending on the type, fruits may be pitted, trimmed, sliced, or left whole.

Antidarkening Treatments

Some fruits need treatment other than sugar to prevent darkening. Ascorbic acid and ascorbic acid mixtures are used most often to prevent darkening of frozen fruits.

Ascorbic acid is a food additive that prevents color and flavor loss. It also adds nutritive value. (Ascorbic acid is another name for vitamin C.)

Ascorbic acid is available in crystalline form in drugstores. Dissolve ascorbic acid in cold water before using it.

Ascorbic acid mixtures contain ascorbic acid mixed with sugar or with sugar and citric acid. These products may be more expensive than ascorbic acid in its pure form. Follow manufacturer's instructions for use.

Packing Fruits

You may pack fruits by one of three methods: dry (unsweetened) pack, sugar pack, or syrup pack. Frozen sweetened fruits, however, usually have a better texture than unsweetened fruits.

For the *dry pack,* place prepared fruit in a shallow pan. If necessary, treat fruit to prevent darkening. Carefully pour fruit into freezer container. Gently tap container to pack fruit closely without crushing. Leave 1 inch (2.5 cm) head space to allow for expansion. Wipe top of container with a clean, damp cloth. Seal tightly and label with name of fruit, type of pack, and date.

For the *sugar pack* method, place prepared fruit in a shallow pan. Treat fruit to prevent darkening, if needed. Add sugar. Turn pieces of fruit gently until the sugar dissolves and forms a syrup. Carefully pack fruit into freezer containers. Gently tap each container to exclude air. Leave 1 inch (2.5 cm) head space. Wipe the top. Seal tightly and label.

For the *syrup pack,* prepare syrup and chill. A medium syrup is recommended for most fruits. You can use a lighter syrup for mildly flavored fruits. Place prepared fruit directly into container. Pour chilled syrup over fruit. (If needed, add dissolved ascorbic acid to chilled syrup.) Allow 1 inch (2.5 cm) head space. Wipe top of container. Seal tightly and label.

Freeze all foods at 0°F (-18°C) or lower immediately after packing. When food freezes too slowly, a loss in quality or food spoilage may occur. Limiting the amount of food placed in the freezer at one time will keep freezer temperature constant. Follow manufacturer's instructions concerning quantity and placement of foods.

Freezing Vegetables

Preparing vegetables for freezing is similar to preparing fruits. The main difference is that you must blanch most vegetables before freezing. This inactivates the enzymes.

Select young, tender vegetables of high quality. Ideally, you should get fresh-picked vegetables into the freezer within two hours. Freezing will toughen the texture and change the flavor of overmature vegetables.

Wash vegetables thoroughly in cold water. Sort according to size.

Blanching Vegetables

You can blanch vegetables with boiling water or steam. To blanch with boiling water, use at least 1 gallon (4 L) of water for each 1 pound (450 g) of vegetables. Place vegetables in a large strainer or basket. Lower the basket into the boiling water. Start counting time when vegetables are in the boiling water. When time is up, cool vegetables quickly. This prevents vitamin loss and spoilage. Plunge basket immediately into a large quantity of ice water. Cool thoroughly. Drain well.

To steam blanch vegetables, you will need a kettle with a tight-fitting lid and a rack. The rack must hold the steaming basket at least 3 inches (7.5 cm) above the water. Put an inch or two (2.5 to 5 cm) of water in the bottom of the kettle. Bring the water to a boil. Put vegetables into the basket in a single layer so steam will penetrate evenly. Cover the kettle and keep the heat high. Begin timing when the lid is on the kettle. Steam blanching takes about one and a half times longer than boiling-water blanching. When blanching is complete, cool vegetables quickly and drain well.

Packing Vegetables

Pack vegetables closely to remove as much air as possible. Do not add any liquid. Label with product, lot number (if you freeze more than one lot in a day), and date. Freeze promptly.

Freezing Meat, Poultry, and Fish

Meats require no special preparation before freezing. You may, however, wish to trim large cuts and package them in serving-sized pieces. Choose only top quality meat cuts for freezing.

Examine poultry for hairs and feathers. Wash and dry thoroughly. You may freeze poultry whole or in pieces.

Purchased fish also require washing and drying before freezing. You must scale and eviscerate (remove entrails) game fish before freezing. You should also remove their heads and fins.

Do not freeze meat, poultry, or fish in their original wrappers. Rewrap them in moistureproof and vaporproof paper, excluding as much air as possible. Seal and label with product name, weight, and date, 25-8.

Deni/Keystone Manufacturing Company, Inc.

25-8 Like other foods, meats and fish should be wrapped carefully and labeled clearly before freezing.

Freeze as soon as possible. Turn the freezer control to its lowest possible setting for the first 24 to 48 hours. Then maintain the temperature at 0°F (-18°C) as for fruits and vegetables.

Freezing Prepared Foods

You can also freeze many other foods. Baked pastry, cookies, breads, and cakes all freeze well. Wrap these items carefully in moistureproof and vaporproof wrapping. (To freeze frosted cakes, first place cake uncovered in the freezer long enough to set the frosting. Then wrap tightly and freeze. Frosting will not stick to the wrapping.)

You can freeze casseroles and stews in their baking dishes. To save space, line the baking dish with foil. Fill the dish with food, wrap well, and freeze. When frozen, remove the food from the dish. Wrap it well, label it, and return it to the freezer. You can then use the casserole dish for other foods.

Be sure to label all prepared foods with the name of the product and the date. Freeze promptly and use within the recommended time.

Some foods do not freeze well. These include: lettuce, salad greens, custards, gelatin products, meringues, sour cream, and hard-cooked egg white. Sandwiches containing salad dressing or mayonnaise do not freeze well, either.

You can store some foods longer than others. Beef, cheese, whole turkeys, and vegetables, for example, can be stored for a year. You can store cookies and soups for six months and unbaked pies for three months.

Thawing Frozen Foods

You should cook some frozen foods, such as vegetables, without thawing. Thaw fruits in their original covered container to prevent *enzymatic browning* (discoloration caused by exposure to air). Fruits have the best flavor if served with a few ice crystals remaining.

You can cook meats, poultry, and fish either frozen or thawed. Cooking frozen food, however, takes longer than cooking fresh or thawed foods. You must consider the extra cooking time when planning meals.

Thaw prepared and baked products in their original wrappers to prevent dehydration.

Occasionally, foods you do not want to thaw will thaw. This can happen when a power failure lasts for a long time. If food is partially thawed but still firm, you can refreeze it. The food will suffer a loss in quality, but it will still be safe to eat. Refreeze it and use it as soon as possible. If the food is fully thawed but still very cold, refrigerate it and use it immediately. Do not refreeze.

Drying Foods

Food drying is one of the oldest and simplest methods of food preservation. Microorganisms that cause food spoilage need moisture to grow. Drying removes moisture, thus stopping the growth of microorganisms. When drying foods, speed is important. Using a temperature that will not seriously affect the flavor, texture, and color of the food is important, too.

People originally dried fruits, vegetables, meats, and fish to provide a dependable food supply for the winter. In Colonial America, hams hung in the smokehouse. Onions, peppers, and herbs hung from the kitchen ceiling. All were dried by a combination of heat and air.

Today, a wide variety of foods are dried commercially. These include milk, eggs, coffee, fruit drinks, dessert mixes, salad dressing mixes, fruits, vegetables, meats, and complete meals.

The many advantages of dried foods make them especially popular with campers, hikers, and backpackers. Dried foods are lightweight. They take up less space than fresh foods, and they taste good. See 25-9.

Campers are not the only ones who use dried foods. In the home, many people add dried vegetables to soups. A variety of dried mixes are popular convenience products. People enjoy jerky and dried meat sticks as snacks. You can add dried fruits to salads, desserts, and a variety of other foods.

Fruit leathers are pliable sheets of dried fruit puree. You can make them from almost any fruit. Fruit leathers are nutritious and lightweight for packing in school lunches or taking on camping trips.

Preparing Fruits and Vegetables for Drying

You must dry vegetables completely to prevent spoilage. Fruits, because of their high sugar

Play It Safe

Organisms that cause food-borne illnesses multiply quickly at room temperature. Therefore you should never thaw foods, especially meat, poultry, and fish, at room temperature. Allow them to thaw overnight in a refrigerator. Use the defrost setting on a microwave oven to thaw foods more quickly. You can also allow them to thaw during the cooking process.

content, may retain more moisture than vegetables. Promptness in drying is one of the most important considerations.

Select young, tender vegetables in prime condition. Wash vegetables thoroughly and drain. Trim and cut them into small pieces. Smaller pieces dry more quickly and evenly. Blanch prepared vegetables using steam or boiling water. Drain well and dry with a towel.

Choose fruits at optimum maturity. Wash, sort, and discard bruised, overripe fruit. Peel, and core fruits, if necessary. You can dry berries and other smaller fruits whole. Larger fruits will dry more evenly and quickly if cut into halves, quarters, or ¼-inch (6 mm) slices.

Sulfuring is an antidarkening treatment used on some fruits before they are dried. Prepare a sulfuring solution with 3 tablespoons (45 mL) sodium metabisulfite and 1 gallon (4 L) of water. You can buy sodium metabisulfite at the drugstore or at stores that sell wine-making equipment. Soak fruits for 15 minutes. Drain. Spread fruit to dry.

You can also use a salt solution to keep fruit from darkening. Make the solution by dissolving 3 to 6 tablespoons (45 to 90 mL) salt in 1 gallon (4 L) of water.

Procedure for Drying

Two popular methods of drying fruits and vegetables at home are sun drying and oven drying. Sun drying is the oldest form of food drying. It also is the least costly, but it does rely on the weather.

If you choose to dry foods in the sun, you will need trays and cheesecloth. Cookie sheets or shallow pans will work. However, trays with screen bottoms will allow air to circulate around the food. This will cause the food to dry faster.

25-9 Bicyclers find dried foods like these apricots lightweight and easy to carry.

irradiation has not caught on as a trend in the food industry. Currently, irradiation in the United States is only being used to a limited degree to preserve spices. Use of irradiation may increase in the future if it becomes more economical for food processors.

Irradiated food products are labeled with the statement "treated with radiation" or "treated by irradiation." A special logo also appears on the label of irradiated foods.

Food preservation techniques allow you to store foods for long periods of time. However, you cannot keep preserved foods forever. Chart 25-12 shows how long you can store various foods in the refrigerator, in the freezer, and on a shelf.

Storage Life of Foods

Foods Kept in the Refrigerator	
beef, pork, lamb	2 to 4 days
poultry, fish	1 to 2 days
bacon, ham	5 to 7 days
milk	1 week
butter	2 weeks
natural, process cheeses	4 to 8 weeks
fruits and vegetables	varies according to type

Foods Kept in the Freezer	
beef	6 to 12 months
pork	3 to 6 months
lamb	6 to 9 months
ground beef, pork, lamb	3 months
ham, hot dogs	2 months
poultry	6 to 8 months
fish	3 to 4 months
fruits and vegetables	9 to 12 months
bread	2 to 3 months
ice cream	2 months

Foods Kept on Shelves	
dried fruits and vegetables	1 year
staple items (creal, flour, sugar)	1 year
home-canned foods	1 year
onions and potatoes	4 weeks
commercially packaged foods in unopened cans and jars	1 year
aseptically packaged products (milk products, juices, soups)	6 months
freeze-dried foods	1 year
shelf-stable entrées	6 months

25-12 Even preserved foods have a limited storage life.

Summary

Enzymes and microorganisms cause food spoilage. Food, moisture, and favorable temperatures need to be present for spoilage to occur. Removing any one of these items will help preserve food.

Canning uses high temperatures to preserve foods. Home-canned foods are stored in jars with two-piece vacuum caps used as closures. You need to process low-acid foods in a pressure canner. You can process high-acid foods in a boiling water bath. Experts do not recommend any other methods of home canning. After canning, you need to check the lids on canning jars to be sure they formed a good seal. Label canned foods clearly and store them in a cool, dry, dark place. Always check for signs of spoilage before using home-canned foods.

Jellied products are popular home-canned foods. The four basic ingredients in jelly are fruit juice, pectin, acid, and sugar. Besides jelly, you can make marmalade, jams, preserves, conserves, and fruit butters.

Freezing uses low temperatures to preserve foods. A freezer and food storage containers are all you need to keep foods on hand for months. Some fruits need an antidarkening treatment before freezing. Most vegetables need blanching before freezing. You must thaw some frozen foods before preparing them. You can cook others in their frozen state.

Drying removes moisture to preserve foods. You need to blanch vegetables and sulfur some fruits before drying. You can dry foods in the sun or in a conventional oven. You should store dried foods in tightly sealed containers to prevent moisture from affecting them.

Commercial food preservation follows the same principles as home preservation. Freeze-drying, aseptic packaging, retort packaging, and irradiation are all commercial preservation techniques.

Review What You Have Read

Write your answers on a separate sheet of paper.
1. True or false. Bacteria, mold, and yeast can have good effects on food.
2. What three factors must be present for microorganisms to grow?
3. What type of jar closure is used in home canning?
4. Space between the food and the closure of a food-storage container is called _____.
5. What canning method should be used to process low-acid foods?
6. List three factors that can cause home-canned foods to lose eating quality during storage.
7. What are five signs of spoilage in home-canned foods?
8. What are the four basic ingredients needed to make good jelly?
9. A tender jelly containing small pieces of fruit and fruit rind is _____.
10. Describe the advantage quick-frozen foods have over foods frozen more slowly.
11. What are the three packing methods that may be used when freezing fruits?
12. List five foods that do not freeze well.
13. What are two popular methods for drying fruits and vegetables at home?
14. What type of commercial food preservation involves separate sterilization of a food and its packaging material?
    A. Aseptic packaging.
    B. Commercial canning.
    C. Freeze-drying.
    D. Retort packaging.

Build Your Basic Skills

1. Design a brochure about the safe use of home-canned foods. The brochure should describe how to check for spoilage. Also list types of spoilage of which people should be aware. Explain what to do with spoiled food. Finally, discuss how to prepare foods that appear to be wholesome.
2. Prepare an oral report explaining how the food industry prevents food spoilage by microorganisms and enzymes.

Build Your Thinking Skills

1. Make two batches of a jellied product. Add commercial pectin to one batch. Do not add pectin to the other batch. Compare the flavor, consistency, cooking time, yield, and appearance of the two products.
2. Make a batch of cookies. Sample and evaluate for quality. Package and freeze half of the remaining cookies in a loosely rolled paper bag. Package and freeze the other half of the cookies in a tightly sealed plastic container. After one month, thaw, sample, and compare the cookies. Which type of container best preserved the flavor, texture, and appearance of fresh cookies?
3. Compare the flavor, texture, appearance, and drying time of oven-dried and sun-dried apples.

Part 4
Foods of the World

In many regions of the United States, people serve baked ham as the main course at holiday meals.

Chapter **26**

Regional Cuisine of the United States

A "Taste" of the World of Work

Restaurant Critic
Writes critical reviews of restaurants for broadcast and publication.

Tourist-Information Assistant
Provides travel information and other services to tourists at State Information Centers.

Travel Writer
Travels to various locations to gather information in order to write articles about rates and amenities of lodging and dining facilities and local points of interest.

NYS Department of Economic Development

Terms to Know

Pennsylvania Dutch	jambalaya
soul food	Cajun cuisine
okra	potluck
yam	sourdough
Creole cuisine	luau
filé	imu
gumbo	

Objectives

After studying this chapter, you will be able to
❑ trace the development of cuisine of the United States.
❑ prepare foods that are representative of the seven main regions of the United States and identify their origins.

The food customs of the United States are as diverse as its inhabitants. People who live in the United States have roots that stretch around the globe.

A Historical Overview

Since shortly after Columbus' discovery in 1492, people began leaving their homelands to move to the New World. They had many reasons for making this major life change. Some moved to escape debtor's prison. Others sought religious freedom. Many fled famine and disease. Some came as forced laborers, whereas others came in search of fame and fortune.

The abundance of land and opportunity they found amazed most of the immigrants to the United States. Each group of settlers had to adjust to the climate and geography of the area in which they settled. However, they were able to adapt many of their food customs to take advantage of what the New World had to offer.

The Native Americans

Food customs of the United States began with the Native Americans. The Native Americans settled in organized groups, or tribes. Each tribe had its own language, religion, and crafts. Tribes engaged in trade with one another to obtain the goods they lacked.

The Native Americans were excellent farmers. They were the first to cultivate potatoes, pineapple, tomatoes, peppers, and many other familiar vegetables and fruits. These foods make up about 50 percent of the plant foods in the world today.

During the time of Christopher Columbus, Native Americans grew beans, corn, and squash to supply the basis of their diet. They hunted wild game, gathered nuts and berries, and fished to supplement these staple foods. The high nutritional quality of their diet made the Native Americans healthier than the Europeans of that time.

The First Colonists

The British and Spanish were the first permanent colonists in the United States. They established the early settlements of Jamestown and Plymouth (British) and St. Augustine (Spanish). The French who settled in the United States established provinces in Louisiana and along the St. Lawrence River. A little later, the Dutch arrived and established the New Netherland Colony, which later became New York.

The life of the first colonists was a struggle for survival. Survival meant learning how to provide shelter and food, prevent sickness, and get along with the Native Americans.

The Native Americans contributed to the success of the first colonial settlements in the New World. They taught the colonists how to hunt; fish; and plant corn, squash, and beans. Within a few years, the colonists had cleared land, built small groups of homes, and planted simple gardens. The colonists grew a variety of vegetables and fruits and learned to eat animals and fish that had been unfamiliar to them.

As the colonists' knowledge grew, they added many new dishes to their diets. They used local lobster, crab, and other fish in seafood chowders. They served preserved beef as creamed dried beef. They used pumpkin to make pies, puddings, and cakes. They used corn to make johnnycakes, corn sticks, hasty pudding, Indian pudding, and succotash. They baked squash and beans with molasses and serve them with thick slices of brown bread and Sally Lunn (a slightly sweetened yeast bread). They used wild blueberries to make blueberry grunt. They used other wild berries to make a variety of fruit cobblers and puddings.

The Immigrants

As more and more people came to the New World, communities sprang up along the east coast. People also began to settle on more fertile lands farther inland. Many immigrants stayed together in groups and settled in particular regions of the country. Many British, Dutch, German, and French people settled in the Northeast. British, French, and Spanish immigrants settled in the Deep South. Other Spanish settlers chose to live in the Southwest. As the South was settled, the slave trade became established. Africans were brought to the United States to work on Southern plantations.

During the 1800s, many people came to the United States in search of economic opportunities. Most of these people arrived in the United States with little more than the clothes they were wearing and a few prized possessions. They did not find the streets paved with gold as they had hoped. However, the new immigrants were not afraid of hard work. Slowly they learned the new language and found jobs so they could support their families.

Most of these immigrants tended to settle in areas with climates similar to those of their homelands. Chicago, Detroit, New York City, and other large industrial cities attracted large groups of Poles, Irish, Italians, and Lithuanians who worked as unskilled laborers. Scandinavians and Germans traveled to Minnesota, Illinois, Iowa, and Wisconsin to farm. Japanese and Chinese settled along the Pacific coast where they mined and worked on the railroads.

The new immigrants brought their native food customs with them to the United States, 26-1. They adapted their recipes to the foods that were readily available. The Italian immigrants made rich spaghetti sauce from ripe tomatoes, fresh basil, and onions sold by street vendors in New York. The Chinese used chicken, bamboo shoots, and water chestnuts to make their chow mein. The Poles made cabbage rolls like those served in their homeland from cabbage leaves stuffed with ground beef and tomato sauce. In this way, these new Americans helped to create the cuisine eaten in the United States today.

Good Manners Are Good Business

Regional foods, perhaps arranged in an attractive basket, make a thoughtful business gift. International business associates or those living in other regions will especially enjoy foods from your region.

Business people often send gifts to celebrate successes, such as mergers and promotions. They also send them to thank people for their help. For instance, you might send a gift to someone who helps you get a job or increase business.

Springfield Illinois Convention & Visitors Bureau

26-1 The foods and cooking techniques of immigrant settlers became part of the cuisine eaten in the United States today.

New England

Maine Office of Tourism

Lobster boats are a common sight in Maine harbors.

The British were the first people to settle in the area now called New England. Much of the land was rocky, mountainous, or forested, and winters were long and severe. The early colonists had to work hard to survive.

The Pilgrims were frugal, sober, hard-working people. They did not believe in overindulgence of any kind. Food was merely nourishment for the body.

The character of the people and the land they inhabited shaped the character of New England cooking. Most of the farms that sprang up were isolated and self-sufficient. Seafood and wild game supplemented the foods that New Englanders could grow at home. The waters provided lobsters, crabs, clams, and other shellfish, which later became New England specialties. The forest provided wild turkeys, geese, ducks, and pheasants.

Each home had a large fireplace that the family used for cooking. New Englanders prepared most foods in iron pots that hung over the fire. They made baked goods in covered Dutch ovens over the coals of the fireplace or in beehive ovens. These baked goods included Indian bread, Sally Lunn, and johnnycakes.

New England cooks used foods that were readily available to create hearty, substantial meals. For instance, they used corn to make corn sticks, Indian pudding, and cornmeal mush. They also used it for succotash (a combination of corn and lima beans).

To survive the long, cold winters, the early New Englanders learned to dry and salt foods to preserve them. They commonly dried beans, corn, and apples. Later, they soaked these foods in water and cooked them until tender. Early New Englanders made baked beans in this way. The Native Americans taught the early settlers how to soak the dried beans overnight. Then they would flavor them with molasses and salt pork and cook them slowly in big pots.

One dish meals were popular in New England because they gave the cooks more time to do other tasks. One of the most common one dish meals of that time, the *New England boiled dinner,* is still popular today. It is a combination of meat (usually corned beef), potatoes, onions, carrots, beets, cabbage, and other available vegetables. The ingredients cook together slowly until they are tender.

The colonists used a variety of meats, seafood, and vegetables to make stews and chowders. *Clam chowder* was one of the most popular. Many people continue to associate New England cooking with this creamy soup made with potatoes and clams.

From the sap of New England's sugar maple trees came maple syrup. Native Americans taught the New Englanders how to tap the maple trees.

After the colonists boiled down the sap, they used the syrup to make cakes, candies, sauces, and puddings. They also used it as a flavoring in baked beans, squash, and other vegetables.

Blueberries, cranberries, blackberries, and other fruits were another important food source. New England cooks gathered the berries and used them to make a variety of nourishing desserts. Two examples are *blueberry mush* (a steamed pudding)

and *blueberry grunt* (berries simmered in a thickened sauce and topped with fluffy dumplings).

New Englanders used leftovers in creative ways. For instance, they would grind the leftovers from a boiled dinner and fry them in a large iron skillet. Beets give this dish a red color, which reminded the New Englanders of red flannel underwear worn during the cold winters. Thus, the dish earned the name *red-flannel hash*.

U.S. Department of Agriculture

New Englanders still tap maple trees to collect sap, which they make into syrup.

New England Menu
New England Clam Chowder
Boiled Dinner
Boston Baked Beans
Brown Bread
Blueberry Muffins
Pumpkin Pie
Tea

New England Clam Chowder
Serves 5 to 6

4   slices bacon
2   cans minced clams, 8 ounces each
1   large potato, peeled and cubed
1   medium stalk celery, chopped
½   cup finely chopped onion
¼   teaspoon pepper
⅛   teaspoon thyme
1   cup skim milk
2   cups milk

1. In large, heavy saucepan, cook bacon until crisp.
2. Remove bacon to a piece of absorbent paper to drain.
3. Drain clams, reserving liquid. Set clams aside.
4. Add potato, celery, onion, pepper, and thyme to liquid from clams. Bring to a boil; simmer covered, until vegetables are tender (about 10 minutes).
5. Add skim milk, milk, and clams and heat almost to the boiling point. Taste to see if additional seasonings are needed. Serve immediately.

Per serving: 230 Cal. (32% from fat), 21 g protein, 16 g carbohydrate, 8 g fat, 76 mg cholesterol, 1.3 g fiber, 286 mg sodium.

Boiled Dinner
Serves 8

4   pounds corned beef
8   medium-sized beets*
2   pounds green cabbage, cored and quartered
8   medium-sized red potatoes, scrubbed, peeled, and cut in half
8   small carrots, scraped
16 small white onions, peeled and trimmed
    parsley, chopped

1. Place corned beef in a large kettle of cold water (water should rise at least 2 inches above meat). Bring to a boil and skim off any scum that rises to surface.

2. Cover kettle and reduce heat to slow simmer; cook corned beef 3 to 4 hours or until tender. (Check water level during cooking.)
3. Scrub beets, cut off tops leaving 1 inch and cover with water. Simmer until tender. Cool slightly and slip off skins.
4. Cook cabbage, potatoes, carrots, and onions in salted, simmering water until tender.
5. To serve the dinner, slice the meat and arrange on serving platter. Surround meat with vegetables and top with chopped parsley. Serve with horseradish sauce or mustard.

*One medium can whole beets can be substituted for fresh.

Note: Vegetables (with the exception of the beets) can be added to the corned beef about 30 to 40 minutes before serving as is done in New England. However, some people object to the salty flavor the corned beef gives to the vegetables.

Per serving: 486 Cal. (31% from fat), 41 g protein, 42 g carbohydrate, 17 g fat, 133 mg cholesterol, 6.5 g fiber, 1403 mg sodium.

Boston Baked Beans
Serves 8

2   cups great northern or navy beans
8   cups water
½   cup molasses
½   cup brown sugar
⅓   cup onions, coarsely chopped
2   teaspoons dry mustard
½   teaspoon pepper
2   slices Canadian bacon

1. Place beans in large saucepan and cover with cold water (water should be at least 2 inches higher than the beans). Bring beans to a boil and let boil 2 minutes.
2. Remove pan from heat and let beans soak about 1 hour.
3. Return pan to heat, bring water to a boil and slowly simmer beans until almost tender (about 1 to 1 ½

3. Return pan to heat, bring water to a boil and slowly simmer beans until almost tender (about 1 to 1 ½ hours); drain and reserve liquid.
4. Preheat oven to 300°F.
5. Place beans in 2-quart bean pot or heavy casserole.
6. Add enough water to bean liquid to make 2 cups.
7. Combine bean liquid, molasses, brown sugar, onions, dry mustard, and pepper; pour over beans.
8. Cut Canadian bacon into bite-sized pieces and add to beans.
9. Cover pot tightly; bake beans 1½ to 2 hours, stirring occasionally and adding water if needed.
10. Remove cover and bake beans an additional 30 minutes without stirring.

Per serving: 266 Cal. (4% from fat), 12 g protein, 54 g carbohydrate, 1 g fat, 3 mg cholesterol, 4.8 g fiber, 142 mg sodium.

Brown Bread
Makes 3 small loaves

1   cup whole wheat flour
1   cup rye flour
1   cup cornmeal
1½ teaspoons baking soda
½   teaspoon salt
¾   cup raisins
2   cups buttermilk
¾   cup dark molasses
2   tablespoons melted shortening

1. Preheat oven to 350°F.
2. Grease three 1 pound coffee cans.
3. In large mixing bowl, combine flours, cornmeal, soda, salt, and raisins; mix well.
4. Combine buttermilk, molasses, and melted shortening; add to dry ingredients mixing well.
5. Pour batter into greased cans filling 2/3 full; cover with foil.
6. Place cans on rack in shallow pan; add boiling water to depth of 2 ½ inches.
7. Steam breads 3 hours until toothpick inserted in center comes out clean.
8. Cool 15 minutes and remove from cans. Serve warm.

Per slice: 85 Cal. (13% from fat), 2 g protein, 17 g carbohydrate, 1 g fat, 1 mg cholesterol, 1 .7 g fiber, 103 mg sodium.

Blueberry Muffins
Makes 12 muffins

2   cups all-purpose flour
2½   teaspoons baking powder
3   tablespoons sugar
½   teaspoon salt
3   tablespoons shortening
1   egg, well beaten
1   cup skim milk
1   cup blueberries

1. Preheat oven to 400°F.
2. Sift dry ingredients together in mixing bowl.
3. Melt shortening; cool.
4. Combine egg and milk; add cooled shortening.
5. Add liquid ingredients to dry ingredients all at once. Stir only until blended. (Batter will be lumpy.)
6. Gently fold in blueberries.
7. Fill greased muffin pans 2/3 full of batter.
8. Bake muffins 20 to 25 minutes or until brown.

Per muffin: 173 Cal. (26% from fat), 3 g protein, 22 g carbohydrate, 4 g fat, 23 mg cholesterol, 1.0 g fiber, 167 mg sodium.

Pumpkin Pie
Makes one 9-inch pie

1   unbaked pastry shell, 9-inch (See Chapter 23)
2   eggs
¾   cup light brown sugar, packed
2   cups canned pumpkin
1½   cups evaporated skim milk
½   teaspoon salt
1   teaspoon cinnamon
½   teaspoon ground cloves
½   teaspoon ginger
½   teaspoon nutmeg

1. Preheat oven to 450°F.
2. In large mixing bowl, beat eggs slightly; add remaining ingredients and mix well.
3. Pour custard into pastry shell.
4. Bake 10 minutes.
5. Reduce temperature to 300°F and continue baking until knife inserted in center comes out clean, about 40 to 50 minutes.
6. Cool. Serve with whipped cream.

⅙ of pie: 394 Cal. (28% from fat), 10 g protein, 63 g carbohydrate, 13 g fat, 94 mg cholesterol, 2.0 g fiber, 478 mg sodium.

Mid-Atlantic

Horse-drawn buggies of the Amish are often seen along the roadways of Lancaster County, Pennsylvania.

South of New England, the climate was more mild. Large groups of Dutch settled in what today is New York. German, Swedish, and British people settled with the Dutch farther down the coast in what is now New Jersey.

The land in the mid-Atlantic region was rich and fertile, and farming was profitable. New Jersey still is a major center of fresh fruit and vegetable production. New Jersey ships apples, peaches, beans, cranberries, tomatoes, onions, asparagus, cucumbers, peas, and melons to many parts of the country.

The Dutch were excellent farmers. They had large vegetable gardens and kept their root cellars well stocked. Many had their own orchards, too.

The Dutch were also excellent bakers. Cookies (koekjes), doughnuts (olykoeks), molasses cake, and gingerbread figures all have Dutch origins. The Dutch also introduced waffles, coleslaw, cottage cheese, and griddle cakes.

Today, the foods of the mid-Atlantic region go far beyond the seafood, fresh produce, and traditional foods of northern Europe. This area is now the home of a huge melting pot of people and cuisines. In New York City, restaurant specialties range from Asian food to South American cuisine. Visitors can satisfy a taste for everything from lasagna to hot dogs.

The Pennsylvania Dutch

One group of mid-Atlantic settlers, the Pennsylvania Dutch, deserves special mention. The *Pennsylvania Dutch* were a group of German immigrants who settled in the southeast section of Pennsylvania. (The word *Dutch* comes from the word *Deutsch*, which means *German*.) These immigrants came from the Rhine Valley, where they were farmers. When they came to the United States, they were successful in adapting their farming techniques to the soil in Pennsylvania.

The food customs of the Pennsylvania Dutch were very different from those of their neighbors. They developed a style of cooking that was rural, hearty, and inventive. They based it on cooking techniques practiced in the Old World. The thrifty *hausfraus* (housewife) canned, pickled, and dried the produce, meat, and poultry raised on the farm. They did not waste anything. They used their thriftiness and inventiveness to create many new dishes. Examples are pickled pigs' feet, blood pudding, *scrapple* (pork combined with cornmeal), smoked beef tongue, stuffed heart, sausages, and bologna.

Soup was one of the most popular dishes. The Pennsylvania Dutch made it from whatever foods were available. Since they were especially skillful in the production of vegetables and poultry, they served vegetable and chicken soups often. *Chicken corn soup* remains a traditional favorite.

Hearty German foods, such as sauerbraten, sauerkraut, liverwurst, and pork, were mainstays of the Pennsylvania Dutch diet. They served noodles, dumplings, potato pancakes, and other filling foods as accompaniments.

Each meal included seven sweets and seven sours. These usually were in the form of pickled vegetables and fruits, relishes, jams, preserves, salads, and apple butter. Homemakers made all of these foods during the summer and stored them in cellars for the winter.

The Pennsylvania Dutch were excellent bakers. Coffee cakes, sticky buns, funnel cakes, crumb cakes, and *shoofly pie* (pastry with a filling made of molasses and brown sugar) are some of their specialties, 26-2.

Several religious groups, including the Amish and the Mennonites, shared a German heritage with the Pennsylvania Dutch. However, these peoples chose to live in isolated groups. Their isolation, however, helped to preserve their hearty homestyle cooking and native crafts. Some small colonies of these peoples still exist throughout the country.

Pennsylvania Dutch Convention & Visitors Bureau, Lancaster, PA

26-2 Molasses and brown sugar are used make the rich filling of shoofly pie.

Buttermilk Biscuits
Makes about 15 biscuits

2   cups unsifted all-purpose flour
1   tablespoon baking powder
½   teaspoon salt
¼   cup shortening
⅔ to ¾ cup buttermilk

1. Preheat oven to 425°F.
2. In large mixing bowl, combine flour, baking powder, and salt.
3. Using a pastry blender, two knives, or fingers, cut in shortening until mixture resembles small peas.
4. Add buttermilk, stirring gently with fork until soft dough forms.
5. Turn dough out onto lightly floured board. Knead 8 to 10 times.
6. Roll to ½ inch thickness. Cut into rounds with 2-inch biscuit cutter.
7. Place close together on an ungreased baking sheet.
8. Bake 10 to 12 minutes or until golden brown. Serve hot.

Per biscuit: 97 Cal. (34% from fat), 2 g protein, 14 g carbohydrate, 4 g fat, 0 mg cholesterol, 0.5 g fiber, 147 mg sodium.

Pecan Pie
Makes one 9-inch pie

1   unbaked pastry shell, 9-inch (See Chapter 23)
4   eggs
⅓   cup light brown sugar, packed
¼   cup melted margarine
1¼   cups dark corn syrup
½   teaspoon salt
1½   teaspoons vanilla
1¼   cups chopped pecans

1. Preheat oven to 350°F.
2. In large mixing bowl, beat eggs and brown sugar together until blended.
3. Add melted butter or margarine, corn syrup, salt, vanilla, and chopped pecans, and mix thoroughly; pour into unbaked pie shell.
4. Bake until filling is puffed and golden brown, about 35 to 40 minutes.
5. Serve pie slightly warm or cool and top with whipped cream.

1/8 of pie: 426 Cal. (56% from fat), 6 g protein, 42 g carbohydrate, 28 g fat, 137 mg cholesterol, 1.6 g fiber, 388 mg sodium.

National Live Stock and Meat Board

Andouille sausage is served with Hoppin' John, a combination of black-eyed peas and rice.

Midwest

National Corn Growers Association

Corn grows abundantly in the rich soil of the Midwest.

The part of the United States called the Midwest developed as the pioneers pushed westward across the Mississippi River. People from a variety of backgrounds settled this area. Therefore, Midwestern cooking is diverse.

People often call the Midwest the "breadbasket" of the nation. Rich soil, good climate, and advanced farming techniques have made the Midwest one of the world's most agriculturally productive regions. Corn, wheat, and soybeans grow in large enough quantities to be exported to many parts of the world.

Beef, pork, lamb, and poultry are produced in large quantities in the Midwest. Lakes and streams in this region provide a variety of fish. People throughout the United States recognize Wisconsin and Minnesota for their dairy products. Small farms throughout the Midwest grow many kinds of fruit and vegetables.

Fairs, festivals, and picnics are popular in the Midwest. At all of these gatherings, food plays an important part. Homemade breads, cakes, pies, cookies, jams, and jellies are judged at county and state fairs. Cities and towns in many parts of the Midwest hold festivals centered on apples, pumpkins, strawberries, and other fruits and vegetables.

The Midwest has a tradition of friendliness and hospitality. This tradition is seen in gatherings like buffet dinners and potlucks. For a buffet dinner, cooks fill a large table with meat dishes, potatoes, other vegetables, fruits, and baked goods. Buffet dinners were originally created to satisfy the hunger of farmers during harvest time. After working together all day to harvest one another's crops, farmers needed a hearty meal.

Potlucks are popular Midwestern social gatherings with church groups, clubs, and relatives. A *potluck* is a shared meal to which each person or family brings food for the whole group to eat. These meals get their name from a tradition of hospitality in which a prepared meal would be shared with an unexpected guest. Since the cook did not know the guest was coming, the guest would have to take "the luck of the pot."

Midwestern cooking, as a whole, is hearty and uncomplicated. Broiled steak, roast beef, baked and hash brown potatoes, and corn on the cob are staples of the Midwestern diet. Coleslaw, fresh tomatoes from the garden, home baked rolls, apple pie, and brownies also belong to the Midwest. Fruit, hot cereal or cornmeal mush, pancakes, bacon, eggs, toast, and coffee might be served at a filling Midwestern breakfast.

Ethnic foods from immigrants who settled in large Midwestern cities have been added to the foods of the farm. Swedish meatballs, Greek moussaka, German bratwurst, Polish sausage, and Italian lasagna have become almost as common as steak and potatoes.

Midwestern Menu
Broiled Steak
Baked Potatoes
Corn on the Cob
Fresh Green Beans
Sliced Tomatoes
Warm Whole Wheat Bread
Apple Pie
Milk   Coffee

Broiled Steak
Serves 8

2   sirloin steaks, each about 1 inch thick and
      weighing 1 pound, 10 ounces*
    salt
    pepper
    garlic powder

1. Preheat broiler.
2. Wipe steaks with damp paper towels; place on broiler pan.
3. Slash fat edges of steaks with a sharp knife.
4. Broil steaks 2 to 3 inches from the heat until brown.
5. Season and turn; finish broiling. Total broiling time will vary according to desired degree of doneness. Estimated broiling time for rare is 15 to 20 minutes; for medium, 20 to 25 minutes.

*Hamburgers may be substituted for steaks, if desired.

Per serving: 196 Cal. (38% from fat), 29 g protein, 0 g carbohydrate, 8 g fat, 83 mg cholesterol, 0 g fiber, 240 mg sodium.

Baked Potatoes
Serves 6

6   medium baking potatoes
    margarine
    pepper
    salt

1. Preheat oven to 350°F.
2. Scrub potatoes under cold, running water.
3. Pierce skins in several places with the tines of a fork.
4. Place potatoes in oven and bake until fork pierces potato easily, about 45 minutes to 1 hour.
5. Remove from oven.
6. Using pot holders, roll potatoes gently between hands for a minute or two.
7. Make a slit in the top of each potato and push gently.
8. Top with margarine and salt and pepper. If desired, serve potatoes with crisp bacon bits, shredded cheese, sour cream and chives, or whipped cream cheese.

Per potato: 180 Cal. (19% from fat), 3 g protein, 34 g carbohydrate, 4 g fat, 0 mg cholesterol, 3.3 g fiber, 410 mg sodium.

Corn on the Cob
Serves 6

6   ears fresh sweet corn*
    margarine
    salt

1. Remove the husks and silk from each ear of corn; trim the ends.
2. Remove the remaining silks under cool, running water with a vegetable brush.
3. In a large kettle, bring a large amount of salted water to a boil.
4. Drop in the ears of corn. Return the water to a boil; reduce the heat and simmer the corn until it is tender, about 3 to 5 minutes.
5. Drain the corn and serve it immediately with margarine and salt.

*Frozen ears of corn may be substituted for fresh. Follow the directions on the package for cooking.

Per ear: 118 Cal. (32 % from fat), 3 g protein, 19 g carbohydrate, 5 g fat, 0 mg cholesterol, 3.6 g fiber, 412 mg sodium.

Whole Wheat Bread (cool rise)
Makes 2 loaves

5½ to 6   cups unsifted all-purpose flour
      2   cups unsifted whole wheat flour
      3   tablespoons sugar
      2   teaspoons salt
      2   packages active dry yeast
      2   cups skim milk
      ¾   cup warm water
      ¼   cup softened margarine

1. On a large sheet of waxed paper, combine all-purpose and whole wheat flours.

2. In large mixing bowl, combine 2½ cups flour mixture, sugar, salt, and dry yeast.
3. In small saucepan, combine milk, water, and margarine.
4. Heat over low until very warm (120° to 130°F). Margarine does not need to completely melt.
5. Gradually add warm liquids to dry ingredients; beat at medium speed of electric mixer two minutes.
6. Add 1 cup flour mixture and beat mixture on high speed another 2 minutes, scraping bowl occasionally.
7. Stir in enough additional flour mixture to make a stiff dough.
8. Turn dough out onto lightly floured board or pastry cloth. Knead until smooth and elastic, about 8 to 10 minutes.
9. Cover with plastic wrap and then a towel. Let rest 20 minutes.
10. Divide dough in half. Roll each half into a rectangle.
11. Shape into loaves and place in two greased 9 by 5-inch loaf pans.
12. Brush tops with oil.
13. Cover with plastic wrap and refrigerate 2 to 24 hours.
14. When ready to bake, remove dough from refrigerator; let stand 10 minutes.
15. Using a greased toothpick, prick any bubbles which may have formed.
16. Bake bread at 400°F about 40 minutes or until loaves are golden and sound hollow when tapped with knuckles.
17. Remove bread from pans and cool thoroughly before storing.

Per slice: 134 Cal. (12% from fat), 4 g protein, 25 g carbohydrate, 2 g fat, 0 mg cholesterol, 2.1 g fiber, 159 mg sodium.

Green Beans
Serves 6

2   pounds fresh green beans*
    margarine
    salt and pepper

1. Wash beans under cool running water. Snap off ends; then snap beans in half.
2. Bring a small amount of salted water to a boil.
3. Add beans. Return to a boil, then reduce heat and simmer beans gently just until crisp-tender, about 10 to 15 minutes.
4. Drain and top with margarine. Serve immediately.

* Two 10-ounce packages of frozen green beans may be substituted for fresh. Follow package directions for cooking.

Per serving: 47 Cal. (36% from fat), 1 g protein, 7 g carbohydrate, 2 g fat, 0 mg cholesterol, 2.8 g fiber, 202 mg sodium.

Apple Pie
Makes one 9-inch pie

Pastry for a double-crust, 9-inch pie (See Chapter 23)
6   cups sliced tart apples
½   cup granulated sugar
¼   cup light brown sugar, packed
2   tablespoons all-purpose flour
1   teaspoon cinnamon
¼   teaspoon nutmeg
1   tablespoon lemon juice
1   tablespoon margarine, cut into chunks
    cinnamon and sugar (optional)

1. Preheat oven to 425°F.
2. In large mixing bowl, combine apples, sugars, flour, cinnamon, nutmeg, and lemon juice; mix well.
3. Pour fruit into pastry-lined pie plate.
4. Dot with margarine.
5. Roll remaining pastry and fit pastry circle on top of filling.
6. Seal and flute edges of pastry and make steam vents.
7. Sprinkle crust lightly with cinnamon and sugar, if desired.
8. Bake until juice is bubbly and apples are tender, about 40 to 45 minutes.

⅙ of pie: 492 Cal. (40% from fat), 4 g protein, 70 g carbohydrate, 22 g fat, 0 mg cholesterol, 4.0 g fiber, 394 mg sodium.

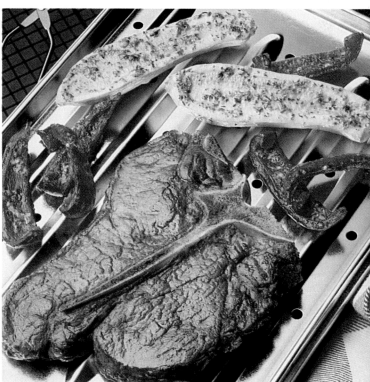

National Live Stock and Meat Board

Broiled steak is a prime example of traditional Midwestern fare.

West and Southwest

Jack Lewis/TxDOT

Rodeo competitions are popular in the Southwest.

The western part of the United States is a land of contrasts. Abandoned mining towns, desolate deserts, sprawling ranches, mountains, plateaus, and oil fields make up much of the landscape.

Big cities like Dallas, Houston, and Denver now dot the countryside. However, the West continues to be the home of wide open spaces and solitude. Many Westerners still live great distances from their nearest neighbors. During the summer, they think nothing of traveling two or three hours to visit friends or shop. In the winter, however, snowstorms can keep them homebound for weeks at a time.

Westerners tend to eat simply. They enjoy meat and game, homemade breads and biscuits, and locally grown fruits and vegetables.

Beef plays an important part in Western cooking. Western cooks grill, spit barbecue, and pit barbecue. Depending on the occasion, they might roast a whole steer at one time.

Lamb is also quite popular in some parts of the West. It usually is roasted or stewed. In remote areas, wild game accounts for quite a bit of the meat in the diet. Antelope, rabbit, deer, and pheasant are among the game animals used for meat.

Many people associate chuck wagons and cowboys with the Southwest. However, Native Americans, Mexicans, and Spaniards also influenced the development of Southwestern cuisine.

During the sixteenth century, the Spaniards explored the southwestern part of the United States. They later ruled this area of the country for 200 years before Mexico gained control. In 1848, Mexico ceded Texas, California, and the land between them to the United States. Until then, Mexicans and Native Americans made up most of the population in the area.

The foods of Native Americans in this region included corn, squash, and beans. To these, the Spanish added cattle, sheep, saffron, olive oil, and anise. The Aztecs of Mexico introduced red and green peppers.

The cattle introduced by the Spanish eventually developed into the longhorn breed. They roamed the plains from Texas to California and north into the Dakotas. Long cattle drives ended at the railroad yards where the cattle were shipped east. Here, stories of the cowboy and the chuck wagon originated.

Beef has always been an important staple food in the Southwest. Trail cooks used the tongue, liver, sweetbreads, and heart of a freshly slaughtered steer to make "Son-of-a-Gun Stew," a favorite of the cowboys. They often served beans and homemade biscuits with the spicy stew. They used chunks of beef in chili, chuck wagon beans, and many other filling dishes. Although some people think of chili as a Mexican dish, Texans claim to have originated it. They made the first chili with cubes of beef, peppers, and seasonings. It did not include beans, 26-5.

From across the Rio Grande came the spicy Mexican foods, which the Southwesterners quickly adopted. Beans, corn, and dishes like tortillas, tostadas, and tacos all have Mexican origins. Other popular Southwestern foods that originated in Mexico are *tamales* (a mixture of cornmeal and peppered ground meat that is wrapped in corn husks and steamed) and *sopapillas* (sweet fried pastries).

Barbecues continue to be an important part of Southwestern cooking. People in this region often baste their meat with a spicy tomato-based sauce during grilling.

The climate of the Southwest is hot and sunny, so many fruits and vegetables grow year-round. Texas produces large quantities of grapefruit, oranges, and strawberries. Farmers in the Rio Grande valley grow early season melons, lettuce, and other fruits and vegetables. Refrigerated trucks transport these fruits and vegetables to all parts of the United States.

National Live Stock and Meat Board

26-5 Spicy Texas chili originated in the Southwest.

Southwestern Menu

Nachos
Barbecued Beef Short Ribs
Three Bean Salad
Tossed Greens with Ranch Dressing
Mexican Cornbread
Sopapillas
Coffee

Nachos
Makes 24 appetizers

6   tortillas
    vegetable oil or shortening for frying
¼   pound sharp Cheddar cheese
3   jalapeno peppers
½   cup sour cream

1. Heat 1½ to 2 inches of oil or shortening in a heavy skillet until hot but not smoking.
2. Cut tortillas into quarters.
3. Fry wedges a few at a time until crisp and golden brown; drain on paper towels.
4. Preheat broiler.
5. Top each tortilla wedge with a piece of cheese and a sliver of pepper.
6. Broil 2 inches from heat just until cheese melts.
7. Top with a small spoonful of sour cream. Serve immediately.

Per nacho: 64 Cal. (63% from fat), 2 g protein, 4 g carbohydrate, 5 g fat, 7 mg cholesterol, 0.3 g fiber, 33 mg sodium.

Barbecued Beef Short Ribs
Serves 6

4½ pounds beef short ribs, cut into serving-sized
        pieces
1½ cups tomato sauce
1   teaspoon beef bouillon granules
⅓   cup red wine vinegar
¼   cup brown sugar, firmly packed
2   tablespoons Worcestershire sauce
1½ teaspoons garlic salt
1½ teaspoons prepared mustard
2   lemons, thinly sliced
1   medium onion, thinly sliced

1. Preheat oven to 350°F.
2. Place short ribs in a deep roasting pan.

3. In small bowl, combine tomato sauce, bouillon granules, red wine vinegar, brown sugar, Worcestershire sauce, garlic salt, and prepared mustard.
4. Pour sauce over ribs; place lemon and onion slices over sauce.
5. Bake ribs, covered, until tender, 1½ to 2 hours.
6. Serve ribs with sauce.

Per serving: 374 Cal. (43% from fat), 36 g protein, 19 g carbohydrate, 18 g fat, 98 mg cholesterol, 2.2 g fiber, 456 mg sodium.

Three Bean Salad
Serves 6 to 8

1½ cups canned red kidney beans, drained
1   cup canned chick-peas, drained
1   cup canned green beans, drained
½   cup finely chopped onion
¼   teaspoon garlic powder
1½ tablespoons chopped parsley
2   small green peppers, seeded and chopped
½   teaspoon salt
    dash pepper
⅓   cup red wine vinegar
1   teaspoon sugar
⅓   cup vegetable oil

1. Using a strainer or colander, rinse drained beans and chick-peas under cold running water; drain and rinse beans, again. Pat beans dry with paper towels.
2. In large bowl, combine beans, chick-peas, onion, garlic powder, green pepper, and salt and pepper; mix well.
3. In small bowl, combine vinegar, sugar, and oil.
4. Pour dressing over beans and toss.
5. Let salad stand for an hour before serving. (If salad must stand longer, refrigerate.)

Per serving: 171 Cal. (50% from fat), 5 g protein, 17 g carbohydrate, 10 g fat, 0 mg cholesterol, 4.9 g fiber, 318 mg sodium.

Tossed Greens with Ranch Dressing
Serves 6

¾ cup plain nonfat yogurt
1½ teaspoons prepared mustard
1½ teaspoons lemon juice
1 tablespoon chopped green onion (tops and bottoms)
3 teaspoons chives
5 to 6 cups assorted salad greens

1. In small bowl, combine yogurt, mustard, lemon juice, and chives.
2. Cover and refrigerate dressing until well chilled.
3. Clean salad greens and tear into bite-sized pieces.
4. When ready to serve, place greens in large salad bowl. Toss with dressing and serve immediately.

Per serving: 33 Cal. (17% from fat), 3 g protein, 5 g carbohydrate, 1 g fat, 2 mg cholesterol, 1.3 g fiber, 60 mg sodium.

Mexican Cornbread
Serves 8

1 cup cornmeal
1 cup buttermilk
¾ teaspoon baking soda
1 teaspoon salt
1 chopped onion
2 eggs, beaten
¼ cup cooking oil
1 can cream-style corn
1 large green pepper, chopped
½ pound Cheddar cheese

1. Preheat oven to 350°F.
2. In medium bowl, combine all ingredients except cheese.
3. Pour half of the batter in a 2½-quart casserole.
4. Cover with half of the grated Cheddar cheese.
5. Add the other half of the batter and cover with the remaining cheese.
6. Bake until cornbread is golden brown and tests done, about 40 minutes.

Per serving: 293 Cal. (56% from fat), 12 g protein, 21 g carbohydrate, 19 g fat, 99 mg cholesterol, 4.4 g fiber, 438 mg sodium.

Sopapillas
Makes about four dozen pastries

2 cups all-purpose flour
2½ teaspoons baking powder
½ teaspoon salt
1 tablespoon shortening
½ cup lukewarm water
shortening or oil for frying

1. In large mixing bowl, sift dry ingredients together.
2. Cut in shortening until mixture resembles coarse cornmeal.
3. Add water gradually, stirring with a fork until dough clings together.
4. Turn dough out onto lightly floured board or pastry cloth. Knead until smooth.
5. Divide dough in half. Let rest for 10 minutes.
6. Roll each half into a 10 x 12-inch rectangle about ⅛-inch thick.
7. Cut into 2-inch squares.
8. In deep fryer or large saucepan, heat shortening or oil until it reaches 375°F.
9. Add sopapillas, a few at a time. Fry about ½ minute on each side.
10. Serve warm with butter and honey or sprinkle with confectioner's sugar.

Per sopapilla: 31 Cal. (41% from fat), 1 g protein, 4 g carbohydrate, 1 g fat, 0 mg cholesterol, 0. 1 g fiber, 39 mg sodium.

National Honey Board

Barbecued beef is a favorite in the West and Southwest where herds of cattle are raised on sprawling ranches.

Pacific Coast

Photo courtesy of Northwest Cherry Growers

Majestic Mount Rainier is the highest mountain in the state of Washington.

The Pacific Coast includes the states of California, Oregon, Washington, and Alaska. Along the miles of coastline are sandy beaches, rocky shores, and breathtaking scenery. Farther inland are dense forests, snowcapped mountains, and rushing rivers and streams.

The Pacific states are the most diverse group of states in the country. They vary widely in geography, climate, culture, and food customs.

Most parts of California have rich, fertile soil; a warm, sunny climate; and adequate rainfall. Fruits and vegetables of all kinds grow in abundance. Avocados, papayas, pomegranates, dates, Chinese cabbage, kale, and okra are common, as are oranges, grapefruit, lettuce, and tomatoes.

The ocean and inland lakes provide a bounty of fish and shellfish. Shad, tuna, salmon, abalone, lobsters, crabs, shrimp, and oysters are especially popular.

Few rules or traditions hamper California-style cuisine. California cooks prepare the many fresh, locally produced foods in conventional as well as unconventional ways. They might simply broil salmon steaks and top them with a fresh dill sauce. However, more unusual combinations, such as crab and artichoke hearts or chicken and anchovies, are also popular.

Many of the foods that are part of California's cuisine also are available in Oregon and Washington. Many fruits, including peaches, apples, apricots, strawberries, raspberries, blackberries, blueberries, and boysenberries, grow in Washington and Oregon. Other fruits and vegetables are shipped there from California.

Steaks, chops, and other standard fare of the United States make up much of the diet of the Pacific Northwest. These foods are supplemented by wild game, fish, and seafood. Dungeness crabs, butter clams, Columbia River salmon, and Olympia oysters are especially popular.

Cooking techniques of all the Pacific states are, for the most part, simple. They take advantage of the natural flavors and colors of the foods. Cooks usually bake or broil fresh fish and shellfish. They serve vegetables raw in large salads or cooked just until crisp-tender. They often serve fresh fruits for dessert.

The people who settled the Pacific Coast influenced California's cuisine (and to a lesser extent that of Oregon and Washington). From the Far East came Chinese, Japanese, and Koreans, and from the South Pacific came Polynesians. Many of these immigrants worked as cooks, thus contributing native foods and dishes. Chop suey, for example, was supposedly invented in California by a Chinese cook. When asked to name the dish he had created, he hesitated and then said "chop suey," which means "everything chopped up."

The Mexicans who settled in Southern California brought native dishes with them. Tacos, tamales, enchiladas, guacamole, chili, and refried beans all are popular in this area of the state. The Spanish brought a type of stew called *cocido* (a mixture of vegetables, beef, lamb, ham, fowl, and a sausage called *chorizo*).

The prospectors who flocked to the Pacific states in search of gold brought sourdough with them. **Sourdough** is a dough containing active yeast plants. It is used as a leavening agent. The prospectors made sourdough by mixing together flour, water, and salt. They exposed the mixture to the air to absorb yeast plants. Then they added the dough to flour, water, and other available ingredients to make a variety of baked products. They always kept a small amount of the dough after each baking to serve as a starter for the next batch. They replenished the starter by adding more flour and water.

Sourdough bread was a staple food of the prospectors and pioneers. By the time the Gold Rush reached Alaska, sourdough was so established that people traveling north were given the nickname "sourdoughs." Much of the frontier cooking they took with them to Alaska remains in the state today.

Only that part of Alaska that lies within the Arctic region has the long, frigid winters many people associate with the state. Farther south, the climate is more mild, and vegetable, grain, and dairy farms dot the countryside.

Alaskans enjoy caribou, reindeer, rabbit, and bear hunted in the wilderness. Caribou sausage and reindeer steak are specialties. The icy, clear waters of the Pacific Ocean provide Alaskan king crab. Glacier-fed lakes and streams provide delicious salmon and trout, 26-6.

Alaskan cooks use the blueberries, huckleberries, and cranberries that grow wild to make pies and sauces. Other Alaskan specialties include fiddlehead ferns (young leaves of certain ferns eaten as greens), raw rose hips (the ripened false fruit of the rosebush), and cranberry catsup.

Be a Clever Consumer

If your vacation budget is limited, consider traveling in the off-season. Many facilities offer lower rates at this time. Off-season travel has the added benefit of smaller crowds at attractions and shorter waits at restaurants. However, some businesses reduce their operating hours in the off-season. Therefore, you would be wise to call ahead before going to shop, eat, or sightsee.

Alaska Seafood Marketing Institute

26-6 Salmon steak topped with salsa butter would be a unique listing on a Pacific coast menu.

Hawaiian Islands

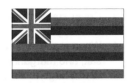

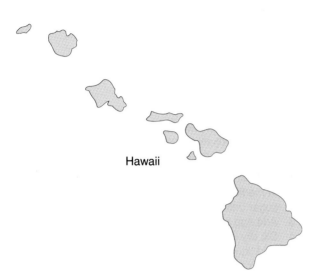

Hawaii

Hawaii Visitors Bureau

Visitors to Waikiki Beach can see Diamond Head rising in the distance beside the clear, blue Pacific waters.

The Hawaiian Islands are much more than a tourist's paradise. They have a rich history and colorful culture. They also have beautiful scenery and delicious food.

Historians believe Hawaii's first settlers were Polynesians from other Pacific islands. After their arrival, Hawaii was isolated from the rest of the world for many years. Although no written records exist, the Hawaiians have a rich heritage of songs and stories.

As Hawaii's population grew, rivalries for power took place. These resulted in a societal structure based on chieftains and kings, common people and aristocrats. Judges and priests defined codes and taboos. Early Hawaiians based their religion on nature worship. They were practicing both polygamy and infanticide at the time of Captain Cook's arrival in the late eighteenth century.

One of the outstanding figures in Hawaiian history is Kamehameha. Kamehameha eventually captured all of the islands and became king. He was able to establish order and peace throughout the islands. He made laws that forbade murder, robbery, and human sacrifice. He also worked to set up a prosperous sandalwood trade with the Orient.

Christian missionaries came to Hawaii in the early 1800s. They brought schools and a printing press to the islands. They also introduced the loose garment called a *muumuu*.

As the islands grew, enterprising foreigners began large sugar plantations. The increasing numbers of Europeans slowly weakened the traditional monarchy. It finally ended with the death of Kamehameha V. Then, in 1898, the United States annexed Hawaii. Hawaii became a state in 1959.

Since annexation, Hawaii has grown rapidly. Pineapple, sugarcane, and tourism are Hawaii's three largest industries.

Hawaii's food customs are as diverse as its people. The first Polynesians are thought to have brought coconuts, breadfruit, and taro root. European traders are believed to have introduced chicken and pork. The missionaries brought the stews, chowders, and corn dishes of their native New England.

Sugar plantation owners found that Hawaiians did not like to labor in the fields. Therefore, the plantation owners imported large groups of Chinese as workers. The Chinese brought rice, bean sprouts, Chinese cabbage, soybeans, snow peas, and bamboo shoots. They also introduced the stir-fry technique for cooking foods quickly over high heat.

A number of Japanese immigrated to the Hawaiian islands. They brought with them a variety of rice and fish dishes, *teriyaki* (a marinade made with soy sauce), seaweed, and pickled foods.

Because water surrounds Hawaii, fishing is an important industry. Hawaiian cooking uses fish and shellfish of all types. Cuttlefish, squid, convict fish, bone fish, crabs, and *opihi* (a clamlike mollusk) are especially popular.

The tropical climate of the islands makes the production of many fresh fruits and vegetables possible year-round. Many of the fruits, such as pineapples, mangoes, coconuts, and papayas, are important to Hawaiian cooking.

The variety of foods amazes visitors to Hawaiian markets. Snow peas, water chestnuts, bean sprouts, watercress, Chinese cabbage, squash, and lotus root are just a few of the many vegetables sold. Papayas, mangoes, and pineapples are among the many locally grown fruits. Dried bonito chips, lobsters, crabs, catfish, frogs, eels, oysters, tuna, snapper, and salmon come from the bounty of the surrounding waters. Other popular items are fresh *tofu* (bean curd), soybean cakes, Japanese fish cake, Korean kim chee, and persimmon tea.

The native Hawaiians held lavish feasts on special occasions. **Luaus** are elaborate outdoor feasts that are still popular in the islands today, 26-7. At these feasts *kalua pig* is served as the main course. This is a whole, young pig that is dressed, stuffed, and cooked in a pit called an **imu**. The imu is lined with hot rocks covered with banana leaves. The dressed pig is stuffed with hot rocks and placed on a wire rack. More leaves are placed over the top of the imu followed by more hot rocks and earth. Bananas, sweet potatoes, and meat or seafood dishes wrapped in leaves may be roasted with the pig.

The pig is served with other traditional Hawaiian foods. These foods include *lomi-lomi salmon* (salted salmon that is mashed with tomatoes and green onions); *poi* (a smooth paste made from the taro plant); shrimp; and fresh pineapples, mangoes, papayas, and coconuts. *Haupie* (a pudding made of milk, sugar, cornstarch, and grated fresh coconut) and macadamia and kukui nuts often are served for dessert.

Musical entertainment, singing, and dancing usually accompany a luau. Guests often join in the festivities.

Hawaii Visitors Bureau

26-7 The table for a luau is lavishly set with fresh flowers, fruits, and traditional Hawaiian dishes.

Hawaiian Menu
Tahitian Pork
Fried Rice
Waimea Salad
Aloha Loaf
Macadamia Nut Chiffon Pie
Sweet Lelani

Tahitian Pork
Serves 6

3   tablespoons cornstarch
2   tablespoons soy sauce
2   pounds lean pork, cut into 1-inch cubes
1   tablespoon vegetable oil
1   can pineapple chunks, 20 ounces
⅓   cup cider vinegar
¼   cup brown sugar, firmly packed
1   teaspoon garlic salt
¼   cup water
½   head cabbage, shredded

1. In medium mixing bowl, combine 2 tablespoons cornstarch with soy sauce.
2. Add pork cubes and toss until all pieces are coated.
3. Heat oil in a heavy skillet until hot but not smoking.
4. Add pork cubes and fry until browned.
5. Remove browned pork to absorbent paper to drain.
6. Remove any remaining oil from skillet.
7. Drain pineapple, reserving juice.
8. Return meat cubes to skillet.
9. Add pineapple juice, vinegar, brown sugar, and garlic salt.
10. Bring pork mixture to a boil; reduce heat and simmer 45 minutes.

Hawaii Visitors Bureau

Poi, lomi-lomi salmon, and haupie are traditional Hawaiian foods that might be served at a luau.

11. Dissolve remaining tablespoon of cornstarch in a small amount of cold water.
12. Add dissolved cornstarch to meat mixture.
13. Cook, stirring constantly, until sauce is thickened and translucent.
14. Add pineapple and heat through.
15. Serve Tahitian pork on a bed of shredded cabbage.

Per serving: 371 Cal. (32% from fat), 33 g protein, 30 g carbohydrate, 14 g fat, 111 mg cholesterol, 1.3 g fiber, 281 mg sodium.

Fried Rice
Serves 8 to 10

3   eggs, slightly beaten
8   slices bacon, cut into ¼-inch pieces
¼   cup bacon drippings
⅓   cup chopped onions
6   cups cooked rice
2   tablespoons soy sauce
¼   teaspoon pepper
½   cup whole green onions, thinly sliced

1. In medium skillet, scramble eggs, set aside.
2. In large skillet, fry bacon until cooked, but not crisp. Reserve drippings and set bacon aside.
3. Sauté chopped onion in drippings.
4. Add rice. Cook over moderate heat, stirring constantly until hot.
5. Add soy sauce, salt, pepper, and green onions; stir to combine.
6. Add scrambled egg and bacon. Toss gently with two forks. Serve immediately.

Per serving: 270 Cal. (29% from fat), 8 g protein, 39 g carbohydrate, 9 g fat, 111 mg cholesterol, 0.4 fiber, 384 mg sodium.

Waimea Salad
Serves 8 to 10

2   cans pineapple chunks, 20 ounces each
2   cans oranges, drained, 11 ounces each
4   cups halved strawberries
3   tablespoons fresh lime juice
3   tablespoons vegetable oil
1   teaspoon mint
½   teaspoon curry powder
¼   teaspoon salt

   crisp salad greens
4   bananas, sliced

1. Drain pineapple, reserving ¾ cup juice.
2. Chill pineapple, oranges, and strawberries.
3. Blend reserved pineapple juice, lime juice, oil, mint, curry powder, and salt in a small bowl and refrigerate covered.
4. When ready to serve salad, arrange crisp greens on large serving platter.
5. Add bananas to other fruits.
6. Attractively arrange fruits on greens.
7. Serve with dressing.

Per serving: 228 Cal. (24% from fat), 2 g protein, 44 g carbohydrate, 6 g fat, 0 mg cholesterol, 4.9 g fiber, 72 mg sodium.

Aloha Loaf
Makes 1 loaf

1½   cups all-purpose flour
2   teaspoons baking powder
½   teaspoon salt
3   tablespoons margarine
½   cup sugar
2   eggs
½   cup skim milk
1   tablespoon orange juice
   grated rind of one orange
½   cup flaked coconut

1. Preheat oven to 350°F.
2. Sift together flour, baking powder, and salt onto a sheet of waxed paper; set aside.
3. In medium mixing bowl, cream margarine, add sugar gradually, beating well after each addition.
4. Add eggs one at a time; continue beating until mixture is light and fluffy.
5. Add orange juice to milk.
6. Add liquid ingredients to creamed mixture alternately with dry ingredients, beginning and ending with dry ingredients.
7. Fold in grated rind and coconut.
8. Pour batter into greased and floured loaf pan.
9. Bake until bread tests done and is golden brown, about 1 hour.
10. Remove from pan to cooling rack.

Per slice: 108 Cal. (31 % from fat), 2 g protein, 16 g carbohydrate, 4 g fat, 34 mg cholesterol, 0.7 g fiber, 144 mg sodium.

Macadamia Nut Chiffon Pie
Makes one 9-inch pie

1	baked pastry shell, 9-inch (See Chapter 23)
1	package unflavored gelatin
1½	cups cold water
4	eggs, separated
½	cup sugar
½	cup boiling water
1	tablespoon rum extract
½	teaspoon lemon extract
1	teaspoon grated fresh lemon rind
⅛	teaspoon salt
1½	cups chopped macadamia nuts
½	cup heavy cream
2	tablespoons confectioners' sugar
½	teaspoon vanilla

1. In custard cup, soften gelatin in cold water. Set the cup in hot water until the gelatin dissolves.
2. In small mixing bowl, beat egg yolks until thick and lemon-colored.
3. Slowly add one half of the sugar and continue beating until yolk mixture forms ribbons when beaters are lifted.
4. Add the boiling water while beating constantly.
5. Pour mixture into a medium saucepan, and place over low heat. Stir until custard will coat the back of a spoon. (Do not let custard boil.)
6. Remove custard from heat and stir in gelatin.
7. Add rum and lemon extracts and lemon rind.
8. Chill, stirring occasionally until mixture mounds when dropped from a spoon.
9. In large mixing bowl with clean beaters, beat egg whites and salt until frothy.
10. Sprinkle in remaining sugar gradually and beat until egg whites form stiff peaks.
11. Stir about one fourth of the egg whites into the custard.
12. Pour the remaining custard over the egg whites, folding in gently.
13. Fold in 1¼ cups of the macadamia nuts.
14. Pour filling into pie shell and refrigerate, at least several hours.
15. Just before serving, whip the heavy cream in small, chilled bowl until thick.
16. Add sugar gradually, then vanilla.
17. Spread whipped cream over pie and garnish with remaining nuts.

⅛ of pie: 441 Cal. (69% from fat), 7 g protein, 28 g carbohydrate, 35 g fat, 157 mg cholesterol, 0.4 g fiber, 214 mg sodium.

Sweet Lelani
Serves 12

2	small cans frozen orange juice
1	large can pineapple juice
1⅓	cups lemon juice
1	bottle ginger ale, 1 liter
	pineapple spears
	maraschino cherries

1. Combine all ingredients except ginger ale, pineapple spears, and cherries. Stir.
2. Add ginger ale just before serving.
3. Pour drink into ice filled glasses.
4. Garnish each glass with a pineapple spear and a maraschino cherry.

Per serving: 154 Cal. (1% from fat), 1 g protein, 38 g carbohydrate, 0 g fat, 0 mg cholesterol, 0.6 g fiber, 9 mg sodium.

Summary

The Native Americans and the first explorers laid the foundations of cuisine in the United States. As immigrants came from many parts of the globe, they added foods and cooking techniques from their homeland. This blend of cultures and traditions has evolved into the cuisine found in the United States today.

Because immigrants from certain countries tended to settle together, the cuisine of the United States has some regional characteristics. For instance, hearty one-dish meals are popular in New England, as are foods made with locally produced maple syrup. German foods of the Pennsylvania Dutch can be found in the mid-Atlantic region. The South is known for fried chicken and buttermilk biscuits. Soul food and Creole cuisine also originated in the South. In the Midwest, where much of the nation's grain is grown, meat and potatoes are standard fare. Native Americans, Mexicans, and Spaniards influenced the foods of the West and Southwest, where chili and barbecued meats are favorites. Sourdough bread introduced by the prospectors, Alaskan seafood, and fresh fruits and vegetables are typical of the Pacific coast. Tropical fruits and vegetables, often prepared with an Asian influence, are common in Hawaii.

Review What You Have Read

Write your answers on a separate sheet of paper.
1. Name three reasons immigrants came to the New World.
2. How did New Englanders preserve foods for winter?
3. Name three culinary contributions of the Pennsylvania Dutch.
4. Name two distinct forms of cooking that developed in the South.
5. Name six agricultural products of the Midwest.
6. What four groups of people had the most influence on cooking in the Southwest?
7. True or false. The complex cuisine of the Pacific coast includes many sauces, herbs, and spices.
8. How did the prospectors make and use sourdough?
9. Briefly discuss the contributions made by the Polynesians, the European traders, the New England missionaries, and the Chinese and the Japanese immigrants in Hawaii.
10. Describe a luau.
11. Match the following foods to the regions with which they are associated:
    ___ poi
    ___ baked beans
    ___ salmon
    ___ tamales
    ___ corn on the cob
    ___ gumbo
    ___ shoofly pie
    A. New England
    B. mid-Atlantic
    C. South
    D. Midwest
    E. West and Southwest
    F. Pacific coast
    G. Hawaii

Build Your Basic Skills

1. Research the first Thanksgiving. Write a report about the foods that were served. Note how many of these foods are still served today.
2. Visit a local butcher to learn more about the parts of the hog used in the preparation of soul food. Then find some interesting recipes using chitterlings or jowls and prepare them.
3. Prepare a time line illustrating important dates in Hawaii's history.

Build Your Thinking Skills

1. Divide into seven groups, one group for each major region of the United States. Research the history and foods of your region. Then plan and prepare a typical meal for the other class members.
2. Work with your school's music and athletic departments to plan a fund-raising luau. Your class can prepare the food, while the other groups furnish the entertainment.

Ruins of ancient civilizations are found throughout Latin America.

Chapter 27
Latin America

A "Taste" of the World of Work

Spanish Interpreter
Translates spoken passages from Spanish into one or more other languages.

Mexican-Food-Machine Tender
Tends machine that automatically dispenses cheese onto tortillas to form enchiladas or ground meat onto taco shells to form tacos.

Mexican Food Cook
Supervises and coordinates activities of workers engaged in preparing, cooking, portioning, and packaging ready-to-serve Mexican food specialties, such as chili, tamales, enchiladas, and tacos.

Terms to Know

Latin America
Aztecs
conquistador
tortilla
frijoles refritos
chilies
guacamole
mole
plantain
comida
siesta

Inca
manioc
cassava
arepa
ají
ceviche
gaucho
empanada
dendé oil
feijoada completa

Objectives

After studying this chapter, you will be able to
❑ identify the geographic, climatic, and cultural factors that have influenced the food customs of Mexico and the South American countries.
❑ prepare foods native to Latin America.

Mexican Government Tourism Office

461

The land mass that stretches southward from the Rio Grande to the tip of South America is known as *Latin America.* It is called Latin America because the official language of most of the countries is either Spanish or Portuguese, both of which are based on Latin.

Latin America was first explored and settled by the Spanish. Later, other Europeans established settlements. A large number of Portuguese settled along the eastern shores of South America in what today is Brazil.

Extremes are the rule rather than the exception in Latin America. Dense, tropical rain forests are as common as snow-capped mountains. Large, modern cities may not be far away from wild jungles.

The food customs of Latin America are rich and varied. They reflect the culture, climate, and geography of each country. The ancient Aztecs and the Spanish conquistadores influenced Mexico. The foods of Peru reflect the ancient Inca civilization. The foods of Argentina are an unusual mixture of European influences and native foods grown in the rich soil. The foods of Brazil reflect strong African and Portuguese heritage.

Mexican Government Tourism Office

Mexican women have been weaving beautiful, multicolored blankets for centuries.

Mexico

Mexican Government Tourism Office

This street vendor in Mexico City has a colorful array of trinkets and souvenirs to sell to tourists.

Of all the Latin American countries, Mexico is most familiar to people in the United States. The close proximity of Mexico has made possible a rich cultural exchange.

Thousands of United States tourists visit Mexico each year. Mexican foods, such as tacos, enchiladas, and refried beans, are popular in the Southwest and throughout the United States.

Climate and Geography of Mexico

Mexico is a land of deserts, mountains, grasslands, woodlands, and tropical rain forests. The Rio Grande separates Mexico from Texas. The Pacific Ocean, Gulf of California, Caribbean Sea, and Gulf of Mexico form its coastline. Although the climate in a few regions is wet and humid, nearly half of Mexico is arid or semiarid.

Much of Mexico is mountainous, with valleys separating the different ranges. The height of the Western and Eastern Sierra Madres has made both communication and travel difficult. This has slowed cultural and economic development.

Both climate and geography have affected food customs in Mexico. In those sections of the country bordered by water, fish is an important part of the cuisine. The areas that border the United States have land that is too dry for large scale crop production. However, it is suitable for raising cattle. As a result, beef is a staple food in these areas. A variety of tropical fruits and vegetables grow along the southern Gulf Coast where rainfall is adequate. In the central plateau, the level land, adequate moisture, and cool temperatures make the production of crops like corn and beans profitable.

Mexican Culture

The *Aztecs* were the original inhabitants of Mexico. They had a very advanced civilization for their time in history. They had picture writing, a number system, and elaborate architecture. In 1520, Hernando Cortes became the first known white man to explore Mexico. Cortes and the Spanish *conquistadores* (conquerors) were impressed by the highly evolved Aztec society. However, they were more interested in the gold and other precious metals that decorated Aztec palaces and temples. Their greed led them to plunder Aztec villages and destroy much of the Aztec civilization.

The Spanish controlled Mexico, except for a few years, until the middle of the nineteenth century. Their influence greatly affected the development of Mexican culture, especially architecture, language, and food customs.

Mexican Lifestyle

Today, Mexico's population is a mixture. *Mestizos* (persons of mixed European and Native American ancestry) make up the largest percentage. Native Americans are the next largest group, and people of European descent are the smallest group.

A typical Mexican home is made of adobe brick and has a thatched or tiled roof. The walls often are whitewashed or painted a pastel color.

Living quarters in all but the wealthiest Mexican homes are simple. Beds, tables, and chairs often are hand-carved. Many dishes and cooking utensils are handmade. Many homes have an altar in one corner where family members place candles, flowers, and pictures of the Virgin Mary.

Traditionally, Mexican families are close-knit. Children learn to help their parents at an early age. The children of rural families work in the fields, help with housework and take care of their younger brothers and sisters. Many city children must work to supplement the family income. They may sell handmade baskets, fruit, or postcards.

Mexican Economy

A little more than half of Mexico's people are farmers. Because good, rich soil is scarce, farming is difficult. Most farmers are too poor to afford modern machinery or fertilizers. As a result, crop yields are poor. In recent years, the government has been trying to help farmers improve yields.

They have begun intensive irrigation projects and have extended credit to farmers for the purchase of machinery and fertilizers.

Corn is Mexico's major crop. Bean production is second. Other important crops include sugarcane, tobacco, coffee, tomatoes, green peppers, peas, melons, citrus fruits, strawberries, and cacao beans. Wheat and cotton are grown in the North as are smaller amounts of barley, rice, and oats. Cattle graze on northern pastures. See 27-1.

Coastal waters provide a variety of seafood. Large quantities of shrimp are caught and exported. Sardines, tuna, turtles, and mackerel also are important.

Mexico has many raw materials needed for industry, and industrial growth has been rapid in recent decades. Industries include the manufacture of glass, paper, textiles, steel, and tequila. Gold, silver, zinc, sulfur, lead, and manganese are exported from Mexican mines.

Good Manners Are Good Business

You will make a better impression when dealing with business associates in other countries if you demonstrate sensitivity to cultural differences. Do not expect everyone to speak English and conduct business as it is conducted in the United States.

In Mexico, for instance, executives often take a rather relaxed view of scheduling. Just because you have an appointment and are waiting outside, a manager is not likely to rush through an earlier meeting. Rather than getting upset, you would be wise to schedule your appointments for early in the day. This will help you avoid being kept waiting.

USA Rice Council

27-1 This burrito is overflowing with traditional Mexican ingredients, including corn, beans, tomatoes, peppers, and rice.

Mexican Cuisine

Both the Aztecs and the Spaniards made many contributions to Mexican cuisine. The Aztecs contributed chocolate, vanilla, corn, peppers, peanuts, tomatoes, avocados, squash, beans, sweet potatoes, pineapples, and papayas. The Aztecs boiled, broiled, or steamed their food or ate it raw. Their more elaborate dishes were similar to modern stews.

The Spanish added oil, wine, cinnamon, cloves, rice, wheat, peaches, apricots, beef, and chicken. With the introduction of oil, many of the early Aztec foods could be fried. Today, frying is an important part of Mexican cooking. Mexican cooks fry foods in deep fat or on lightly greased griddles.

A final contribution to Mexican cuisine was made during the short reign of Maximilian and Carlotta. At this time, more sophisticated French, Italian, and Austrian dishes were introduced.

Characteristic Foods of Mexico

Corn, beans, and peppers are staple ingredients in Mexican cuisine. Mexican cooks use a variety of locally grown vegetables and fruits, too. Flavorful sauces and stews, as well as some distinctive desserts and beverages, are also typical foods of Mexico.

Corn

Corn has formed the basis of Mexican cuisine since the days of the Aztec civilization. Mexican cooks use corn in many ways, but its most important use is in the production of tortillas. A *tortilla* is a flat, unleavened bread made from cornmeal and water. The dough is shaped into a thin pancake in a tortilla press. Then it is cooked on a lightly greased griddle called a *comal.* You can eat tortillas plain, but most people eat them with other foods. You can roll any semisolid food inside the tortilla and eat the entire package like a sandwich.

Mexican cooks make many popular dishes from tortillas. They fill tortillas with a mixture of shredded meat or sliced chicken, onions, garlic, and chilies to make *enchiladas.* Then they bake and serve the enchiladas with cheese and a red or green tomato sauce. Mexicans fry tortillas until crisp and garnish them with chopped onion, chilies, beans, shredded lettuce, meat, and cheese to make *tostadas. Quesadillas* are deep-fried turnovers made of tortillas filled with meat, sauce, cheese, beans, or vegetables. Tortillas wrapped around a meat or bean filling are called *burritos.* Crisp, fried tortillas filled with meat, beans, shredded lettuce, and cheese and seasoned with chili are called *tacos.*

Mexican cooks never waste corn. They do not even discard the husks. They use the husks to make *tamales.* The cooks stuff small amounts of corn dough with meat and beans and tuck it into the corn husks. They fold the husks into small parcels and steam them or roast them over an open fire.

Beans

Like corn, beans are a staple food in Mexico. Local farmers grow many varieties of beans. Sometimes people boil the beans and eat them from the pot as was done during Aztec times. Often they cook the beans until they are soft, then they mash the beans and fry them slowly. The Mexicans call this dish *frijoles refritos* (refried beans) and frequently serve the beans with grated cheese.

Peppers

People throughout Latin America use peppers, but they are especially important in Mexico. Strings of peppers hang outside many Mexican homes to dry.

Mexican cooks use over 30 varieties of peppers. The peppers range in size from $1/8$ to 8 inches (3 mm to 20 cm) in length. Their colors vary from light to dark green, from bright to brick red, and from yellow to orange. They can be sweet, pungent, or burning hot. Generally, the mild peppers are called *sweet peppers,* and the hot ones are called **chilies.**

The peppers used most often in cooking can be divided into two groups according to color—red and green. Mexican cooks use red peppers dried, except for ripe red bell peppers and pimientos. They use green peppers fresh. See 27-2.

Mexican Vegetables and Fruits

Mexican farmers grow a variety of vegetables. Mexicans usually do not eat vegetables plain. Instead, they add them to casseroles and use them as garnishes for other dishes.

Mexican vegetables that are common in the United States include zucchini, artichokes, white potatoes, spinach, chard, lettuce, beets, cauliflower, and carrots. Less common are *huazontle* (wild broccoli), *jicama* (a large, gray root), *nopole* (tender cactus leaves), and *chayotes* (the fruit of a climbing vine).

Many fruits grow in Mexico. Avocados are both plentiful and inexpensive. They have a bland flavor and are often added to other foods. **Guacamole,** for example, is a spread made from mashed avocado, tomato, and onion. It may be served with tortillas or crisp corn chips. It is popular in the United States as well as in Mexico. Bananas, pineapples, guavas, papayas, and prickly pears are other tropical fruits that are popular in

27-2 Mexican cooking is flavored with a variety of chilies.

Mexico. The fruits are often served alone or in a heavy syrup as a light, refreshing dessert.

Sauces and Stews

Mexican cooks often use thick sauces. They pour some sauces over other foods. Other sauces contain pieces of meat, vegetables, tortillas, or beans and are served as main dishes.

Very simple sauces are made from chilies or sweet peppers or several varieties of chilies and sweet peppers mixed with finely chopped onions and tomatoes. More complex sauces are called **moles.** The word *mole* is derived from the Aztec word, *molli,* which means a chili-flavored sauce. Cooks make one type of mole from a variety of chilies, almonds, raisins, garlic, sesame seeds, onions, tomatoes, cinnamon, cloves, coriander seeds, and anise seeds. They finely chop these ingredients and add them to chicken stock. They add the final ingredient, unsweetened chocolate, just before serving. This type of mole is part of turkey mole, which is a traditional dish.

Mexican stews are as unique as moles. Stews begin with a sauce. Cooks grind dried peppers and

mix them with ground spices and vegetables. They add some meat or poultry stock to the ground mixture to make a thick paste. Then they fry the paste, thin it to the consistency of a medium white sauce, and add it to cooked meat or poultry.

Long, slow cooking gives Mexican stews their characteristic flavors. Because of the high altitude, the boiling point in many parts of Mexico is lower. As a result, stews can be simmered for many hours to develop flavor without becoming overcooked.

Mexican Desserts

Other than fresh fruits and sweet tamales, the Aztecs had few desserts. Catholic convents begun by the Spaniards developed many of the desserts and sweets eaten in Mexico today. Early Spanish and Portuguese cooks influenced those desserts that use large amounts of egg and sugar, such as *flan* (a caramel custard).

Mexican Beverages

Chocolate drinks and coffee are popular Mexican beverages. The cacao bean, known since the days of the Aztecs, is toasted and ground into cocoa or made into chocolate. Mexican chocolate is similar to the hot chocolate drink served in the United States. However, it has a different texture and is lighter than the chocolate served in other Latin American and European countries. A tool called a *molinillo* is used to beat the chocolate into a foam before serving. Coffee often is served with milk and called *café con leche*. It also can be boiled to a thick syrup and served black or with sugar.

Mexican Regional Cuisine

Although many foods are common throughout Mexico, regional differences do exist. These occur mainly as a result of geographic and climatic conditions.

In northern Mexico, the climate is such that farmers can grow wheat and raise cattle. Therefore, tortillas in this area are made from wheat rather than corn. People commonly eat beef, which they may dry or cook with onions, peppers, and tomatoes and serve with beans. Cheese is also popular in several northern states. In Chihuahua, for example, people fry beans in lard and then carefully heat them with cheese. In Senora, cooks cover a potato soup with a thick layer of melted cheese.

Finfish and shellfish are important protein sources for people living in coastal areas. They use seafood in appetizers, soups, and main dishes. Cooks near the Gulf coast make a popular dish from **plantains** (green, starchy fruits that have a bland flavor and look much like large bananas) fried with onions and tomatoes and served with shrimp (or other seafood) and chili sauce. *Paella*, derived from the Spanish dish with the same name, contains seafood, chicken, and peas cooked in chicken broth and served with rice.

Wild duck is popular in eastern Mexico. Turkey is one of the most important foods of the Yucatan (peninsula that forms Mexico's southern tip).

Squash blossoms and sea chestnuts (a type of crustacean) are popular in southern Mexico. Because banana trees are abundant, tamales in this region are wrapped in fresh banana leaves rather than in corn husks.

Mexican Meals

Mexican meal patterns differ somewhat from those of the United States. Families with ample incomes often eat four meals a day.

The first meal of the day, *desayuno*, is a substantial breakfast. Fruit, tortillas, bread or sweet rolls, eggs or meat, and coffee or chocolate are served. *Huevos rancheros* (eggs prepared with chilies and served on tortillas) are a popular breakfast dish.

The main meal of the day, **comida**, is served in the middle of the day between one and three o'clock. Six courses are not unusual. These may consist of an appetizer, a soup, a small dish of stew, a main course, beans, dessert, and coffee. Tortillas are traditionally served, but bread sometimes is substituted. A **siesta** (rest period) usually follows comida. See 27-3.

A light snack, *merienda*, is served around five or six o'clock. Merienda is similar to the English high tea. It includes chocolate or coffee, fruit, and *pan dulce* (sweet breads).

Mexicans may eat *cena*, supper, between eight and ten o'clock. Cena is similar to comida, but smaller and lighter. (Many Mexican families combine merienda and cena and eat one meal in the early evening.)

27-3 These quesadillas, made with beef, onions, peppers, tomatoes, and cheese, might be served as a main course in northern Mexico.

Chapter 27

group of Native South Americans, the *Inca,* built a large empire in the Andes Mountains. The Inca had no written language or system of money. However, they were advanced in many ways. The Inca built roads and bridges to facilitate travel throughout the empire. They used an irrigation system to increase the productivity of their farmlands. They wove fine cloth and crafted beautiful items from metal and pottery.

When Spanish explorers discovered the Incan empire, they were amazed by the level of civilization. Like the explorers in Mexico, however, the explorers of South America were more fascinated by gold and silver. The Incan empire was unable to survive the Spanish conquest. However, Inca influence is still felt in South America today.

Explorers from Portugal landed in the area that is now Brazil. The Portuguese stayed in the area and built large plantations where they grew sugarcane. Today, Portuguese is the official language of Brazil.

The Portuguese brought Africans to Brazil to work in the sugar fields. The Africans influenced the development of South American cuisine. They raised crops of foods from their homeland, including bananas, yams, and coconuts. African women used some of their native foods and cooking techniques in the kitchens of the Portuguese.

Following the Portuguese, small groups of French and Dutch settlers established colonies along the northern coast of South America. Their influence is still evident in French Guiana and Suriname.

Modern Culture in South America

Since the days of the early explorers, racial groups in South America have intermingled. A few direct descendants of the native tribes, Europeans, and Africans are scattered throughout the continent. However, many South Americans are of mixed blood.

Today, South America is in a process of evolution. Most South American countries are experiencing rapid population growth. However, South America still is not as heavily populated as other continents. As in other developing areas of the world, the population movement is toward the cities.

South America has made great economic and technological progress in recent years. Skyscrapers, modern highways, and industrial plants are becoming more and more common. The old and the new are apparent throughout the continent. Brasilia, Rio de Janeiro, Caracas, and Buenos Aires are modern cities. Their architecture and transportation systems resemble those of cities in Europe and the United States. However, intermingled with modern

buildings are churches that date back to the Spanish conquistadores and the Inca, 27-4.

South America has both great wealth and great poverty. Some landowners control vast amounts of the most productive farmland. However, most farmers barely survive on small plots with poor soil. The members of the upper classes enjoy the best foods, entertainment, and housing. At the same time, the lower classes are hindered by illiteracy, lack of transportation, antiquated farming methods, and poor wages.

South American Cuisine

South American cuisine combines influences of native tribes with those of the Spanish, Portuguese, and Africans. Many staple foods, such as corn, potatoes, and manioc, are found throughout the continent. (*Manioc,* known as *cassava* in some regions, is a starchy root plant eaten as a side dish and used in flour form in cooking and baking.) However, most food customs have developed on a regional basis because of geographic isolation. Each region reflects cultural influences as well as geographic and climatic ones.

The following discussion briefly describes the cuisine of several South American countries. This discussion will give you an overview of some of the unique dishes typical of this continent.

Be a Clever Consumer

Many hotels, restaurants, and shops in other countries may be willing to accept U.S. currency. However, it is more convenient and economical to use local currency when you travel.

The value of U.S. dollars in other countries changes frequently. You may want to exchange some money (perhaps $50) at a bank before leaving home. This will allow you cover small expenses when you first arrive in another country. However, you should wait until you reach your destination before exchanging most of your money. This will allow you to get a better exchange rate (more foreign currency in exchange for U.S. currency). You will also get a better exchange rate at a bank than you will at a store or hotel.

Those people living in the tropical lowlands make good use of the banana, plantain, and coconut. Bananas and plantains are boiled, fried, baked, and added to stews and soups. Plantains, thinly sliced and fried until crisp, are a popular Venezuelan snack. Banana leaves are used to wrap *hallacas,* Venezuela's national dish, which is cornmeal dough filled with other foods. Candies, puddings, and cakes are made from coconuts. Coconut and coconut milk are also added to stewed meats. A sponge-type cake moistened with muscatel (a type of wine) and covered with coconut cream is a famous Venezuelan dessert.

Colombia

Potatoes, which are grown high in the mountains, are especially important in the diet of northern Colombians. Farther south, cassavas are used instead of potatoes.

Poor Colombians eat little meat. However, stews and thick soups are popular in Colombia. Cooks make one soup, *ajiaco,* with potatoes, chicken, corn, and cassava.

Colombia is an important coffee-producing country. The coffee trees thrive on the cool slopes of the Andes Mountains. The coffee served in Colombia is much stronger than that served in the United States. However, Colombians do not drink as much coffee as people in the United States.

Ecuador

Because Ecuador is a large producer of bananas, local dishes often feature bananas. Ecuadorian people make bananas into flour, which they use to make breads and pastries. They cut firm green bananas and plantains into chips and deep-fry them. The simplest and most common banana dessert is made by slowly frying ripe bananas in butter. As the slices begin to brown, sugar is added little by little until the bananas are brown on both sides. Before serving, the sautéed banana slices are splashed with brandy and dusted with powdered sugar.

Peru

The descendants of the Inca still live in Peru. They have retained many of the customs of their ancestors. Their cuisine reflects both Inca and Spanish traditions.

Since the days of the Inca, the *papa* (potato) has been the staple food of the Peruvian people. The Inca developed over 100 potato varieties. To preserve their potatoes, they freeze-dried them. The cold night air of the Andes quickly froze the

Consulado General de Chile

27-4 Remains of churches built centuries ago can still be found in South America.

Venezuela

The Spanish who explored Venezuela found rich, fertile soil and a temperate climate in the valleys formed by the Andes. The cuisine of this country reflects these two factors. It also reflects the tropical climate found in the jungle lowlands just south of the valleys and the food customs of the Spanish explorers.

Caracas, the capital city, is filled with modern buildings exhibiting a cosmopolitan lifestyle. However, much of Venezuela is less developed and is inhabited by small farming families.

Arepa, a corn pancake similar to a tortilla, is a traditional Venezuelan bread. It forms the basis of the small farmer's diet. Cooks make arepa by mixing corn flour with water and salt. They shape the stiff dough into balls or patties and toast it on a lightly greased griddle. Although people often eat arepa plain, they also use it to make more elaborate dishes. *Bollos pelones,* for example, are balls of arepa dough stuffed with a meat mixture. These dumplings are then deep-fried or simmered in soup or sauce.

potatoes. When the sun came out, the potatoes thawed. At night, they froze once again. The moisture that formed evaporated. Soon the potatoes became hard as stone but very lightweight. The Inca could then store the potatoes indefinitely.

The poorest people of Peru eat boiled potatoes alone or with a few local herbs or chilies, which the Peruvians (and Chileans) call *ají*. Those who are not quite so poor prepare potatoes in many unusual and delicious ways. One popular potato dish is made by pouring a thick sauce made of cheese, milk, ají, and various local spices over boiled potatoes. Another flavorful potato dish of Inca origin is *causa a la limena*. A mixture of stiff mashed potatoes, olive oil, lemon juice, salt, pepper, chopped onions, and ají is pressed into small molds. The unmolded dish is garnished with hard-cooked eggs, cheese, sweet potatoes, prawns (a shrimplike crustacean), and olives.

Peruvians often make *cuy* (guinea pig) into a stew. They also brush cuy with olive oil and garlic and roast it. Vendors on Peruvian streets sell another popular meat dish called *anticuchos*. They marinate small strips of beef heart overnight and thread them on skewers. They baste the meat with a sauce and grill it over hot coals.

Peruvians who live along the coast eat a variety of seafood. Shrimp is especially popular in both appetizers and main dishes. *Chupe,* a thick soup made from milk, vegetables, and shellfish, is served as a main dish.

Peruvians invented **ceviche**, a marinated raw fish dish, 27-5. However, people throughout South America enjoy it. Cooks usually make ceviche from *corvinas* (a type of whitefish found off the Peruvian coast), but they can use other types of whitefish. They cut the fish into small cubes. Then they cover it with a marinade made of lime juice, lemon juice, salt, pepper, garlic, onion, and ají. After the fish has marinated for several hours, its texture becomes similar to that of cooked fish. The ceviche is then ready to eat. Peruvians often serve ceviche with corn and sweet potatoes. People in other South American countries often serve it as an appetizer.

Peruvian tamales contain a variety of foods including meat, chicken, sausage, eggs, peanuts, raisins, and olives. Unlike Mexican tamales, they often are somewhat sweet.

Chile

Chile is a long, thin country. The upper third of Chile is arid desert, and the lower third is mountainous. The central region has fertile valleys, irrigated fields, and forests.

Almond Board of California

27-5 Although it is Peruvian in origin, ceviche is enjoyed by people throughout South America.

Because the land is not suitable for raising cattle or sheep, Chileans eat little meat. Instead, seafood, beans, and small amounts of meat are combined with vegetables in many delicious stews. *Porotos granados,* for example, contains cranberry beans, corn, squash, garlic, and onion.

Another popular dish in Chile is *pastel de choclo*. It is a meat pie made with a sugar coated topping of ground fresh corn. Beef, or a combination of beef and chicken, usually is used in the filling. Raisins and olives may be added. Some cooks also add pepper or ají. However, most Chilean dishes are not peppery.

Of all the South Americans, Chileans probably eat the most seafood. Seafood is both plentiful and inexpensive, and shellfish are particularly popular. Crabs, lobsters, clams, scallops, and sea urchins are used in many dishes. *Chupe de marisco* (scallop stew) is baked in a deep dish. A creamy cheese sauce flavored with paprika, nutmeg, pepper, and onion complements the flavors of scallops and rice.

Argentina

The Pampas are the richest lands in South America. They cover the southeastern part of the continent and reach into the countries of Argentina and Uruguay. Here, large herds of cattle and sheep graze until they are ready for market.

Because it is so readily available, the people of Argentina eat large amounts of meat. Much of the meat is roasted in the style of the gauchos. The *gauchos* were nomadic herders of the Pampas during the eighteenth and nineteenth centuries. They put meat from freshly slaughtered cattle on large stakes placed at an angle around a fire. (This prevented the juices from dripping into the coals.) A peppery herb and parsley sauce called *chimichurri* accompanied the freshly roasted meat.

Argentine cooks also prepare meat in other ways. They make one popular dish, *metambre,* by layering spinach, hard-cooked eggs, carrots, and onions on top of a marinated flank steak. Then they roll the metambre, tie it, and either poach it or roast it until tender.

Argentine appetizers are called **empanadas.** They are small turnovers filled with chopped meat, olives, raisins, and onions.

Although most of the foods of Argentina have a strong flavor, mild-flavored squashes and pumpkins have been popular for centuries. Cooks use squash to make fritters, soups, and puddings. They sometimes thicken and decorate stews with squash. *Carbonada criolla,* a colorful stew, contains pieces of beef, squash, tomatoes, corn on the cob, and fresh peaches. It sometimes is served in a squash or pumpkin shell.

Humitas are similar to Mexican tamales. Unripe kernels of corn are mixed with onions, tomatoes, salt, pepper, sugar, and cinnamon. Sometimes cheese is also added. Humitas may be cooked with milk until tender and served plain. They may also be rolled into corn husks, tied, and boiled or steamed.

Brazil

Brazilian culture is a mixture of Native South American, Portuguese, and African cultures.

The native inhabitants of Brazil were more primitive than the Inca of the Andes. They did not practice agriculture on a wide scale. However, they did produce manioc, which is still a staple food in Brazil.

The Africans brought to Brazil by the early Portuguese made a great impact on Brazilian cuisine. The *dendé oil* (palm oil that gives Brazilian dishes a bright yellow-orange color), red pepper, bananas, and coconuts used in many Brazilian dishes were first used by the African cooks.

The African women were skilled cooks and made use of the readily available shrimp and fish. *Vatapa,* for example, is a delicious stew made of pieces of shrimp and fish cooked with coconut milk, palm oil, and pieces of bread. Vatapa is usually served over rice.

The Brazilians serve rice, a second staple food, in a variety of ways. One popular dish is a casserole made of layers of rice, shrimp, ham, chicken, cheese, and tomato. A popular Afro-Brazilian coconut pudding also contains rice.

Beans, a third staple food, are as important to Brazilian cooking as they are to Mexican cooking. Brazilians prefer shiny black beans that they can cook to a paste. They use these beans to make *feijoada completa,* Brazil's national dish. Feijoada completa is made with meat and beans. It can be simple or elaborate depending on the ingredients used. Traditional feijoada completa includes dried beef and smoked tongue. Other meats, such as fresh beef, pork, bacon, sausage, and pigs' feet, can also be added. The meats are cooked until tender and then arranged on a large platter. The black beans, cooked to a pulp, are served in a separate pot. Bowls of hot sauces, cooked rice, manioc meal, shredded kale or collard greens, and orange slices accompany the beans and meat. See 27-6.

A Brazilian version of the tamale, called *abara,* is African in origin. Abara is a mixture of cowpeas, shrimp, pepper, and dendé oil rolled into banana leaves and cooked over an open fire.

Cuscuz, a steamed grain dish, is either Arabian or North African in origin. The Brazilians adopted it and developed two different forms of it.

One kind of cuscuz is sweet and is served as a dessert. Cooks mix tapioca, freshly grated coconut, coconut milk, sugar, and water together with boiling water. They pour the mixture into a mold and refrigerate it. Later, they slice and serve the chilled cuscuz. The other type of cuscuz, often called *cuscuz paulista,* is served as a main dish. Cuscuz paulista is made with specially prepared cornmeal mixed with shredded vegetables and meat and a small amount of fat. The mixture is steamed and garnished decoratively.

27-6 Feijoada completa, a hearty mixture of meat and black beans, is Brazil's national dish.

South American Menu

Empanadas
(Turnovers)
Carbonada Criolla
(Beef Stew)
Couve à Mineira
(Shredded Kale)
Tortillas de Maiz
(Corn Pancakes)
Plàtanos Tumulto
(Broiled Bananas)
Brasileiras
(Brazilian Coconut Cookies)
Café
(Coffee)

Empanadas
(Turnovers)
Makes about 24

Filling:
 1 pound lean ground beef
 1 onion, finely chopped
 ½ clove garlic, chopped
 2 medium tomatoes
 8 large green olives, cut in half
 ½ cup raisins
    salt
    pepper

1. In large, heavy skillet, brown ground beef.
2. Add onions and garlic.
3. When browned, add tomatoes, olives, raisins, and salt and pepper to taste.
4. Simmer mixture uncovered, until cooked, about 20 minutes.
5. Remove from heat and refrigerate until you are ready to fill empanadas.

Pastry:
 2 cups all-purpose flour
 ½ teaspoon salt
 1 teaspoon baking powder
 ½ cup shortening
 ⅓ cup ice water

1. Sift flour, salt, and baking powder into a large mixing bowl.
2. With pastry blender, two knives, or fingers, cut shortening into dry ingredients until particles are the size of coarse cornmeal.
3. Add ice water, stirring gently with a fork until dough forms a ball.
4. On lightly floured board or pastry cloth, roll out dough.
5. Using a 2-inch biscuit cutter, cut dough into circles.

6. Place about 1 tablespoon of filling in the center of each circle. Seal edges well with a little cold water.
7. Bake in a 450°F oven until lightly browned, about 10 to 15 minutes. (For a more authentic dish, empanadas can be fried, a few at a time, in 375°F oil until golden brown.)

Per serving: 126 Cal. (50% from fat), 5 g protein, 11 g carbohydrate, 7 g fat, 11 mg cholesterol, .8 g fiber, 95 mg sodium.

Carbonada Criolla
(Beef Stew)
Serves 10

 2   tablespoons vegetable oil
 2½   pounds beef chuck, cut into 1-inch cubes
 ¾   cup coarsely chopped onions
 ½   cup coarsely chopped green pepper
 ½   teaspoon finely chopped garlic
 4½   cups beef stock
 3   medium tomatoes, seeded and chopped
 ½   teaspoon oregano
 1   bay leaf
 1¼   teaspoons salt
 ½   teaspoon pepper
 4½   cups sweet potatoes cut into ½-inch cubes (about 1½ pounds)
 4½   cups white potatoes, cut into ½-inch cubes (about 1 ½ pounds)
 ¾   pound zucchini, scrubbed but not pared
 4   small ears sweet corn, shucked and cut into rounds, 1 inch wide
 6   canned peach halves, rinsed in cold water

1. Heat oil in a large Dutch oven.
2. Add meat and brown.

3. Transfer browned meat to a platter. In the same Dutch oven, cook onions, green peppers, and garlic until lightly browned.
4. Add beef stock and bring to a boil.
5. Return meat to stock and add tomatoes and seasonings.
6. Cover Dutch oven and reduce heat to low. Simmer stew for 15 minutes.
7. Remove cover and add sweet potatoes and white potatoes. Simmer for 15 minutes more.
8. Remove cover and add zucchini. Cover and cook 10 minutes more.
9. Remove cover and add corn and peach halves, cover and cook 5 minutes more. Serve.
10. To serve stew in a traditional style, remove seeds and fiber from inside of a 10 to 12 pound pumpkin.
11. Rub insides with softened margarine; sprinkle with a mixture of granulated and light brown sugars.
12. Cover pumpkin shell with lid and place on baking sheet. Bake at 375°F for 45 minutes or until a sharp knife easily pierces the skin.
13. Pour stew into pumpkin shell and place in 375°F oven for 15 minutes.
14. Place filled pumpkin on a serving platter and serve immediately.

Per serving: 312 Cal. (32% from fat), 20 g protein, 34 g carbohydrate, 11 g fat, 53 mg cholesterol, 4.4 g fiber, 403 mg sodium.

Couve à Mineira
(Shredded Kale)
Serves 6

1½   pounds kale*
¼   cup bacon drippings
½   teaspoon salt
     dash pepper

1. Under running water, carefully wash kale. With a sharp knife, remove any bruised spots and cut tender leaves from tough stems. Discard stems. Shred kale into strips about ½ inch wide.
2. In large sauce pan, bring 2 quarts of water to a boil.
3. Add kale and cook uncovered 3 minutes.
4. Drain kale in a colander removing as much water as possible.
5. In a large, heavy skillet, melt bacon drippings.

6. When hot, add kale. Cook, stirring frequently, until kale is tender, about 30 minutes. (Kale should still be slightly crisp.)
7. Add salt and pepper and serve immediately.

*Collard greens may be substituted for kale.

Per serving: 97 Cal. (82% from fat), 1 g protein, 4 g carbohydrate, 9 g fat, 8 mg cholesterol, 3.3 g fiber, 193 mg sodium.

Tortillas de Maiz
(Corn Pancakes)
Makes 8 pancakes

1   cup frozen corn kernels, thawed
1   egg
2   tablespoons all-purpose flour
¼   teaspoon salt
3 to 4   tablespoons margarine
½   cup plain yogurt
1½   tablespoons chopped fresh parsley

1. Using paper towels, pat corn completely dry.
2. Heat a large, heavy skillet, sprayed with no-stick cooking spray.
3. Add corn and cook until lightly browned.
4. Remove corn to plate lined with paper towels.
5. In large mixing bowl, beat egg until foamy; add flour, salt, and corn.
6. In small skillet or crepe pan, heat 1 tablespoon margarine until it foams.
7. Pour in ⅛ cup batter. As tortilla cooks, gently lift edges to allow uncooked batter to flow underneath.
8. When tortilla is brown on the bottom, flip with spatula and cook other side 1 minute.
9. Slide tortilla onto a heated platter and keep warm in a 225°F oven.
10. Continue making tortillas, adding a teaspoon of margarine before frying each.
11. Serve tortillas topped with 1 tablespoon of yogurt and chopped parsley.

Per tortilla: 79 Cal. (55% from fat), 2 g protein, 7 g carbohydrate, 5 g fat, 35 mg cholesterol, .9 g fiber, 137 mg sodium.

Plàtanos Tumulto
(Broiled Bananas)
Serves 6

6 firm, medium bananas
  lemon juice
3 tablespoons margarine
3 tablespoons light brown sugar, packed
¾ teaspoon cinnamon

1. Preheat broiler.
2. Peel bananas and slice in half lengthwise.
3. Place banana halves cut side up on broiler pan; sprinkle with lemon juice.
4. Combine brown sugar and cinnamon in small bowl; cut in margarine until mixture resembles large peas. Sprinkle over banana halves.
5. Place bananas 2 inches from heat and broil until sugar has melted. (Watch carefully.) Serve immediately.

Per serving: 198 Cal. (29% from fat), 1 g protein, 34 g carbohydrate, 7 g fat, 0 mg cholesterol, 2.1 g fiber, 71 mg sodium.

Brasileiras
(Brazilian Coconut Cookies)
Makes about 3 dozen

1 cup granulated sugar
½ cup water
4 egg yolks, slightly beaten
¼ cup all-purpose flour
2¼ cups freshly grated or packaged coconut
½ teaspoon vanilla

1. In heavy saucepan, combine sugar and water. Cook over moderate heat, stirring until sugar dissolves.
2. Cook syrup undisturbed until candy thermometer reads 230°F. (A small amount of syrup dropped into ice water should immediately form a hard thread.)
3. In small mixer bowl, combine egg yolks and flour until well blended.
4. Add 2 tablespoons of the hot syrup, stirring constantly.
5. Slowly add this mixture to the syrup remaining in the pan, stirring constantly.
6. Add coconut and simmer over low heat, stirring constantly, until mixture becomes thick. (Do not let it boil.)
7. Remove from heat and quickly stir in vanilla. Let mixture cool to room temperature.
8. Preheat oven to 375°F.
9. Shape cookie dough into small balls.
10. Arrange balls 1 inch apart on lightly greased baking sheets.
11. Bake 15 minutes or until cookies are a delicate golden brown.
12. Remove to wire racks to cool.

Per serving: 50 Cal. (41% from fat), 1 g protein, 7 g carbohydrate, 2 g fat, 30 mg cholesterol, .7 g fiber, 2 mg sodium.

USA Rice Council

Empanadas are served as appetizers in Argentina.

Summary

The Aztecs and the Spanish conquistadores played a role in Mexico's history. They also contributed to Mexico's cuisine. Many Mexicans are farmers. The corn and beans they grow are important to the economy. These foods are important ingredients in Mexican cuisine, too. Mexican cooks also make much use of peppers, fruits, and vegetables in their cooking. They prepare a variety of flavorful sauces and stews and unique desserts and beverages. Many of these dishes have evolved on a regional basis due to Mexico's varied climate and geography.

Spanish, Portuguese, and African influences are blended with foods of native tribes to form South American cuisine. Throughout the continent, corn, potatoes, and manioc are used as staple foods. However, geographic isolation has caused the way these foods are used to vary from region to region.

Review What You Have Read

Write your answers on a separate sheet of paper.
1. How have climate and geography affected Mexican food customs?
2. The Aztecs and the Spaniards made many contributions to Mexican cuisine. Name four contributions of each.
3. What is a tortilla and how is one made? Describe three different Mexican foods made from the tortilla.
4. What are the colors of peppers used in Mexican cooking, and how are they used?
5. True or false. Guacamole is a popular spread made from mashed bananas.
6. Describe one type of mole.
7. In Mexico, the main meal of the day is called _____. What foods are usually served at this meal?
8. A corn pancake similar to a tortilla that is a traditional Venezuelan bread is _____.
9. What has been the staple food of the Peruvian people since the days of the Inca? How did the Inca preserve this food?
10. With which South American country are the following words associated: *Pampas, gaucho, chimichurri,* and *carbonada criolla?*
    A. Argentina.
    B. Brazil.
    C. Chile.
    D. Venezuela.
11. Brazilian culture is a mixture of three different cultures. Name them.
12. True or false. Feijoada completa is a Peruvian national dish made of meat and beans.

Build Your Basic Skills

1. Research the history of the Aztecs and write a two-page report summarizing your findings.
2. Borrow several travel films from your local library to learn more about South America. Then discuss how the countries of South America are similar to and different from the United States.

Build Your Thinking Skills

1. Plan and prepare a Mexican meal. Set the mood with appropriate decorations.
2. Plan and prepare a buffet with foods representing each of the South American countries you have studied.

Chapter 28

Europe

A "Taste" of the World of Work

Tea Taster
Tastes samples of tea to determine palatability of product or to prepare blending formulas.

Sommelier
Selects, requisitions, stores, sells, and serves wines in a restaurant.

Tour Guide
Arranges transportation and other accommodations for groups of tourists, following planned itinerary, and escorts groups during entire trip, within single area or at specified stopping points of tour.

Terms to Know

fish and chips	escargot
pudding basin	quiche
tea	braten
clan	kartoffelpuffer
haggis	sauerkraut
colcannon	spätzle
cockles	strudel
haute cuisine	smørrebrød
provincial cuisine	lutefisk
nouvelle cuisine	smörgåsbord
fines herbes	husmankost
hors d'oeuvres	lingonberry
croissant	crayfish
crêpe	sauna
truffles	

Objectives

After studying this chapter, you will be able to
- ❏ describe the food customs of the British Isles, France, Germany, and the Scandinavian countries.
- ❏ explain how and why these customs have evolved.
- ❏ recognize and prepare foods native to each of these countries.

Courtesy of the Danish Tourist Board

481

Europe is the second smallest continent in terms of land area. It stretches from the Atlantic Ocean to the Ural Mountains. It reaches from the Scandinavian peninsula to the tips of Italy and Greece. Despite its small size, it is one of the most heavily populated continents. Nearly one-fifth of the world's people live in Europe.

Europe has been a cultural, political, and economic leader for centuries. Its history is rich and varied.

Europeans have made many contributions to Western culture. Galileo, Bach, Luther, Rembrandt, Gutenberg, Moliere, the Curies, Einstein, and Churchill are all eminent Europeans. Their achievements have enriched the world.

Because so many countries are part of Europe, you will read about them in two groups. This chapter will discuss the British Isles, France, Germany, and Scandinavia. The following chapter will discuss Spain, Italy, and Greece.

Healthy Living

When flying to Europe, or anywhere else, be sure to drink plenty of beverages on the plane. The air on airplanes is dry. An adequate fluid intake will help you prevent dehydration.

Courtesy of the Danish Tourist Board

Quaint homes and grassy meadows dot much of the European countryside.

British Isles

George A. Fischer

Visitors to England today can still see Stonehenge, which was built by prehistoric people.

The British Isles are a group of two large islands and several small islands. They are located northwest of mainland Europe by the English Channel. The largest island includes England, Scotland, and Wales. The second largest island includes Northern Ireland (part of the British Commonwealth) and Ireland or Eire (independent).

The people of the British Isles share a common ancestry and culture. This culture has ancient Celtic, Germanic, and Norman roots. Due to geographic isolation, however, many customs have formed on a regional basis. As a result, each country of the British Isles has separate proud traditions.

Climate and Geography of the British Isles

Water surrounds the British Isles. The Atlantic Ocean, the North Sea, and the Irish Sea form the major coastlines. The English Channel separates England from France.

Fertile farmlands, windswept plains, thick forests, and rugged mountains make up the varied terrain. The Pennine Chain is a mountain range that runs northward through the center of England into Scotland. It divides the wide open flatlands of the Northeast from the flatlands of the Northwest.

Just beyond these flatlands lie the beautiful, mountainous lands of Cornwall, Wales, and Scotland.

The weather changes in Britain from hour to hour and from village to village. England, Scotland, Ireland, and Wales do not have the severe cold of northern Scandinavia. However, fog along the coasts is common, and the air often is raw and bone-chilling.

British Culture

The Germanic invaders (Angles, Saxons, and Jutes) came from northern Europe in the fifth century. They settled in southeastern England where food was readily available.

The early Anglo-Saxons hunted, fished, and gathered nuts and berries for food. They eventually made small gardens and grew grain along the edges of the forests.

The Anglo-Saxons introduced brewing, baking, and butter- and cheese-making techniques they had brought from their homelands. They used barley to make ale, and ground grain for use in baking bread. They made the milk of sheep and cattle into cheese and butter. The Anglo-Saxons also grew apple trees for cider and kept bees for honey. They either roasted the meat from freshly caught game or cooked it in large iron pots.

At the end of World War II, the inhabitants of the southern part of the island voted for independence. The people living in the northern part of Ireland chose to remain part of Great Britain. Thus, two countries were formed.

The people of Northern Ireland are predominantly Protestant. However, groups of Catholics also live there. Conflict between Catholics and Protestants in Northern Ireland periodically erupts in outbreaks of bitter fighting.

Beyond the political strife, Ireland is a picturesque land of bright green fields, whitewashed cottages, country lanes, and horse-drawn carts. The Irish enjoy festivity, which includes a great deal of singing and dancing. St. Patrick's Day is a national celebration. Celebrations would not be complete without the shamrock and the mythical leprechaun, who enjoys playing tricks and having fun. See 28-3.

Because water surrounds Ireland, fishing is an important industry. The Irish export shellfish in large numbers to hotels and restaurants of mainland Europe.

Beef cattle also are important commodities. Ireland has always been known for its excellent cattle, and Irish pedigree bulls are traded all over the world.

Irish whiskey is equally famous. It is the basis of such popular drinks as Irish coffee. (*Irish coffee* is strong coffee flavored with Irish whiskey and sugar and topped with whipped cream.)

Irish Cuisine

The Irish people have held tightly to their heritage. As a result, Ireland has retained much of the flavor and character of earlier centuries. Strictly local dishes are still prepared with recipes that have been handed down from generation to generation.

Irish Vegetables

Of all foods, potatoes have been the mainstay of the Irish diet for centuries. Since their introduction in the seventeenth century, potatoes have been Ireland's largest resource. Their importance can best be seen in the results of the 1847 potato crop failure. Thousands of Irish people died, and over a million fled to the United States to escape the "black famine."

The Irish eat potatoes every day as a vegetable. They also use potatoes in soups, stews, breads, rolls, and cakes. New potatoes, dug from an Irish garden, are so fresh the skins can be peeled with the fingers. The Irish cook them in a small amount of salted water and serve them with butter. Other

George A. Fischer

28-3 Blarney Castle, situated in the lush green countryside near Cork, houses the source of another Irish myth—the Blarney stone. According to legend, those who kiss the stone will become skilled in flattery.

potato dishes are popular too. Crisp, fried cakes made from grated raw potatoes, flour, salt, and milk are called *boxty.* Potatoes mashed with finely chopped scallions and milk and served with melted butter are called *champ.* Mashed potatoes mixed with chopped scallions, shredded cooked cabbage, and melted butter are called **colcannon.**

A variety of other vegetables are also grown in small gardens across Ireland. Cabbage, onions, carrots, cauliflower, parsnips, turnips, and peas are plentiful. The Irish may cook them in water, cream them, or bake them. Mushrooms gathered from the fields are sautéed in butter or added to soups and stews. Garlic and parsley add both color and flavor to meats, poultry, soups, and stews.

Irish Main Dishes

The excellent beef cattle produced in Ireland account for the popularity of *corned beef and cabbage.* This Irish dish is economical because it is made with the beef brisket. The Irish also use beef for roasting, braising, and adding to stews. The Irish steak and kidney stew is similar to the steak and kidney pie served in England.

Sheep thrive in the mountainous areas of Ireland where the land is too poor for farming. The Irish serve the first lamb of the year on Easter Sunday to mark the beginning of spring. They usually roast the leg of lamb. However, they use less tender parts of the animal to make Irish stew. (*Irish stew* is pieces of lamb and potatoes in a hearty gravy.)

The Irish eat pork both fresh and cured, but Ireland is best known for its boiled hams. Traditionally, the Irish covered a whole boiled ham with sugar and bread crumbs and studded it with cloves.

The Irish who live close to the sea carry home buckets of seafood from the fishing boats on the wharf. The seafood they carry includes crabs, mussels, prawns, and scallops. Most kinds of seafood are inexpensive because they are readily available.

Irish Baked Goods

Many people consider Irish breads to be some of the best in the world. Some Irish farm families still bake *soda bread* and *brown bread* every day.

Baking is most important at tea. The Irish sometimes serve eggs, cold meats, and salads at tea. However, they always serve a variety of breads and cakes. They spread soda bread, brown bread, oatcakes, and scones thickly with butter. *Barmbrack,* a light fruitcake served with butter, is one of the most popular Irish cakes. On Hallow's Eve (October 31), the family baker adds a wedding ring wrapped in paper to the batter before baking. Legend says that the person who receives the slice of cake with the ring will marry before the year ends. Irish whiskey cake and sponge cake are other popular desserts served for tea.

Irish Meals

In Ireland, as in other parts of the British Isles, the day begins with a hearty breakfast. Breakfast commonly includes porridge, eggs, bread, butter, and tea. The Irish serve dinner in the middle of the day. It is the main meal for many people, especially those who live in rural areas. See 28-4. They serve tea at about six o'clock in the evening.

Wales

Wales is a small country that borders the southwestern corner of England. Wales can be divided into two parts—North Wales and South Wales. There is a certain amount of rivalry between the two.

North Wales is mountainous country with valleys and coastal plains. Remains of the early Roman occupation are still apparent. The Welsh tell stories of a pink-colored pearl found in the Conway River. They believe the pearl was the reason Julius Caesar invaded Wales.

South Wales is known for its coal. Several generations of some Welsh families have worked in the coal mines.

Monks established monasteries in Wales centuries ago. The remains of ancient monasteries, castles, and fortifications, some in ruins and some maintained, can be seen throughout South Wales.

Cockles, a type of mussel, have flourished along the Welsh coast for hundreds of years. People still go to the shallow waters of the shore and dig cockles out of the sand. They take the cockles to market in nearby towns.

Welsh ponies are a cross between a Palomino and a Welsh cob. They are popular in many parts of the world. Because they are so small, children usually ride them.

Wales has been united politically with England for over 400 years. Therefore, the Welsh systems of law, government, and land tenure are the same as those of England. Welsh leaders sit in the House of Commons and the Secretary of State for Wales represents them.

Welsh Cuisine

Welsh food is similar to the foods of England, Scotland, and Ireland in its simplicity. The Welsh use homegrown foods to prepare dishes that are substantial yet plain and economical.

The rugged hills found in much of Wales are suitable for sheep production. The finest spring lambs in the British Isles graze on the grasses in the Brecon Beacons of Wales.

Lamb and mutton are prominent in the Welsh diet. The Welsh also eat beef, pork, veal, and seafood. *Cawl* is a hearty soup made from mutton, leeks, and other vegetables. The Welsh often serve ham boiled, as the Irish do. The Welsh eat cockles with a dash of vinegar.

The Welsh grow potatoes, carrots, and other vegetables in local gardens and add them to soups and stews. *Tatws slaw* (potatoes mashed with buttermilk) frequently accompanies ham.

The Welsh serve tea in late afternoon or early evening. Various baked goods accompany cups of steaming tea. *Crempog* (buttermilk cakes) and *bara ceirch* (oatcakes spread with butter and eaten with buttermilk) are especially popular. Sponge cake and *bara brith* (a bread filled with currants) are enjoyed, as well.

Familiar to most Americans is Welsh rabbit (or rarebit). *Welsh rabbit* is toast covered with a rich cheese sauce. According to legend, long ago the Welsh peasants were not allowed to hunt on the estates of the nobility. Instead of rabbit, they served a cheese dish and called it "Welsh rabbit."

National Live Stock and Meat Board

28-4 Corned beef, cabbage, and soda bread are traditional Irish dishes that might be served at the main meal of the day.

British Menu

Welsh Rabbit
Corned Beef and Cabbage
Parsley-Buttered Potatoes and Carrots
Scones and Marmalade
English Trifle
Tea

Welsh Rabbit
Serves 6

2   tablespoons margarine
2   tablespoons all-purpose flour
1/8   teaspoon pepper
1/4   teaspoon dry mustard
1/2   teaspoon Worcestershire sauce
3/4   cup skim milk
1   cup shredded Cheddar cheese
6   slices toast, cut into quarters

1. Melt margarine over low heat.
2. Blend in flour and seasonings, stirring until mixture is smooth.
3. Add milk slowly, stirring constantly.
4. Cook sauce until it is smooth and thick.
5. Remove sauce from heat and add cheese, stirring constantly until the cheese is melted.
6. Serve over toast points. Garnish with hard-cooked egg wedges, parsley, or paprika.

Per serving: 195 Cal. (51% from fat), 8 g protein, 16 g carbohydrate, 11 g fat, 20 mg cholesterol, .6 g fiber, 337 mg sodium.

Corned Beef and Cabbage
Serves 6 to 8

3 to 4   pounds corned beef
     cold water
1   sprig thyme
1   onion studded with 6 cloves
     pepper
1   bay leaf
1   whole carrot
2   pounds cabbage, cut into wedges

1. Place beef and all other ingredients except cabbage in a large pot. Cover with cold water. Slowly bring to a boil. Do not cover. Simmer for 3 hours, skimming when necessary.
2. Remove spices and add cabbage. Simmer for another 10 to 15 minutes or until the cabbage is crisp-tender.

3. Remove corned beef to heated serving platter surround with cabbage wedges.

Per serving: 333 Cal. (46% from fat), 38 g protein, 6 g carbohydrate, 17 g fat, 133 mg cholesterol, 2.1 g fiber, 1350 mg sodium.

Parsley Buttered Potatoes
Serves 6 to 8

2 1/2   pounds small new potatoes*
2   tablespoons margarine
     fresh parsley, coarsely chopped

1. Carefully scrub potatoes. Remove one strip of peel around the center of each potato.
2. Place potatoes in a large pan filled with cold water. Bring to a boil. Gently simmer 35 to 40 minutes or until potatoes are tender.
3. Drain potatoes well. Add margarine and parsley; stir gently until potatoes are coated. Serve immediately.

*Red potatoes may be substituted for the new potatoes.

Per serving: 134 Cal. (25% from fat), 3 g protein, 23 g carbohydrate, 4 g fat, 0 mg cholesterol, 1.2 g fiber, 49 mg sodium.

Carrots
Serves 6 to 8

2   pounds carrots
1 1/2   tablespoons margarine
     salt and pepper

1. Wash carrots and remove peel with a vegetable peeler. If the carrots are small, leave them whole. Otherwise, slice or dice.
2. Bring a small amount of salted water to a boil in saucepan; add carrots.
3. Bring water again to a boil and let carrots gently simmer until crisp-tender, about 10 to 15 minutes.

4. Drain carrots well and toss with margarine. Season with salt and pepper to taste. Serve immediately.

Per serving: 75 Cal. (33% from fat), 2 g protein, 12 g carbohydrate, 3 g fat, 0 mg cholesterol, 3.9 g fiber, 75 mg sodium.

Scones
Makes 8 scones

3 tablespoons margarine
1 egg
1 cup skim milk
2½ cups all-purpose flour
2½ teaspoons baking powder
½ teaspoon salt
1 tablespoon sugar

1. Preheat oven to 400°F.
2. Grease a baking sheet and set aside.
3. In a large bowl, combine the dry ingredients.
4. Cut in margarine until mixture resembles coarse cornmeal.
5. Beat the egg until frothy, reserving 1 tablespoon.
6. Add the milk to the beaten egg and pour into the flour mixture.
7. Stir dough lightly with a fork until it forms a soft ball.
8. On a floured board, roll the dough into a square ½ inch thick. With a sharp knife, cut the square into quarters. Then cut each quarter diagonally into a triangle.
9. Place the triangles about 1 inch apart on the baking sheet; brush the tops with reserved beaten egg.
10. Bake scones for 15 minutes or until light brown. Serve at once.

Per scone: 207 Cal. (23% from fat), 6 g protein, 33 g carbohydrate, 6 g fat, 35 mg cholesterol, 1.0 g fiber, 306 mg sodium.

English Trifle
Serves 12

1 pound cake (homemade or packaged)
4 tablespoons raspberry jam
1 cup blanched almonds, halved
2 cups fresh raspberries or 2 packages frozen raspberries, 10 ounces each
2 cups custard sauce (See Chapter 16)
2 cups heavy cream
2 tablespoons confectioners' sugar

1. Cut the pound cake into slices, ½ inch thick.
2. Coat about half of the slices with jam and place them, jam side up, along the bottom and sides of a glass bowl.
3. Cut the remaining slices into cubes and scatter the cubes over the jam covered slices.
4. Sprinkle ½ cup of the almonds over the cake.
5. Drain juice from frozen berries. Reserve 12 of the best raspberries. Sprinkle the remaining berries over the cake.
6. Using a rubber spatula, gently spread the custard sauce over the fruit.
7. In a small, chilled bowl, whip cream until slightly thick.
8. Add sugar gradually, beating until cream forms soft peaks.
9. Spread half of the whipped cream over the custard sauce.
10. Using a pastry bag, pipe the remaining cream decoratively around the edge of the trifle. Garnish with reserved berries and almonds.

Per serving: 436 Cal. (59% from fat), 8 g protein, 38 g carbohydrate, 30 g fat, 147 mg cholesterol, 3.4 g fiber, 179 mg sodium.

National Live Stock and Meat Board

Roast beef is typical of the British, who perfected the art of roasting.

France

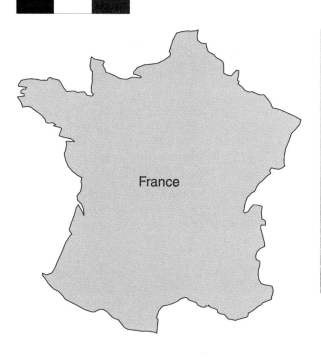

French Government Tourism Office

Vineyards throughout France produce grapes used to make world-famous wines.

France is the largest country in Western Europe. France also is the oldest unified nation in Europe. It has been an important world power for centuries. The French have had an impact on the development of the entire Western civilization. They have made many contributions in art, science, government, and philosophy.

Climate and Geography of France

The Atlantic Ocean, the Mediterranean Sea, and the English Channel border France. Belgium, Luxembourg, Germany, Switzerland, Italy, and Spain also border France. All of these nations have influenced the development of French culture.

The French Alps, the Juras, and the Pyrenees form the mountainous areas of eastern and southwestern France. The northern and western parts of the country are rolling plains. Both highlands and lowlands are found in the central provinces.

Busy ports dot the Atlantic Ocean and Mediterranean Sea. The Seine, Loire, Garonne, and Rhône-Saône Rivers are the basis of an excellent waterways system throughout France.

The climate of France is moderate. In the higher elevations, snow falls during the winter. However, most of the country has cool, rainy weather instead of snow. Throughout much of France, spring is humid, summer is moderate, and autumn is long and sunny. These climatic conditions are especially favorable for the production of the grapes used to make famous French wines.

French Culture

The French are a mixture of many different peoples. The original inhabitants of France were the Ligurians, the Iberians, and the Celts. The Ligurians lived in the Alpine region. The Iberians lived in the Pyrenees and the Aquitaine Basin. The Celts inhabited much of the remaining area. The Romans called these peoples *Gauls* when they invaded and conquered the land between 58 and 51 B.C.

When the Roman Empire fell, Germanic tribes conquered the territory. Later, other groups of people filtered into France. The Moors came from Spain, and the Vikings came from Scandinavia. Italians and Germans also made their way to France. Each group settled in a different part of the country.

During the feudal period, France was divided into small areas called *domains*. A member of the nobility ruled each domain and peasants worked it. Once France was unified, these areas became *provinces.* The people of many of the new provinces did not think of themselves as French citizens. Instead, they still considered themselves Bretons or Gascons or Burgundians. Today, regional ties continue to be strong in many parts of France, especially in rural areas.

France is now a republic headed by a president. Paris, France's largest city and marketing and distribution center, is the seat of government. The official language is French. The greatest percentage of the population is Roman Catholic.

Manufacturing has become the leading industry in France. It is highly diversified. The French produce appliances, automobiles, railway equipment, textiles, and perfumes. Chemical and steel production and coal mining are other major industries. France is also well known for its fashion industry.

Fishing and agricultural industries are important to France. Fishers catch large amounts of cod, crab, herring, lobster, mackerel, oysters, sardines, shrimp, and tuna along the French coastlines. Grapes grow throughout much of the southern part of the country. They are used in wine production. Cattle provide meat and dairy products. Wheat, corn, oats, and barley are important grain crops. Sugar beets, fruits, vegetables, flax, flowers, and other livestock also are important agricultural commodities.

French Cuisine

In France, good food and wine are an important part of daily life. French children learn at an early age to appreciate food. They look forward to mealtime as a time to enjoy both food and conversation.

In many parts of France, cooks buy food fresh each day, and they take great care in selecting it. The French usually shop in small specialty shops rather than in large supermarkets.

French cooking can be divided into two main classes: haute cuisine and provincial cuisine. A newcomer to French cooking is the style called *nouvelle cuisine.*

Haute cuisine is characterized by elaborate preparations, fancy garnishes, and rich sauces. Chefs make lavish use of eggs, cream, and butter in this style of French cooking.

Haute cuisine was perfected by a few distinguished chefs originally employed by French nobility. Two chefs, Antoine Carême and George August Escoffier, had tremendous influence on the development of haute cuisine. Today, haute cuisine is seen most often in leading restaurants and hotels.

Provincial cuisine is the style of cooking practiced by most French families. Provincial cooks make fewer fancy sauces and lavish creations. Instead, the flavors of locally grown foods are enhanced by simple cooking methods. Many provincial dishes were once regional specialties. See 28-5.

Nouvelle cuisine emphasizes lightness and natural taste in foods. It is a product of recent years. Flavor, color, texture, and presentation are as important in nouvelle cuisine as they are in haute cuisine. However, nouvelle cooks believe the richness and heaviness of haute cuisine spoil the natural flavors of food. The idea behind nouvelle cuisine is to preserve the nutrients and natural taste of foods. Nouvelle cuisine appeals to people who love French food but are concerned about fat and calories.

Nouvelle cooks serve less butter, cream, and other high calorie (kilojoule) foods. They use fewer starches and sauces. When they do serve a sauce, they do not thicken it with flour. Instead, nouvelle cooks use vegetable purees to thicken sauces. Nouvelle cuisine includes more fresh fruits and vegetables. (The vegetables are served nearly raw.) Meat, fish, and poultry are often broiled or poached.

Foundations of French Cooking

Two basic points form the secret of good French cooking. First, the ingredients used must be of top quality. Bread, for example, is baked twice a day in French bakeries to ensure its freshness. Second, successful cooks are very patient. Patience can make the difference between a dish that is good and one that is excellent. Cooks may simmer some sauces for hours to develop the flavors of all their ingredients.

French Sauces

The French use a variety of sauces. A sauce can be used as the basis for a dish or as a finishing touch.

A *roux* is a mixture of butter (or other fat) and flour. It forms the base of all white sauces. When you add milk to a roux, the mixture becomes a *béchamel* sauce. If you add chicken, veal, or fish stock to a roux, the mixture becomes a *velouté* sauce. You can make many variations of these sauces by adding extra ingredients like mustard or cheese.

The classic French brown sauce is called a *demi-glace* sauce. Cooks make it from a slightly thickened stock-based sauce that they have simmered for a long time. They add additional stock and flavorings to this basic sauce. They may or may not use a thickening agent, such as a roux.

National Live Stock and Meat Board

28-5 This country French beef stew is typical of provincial cuisine.

Hollandaise sauce contains egg yolks, lemon juice, and butter. The cook must warm and gently thicken the beaten egg yolks to prevent curdling. Then the butter must be added slowly to keep the sauce from separating. Hollandaise sauce often accompanies green vegetables such as asparagus.

Oil and vinegar sauces are called *vinaigrettes.* They are made by combining wine vinegar, oil, and seasonings. Many variations are possible. Vinaigrettes are commonly used as dressings on green salads and as marinades for vegetables.

Butter sauces include *cold flavored butters, white butter sauce,* and *brown butter sauce.* Cooks use them when baking and broiling seafood, when preparing vegetables and poultry, and when making sauces.

French Seasonings

Herbs are just as important to French cooking as sauces. Marjoram, rosemary, basil, chervil, parsley, saffron, chives, tarragon, oregano, fennel, bay leaves, thyme, and savory are used most often. **Fines herbes** is a mixture of fresh chives, parsley, tarragon, and chervil. Many French chefs use this combination of herbs to flavor soups and stews.

Cooks add herbs directly to some dishes. For other dishes, such as stews, they tie herbs in a cheesecloth bag and add it to the liquid. (They remove the bag before serving.)

French Appetizers and Soups

A French meal would not be complete without hors d'oeuvres. **Hors d'oeuvres** are small dishes designed to stimulate the appetite. They may be hot or cold, but chefs always plan for them to complement the other menu items.

Soup often follows hors d'oeuvres. French soups fall into four basic categories: consommés, puree soups, cream soups, and velouté soups. *Consommés* have a meat stock base. They are rich and clear and may be served hot or cold. *Puree soups* are made from meat, poultry, fish, or vegetables that have been cooked in liquid and pureed. *Cream soups* generally use a béchamel sauce as a base. Pureed meat, fish, poultry, or vegetables are added to the béchamel sauce along with cream. *Velouté soups* are similar to cream soups. Meat, fish, poultry, or vegetables are added to a velouté sauce. Egg yolks, butter, and cream thicken the soup.

French Main Dishes

Seafood and poultry form the basis of many French main dishes. As a rule, the French eat meat less often than people in the United States.

Many types of freshwater and saltwater fish are popular in France. Escargots (snails), frog legs, crabs, scallops, and mussels are especially popular. Poaching is the preparation technique used most often for fish fillets and whole fish.

The French eat all types of poultry. They often truss and roast chicken, duck, and goose whole with or without a stuffing. They also fricassee chicken and add it to stews. They make game birds, such as pigeons, into *pâté* or gently simmer them until tender.

The French usually broil beef steaks and serve them with a sauce. They often braise other beef and veal cuts, and use some of them in stews. Lamb is particularly popular in the spring. The French consider organ meats of all kinds to be delicacies. See 28-6.

French Vegetables and Salads

Vegetables are an important part of a French meal. The French often serve two or more fresh vegetables with a main dish. They cook vegetables just to the crisp-tender stage and then serve them immediately to preserve their texture.

The French often serve vegetables with just butter and seasonings. Vegetables can also be creamed, braised, glazed, or served with a cheese or hollandaise sauce. Some vegetables, such as spinach, adapt particularly well to soufflés.

The French usually serve a green salad after the main course but before dessert. They often dress it with a vinaigrette sauce. Other salads, such as potato salads and meat salads, are popular additions to lighter and more casual meals. One of the best-known salads of this type is *salade nicoise.* This popular salad is a colorful combination of potatoes, green beans, and tomatoes, served with a vinaigrette sauce.

France is famous for its cheeses, and cheese is an important part of meals. The French serve cheese and fresh fruit after the green salad and before the sweet dessert in a large meal. Many simpler meals include only cheese, sausage, bread, fresh fruit, and wine.

French Baked Goods

The French serve bread at every meal. *Baguette* is the most popular. It contains only yeast, flour, salt, and water. People buy the long, crusty loaves daily from local bakers. Other breads are popular, too. *Brioche* is a rich yeast roll that contains egg. **Croissants** are flaky, buttery yeast rolls shaped into crescents.

The dessert course may be simple or elaborate. Some of the most elegant desserts in the world originated in France. *Napoleons* are layers of puff pastry separated by creamy fillings. *Éclairs* are

28-6 The French roast lamb with herbs to give it a delicately-seasoned flavor.

slender pastry shells filled with custard or a cream filling and iced. *Baba au rhum* is a yeast cake soaked in a rum syrup. Chocolate, vanilla, liqueur, or fruit based soufflés are popular. Crêpes filled with fruit, custard, or other sweet filling and fruit tarts are also favorite desserts.

Regional Nature of French Cuisine

French cuisine is regional in nature. A visitor can travel throughout the country and never eat the same dish prepared in the same way twice. A traveler can even identify certain regions by their local dishes.

Normandy is located in the northwestern corner of France. Cattle graze in the fertile green pastures, and apple orchards dot the countryside. Normandy is known for tender veal, rich cream and butter, and apples. *Calvados,* a liquor made from apple cider, is produced locally for export around the world.

Brittany, Normandy's neighbor to the southwest, is relatively poor. Much of the land is rocky and wooded. Because agriculture is difficult, much of the local food comes from the sea. People in Brittany eat most seafood fresh. They use simple preparation methods, such as poaching. In early spring, vegetables are harvested from small gardens throughout Brittany. The asparagus, artichokes, and cauliflower are reported to be the best in France. Brittany is also known for its **crêpes** (thin, delicate pancakes usually rolled around a filling).

To the southwest, in the *Aquitaine* region, the finest pâté is produced. It is made from expensive goose liver and truffles. **Truffles** are a rare type of fungi that grow underground near oak trees. Each November, people use pigs to sniff the ground and find the rare fungi for harvesting. They are very expensive and appear in many French recipes. This region is also known for its poultry, veal, and pork.

Languedoc, also located in southern France, is the cradle of French civilization. Here, the first distinctive French music and literature were created. *Cassoulet* is a traditional stew of the region. It is made with white beans, goose or chicken, pork, bacon, and herbs.

Provence is a rich agricultural region in southeastern France. Fresh vegetables are used in many colorful dishes. One of the most popular vegetable dishes is *ratatouille.* It is a vegetable casserole containing tomatoes, eggplant, green pepper, zucchini, onions, and seasonings. The olive trees that grow on the sunny slopes along the Mediterranean Sea provide the oil needed to make aioli. (*Aioli* is a regional sauce made from olive oil and garlic.) *Bouillabaisse* (a seafood stew), leg of lamb, grilled fish, and chicken are equally popular. Many of the dishes of Provence are flavored with locally grown herbs.

Burgundy, located in central France, is famous for its vineyards and the wines they produce. Many Burgundy dishes are flavored with the local wines. *Boeuf à la Bourguignonne* (beef Burgundy) is one of the most famous of these dishes. **Escargots** (snails eaten as food) are another Burgundy specialty. They often are served in their shells with garlic butter.

For centuries, the people of the *Rhône-Alpes* region have based their diet on local foods. Potatoes grow in the hilly land. The cows that graze on mountain grasses provide milk and cheese. Many Alpine dishes combine these three staple foods.

Lyon is a major industrial city located in the east central part of the Rhône-Alpes region. Some people refer to Lyon as the "gastronomical center of France." Here, the best of everything is available—fruits, vegetables, meats, and poultry. Lyon has many restaurants featuring the specialties of the greatest French chefs. *Méres* are a group of French women who own small restaurants where they do all the cooking themselves. They are also part of Lyon's culinary heritage.

The Germans have influenced the foods of the *Alsace* and *Lorraine* regions. (These regions of France border Germany. They have gone back and forth between Germany and France several times throughout history.) Sausages and smoked hams are popular throughout these regions, as are fruit pies and tarts. Fine white wines are produced in Alsace. **Quiche,** a custard tart served in many variations as an appetizer and a main dish, originated in Lorraine. The most famous type of quiche is called *Quiche Lorraine.* It contains grated Swiss cheese, crumbled bacon, and diced onions along with eggs and cream. See 28-7.

French Meals

Most French people eat three meals a day. *Le petit dejeuner* (breakfast) usually is light. The French often have *café au lait* (hot milk and coffee) and brioche or crusty bread with butter and jam.

Traditionally, *le dejeuner* (the midday meal) was the main meal of the day. People ate it leisurely. In many parts of France this is still the case.

People in the major cities, however, often eat the heavier meal in the evening. A traditional midday meal might include hot or cold hors d'oeuvres, soup, and a main dish. A vegetable, a green salad, bread and butter, dessert, and wine would also be served. If the main dish contains vegetables, a separate vegetable usually would be eliminated.

In France, bread usually remains on the table through the end of the meal. The salad usually is served after the main course, and coffee usually accompanies dessert.

The traditional evening meal is light. Soup, an omelet, bread and butter, fruit, and a beverage are typical supper dishes. City dwellers, however, may eat a more substantial evening meal. Business hours are later in France than they are in the United States. Therefore, the evening meal usually is not served before eight o'clock.

Wilton Industries

28-7 This quiche is made with fresh vegetables and herbs.

> # French Menu
> Soupe à l'Oignon
> (Onion Soup)
> Poulet au Citron
> (Chicken with Lemon)
> Ratatouille
> (Vegetable Casserole)
> Salade Verte
> (Green Salad)
> Pain
> (French Bread)
> Mousse au Chocolat
> (Chocolate Mousse)
> Café
> (Coffee)

Soupe à l'Oignon
(Onion Soup)
Serves 6

5 to 6 medium onions
2 tablespoons margarine
2 tablespoons all-purpose flour
   salt and pepper to taste
6 cups low-sodium beef broth
6 thick slices French bread
⅓ cup grated Parmesan cheese
½ pound Swiss cheese, grated

1. Clean onions, cut into thin slices.
2. In a large, heavy skillet, melt margarine.
3. Add onions and saute' until golden brown and transparent (about 10 minutes).
4. Add flour, stirring constantly to form a smooth paste. Cook for a minute or two.
5. Add salt and pepper and slowly stir in beef broth. Bring soup to a boil, reduce heat and simmer for 30 minutes.
6. Toast bread slices in the oven.
7. Place one piece of bread in each of six ovenproof soup bowls or use one large tureen; sprinkle with Parmesan cheese.
8. Preheat broiler.
9. Pour soup over bread. Sprinkle Swiss cheese on top.
10. Place soup bowls under broiler and broil until cheese is light brown. Serve soup immediately.

Per serving: 511 Cal. (33% from fat), 25 g protein, 61 g carbohydrate, 19 g fat, 39 mg cholesterol, 6.2 g fiber, 968 mg sodium.

Poulet au Citron
(Chicken with Lemon)
Serves 6

2 tablespoons margarine
1 tablespoon vegetable oil
2 broilers, 2 pounds each, cut-up, skin removed
¾ teaspoon salt
   pepper to taste
2 tablespoons finely chopped parsley
1 tablespoon minced chives
1 teaspoon marjoram
2 teaspoons paprika
   grated rind and juice of two lemons
1 cup chicken broth
2 tablespoons cornstarch
3 tablespoons cold water

1. Preheat oven to 350°F.
2. Heat margarine and oil together in large skillet.
3. Brown chicken pieces.
4. Place chicken in a large casserole or baking pan. Season with salt and pepper, parsley, chives, marjoram, and paprika, and sprinkle with lemon juice and rind.
5. Cover pan tightly, and bake chicken until tender, about 45 minutes.
6. Remove chicken to a heated platter.
7. Pour juices into a small saucepan. Add chicken broth and bring to a boil.
8. Quickly whisk in cornstarch dissolved in cold water.
9. Simmer sauce until thickened, about 2 minutes. Serve with chicken.

Per serving: 293 Cal. (37% from fat), 41 g protein, 4 g carbohydrate, 11 g fat, 134 mg cholesterol, 0 g fiber, 470 mg sodium.

Ratatouille
(Vegetable Casserole)
Serves 6 to 8

1 medium eggplant
1 tablespoon salt
2 tablespoons vegetable oil
1½ large onions, cut into rings
2 cloves garlic, crushed
2 green peppers, cut into strips
3 medium zucchini, cut into bite-sized pieces
2 medium tomatoes, cut in wedges
1 bay leaf
½ teaspoon thyme
¼ teaspoon salt
　 pepper to taste

1. Cut eggplant first into thick slices and then into bite-sized pieces. Sprinkle with salt and let eggplant stand 30 minutes. Rinse and pat dry with paper towels.
2. In a large skillet, heat oil. Sauté onions and garlic until golden.
3. Add green pepper strips and cook for 2 minutes.
4. Add eggplant and cook for 3 minutes, stirring constantly.
5. Add zucchini and continue stirring and cooking another 3 minutes.
6. Add tomatoes and seasonings. Simmer uncovered for 40 minutes or until vegetables are tender.
7. Remove bay leaf. Ratatouille can be served immediately or refrigerated and reheated later.

Per serving: 98 Cal. (46% from fat), 2 g protein, 12 g carbohydrate, 5 g fat, 0 mg cholesterol, 3.3 g fiber, 273 mg sodium.

Salade Verte
(Green Salad)
Makes ½ cup dressing

Tear a variety of salad greens into bite-sized pieces. Toss greens together in a salad bowl with oil and vinegar dressing.

Oil and vinegar dressing:
1 tablespoon lemon juice
1 tablespoon white wine vinegar
　 salt
　 pepper
6 tablespoons olive or vegetable oil

1. In small bowl, whisk together lemon juice, wine vinegar, and salt and pepper to taste.

2. Add oil, a few drops at a time while beating. Continue to beat dressing with whisk until all of the oil has been absorbed.
3. Shake dressing well before using.

Per serving: 129 Cal. (96% from fat), 0 g protein, 1 g carbohydrate, 14 g fat, 0 mg cholesterol, 0.4 g fiber, 2 mg sodium.

Pain
(French Bread)
Makes 2 loaves

2¼ cups water
6½ cups all-purpose flour
2 packages active dry yeast
2 teaspoons salt
　 cornmeal
　 vegetable oil
　 cold water

1. In small saucepan, heat water to 120°F.
2. In large mixer bowl, combine 3 cups flour, yeast, and salt.
3. Add warm liquid and mix by hand or on medium speed of electric mixer for 3 minutes. Gradually add enough remaining flour to form a stiff dough.
4. Turn dough out onto lightly floured board or pastry cloth; knead until smooth and satiny, about 8 to 10 minutes.
5. Place dough in a greased bowl, turning once to grease top. Cover and let rise in a warm place 30 minutes.
6. Punch down and divide into 2 equal parts.
7. Roll each half of dough into a 15 x 8-inch rectangle on a lightly floured board.
8. Beginning with long side, roll dough up tightly, sealing edges and ends well.
9. Place loaves seam side down, diagonally, on a lightly greased baking sheet that has been sprinkled with cornmeal. Brush with oil, cover. Refrigerate 2 to 24 hours.
10. When ready to bake, preheat oven to 400°F.
11. Remove bread from refrigerator, uncover and let stand 10 minutes.
12. Brush bread with water. Slash tops of loaves diagonally at 2 inch intervals just before baking.
13. Bake at 400°F, 35 to 40 minutes.

Per slice: 98 Cal. (6% from fat), 3 g protein, 20 g carbohydrate, 1 g fat, 0 mg cholesterol, 0.7 g fiber, 1 34 mg sodium.

Mousse au Chocolat
(Chocolate Mousse)
Serves 6

¼   pound semisweet chocolate, broken into chunks
4   egg yolks
4   tablespoons margarine, softened
4   egg whites
6   strips orange peel

1. Melt chocolate in the top of a double boiler over barely simmering water.
2. In small bowl of electric mixer, beat egg yolks until thick and lemon-colored (about 10 minutes).
3. Add margarine a tablespoon at a time to chocolate, beating until mixture is smooth.
4. Quickly fold a small amount of the chocolate mixture into the beaten egg yolks.
5. Add the egg mixture to the remaining chocolate mixture and cook, beating constantly, until the mixture has thickened and is smooth, about 5 minutes. (Do not let mixture come to a boil.)
6. Remove pan from the heat. Set top portion of double boiler aside, and cool chocolate mixture to room temperature, about 30 minutes.
7. In large mixer bowl with clean beaters, beat egg whites until soft peaks form.
8. Gently fold chocolate mixture into egg whites, folding until no streaks of white are visible.
9. Pour mousse into a pretty bowl or individual serving dishes and refrigerate until set, at least four hours.
10. Garnish mousse with strips of orange peel.

Per serving: 216 Cal. (72% from fat), 5 g protein, 11 g carbohydrate, 18 g fat, 181 mg cholesterol, 0 g fiber, 129 mg sodium.

French Government Tourism Office

Tourists and locals alike enjoy the food served at Parisian cafés.

Germany

George A. Fischer

Grapes used to make some of Germany's fine white wines come from the vineyards along the Rhine River.

Germany is in the heart of Western Europe. Germany's boundaries have changed several times over the years. Many of these changes were the result of wars. At the end of World War II, Germany was divided into East Germany and West Germany. Then, in 1990, Germany was reunited.

German culture and cuisine developed with more unity than German politics. Common heritage and ingredients have led to the origin of dishes that are liked throughout Germany. However, Germany also has many regional dishes.

Climate and Geography of Germany

To the north of Germany are the Baltic and North Seas. The Rhine and the Elbe are the most important rivers in Germany.

Lowlands (flat, sandy plains) make up much of the northern part of the country. Highlands are in the central and southern regions. Two other important geographical regions, the Bavarian Alps and the Black Forest, are in southern Germany. These two regions are popular vacation spots.

Germany's climate is generally moderate. However, the Baltic region has extremes of temperature. Also, the higher elevations in the southern mountains receive large amounts of snow.

German Culture

The first peoples to inhabit Germany were from the Germanic tribes. They swept across Europe between 200 B.C. and A.D. 500. They left few records of their civilization, so historians know little about that era.

After the collapse of the Roman Empire, a series of empires rose and fell. Each one brought new peoples to Germany. Many of these peoples

Protect the Planet

Before leaving for a trip, turn off your hot water heater. Empty your refrigerator and set the control on the least cool setting. Turn air conditioning off in the summer and adjust your thermostat to about 55°F (13°C) in the winter. These steps will save energy and energy costs while you are away.

came from what is now Poland, Denmark, Switzerland, Austria, and France.

Today, many northern Germans are tall, blue-eyed, and fair-haired like their Nordic ancestors. Many southern Germans are shorter, heavier, and darker. They are more like members of the tribes that came from southern Europe.

Music is one of Germany's many contributions to Western civilization. Bach, Beethoven, and Brahms, often called the three Bs of classical music, were German. Other well-known German composers include Wagner, Mendelssohn, Handel, and Schumann.

Germany has been a major industrial nation for many years. Large amounts of coal as well as several lesser minerals are mined. Shipbuilding and publishing are important to the German economy. The Germans also make automobiles, optical instruments, cameras, textiles, toys, and porcelain.

The northern lowlands and southern highlands are primarily agricultural. Potatoes and sugar beets are the main crops of the northern lowlands. In addition, farmers grow some rye, oats, wheat, and barley and raise some cattle. The southern highlands are known for their cattle, wheat, and dairy products. Tobacco, grapes, and other fruits grow in the west and southwest regions. Hops grow in Bavaria, the center of the German brewing industry.

Until the last half of the nineteenth century, Germany was a loose mixture of states, kingdoms, duchies, and principalities. Following the unification of these territories, Germany became involved in the two World Wars. Both wars left much of the country devastated. World War II resulted in the split of the country. West Germany had a democratic government. East Germany had a communistic government.

For years, the people of both German nations longed to live under a common flag. In 1989, they tore down the Berlin Wall—a symbol of the political division between the countries. In the following year, the two nations were reunited under a single democratic government.

German Cuisine

German cuisine is characterized by roasted meats, filling side dishes, and delicious baked goods. World-famous beers and fine white wines are also typical German fare.

German Main Dishes

Meat has been the foundation of German cuisine for centuries. The **braten** (roast) is Germany's national dish. A variety of traditional German dishes contain pork, beef, veal, and game.

Pork, both fresh and cured, is the most popular of all meats. Hams are roasted, marinated in wine, or cut in slices and then fried and served with a sauce. One of the most popular pork dishes is called *kasseler rippenspeer*. It is a whole smoked pork loin that is roasted. It is served with sauerkraut, apples or chestnuts, peas, white beans, mushrooms, and browned potatoes. See 28-8.

Boiled beef served with a horseradish sauce is one of the most popular beef dishes. *Sauerbraten,* a sweet-sour marinated beef roast, is popular, too. The marinating process used to make sauerbraten is similar to the process the ancient Romans used to preserve their meat. The ingredients used in the marinade vary from one region to another. One method uses red wine, wine vinegar, onion, peppercorns, juniper berries, and bay leaves. Sauerbraten gravy may be thickened and flavored with crushed gingersnaps and raisins.

Hasenpfeffer (braised rabbit) is also marinated. The meat is first marinated in wine, vinegar, onions, and spices and then stewed in the marinade. Sour cream is often added to the stew for thickening and flavor.

Many German meat dishes have regional origins. One such dish is schnitzel. *Schnitzel* is a breaded, sautéed veal cutlet. Schnitzel originated in Holstein where it is served with a fried egg. A richly flavored, smoked uncooked ham originated in Westphalia. *Westphalian ham* is served throughout Germany.

The German people use leftovers to make hearty soups and one dish meals. Filling lentil soups and *eintopf,* a popular stew, are both made with leftover meats.

Sausages

A discussion of German meat dishes would not be complete without mentioning sausage. The Germans produce hundreds of types of sausages. Some are ready-to-eat. Others must be grilled, boiled, or fried. Some sausages are soft, and others are hard. Some sausages are smoked, and a few are pickled.

Some sausages bear the names of the cities where they were first produced. *Braunschweiger,* for example, is a type of liver sausage. It was first produced in Braunschweig. The *frankfurt* (hot dog) originated in the German city of Frankfurt. Other well-known German sausages include blutwurst, bratwurst, knockwurst, and schinkenwurst. *Blutwurst* is blood sausage. *Bratwurst* is sausage made of freshly ground seasoned pork that is usually cooked by grilling. *Knockwurst* is smoked,

National Pork Producers Council

28-8 These German-style pork chops are served with spätzle, which are small dumplings.

precooked sausage made of beef and pork. *Schinkenwurst* is a ready-to-eat pork sausage that contains pieces of ham.

German Seafood

Open air fish markets scattered throughout northern Germany sell a variety of seafood obtained from the North and Baltic Seas. Smoked eel, enjoyed by many northern Germans, is inexpensive. Herring is prepared in a variety of ways. One salty, sharp, pickled herring dish bears the name of Otto von Bismarck. Bismarck, called the Iron Chancellor, helped unify the German territories.

German Side Dishes

Germans usually serve fruit accompaniments with pork and game dishes. Apples, prunes, raisins, and apricots accompany pork. Tart fruits like currants and *preiselbeeren* (small, cranberry-like fruits) accompany game.

Another staple in the German diet is potatoes. Germany has produced large amounts of potatoes since the days of Frederick the Great. Faced with huge food shortages, Frederick ordered all of the farmers to plant potatoes. At least one meal a day in Germany still includes potatoes.

Potatoes cooked in salted water, drained, and steamed until dry are known as *salzkartoffeln*. Salzkartoffeln are served most often as a side dish with melted butter, parsley, and bits of bacon. *Kartoffelsalat* is potato salad made with a vinegar dressing and bits of cooked bacon. Kartoffelsalat can be served either hot or cold. *Kartoffelpuffer* are the famous potato pancakes enjoyed throughout Germany. They are served with mixed stewed fruit or applesauce. *Kartoffelklösse* are potato dumplings.

Sauerkraut, another German specialty, is fermented or pickled cabbage. It is prepared by layering freshly shredded cabbage with coarse salt in crocks or large barrels. German cooks usually flavor sauerkraut with caraway, apple, onion, or juniper berries and serve it hot. The Germans eat sauerkraut with a variety of dishes. It is especially popular with pig's knuckles, spareribs, pork chops, and pork roasts.

The Germans may serve vegetables as side dishes or add them to stews. Cabbage and root vegetables are especially popular during winter months. Asparagus and mushrooms are spring delicacies. Cooks use fresh greens to make delicious salads, which they often serve with a vinegar dressing flavored with bacon. See 28-9.

Spätzle (small dumplings made from wheat flour) are another popular side dish. Spätzle can be made in many shapes and forms. Cheese spätzle and liver spätzle are just two of the many kinds of spätzle eaten in Germany.

German Baked Goods

The German people serve bread at nearly every meal. Many breads and rolls are produced all over the country, while others are strictly regional. Some breads are baked in round or oblong rolls. Others are made into fanciful shapes and called *gebildbrote* (picture breads).

Rye, pumpernickel, and other dark breads are favorites. Bakers make *pumpernickel bread* from unsifted rye flour. They allow it to rise and bake for long periods of time. This is so the natural sugars in the rye will sweeten the bread evenly.

Sweet baked goods are also popular in Germany. Sweet rolls, breads, and coffee cakes are served at coffee time. Snail-shaped *schnecken*, streusel-topped coffee cakes, and *apfelkuchen* (apple cake) are served throughout Germany. *Stollen* is a rich yeast bread filled with almonds, raisins, and candied fruit. It usually is served at Christmastime.

German bakers have traditionally made cakes with honey or honey and spices. This is because sugar was not commonly available in Europe until the seventeenth century. The early honey cakes and cookies were eaten as sweets and used for religious and ceremonial celebrations. Cakes were baked in different shapes and decorated. *Lebkuchen*, one of Germany's best known honey-spice cakes, has a long history. For centuries, the Germans have used decorated lebkuchen to celebrate weddings, birthdays, and anniversaries. Sometimes young men and women have given lebkuchen to their sweethearts as gifts.

Glamorous *torten* (tortes) are made of layers of cake separated by sweet fillings. The most famous German torten is the *Schwarzwälder Kirschtorte* (Black Forest cherry cake). Bakers make this rich dessert with three layers of chocolate sponge cake. They moisten the cake with *Kirschwasser*, which is a potent, colorless brandy made from a special variety of cherry. They spread kirsch-flavored whipped cream and cherries between the cake layers. They then decorate the torten with tart cherries, chocolate curls, and more whipped cream.

Another popular German dessert with a regional origin is strudel. *Strudel* is paper-thin layers of pastry filled with plums, apples, cherries, or poppy seeds. It usually is sprinkled with confectioners' sugar and served warm. (People in some parts of Germany also make strudel with a protein-based filling and serve it as a main dish.)

German Beverages

Beer drinking is one of Germany's oldest customs. Germans drink beer by itself and with meals. Beer halls are familiar sights in all German cities and towns.

Many wine experts agree that the finest table wines are produced in France and Germany. They also agree that the best German wines are white wines. Most of the grapes used to make Germany's white wines grow in the valleys bordering the Rhine and Moselle Rivers.

National Live Stock and Meat Board

28-9 Red cabbage is a colorful accompaniment to these German sausages.

The Germans serve table wines with meals and snacks. Both wine and beer festivals are common in many parts of the country.

German Meals

Traditionally, Germans who could afford to do so ate five meals a day. Many Germans still follow this custom.

Frühstück (breakfast) is hearty. The Germans serve eggs with dark bread and freshly baked crisp rolls. They eat butter and jams with the breads, and serve their coffee with milk. People in northern Germany often serve ham, sausage, and cheese with the eggs.

The Germans eat *zweites frühstück* (second breakfast) during midmorning. Office workers often eat thick sandwiches made of sausage and cheese. Other Germans leave their morning's work for a snack of beer and sausage at a beer hall. Still others prefer fresh pastries at the *bäckerei* (bakery) or cheese sandwiches at the *mölkerei* (dairy).

Mittagessen is the main meal of the day for those Germans who are able to go home at noon. A typical mittagessen might include soup, eintopf, dumplings, and a simple dessert like rote grutze. *Rote grutze* is a pudding made of raspberry, cherry, or red currant juice thickened with cornstarch.

The Germans eat *kaffee* (a sociable snack) in late afternoon. They serve coffee and a variety of small sandwiches, cakes, and rich pastries. Kaffee is important to the Germans, for it is a time to talk with friends.

The Germans usually serve *abendroft* (light supper) in the early evening. Traditionally, abendroft is nothing more than buttered breads served with a variety of cold meats, sausages, and cheeses. For those who cannot eat a hearty meal at noon, however, abendroft is the main meal of the day. An appetizer, soup, main dish, vegetable, bread, and dessert are typical.

Scandinavia

Norwegian Tourist Board

These Norwegian children are dressed in their traditional national costume.

Scandinavia is a land of rugged wilderness and breathtaking beauty. Lakes made centuries ago by glaciers are crystal clear. Dense forests, snowcapped mountains, and lush valleys dot the landscape once ruled by Vikings.

Climate and Geography of Scandinavia

Scandinavia includes the countries of Denmark, Norway, Sweden, and Finland. Norway, Sweden, and Finland are part of a large peninsula that extends above the Arctic Circle. In the northern sections of these three countries, winters are long and severe. Summers are short and cool, thus making the growing season short. Above the Arctic Circle, however, the sun does not set for about two months during the summer. For this reason, the Scandinavian regions above the Arctic Circle are often called the "Land of the Midnight Sun."

Norway is a long, narrow country. Its rocky, mountainous coast makes up much of its land area. Norway is known for its *fjords,* which are slender, deep bays that cut deeply into the land. Norway's greatest wealth is in timber and seafood.

Mountains separate Sweden from Norway, and forests cover much of the northern part of the country. The most fertile areas are located in the southern tip of the peninsula.

Glaciers have left much of Finland stony, rough, and dotted with over 60,000 lakes. The glaciers also formed large marshy areas. These areas give the country its Finnish name, *Swomi,* which means swamp. Forests cover much of the rest of the land.

Of the four Scandinavian nations, Denmark has the most moderate climate and the least rugged geography. A large peninsula (called *Jutland*), two large islands, and 500 smaller islands make up Denmark. The North Sea forms the large peninsula's western coast, and the Baltic Sea forms the eastern coast. Forests fringe the eastern shore, and irregular hills cut through the central part of the country. The climate is mild with plenty of rainfall. The average winter temperature is 32°F (0°C), which is considerably warmer than the rest of Scandinavia.

Scandinavian Culture

The *Vikings* are the ancestors of the Scandinavian peoples. (The Finns' origins are found in the Central Asian steppes, but Viking influence is present.) The Vikings were both industrious and warlike. They sailed to all parts of the known world during the eighth, ninth, and tenth centuries. At one time, the Vikings controlled many lands. These included Scandinavia, the British Isles, Iceland, Greenland, the Baltic states, Sicily (part of Italy), and Normandy (part of France).

As the Viking Age was ending, the people of Norway, Sweden, Denmark, and Finland began a series of governments. (Russia also ruled Finland.) Some of these were joint governments; others were single. These governments lasted into the nineteenth century.

Today, governments in Sweden, Norway, and Denmark differ in form but are similar in effect. Denmark and Norway have constitutional monarchies, and Sweden has a limited monarchy. Finland has a representative government headed by a President. All four nations are peace-loving, and all are known for their advanced forms of social welfare. Each government provides for its people, ensuring that each citizen has an ample livelihood. Each government makes provisions for old age pensions and health care, hospitalization, disability, and survivor's insurance.

Scandinavians, for the most part, have the height, light hair, and blue eyes of their Viking forebears. They are industrious, hard-working people with deep family ties. Scandinavians enjoy singing, dancing, and a variety of sports. They like to ski and skate in the winter. They enjoy swimming, sailing, and hiking in the summer.

Scandinavian Economy

Many Scandinavians make their living in the large fishing industries found in all four countries. They catch herring, cod, haddock, salmon, and a variety of other fish and shellfish. They sell some locally, but they export much of their catch.

In Norway, Sweden, and Finland, logging is an important and profitable industry. The Scandinavians ship lumber and wood products, including paper, pulp, matches, and furniture, all over the world. The governments of all three countries supervise both logging and replanting. Other manufactured products of Scandinavia include textiles, glass, ceramics, metal products, electrical appliances, and machinery. People throughout the world recognize the simplicity, beauty, and quality of Scandinavian furniture, glassware, and ceramics.

All the Scandinavian countries obtain as many agricultural products as possible from the land. Denmark's climate and geography help make it the most agriculturally prosperous. In Denmark, the climate is mild and about 75 percent of the land

can be farmed. (Only 8 percent of the land in Finland and 10 percent of the land in Sweden can be farmed.) Denmark's main wealth is in pigs, cows, and chickens. These animals provide bacon, dairy products, and eggs, which the Danes export. Danish farmers grow grain and other crops for home use and to feed livestock.

Grain and livestock (including dairy cattle) are the main agricultural products of the other Scandinavian countries. Norway also produces large quantities of potatoes. Small family gardens provide fresh vegetables and fruits that can grow in the short growing season. People in the northern parts of Finland, Norway, and Sweden gather wild berries, including lingonberries and cloudberries. They use the berries to make sauces, puddings, cordials, and desserts.

Scandinavian Cuisine

Three major factors have affected Scandinavian cuisine. The first of these is geography. The geography of Scandinavia has made it hard to produce food. (Denmark is an exception.) Scandinavians have had to work to gain enough food from the water, forests, and tillable land.

Human isolation is the second factor affecting Scandinavian cuisine. Mountains and seas have separated the Scandinavian countries from most of Europe. As a result, other European countries have had little impact on Scandinavian cuisine. Geography has also kept the Scandinavian people apart from one another. Therefore, many local and regional dishes can be found. See 28-10.

The third factor affecting Scandinavian cuisine is climate. The Scandinavian climate includes long winters. The growing seasons are short. Therefore, much effort has to be put into preserving food. Pickled, dried, and salted foods are common.

The basic diets of the Danes, Norwegians, Swedes, and Finns are all rather plain and hearty. However, preparation and serving methods differ.

Danish Foods

Of all Scandinavian foods, Danish foods are the richest. The Danes use butter, cream, cheese, eggs, pork, and chicken in large quantities. Fish is not nearly as popular in Denmark as it is in the other Scandinavian countries.

The Danes are famous for their smørrebrød, which is literally translated as *buttered bread*. *Smørrebrød* are open-faced sandwiches usually made with thin, sour rye bread spread thickly with butter. (Soft white bread is used for smørrebrød

28-10 Mountains and waterways have isolated Scandinavian cuisine from the influence of other European countries.

with shellfish toppings.) Toppings can be nearly any type of meat, fish, cheese, or vegetable. Danish blue cheese with raw egg yolk is a typical topping. Sliced roast pork garnished with dried fruit and smoked salmon and scrambled eggs garnished with chives are also popular toppings. Both young and old Danes eat smørrebrød for lunch.

The Danes frequently accompany their smørrebrød with glasses of chilled aquavit. *Aquavit* is a clean, potent spirit distilled from grain and potatoes and flavored with caraway seeds. It is served throughout Denmark, Sweden, and Norway.

Danish cheeses are exported and used in Danish homes to make smørrebrød. Tybo, Danbo, Danish brie, havarti, Danish blue, and Danish Camembert are particularly well known.

Danes eat a great deal of pork. They often stuff pork roasts with dried fruits. They mix ground pork with ground veal to make *frikadeller* (meat patties). The Danes use pork liver to make liver paste, which is an important part of the Danish cold table. This cold table, which is a buffet similar to the Swedish smörgåsbord, is called *koldebord*.

Most Danes love desserts. Fruit pudding, apple cake, rum pudding, and pancakes wrapped around ice cream are favorites.

The Danes often begin their day with a substantial breakfast. This meal consists of several dairy products, such as yogurt, sour milk served with cereal, and ymer. *Ymer* is a high-protein milk product. This may be followed with cheese, bread, a boiled egg, juice, milk, strong coffee, and weinerbrød. *Weinerbrød* are layers of buttery pastry filled with fruit or custard and sprinkled with sugar or nuts. The famous smørrebrød are eaten for lunch. Dinner may include a roast, vegetables, bread, and a rich fruit and cream dessert.

Norwegian Food

The rugged land of Norway is ideally suited to the outdoor sports loved by the Norwegians. Outdoor activity requires hearty foods, and Norwegians begin the day with a big breakfast. They may eat herring, eggs, bacon, potatoes, cereals, breads, pastries, fruit, juice, buttermilk, and coffee.

The Norwegians work from early in the morning to midafternoon. This gives them time to take the family skiing, skating, or sailing. Because of their active lifestyles, Norwegians enjoy foods that are quick to prepare, yet filling and nourishing. Such foods include hearty soups like Bergen fish soup and rich desserts like sour cream waffles. *Lefse*, a thin potato pancake, is also a traditional Norwegian food.

Because agriculture is difficult in Norway, Norwegians have relied on seafood as a staple in their diet, 28-11. Herring (smoked, pickled, and fresh), halibut, cod, and salmon all are popular. The Norwegians often poach fish or add it to nourishing stews and soups. *Lutefisk* (dried cod that have been soaked in a lye solution before cooking) is a traditional Norwegian fish dish.

The Norwegians raise both goats and sheep on their mountainous land. They use goats' milk to make cheese. They use lamb and mutton in a variety of dishes. The Norwegians make a stew called *får i kål* from mutton and cabbage. One of the most popular smoked meat dishes is *fenalår*, which the Norwegians make from smoked mutton.

Danish cooks use sweet and whipped cream, but Norwegian cooks traditionally use sour cream. Soups, sauces, salads, and meat dishes are all likely to contain sour cream. Sour cream spread on bread or crackers is a popular snack.

Norwegians take great pride in their baked goods. They serve many traditional cookies and cakes at Christmastime. *Krumkaker* are thin, delicate cookies baked on a special iron and rolled around a wooden spoon while still warm. The cooled cookies are eaten plain or filled with whipped cream and fruit. *Rosettes* are light and airy cookies cooked on the ends of special irons in hot fat. *Fattigmand*, diamond-shaped cookies, are also fried in fat. *Kringla* are rich with sour cream or buttermilk and tied in figure eights or knots.

Swedish Food

The famous smörgåsbord originated in Sweden where it is served in private homes as well as in restaurants. A *smörgåsbord* is a buffet that includes a wide variety of hot and cold dishes. One legend traces the smörgåsbord to large country gatherings when each guest brought a dish for the table. The word *smörgåsbord* means "bread and butter table." However, smörgåsbords can be elegant and are likely to include 30 or more dishes. The kind and number of dishes depend on the occasion. Typical smörgåsbord dishes include herring dishes; cold fish, meats, and salads; hot meats, eggs, or fish; breads; cheeses; and desserts.

Diners return to the smörgåsbord several times to partake of the different courses. They take a clean plate each time. Generally, they eat the herring dishes first. Then they eat the fish, meats, and salads; the hot dishes; the cheeses; and the desserts, in that order.

Generally, people save the smörgåsbord for large gatherings and special occasions. The traditional, everyday style of cooking, called **husmankost**, is very simple. Visitors of Swedish homes are still likely to see rich yellow pea soup and salt pork served for supper. Traditionally, these foods are followed by Swedish pancakes and *lingonberries* (tart, red berries) for dessert.

Norwegian Tourist Board

28-11 Seafood plays an important role in the diet and the economy of Norway.

Baked brown beans, herring and sour cream, fried pork sausages, pickled beets, and fruit soups are other traditional Swedish foods. *Nyponsoppa* is a fruit soup made with rose hips (the orange seed capsules of the rose). It is served with whipped cream and almonds and is a Swedish specialty.

Reindeer is not exclusively Swedish, for reindeer herds roam the northern sections of Norway, Finland, and Sweden. However, reindeer is becoming increasingly popular in Sweden. Reindeer feed on young leaves and buds, mushrooms, and lichens. This makes the flavor of their flesh wild but still mild. Shaving reindeer meat into hot fat and frizzling it is one popular preparation method.

Some Swedes consider dessert to be the best part of a meal. Ostkaka and spettekaka are two of their favorites. They make *ostkaka*, a rich pudding-like cake, from milk, heavy cream, eggs, sugar,

rennet, and flour. The Swedes can buy ostkaka in local shops, but some still make the dish at home. Strawberries, lingonberries, or raspberries are common accompaniments. *Spettekaka* is a delicate cake made of eggs, sugar, and flour. Swedish bakers slowly pour the batter onto a cone-shaped spit placed in front of a fire. As they rotate the cone, the batter dries in layers and forms a delicate pattern. *Pepparkakor* (spicy gingerbread cookies) are a traditional Christmas treat.

Finnish Food

In Finland, forests are everywhere. Forests surround Helsinki, the capital of Finland. The berries, mushrooms, and potatoes sold at the large open-air market in Helsinki come from the nearby forests, 28-12.

Finnish Tourist Board

28-12 Finns buy a variety of fresh fruits and vegetables at the market square in Helsinki.

The Finns gather raspberries, strawberries, lingonberries, arctic cloudberries, Finnish cranberries, and mesimarja from the forests. (Finnish cranberries are smaller than those grown in the United States. *Mesimarja* are small, delicate fruits similar to raspberries.) The Finns use berries to make liqueurs, puddings, tarts, and snows (light puddings containing beaten egg whites). One popular fruit pudding is called *vatkattu marjapuuro.* Finnish cooks make it by whipping fruit juice, sugar, and a cereal product similar to farina until light and fluffy.

Finnish foods are hearty, often in a primitive way. *Vorshmack,* which is ground mutton, salt herring, and beef combined with onions and garlic, is a traditional Finnish dish. Pork gravy, black sour rye bread, and rutabagas and other root vegetables help warm the Finns during the bitter winters. The Finns add mushrooms to soups, sauces, salads, gravies, and stews. They make porridges and gruels from whole grains, just as their ancestors did centuries ago. *Mämmi* is a pudding made of molasses, bitter orange peel, rye flour, and rye malt. The Finns serve it at Easter with sweet cream.

At one time, the Finns lived under Russian rule. As a result, some Russian foods have become part of Finnish cuisine. Two of the most popular Finnish dishes with Russian origins are pasha and piirakka. *Pasha* is a type of cheesecake and *piirakka* are pastries or pies. The Finns fill piirakka with meat, fish, vegetables, and fruits. They serve the piirakka as appetizers, side dishes, or desserts.

Finns have many traditions. The Swedes also claim one of these—the crayfish party. The Finns hold their crayfish party in the summer under a full moon. **Crayfish** are crustaceans related to the lobster. The Finns drop the crayfish one-by-one into a pot of boiling water flavored with fresh dill. As they cook, the crayfish turn bright red. Served with toast, butter, vodka, and beer, the crayfish are messy to eat. As a result, the meal is extremely casual and fun.

Another Finnish tradition is the sauna. The **sauna** is a steam bath in which water is poured on hot stones to create steam. Finns follow the heat of the sauna with a quick dip in a chilly lake or swimming pool. They serve snacks during the sauna. They often serve salty fish to help replace the salt lost by the body during the sauna. After the sauna, the Finns eat a light meal. Grilled sausages, piirakka, poached salmon, salads, and Finnish rye bread are popular after-sauna supper dishes. The Finns may serve chilled vodka or beer with the meal.

Scandinavian Menu

Sill med Kremsaus
(Herring in Cream Sauce)
Kesäkeitto
(Summer Soup)
Frikadeller
(Danish Meat Patties)
Brunede Kartofler
(Caramelized Potatoes)
Smordampete Erter
(Buttered Peas)
Syltede Rødbeder
(Pickled Beets)
Limpa
(Swedish Rye Bread)
Kringla
(Double-Ring Twist Biscuits)
Fattigmand
(Poor Man's Cookies)
Kaffe
(Coffee)

Sill med Kremsaus
(Herring in Cream Sauce)
Serves 6

2½ cups coarsely chopped herring
       (salt, pickled, or Bismark herring)
2 tablespoons finely chopped onion
2 tablespoons fresh dill, divided in half
   salt
   pepper
1½ tablespoons white wine vinegar
2 chilled hard-cooked egg yolks
1 teaspoon prepared mustard
1½ tablespoons white wine vinegar
3 tablespoons vegetable oil
1½ to 3½ tablespoons evaporated skim milk

1. In small mixing bowl, combine herring, onion, 1 tablespoon dill, salt and pepper to taste, and 1½ tablespoons white wine vinegar; set aside.
2. In another bowl, mash egg yolks with a wooden spoon.
3. Add remaining vinegar, oil, and prepared mustard, beating until smooth.
4. Gradually add evaporated milk, beating constantly, until sauce is the thickness of heavy cream.
5. Pour sauce over herring mixture and refrigerate, covered, at least two hours.
6. Garnish with remaining fresh dill just before serving.

Per serving: 260 Cal. (73% from fat), 17 g protein, 2 g carbohydrate, 21 g fat, 166 mg cholesterol, 0.1 g fiber, 774 mg sodium.

Kesakeitto
(Summer Soup)
Serves 6 to 8

1 cup fresh green peas*
1 small head cauliflower, separated into small florets
5 small carrots, diced
2 small potatoes, diced
½ pound fresh string beans, cut into narrow strips*
¼ pound fresh spinach, finely chopped*
¾ teaspoon salt
   white pepper to taste
2 tablespoons margarine
2 tablespoons all-purpose flour
1 cup skim milk
¼ cup evaporated skim milk
1 egg yolk

1. With the exception of the spinach, place vegetables in a large saucepan, cover with cold water, and simmer until just tender, about 5 minutes.
2. Add spinach and cook another 5 minutes.
3. Remove from heat and strain liquid into a bowl; set aside.
4. Place vegetables in a second bowl.
5. In same saucepan, melt margarine over low heat.
6. Stir in flour to form a paste.
7. Add hot vegetable stock slowly, stirring constantly, then add skim milk.
8. In a small bowl combine the evaporated skim milk and egg yolk.

9. Add a few tablespoons of hot soup, beating constantly. Then add the warmed cream mixture to the hot soup.
10. Add vegetables and bring soup to a simmer. Simmer uncovered over low heat for 3 to 5 minutes.
11. Taste and add salt and pepper as needed.
12. Pour into a tureen and garnish with chopped parsley.

* If fresh peas, string beans, or spinach are not available, substitute frozen June peas, French-style green beans, and chopped spinach. Adjust cooking time accordingly.

Per serving: 182 Cal. (24% from fat), 7 g protein, 28 g carbohydrate, 5 g fat, 46 mg cholesterol, 6.6 g fiber, 407 mg sodium.

Frikadeller
(Danish Meat Patties)
Makes about 15 meat patties

½ pound ground pork shoulder or fresh ham
½ pound ground shoulder of veal
½ cup flour
2 eggs
1 large onion, chopped
⅔ cup skim milk
salt and pepper, to taste
margarine for frying

1. Mix the meats with the flour, salt, pepper, eggs, and onion in a bowl.
2. Add milk gradually and mix thoroughly. Let the mixture stand 15 minutes to allow the flour to absorb the milk.
3. Shape the mixture into small meat patties.
4. Melt margarine in electric skillet or frying pan over medium heat.
5. Fry patties about 5 minutes on each side.
6. Drain on paper toweling.

Per meat patty: 98 Cal. (50% from fat), 7 g protein, 5 g carbohydrate, 5 g fat, 58 mg cholesterol, 0.4 g fiber, 40 mg sodium.

Brunede Kartofler
(Carmelized Potatoes)
Serves 6 to 8

2 pounds small red potatoes
½ cup sugar
½ cup melted margarine

1. Scrub potatoes carefully. Do not remove skins.
2. In a heavy 2- to 3-quart saucepan, bring water to a boil.

3. Add potatoes and simmer 15 to 20 minutes or until potatoes are tender.
4. Cool potatoes slightly; slip off skins.
5. In a large heavy skillet, melt sugar. Use a low heat and stir sugar constantly until it turns into light brown syrup. (Heat must be low or sugar will scorch.)
6. Add melted margarine.
7. Add potatoes, a few at a time, shaking pan to coat all sides with syrup. Serve immediately.

Per serving: 318 Cal. (42% from fat), 3 g protein, 44 g carbohydrate, 15 g fat, 0 mg cholesterol, 1.4 g fiber, 181 mg sodium.

Smordampete Erter
(Buttered Peas)
Serves 6 to 8

¾ cup water
salt
2 packages frozen peas, 10 ounces each
1 tablespoon butter

1. Place water and salt in a medium saucepan; bring to a boil.
2. Add peas and return to a boil. Simmer peas until tender.
3. Drain and serve with butter.

Per serving: 79 Cal. (22% from fat), 4 g protein, 12 g carbohydrate, 2 g fat, 5 mg cholesterol, 4.6 g fiber, 267 mg sodium.

Syltede Rodbeder
(Pickled Beets)
Makes 2½ cups

¼ cup cider vinegar
¼ cup white vinegar
½ cup sugar
1 teaspoon salt
dash pepper
2½ cups thinly sliced canned beets

1. In a 1½-to 2-quart stainless steel saucepan, combine all ingredients but beets. Boil briskly for 2 minutes.
2. While marinade boils, place beets in a deep stainless steel or glass bowl.
3. Pour hot marinade over beets; let cool to room temperature, uncovered.
4. Cover bowl and refrigerate at least 12 hours, stirring occasionally.

Per serving: 105 Cal. (0% from fat), 1 g protein, 28 g carbohydrate, 0 g fat, 0 mg cholesterol, 2.2 g fiber, 466 mg sodium.

Limpa
(Swedish Rye Bread)
Makes 2 loaves

  1 package active dry yeast
  ¼ cup warm water
  ½ cup light brown sugar, firmly packed
  ½ cup light molasses
 1½ teaspoons salt
  2 tablespoons shortening
 1½ cups hot water
 2½ cups sifted rye flour
  ½ cup dark seedless raisins
  1 tablespoon grated orange peel
3½ to 4 cups sifted all-purpose flour

1. Soften yeast in warm water.
2. In a large bowl, combine brown sugar, molasses, salt, and shortening.
3. Add hot water (120° to 130°F) and stir until the sugar dissolves; cool mixture to lukewarm.
4. Stir softened yeast and rye flour into liquid mixture; beat well.
5. Add raisins, orange peel, and enough all-purpose flour to make a soft dough.
6. Turn dough out onto a lightly floured board or pastry cloth. Cover; let rest 10 minutes.
7. Knead dough until smooth and elastic, about 10 minutes.
8. Place dough in a lightly greased bowl, turning once to grease surface. Cover with a towel. Let dough rise in warm place until doubled in bulk (about 1½ to 2 hours).
9. Punch dough down. Turn dough out on lightly floured board or cloth and divide into 2 portions.
10. Shape each portion into a ball; cover, let rest 10 minutes.
11. Pat balls of dough into 2 round loaves and place on a greased baking sheet. Cover loaves and let rise in a warm place until double (about 1½ to 2 hours).
12. Bake loaves at 375°F for 25 to 30 minutes.
13. Remove bread from pans to cooling racks. For a soft crust, butter tops of loaves while hot.

Per slice: 119 Cal. (8% from fat), 3 g protein, 25 g carbohydrate, 1 g fat, 0 mg cholesterol, 2.3 g fiber, 107 mg sodium.

Kringla
(Double-Ring Twist Cookies)
Makes about 2 dozen cookies

1 cup sugar
1 cup plain yogurt
1 cup sour milk
1 egg
1 teaspoon baking soda
  pinch salt
½ teaspoon cinnamon
  all-purpose flour (enough to make a fairly stiff dough)

1. Preheat oven to 375°F.
2. Combine sugar, yogurt, sour milk, egg, soda, salt, and cinnamon in a large bowl.
3. Add enough flour to make a fairly stiff dough.
4. Roll dough between palms to form pencil-sized rolls; shape rolls into figure eights.
5. Place cookies on lightly greased baking sheet and bake until lightly browned, about 10 to 12 minutes.

Per cookie: 92 Cal. (4% from fat), 2 g protein, 20 g carbohydrate, 0 g fat, 12 mg cholesterol, 0.4 g fiber, 51 mg sodium.

Fattigmand
(Poor Man's Cookies)
Makes about 3 dozen cookies

4 eggs
½ cup sugar
  dash salt
4 tablespoons evaporated skim milk
  all-purpose flour (enough to make a soft dough)
  shortening or oil for frying
  granulated sugar

1. Beat eggs, sugar, and salt until thick and light.
2. Add evaporated milk and enough flour to make a soft dough. Chill dough.
3. Roll dough ¹⁄₁₆ inch thick
4. Cut dough into diamond shapes and fry in hot fat (375°F).
5. While warm, sprinkle cookies with granulated sugar.

Per cookie: 53 Cal. (13% from fat), 2 g protein, 10 g carbohydrate, 1 g fat, 31 mg cholesterol, 0.2 g fiber, 10 mg sodium.

Finnish Tourist Board

This table is spread with cheeses, breads, fish, and fresh produce typical of Scandinavia.

Summary

The British Isles include the countries of England, Scotland, Ireland, and Wales. These countries have a common climate and culture. However, each has unique aspects to its cuisine. Roasted meats, baked apples, main dish pies, and steamed puddings are among the popular foods in England. Simple, wholesome foods of the Scots often include such basic ingredients as oats, barley, lamb, and fish. Potatoes are the staple of the Irish diet. The hearty fare of Wales is similar to that of its neighbors. Tea is a popular beverage throughout the British Isles. It is also the name of a light meal served in the late afternoon or early evening.

France has long been known for its fine cuisine. French cooks use one of three main cooking styles: haute cuisine, provincial cuisine, and nouvelle cuisine. A variety of sauces and delicate seasonings characterize French cooking. Local dishes are popular throughout the various regions of France.

German cuisine is filling and flavorful. Roasted meats and a variety of sausages are common main dishes in Germany. Potatoes, sauerkraut, and dumplings are popular as hearty side dishes. Delicious breads as well as sweet rolls and cakes are the pride of German bakers. Of course, people throughout the world know Germany for its beers and wines.

Denmark, Norway, Sweden, and Finland are all part of Scandinavia. Much of Scandinavia is characterized by rugged terrain. This has made farming difficult in many areas and has isolated one region from another. Scandinavia is also typified by a cold climate. These factors have all affected the development of Scandinavian cuisine. Danish foods tend to be rich, often containing butter, cream, cheese, eggs, and pork. The Norwegians eat much fish and use sour cream in many of their recipes. Special occasions in Sweden often feature a smörgåsbord, but the everyday style of cooking is much simpler. Some Finnish dishes have Russian origins, and many include berries, mushrooms, and potatoes gathered from local forests.

Review What You Have Read

Write your answers on a separate sheet of paper.

1. What foods eaten by the early Anglo-Saxons and other Germanic tribes became staples of the British diet?
2. Describe a typical breakfast in England.
3. How is the word *tea* used in the British Isles?
4. True or false. Haggis is an Irish porridge made with potatoes and cabbage.
5. What food has been the mainstay of the Irish diet for centuries?
6. Define haute cuisine, provincial cuisine, and nouvelle cuisine.
7. Name and describe three types of French sauces.
8. True or false. The French serve the salad as a first course.
9. Name three foods that are eaten in the Provence region of France.
10. Describe three popular German potato dishes.
11. True or false. German bakers have traditionally made their cakes with molasses.
12. How do German meal patterns differ from those in the United States?
13. What are two specific toppings commonly eaten on Danish smørrebrød?
14. Describe three kinds of Norwegian cookies.
15. What dishes are typically included at a smörgåsbord?
16. True or false. Some Russian foods have become part of Finnish cuisine.

Build Your Basic Skills

1. Investigate the production and economic importance of one of Germany's primary industrial products. Share your findings in a brief oral report.
2. Europeans use the metric system of measurement. List the metric equivalents for each ingredient in either the British, French, German, or Scandinavian recipes found in this chapter. You may wish to refer to Chapter 12, "Getting Started in the Kitchen," for more information on metric measurements.

Build Your Thinking Skills

1. Work in a small group to thoroughly research one of the regions of France. Each member of the group should be responsible for a different part of the research. Research topics should include the geography, economy, culture, and cuisine of the region. Then prepare a meal that is typical of the region. As your classmates sample the meal, present your research findings in a team report.
2. Plan and prepare a Scandinavian dessert buffet. Be sure to include Danish pastries, Norwegian cookies, Swedish rice pudding, and Finnish vatkattu marjapuuro.

Chapter 29

Mediterranean Countries

A "Taste" of the World of Work

International Airplane-Flight Attendant
Performs a variety of personal services to provide for safety and comfort of international airline passengers during flight.

Press Tender
Tends battery of presses that automatically mix ingredients, and knead and extrude dough for use in making macaroni products.

Italian Chef
Supervises, coordinates, and participates in activities of cooks and other kitchen personnel engaged in preparing and cooking Italian foods in hotel, restaurant, or other establishment.

George A. Fischer

Terms to Know

eggplant	risotto
del pueblo	antipasto
tapas	minestrone
gazpacho	taverna
chorizo	avgolemono
paella	phyllo
sangria	mezedhes
al dente	

Objectives

After studying this chapter, you will be able to
❏ describe the food customs of Spain, Italy, and Greece.
❏ discuss how climate, geography, and culture have influenced these customs.
❏ recognize and prepare foods that are native to each of these countries.

The Mediterranean Sea is a warm, salty body of water that lies south of Europe. The Mediterranean region supports crops like citrus fruit, olives, grapes, wheat, barley, peaches, and apricots. The sea itself harbors a variety of fish as well as sponges and coral. For ages, people in the Mediterranean region have harvested these products and the sea salt to earn a living.

The climate in this region is balmy with plenty of sunshine throughout the year. The winters are mild with average rainfall. The summers are hot and dry. This weather makes the Mediterranean a popular vacation area.

Three European countries that lie along the Mediterranean Sea are Spain, Italy, and Greece. Because of their similar climates and resources, the cuisines of these countries resemble one another. Vegetables like tomatoes, eggplant, and green peppers are used in many dishes in each of these countries. (**Eggplant** is a fleshy, oval-shaped vegetable with a deep purple skin.) Seafood is also common in each of these cuisines.

As you read about Spain, Italy, and Greece, you will recognize how their food customs are similar. You will also note unique aspects of each cuisine.

Italian Government Travel Office

Visitors to the Mediterranean countries find traces of history in remains of structures built by people centuries ago.

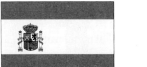

Spain

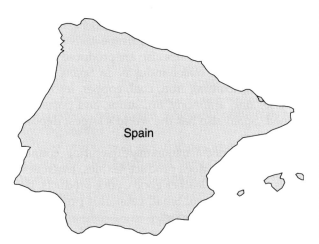

Tourist Office of Spain

These Spaniards are celebrating a fiesta in traditional costume.

The Iberian Peninsula lies between the Mediterranean Sea and the Atlantic Ocean. This land mass forms the southwestern corner of Europe. Spain and Portugal share the peninsula. Spain occupies the largest part.

The rough terrain of the Iberian Peninsula has shaped the development of Spanish culture. In the past, Spain's geography made it hard for people to travel and communicate. Thus, the people had to be self-reliant. Today, the people of Spain are proud and independent. These traits carry through to their cuisine.

Climate and Geography of Spain

The two main geographic features of Iberia are water and mountains. Water nearly surrounds the peninsula, and several mountain ranges crisscross the land.

Most Spaniards live along the coast of the Bay of Biscay and the Mediterranean Sea. There the land is fertile and agriculture is prosperous.

In the North, the Pyrenees separate Spain from France and the rest of Europe. Four other mountain ranges divide the rest of the land into isolated units. These are the Cantabrians, the Sierra de Guadarrama, the Sierra de Credos, and the Sierra

Guadalupe. Some of these areas are so private and beautiful that some people call Spain the "land of romance."

Within the circle formed by the mountain ranges is the *Meseta*. The Meseta is a large plateau. It occupies more than half of the total area of Spain.

Spain has a surprising range of climates for a country that is relatively small. Much of Spain has a Mediterranean climate with hot, dry summers, mild winters, and light rainfall. Northern Spain has cool summers with mild, damp winters. The Meseta of central Spain has the most severe climate with extremes of both heat and cold. The southernmost tip of Spain is semidesert with virtually no winter.

Spanish Culture

Spain has a rich cultural heritage that has influenced life in the country today.

Influences on Spanish Culture

The Phoenicians established colonies in Spain along the Mediterranean coast, perhaps as early as 1100 B.C. They brought a written language, money, and advanced mining techniques with them. The Carthaginians followed the Phoenicians about 600 years later. They held Spain for about 200 years attractive arrangement of raw vegetables on a plate. Spaniards never toss their salads. Tossing would destroy the color, line, and form so important to Spanish cuisine.

Soups are popular throughout Spain. Spanish soups may be light and refreshing or thick and hearty. One of the heartiest soups is a fish soup called *sopa al cuarto de hora,* or 15 minute soup. It is made with mussels, prawns, whitefish, rice, peas, hard-cooked eggs, saffron, salt, pepper, and meat broth. All the ingredients cook together for 15 minutes—just long enough to blend the flavors.

People throughout Spain enjoy garlic soup. Cooks prepare one of the simplest versions by slowly sautéing two cloves of garlic in olive oil. Once the garlic browns, a few slices of bread, salt, pepper, and water are added. Then the soup cooks for just a few minutes. Other versions include a small amount of minced ham and tomatoes.

Another popular Spanish soup is **gazpacho.** This soup is often made with coarsely pureed tomatoes, onions, garlic, and green peppers; olive oil; and vinegar. It can be thick or thin; served icy cold or at room temperature. Some Spanish farm workers eat gazpacho prepared in the fields as their noon meal. See 29-2.

Spanish Main Dishes

Most culinary experts agree that few cooks can prepare seafood as well as the Spaniards. Mussels, shrimp, and crab are popular shellfish in Spain. Tuna, hake, sole, squid, and cod are also caught off Spain's coasts. Cooks bake, fry, and poach fish and shellfish. In some parts of Spain, they serve seafood with *all-i-oli* (garlic mayonnaise).

Although methods for cooking meat are not as refined as those for seafood, Spain produces some excellent meat dishes. Veal, lamb, and pork are the most popular meats. The lean, dark Spanish pig is used in many ways. Raw ham, which is air cured high in the mountains, is a specialty. Filet of cured pork is sliced thinly and served as an appetizer. However, the best known pork product is **chorizo,** a dark sausage with a spicy, smoky flavor.

People throughout Spain eat poultry. Although Spaniards eat pigeon, pheasant, and partridge, chicken is by far the most popular type of poultry. Cooks stew and roast chicken. They also use it in the famous Spanish dish called paella. **Paella** is a Spanish rice dish that has many variations. All versions of paella, however, are colorful and delicious. The version most often seen in the United States contains chicken, shrimp, mussels, whitefish, peas, and rice. It is flavored with saffron, salt, pepper, and pimiento.

Tourist Office of Spain

29-2 Peppers, tomatoes, and cucumbers are among the fresh vegetables used to make this delicious gazpacho.

Two of the most important points to remember when preparing paella (and most other Spanish rice dishes) are cooking time and temperature. When Spanish cooks prepare rice, the rice is tender and fluffy without being dry.

When cooks prepare paella, they begin by cooking chicken and seafood. Then they add rice and stir constantly while it absorbs some of the sauce. The next step is to add boiling water or broth and lower the heat to prevent scorching. The rice continues to cook without stirring until it has absorbed most of the liquid.

Spanish Accompaniments

The Spanish serve bread with soups, salads, and main dishes. A variety of breads are popular. Some breads are dark and heavy; others are light. A few breads are sweet. *Pan de Santa Teresa* (fried cinnamon bread), for example, is similar to French toast. *Picatostes* (fried sugar bread) are more like a pastry. They are served as an afternoon snack with coffee.

Tortillas (Spanish omelets) may be served as a separate course or as an accompaniment. Spanish cooks use a variety of fillings for tortillas. Potato, onion, white bean, and eggplant are the most popular. Sometimes cooks pile several tortillas with different fillings on top of one another. They serve them the way people serve pancakes in the United States.

Spaniards generally serve vegetables as a separate course. However, potatoes or grilled tomatoes may accompany a dish. Vegetables served alone are often cooked in a tomato sauce or coated with a batter and deep-fried. Two or more vegetables are often combined and cooked in liquid. Many Spanish vegetable dishes contain artichokes, cauliflower, and eggplant. Spaniards also enjoy dried beans, lentils, and chick-peas, which they call *pulses.* Dried beans often appear in one-dish meals with meat, poultry, and fish.

Spanish Desserts

Simple desserts like fresh fruit, dried figs, cheese, or almonds often follow a meal. Spaniards usually save fancy cakes, cookies, pastries, and other rich desserts for guests. They may also serve these desserts as afternoon snacks. Rice pudding, sponge cake, and *flan* (caramel custard) are especially popular.

Spanish cakes and pastries contain very little baking powder or butter. However, they do contain many eggs and powdered almonds. They are flavored with cinnamon, anise, and orange and lemon peel. Spaniards fry rather than bake many cakes and pastries. This is because most Spanish homes did not have ovens until recent years.

Spanish Meals

Spanish meals are similar to Mexican meals with the same names. The people of Spain begin each day with *desayuno* (breakfast). They may just have coffee or a chocolate drink. Sometimes they have bread and jam or a sweet roll. *Churro,* a thin pastry fried in deep fat, is especially popular at breakfast. Vendors on the streets of many Spanish cities sell churros, 29-3.

People who have slept late or workers who find themselves hungry around 11 o'clock eat a second morning meal, *almuerzo.* It is more substantial than desayuno. This meal varies depending on locale and personal taste. It may include an omelet, grilled sausage, fried squid, open-faced sandwiches, fish, or lamb chops.

The *comida* is the main meal of the day. Spaniards eat this meal in the middle of the afternoon, around two or three o'clock. Most businesses close to escape the hottest part of the day, and workers come home to eat. A main course of fish, poultry, or meat usually follows salad or soup. Fruit or another light dessert ends the meal.

Spaniards serve *merienda* around six o'clock. It usually is a light snack of cakes and cookies or bread and jam. If a family has visitors, however, the meal may be more substantial.

Dusk is a pleasant time of day in Spain. At this time, the air becomes cooler, and the day's work ends. The sidewalk cafés fill with people, and the odors of the tapas drift out to the streets. Around nine o'clock, the streets empty, and everyone goes home for *cena* (supper). Cena is a light meal similar to almuerzo.

Wine is Spain's national drink, and both the rich and the poor serve it with every meal. Two popular Spanish wines are *malaga* and *sherry,* a perfumed type of wine almost in a class by itself. Restaurants and taverns throughout Spain serve **sangria,** a wine-based punch. There are many versions of the punch, but they all include red wine, fruit juice, and sparkling water.

Mazola Corn Oil

29-3 Deep-fried churros are a popular Spanish breakfast food.

Summers are sunny and dry with most of the rainfall occurring in the winter. In the North, however, temperatures are cooler, and the rains can come during any season. As a result, Italy has a range of vegetation. Pine trees grow in the North. Citrus fruits grow in the South.

Italian Culture

Italy has been the site of many major historical and cultural events. At one time in ancient history, Rome ruled the Western world. Centuries later, Italy led the rest of Europe in the Renaissance. The Renaissance was a time of a great rebirth in art and learning.

Influences on Italian Culture

A number of factors have influenced Italian culture. The early occupants, the rise and fall of the Roman Empire, and the Catholic Church all had an impact.

The Etruscans and the Greeks

The Etruscans and the Greeks were the two most powerful peoples of early Italy. Historians believe the Etruscans came from the eastern Mediterranean area around 1000 B.C. They developed a refined society in Northern and Central Italy.

The Greeks colonized Southern Italy and the island of Sicily. Their colonies served as centers for Hellenic society. Remains of the beautiful temples, palaces, and theaters built by the Greeks still stand.

The Roman Empire

At the height of the Etruscan and Greek periods, another group of people began exerting power. The Latins were farmers on the hills that bordered the Tiber River. Gradually, the Latins gained more and more power. They made Rome their capital. Rome prospered and in time became the head of the mighty Roman Empire. During the Roman Empire's Golden Age, Rome ruled Europe, northern Africa, and western Asia. Roman culture spread throughout the Empire.

The Romans made many achievements in art, architecture, law, and government. They established an excellent system of roads and bridges. They built elaborate temples and theaters. The Romans built their cities around a forum or main square. Homes had interior courtyards and plumbing made of lead pipes.

The fall of the Western Roman Empire (the part located in Europe) began in A.D. 330. This was when Emperor Constantine moved his capital from Rome to Constantinople. Before long, waves of barbarians came from the North. They first invaded Northern Italy and later destroyed the city of Rome.

The Roman Catholic Church

As civil rule declined in the Roman Empire, the Roman Catholic Church slowly gained power. The Church met the people's need for leadership. The structure of the Church became more governmental. Then in the fifth century, the Bishop of Rome became Pope. See 29-4.

With the support of the papacy and wealthy Italian families, the *Renaissance* began in Italy in the fourteenth century. The movement spread all through Europe. It lasted into the seventeenth century. It marked the end of medieval times and the beginning of modern times. Arts, literature, and science flourished. This was the age of Leonardo da Vinci, Michelangelo, Raphael, and Galileo.

As the Renaissance began to fade, struggles between local rulers and the papacy tore at the Italian city states. Italy finally became independent in the nineteenth century.

Italian Government Travel Office

29-4 The Roman Catholic Church has been an important part of Italian culture for centuries.

Modern Culture in Italy

Italy has been involved in wars of modern times. However, its republican form of government is at peace today. Italy is aligned with nations of the Western world. Industrial and agricultural growth is under way. The lives of the poor are slowly improving. Italian culture seems to be experiencing a rebirth.

Italian Economy

Agriculture is vital to Italy's economy. About half of the nation's land is used for farming. In many areas, farmers cannot use machines to do farm work. Therefore, they must do it by hand.

The richest and most productive farmland is located in Northern Italy in the Po River Valley. Leading crops are wheat, corn, rice, sugar beets, and flax. The many dairy herds make this region the largest cheese-producing region in the country. Olive trees thrive in Southern Italy. Farmers grow vegetables and fruits for local use and for export to other European countries.

Vineyards are scattered throughout the country. They supply grapes for Italy's large wine industry. Italian wine makers produce a variety of red, white, and sparkling wines for domestic use and export.

Northern Italy produces much of the nation's total industrial output. Steel and textiles are two of the major manufactured products. Other leading products include: typewriters, ball bearings, electronic equipment, precision tools, and chemical and petroleum products. Clothing design and manufacturing and motion-picture making have grown greatly in recent years.

Italian Lifestyle

Italians have always had great respect for the fine arts. Many of the world's most beautiful paintings, sculptures, and architectural works are in Italy.

Conversation is a popular pastime in Italy. Italians also enjoy card games, tennis, soccer, and water polo. Skiing, bicycle racing, auto racing, fencing, and hunting are popular, too.

Almost all Italians are Roman Catholics. Catholicism is the state religion. It is taught in the public schools. Religion plays an important part in the daily lives of most Italians. Many holidays and festivals are religious.

Italian Cuisine

During the Renaissance, Italian cooking became the "mother cuisine." It is the source of all other Western cuisines.

History of Italian Cuisine

The beginning of Italian cuisine belongs to the Greeks. Ancient Rome was known for its elaborate feasts. Romans paid high prices for Greek chefs because good food was a status symbol.

Cooking declined somewhat after the fall of the Roman Empire. Cooking and food experienced a rebirth during the Renaissance. Many people say the French have the greatest Western cuisine. However, even they grudgingly give Italy credit for laying the foundation for haute cuisine. Catherine de Medici, an Italian, brought her cooks to France when she married the future French king, Henri II. These cooks taught new cooking skills to the French. They also introduced new foods like peas, haricot beans, artichokes, and ice cream.

Characteristics of Italian Cuisine

Italian food, as a whole, is lively, interesting, colorful, and varied, yet it is basically simple. The Italians believe in keeping the natural flavors of food, and they insist upon fresh, high quality ingredients. Many Italian cooks shop daily so that foods will be as fresh as possible. They do not indulge in convenience foods. If a particular food is too costly or out of season, an Italian cook substitutes whatever is available.

Italian cooks use many kinds of herbs, spices, and other seasonings. They stock their kitchens with parsley, marjoram, sweet basil, thyme, sage, rosemary, tarragon, bay leaves, oregano, and mint. Other commonly used seasonings include cloves, saffron, and coriander; celery, onions, shallots, and garlic; vinegar, olives, and lemon juice.

Fresh fruits and vegetables are as important to the Italian kitchen as herbs and spices. Those who live in the country grow many of the fruits and vegetables they use. City dwellers make trips to the local market each day. There, they select the ripest and freshest tomatoes, artichokes, peas, beans, and other produce.

Italian cooks prepare many dishes on top of the range, either by simmering or frying. Because fuel is relatively expensive, they use the oven as little as possible.

Italian Staple Foods

People throughout Italy eat pasta. *Pasta* refers to any paste made from wheat flour that is dried in various shapes. In Italy, the pasta may be made from just flour and water. However, pasta may have added ingredients like eggs. It may be made at home, or it may be made commercially.

Italians serve pasta in many different ways, but they always serve it cooked *al dente* (slightly resistant to the bite). They may serve it with butter and a sprinkling of grated cheese. They may add it to soups or stews. They may serve it with any of a variety of sauces. They may also stuff it with meat, poultry, vegetables, or cheese. See 29-5.

After pasta, Italy's most important staple food is seafood. Every locale with a coastline has developed unique methods of preparing and serving

Del Monte Corporation

29-5 Pasta is a staple food in Italy, and rich tomato sauces are a traditional accompaniment.

fish. Sole, sea bass, anchovies, sardines, mackerel, tuna, eel, squid, and octopus are some of the varieties of fish caught. Equally popular are the shellfish, including oysters, clams, mussels, spiny lobsters, shrimp, and crayfish.

Rice is both an important agricultural product and a staple food. Italy is Europe's largest rice producer. Italians cook the rice so the grains remain separate with a slight firmness.

Pork, lamb, veal, and beef are produced and eaten in Italy. Sausage, wild game, and poultry are equally popular. Meat is relatively expensive so many Italian dishes rely on meat extenders. The sauces for many pasta dishes contain little meat. If large cuts of meat are served, they usually are roasted.

Italian Dairy Products

Italy produces cheeses that rival those of the French. Among the best-known Italian cheeses sold in the United States are Parmesan, mozzarella, Romano, ricotta, provolone, and Gorgonzola.

Some varieties of cheese, such as Parmesan, are named after their place of origin.

The Italians introduced ice cream to the rest of Europe. Ice cream is served in restaurants, in private homes, and by street vendors throughout Italy. There are two basic varieties. *Granita* is a light and delicate sherbet made with powdery ice and a syrup. The syrup usually is coffee or fruit-flavored. *Gelati* is made with milk. It resembles the vanilla and chocolate ice creams familiar to people in the United States.

Italian Beverages

Caffe espresso is a rich, dark, flavorful coffee served throughout Italy. It is made in a special type of coffeemaker called a *caffettiera*. Darkly roasted, finely ground coffee beans must be used. (This type of coffee is often called *French roast* in stores in the United States.) See 29-6.

Even more important to the Italians than caffe espresso is *vino* (wine). Even children drink it. Usually a mild burgundy or Chianti replaces water at Italian meals.

Libbey

29-6 Italians combine espresso with frothed milk to make cappuccino, which they might serve with crisp biscotti.

Regional Italian Specialties

Thanks to modern transportation, people throughout Italy can now buy foods that were once strictly regional. Pizza, for example, originated in Naples. Today it is eaten all over Italy and much of the rest of the world as well. Likewise, Bolognese meat sauces and stuffed pastas are found in towns thousands of miles from Bologna. Despite this, Italian cooking is regional cooking. Most culinary experts agree the best regional foods still are found within their home region.

The largest culinary division occurs between the North and the South. This difference is due primarily to geography and climate.

Northern Italy has more resources than Southern Italy. Meat is easier to obtain and less expensive. Dairy products are more common. Foods are not as heavily spiced as they are in the South. Cooks use delicate sauces instead of heavier tomato sauces.

Most of the farming and grazing land in Southern Italy is of poor quality. This region is rather sparsely populated and many of the people are poor. Meat is expensive and eaten in small amounts. Dairy products, except for cheese, are rare. Most foods are hearty, filling, and economical. Southern Italian cooking is the cooking with which most people in the United States are familiar. This is because most Italian restaurants in the United States are Neapolitan, and Naples is the heart of Southern Italian cooking.

Cooking fats and pasta varieties also differ between the North and the South. Northern Italy is too cold to raise olive trees but has excellent grazing land for dairy cattle. Southern Italy is warm enough for olive trees but has poor grazing land. Therefore, butter is the favored cooking fat in the North. In the South, cooks prefer olive oil.

Northern Italy is the home of the fat, ribbon-shaped groups of pastas called *pasta bolognese*. These pastas usually are made at home and contain egg. Southern Italy is the home of the tubular-shaped groups of pastas called *pasta naploetania*. These pastas are usually produced commercially. They do not contain egg, and they have a longer shelf life.

Specialties of Northern Italy

The specialties of Northern Italy include the simple *minestras* (soups) of the Friuli-Venezia region. The elegant stuffed pastas and rich meat sauces of the city of Bologna are also part of this fare.

The North is known for its sausages and other pork products. Bologna's *mortadella* is one of the best-known Italian sausages in the United States. It is made with beef and pork and seasoned with pepper and garlic. Delicately-flavored *Parma ham* is a popular appetizer.

In the North, people often serve risottos, gnocchi, and polenta instead of pasta. **Risottos** are rice dishes made with butter, chopped onion, stock or wine, and Parmesan cheese. They may have meats and vegetables added. Because many of the northern regions lie along the sea, risottos in this area often contain seafood. *Gnocchi* are dumplings. They may be made of potatoes or wheat flour. *Polenta* is a porridge made of cornmeal. It sometimes is combined with butter and cheese and served as a filling side dish.

In several of the northeastern regions, Austrian influences are evident. Foods such as *apfelstrudel* (apple strudel) and *crauti* (sauerkraut) have retained their original names.

Other Northern Italian specialties popular in the United States are chicken cacciatore, minestrone soup, and osso buco. *Pollo alla cacciatore* (chicken hunter-style) is prepared by simmering pieces of chicken with tomatoes and mushrooms. *Minestrone alla milanese* (minestrone soup) is a rich soup. It is made with butter, bacon, potatoes, onions, carrots, zucchini, celery, cabbage, rice (or pasta), and seasonings. It is served with butter and Parmesan cheese. *Osso buco* is the portion of a calf's leg between the knee and hock. It is served with the marrow that fills the center of the bone. The flavorful marrow is eaten with rice. See 29-7.

Famous Northern Italian sweets include zabaglione and panettone. *Zabaglione* is fluffy egg custard flavored with Marsala wine. *Panettone* is a sweet cake filled with fruit and nuts. It is often served for breakfast.

Specialties of Central Italy

Several of Central Italy's specialties have Roman origins. Roman cooks serve spaghetti in at least 25 ways. People in the United States are most familiar with the spaghetti dish called *spaghetti alla carbonara*. The sauce for this dish contains eggs, pork, pepper, and cheese.

Of all meats, Romans enjoy lamb the most. Cooks rub young lambs with garlic, rosemary, pepper, and salt. Then they cover the lambs with rosemary and roast them until tender.

The Romans must be given credit for inventing cheesecake. The early Romans made their *crostata di ricotta* (cheese pie) without any sweetening. It contained flour, cheese, and eggs. Today's cooks sweeten crostata di ricotta with sugar and flavor it with candied fruits, almonds, and vanilla.

In the rich countryside of Tuscany, home-grown vegetables, beans, and charcoal-grilled meats are specialties. Tuscan cooks grill a large beefsteak on a gridiron. They sprinkle it with coarse salt and pepper to make *bistecca alla fiorentina*. They add beans to minestras. They also cook beans with garlic and tomatoes or flavor them with sage and cheese. They prepare beans *nel fiasco* by cooking them with garlic, water, and olive oil in an empty wine flask.

Cenci and panforte are sweets with Central Italian origins. *Cenci* are deep-fried pastry strips shaped like bows. *Panforte* is a honey cake flavored with cinnamon and cloves.

National Live Stock and Meat Board

29-7 Osso buco, or braised veal shanks, served with risotto is a typical dish of Northern Italy.

Specialties of Southern Italy

Southern Italy is pasta country at its best. Southern Italian cooks serve their pasta with rich tomato sauces. They may flavor the sauces with meat, seafood, or vegetables.

Spaghetti and lasagne are the southern pastas with which people in the United States are most familiar. However, Southern Italian cooks do not limit themselves to just these varieties. Fusilli (pulled out spirals), orecchietta (little ears), ricci di donna (ladies' curls) are equally popular. Large tubular pastas like cannelloni and rigatoni are used as well.

With pasta, the Southern Italians love rich tomato sauces. The traditional Neapolitan tomato sauce is simple. Cooks combine fresh tomatoes with fried onions, larded filet of beef, and a sprig of basil. The mixture simmers in an earthenware pot for several hours to bring out all the flavors.

One popular Neapolitan dish is *stuffed lasagne.* Long, wide noodles are layered with cheeses and meats. Cheeses include ricotta, mozzarella, and grated Parmesan. Pieces of sausage, minced pork, and strips of ham are the meats used, along with hard-cooked egg slices. A thick tomato sauce is poured over the mixture and the lasagne is baked until bubbly. This dish makes good use of the many fine types of cheese produced in Southern Italy.

Tomatoes and mozzarella cheese are two of Southern Italy's major agricultural products. They also are key ingredients in the popular Neapolitan dish called *pizza.* Pizza has been part of Neapolitan cooking since the 1500s when the tomato was brought to Naples. The Italians make many kinds of pizza. Many pizzas bear the name of the pizza maker. All pizzas contain tomato sauce, cheese, and a crust made from a yeast dough. Sausage, anchovies, mushrooms, green peppers, olives, and other ingredients are optional.

Spaghetti with clam sauce is one of the many other Southern Italian specialties. *Soffritti* is lightly fried onions and other vegetables mixed with a small amount of meat. *Eggplant Napoli* is eggplant layered with tomato sauce and cheese. *Zucchini Parmesan* is sliced zucchini and cubed tomatoes tossed with Parmesan cheese.

Italian Meals

Like many Europeans, Italians typically eat a light breakfast and a hearty noon meal. The noon meal is the largest meal of the day and people usually eat it at home.

The well-known *antipasto* is an appetizer course that often begins the meal. It may include a variety of meats and vegetables. Regardless of the selection of foods, the tray must have both color and taste appeal. Foods in an antipasto may include salami, Parma ham, anchovies, and hard-cooked eggs. Celery, radishes, pickled beets, black olives, marinated red peppers, and stuffed tomatoes are popular antipasto foods, too.

Minestra (soup) follows the antipasto. (Some people skip antipasto and begin the meal with soup.) Each region has its favorite soups. ***Minestrone,*** one of the most popular, is a vegetable soup thick with pasta. *Pasta in brodo* is a simple broth with pasta.

A main course of a meat, poultry, or fish dish usually follows the soup. Italians often roast their meat, and lamb is particularly popular when roasted. Poultry often is served in a sauce, whereas fish is baked or broiled. (If meat is too costly, a large serving of pasta may replace the main dish. Pasta is usually served with a sauce containing small pieces of meat or fish.) A vegetable or salad usually accompanies the main dish. Salads always contain tomatoes and other vegetables.

Fruit and cheese end a typical meal. Italians reserve fancier desserts for special occasions.

The evening meal usually is light. Soup, omelets, and risottos are popular supper dishes. Bread, wine, and a simple fruit dessert complete the meal.

Good Manners Are Good Business

It would be ungracious for you to refuse an invitation to dine in the home of an Italian business associate. When you go, you might take flowers as a gift for your host. Avoid taking chrysanthemums, however, as Italians consider them to be funeral flowers. You are probably safest with a mixed bouquet, which should contain an odd number of flowers.

Italian Menu

Antipasto
(Appetizers)
Minestrone
(Vegetable Soup)
Pollo alla Cacciatore
(Chicken Hunter-Style)
Fettuccine Verde al Burro
(Green Noodles with Butter and Cheese)
Panne
(Italian Bread)
Spumoni with Cenci
(Three-Flavored Ice Cream with Deep-
Fried Sweet Pastry)
Caffe Espresso
(Rich Coffee)

Antipasto
(Appetizers)

Many different foods can appear in an antipasto. Regardless of the number of types of foods chosen, however, all antipasto ingredients should be attractively arranged on the serving platter. The following foods frequently are part of an antipasto.

Anchovy fillets
Artichoke hearts
Sautéed cold mushrooms marinated in vinegar and oil
Black olives
Roasted red peppers
Prosciutto (dry-cured spiced Italian ham)
Salami
Celery hearts
Radishes
Peperoncini (small green peppers pickled in vinegar)
Sliced hard-cooked eggs
Finocchio (Italian celery)
Sliced tomatoes
Provolone

Minestrone
(Vegetable Soup)
Serves 8

2   quarts low-sodium chicken bouillon
1   can Italian peeled tomatoes, 16 ounces
1   medium onion, chopped
2   ribs celery, cut into 1-inch pieces
¼   cup chopped parsley
1   teaspoon salt
½   teaspoon oregano
⅛   teaspoon pepper
1   clove garlic, minced
1   can chick-peas, 16 ounces, drained and rinsed
1   cup cubed zucchini
1   cup fresh or thoroughly defrosted frozen peas
1   cup diced carrots
1   cup chopped cabbage
½   cup uncooked white rice or orzo pasta
1   cup grated Parmesan cheese
    chopped fresh parsley

1. In kettle, combine bouillon, tomatoes, onion, celery, ¼ cup parsley, salt, oregano, pepper, and garlic, Simmer, stirring occasionally, 20 to 30 minutes.
2. Add chick-peas, zucchini, peas, carrots, cabbage, and rice or pasta; simmer an additional 20 to 25 minutes or until vegetables and rice or pasta are tender.
3. Before serving, taste soup and add additional salt and pepper if needed.
4. Pour soup into large tureen or individual soup bowls. Pass bowls of grated Parmesan cheese and chopped parsley separately.

Per serving: 229 Cal. (21% from fat), 13 g protein, 34 g carbohydrate, 6 g fat, 10 mg cholesterol, 5.0 g fiber, 554 mg sodium.

Pollo alla Cacciatore
(Chicken Hunter-Style)
Serves 4 to 6

4   pound chicken
½   cup all-purpose flour
½   teaspoon salt
¼   teaspoon pepper
3   tablespoons olive oil

2   medium onions, chopped
1   clove garlic, finely minced
1   cup canned whole tomatoes
1   cup sliced green pepper
1½ cups sliced fresh or canned mushrooms
    salt
    pepper

1. Rinse chicken; pat dry with paper towels. Cut into serving-sized pieces and remove skin.
2. Combine flour, salt, and pepper.
3. Coat chicken pieces with seasoned flour.
4. In large skillet, heat oil until hot but not smoking.
5. Add chicken pieces, a few at a time, and fry until golden brown.
6. Combine onions, garlic, tomatoes, and green peppers in a mixing bowl; add to chicken.
7. Cover skillet and simmer chicken slowly until tender, about 40 minutes.
8. Add mushrooms and simmer an additional 10 to 15 minutes.
9. Taste; add additional seasonings if needed. Serve immediately.

Per serving: 433 Cal. (33% from fat), 48 g protein, 23 g carbohydrate, 16 g fat, 135 mg cholesterol, 4.4 g fiber, 425 mg sodium.

' Fettuccine Verde al Burro
(Green Noodles with Butter and Cheese)
Serves 8

2   packages frozen chopped spinach, 10 ounces each
2   cups all-purpose flour
1   teaspoon salt
2   eggs
6 to 8 quarts water
⅓ cup margarine, softened
⅓ cup evaporated skim milk
⅔ cup freshly grated Parmesan cheese

1. In medium saucepan, cook spinach in a small amount of simmering salted water until tender. Drain well and squeeze dry.
2. Using fine blade of food processor, grind spinach 2 or 3 times.
3. Transfer chopped spinach to mixing bowl. Add flour, salt, and eggs.
4. Using hands, mix to form a soft dough.
5. Turn dough out onto a floured board and knead until smooth and no longer sticky, adding additional flour if needed.
6. Roll dough into a very thin rectangle. Cover with damp towels and let stand 1 hour.
7. Starting at the narrow end closest to you, fold dough over and over until it is about 3 inches wide.
8. Using a sharp knife, cut into very thin strips, about ¼ inch wide.

9. Unroll strips on flat surface and let dry 2 to 3 hours or overnight.
10. When ready to cook, bring water to boil in a large kettle. Add noodles and simmer until tender.
11. Meanwhile, combine softened margarine, evaporated milk, and cheese in small bowl; beat until smooth.
12. When noodles are tender, drain well. Toss with cheese mixture and serve immediately.

Per serving: 267 Cal. (39% from fat), 11 g protein, 29 g carbohydrate, 12 g fat, 75 mg cholesterol, 2.4 g fiber, 601 mg sodium.

Panne
(Italian Bread)
Makes 2 loaves

4½ to 5½ cups unsifted all-purpose flour
1   tablespoon sugar
1½ teaspoons salt
2   envelopes active dry yeast
1   tablespoon softened margarine
1¾ cups very warm water (120° to 130°F)
    cornmeal
    vegetable oil
1   egg white
1   tablespoon cold water

1. In large mixing bowl, combine 1½ cups flour, sugar, salt, and dry yeast.
2. Work in margarine.
3. Gradually add warm water and beat 2 minutes on medium speed of electric mixer, scraping bowl occasionally.
4. Add ¾ cup flour and beat 2 more minutes on high speed. Stir in enough additional flour to make a stiff dough.
5. Turn dough out onto lightly floured board or pastry cloth. Knead until smooth and elastic, about 8 to 10 minutes.
6. Place dough in greased bowl and turn once to grease top. Cover with plastic wrap and a clean towel and let rest 20 minutes.
7. Divide dough in half and shape into two long loaves. (Shape by rolling each piece into an oblong. Beginning at wide end, roll tightly, like a jelly roll, and seal edges well.)
8. Place loaves on lightly greased baking sheets that have been sprinkled with cornmeal. Brush loaves lightly with oil and cover with plastic wrap. Refrigerate dough 2 to 24 hours.
9. When ready to bake, remove dough from refrigerator. Uncover dough carefully and let stand at room temperature 10 minutes.
10. Meanwhile, preheat oven to 425°F.
11. Slash loaves 4 to 5 times with a sharp knife on the diagonal.

12. Bake at 425°F for 20 minutes.
13. Remove from oven and brush with beaten egg white mixed with water.
14. Return to oven and bake an additional 5 to 10 minutes longer or until loaves are golden brown and sound hollow when tapped with the knuckles.
15. Remove to cooling racks.

Per slice: 73 Cal. (8% from fat), 2 g protein, 14 g carbohydrate, 1 g fat, 0 mg cholesterol, 0.6 g fiber, 106 mg sodium.

Cenci
(Deep-Fried Sweet Pastry)
Makes about 4 dozen pastries

2 cups all-purpose flour
2 whole eggs
2 egg yolks
1 teaspoon rum extract
1 tablespoon sugar
¼ teaspoon salt
  confectioners' sugar
  vegetable shortening for frying

1. Place flour in a large mixing bowl. Make a well in the center and add the eggs, egg yolks, rum extract, and 1 tablespoon sugar.
2. Using a fork or fingers, mix until soft dough forms.
3. Turn dough out onto a lightly floured board or pastry cloth. Knead until dough is smooth, adding more flour if needed.
4. Refrigerate for one hour.
5. Heat 4 inches of shortening to 350°F.
6. Roll the dough until paper thin.
7. Cut into strips six inches long and ½ inch wide. Tie the strips into loose knots and fry until golden brown.
8. Drain on absorbent paper and sprinkle with confectioners' sugar. Serve immediately.

Per pastry: 40 Cal. (37% from fat), 1 g protein, 5 g carbohydrate, 2 g fat, 23 mg cholesterol, 0.1 g fiber, 14 mg sodium.

Chapter 29

National Live Stock and Meat Board

Lasagne, a Southern Italian specialty, is also quite popular in the United States.

Greece

Greece

George A. Fischer

Remnants of Ancient Greek architecture can still be seen at the sight of the first Olympic Games.

Greece is a land of terraced gardens, busy seaports, and ancient temples. In this sunny land, the art, literature, science, and philosophy that form the basis of Western civilization began. Greece is also an important part of the much older civilization of the East. Parts of Greek culture, such as some Greek foods, have their roots in the Middle East. The foods moussaka and baklava are examples.

Climate and Geography of Greece

Greece forms the southern tip of Europe's Balkan Peninsula. The country is made up of one large landmass (mainland Greece) and many islands. The islands make up one-fifth of the total land area. Crete and Rhodes are the largest of the islands. Water surrounds Greece on three sides. The Ionian Sea is to the west, the Aegean Sea to the east, and the Mediterranean Sea to the south.

The geography is varied. The Pindus Mountains form the backbone of Greece. Spurs (ridges) that jut out from these mountains form the jagged coastline, which adds to the beauty of the land. To the east lie Mount Olympus and another strip of mountains separated by fertile valleys.

The short, swift rivers of Greece are not useful for transportation. However, the Greeks do travel

by way of the seas that surround much of their homeland. Early in their history, the Greeks became a seafaring people. They made early contact with Asia, Africa, and the rest of Europe by making the first long voyages.

The mountainous land with its stony, dry soil makes farming difficult. However, olive trees and grapevines, with their deep roots, can be cultivated in this terrain. Sheep thrive on the short grasses of the more mountainous areas.

Greece has mild winters and warm, sunny summers. Rainfall rarely exceeds 20 inches (50 cm)

Be a Clever Consumer

When traveling to an unfamiliar area, you may want to look into package tours. However, be sure to read all information carefully before signing any contracts or paying any money. Be sure you know exactly what your package includes. Find out about cancellation policies, too. Canceling a prepaid trip often means losing a large portion of the money you paid.

per year, and most of the rain falls in the winter. Because Greece has little or no frost, subtropical fruits and flowers can be grown.

Greek Culture

Greek history spans centuries. It usually is divided into two stages: the history of *Ancient Greece* and the history of *Modern Greece.* (Ancient Greece is sometimes called *Classical Greece.)*

Ancient Greek Culture

The Minoans established the first Greek society on the island of Crete around 3000 B.C. About a thousand years later, people came to the Greek mainland from the north. These early Greeks set up small farming villages. These people adopted some of the Minoan ways. Their culture thrived for several hundred years. Then the society underwent an unexplained destruction. Greece fell into a period known as the *Dark Age,* which lasted about 400 years. During this time, knowledge of writing was lost, and history was kept alive through songs and legends.

Before the end of the Dark Age, Ancient Greece was divided into small units called *city states.* Although Greece never became unified, two of the city states, Athens and Sparta, became seats of power. Athens was democratic, and the Athenians originated the basic concepts of Western law. The right of appeal and the validity of wills, for example, both originated in Ancient Greece. Sparta, on the other hand, was not democratic. Spartans lived a strict, military life with stern laws. All boys were taken from their homes at an early age to train as soldiers. The Spartan ideal was individual sacrifice for community welfare.

Minor wars occurred now and then among the different city states. Wars also occurred between Greece and Persia. Finally, the city states fell to the Roman Empire. After the seat of Roman government moved to Constantinople, Greece lost much of its importance. Invaders, including the Visigoths, Slavs, and Bulgurs, later overran it. In 1453, the Turks seized Constantinople and in time took control of all of Greece.

Achievements in art, literature, science, and philosophy mark the history of Ancient Greece. The philosophers Socrates, Aristotle, and Plato and the jurist Solon were products of Ancient Greece. The dramatists Sophocles, Aristophanes, and Euripides and the scientist Hippocrates were from this culture, too. The Acropolis, the Parthenon, and the Theatre of Dionysis also belong to this early age.

From the middle of the fifteenth century until the nineteenth century, Turkey ruled Greece. Turkey granted liberty to a large part of the Greek peninsula in 1829. Then the Greeks began their fight to regain those parts of their country that remained under foreign rule. Today the Greeks take great pride in their heritage. They are proud of the achievements of the Classical Age. They are also proud of their brave struggles for freedom in later centuries.

Modern Greek Culture

Greece has always been a crossroad for migrating groups. Some modern Greeks may be able to trace their heritage to the early people who came from the north. However, most have a mixed heritage. As the Romans, Bulgurs, Slavs, Albanians, Turks, and other invading groups eventually settled down, they intermingled with the Greeks.

The people of Greece share a common language, Greek, and a common religion, Christianity. The majority of Greeks belong to the Greek Orthodox Church. Religious holidays hold great importance for the Greeks, who devote much time and energy to their celebrations. See 29-8.

John F. Flanagan

29-8 The Greeks are a hard-working people who are proud of their heritage.

Greece is a relatively poor country, and many of its people must work hard to make a living. Many Greeks are farmers, despite the lack of fertile farmland. They produce wheat and corn on small acreages. They raise vegetables in terraced gardens. Grapes, olives, and citrus fruits grow in more fertile areas. Goats and sheep, which graze in the mountains, provide milk, cheese, and meat. Farming is difficult, and many families are able to provide only enough food for themselves. With new agricultural methods, however, food production in Greece's fertile areas has increased tremendously in recent years.

The Greek people are skilled mariners. Greek ships carry foreign as well as domestic cargo to ports all over the world. (Many of Greece's wealthiest citizens are involved in shipping.) Fishing is an important industry on the islands and in coastal areas. Much of the seafood that is caught is eaten in Greece. However, some is exported along with tobacco, olive oil, and raisins.

Although mining and manufacturing industries are relatively small, a few minerals and industrial products are produced for export. These include iron ore, lead ore, manganese, chromite, textiles, canned goods, wine, and cigarettes. In recent years, the textile industry has seen the greatest growth.

The Greeks enjoy singing and dancing, large family gatherings, and storytelling. They also enjoy good conversation.

In small communities, the *tavernas* are cafés that serve as public meeting places. Guests who gather in the tavernas often order glasses of *retsina* or *ouzo*. (Retsina is a resin-flavored wine. Ouzo is a strong spirit with the flavor of anise.) Often, someone will play a mandolin-like instrument called a *bouzoukia* while the other guests talk, play games, or dance.

Just under half of the Greek population lives in urban areas. Athens, the capital of Greece, is the largest and most modern city in the country. It once was a town with just 300 houses. However, it has grown to a city with a population of over two million since Greece regained its independence. Athens has many modern buildings and busy streets. It is Greece's commercial, political, and cultural center.

Greek Cuisine

For 2,000 years, the Greeks have been developing their cuisine. Early records show that the Greeks cooked foods while the rest of the world ate raw foods. Early Greek foods included roast lamb with capers, wild rice with saffron, and honey cakes. As Greek civilization spread throughout the Mediterranean, so did Greek cuisine. The Greeks taught the Romans how to cook, and a Greek named Hesiod wrote one of the first cookbooks.

Greek cooking has a rich and varied past. A pre-Greek people belonging to the Stone Age brought foods like lamb and beans to Greece. Other foods, like olives, grapes, and seafood, are native to the area. Invading groups of peoples added their food customs to these native foods. The many Greek pasta dishes, for example, are Italian in origin. Layers of pasta, ground lamb, and cheese covered with a rich custard and baked is called *pastitsio,* 29-9. Kebabs, yogurt, Greek coffee, and rich sweet pastries are Turkish in origin. (*Kebabs* are pieces of meat, poultry, fish, vegetables, or fruits threaded onto skewers and broiled.)

Greek Staple Foods

A number of foods are basic to Greek cooking. Greek cooks make liberal use of lemon juice, tomatoes, green peppers, and garlic. *Avgolemono,* one of the most popular Greek sauces, is a mixture of egg yolks and lemon juice. The Greeks use it to flavor soups and stews. They serve it with vegetables and fish, too. Tomatoes and green peppers add both color and flavor to Greek dishes. Greek cooks stuff them with meat and other vegetables. They also thread them on skewers and broil them and add them to soups and stews. Tomato sauces are used with both meat and fish dishes.

Greek cooks use many herbs and spices to bring out the natural flavors of lamb, fish, and vegetables. The most widely used herbs and spices include cinnamon, basil, dill, bay leaves, garlic, and oregano.

The Greeks serve eggplant as a side dish or add it to main dishes. Cooks prepare *moussaka* by layering slices of eggplant, ground lamb, and cheese. (They often cook the lamb with tomato paste, wine, cinnamon, and onion.) They pour a rich cream sauce over the meat, vegetable, and cheese mixture before baking.

Lamb

Sheep have been raised in Greece since prehistoric times. Greek cooks roast lamb whole or thread it onto skewers and broil it. They also grind and layer it with other ingredients in casseroles. They use lamb as a filling for vegetables and add it to soups and stews, too.

A seven-week fast characterizes the Lenten season in Greece. When this fast is broken, lamb is

29-9 Pastitsio is a Greek dish with Italian origins.

served as mayeritsa. (*Mayeritsa* is the internal organs of a lamb cooked in a seasoned broth.) Early the next morning, the rest of the lamb is roasted whole and served for Easter dinner.

Seafood

Because of Greece's location, seafood is an important part of the Greek diet. Fishers catch red mullet, crawfish, cuttlefish, sea bass, red snapper, swordfish, squid, and shrimp in the Mediterranean Sea.

Greek cooks prepare freshly caught seafood simply, usually by baking or broiling. They often bake fresh vegetables, such as tomatoes and zucchini, with the fish. Squid is particularly popular. Fresh squid, stuffed with rice, onions, nuts, and seasonings, is poached and served as a favorite main dish. Raw squid served with raw green beans or artichokes is eaten as an appetizer. Another popular appetizer or snack is *taramasalata*, a pâté made from fish roe (eggs).

Olives

Olives grow in abundance in Greece. Their many sizes, shapes, and colors often amaze people from the United States. The flavor of olive oil dominates Greek cuisine. People throughout Greece eat olives as appetizers and snacks or add them to other dishes. The popular *salata horiatiki* (rural salad) contains olives, a variety of greens, tomatoes, and feta cheese. (*Feta cheese* is a slightly salty, crumbly, white cheese made from goat's milk.)

Honey

Greek honey is world famous. The writings of Aristotle describe the different types of honey that were available in Ancient Greece. During this time, people used honey to make *melamacarons* (honey cakes), which they offered as gifts to the gods. Today, Greek bakers prepare the same honey cakes to celebrate New Year. Honey is the basic sweetener used in the preparation of many Greek desserts, pastries, and cakes. See 29-10.

Although the Greeks enjoy sweets, they usually serve sweets only on special occasions. The Greeks make many of their desserts with **phyllo,** a paper-thin pastry made with flour and water. Some Greek cooks still make phyllo, although the task is both difficult and time-consuming. Others prefer to buy sheets of phyllo ready-made. (Many large supermarkets in the United States sell phyllo in frozen form.) They use phyllo to make baklava, galat oboureko, and kopenhai. *Baklava* is thin layers of pastry filled with nuts and soaked with a honey syrup. *Galat oboureko* is phyllo layered with rich custard, honey, and nuts. *Kopenhai* is a nut cake with phyllo.

Other popular sweets contain flour, eggs, and oil rather than phyllo. They are deep-fried and are similar to fritters. *Diples,* for example, are small thin sheets of dough that are rolled with two forks as they are fried. They may be coated with a honey and nut syrup flavored with cinnamon.

Greek Meals

The Greeks appreciate simple pleasures. Their meals reflect this simplicity.

Breakfast is often no more than a slice of dry bread and a cup of warm milk. Sometimes, eggs or cheese accompanies the bread.

Both lunch and dinner are hot meals. The Greeks eat lunch at noon and dinner late in the evening.

Early evening is generally the most pleasant and enjoyable time of the day. Many Greek families go for an evening walk. Some choose to sit at small outdoor cafés and enjoy a variety of appetizers called **mezedhes**. Olives, feta cheese, pistachio nuts, garlic-flavored sausage, shrimp, and hard-cooked eggs are popular mezedhes. Ouzo and conversation accompany this early snack.

Later, families gather at home for the evening meal. This meal might include either baked or broiled fish, a vegetable, and bread. Fresh fruit would complete the meal.

John F. Flanagan

29-10 Greek honey, along with other typical Greek foods like olives, almonds, and dried fruits, is sold at shops throughout Greece.

Greek Menu

Soupa Avgolemono
(Egg-Lemon Soup)
Moussaka
(Baked Eggplant, Lamb, and Tomatoes
with Cream Sauce)
Salata Horiatiki
(Rural Salad)
Psomi
(Greek Bread)
Kourambiedes
(Walnut Cookies)
Kafés
(Greek Coffee)

Soupa Avgolemono
(Egg-Lemon Soup)
Serves 6 to 8

8	cups low-sodium chicken bouillon
½	cup uncooked white rice
3	eggs
2 to 3	tablespoons lemon juice
	salt
	pepper
	finely chopped parsley

1. In a large saucepan, bring chicken bouillon to a boil.
2. Add rice and simmer until tender.
3. Drain excess bouillon from rice and set aside.
4. Put eggs and lemon juice into blender container. Cover and process at high speed until frothy.
5. Remove cover and slowly pour the hot bouillon into the egg mixture while processing at low speed.
6. Pour soup into saucepan with rice. Cook over low heat until thoroughly heated. Do not let soup boil.
7. Season soup with salt and pepper. Serve immediately garnished with parsley.

Per serving: 114 Cal. (28% from fat), 5 g protein, 16 g carbohydrate, 4 g fat, 137 mg cholesterol, 0.4 g fiber, 43 mg sodium.

Salata Horiatiki
(Rural Salad)
Serves 6 to 8

6	cups assorted salad greens
3	medium tomatoes, washed and cut into wedges
½	cup chopped green onion
1	medium cucumber, washed and sliced thinly
⅓	cup oil (part olive, part corn)
2	tablespoons lemon juice
2	teaspoons sugar
½	teaspoon salt
	few dashes pepper
6	ounces feta cheese
1	can flat anchovy filets, drained, 2 ounces
⅔	cup whole pitted ripe olives
	crumbled dry oregano

1. Wash greens; pat dry and refrigerate until ready to use.
2. Prepare other vegetables.
3. In large salad bowl, combine greens with tomatoes, onions, and cucumber.
4. In small bowl, mix oil, lemon juice, sugar, salt, and pepper to taste. Toss with greens mixture.
5. Crumble cheese coarsely and sprinkle over salad in a ring.
6. Wrap each anchovy around an olive and place inside ring of cheese.
7. Sprinkle oregano over all.

Per serving: 252 Cal. (74% from fat), 8 g protein, 9 g carbohydrate, 21 g fat, 34 mg cholesterol, 2.7 g fiber, 620 mg sodium.

Moussaka
(Baked Eggplant, Lamb, and Tomatoes with Cream Sauce)
Serves 8 to 10

4	medium eggplants
	salt
2	pounds ground lamb
3	onions, chopped
2	tablespoons tomato paste
½	cup tomato sauce
¼	cup parsley, chopped
	salt and pepper to taste

½ cup water
  dash cinnamon
½ cup grated Parmesan cheese
½ cup bread crumbs
3 tablespoons margarine
3 tablespoons all-purpose flour
3 cups skim milk
  salt and pepper to taste
  dash nutmeg
4 egg yolks, lightly beaten
  olive oil
  grated Parmesan cheese

1. Remove ½-inch wide strips of peel, lengthwise, from eggplants, leaving ½ inch peel between the strips.
2. Cut eggplant into thick slices. Sprinkle slices with salt and let stand between two heavy plates while browning meat and making sauce.
3. In large skillet, sautè ground lamb and onions until meat is browned.
4. Add tomato paste, tomato sauce, parsley, salt, pepper, and water. Simmer until liquid is absorbed; cool.
5. Add cinnamon, cheese, and half of the bread crumbs to meat mixture. Set aside.
6. In a medium saucepan, melt the margarine over low heat.
7. Add flour and stir until well blended.
8. Remove from heat. Gradually stir in cold milk.
9. When mixture is smooth, return to heat and cook, stirring until sauce is thick and smooth.
10. Add salt, pepper, and nutmeg to taste.
11. Combine egg yolks with a little of the hot sauce, then stir egg mixture into sauce and cook over very low heat for 2 minutes, stirring constantly. Set aside.
12. Preheat oven to 350°F.
13. In large skillet, heat oil.
14. Brown eggplant slices on both sides.
15. Grease an ovenproof casserole and sprinkle bottom with remaining bread crumbs. Cover with layer of eggplant slices, then a layer of meat. Repeat layering until all eggplant and meat have been used, finishing with a layer of eggplant.
16. Cover with sauce, sprinkle with grated cheese and bake 1 hour or until hot and bubbly.

Per serving: 330 Cal. (43% from fat), 25 g protein, 22 g carbohydrate, 16 g fat, 190 mg cholesterol, 4.2 g fiber, 399 mg sodium.

Psomi
(Greek Bread)
Makes 2 loaves

3¾ to 4¼ cups all-purpose flour
       1 package active dry yeast
     1⅓ cups skim milk
       2 tablespoons sugar
1 tablespoon plus 1 teaspoon shortening
     1½ teaspoons salt
         melted margarine
         sesame seeds

1. In large mixing bowl, combine 1½ cups flour and yeast.

from *The Foods of Greece* by Aglaia Kremezi

Typical ingredients in Greek cuisine include peppers, tomatoes, onions, lemons, and olive oil.

2. Combine milk, sugar, shortening, and salt in saucepan and heat until warm (110° to 115°F) (Shortening does not need to be completely melted.)
3. Add warm milk mixture to yeast and flour. Beat on low speed of electric mixer (or with wooden spoon) ½ minute (75 strokes) scraping the sides of the bowl often.
4. Beat an additional 3 minutes at high speed (900 strokes). Add enough additional flour to make a soft dough.
5. Turn dough out onto lightly floured board or pastry cloth and knead until smooth and elastic (about 8 to 10 minutes).
6. Place dough in lightly greased bowl, turning once to grease top. Cover with a clean towel and let rise in a warm place until doubled in bulk (about 1½ hours).
7. Punch dough down and divide in half. Shape each half into a round loaf.
8. Place loaves on a lightly greased baking sheet. Brush tops with melted margarine and sprinkle with sesame seeds. Cover with a clean towel and let rise in a warm place until almost doubled in bulk (about 1 hour).
9. Bake loaves at 375°F until they are golden brown and sound hollow when gently tapped with the knuckles.
10. Remove breads to cooling racks and cool thoroughly before storing.

Per slice: 65 Cal. (10% from fat), 2 g protein, 13 g carbohydrate, 1 g fat, 0 mg cholesterol, 0.4 g fiber, 106 mg sodium.

Kourambiedes
(Walnut Cookies)
Makes 3 dozen cookies

¾ pound margarine
3 tablespoons confectioners' sugar
½ teaspoon vanilla
1½ teaspoons baking powder
3½ cups all-purpose flour, minus 1 tablespoon
½ cup finely chopped walnuts
½ cup confectioners' sugar

1. Melt margarine in small saucepan and cool to lukewarm.
2. Preheat oven to 350°F.
3. In large mixing bowl, combine melted margarine, 3 tablespoons sugar, vanilla, and baking powder; stir with a wooden spoon until mixed.
4. Add flour, ¼ cup at a time, beating well after each addition.
5. Add walnuts, stirring until mixed.
6. On lightly floured board, roll about 2 tablespoons of dough into an S-shaped rope, 6 inches long and ¼ inch thick. Repeat with remaining dough.
7. Place cookies 1 inch apart on baking sheet. Bake until light brown, about 15 minutes.
8. Sprinkle with remaining confectioners' sugar.

Per cookie: 130 Cal. (60% from fat), 2 g protein, 12 g carbohydrate, 9 g fat, 0 mg cholesterol, 0.4 g fiber, 102 mg sodium.

Summary

The mild climate of the Mediterranean region is favorable for the growth of a bounty of fruits and vegetables. These foods, along with fish from the sea, appear in a variety of dishes throughout Spain, Italy, and Greece. Despite common ingredients, however, each of these countries has a distinct cuisine.

Spanish cuisine is simple and colorful, focusing on the natural flavors of fresh ingredients. Spaniards enjoy an assortment of tapas at the beginning of meals or while socializing with friends. Attractive salads and flavorful soups are popular throughout Spain. Main dishes like cocido and paella include a variety of ingredients cooked together to produce a blend of flavors. Breads, tortillas, vegetables, and desserts round out Spanish meals.

Italy was the center of the Roman Empire, the birthplace of the Renaissance, and the home of the Roman Catholic Church. The foods of Italy are as notable as its cultural heritage. Italian cuisine focuses on fresh fruits and vegetables, a variety of seasonings, and rangetop cooking methods. Pasta, rice, and seafood are staples of the Italian diet.

The cuisine in each of Italy's three main geographic regions has distinct features. In Northern Italy, foods are cooked in butter, and homemade, ribbon-shaped pastas are popular. This region is also known for its soups, sausages, and risottos. The Central region is known for roasted lamb and cheesecake from Rome and grilled meats and bean dishes from Tuscany. In the South, cooks use olive oil and tubular pastas. This region is the home of rich tomato sauces, stuffed lasagne, and pizza.

Greek cuisine has been evolving for centuries. Staple foods of the Greek diet include lamb, seafood, olives, and honey. Lemon juice, tomatoes, green peppers, garlic, and eggplant also appear in many Greek dishes. Greek cooks flavor their foods with a number of herbs and spices.

Review What You Have Read

Write your answers on a separate sheet of paper.
1. Name the three culinary advances the Moors made to Spanish cuisine.
2. Spanish meals often begin with appetizers called _____.
3. What is the difference between tortillas in Spain and tortillas in Mexico?
4. Why is Italian cuisine known as the "mother cuisine?"
5. Describe three different ways Italians may serve pasta.
6. True or false. Northern Italian cooks favor olive oil for cooking, but Southern Italian cooks prefer butter.
7. List the courses that would make up a typical noon meal in Italy. Give an example of a food that might be served for each course.
8. Name three dishes invading groups of people contributed to Greek cuisine and two foods that are native to Greece.
9. Which of the following foods would most likely be served as a main dish in Greece?
   A. Avgolemono.
   B. Diples.
   C. Moussaka.
   D. Taramasalata.
10. What is the basic sweetener used in the preparation of many Greek desserts, pastries, and cakes?

Build Your Basic Skills

1. Research the similarities and differences between Spanish and Mexican cuisine. Summarize your findings in a two-page written report.
2. Prepare a time line illustrating major events in Italian history from the Roman Empire to today. Explain to the class the significance of one of the events shown on your time line.

Build Your Thinking Skills

1. Working in lab groups, research and prepare a regional version of paella. Each group should choose a different version. Serve all the paellas buffet-style. Analyze the major differences that are apparent among the dishes.
2. Plan to turn your classroom into a Greek taverna. Divide the class into four groups. One group should find appropriate music and learn a traditional Greek dance to teach the rest of the class. One group should be responsible for decorations. One group should learn a few Greek games to teach the rest of the class. The fourth group should choose a menu of Greek appetizers and find recipes to distribute. Each group should prepare one of the appetizer recipes.

Chapter 30
Middle East and Africa

A "Taste" of the World of Work

Foreign Correspondent
Collects and analyzes information about newsworthy events to write news stories for publication or broadcast.

Travel Clerk
Plans itinerary and schedules travel accommodations for military and civilian personnel and dependents according to travel orders, using knowledge of routes, types of carriers, and travel regulations.

Moshgiach
Supervises workers engaged in storing, preparing, and cooking meats, poultry, and other foods in restaurants, catering halls, hospitals, or other establishments to ensure observance of Hebrew dietary laws and customs.

Terms to Know

bulgur	pareve foods
mazza	matzo meal
chelo kebab	felafel
kibbutzim	cacao
kashrut	Kwanzaa
kosher	pita bread
shohet	injera
milchig foods	teff
fleishig foods	wat

Objectives

After studying this chapter, you will be able to
❏ describe the food customs of the Middle East and Africa.
❏ discuss how climate, geography, and culture have influenced these customs.
❏ recognize and prepare foods that are native to each of these countries or regions.

The Consulate General of Israel to the Midwest
Baruch Gian, photographer

The Middle East and Africa cover a large area. These regions are home to people of several races and many nationalities. They speak a number of major languages and hundreds of dialects.

Geographical features in the Middle East and Africa vary widely. In Egypt, the hot, dry, sandy desert stretches for miles. In Eastern Africa, rugged, snowcapped mountains rise above the arid plains. Along the equator, tropical rain forests boast lush vegetation.

The climate limits the types of foods that are available in each of the countries in this area. Strict religious doctrines also restrict the foods that many Middle Eastern and African people can eat. These factors have caused a number of distinct cuisines to emerge in these regions.

Cooking styles vary. However, there are some similarities in foods from this part of the world. For instance, many foods eaten in Israel originated in Africa and other Middle Eastern countries.

Play It Safe

Before leaving for a trip, contact the post office to have your mail held. Also stop delivery of any newspapers you receive. Set timers to turn lights on and off and play the TV or radio. Arrange to have someone care for your lawn, too. Making these arrangements will create the appearance that someone is in your home. This will make your home seem less inviting to would-be intruders.

As you read about these regions, you will become more familiar with their cultures, climates, and customs. You will begin to identify differences and similarities in their cuisines.

George A. Fischer

In the Middle Eastern country of Turkey, over 98 percent of the people are Muslims. Beautiful Islamic houses of worship, called mosques, *were built throughout Turkey in the thirteenth century.*

Middle East

Turkish Tourism Office, Washington, DC

Open-air bazaars filled with carpets, baskets, metal wares, and food are common throughout the Middle East.

The Middle East forms a large horseshoe from the eastern edge of the Mediterranean Sea to North Africa. History in this part of the world dates back for centuries. This land is the cradle of civilization. Christianity, Judaism, and Islam began in this region. This is where the Byzantine, Persian, Arab, and Ottoman Empires flourished.

Much of the land in the Middle East is arid and desolate. However, fertile oases dot the deserts, mountain valleys, and treeless plateaus.

The exact boundaries of the Middle East are sometimes disputed. However, the countries of Turkey, Iran, Iraq, Syria, Lebanon, Jordan, Israel, and Egypt form its center. (Because the foods of Israel have unique characteristics, Israel will be discussed separately.) Trading and shipping in these countries are as important today as they were in the days of the Turkish sultans.

Climate and Geography of the Middle East

Seven major bodies of water border the eight nations that form the core of the Middle East. These are the Mediterranean, Aegean, Black, Caspian, and Red Seas; the Persian Gulf; and the Indian Ocean.

Mountains and high plateaus are important geographical features of all the countries, and deserts are located in all but Turkey. Three of the world's most famous rivers, the Nile, the Tigris, and the Euphrates, are in the Middle East. The Dardanellas and Bosporus Straits in western Turkey form a gateway between Europe and Asia.

Much of the Middle East is dry and hilly. Scattered throughout the area are naturally fertile areas. The lands along the banks of the Nile, Tigris, and Euphrates Rivers are among the world's richest. Coastal lands and inland mountain valleys also are excellent farming areas.

Rainfall varies in the Middle East. Villages in northern Egypt may not have rain for 10 or 20 years. However, cities along the coasts of Turkey may have 20 to 30 inches (50 to 70 cm) of rain during one season. As a whole, however, much of the Middle East is hot and dry, so irrigation is essential. When rain does fall, it is often so heavy that flooding occurs.

The climate along the Mediterranean coasts is subtropical with warm, dry summers and mild, rainy winters. Mountain valleys have hot, dry summers and cool winters. Desert areas have daytime temperatures above 100°F (38°C) and little if any rain.

Middle Eastern Culture

Egypt has one of the world's oldest civilizations. Thousands of years before the birth of Christ, the Egyptians had reached a high level of civilization. They had an orderly government and a written language. They traded with other parts of the world and built great structures of stone.

Ancient Empires of the Middle East

Much of the history of the Middle East centers around large empires that rose to power, weakened, and fell. As each new group of people gained power, a great intermingling of cultures took place. The conquerors shared their manner of dress, food customs, religion, and way of life with those they conquered.

The first of the four greatest Middle Eastern empires was the Persian Empire. At its height, the Persian Empire stretched from the Aegean Sea to the Indus River and included Egypt. Today, the country of Iran is all that remains of this once mighty empire. However, beautiful Persian rugs, tapestries, metalwork, and architecture have been preserved.

The second great empire, the Byzantine Empire, formed when the Roman Empire split into East and West. It did much to preserve the many achievements of Ancient Greece and Rome. Its headquarters were in Constantinople, which later became the capital of the Ottoman Empire.

The followers of the prophet Muhammad formed the Arab Empire. This empire extended from Spain across North Africa and the Middle East into India. People in Middle Eastern countries where Islam is the primary faith still speak the Arabic language.

Eventually, the Ottoman Turks combined the Middle Eastern parts of the Persian, Byzantine, and Arab Empires. The last of the great empires, the Ottoman Empire, extended as far west as the Balkan States. As a result, Turkish foods and customs are evident in many parts of the Middle East.

Modern Culture in the Middle East

Today, many Middle Easterners make their living as farmers or herders. Sheep, goats, and camels graze on the short, stubby grasses of the arid regions, 30-1. They supply meat, milk (used to make yogurt and cheese), and hides. The Angora goat of Turkey is also the source of mohair fibers.

A variety of crops grow in areas where there are irrigation systems or where there is enough rain. Wheat and barley are the major grain crops. Corn grows in some areas, and large amounts of cotton grow in Egypt. Citrus fruits, Persian melons, olives, bananas, figs, grapes, and other fruits grow in the subtropical climate of the coastal regions. Other important agricultural products include sugar beets, rice, tobacco, and poppies. Families grow vegetables for home use on small plots of land.

As a whole, the Middle East is not highly industrial. Oil is the major natural resource. Iron ore and copper are mined in small amounts throughout the area. Textile and food processing industries are important in Lebanon and Turkey. Caviar and hand-woven rugs and other handicrafts are important Iranian exports. Trade has always been an important industry for the Middle East. Today, Beirut, the capital of Lebanon, is a busy port. Much of Lebanon's prosperity depends on trade with nations in the Middle East and elsewhere.

Cairo, Alexandria, Istanbul, Beirut, Teheran, and Baghdad are major cities of the Middle East. They are filled with modern buildings and businesses. However, visitors can still find narrow streets lined with open-air booths. There, vendors sell spices, metalwork, colorful fabrics, and native foods.

Middle Eastern Cuisine

Middle Eastern cuisine has been developing for centuries. As traders crossed the deserts and one group of people conquered another, recipes were exchanged and modified. As a result, it is often difficult to determine the exact origin of a particular dish.

Foods Found Throughout the Middle East

Basic to all Middle Eastern cooking are five ingredients: garlic, lemon, green pepper, eggplant, and tomato. These ingredients appear again and again in dishes served throughout the area. Also basic is the taboo against eating pork. Both Judaism and Islam forbid their followers to eat the meat of swine.

Both olives and olive oil are common in Middle Eastern cuisine. Olives come in a variety of shapes, sizes, and colors. People eat them as appetizers and snacks. They use olive oil in place of butter or lard for cooking. Fresh olive oil gives a special flavor to Middle Eastern foods.

Spice caravans were once a common sight in the Middle East. Therefore, it seems only natural to expect cooks to use spices liberally. Middle Eastern foods are not spicy hot. Instead, spices and herbs add delicate flavor to foods.

In the Middle East, lamb is the staple meat. It is often roasted whole. Chunks of lamb sometimes are threaded on skewers and served as *shish kebabs* or added to hearty stews. Ground lamb is used to make dolmas. *Dolmas* are a mixture of ground meat and seasonings wrapped in grape leaves or stuffed into vegetables.

Middle Eastern yogurt is curdled milk with a tangy flavor. It is not at all like the yogurt eaten in the United States. People throughout the Middle East eat it as a side dish, snack, and dessert. They also use it to make cakes and hot and cold soups. In some areas, people serve diluted yogurt as a beverage.

Middle Eastern Grains and Legumes

Wheat, beans, rice, lentils, and chick-peas are the staple grains and legumes of the Middle East. Middle Easterners use wheat flour to make bread. In Middle Eastern countries, bread is holy. If someone drops it on the floor, he or she must pick it up and kiss it. Middle Eastern people serve bread at every meal and often buy it from the village baker twice a day.

Courtesy of Abercrombie & Kent

30-1 Many Middle Easterners herd camels and other animals.

Middle Eastern people also serve wheat as bulgur. **Bulgur** is a grain product made from whole wheat that has been cooked, dried, partly debranned, and cracked. Midddle Easterners add bulgur to soups, stews, stuffings, and salads. They also serve it as a side dish with ground lamb, 30-2. *Felafel* is a deep-fried mixture of bulgur, ground chick-peas, and spices. Street vendors sell felafel and people eat it much as people in the United States eat hot dogs.

Rice is as popular as bulgur, and in Iran, it is even more popular. People in the Middle East often serve rice plain. However, they may cook it with tomato juice or saffron and make it into *pilav* (rice pilaf).

Middle Eastern Dessert and Coffee

Middle Eastern people, as a group, enjoy sweets and rich desserts. However, they usually eat these foods as snacks or serve them on special holidays. They eat fruit at the end of most meals. Quince, pomegranates, figs, and melons are particularly popular.

People throughout most of the Middle East drink coffee. (Iran is an exception. There, tea is the main beverage.) All Middle Eastern coffee is strong, but it can be prepared in several ways. People who make *khave* (Turkish-style coffee) use a long-handled pot with a wide bottom and thin neck. They combine and heat water, coffee, and sugar just until the mixture begins to foam. They quickly remove the pot from the heat. Then they return the pot to the heat once or twice to again build up the foam. Finally, they pour the foaming liquid into small cups and top it with the remaining coffee, grounds and all. More sugar can be added if desired. *Arab-style coffee* rarely contains sugar. People who make this type of coffee bring it to a boil only once. They pour it into a second pot to get rid of the grounds and sediment. They may add cloves and cardamom seeds before serving.

Middle Eastern cuisine tends to bridge differences among the people of the region. Even so, each Middle Eastern country has developed a distinct style of cooking.

Turkish Foods

Turkish food customs had their beginnings in the days of the Ottoman sultans. The cooking of modern Turkey still is richly varied, somewhat exotic, and often extravagant.

30-2 Bulgur is a filling Middle Eastern side dish made from wheat.

The waters that border Turkey on three sides provide a variety of fish and shellfish. Seafood vendors in Istanbul sell lobster, salty red caviar, jumbo shrimp, mussels, haddock, bass, and mackerel.

Lamb is the most readily available and most popular meat. Lamb cubes marinated in a mixture of olive oil, lemon juice, and onions are threaded onto skewers and charcoal-broiled. Rice, sliced tomatoes, and bread often accompany this dish, which is called *shish kebab*. Another type of kebab, the *döner kebab,* is a large cone made of thin pieces of lamb. As the cone rotates over a bed of charcoal, the outside slices of meat become crisp and flavorful. Turkish cooks slice these crisp pieces from the cone with large knives. They serve the meat with a salad, onion rings, cucumbers, and tomato slices. By the time they serve one helping, the next layer of meat has become crisp.

Stuffed vegetables, cacik, and pilav are other common Turkish foods. *Cacik* is slices of cucumber in a yogurt sauce flavored with mint; *pilav* is rice pilaf. Turkish cooks may serve pilav plain or mix it with currants, nuts, and tomato sauce.

Snacking is popular in Turkey. Nuts, pumpkin seeds, and toasted chick-peas are favorite snack foods. The cry, "Semit!" is heard in the streets of Istanbul as vendors sell crisp bracelets of bread from the long poles they carry. Other vendors look like walking refreshment stands. Each carries a container of a sweet, fruit-flavored syrup, a jug of water, and a rack of glasses. The vendor mixes a little of the syrup with some of the water and sells the beverage by the glass.

Sweets are popular in Turkey. *Halva* is a candylike sweet made from farina or semolina and sugar. *Baklava* is a sweet pastry made from phyllo, nuts, and honey. *Kurabiye* is a rich butter cookie. *Rahat lokum* (Turkish delight) is a candylike sweet made from grape jelly coated with powdered sugar. Other sweets have even more exotic names. The "vizier's finger" is a sweet roll fried in olive oil until crisp. A "lady's navel" is a deep-fried fritter with a depression in the center. "Sweetheart's lips" are rounds of dough filled with nuts and folded in a way that resembles human lips.

Foods of the Arab States

The countries of Lebanon, Iraq, Jordan, Syria, Saudi Arabia, and Egypt are often called the *Arab States*. The Arab States include the area once called the *Fertile Crescent*. This is where people first learned to grow crops.

People can buy a variety of spices at bazaars throughout the Arab world. Vendors scoop cinnamon, cumin, ginger, coriander, allspice, and hot peppers onto pieces of paper, which they roll into cones. Arab cooks add spices to many dishes. They use rose water and orange-flower water to flavor their sweets.

No Arab meal is complete without **mazza** (appetizers). *Arak,* an anise-flavored liquor, is usually served with the mazza. One kind of mazza, called *tabbouleh,* is actually a salad. It is made of chopped tomatoes, radishes, green and white onions, parsley, mint, and bulgur. See 30-3. People break off pieces of *shrak* (a flat bread) and use them to scoop up the tabbouleh.

Islam law forbids the eating of pork, but the Arabs enjoy both camel and lamb. Camel, boiled in sour milk until it is tender, is popular among the nomadic Bedouin people. Most other Arabs prefer lamb.

Kibbi (called *kibbi* in Syria, *kobba* in Jordan, and *kubba* in Iraq) is a popular Arab lamb dish. Arab cooks pound raw lamb and bulgur into a paste and shape it into flat patties or hollow balls. They fry the patties. They stuff the hollow balls with ground lamb, pine nuts, rice, or vegetables and either bake or broil them.

Arab cooks love both color and pattern, and they use both lavishly. For example, they often garnish hummus with red pepper, green parsley, and brown cumin. *Hummus* is a mixture of chick-peas and sesame paste. They serve torshi the way people serve pickle relish in the United States. *Torshi* is a mixture of pickled turnips, onions, peppers, eggplant, cucumbers, and occasionally beets. They use saffron to give a bright gold color to a variety of dishes.

Along the eastern Mediterranean coastline, fishers catch a variety of fish daily. Cooks quickly clean mullet, sea bass, turbot, swordfish, cod, sardines, and other fish. Then they bake or poach the fish or cook them over charcoal. Restaurants that line the riverbanks of the Tigris serve smoked shabait (a kind of trout).

Bedouins are a nomadic group of Arabs. In the tent of a Bedouin *sheikh,* or chief, it is customary to dine on the rug-covered floor. The sheikh's family members serve trays covered with Arab bread, rice, pine nuts, almonds, and lamb. According to Arab custom, diners must eat the food with the right hand only. At the end of the meal, coffee and tea are served in small cups.

Iranian Foods

The Persians (predecessors of the present day Iranians) laid the foundation for Middle Eastern cooking. Scholars believe that wine, cheese, sherbet, and ice cream were first made in Persia. The Persians

National Live Stock and Meat Board

30-3 Tabbouleh, served here with lamb kebabs, is a Middle Eastern salad.

were also the first to extract the essence of roses and combine exotic herbs and spices with foods.

For centuries, rice has been the staple food of the Iranians. They serve many different kinds of rice dishes. All of these dishes belong to one of two groups: chelo or polo. *Chelo* is plain boiled, buttered rice served with *khoresh* (a topping made of varied sauces, vegetables, fruits, and meats). *Polo* is similar to pilaf in that all the accompaniments cook with the rice.

Iran's national dish is called **chelo kebab.** The kebab consists of thin slices of marinated, charcoal-broiled lamb. Three accompaniments are served with the chelo: a pat of butter, a raw egg, and a bowl of sumac. Each diner combines these accompaniments with the chelo.

Iran's proximity to the Caspian Sea with its many sturgeon makes caviar a bargain. (*Caviar* is the processed eggs of a large fish, often the sturgeon.) Over 95 percent of the world's caviar comes from the Caspian Sea.

Iranians use yogurt to make a variety of hot and cold soups. One popular version contains grated cucumber and is served with a topping of raisins and fresh mint leaves. When combined with plain or carbonated water, yogurt becomes a refreshing drink.

Iranians are not quite as fond of rich pastries as other Middle Easterners. They eat fresh fruits instead. Iran produces some of the finest Persian melons, watermelons, peaches, pomegranates, apricots, quinces, dates, pears, and grapes. Iranians often eat these fruits plain. However, sometimes they slice and sweeten the fruits and serve them with crushed ice or make them into sherbets.

Good Manners Are Good Business

Follow the lead of your host when dining with a Middle Eastern business associate. Be ready to eat with your fingers if he or she does so. Also, remember to eat only with your right hand.

Middle Eastern Menu

Shish Kebab
(Chunks of Meat Threaded on Skewers)
Pilav
(Rice Pilaf)
Mast va Khiar
(Cucumber and Yogurt Salad)
Pita Bread
(Pocket Bread)
Baklava
(Layered Pastry with Walnuts and Honey Syrup)
Khave
(Turkish Coffee)

Shish Kebabs
(Chunks of Meat Threaded on Skewers)
Serves 8

1   large onion
4   tablespoons vegetable oil
½   cup lemon juice
1   teaspoon salt
½   teaspoon pepper
½   teaspoon garlic powder
2   pounds lean, boneless lamb cut into 2-inch cubes
4   large tomatoes, quartered
4   large green peppers, cut into chunks
¼   cup evaporated skim milk

1. Remove papery covering from onion and slice into rings.
2. Put onion rings into deep pan. Add oil, lemon juice, salt, pepper, and garlic powder.
3. Add lamb cubes to marinade and stir well. Cover and place in refrigerator for at least 4 hours, turning lamb occasionally.
4. Preheat broiler.
5. Thread lamb cubes on eight long skewers.
6. Thread tomato quarters and green pepper chunks on two more skewers.
7. Place skewers of meat side by side along the length of a deep roasting pan. Brush meat with evaporated milk.
8. Broil 4 inches from the heat, turning occasionally, until meat reaches the desired degree of doneness, about 10 minutes for pink lamb and 15 minutes for well-done lamb.
9. Add vegetables to roasting pan about a third of the way through the cooking period. Watch carefully and remove when tender. Serve lamb with broiled vegetables and pilav.

Per serving: 157 Cal. (42% from fat), 16 g protein, 7 g carbohydrate, 7 g fat, 50 mg cholesterol, 1.8 g fiber, 133 mg sodium.

Pilav
(Rice Pilaf)
Serves 6 to 8

2   tablespoons margarine
1½   cups raw white rice
3   cups chicken stock
     salt
     pepper
1   tablespoon melted margarine

1. In heavy saucepan, melt 2 tablespoons margarine.
2. Add rice and stir for several minutes to evenly coat rice with fat. (Do not let rice brown.)
3. Add chicken stock and salt and pepper to taste.
4. Bring mixture to a boil, stirring constantly.
5. Cover pan and simmer rice slowly for 20 minutes or until all the liquid has been absorbed.
6. Add melted margarine, stir with a fork.
7. Let rice stand, covered with a clean towel, for 20 minutes before serving.

Per serving: 224 Cal. (24% from fat), 3 g protein, 38 g carbohydrate, 6 g fat, 0 mg cholesterol, 1.2 g fiber, 160 mg sodium.

Mast va Khiar
(Cucumber and Yogurt Salad)
Serves 8

2   medium cucumbers
4   tablespoons finely chopped green pepper
3   tablespoons finely chopped green onion
2   tablespoons dried taragon or dill
1   teaspoon lime juice
½   teaspoon salt
2   cups plain yogurt

1. Wash cucumbers and peel.
2. Slice each cucumber in half lengthwise. Scoop out seeds, and chop cucumber coarsely.

3. Put cucumber in a deep bowl and add green pepper, green onion, tarragon or dill, lime juice, and salt. Mix well.
4. Add yogurt and stir to coat vegetables.
5. Chill at least one hour before serving.

Per serving: 40 Cal. (4% from fat), 4 g protein, 6 g carbohydrate, 0 g fat, 1 mg cholesterol, 0.3 g fiber, 178 mg sodium.

Pita Bread
(Pocket Bread)
Makes 18

5 to 6 cups all-purpose flour
    1 package active dry yeast
    2 cups water
    2 tablespoons sugar
  1½ teaspoons salt

1. In large mixing bowl, stir together 2 cups flour and yeast.
2. Heat water, sugar, and salt over low heat until warm (105° to 115°F), stirring to blend.
3. Add liquid ingredients to flour mixture and beat until smooth, about 2 minutes on medium speed of electric mixer.
4. Add 1 cup flour and beat 1 minute more.
5. Stir in enough additional flour to make a moderately stiff dough.
6. Turn dough out onto lightly floured board or pastry cloth and knead until smooth and satiny, about 18 to 20 minutes.
7. Divide dough into 18 portions. Roll each into a 3-inch circle.
8. Place circles on lightly greased baking sheet. Cover with a clean towel and let rise in warm place until doubled, about 45 minutes.
9. Bake on middle shelf of preheated 450°F oven, 10 to 12 minutes or until lightly browned. Cool.

Per pita: 133 Cal. (2% from fat), 4 g protein, 28 g carbohydrate, 0 g fat, 0 mg cholesterol, 1.0 g fiber, 179 mg sodium.

Baklava
(Layered Pastry with Walnuts and Honey Syrup)
Makes about 3 dozen

  4 cups walnuts
  5 tablespoons sugar
  1 teaspoon cinnamon
    dash ground cloves
  1 pound phyllo (30 sheets Greek pastry dough)
1½ cups melted margarine
  2 cups sugar

  1 cup water
  1 tablespoon lemon juice
 ½ cup honey
  4 thin slices lemon
    3-inch cinnamon stick, broken
  2 teaspoons vanilla

1. Butter a 13 x 9 x 2-inch pan.
2. Finely chop walnuts.
3. In mixing bowl, combine walnuts, sugar, cinnamon, and cloves; set aside.
4. Place 2 sheets of phyllo pastry in pan, folding edges to fit pan. Brush evenly with melted margarine. Continue layering phyllo until 10 sheets of phyllo have been used.
5. Sprinkle 1 cup nut mixture over the buttered top sheet. Repeat; layering three times using 5 sheets to form pastry layers and ending with 5 sheets on top.
6. Preheat oven to 350°F.
7. With a very sharp knife, cut the baklava into diamond-shaped pieces.
8. Heat remaining margarine until very hot and pour over top.
9. Bake baklava for 30 minutes.
10. Reduce heat to 300°F and continue to bake for 45 minutes more.
11. While baklava is baking, prepare syrup. In medium saucepan, combine sugar, water, lemon juice, honey, lemon slices, and cinnamon. Bring to a boil, stirring until sugar is dissolved.
12. Simmer syrup uncovered 10 minutes.
13. Remove lemon slices and cinnamon stick.
14. Add vanilla and pour syrup over hot pastry. Cool.

Per serving: 267 Cal. (62% from fat), 3 g protein, 24 g carbohydrate, 19 g fat, 0 mg cholesterol, 0.9 g fiber, 152 mg sodium.

Turkish Tourism Office, Washington, DC

As this döner kebab rotates near a heat source, the outer layer of the lamb meat becomes crisp and tasty. The cook then slices off pieces of the meat to serve as a popular Turkish food.

Israel

The Consulate General of Israel to the Midwest
Baruch Gian, photographer

Three fourths of the people in Israel are Jewish. These men are ultra-Orthodox Jews.

To Jewish people throughout the world, the date May 14, 1948, has a special meaning. On this date, the state of Israel was established. Israel was founded on the land that had been called *Palestine* for centuries. This land was the birthplace of the Jews. For the first time in more than 2,000 years, Jews were able to govern themselves.

Since 1948, Israel has grown at a tremendous rate. Irrigation systems and modern farming techniques have increased agricultural production. Heavy industry flourishes in Haifa, Israel's largest seaport. Tel Aviv is one of the most modern cities in the world. As the home of many talented writers, artists, and musicians, Israel also has flourished as a cultural center.

Climate and Geography of Israel

The Mediterranean Sea forms Israel's western border. Along this coast are three of Israel's major cities—Haifa, Tel Aviv, and Jaffa. The northern part of the country borders Syria and Lebanon. There the land rises from a fertile coastal plain to the hills of Galilee. Galilee's scattered green valleys are suitable for agriculture. To the east is the Jordan River, which separates Israel from Jordan. To the south lies the triangular Negev Desert bordered by Egypt and the Red Sea.

Israel has four climatic regions. Along the Mediterranean Sea, summers are warm, and winters are mild with occasional rain. In the central highlands, summers are again warm and dry, but the winters are cold and wet. The Negev Desert is hot and dry in the summer and cool and dry in the winter. The Jordan Valley has hot, dry summers and mild winters. Almost no rain falls in Israel from May to October. This makes irrigation necessary for the production of most crops.

Israeli Culture

Over 80 percent of Israel's citizens are Jewish. According to the Bible, the Jews are the descendants of Abraham. Around 5,000 years ago, the descendants of Abraham, known as the Hebrew tribes, settled in Canaan (later called Palestine). Several centuries later, the Hebrew tribes became slaves of the Egyptian pharaohs. Under the leadership of Moses, the Hebrews completed their long journey out of Egypt into the Promised Land of Palestine.

Periods of peace followed by revolts, invasions, and foreign rule mark the history of Palestine. The Jewish population gradually dwindled. Some Jews were killed or sold into slavery. Some fled to nearby Middle Eastern countries and to other countries around the world. The Jews were physically separated from their homeland and from one another. Even so, they were able to keep their identity and religion. Jews around the world waited for the time when they could return to the place of their birth.

The movement of Jews back into Palestine began in the second half of the nineteenth century. However, the present state of Israel was not declared until 1948. Since that time, territorial disputes with neighboring Arabs have marked Israeli history. Even so, growth and progress continue at a rapid rate.

Almost all the fruits and vegetables eaten in Israel are grown there. Guavas, citrus fruits, mangoes, dates, bananas, avocados, and melons are some of the most popular fruits. Cattle, sheep, poultry, and fish are also available from local sources. Cattle breeds that are suitable for the semiarid land are raised. Fresh fish and ducks are scientifically raised on farm ponds.

Many of the farms in Israel operate as collective communities called *kibbutzim*. Members of a kibbutz own their property collectively and live together in a cluster of dwellings. They receive no wages for their work, but all of their needs are met. Food, clothing, medical care, entertainment (movies, concerts, plays, and lectures), and even haircuts and newspapers are supplied. Children who live in a kibbutz are educated communally according to age. A kibbutz may have from 30 to 2,000 members and may or may not have a few small industries.

About 90 percent of Israelis are town dwellers. Roughly 25 percent live in the three major cities of Haifa, Tel Aviv, and Jerusalem.

Jerusalem, Israel's capital, has been an important city to people of many nationalities and religions for centuries. Millions of men, women, and children have fought over it and died for it. Jerusalem is called the "Holy City" by Christians, Jews, and Muslims.

Israeli Cuisine

When the Jews fled from Palestine, they settled in many parts of the world. Thus Jewish cuisine is multinational. This is most noticeable in Israel. For there, people of 80 nationalities have added their foods to the area's native Middle Eastern cuisine. Borscht, sauerbraten, and shish kebab might be listed in an Israeli cookbook along with kreplach, challah, and blintzes.

Besides this mixture of native and ethnic Jewish foods, Israeli cooks have developed totally new dishes. These dishes are based on foods readily available in Israel. Many of them contain fish, poultry, and fresh fruit.

Jewish Dietary Laws

People in most Israeli homes and restaurants observe the Jewish *kashrut* (dietary laws). Foods prepared according to the dietary laws are considered *kosher*. See 30-4.

The first of these laws concerns foods that are suitable for eating. Only animals that have cloven (split) hoofs and chew their cud are considered fit to eat. Therefore, Jews cannot eat pigs because pigs do not chew their cud. Fish must have both scales and fins. Therefore, people cannot eat shellfish. They can eat domestic fowl, but not wild fowl. Cooks must carefully check vegetables and cereals to be sure they are free of insects. They must break eggs into a separate dish and inspect them for blood spots before using them. Manufactured products must not contain any nonkosher ingredients.

Other dietary laws describe the proper methods of slaughter. According to these laws, a *shohet* (licensed slaughterer) must slaughter all animals and fowl. The shohet slashes the jugular vein of the

The Consulate General of Israel to the Midwest
Baruch Gian, photographer

30-4 Many restaurants in Israel serve kosher foods.

animal with one stroke of a sharp knife. All blood must then be drained. The meat or poultry first is soaked in water. Then it is salted and rinsed in several changes of clean water.

There are distinctions between *milchig* (dairy) and *fleishig* (meat) foods. People cannot cook or eat milchig and fleishig foods together. For this reason, kosher kitchens contain two complete sets of eating, serving, and food preparation utensils. Cooks use one set for milchig foods. They use the other set for fleishig foods. People may eat fleishig foods after milchig foods—but only if they thoroughly cleanse their mouth first. They cannot eat milchig foods for three hours after fleishig foods.

Foods that are neither milchig nor fleishig are called *pareve* foods. Pareve foods include eggs, fruits, vegetables, cereals, fish, and baked goods made with vegetable shortening. Except for fish, pareve foods can be prepared and eaten with both milk and meat dishes.

Traditional Jewish Dishes

Some Jewish foods are considered traditional. Most of these foods are very old. Jewish cooks all over the world prepare and serve them.

For centuries, soups have played an important part in Jewish cooking. They are hot, filling, and relatively inexpensive. Soups may be clear or thick. Chicken soup is perhaps the best-known clear soup. Lentil soup is perhaps the best-known thick soup. Other popular soups include borscht, barley and bean, and fruit soup.

Jewish cooks serve many Jewish soups with *knaidlach* or *mandlen*. Both are similar to dumplings and are frequently made with **matzo meal** (meal made from unleavened bread called matzos).

Gefilte fish is another popular Jewish dish. A variety of freshwater fish may be used to make gefilte fish. However, pike, carp, and whitefish are most common. First, the cook simmers the bones, skin, and heads of the fish in a seasoned stock. Then he or she minces the fish and mixes it with matzo meal, eggs, onion, sugar, seasonings, and water. The cook forms the mixture into balls the size of small dumplings. Then he or she either bakes the gefilte fish or simmers it in the fish stock with a few vegetables. See 30-5.

Chicken is both versatile and economical. Cooks boil and roast chicken and use it to make soup. Other popular Jewish chicken dishes include gizzards simmered in seasoned gravy. Chopped

The B. Manischewitz Company, Jersey City, NJ

30-5 Baked gefilte fish is a popular Jewish dish.

chicken liver and neck skin stuffed with seasoned bread crumbs are well-liked chicken dishes, too.

Homemade noodles and dumplings are frequent additions to soups, main dishes, and puddings. They also are used to make the popular kreplach. *Kreplach* are squares of noodle dough stuffed with a filling made of meat, cheese, potato, chicken, or chicken liver. Kreplach may also be stuffed with kasha, which is cooked buckwheat groats.

The Jewish *kugel* developed during the Middle Ages when vegetables were available only during harvest time. Kugels, which resemble puddings, were served in place of vegetables as side dishes. Today, kugels may contain vegetables, fruits, noodles, rice, or fish. A kugel may be a separate course or a side dish. Sweet kugels are often served for dessert.

Tzimmes literally means *fuss* or *excitement.* In the Jewish kitchen, however, tzimmes are combinations of meats, vegetables, and fruits. Although the cook's imagination determines the choice of ingredients, long, slow cooking improves the flavor of all tzimmes.

Blintzes, knishes, latkes, and challah have been Jewish specialties for centuries. *Blintzes* are thin pancakes similar to French crêpes. They contain eggs, milk (or water), oil, salt, and flour. Blintzes are browned on one side only. Then they are filled with a cheese or fruit filling and folded like a napkin with the browned side up. *Knishes* are dumplings. They may be filled with potato, cheese, meat, or chicken. *Latkes* (pancakes) can be made from matzo meal, buckwheat, or wheat flour. However, potato latkes, which are similar to German potato pancakes, are particularly popular. *Challah* is a braided, rich egg bread. Jewish people often serve it at holiday meals.

Middle Eastern Foods

Many of the foods found in Israel originated in other Middle Eastern countries. One of these foods, felafel, has become one of Israel's national dishes. **Felafel** is a mixture of ground chick-peas, bulgur, and spices that is formed into balls and deep-fried. The warm balls of felafel are tucked inside a half slice of Arab bread and served with a salad.

A variety of salads and colorful, spicy hot hashes have North African origins. *Couscous,* for example, is a thick, steamed semolina and porridge flavored with chicken and spices.

Leben is an Israeli delicacy. It is a type of cheese made from sour milk. Jewish people often serve it with crackers as an appetizer.

Israeli Additions

The citrus fruits, figs, dates, almonds, grapes, and melons that grow abundantly in Israel have inspired many new dishes. Turkey pieces coated with flour, browned, and stewed in orange juice with peas and mushrooms is uniquely Israeli. Avocado halves stuffed with a mixture of walnuts, pistachios, sour cherries, and marinated herring is a new native dish, too.

Two desserts are also uniquely Israeli. Sabra liqueur has the flavor of the Jaffa orange. Jewish cooks use it to make a rich dessert. They dip chocolate cookies into hot, strong coffee. Then they arrange the cookies in layers with whipped cream flavored with the liqueur. After chilling, the dessert is cut into pieces and served like a cake. The traditional honey cake is made in Israel with a new ingredient—instant coffee.

Israeli Menu

Lentil Soup
Gefilte Fish with Horseradish
Roasted Chicken
Noodle Kugel
(Noodle Pudding)
Avocado, Carrot, and Orange Salad
Challah
(Braided Egg Bread)
Honey Cake
Coffee

Lentil Soup
Serves 6 to 8

3   cups sliced onions
3   tablespoons vegetable oil
¾   pound ground lamb
2½   cups canned whole tomatoes, mashed slightly
1   cup diced celery
¾   cup diced carrots
¾   cup diced parsnips
¾   cup green pepper
3½   cups cold water
1   pound lentils
1   teaspoon salt
½   teaspoon pepper

1. In Dutch oven or large saucepan, sauté onions in oil until browned.
2. Add ground lamb and cook until lamb loses its pink color.
3. Add tomatoes, celery, carrots, parsnips, green pepper, water, lentils, and seasonings. Bring to a boil.
4. Reduce heat and cover pan. Simmer soup about 1½ hours or until lentils are tender.

Per serving: 394 Cal. (27% from fat), 27 g protein, 46 g carbohydrate, 12 g fat, 36 mg cholesterol, 11.1 g fiber, 449 mg sodium.

Gefilte Fish
Makes 6 to 8 appetizer servings

3   pounds whitefish
3   medium onions
2   eggs
1   teaspoon salt
½   cup cold water
3   onions
2   scraped carrots, diced
2   stalks celery, diced
3   teaspoons parsley
     boiling water

1. Slice fish into 2-inch strips, Remove all skin and bones.
2. Chop fish with onions.
3. Add eggs, ½ teaspoon salt, and cold water.
4. Shape into balls. Wrap a piece of fish skin around each ball.
5. In a large saucepan, place onions, carrots, celery, parsley, and remaining salt. Place the fish balls on top.
6. Slowly add boiling water, trying not to disturb fish balls. Bring to a boil.
7. Reduce heat and simmer for 2 hours without stirring.
8. Remove fish carefully to a bowl. Strain gravy over it and chill. Serve with horseradish.

Per serving: 300 Cal. (15% from fat), 50 g protein, 11 g carbohydrate, 5 g fat, 251 mg cholesterol, 4.6 g fiber, 681 mg sodium.

Roasted Chicken
Serves 8

2   roasting chickens, 2 pounds each
     margarine, softened
     salt and pepper

1. Preheat oven to 350°F.
2. Remove heart, liver, and giblets from chickens.
3. Rinse chickens under cool running water. Pat dry with paper towels.
4. Place breast side up on rack in roasting pan.
5. Rub skin with margarine. Sprinkle with salt and pepper.
6. Roast, uncovered, about 1 ½ hours or until juices run clear and drumstick moves easily.

Per serving: 345 Cal. (59% from fat), 34 g protein, 0 g carbohydrate, 22 g fat, 135 mg cholesterol, 0 g fiber, 146 mg sodium.

Noodle Kugel
(Noodle Pudding)
Serves 8

3   eggs
4   tablespoons light brown sugar
¼   teaspoon nutmeg
½   teaspoon cinnamon
4   cups cooked wide egg noodles
⅔   cup seedless raisins
½   cup sliced blanched almonds
1   tablespoon lemon juice
2   tablespoons melted margarine
3   tablespoons bread crumbs

1. Preheat oven to 350°F.
2. In large bowl, beat eggs until foamy.
3. Add brown sugar, nutmeg, and cinnamon and continue beating until well mixed.
4. Fold in noodles, raisins, almonds, lemon juice, and melted margarine.
5. Pour into a 1½ quart greased casserole or ring mold.
6. Sprinkle with bread crumbs.
7. Bake for 50 minutes or until browned.

Per serving: 277 Cal. (34% from fat), 8 g protein, 39 g carbohydrate, 11 g fat, 128 mg cholesterol, 2.5 g fiber, 83 mg sodium.

Challah
(Braided Egg Bread)
Makes 2 loaves

4½ to 5½   cups unsifted all-purpose flour
2   tablespoons sugar
1½   teaspoons salt
1   package active dry yeast
⅓   cup softened margarine
    pinch powdered saffron (optional)
1   cup very warm water (120° to 130°F)
3   eggs (at room temperature)
1   teaspoon cold water
1   teaspoon poppy seeds

1. In large mixing bowl, combine 1¼ cups flour, sugar, salt, and dry yeast.
2. Work in softened margarine with pastry blender or two knives.
3. Dissolve saffron in the very warm water. Gradually add water to dry ingredients, beating on medium speed of electric mixer for 2 minutes, scraping bowl occasionally.
4. Divide one of the eggs and set aside the yolk. Add the egg white and the other two eggs to the dough mixture along with ½ cup flour. Beat at high speed for 2 minutes.
5. Stir in enough additional flour to form a stiff dough.

6. Turn dough out onto a lightly floured board or pastry cloth. Knead until smooth and elastic, about 8 to 10 minutes.
7. Place dough in a greased bowl, turning once to grease top.
8. Cover with a clean towel and let rise in a warm place until doubled in bulk, about 1 hour.
9. Punch dough down and divide it in half. Divide each half into three strips. Place strips side by side on a lightly greased baking sheet and braid, pinching ends to seal.
10. Braid the second loaf.
11. Beat together reserved egg yolk with 1 teaspoon cold water.
12. Brush loaves with egg wash and sprinkle with poppy seeds.
13. Let rise in a warm place until doubled in bulk, about 1 hour.
14. Bake at 400°F for 20 to 25 minutes or until loaves sound hollow when tapped with knuckles.
15. Remove loaves from baking sheets and place on cooling racks.

Per slice: 92 Cal. (25% from fat), 2 g protein, 14 g carbohydrate, 3 g fat, 26 mg cholesterol, 0.5 g fiber, 129 mg sodium.

Avocado, Carrot, and Orange Salad
Serves 8

2   cups fresh orange juice
¼   teaspoon powdered ginger
1   teaspoon salt
4   cups coarsely grated carrots
2   navel oranges
2   large, ripe avocados
¼   cup lemon juice
    salad greens

1. In small bowl, mix together orange juice, powdered ginger, and salt.
2. Pour over carrots and marinate for at least an hour.
3. When ready to serve, peel and section oranges.
4. Cut avocado in half. Remove pits and skin.
5. Slice each half lengthwise into 2 pieces and brush with lemon juice.
6. Line 8 small salad plates with salad greens.
7. Place two pieces of avocado side by side on each plate with the narrow ends touching.
8. Fill cavity with grated carrots.
9. Garnish with orange sections. Serve at once.

Per serving: 152 Cal. (42% from fat), 3 g protein, 21 g carbohydrate, 8 g fat, 0 mg cholesterol, 4.4 g fiber, 298 mg sodium.

Honey Cake
Serves 12

2 tablespoons vegetable oil
1 cup sugar
3 eggs
⅔ cup cold strong coffee
1 cup honey
3 cups cake flour, sifted
2 teaspoons baking powder
1 teaspoon soda
1 teaspoon cinnamon
½ teaspoon ginger
½ teaspoon nutmeg
½ cup blanched almonds, chopped (reserve a few for the top)
½ cup seedless raisins

1. Preheat oven to 350°F.
2. In large mixer bowl, combine oil, sugar, and eggs. Beat until light and fluffy.
3. In small bowl, combine coffee and honey.
4. Sift dry ingredients together.
5. Add dry ingredients alternately with liquid ingredients to egg mixture.
6. Fold in almonds and raisins.
7. Pour batter into a greased and floured 9-inch tube pan.
8. Sprinkle batter with the reserved almonds.
9. Bake for 45 minutes to 1 hour, or until toothpick inserted in center comes out clean.

Per piece: 332 Cal. (18% from fat), 5 g protein, 66 g carbohydrate, 7 g fat, 69 mg cholesterol, 1.7 g fiber, 143 mg sodium.

The B. Manischewitz Company, Jersey City, NJ

Jewish people eat a ceremonial seder meal on the first evening of Passover. Each of the traditional foods on the seder plate has a special symbolism.

Chapter 30

Africa

Courtesy of Abercrombie & Kent

The beauty and strength of African wildlife deserve respect and protection.

Africa is the second largest continent; only Asia is larger. Africa shares the title of warmest continent with South America. The geographic extremes of Africa range from sandy deserts to tropical forests.

The countries of Africa are as varied as its geography. Much of Africa is in a state of political, economic, and cultural development. Therefore, Africa does not have a typical cuisine. Each African nation has unique foods.

Climate and Geography of Africa

Since the equator runs through the middle of Africa, both the extreme northern and southern countries have subtropical climates. Summers are dry, with the highest monthly average temperature

above 72°F (22°C). Monthly winter temperatures average above 50°F (10°C). In these areas, grains such as millet, teff, and sorghum grow well.

Along the equator in central and western Africa, temperatures range between 64°F (18°C) and 80°F (27°C) year round. This area has rainfall throughout the year. In these tropical, humid sections, root crops and vegetables are grown. Other products include palm oil, groundnuts (peanuts), bananas, dates, figs, plantains, citrus fruits, sugarcane, tobacco, coffee, and cacao. (*Cacao* is a plant that produces beans that are ground into cocoa or made into chocolate.)

The majority of the people in Africa live on the savannas, or grasslands. These are the broad areas above and below the equatorial belt. They receive less precipitation and have greater temperature ranges. Raising crops is difficult and unprofitable on the savannas because the soil is poor. The soil has little humus, a substance formed by decayed matter. Humus holds water near the ground surface, within reach of plant roots.

North and south of the savannas are the deserts. The Sahara and the Kalahari are the two major African deserts. Average summer temperatures may reach 98°F (37°C) and winter temperatures never drop below 59°F (15°C). Rain, when it falls, is brief. In the deserts, there are places called oases where water is available. Groups of people known as nomads still move from one oasis to another. They herd sheep, goats, and camels as was done in primitive times.

African Culture

Native Blacks, including the pygmies, Bushmen, and Hottentots, make up over 70 percent of Africa's population. Over five million people of European descent also live in Africa.

More than 800 languages are spoken in Africa. Most Africans speak a local language in their home village. They also speak an interchange language to communicate with people outside their village. The interchange languages most often used are English, French, Portuguese, Dutch, and Swahili.

Over half of the people in Africa have not had an opportunity to attend school. Therefore, few Africans can read or write. This has made it hard for African governments to communicate modern ideas to their people. To help solve this problem, African governments send some students to schools in Europe and the United States. In payment, the governments expect students to return to their native lands and help educate others.

One of the two major religions practiced in Africa is Islam. The other religion is Christianity. People who practice Islam are called *Muslims.* Islam greatly affects the lifestyle and food choices of the Muslims.

The Koran is a book of sacred writings in the Islamic religion. It specifies foods Muslims should and should not eat. It forbids the eating of animals that have died from disease, strangulation, or beating. Only animals that have been slaughtered by a proper ritual are considered to be edible. The Koran also forbids Muslims to eat pork and drink wine and other alcoholic beverages.

During the entire ninth calendar month, Muslims are required to fast (abstain from food) from sunrise to sunset. This is called the *Fast of Ramadan.* Meals eaten after sunset are supposed to be light. Several other fast days exist, but none are as important as the Fast of Ramadan.

An important holiday in African culture is Kwanzaa. **Kwanzaa** is a family-centered observance of cultural unity among African people. It is celebrated not only in Africa, but by African people throughout the world. This week-long celebration occurs between Christmas and New Year's Day. African people use this time to think about their ancestry, family, and community. On the next to the last night of Kwanzaa, families hold the *karamu,* which is a ritual feast.

African Cuisine

Since Africa is a continent of many nations, it does not have a typical cuisine. Each separate nation has dishes of its own. However, certain foods are common in many areas of Africa.

A wide variety of fruits and vegetables grow in Africa. A *papaya* is a small melonlike fruit. A *guava* is a small fruit with many seeds. A *plantain* is like a banana, but it is much larger and has a bland flavor. *Cassava* is a root vegetable much like a sweet potato. *Okra,* which also grows in the United States, is a native African vegetable. African slaves brought it to the southeastern United States. See 30-6.

Some of the breads and pastries prepared in Africa are kesra, brik, and pita. *Kesra* is a round oven bread made in mountain villages. A *brik* is a pastry that is filled and then deep-fried. **Pita bread** is found throughout Africa as well as the Middle East. It is a flat, round, hollow bread. When cut in half, each half opens like a pocket and can be filled with meat or vegetables.

The French influenced the foods of the North African countries of Morocco, Senegal, and Algeria. In ancient times, the French invaded these countries and brought their European customs to the region. A common meat in Algeria is lamb. It is usually grilled or stewed. *Mechoui* is lamb that has smoldered and cooked over a fire for many hours. The smoked head of a sheep is a delicacy.

Brooks Tropicals

30-6 Papayas are one of the many tropical fruits that grow in Africa.

Ghana, a country on the midwestern coast, is the world's greatest exporter of cacao. The English influence is evident here in the drinking of tea and the speaking of the English language.

Another country along the western coast is Liberia. Freed slaves from the United States founded Liberia in the late 1800s after the Civil War. Its capital and most important city is Monrovia. Monrovia was named after President Monroe, who was president of the United States at the time Liberia was established. The food of Liberia is similar to soul food in the United States. It is a combination of American and African cooking.

One of the oldest countries in Africa is Ethiopia, located in eastern Africa. Christians founded Ethiopia in an otherwise Muslim world. Therefore, Ethiopia has a different cuisine from the rest of Africa. Ethiopia's main dish is *injera*, which is a large, sourdoughlike pancake made from teff. *Teff* is a milletlike grain grown only in Africa and the Middle East. Injera is served with *wat*, a spicy sauce or stew. Diners tear the injera into pieces, roll it around in the wat, and eat it with their fingers.

South Africa is an African country with many contrasts. White South Africa was first settled in the seventeenth century. The English, Germans, Dutch, and Portuguese formed colonies in this country. Colonists brought foods from each of these nations, which have been blended with native foods over the years.

The Portuguese influence can also be seen in the foods of Mozambique, a country in southeastern Africa. Chicken is cooked the Portuguese way with tomatoes and wine. Hot curries are another food typical of Mozambique.

African Meals

Africans often serve meals on low tables with pillows, folded carpets, or the floor used as seats. They usually arrange the food on one large tray and place it in the center of the table. Then each household member takes his or her individual share. Although diners do not use knives and forks, they may use spoons. However, they use their fingers to eat most foods. They use flat breads to sop up the stews and sauces. See 30-7.

In most of Africa, a hand-washing ritual takes place before and after meals. A servant or member of the household brings in a long-necked pitcher of water and a bowl or basin. This person pours water over the hands of each household member and catches it in the basin. He or she then offers a small towel to dry the hands. Since diners eat most of the food with their fingers, this ritual is usually repeated after the meal.

Courtesy of Abercrombie & Kent

30-7 This area is set for a traditional South African "Boma" feast.

African Menu

Brik bil Lahm
(Lamb Turnovers)
Sopa de Feija Verde
(String Bean Soup)
Couscous
(Semolina with Meat Stew Filling)
Monrovian Collards and Cabbage
Ground Nut Ice Cream
(Peanut Ice Cream)
Makroud el Louse
(Soft Almond Cookie)

Brik bil Lahm
(Lamb Turnovers)
Serves 8

1	pound ground lamb
½	cup finely chopped onions
¼	cup parsley
¾	teaspoon salt
½	teaspoon pepper
2	tablespoons margarine
½	cup grated Parmesan cheese
8	sheets phyllo pastry
¼	cup margarine, melted
8	eggs
1	egg, beaten
	vegetable or olive oil for frying
2	lemons

1. Combine ground lamb, onions, parsley, salt, and pepper and mix well.
2. Place the 2 tablespoons margarine in a skillet.
3. Add the lamb mixture. Break up the mixture with a fork as it cooks.
4. When no pink remains, remove from heat and stir in cheese.
5. To assemble with phyllo pastry, spread one sheet of pastry flat and brush with melted margarine. Repeat with seven more sheets of pastry.
6. Fold in the 8-inch sides by 2 inches to make 6-inch squares.
7. Spoon ⅛ of the lamb mixture onto a corner of each square.
8. Make a well in the lamb mixture. Break an egg (intact) into the well.
9. Moisten the edges with the beaten egg and fold the square diagonally. Seal edges. Repeat the process to make a total of 8 briks.
10. Heat the oil until hot but not smoking.
11. Fry two briks at a time for 2 or 3 minutes on each side until light brown.
12. Drain on paper towels. Serve hot, garnished with lemon slices.

Per serving: 346 Cal. (66% from fat), 21 g protein, 8 g carbohydrate, 26 g fat, 347 mg cholesterol, 1.0 g fiber, 549 mg sodium.

Sopa de Feija Verde
(String Bean Soup)
Serves 8

1	pound fresh green beans
1½	quarts water
1	teaspoon salt
½	teaspoon pepper
4	large potatoes, peeled and cut into chunks
2	large onions, peeled and sliced
3	tomatoes, peeled and cut into chunks

1. Wash green beans and cut French style. (Frozen French style green beans may be used.)
2. Bring water to a boil and add all ingredients except green beans.
3. Simmer until all vegetables are tender.
4. Remove from heat and puree in blender.
5. Pour pureed mixture back into the pot. Add green beans.
6. Simmer 10 minutes or until beans are tender.

Per serving: 98 Cal. (3% from fat), 3 g protein, 22 g carbohydrate, 0 g fat, 0 mg cholesterol, 3.8 g fiber, 276 mg sodium.

Couscous
(Semolina with Meat Stew Filling)
Serves 8 to 10

2   pounds meat, cubed (may use lamb, beef, or
      poultry)
2   cups onions, chopped
2   tablespoons olive oil
¼   cup parsley
¼   cup fresh coriander
1   can garbanzo beans or chick-peas, drained
1   pound turnips, cubed
1   pound carrots, cut into strips
1   pound zucchini, cut into chunks
4   fresh tomatoes, peeled and cut into chunks
2   green peppers, cut into strips
1   package instant couscous
1   tablespoon margarine

1. In a large pot, brown the meat and sauté the
   onions in the olive oil.
2. Add the parsley and coriander and cover with
   water.
3. Add the garbanzo beans. Simmer for 1 hour.
4. Add turnips, carrots, and zucchini to the meat mixture. Simmer for another hour.
5. Add tomatoes and green peppers and simmer 30
   minutes longer.
6. Prepare couscous according to package directions. Toss with margarine.
7. To serve, place the couscous on a warm platter.
   Place the vegetables around the edge and the
   meat in the center. Pour the broth over the dish.

Per serving: 372 Cal. (24% from fat), 27 g protein, 45 g
carbohydrate, 10 g fat, 53 mg cholesterol, 5.7 g fiber,
387 mg sodium.

Monrovian Collards and Cabbage
Serves 8

1   quart water
1   bunch collards or 2 pounds spinach
½   pound bacon, cut into pieces
1   onion, sliced
½   teaspoon salt
½   teaspoon pepper
¼   teaspoon red or cayenne pepper
1   tablespoon margarine
2   pounds cabbage, cut into wedges

1. Bring water to a boil.
2. Add all ingredients and simmer for 10 to 15 minutes, or until vegetables are tender.
3. Drain and serve hot with extra margarine.

Per serving: 84 Cal. (55% from fat), 4 g protein, 6 g
carbohydrate, 5 g fat, 7 mg cholesterol, 3.3 g fiber, 301
mg sodium.

Ground Nut Ice Cream
(Peanut Ice Cream)
Serves 8

1   8-ounce container of whipped topping
4   tablespoons lemon juice
¼   cup sugar
1   cup peanut butter
1   can condensed milk
½   cup skim milk

1. Add lemon juice and sugar to the whipped topping.
2. Combine peanut butter, condensed milk, and skim
   milk.
3. Fold the whipped mixture into the peanut butter
   mixture.
4. Pour into freezer trays and freeze. Stir occasionally as the mixture freezes.

Per serving: 434 Cal. (52% from fat), 14 g protein, 41
carbohydrate, 27 g fat, 13 mg cholesterol, 2.2 g fiber,
215 mg sodium.

Makroud el Louse
(Soft Almond Cookies)
Makes 5 dozen cookies

2   pounds whole almonds, blanched and finely
      ground
2   cups sugar
3   tablespoons grated lemon peel
4   eggs

1. Mix almonds, sugar, and lemon peel together.
2. Add eggs one at a time and beat until smooth.
3. On a heavily floured board, divide the dough into
   quarters. Roll each quarter with no hands into a
   1½ by 16-inch cylinder.

4. Flour hands repeatedly. Flatten each cylinder into an oblong roll, about 2 inches wide.
5. Using a sharp knife, cut each roll into 1-inch slices.
6. Dust with flour and place about 1 inch apart on an ungreased baking sheet.
7. Bake at 350°F for 15 minutes.
8. Dust off any excess flour and cool on a wire rack.

Syrup:
2   cups water
½   cup sugar
1   tablespoon orange blossom water or 1 teaspoon orange extract

2   boxes powdered sugar

1. Combine water and sugar and boil for 15 minutes.
2. Cool and add the orange blossom water.
3. Spread the powdered sugar on paper towels.
4. Dip each cookie into the syrup and then into the powdered sugar. Place the cookies on cooling racks to dry.

Per cookie: 116 Cal. (37% from fat), 2 g protein, 17 g carbohydrate, 5 g fat, 18 mg cholesterol, 1.2 g fiber, 6 mg. sodium.

Almond Board of California

Couscous is a typical grain dish eaten in Africa.

Summary

The climate throughout much of the Middle East and Africa is hot and dry. Irrigation is essential for growing crops in many Middle Eastern and African countries. Religion is an important part of the culture in this part of the world. Religious laws as well as the climate have an impact on the foods of this region.

A number of ingredients and foods are common throughout the Middle East. However, unique dishes are found in each Middle Eastern country. Lamb is the staple meat of this region and bulgur and rice are often served as side dishes. Fish is popular in coastal countries. Middle Eastern cooks use a variety of spices to season foods. Fruits and rich pastries are common desserts. Coffee is a favorite beverage, although Iranians prefer tea.

Israel has a rather eclectic cuisine. Jewish people from many parts of the world have made contributions to the foods of Israel. The neighboring Middle Eastern and African countries have had an influence, too. Of course, Jewish dietary laws also affect many foods.

The Islamic religion influences food habits throughout much of Africa. European countries that colonized various parts of Africa also left their mark on the cuisine. Although each African country has unique dishes, some foods are common all over the continent. Such foods include a variety of fruits and vegetables and several breads and pastries.

Review What You Have Read

Write your answers on a separate sheet of paper.
1. List the five ingredients basic to all Middle Eastern cooking.
2. True or false. Both Islam and Judaism forbid their followers to eat poultry.
3. Describe three Turkish sweets.
4. Which of the following is an Arabian mazza?
   A. Hummus.
   B. Kibbi.
   C. Tabbouleh.
   D. Torshi.
5. Name and describe the two types of rice dishes served in Iran.
6. Collective community farms in Israel are called _____.

7. Match the following terms and definitions associated with Jewish dietary laws:
   ___ Someone who, in accordance with Jewish dietary laws, is licensed to slaughter all animals and fowl used as food.
   ___ Foods that are prepared according to Jewish dietary laws.
   ___ Dairy foods.
   ___ Meat foods.
   ___ Fruits, vegetables, cereal, fish, and baked goods made with vegetable shortening.
   A. fleishig
   B. kosher
   C. milchig
   D. pareve
   E. shohet
8. Name five foods used to stuff kreplach.
9. Most of the world's chocolate is made from a plant grown in Africa called _____.
10. How do Muslims observe the Fast of Ramadan?
11. What is injera? How is it served and eaten?
12. On what do Africans sit during a meal?

Build Your Basic Skills

1. Many spices grow in the Middle East. Make a list of five spices that come from this area. Find both Middle Eastern and American recipes that include each of these spices. Compare the two types of recipes. Discuss in class what foods are typically flavored with these spices in each cuisine.
2. Use library resources to read about the establishment of the state of Israel. Summarize your findings in a brief written report.

Build Your Thinking Skills

1. Investigate the average annual rainfall in various regions of the Middle East. Analyze how rainfall affects agricultural production in these regions.
2. Work in a small group to research the specific food customs of one African country. Use visual aids to give a presentation about the ingredients, cooking methods, eating habits, and meal patterns in your chosen country. Each member of the group should be responsible for a different part of the presentation. Following the group presentations, each group should prepare a dish typical of their country to serve as part of an African banquet.

Asia

A "Taste" of the World of Work

Travel Agent
Plans itineraries and arranges accommodations and other travel services for customers of travel agency.

Japanese Translator
Translates documents and other materials from Japanese into one or more other languages.

Chinese-Style Food Cook
Plans menus and cooks Chinese-style dishes, dinners, desserts, and other foods, according to recipes.

Terms to Know

kasha	korma
zakuska	vindaloo
caviar	chasnidarth
schi	wok
borscht	stir-frying
beef stroganov	congee
paskha	chopsticks
kulich	gohan
caste system	soybean
curry	tofu
ghee	sukiyaki
masala	nihon-cha
chapatis	kaiseka
tandoori	tsukemono

Objectives

After studying this chapter, you will be able to
❑ discuss how climate, geography, and culture have influenced the food customs of Russia, India, China, and Japan.
❑ recognize and prepare foods that are native to each of these countries.

Courtesy of Abercrombie & Kent

Asia is the largest continent in the world. It covers nearly a third of the earth's total land surface. Asia also is the home of over three fifths of the world's people. Deserts, jungles, swamps, and mountains cover much of Asia. Therefore, most of its people are crowded into small areas that can better support vegetation.

When people in the rest of the world were making crude tools, Asian art, architecture, and technology were highly advanced. The Eastern world laid the groundwork for the later development of Western civilization.

Russia, India, China, and Japan dominate the Asian continent, both in area and population. (The largest portion of Russia lies in Asia. The smaller portion lies in Europe.) Interest in these nations, however, goes far beyond size and population statistics. For each of these nations has a culture that is totally unique. The culture of Russia is a mixture of Eastern and Western influences. The cultures of India, Japan, and China are far different from those of any Western nation. Despite growing Western influence, many of their native customs have been preserved.

Healthy Living

When you are traveling, be sure to start every day with a good breakfast. Do not skip lunch, either. Sightseeing requires energy. You might want to keep some bread and fruit in your travel tote. This will allow you to grab a quick bite while you are on the go.

Courtesy of Abercrombie & Kent

Asia is a large and diverse continent. Although this architecture is typical of Russia, it is significantly different from the architecture of other Asian nations.

Russia

Courtesy of Abercrombie & Kent

Many Russian people buy fresh fruits and vegetables at outdoor markets.

Inside Russia's borders are vast natural resources. Forests provide timber. Thousands of rivers provide power, food, water, and transportation. A large population representing a range of cultures has added to the diversity of Russian cuisine.

Climate and Geography of Russia

Russia is the largest country in the world. It is almost twice the size of the United States. It extends from the Baltic Sea on the west to the Pacific Ocean on the east. It reaches from the Arctic Ocean on the north to Kazakhstan and Mongolia on the south.

Most of Russia is a vast lowland, but mountains are important too. The Ural Mountains are considered to be the dividing line between Europe and Asia. The other important mountain ranges form a large arc along the southern and southwestern borders. These include the Caucasus Mountains, where Europe's highest peak is located.

The rivers of Russia are important transportation arteries. Because many of the rivers run north and south, canals have been built to improve east-west transportation.

The climate in a large portion of Russia is marked by short, cool summers; long, severe winters; and light precipitation. Much of the European part of Russia (including Moscow) has short, mild summers. The winters are long and cold, and precipitation is moderate. In the northern Arctic regions, summers are short and chilly, and winters are long and bitterly cold. Temperatures of -94°F (-70°C) have been recorded in northeastern Siberia. The Pacific Ocean brings monsoons to the far southeastern portion of the country.

Russian Culture

Russian history dates back for centuries. However, Russia has been an independent country for only a few years.

Influences on Russian Culture

Little is known about Russia's earliest beginnings. However, during the eighth and ninth centuries, the Rus civilization began to develop. In the tenth century, a ruler named Vladimir worked to unite the land of Rus. After Vladimir's baptism in the Byzantine church, the Russian Orthodox faith was founded in Russia. The alphabet, art, and architecture of the Byzantine Empire were also brought to Russia.

During the thirteenth century, Mongolian Tatars invaded from the south. Their customs had an influence on Russian culture. During their rule, Moscow became an important political center.

In 1547, Ivan the Terrible became the first czar of Russia. (The word *czar* means ruler.) He fought against the Tatars and ended their rule. Ivan's military successes led to territorial growth. Following Ivan's rule, internal strife spread throughout the empire. This strife ended in 1613 with the election of Michael Romanov as czar. The Romanov family ruled the Russian Empire until 1917. See 31-1.

In 1917, Vladimir Lenin led a revolutionary group, called the *Bolsheviks*, that took control of the

31-1 The Church of the Resurrection in St. Petersburg, Russia, was built during the Romamov rule.

government. Following a civil war, the Union of Soviet Socialist Republics (U.S.S.R., or Soviet Union) was formed. The Russian S.F.S.R., based in Moscow, was the main republic in the Soviet Union.

Modern Culture in Russia

With the establishment of the U.S.S.R., a communist dictatorship replaced rule by the czars. The Communist Party controlled the government until 1991. In that year, the Communist Party was dissolved. The Soviet Union was broken up into 15 independent countries, one of which is Russia.

About 80 percent of the people in Russia are Russian. However, members of more than 60 other ethnic groups also live there. Three fourths of the people live in urban areas.

Russian Economy

Wheat is the major grain crop, followed by rye, barley, oats, and corn. Other important crops include sugar beets, sunflower seeds, and flax. Fruit and vegetable crops are not as varied as they are in the United States. However, hardy fruits and vegetables, such as cabbage, potatoes, and apples, grow where climate and soil are suitable.

Russia has some of the world's richest natural resources. They include natural gas, coal, oil, copper, lead, zinc, nickel, and iron ore. These resources form the base of Russian industries.

Metallurgy, coal mining, oil refining, and shipbuilding are major industries in Russia. Production of building materials, aircraft, and chemicals are important to the economy, too. The production of food products, clothing, and other consumer goods is secondary.

Russian Cuisine

Russians are a Slavic people. Therefore, Russian cuisine has Slavic origins. Russian cuisine is, for the most part, hearty and filling.

Contributions to Russian Cuisine

The first Slavs depended on the forests, mountains, and waters for most of their food. Cream sauces and the queen cake are examples of Scandinavian foods contributed by these early people. (*Queen cake* is apples and cherries baked between layers of sweet pastry and topped with meringue.) Later, people of the Russian Orthodox faith added other special foods and customs to celebrate their religious holidays.

The next major contribution to Russian cuisine came from the Mongols. The Mongols taught the Slavs how to broil meat and how to make sauerkraut, yogurt, kumys, and curd cheese. (*Kumys* is a mild alcoholic beverage.) The Mongols also introduced tea drinking and the *samovar* (a special piece of equipment used to make Russian tea).

The czars staged elaborate banquets and introduced European foods to Russia. For instance, Peter the Great brought French soups and Dutch cheeses to the Russian court. He also introduced the custom of serving fruit preserves with meat.

Staple Foods of Russian Peasants

Few Russians ate like the czars. Most were peasants who ate foods they could grow themselves or obtain from the forests or rivers. Bread, kasha, and soup formed the basis of their diet.

Peasant bread was dark, nourishing, and filling. Peasants usually made it from rye flour because they could grow rye in the short, cool growing season.

Kasha was another staple food. The peasants usually made **kasha** from buckwheat, but they also used other grains. They first fried the raw grain. Then they simmered it until tender. The peasants could eat the kasha alone. However, those who could afford to do so added vegetables, meat, eggs, or fish.

The third staple food of the peasants was soup. Cabbage, beet, and fish soups were the most common.

Some peasant families had enough money to have a small vegetable garden and some livestock. The garden supplied potatoes, cabbage, cucumbers, beets, carrots, and turnips. A cow provided milk and milk products. Chickens gave eggs, and hogs and cattle provided meat.

Modern Russian Cuisine

The Russian cuisine of today combines native Russian foods with foods of neighboring European and Asian countries.

Russian Appetizers and Soups

Zakuska (appetizers), such as smoked salmon, pickled herring, fish in aspic, and sliced cold meats, begin many Russian meals. Pâtés, salads, cheese, pickles, and breads are also among the many foods that appear on a zakuska table. However, the star of the table always is caviar.

Caviar is the processed, salted roe (eggs) of large fish. The roe of the sturgeon are used most often. The best caviar is hand sieved to remove the egg membranes. The light salting that follows acts as a preservative. The caviar requires proper storage to prevent spoilage by cold, heat, or air. Russians serve their fine black caviar on small pieces of white bread.

Soup usually follows the zakuska. *Schi* (cabbage soup) is one of the most popular Russian soups. Cooks obtain different flavors by varying the vegetables and broth. **Borscht** (beet soup) can be thin and clear or thick with chunks of beets and other vegetables. Russians often top borscht with a dollop of sour cream, 31-2. Other popular soups include ouba, rasolnik, and solianka. *Ouba* is a clear fish broth. *Rasolnik* is a mixture of vegetables garnished with chopped veal or lamb kidneys. *Solianka* contains meat or fish and salted cucumber.

National Live Stock and Meat Board

31-2 Borscht, a soup made with beets and topped with sour cream, is traditional in Russian cuisine.

Russian Main Dishes

Beef has been the traditional meat of Russian cuisine. However, those of Eastern descent prefer lamb and mutton. They also eat pork, which they usually serve salted. On special occasions, however, roast suckling pig is traditional.

Many meat dishes have regional origins. *Shashlik* (cubes of marinated lamb grilled on skewers), for example, developed in Georgia (a country that borders Turkey).

One of the best-known Russian meat dishes was created for a Russian count of the late nineteenth century. **Beef stroganov** is made with tender strips of beef, mushrooms, and a seasoned sour cream sauce.

Other Russian main dishes are made with chicken. *Chakhokhbili* is stewed chicken with tomato sauce, onions, vinegar, wine, peppers, and olives. *Kurnik* is a chicken and rice pie and *kotmis satsivi* is roasted chicken with walnut sauce. *Kotlety po-kyivskomu* (Chicken Kiev) has become popular in American kitchens. To prepare Chicken Kiev, wrap pounded chicken breasts around pieces of sweet butter. Then carefully bread them and fry them in deep fat until golden brown. When a fork pierces the golden coating, the butter spurts out and serves as a sauce.

More than 100 types of fish live in the waters that border Russia. Sturgeon, pike, carp, bream, salmon, and trout were favorites of the Russian czars. A branch of Russian cuisine developed around these and other varieties of fish. In one region, sturgeon and swordfish are prepared on skewers. White-fleshed fish are served in aspic, and crisp fish cakes are eaten with a mustard sauce.

Russian Side Dishes

Russian vegetable dishes have always changed with the seasons. During the cold winters, rutabagas and other root vegetables, potatoes, pickles, dried mushrooms, and sauerkraut are eaten. During the summers, asparagus, peas, fresh cabbage, berries, melons, and other fruits are more common.

Cereals are available year-round. Because they are both filling and inexpensive, they serve as staples in the Russian diet. Russian cooks use cereals in many ways. They use cereals to make dark breads, white breads, and sweet breads. They use cereals to make kasha, which is still popular in Russia. Russians may serve kasha plain or add it to soups. They may combine it with other foods and serve it as a side dish or a puddinglike dessert. *Blini* are pancakes made from buckwheat flour.

Russians fry them in butter and serve them with butter and sour cream, caviar, smoked fish, or jam. Russian cooks use flour doughs to make noodles, dumplings, and pirozhki. *Pirozhki* are pastries filled with protein-based or sweet fillings.

Milk and milk products are an important part of Russian cooking. Russian cooks use *smetana* (sour cream) on top of borscht and in cakes, pastries, salads, sauces, and main dishes. They also use *prostokvasa* (sour milk), *kefir* (a type of yogurt), and *koumys* (sour mare's milk).

Russian Desserts

Russian desserts have varied origins. Some Russian desserts, like *charlotte russe* (ladyfinger mold with cream filling) and fruit tarts, were favorites of the czars. Other desserts, like *kisel* (pureed fruit), were eaten by the peasants. Many desserts are strictly regional in origin. These include *samsa* (sweet walnut fritters) and *medivnyk* (honey cake).

Two of the most popular Russian desserts are part of the Easter celebrations of the Russian Orthodox Church. **Paskha** is a rich cheesecake. It is molded into a pyramid and decorated with the letters XB. These are the initials of the Greek phrase "Christos voskres" meaning Christ has risen. **Kulich** is a tall, cylindrical yeast cake filled with fruits and nuts. Russians always serve kulich by first removing the top half of the cake and placing it on a serving plate. Then they slice the rest of the cake and arrange the slices around the mushroom-shaped top.

Russian Meals

The average Russian family eats three meals a day. Breakfast generally is simple. Kasha with milk, bread, butter, jam, hot tea, and an occasional egg are typical.

Lunches may be eaten in factory cafeterias or the fields. They may consist of a hearty soup, thick slices of bread with a little cheese or sausage, and tea. In wealthier families, a fish or meat course and vegetables may follow the soup.

Dinner is the main meal of the day. Russians serve a small assortment of zakuska with glasses of vodka or *kvas* (similar to European beers). They often follow zakuska with soup. Then they serve the main course of meat, poultry, or fish. Potatoes, vegetables, and bread usually accompany the main course. A simple dessert, such as kisel and hot tea, follows.

Russian Menu
Pirozhki
(Small Pastries Filled with Meat)
Borscht
(Beet Soup)
Kotlety Po-Kyivskomu
(Chicken Kiev)
Kartoplia Solimkoi
(Deep-Fried Straw Potatoes)
Màslo Garókh
(Buttered Peas)
Chernyi Khlib
(Black Bread)
Paskha
(Easter Cheese Pyramid)
Tchai
(Tea)

Pirozhki
(Small Pastries Filled with Meat)
Makes 20

Pastry:
  2 cups all-purpose flour
  ¼ teaspoon salt
  ¼ cup margarine, cut into small pieces
  ¼ cup vegetable shortening
4 to 6 tablespoons ice water

1. Sift flour and salt into mixing bowl.
2. Using pastry blender, two knives, or fingers, cut in margarine and shortening until mixture resembles coarse cornmeal.
3. Add ice water, stirring gently with fork, until dough forms a ball.
4. Wrap dough in waxed paper and refrigerate at least one hour.
5. On lightly floured board or pastry cloth, roll dough into a strip about 11 inches by 3 inches. Fold the dough into thirds, turn pastry around, and again roll into a lengthwise strip about 11 inches by 3 inches. Fold into thirds, turn and roll again. Repeat this process two more times, ending with folded dough.
6. Wrap dough in waxed paper and refrigerate for at least 1 hour while filling is being prepared.

Filling:
  2 tablespoons margarine
1¼ cups finely chopped onion
  ¾ pound lean ground beef
  1 hard-cooked egg, chopped
  3 tablespoons chopped fresh dill
  ½ teaspoon salt
     dash pepper

1. In medium skillet, melt margarine.
2. Add onions and sauté until golden brown.
3. Add meat. Cook over moderate heat, stirring occasionally, until no pink remains.
4. On wooden cutting board, chop mixture as finely as possible or run through grinder with fine blade.
5. In large bowl, mix meat with eggs, dill, salt, and pepper.
6. Preheat oven to 400°F.
7. On floured board or pastry cloth, roll dough to a thickness of 1/8 inch. With a floured 3-inch biscuit cutter, cut out as many rounds as you can. Reroll scraps.
8. Place 2 tablespoons of filling in the center of each round. Fold one side to center. Fold two ends of dough about ½ inch toward center. Fold remaining edge to center and seal.
9. Place pirozhki side by side, seam sides down, on lightly greased baking sheet.
10. Bake 30 minutes or until golden brown.

Per pastry: 137 Cal. (56% from fat), 5 g protein, 10 g carbohydrate, 9 g fat, 24 mg cholesterol, 0.7 g fiber, 133 mg sodium.

Borscht
(Beet Soup)
Serves 6

  2 pound brisket of beef
  8 medium beets, coarsely grated
  4 medium onions, sliced
  2 medium tomatoes, coarsely chopped
  2 tablespoons sugar
  2 tablespoons lemon juice

1½ teaspoons salt
⅛ teaspoon pepper
½ pound white cabbage, shredded
sour cream

1. Fill a large Dutch oven with water. Add beef, beets, onions, and tomatoes; simmer until meat is tender, about 1½ hours.
2. Remove meat. Add sugar, lemon juice, salt, and pepper to stock. Stir until sugar has dissolved.
3. Add cabbage and simmer an additional 25 minutes.
4. Skim fat.
5. Shred meat and add to soup.
6. Pour into large tureen and serve immediately with dollops of sour cream. (Soup may also be served cold, if desired.)

Per serving: 259 Cal. (37% from fat), 20 g protein, 21 g carbohydrate, 11 g fat, 68 mg cholesterol, 5.9 g fiber, 1030 mg sodium.

Kotlety Po-Kyivskomu
(Chicken Kiev)
Serves 6

6 boneless, skinless chicken breast halves
6 tablespoons chilled margarine
salt
pepper
1½ teaspoons chopped parsley
¼ cup skim milk
2 eggs, beaten
½ cup all-purpose flour
1½ cups dry bread crumbs
vegetable oil for deep-frying

1. Place chicken breasts, one at a time, between two sheets of waxed paper. Flatten with a meat mallet until ¼ inch thick.
2. Cut margarine into 6 equal pieces. Shape each into a cylinder. Wrap in waxed paper and chill.
3. Place one piece of chilled margarine on each breast. Sprinkle with salt, pepper, and parsley.
4. Roll chicken breast; carefully seal edges with toothpicks.
5. Beat milk and eggs until smooth.
6. Dredge rolled chicken breast in flour, dip in milk mixture; then roll in bread crumbs. Repeat coating process until all rolls have been coated. Chill until ready to cook.
7. Heat oil to 375°F. Fry chicken rolls until golden brown. Remove toothpicks and serve immediately.

Per serving: 433 Cal. (43% from fat), 34 g protein, 27 g carbohydrate, 20 g fat, 161 mg cholesterol, 1.5 g fiber, 421 mg sodium.

Chernyi Khlib
(Black Bread)
Makes 2 loaves

4 cups unsifted rye flour
3 cups unsifted all-purpose flour
1 teaspoon sugar
2 teaspoons salt
2 cups whole bran cereal
1½ tablespoons caraway seeds, crushed
2 teaspoons instant coffee
1 teaspoon onion powder
½ teaspoon fennel seed, crushed
2 packages active dry yeast
2½ cups water
¼ cup vinegar
¼ cup molasses
1 square unsweetened chocolate, 1 ounce
¼ cup margarine
1 egg white
1 teaspoon cold water

1. On a sheet of waxed paper, combine rye flour and all-purpose flour.
2. In a large mixer bowl, combine 2⅓ cups flour mixture, sugar, salt, bran cereal, caraway seeds, coffee, onion powder, fennel seed, and dry yeast.
3. In medium saucepan, combine 2½ cups water, vinegar, molasses, chocolate, and margarine. Heat over low heat until very warm (120° to 130°F). (Margarine and chocolate do not need to melt).
4. Gradually add warm liquids to dry ingredients and beat on medium speed of electric mixer 2 minutes, scraping bowl occasionally.
5. Add ½ cup of flour mixture and beat on high speed 2 minutes.
6. Add enough remaining flour to form a soft dough.
7. Turn dough out onto a lightly floured board or pastry cloth. Cover with a clean towel and let rest 15 minutes.
8. Knead dough until smooth and elastic, about 10 to 15 minutes. (Dough will still be a little sticky.)
9. Place dough in greased bowl, turning to grease top. Cover with a clean towel and let rise in a warm place until doubled in bulk, about 1 hour.
10. Punch down; turn out onto lightly floured board. Divide in half and shape each half into a ball about 5 inches in diameter.
11. Place each ball in a greased 8-inch round cake pan. Cover with a clean towel and let rise in a warm place until doubled in bulk, about 1 hour.
12. Bake at 350°F for 45 to 50 minutes or until loaves sound hollow when gently tapped with knuckles.
13. Remove to cooling rack and brush tops with egg white that has been mixed with 1 teaspoon water.

Per slice: 130 Cal. (16% from fat), 4 g protein, 26 g carbohydrate, 3 g fat, 0 mg cholesterol, 5.4 g fiber, 206 mg sodium.

Maslo Garokh
(Buttered Peas)
Serves 6

water
½ teaspoon salt
1½ pounds shelled, fresh peas*
margarine

1. In medium saucepan, bring a small amount of salted water to a boil.
2. Add peas and gently simmer until tender.
3. Drain; add margarine and serve immediately.

*Two 10-ounce packages of frozen peas may be substituted for the fresh peas.

Per serving: 74 Cal. (27% from fat), 4 g protein, 11 g carbohydrate, 2 g fat, 0 mg cholesterol, 5.4 g fiber, 386 mg sodium.

Kartoplia Solimkoi
(Deep-Fried Straw Potatoes)
Serves 6

6 medium-sized baking potatoes
vegetable oil for deep-frying
salt

1. Peel potatoes and cut into strips about 2½ inches long and ⅛ inch thick.
2. Place strips in a bowl and fill with ice water until they are ready to be fried. Then, drain in a colander and place on paper towels. Using more paper towels, pat potatoes until they are thoroughly dry.
3. In large saucepan, heat oil to 375°F.
4. Place potatoes in frying basket and fry for about 15 seconds, occasionally shaking basket to keep potatoes from sticking. Potatoes should be a pale golden brown.
5. Drain well on paper towels. (Potatoes can rest up to an hour.)
6. Just before serving, reheat oil to 385°F.
7. Put potatoes in basket and fry 15 more seconds or until crisp and brown.
8. Drain, transfer to a platter and sprinkle with salt. Serve immediately.

Per serving: 135 Cal. (29% from fat), 2 g protein, 23 g carbohydrate, 4 g fat, 0 mg cholesterol, 1.0 g fiber, 5 mg sodium.

Paskha
(Easter Cheese Pyramid)
(Serves 18)

2 cups sweet butter, softened
2 cups granulated sugar
3 pounds pot cheese
3 egg yolks
1 can orange juice concentrate, 6 ounce can, thawed
1/3 cup toasted slivered almonds, chopped
1 cup chopped, mixed, candied fruit

1. In a large mixing bowl, cream butter and sugar until light and fluffy.
2. Gradually beat in pot cheese and continue beating until mixture is very smooth and creamy.
3. Add egg yolks, one at a time, beating constantly until well blended.
4. Add orange juice concentrate, almonds, and candied fruit.
5. Line a new 6-inch clay flower pot (one with a hold in the bottom) with several layers of cheesecloth.*
6. Turn cheese mixture into pot and pack tightly.
7. Cover with cheesecloth and place pot in a shallow pan. Put weights on top. Refrigerate for 24 hours, pouring off the liquid that accumulates every few hours.
8. To serve, unmold pashka onto a serving platter and remove cheesecloth. Garnish with candied fruits.

*Flower pot should have a 9-cup capacity.

Per serving: 406 Cal. (57% from fat), 11 g protein, 34 g carbohydrate, 26 g fat, 112 mg cholesterol, 1.3 g fiber, 310 mg sodium.

National Broiler Council

Chicken breasts are wrapped around butter, breaded, and deep-fried to make Chicken Kiev.

India

India

Courtesy of Abercrombie & Kent

Many people traveling to India make a point of visiting the beautiful Taj Mahal.

The local people call it *Bharat.* The English call it *India.* Both names belong to the seventh largest country in the world. It is a beautiful country with mountains, jungles, rich valleys, and miles of coastline.

Climate and Geography of India

India is located on a peninsula of southern Asia. The Arabian Sea, Indian Ocean, and Bay of Bengal form its borders.

India has three distinct geographical areas. These are the Himalayan Mountains, the broad river plains, and the plateau.

The giant Himalayas are a natural barrier between India and the rest of Asia. The hilly regions, which stretch out beneath the mountains, are forests or grazing lands.

The Himalayas are the source of India's three great rivers—the Indus, the Ganges, and the Brahmaputra. These rivers form vast river plains. In the Ganges River basin, the soil is rich and deep, and farmers can plant two crops each year. It is one of the most densely settled farming areas in the country.

To the south of the fertile river plains lies a large plateau called the *Deccan.* The Deccan covers most of the peninsula. There, India's richest mineral deposits are located. Agriculture is possible in level areas where rainfall or irrigation systems provide enough moisture.

India has a tropical climate. Cool weather lasts only from about December to March. In June, monsoon season begins. (*Monsoons* are storms with high winds and heavy rains.) The season lasts until the end of September. The monsoon rains provide needed moisture for the dry earth. In just a short time, however, they can force rivers to flood their banks.

Indian Culture

The people of India belong to a variety of races. They speak more than 700 languages and dialects. This variety is the result of foreign invasions that lasted many centuries.

Influences on Indian Culture

Legend and myth surround India's earliest history. However, archaeologists do know that a highly developed society existed in the Indus Valley as long ago as 3000 B.C. These early people knew how to use iron, copper, and other metals. They grew a few crops and raised sheep, elephants, and the humped bull.

A series of invasions began with the Aryans. The Aryans came from the north and conquered the Indians. The Persians, the Huns, the Arabs, the

Turks, and the Mongols followed. During the Persian rule, India actively traded with ports in the Persian Gulf and the Mediterranean and Red Seas. During Mongol rule, Islam became an important religion. Great cities like Delhi were founded, and beautiful monuments like the Taj Mahal were built.

British Rule

During the sixteenth century, European nations began struggling to gain political power in India. In 1848, Great Britain took control and made India the center of its Indian Empire. The British set up a uniform educational system. They made English the official language. They founded a judicial system and passed legislative codes. They modernized harbors and built irrigation systems, factories, mills, and railroads. With these changes, a spirit of nationalism began to emerge in India.

Following World War I, many Indian people began to demand home rule. Mahatma Gandhi became the leader of those Indians who wanted an independent nation. Gandhi developed a program of passive resistance and noncooperation with the government. In this way, he was able to transform the outbursts of social discontent into a passive revolutionary movement.

In 1947, British rule ended, and India and Pakistan emerged as two independent nations. Most of the Muslims chose to live in Pakistan, while the Hindus chose to remain in India.

Indian Social Order

Religion continues to play an important part in the lives of India's people. Most Indians are Hindus. Muslims are the next largest group. Small groups of Christians, Sikhs, Jains, Buddhists, and Parsees also live in India.

The caste system developed from Hinduism. The *caste system* is a social system that has had a great influence on the development of Indian culture. Centuries ago, the Hindus divided themselves into four major groups, or castes. They were the *Brahmins* (priests), the *Kshatriyas* (warriors), the *Vaisyas* (farmers), and the *Sudras* (laborers). These castes were partly religious and partly social. Below the Sudras were the outcasts or "untouchables." The untouchables were forbidden to use public roads or bridges. They were forced to live away from the rest of the people.

Today, the four major castes have been divided and subdivided into thousands of smaller groups. However, many of the old caste restrictions have been relaxed.

Indian Economy

Over 70 percent of India's people are farmers. They live in crowded villages scattered among the fields. They live in sparsely furnished houses and usually cook outdoors. An iron sheet set on clay supports over a fire is the main cooking surface.

Rice is India's major crop. Wheat, barley, millet, corn, and sorghum are grown in areas lacking the moisture needed for rice. Other important crops are chick-peas, beans, peas, and other legumes; cotton; sugarcane; and tea. Smaller quantities of coffee, tobacco, coconuts, and spices also are grown.

Government irrigation and land distribution projects have helped increase total food production in recent years. India is now able to meet most of its needs for food.

Indians raise more cattle than any other type of livestock. Cows provide some milk, but Indians primarily use cattle as work animals. They also raise smaller numbers of goats, hogs, sheep, and water buffalo and export the hides and skins.

Indian manufacturing has progressed far in recent decades. The textile industry has seen the greatest growth. The spinning and weaving of cotton is India's most important industry. Leather, steel, paper, machinery, cement, aluminum, and chemicals are other important manufactured products. See 31-3.

Large mineral deposits are located in eastern India just west of the city of Calcutta. Coal, iron ore, manganese, and sheet mica are plentiful. Smaller amounts of gold, silver, and other precious metals are also mined.

Indian Cuisine

Geography and climate have influenced India's cuisine. Geographically, the major division occurs between the North and the South. Invading groups of people, especially the Mongols, influenced Northern India. The Mongols brought the meat-based cuisine of their central Asian home. Because much of the cuisine developed in the royal kitchens, most foods are rich and heavily seasoned. Foreigners had less influence on Southern India. Its foods are hotter and not as subtle or refined as those of the North.

Climate has played a large part in the development of the two styles of cooking. The heavy rainfall of the South allows large crops of rice, fruits, and vegetables to grow. In the drier North where wheat grows, bread sometimes replaces rice.

31-3 Many Indian people are farmers, and some work in industry. Others, like this stone cutter, are artisans.

Influence of Religion on Indian Cuisine

Religion has been a third major influence on the development of Indian cuisine. Most Indian people are either Hindu or Muslim. Therefore, the dietary restrictions of these two religions have been most influential.

Many Hindu taboos concern food. Hindus cannot eat beef because they consider the cow to be sacred. Most Hindus are vegetarians. However, some Hindus, usually members of lower castes, eat mutton, poultry, goat, and fish. A member of the diner's caste must prepare these foods with cooking utensils belonging to that caste. In addition, food cannot be organically altered. (Artificial color and chemical processes used as preservatives are allowed.)

Although Muslims cannot eat pork, they do eat beef, mutton, lamb, fish, and poultry. These animal foods are more common in Northern India where most Indian Muslims live.

Indian Vegetable Dishes

Vegetable dishes are common in Indian cooking. This is especially true in the South where many people are vegetarians. There, *pulses* (lentils) are an important source of protein.

Indian cooks prepare many vegetable dishes by frying the vegetables with spices. They shape mashed vegetables into balls, deep-fry them, and serve them with a sauce. They skin eggplant; flavor it with oil, pepper, and lemon; and grill it. *Raita*, a salad made of yogurt, vegetables, and seasonings, is a cool accompaniment to spicy dishes. *Rayata*, a potato salad flavored with yogurt, cucumber, tomatoes, cumin, and paprika, is served as a main dish.

Indian Main Dishes

Rice is a staple food throughout much of India. Rice often is served as a side dish. However, it sometimes is used in a variety of main dishes and desserts. Rice also is served as part of a group of dishes called *curry*.

Literally, *curry* is a variation of a word meaning *sauce.* It describes a type of stew. Curry can be prepared in many different ways depending on the region. One common curry is prepared by pounding a variety of Oriental spices. The powdered spices are added to pickled fruit and the mixture is cooked with sugar and vinegar. The curry may be combined with vegetables, meat, poultry, or fish and accompanied by a variety of condiments.

India's many miles of coastline provide a variety of fish. Fish are dried, marinated, and smoked. One specialty is a marinated fish prepared by layering fillets of fish with spices, salt, and tamarind pulp. *Bombil,* a small, nearly transparent fish, is caught in large quantities. When dried, it can be stored for long periods of time. Pomfret often is stuffed with a mixture of spices. It is then wrapped in a banana leaf and steamed, baked, or fried.

Shellfish are also widely available in India. Shrimp and prawns are baked, grilled, or used in curries. Cooks often coat these crustaceans with a spicy batter and deep-fry them. Crabs and lobsters are shredded; mixed with coconut milk, eggs, and spices; and fried in butter.

Most Indian meat dishes are made with mutton. Few Indians eat pork, and beef is both scarce and expensive. Indians prepare meat in many ways. Meat braised in yogurt, cream, or a mixture of the two is called *korma. Bhona* is meat that is first sautéed and then baked. Kebabs are made from mutton that has been spiced, minced, and grilled. *Koftas* are spicy meatballs.

Chicken dishes are also popular in parts of India. People in the North marinate chicken in a mixture of yogurt and spices and roast it on a spit. People in the South add chicken to a spicy, coconut-flavored curry, 31-4.

Indians cook many dishes in oil or fat. *Ghee* (Indian clarified butter) is the preferred cooking fat. To prepare ghee, melt butter over low heat. Then increase the heat and bring the butter to a boil. After gently simmering the ghee for about 50 minutes, strain it through several layers of cheese-cloth. This straining removes solids that could cause ghee to become rancid during storage.

Indian Seasonings

The art of Indian cooking lies in obtaining the right mixture of spices used to make curry. This mixture is called **masala.** The combination of spices can vary. However, each part of the masala must retain its identity without overpowering the other flavors.

Indian cooks use two types of masala: wet masala and dry masala. The spicy dishes of the

Almond Board of California

31-4 This rich, flavorful chicken curry is served over rice.

coastal South use *wet masalas.* These are prepared by mixing the spices with vinegar, coconut milk, or water. They must be used immediately. Northern Indians use *dry masalas.* Dry masalas contain no liquid and cooks can prepare them ahead and store them for a short time.

Indian cooks have a wide variety of spices at their disposal—well over 100 kinds. Six of these spices are basic to Indian cooking. They are saffron, fenugreek, cumin seed, coriander seed, turmeric, and fennel seed.

Other seasonings essential to Indian cooking are garlic, onions, and chili peppers. Chilies are extremely hot. Cooks must use them in small amounts and handle them carefully to prevent burning the skin and eyes.

Fresh herbs add flavor to Indian foods. They are also used to make *chutneys* (condiments containing fruits, onions, spices, and herbs) and sauces. Coriander leaves, mint, and sweet basil are the most popular fresh herbs.

Spices add color as well as flavor to Indian dishes. Saffron and turmeric give rice and potato dishes a bright yellow color. Red and green chilies add vivid color to curries.

Indian Breads

Indians eat several different kinds of *roti*, or bread. Most Indian breads are made from wheat, and they are unleavened and round. The most common is **chapatis**, a flat bread. Indian bakers fry some breads in hot fat. They bake others on a griddle. They make *naan* with yeast or baking powder and bake it in an Indian oven called a *tandoor*. When bakers make *paratha*, they roll and fold it several times so layers form when the bread bakes. Indians often stuff paratha with a meat or vegetable mixture.

Indian Sweets

Indians make many of their sweets from milk. Cooks first simmer the milk until thickened. They combine this thickened mass, called *mawa*, with sugar and cook it a short time longer. Finally, they add flavorings, such as almonds and coconut.

Another group of confections is made from semolina, chick-pea flour, wheat flour, or corn flour. *Halva*, one type of flour-based sweet, is made from semolina.

Indian Cooking Techniques

A number of cooking techniques characterize Indian cuisine. The **tandoori** is the simplest cooking technique. Used most often in Northern India, this technique requires a clay oven called a *tandoor*. Four traditional dishes—tandoori chicken, lamb on skewers, and two types of bread—are prepared in the tandoor. This cooking method has also been extended to include other dishes.

Korma is the second major cooking technique. Foods prepared in this fashion are braised, usually in yogurt. Lamb traditionally is prepared in this way.

Vindaloo is the third major technique. Foods prepared in this way have a hot, slightly sour flavor created by combining vinegar with spices.

Chasnidarth is the fourth major technique. This simply is an Indian version of the Chinese sweet and sour.

Mastering the basic cooking techniques, however, is not enough. The Indian cook also must master the art of using spices—the essence of Indian cuisine.

Indian Meals

During Indian meals, all dishes are served at one time. The serving dishes usually are placed upon a thalis. A *thalis* is a large, round tray made of brass, stainless steel, or silver. (In some parts of India, a banana leaf replaces the thalis. Because it can be discarded after the meal, it is both economical and hygienic.)

In middle class Indian homes, the main meal of the day usually includes a meat or fish dish. (Vegetarian families would omit this dish.) Several vegetable dishes or rice or lentils and bread are also included. Occasionally, *samosas* (small pastries stuffed with vegetables, fish, or meat) may be served as an appetizer. If sweets are served, Indians eat them with the meal rather than afterward.

The rice generally is placed in the center of the thalis. Chutneys, pickles, yogurt, and other condiments surround it. The main dishes are placed around the edges of the tray. Diners help themselves to the food by using their fingers.

Family etiquette requires that the diners wash their hands and rinse their mouth following the meal. They frequently follow this ritual with *paan*. Paan is a betel leaf spread with lime paste and wrapped around chopped betel nuts. As people chew it, it acts as a mouth freshener and a digestive aid.

Indian Menu

Samosas
(Stuffed Savory Pastries)
Badami Gosht Korma
(Lamb and Almond Curry)
Pulao
(Rice)
Raita
(Yogurt with Vegetables)
Chapatis
(Unleavened Bread)
Halva
(Semolina Dessert)
Tea

Ghee
(Clarified Butter)
Makes about 2¾ cups

2 pounds sweet butter

1. In a heavy saucepan, melt butter over very low heat.
2. When butter has melted, increase heat just enough to bring it to a boil.
3. Stir once and reduce the heat to very low. Simmer the butter, uncovered, for 50 minutes.
4. Line a strainer with 3 or 4 layers of cheesecloth.
5. Carefully strain the clear liquid ghee through the cheesecloth. Make sure none of the solids in the bottom of the pan go through the cheesecloth.
6. Pour the ghee into a jar, cover, and store in a cool place.

Per tablespoon: 100 Cal. (100% from fat), 0 g protein, 0 g carbohydrate, 11 g fat, 31 mg cholesterol, 0 g fiber, 2 mg sodium.

Garam Masala
(Indian Spice Mixture)

24 large cardamom seeds
2 ounces coriander seeds
2 ounces black peppercorns
1½ ounces caraway seeds
½ ounce whole cloves
½ ounce ground cinnamon

1. Remove skin from the cardamom seeds.
2. Grind cardamom seeds, coriander seeds, peppercorns, caraway seeds, and cloves until fine.
3. Add cinnamon and mix thoroughly.
4. Seal in airtight container.

Samosas
(Stuffed Savory Pastries)
Makes about 30

Pastry:
1½ cups all-purpose flour, sifted
1 tablespoon vegetable oil
¾ teaspoon salt
½ cup warm water

1. In medium mixer bowl, blend ingredients until soft dough forms.
2. Turn dough out onto lightly floured board. Knead until dough is smooth and elastic, about 10 minutes.
3. Cover and set aside while preparing filling.

Filling:
1 tablespoon ghee
1 clove garlic, chopped
1 teaspoon chopped ginger root
1 medium onion, chopped
½ pound lean ground beef
½ cup hot water
1 teaspoon garam masala
1 tablespoon fresh coriander or mint
1 medium onion, chopped
vegetable oil for frying

1. In large skillet, heat 1 tablespoon ghee, garlic, ginger root, and onion.
2. Add ground beef and sauté until meat no longer is pink.
3. Add hot water. Cover and cook mixture until meat is tender and water is absorbed.
4. Remove from heat and season with garam masala, coriander or mint, and onion.
5. Using fingers, shape small balls of dough and roll each into a flat disk about the size of a saucer.
6. Cut each circle in half. Place 1 teaspoon of filling on one side of each half-circle.
7. Moisten the edge with water. Fold dough over and press edges together to form a triangle.

8. Heat vegetable oil in a deep saucepan.
9. Fry samosas a few at a time, until golden brown.
10. Drain on absorbent paper. Serve immediately.

Per serving: 52 Cal. (43% from fat), 2 g protein, 5 g carbohydrate, 2 g fat, 5 mg cholesterol, 0.5 g fiber, 58 mg sodium.

Raita
(Yogurt with Vegetables)
Serves 6 to 8

3   medium cucumbers
3   tablespoons chopped onions
1   tablespoon salt
3   medium firm ripe tomatoes
3   tablespoons chopped coriander
3   cups plain yogurt
1   tablespoon cumin

1. With a small sharp knife, peel cucumbers. Slice them lengthwise into halves. Scoop out the seeds. Make lengthwise slices about ⅛ inch thick. Then cut slices crosswise into ½-inch pieces.
2. In medium mixer bowl, combine cucumbers, onions, and salt and mix thoroughly. Let rest at room temperature for five minutes.
3. Squeeze gently to remove the excess liquid and transfer to a clean bowl.
4. Add the tomato and coriander and toss together thoroughly.
5. Combine the yogurt and cumin. Pour over the vegetables.
6. Refrigerate until ready to serve.

Per serving: 93 Cal. (10% from fat), 7 g protein, 14 carbohydrate, 1 g fat, 2 mg cholesterol, 1.0 g fiber, 1161 mg sodium.

Badami Gosht Korma
(Lamb and Almond Curry)
Serves 6

1   medium onion
3   garlic cloves
⅔   cup almonds
½   teaspoon ground ginger
½   teaspoon cayenne pepper
1   tablespoon whole coriander seeds
¾   teaspoon salt
1½ pounds boned leg of lamb, cut into 1-inch cubes
¼   cup ghee or butter
1   cup nonfat yogurt
1   cup evaporated skim milk
½   teaspoon powdered saffron

1   tablespoon chopped coriander leaves
4½ cups hot cooked rice

1. Chop the onion.
2. Place chopped onion in blender container with garlic, half of the almonds, ground ginger, cayenne pepper, coriander seeds, and salt.
3. Blend on high speed, gradually adding one or two teaspoons of cold water, until pureed.
4. Place meat cubes in large bowl and rub with puree. Cover and let stand at least 30 minutes.
5. In large skillet, heat ghee (or melted butter).
6. Add meat cubes; stir constantly until browned.
7. Add 3 tablespoons of the yogurt and continue cooking meat over moderate heat until yogurt is absorbed.
8. Add the rest of the yogurt, 1 tablespoon at a time, stirring constantly.
9. Cover skillet and cook mixture over low heat for 30 minutes. (You may need to add a tablespoon or so of water if meat becomes dry.)
10. Grind remaining almonds in blender and mix with evaporated milk and saffron. Add to meat, stirring to blend.
11. Cover and cook low heat 15 to 20 minutes or until thickened and hot. Curry may be served immediately or kept warm in a covered casserole in a 200°F oven.
12. Garnish with coriander leaves and serve over rice.

Per serving: 495 Cal. (36% from fat), 26 g protein, 51 g carbohydrate, 20 g fat, 69 mg cholesterol, 3.7 g fiber, 385 mg sodium.

Chatni
(Mixed Fruit Chutney)
Serves 8

½   pound cooking plums
½   pound cooking apples
½   pound pears or apricots
1   clove garlic
¼   ounce fresh ginger root
2   teaspoons garam masala
1   teaspoon caraway seeds
1   teaspoon salt
2   tablespoons raisins
1½ teaspoons chili powder
½   cup brown sugar
1   cup vinegar

1. Peel, core, and pit fruit; cut into small pieces.
2. Mince garlic and ginger.
3. Put fruit, garlic, and ginger into large saucepan.
4. Add all ingredients except sugar and vinegar. Bring mixture to a boil and simmer over moderate heat for 35 minutes, stirring frequently

5. Remove from heat, stir in sugar and vinegar, and cool. Serve cold as an accompaniment.

Per serving: 106 Cal. (4% from fat), 1 g protein, 29 g carbohydrate, 1 g fat, 0 mg cholesterol, 1.9 g fiber, 278 mg sodium.

Chapatis
(Unleavened Bread)
Makes 8

2   cups whole wheat flour
½   teaspoon salt
4   tablespoons margarine
¾   cup water
1   tablespoon ghee

1. Mix flour and salt together in mixing bowl.
2. With pastry blender, two knives, or fingers, cut margarine into dry ingredients until particles are the size of small peas.
3. Add ¼ cup water all at once. Mix with fingers, gradually adding enough additional water to form a soft dough.
4. Turn dough out onto a lightly floured board or pastry cloth. Knead dough until smooth and elastic, about 10 minutes.
5. Place dough in bowl, cover and let stand at room temperature 30 minutes.
6. Turn dough out onto floured surface. Divide into 8 pieces. Shape each into a thin circle about 5 inches in diameter.
7. Meanwhile, heat heavy skillet over moderate heat.
8. Put chapatis, one at a time, in skillet, When small blisters appear on surface, flatten chapati with hand. Turn and cook other side until golden.
9. Remove from skillet. Brush with ghee and keep warm in 200°F oven until all chapatis are cooked. Serve warm.

Per piece: 163 Cal. (40% from fat), 4 g protein, 21 g carbohydrate, 8 g fat, 4 mg cholesterol, 5.6 g fiber, 201 mg sodium.

Halva
(Semolina Dessert)
Serves 10

1¾   cups sugar
4   cardamom seeds
3   cinnamon sticks
1   cup margarine
2   cups semolina
¾   cup seedless raisins
¾   cup slivered, blanched almonds

1. In a large heavy saucepan, bring 3¾ cups water to a boil.
2. Add sugar and stir until dissolved.
3. Add cardamom and cinnamon.
4. Simmer mixture over moderate heat until syrupy, about 10 minutes.
5. In second saucepan, melt margarine over low heat.
6. Stir in semolina and simmer for 20 minutes, stirring frequently.
7. Add raisins, almonds, and sugar syrup and bring to a boil. Boil for 5 minutes, stirring constantly.
8. Remove cinnamon sticks and cardamom seeds and discard.
9. Pour pudding into shallow pan and cool. Chill well before serving.

Per serving: 473 Cal. (43% from fat), 6 g protein, 64 g carbohydrate, 24 g fat, 0 mg cholesterol, 2.2 g fiber, 260 mg sodium.

USA Rice Council

Indian cooks season their foods with an array of spices.

China

George A. Fischer

Turtle Garden in Xiamen, China, is a beautiful example of classic Chinese architecture.

The People's Republic of China (commonly called *China*) is the home of one of the oldest civilizations. At a time when most of the world's people were barbarians, the Chinese were building beautiful palaces. They were also making pottery and bronze vessels, weaving silk fabrics, and carving jade and marble figures.

Today, this nation has a larger population than any other. In modern history, China has gone through many changes. When studying culinary arts, however, the old Chinese Empire is most interesting.

Climate and Geography of China

China is the third largest country in the world. It occupies nearly one fourth of Asia. Few countries have such clearly defined geography. Geographical features have kept China isolated for much of its history.

The Pacific Ocean and the South China Sea form China's coastlines. Western China is mountainous. The Himalayan and Tien Shan Mountains are most familiar to the Western world. Mount Everest, the world's highest mountain, lies on China's southwestern border. Much of western and southwestern China is barren. The mountains are too high and rugged, and the valleys are too cold and dry for food production.

Eastern China is more suitable for human life. The mountains and hills are lower, and the rolling plains are fairly level. The wide valleys formed by China's great rivers—the Amur, the Yellow, the Yangtze, and the West—have rich soil. Historically, most of China's people have crowded within this geographic area.

Because China's borders extend so far north and south, there are extremes in climate. In China's northernmost regions, the ground stays frozen two thirds of the year. Subarctic conditions keep temperatures below zero for months at a time. Rainfall is scarce. In the southernmost provinces, however, the climate is subtropical with ample rainfall.

The monsoons that come off the Pacific Ocean bring dust storms to the North. They also bring undependable rainfall to much of the eastern third of the country. Both drought and flooding are common.

Chinese Culture

Most modern Chinese people belong to a group known as the *Han* people. This group is a mixture of Mongoloid peoples.

Chapter 31

Influences on Chinese Culture

Much of China's early history is uncertain. However, historians do know that the Chinese lived in a feudal state for many years. Five classes of lords under an emperor ruled them. As the emperor's power weakened, the lords fought among themselves for power. Finally, China was unified under the Ch'in Dynasty in 221 B.C. This was the beginning of the *Chinese Empire.*

The Ch'in Dynasty was short-lived. The Chinese rebelled and overthrew the dynasty. This began a pattern that occurred repeatedly until the birth of the Chinese Republic in 1912. A dynasty came to power, ruled, gradually weakened, and was overthrown. A period of chaos followed, and another dynasty arose to bring peace to China.

During the times of peace, the Chinese made great progress. China's boundaries were extended. The compass, gunpowder, wood block printing, and paper money were invented. The fine arts flourished, and the empire prospered.

Between the fall of one dynasty and the rise of another, foreign invasions often occurred. Most of the invaders came from the north, and the Chinese considered them to be barbarians. They included the Turks, Tunguses, Tibetans, Tatars, Mongols, and Manchus. The Mongols under Kublai Khan conquered all of China and ruled for a time. Eventually, the Chinese absorbed all of these groups. The last invading group, the Manchus, arrived in the seventeenth century. They ruled until the Chinese Republic was declared in 1912.

Modern Culture in China

The Chinese Republic lasted only until 1949. Then, the Chinese Communists gained control. They named the country the *People's Republic of China.* The leaders of the Republic were forced to flee to the nearby island of Formosa (Taiwan). See 31-5.

In pre-Communist days, most Chinese were Buddhists, Taoists, or Confucianists. Taoism and Confucianism both originated in China. They were philosophies as well as religions. Both taught their followers how to live good lives. Buddhism came to China from India. Smaller groups of Chinese Christians and Muslims lived in scattered groups. Today, people do not openly practice religion in China.

George A. Fischer

31-5 These Chinese school children are the bright promise of China's future.

Chinese Economy

Today most of China's people are farmers, just as they were thousands of years ago. Some small family farms still exist. There, the farming methods are primitive. Farmers do nearly all the work by hand or with the help of a single water buffalo or donkey. The government controls other farms and operates them as communes.

China's chief agricultural product is rice. Other important products include wheat, corn, millet, sorghum, oats, rye, barley, soybeans, tea, sugarcane, and cotton. Vegetables are important to the Chinese diet. The Chinese grow vegetables locally to avoid high transportation costs. Chinese celery, turnips, radishes, and eggplant are the most important vegetable crops. The Chinese also grow pears, grapes, oranges, apricots, kumquats, lychee nuts, and figs where weather permits.

The Chinese raise few beef or dairy cattle. Instead, they raise pigs, chickens, ducks, and other small animals that can eat scraps. A few sheep and goats graze in mountainous and grassy areas. China's waters provide an abundance of fish.

Chemicals, porcelain products, and cotton and silk fabrics are China's most important industrial products. Shipbuilding and steel, cement, iron, paper, ball bearing, radio, bicycle, and clock production have grown in recent years. Highly skilled Chinese artisans produce jewelry, lacquer pieces, brushes, and rugs.

Chinese Cuisine

Like all other aspects of Chinese culture, Chinese cuisine developed in isolation. As a result, Chinese cooking is unique.

An old Chinese proverb describes a well-prepared dish. Such a dish must smell appetizing as it is brought to the table. It must stimulate the appetite by its harmonious color combinations. It must sound pleasing as the food is being chewed. It must also taste delicious. Today, the best Chinese dishes still live up to these high standards.

Learning the basics of Chinese cooking is not difficult. Many dishes are simple to prepare. You just need to become familiar with the ingredients, utensils, and cooking methods you will be using.

Chinese Ingredients

In the past, many Chinese ingredients were difficult to obtain in the United States. Today, most large cities have specialty shops that stock Chinese foods.

The ingredients described in 31-6 often appear in Chinese recipes. Besides these ingredients, Chinese cooks use many seasonings. Important seasonings include ginger root, scallions, garlic, sugar, bean paste, and fermented black bean. Monosodium glutamate (MSG), hot pepper, sesame seed oil, star anise, Chinese peppercorns, and five spice powder are also common. (The last three seasonings may be hard to find in the United States. If so, you can substitute anise seed for star anise. You can substitute black peppercorns for Chinese peppercorns. You can substitute a mixture of cinnamon, ginger, cloves, and nutmeg for five spice powder.)

Preparing Ingredients

The Chinese spend more time preparing food to be cooked than they spend cooking. Because most Chinese dishes cook so quickly, cooks must assemble all the ingredients in advance.

Much of the preparation time involves slicing, chopping, shredding, dicing, and mincing vegetables and meats. You can prepare many ingredients hours or even days in advance. You can refrigerate the prepared foods in airtight containers until you are ready to use them.

Chinese Cooking Utensils

You do not need special equipment to cook Chinese food. A large sharp knife; a wooden cutting board; and a heavy, smooth skillet are the most important utensils. However, a few special tools, as shown in 31-7, can be helpful.

Of all Chinese cooking utensils, the wok is the most versatile. A *wok* looks like a metal bowl. It is wider at the top than at the bottom and has sloping sides. The wok originally was used on the Chinese stove, which was similar to a wood burning stove. The wok's curved bottom fit snugly into the openings of Chinese stoves. Today, a metal ring makes it possible to use the wok on a gas or electric range.

Woks are ideal for stir-frying because they conduct heat evenly and rapidly. There are few foods that cannot be cooked in a wok. Other cooking methods, such as deep-frying, can also be done in a wok. If you do not have a wok, you can use a heavy, smooth skillet for this type of cooking.

Woks come in several sizes. A wok with a 12- to 14-inch (30 to 35 cm) diameter should be adequate for an average family. Woks may be made of iron, steel, stainless steel, or aluminum. Some have covers.

A second piece of Chinese cooking equipment is the *steamer*. A steamer looks like a round, shallow basket with openings. Steamers often are sold in sets of five so that several foods can steam at the same time. Most Chinese steamers are made from bamboo. In the United States, aluminum steamers are more common.

Basic Ingredients Used in Chinese Cooking

Ingredient	Description
Bamboo shoots	Cream-colored vegetable available canned in whole or chunk form.
Bean curd	Gelatinous, cream-colored cake made from soybeans. Softened soybeans that are mixed with water to form a milklike substance that is coagulated to form the curd. Bean curd must not be overcooked or it will fall apart. Because bean curd is high in protein and inexpensive, it is a major source of protein in the Chinese diet.
Bean sprouts	The sprouts of the Mung bean. They can be purchased fresh or canned.
Bean threads (cellophane noodles)	Thin, smooth, and translucent noodles. They must be softened in warm water before they are used. Overcooking can cause them to stick together.
Black mushrooms	Very dark mushrooms that are sold dried. Two varieties are available. One is dark, black, and thin. The other is lighter in color and thick. Both must be soaked in boiling water before being used.
Chinese cabbage (bok choy)	Type of cabbage with a white celerylike stalk topped with green leaves. It can be used for cooking and stewing. Another variety called celery cabbage also can be used raw in salads.
Chinese pea pods	Green pod-shaped vegetable that looks something like American sweet pea pods. But the two are very different and cannot be substituted for one another. Whereas sweet pea pods are tough and must be discarded, Chinese pea pods are tender and crisp.
Golden needles	Parts of the tiger lily that look like brown shriveled stems. They are available dried and may be sold pressed into a cake. They must be softened before use.
Hoisin sauce	Sauce that is made from beans, salt, spices, and sugar. Hoisin sauce is thick and dark. It is used in cooking and at the table.
Oyster sauce	Sauce that is made from oysters and seasonings and is dark brown in color. It is used with dark-colored dishes and as a dipping sauce.
Soy sauce	Sauce made from soybeans, wheat, flour, salt, water, and sunshine. (The sunshine gives the sauce its brown color.)
Water chestnuts	Round, cream-colored vegetables that can be purchased either canned or fresh. The canned water chestnuts are ready to use. The fresh water chestnuts first must be cleaned and peeled, but they are sweeter and crisper than the canned ones. Water chestnuts are used whole, sliced, and dried.
Winter melons	Large melons with pale green skins and white flesh. They are not sweet like cantaloupes and watermelons. They are used only for cooking. Winter melon is cut into slices or chunks and cooked with vegetables and meat or added to soup.
Wood ears	Type of fungus that grows on trees. Brown in color, wood ears are sold dried and must be softened in boiling water.

31-6 This chart describes ingredients commonly used in Chinese recipes.

You can improvise a steamer. Place several inches (centimeters) of water in a deep pot. Put the food you are steaming on a plate. Put the plate on a rack in the bottom of the pot. Cover the pot tightly and bring the water to a boil.

A third cooking tool is the *cleaver*. Because the Chinese eat with chopsticks, cooks must cut all the ingredients into pieces that diners can handle easily. Small pieces of food also cook more evenly and rapidly. A beginner may find a cleaver awkward.

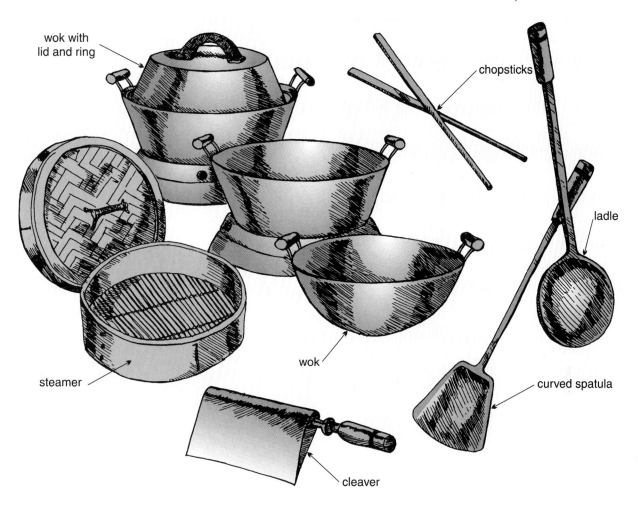

31-7 A few special tools can be helpful when cooking Chinese foods.

With a little practice, however, a cleaver may become more useful than a knife. Chinese cooks use cleavers to perform all cutting tasks as well as crushing and pounding tasks. They use the wide, flat sides of the cleaver blade to scoop and transfer food.

The *Chinese spatula* and *long chopsticks* are other useful tools. The spatula is ideal for stirring and turning foods in the wok. The chopsticks are useful for loosening and mixing food.

Chinese Cooking Methods

The Chinese use four main cooking methods: stir-frying, steaming, deep-frying, and simmering. Less often, they also use roasting as a cooking method.

Stir-Frying

Stir-frying is a cooking method in which foods are cooked over high heat in a small amount of fat. It is the most common Chinese cooking method. Meat, poultry, fish, and vegetables can be stir-fried.

You must cut all ingredients into uniform pieces so they will cook evenly.

To stir-fry foods, heat a small amount of oil in the wok. When the oil becomes hot, add the ingredients. Begin with the ingredients that need the longest cooking time. When the vegetables are crisp-tender, the dish is ready to serve. (Sometimes you might add a little stock or water and seasonings to form a sauce.)

Stir-fried foods cook rapidly, so you must watch them carefully. Stir-fried foods retain their color, texture, flavor, and nutrients. You must serve them immediately, however, or they will lose their texture and flavor. Never overfill a wok. If you are serving more than a few people, you will need to prepare several batches of the same dish. See 31-8.

Steaming

Steaming is the second most common cooking method in China. Because most Chinese do not have ovens, steaming replaces baking. You can steam meats, poultry, dumplings, bread, and rice.

31-8 This beef and vegetable stir-fry cooks in just 15 minutes.

The kettle used for steaming must be large enough to allow the steam to circulate freely around the food. (The water never should touch the food.) Like stir-frying, steaming is economical. Because you can steam several dishes at the same time, you save energy.

Deep-Frying

Deep-frying seals in juices and gives foods a crisp coating. Meat, poultry, egg rolls, and wontons are often deep-fried.

Foods to be deep-fried are first cut into cubes. You can coat the cubes with cornstarch or dip them in a flour and egg batter. (Sometimes you might marinate the cubes before coating them.) Plunge the coated food into hot fat a few pieces at a time. Drain all deep-fried foods on absorbent paper.

Simmering

You may prepare Chinese soups and large pieces of meat by *simmering*. In this method of cooking, you cook the ingredients in simmering liquid over low heat. If you use a clear liquid, such as chicken broth, this method is called *clear-simmering*.

Roasting

The Chinese occasionally use several other cooking methods. Of these methods, *roasting* is most popular. The Chinese sometimes roast pork and poultry. They first rub the meat or bird with oil and/or marinate it. A quick searing over an open flame makes the skin crisp. Then they place the meat or bird on a rack or hang it on a hook to roast slowly. Of all roasted dishes, *Peking Duck* is the best known. The Chinese roll slices of the crisp duck skin and tender flesh inside thin pancakes with scallions and hoisin sauce.

Traditional Chinese Foods

From basic ingredients and cooking methods, the Chinese prepare a variety of traditional foods.

Chinese Grain Products

For centuries, rice has been the backbone of the Chinese diet. This is mainly because rice is both inexpensive and filling.

The Chinese grow two types of rice. One type is glutinous rice. The other type is a variety similar to the long grain rice grown in the United States. The Chinese use glutinous (short grain) rice to make rice flour and translucent rice noodles. They use rice flour to make pastries and dumplings. They serve long grain rice as a side dish and use it to make the main dish called *fried rice.* For this dish, Chinese cooks mix rice with meat, poultry, fish, eggs, vegetables, and seasonings.

The Chinese prepare most rice by steaming. When ready to serve, the rice should be fluffy with firm, distinct grains.

In some parts of China, noodles or flat pancakes made from wheat flour are used in place of rice. One type of noodle is called *lo mein.* It is made from flour and eggs and resembles spaghetti. (Historians believe the Italians learned about pasta from the Chinese.)

The Chinese also use wheat flour to make the skins or wrappers for *wontons* (dumplings) and *egg rolls.* The dough for both contains wheat flour and eggs. The Chinese usually fill egg rolls and wontons with a mixture of minced vegetables and meat, poultry, or shellfish. They prepare wontons by steaming, deep-frying, or boiling them in soups. Egg rolls usually are deep-fried.

Chinese Vegetables

Vegetables are used to a greater extent than meat in the Chinese diet. The Chinese grow many varieties of vegetables. These include Chinese cabbage, broccoli, spinach, pea pods, radishes, mushrooms, and cauliflower. The Chinese eat vegetables alone, in salads, and in soups. They also use vegetables to stretch small amounts of meat, fish, and poultry. Vegetables help make Chinese cooking economical.

Chinese Main Dishes

Although the Chinese eat chicken and duck, they eat little beef. This is partly because beef is scarce and not very good. Also, some religions forbid the eating of beef. Religions may forbid the eating of pork as well. Sweet and sour pork is a popular dish among those allowed to eat pork. *Sweet and sour pork* is a mixture of deep-fried pork cubes, pineapple, and vegetables in a sweet-sour sauce.

Fish are more important to the Chinese diet than meat. Many kinds of fresh and saltwater fish and shellfish are available. The Chinese preserve some fish by drying. This allows them to transport the fish inland or store it for times of need.

The Chinese also like eggs, which they consider a sign of good luck. The Chinese eat both chicken eggs and duck eggs, but they prefer chicken eggs. They use eggs in soups, such as egg drop soup. (*Egg drop soup* is seasoned chicken broth containing

beaten eggs.) They also use eggs in main dishes, such as fried rice and egg foo yung. (*Egg foo yung* is the Chinese version of an omelet.) The Chinese scramble, steam, and smoke eggs, too.

Chinese Soups

Soups are popular throughout China. Some soups, such as *Chinese noodle soup,* are very light. Others, such as *velvet-corn soup,* are heavier. The Chinese use exotic ingredients to make *shark fin soup* and *bird nest soup.*

Most Chinese soups are accompaniments rather than filling main dishes. Soup is the only dish the Chinese eat without chopsticks. They use tiny spoons instead. See 31-9.

Chinese Desserts

Chinese cooks use few dairy products. Chinese recipes rarely call for milk, cheese, butter, or cream. However, some Chinese people now eat ice cream, and they sometimes serve Peking Dust at banquets. *Peking Dust* is a dessert made of whipped cream covered with chestnut puree and garnished with nuts.

Sweet desserts are much less common in China than in other Asian countries. The Chinese reserve sweet desserts for banquets. Then they serve the desserts in the middle of the meal rather than at the end. Fresh or preserved fruits, almond cookies, almond float, and eight treasure rice pudding are popular desserts. (*Almond float* is cubes of almond-flavored gelatin garnished with fruit. *Eight treasure rice pudding* is a molded rice pudding made with candied or dried fruits.)

Chinese Tea

Tea is China's national drink. The Chinese serve black teas, oolong teas, and green teas. (In China, black tea is called *red tea* because black is an unlucky color.) Some teas are scented with fragrant blossoms. The Chinese never add cream, lemon, or sugar to their tea. They usually serve tea at the end of meals. They also offer tea to arriving and departing guests as a sign of hospitality.

Chinese Meals

The Chinese eat three meals a day. Breakfast may be just a bowl of **congee** (a thick porridge made from rice or barley), rice, or boiled noodles. More well-to-do families often serve the congee with several salty side dishes. They may also serve sesame hot muffins, Chinese doughnuts, or pastries bought from a nearby street vendor.

Lunch and dinner are similar. At both meals, all the dishes are served at once. The soup is placed in the center of the table. Four other dishes of pork,

31-9 Hot and sour soup is typical of the spicy cuisine from the Szechwan region of China.

chicken, or fish, with or without vegetables, and one vegetable dish surround the soup. Rice always accompanies the main dishes.

Although the Chinese eat few sweets, they do enjoy snacks. *Dim sum* (steamed dumplings) are delicate pastries filled with meat, fish, vegetables, or occasionally a sweet fruit. Most are steamed, but a few are deep-fried.

The Use of Chopsticks

At a Chinese table, each person's cover is set with a rice bowl, soup spoon, and shallow soup bowl. A shallow sauce dish, a larger dish for main dishes, and a tea cup are also placed at each cover. The Chinese use *chopsticks* as their eating utensils for all dishes except soup and finger foods.

The reason behind the invention of chopsticks is not clear. Perhaps the invention resulted from China's constant fuel shortage. This made it necessary for cooks to cut foods into small pieces that would cook quickly. Diners do not really need a knife and fork to eat such finely cut foods.

The first chopsticks probably were made of bamboo. Later, the wealthy used chopsticks made

of silver and ivory. The chopsticks you will find in Chinese restaurants or in specialty shops will most likely be made of bamboo.

Good Manners Are Good Business

In the United States, people are often coached to accept a portion of all the foods offered to them. Following this practice at a Chinese business dinner, however, could cause you to offend your host. As a sign of his or her generosity, your host is likely to repeatedly refill your empty dish. He or she will probably offer plain rice as the next-to-last course. Eating the rice would indicate that you are still hungry. This would make your host feel as though he or she had failed to meet your needs. You would be wise to refuse the rice course.

Chinese Menu

Ch'un-Chuan
(Egg Rolls)
Tan-Hau-T'ang
(Egg Drop Soup)
T'ien-Suan-Ku-Lao-Jou
(Sweet and Sour Pork)
Chao-Hsueh-Tou
(Stir-Fried Snow Peas with Chinese
Mushrooms and Bamboo Shoots)
Pai-Fan
(Steamed Rice)
Preserved Kumquats
Hsin-Jen-Ping
(Almond Cookies)
Ch'a
(Tea)

Ch'un-Chuan
(Egg Rolls)
Makes 16 to 18 egg rolls

*Wrappers:
 2 cups all-purpose flour
 ½ teaspoon salt
 ¼ cup cold water
 1 egg, lightly beaten

1. To prepare wrappers, sift flour and salt into medium mixing bowl.
2. Using fingers, gradually combine water and beaten egg with flour to form a stiff dough.
3. Knead dough in bowl until smooth, about 5 minutes.
4. Cover with damp towel and let rest 10 minutes.
5. Turn out onto lightly floured board and roll to thickness of 1/16 inch.
6. Using a pastry wheel, cut dough into 7-inch squares.
7. Cover with a slightly damp cloth and set aside while making the filling.

Filling:
 ½ pound ground pork
 1½ teaspoons cornstarch
    dash pepper
 1 tablespoon light brown sugar
 1 tablespoon soy sauce
 3 tablespoons vegetable oil
 3 cups finely chopped celery
 3 cups raw bean sprouts, washed and drained
 ¼ cup sliced mushrooms
 1 tablespoon cornstarch
 2 tablespoons cold water

1. In medium mixing bowl, combine pork, cornstarch, pepper, brown sugar, and soy sauce. Let stand while heating oil.
2. Heat 1 tablespoon oil in wok or large skillet over high heat for 30 seconds.
3. Swirl over bottom and sides of wok and heat another 30 seconds. (If oil begins to smoke, reduce heat.)
4. Add pork and fry 2 minutes stirring constantly. (Meat should lose its reddish color.) Put meat in bowl and set aside.
5. Add the two remaining tablespoons of oil to the wok.
6. Add celery and bean sprouts, stir-fry 3 minutes.
7. Add mushrooms, stir-fry another 2 minutes.
8. Add pork. Stir until all ingredients are combined. Continue cooking over moderate heat until liquid comes to a boil.
9. Remove meat and vegetables. Remove all but 3 tablespoons of the cooking liquid from the wok.
10. Mix cornstarch with cold water. Add to cooking liquid and stir until slightly thickened.
11. Return meat and vegetables to wok to glaze with sauce and then transfer entire contents of wok to mixing bowl. Cool to room temperature.
12. To shape egg rolls, use fingers to shape about ¼ cup of filling into a cylinder about 4 inches long. Place in center of wrapper on the diagonal.
13. To fold, fold corner of wrapper closest to you to the center. Fold the end two edges toward the center. Then, fold the remaining edge to the center and seal well.
14. Place filled egg rolls on a baking sheet and cover with a slightly damp towel.
15. Place 3 cups of oil in wok or deep saucepan. Heat oil to 375°F.

Chapter 31

16. Fry egg rolls, 5 at a time, until crisp and golden brown, about 3 or 4 minutes.
17. Transfer to a paper towel to drain while you finish frying. Serve immediately or keep warm for a short time in a 225°F oven.

*A 1-pound package of commercial egg roll wrappers can be substituted.

Per egg roll: 124 Cal. (31% from fat), 6 g protein, 16 g carbohydrate, 4 g fat, 27 mg cholesterol, 1.2 g fiber, 165 mg sodium.

Tan-Hau-T'ang
(Egg Drop Soup)
Serves 5 to 6

5   cups chicken stock
¾   cup minced chicken
1   tablespoon cornstarch
3   tablespoons cold water
2   eggs, lightly beaten
2   scallions, finely chopped

1. In large saucepan, bring chicken stock to a boil.
2. Reduce heat to medium and add chicken. Simmer 5 minutes.
3. Mix cornstarch with cold water. Add to soup, stirring until soup thickens and becomes clear.
4. Slowly pour in eggs and stir once, gently. Turn off the heat.
5. Taste soup to see if it needs salt.
6. Transfer to a heated soup tureen and garnish with chopped scallions.

Per serving: 120 Cal. (50% from fat), 10 g protein, 5 g carbohydrate, 7 g fat, 127 mg cholesterol, 0 g fiber, 960 mg sodium.

T'ien-Suan-Ku-Lao-Jou
(Sweet and Sour Pork)
Serves 5 to 6

2   eggs, lightly beaten
1½ teaspoons salt
1   teaspoon soy sauce
½   cup cornstarch
½   cup flour
½   cup chicken stock
2   pounds lean pork, trimmed and cut into 1-inch cubes
3   cups vegetable oil

Sauce:
2   tablespoons vegetable oil
3   green onions, finely chopped
3   medium green peppers, cleaned, seeded, and cut into strips

2   cups canned pineapple chunks, drained (reserve liquid)
3   tablespoons brown sugar
½   teaspoon ginger
¾   cup reserved pineapple juice
4½ tablespoons cider vinegar
1½ tablespoons red wine vinegar
3   tablespoons soy sauce
1½ tablespoons cornstarch dissolved in 2 tablespoons cold water

1. In large bowl, combine eggs, salt, 1 teaspoon soy sauce, cornstarch, flour, and chicken stock. Set aside.
2. Prepare and assemble all other ingredients.
3. Just before cooking, add pork cubes to coating batter. With fork or chopsticks, stir to coat cubes evenly.
4. Preheat oven to 250°F.
5. Put 3 cups oil into wok or deep saucepan. Over high heat, heat oil until it reaches a temperature of 375°F.
6. Add pork cubes, a few at a time, fry until crisp and golden.
7. Remove to paper towel-lined baking pan to drain. Then, put in baking dish and keep warm in oven.
8. Pour off remaining oil. Add 2 tablespoons fresh oil to wok or very large skillet and heat over high heat for 30 seconds.
9. Add green onions and green peppers and stir-fry about 2 to 3 minutes.
10. Add pineapple and stir-fry an additional minute.
11. Add brown sugar, ginger, pineapple juice, cider vinegar, red wine vinegar, and soy sauce. Cook until bubbly.
12. Dissolve cornstarch in 2 tablespoons cold water. Add to sauce. Cook, stirring constantly, until sauce thickens and becomes clear.
13. Pour sauce over fried pork cubes and serve immediately.

Per serving: 663 Cal. (46% from fat), 33 g protein, 58 g carbohydrate, 35 g fat, 198 mg cholesterol, 2.1 g fiber, 1861 mg sodium.

Chao-Hsueh-Tou
(Stir-Fried Snow Peas with Chinese Mushrooms and Bamboo Shoots)
Serves 6

⅔   cup dried Chinese mushrooms
1½ pounds fresh snow peas (or thoroughly defrosted frozen snow peas)
1   cup canned bamboo shoots, rinsed and sliced thinly
3   tablespoons vegetable oil
1½ tablespoons soy sauce
2   teaspoons sugar

1. In small bowl, combine mushrooms with ½ cup boiling water. Let soak 15 minutes.
2. Drain, squeezing excess water from mushrooms with fingers. (Reserve soaking liquid.)
3. Cut off stems and cut mushrooms into quarters.
4. Remove tips from fresh snow peas and string from pods.
5. In wok or heavy skillet, heat the oil over high heat.
6. Add mushrooms and bamboo shoots and stir-fry for 2 minutes.
7. Add snow peas, sugar, 2 tablespoons of the reserved soaking liquid, and soy sauce. Cook over high heat, stirring constantly, until water evaporates, about 2 to 3 minutes.
8. Transfer contents of wok to a serving dish and serve immediately.

Per serving: 109 Cal. (58% from fat), 3 g protein, 8 g carbohydrate, 7 g fat, 0 mg cholesterol, 2.1 g fiber, 262 mg sodium.

National Pork Producers Council

The Chinese enjoy steamed dumplings called dim sum *as snacks.*

Pai-Fan
(Steamed Rice)
Serves 6 to 8

1 cup uncooked long grain rice
2 cups cold water

1. Put cold water and rice in heavy saucepan and bring to a boil. Stir once or twice.
2. Cover pan, reduce heat to low and simmer 15 minutes.
3. Remove from heat and let rest 10 minutes. (Do not uncover pan.)
4. Remove cover and fluff rice with chopsticks or a fork. Serve immediately.

Per serving: 112 Cal. (1% from fat), 2 g protein, 25 g carbohydrate, 0 g fat, 0 mg cholesterol, 1.0 g fiber, 2 mg sodium.

Hsing-Jen-Ping
(Almond Cookies)
Makes 5 dozen cookies

4 cups sifted all-purpose flour
1½ cups sugar
½ teaspoon baking powder
1 teaspoon salt
1 cup shortening
1 egg, beaten
1 tablespoon water
1 teaspoon almond extract
  blanched whole almonds
1 egg yolk
2 tablespoons skim milk

1. Preheat oven to 375°F.
2. In large mixing bowl, combine flour, sugar, baking powder, and salt.
3. With pastry blender or two knives, cut in shortening until particles are the size of small peas.
4. In small bowl, combine egg, water, and almond extract.
5. Add to flour mixture all at once. Mix well.
6. Knead dough 1 minute in bowl.
7. Roll into small balls. Place 2 inches apart on ungreased baking sheets.
8. Flatten to about ⅜-inch thickness. Top each cookie with an almond and brush with egg glaze made by combining the egg yolk with milk.
9. Bake until lightly browned, about 12 minutes.

Per cookie: 93 Cal. (46% from fat), 1 g protein, 11 g carbohydrate, 5 g fat, 9 mg cholesterol, 0.6 g fiber, 40 mg sodium.

Japan

The Japanese wear traditional costumes to celebrate the Gion Festival.

Japan is a nation of islands. The four main Japanese islands are Hokkaido, Honshu, Shikoku, and Kyushu. They lie along with thousands of smaller islands near Asia's Pacific Coast.

Japan has successfully adapted to Western ways without losing its sense of identity. Postwar industrial growth brought many changes to cities like Tokyo. However, Japan's traditional values are still alive today. These values include respect for family, love of nature, and belief in hard work. The Japanese word *sappari* means "clean, light, and sparkling with honesty." *Sappari* still describes the Japanese people, their country, and their cuisine.

Climate and Geography of Japan

Three fourths of Japan's total land area is mountainous or hilly. The mountains add great beauty to the land. However, they have made farming difficult and have caused crowded living conditions in the few lowlands. One of the most spectacular mountains is the volcanic peak, Mount Fuji. Although Mount Fuji is dormant, at least 30 volcanoes are still active in Japan.

Swift-flowing rivers and crystal clear lakes dot Japan's landscape. Many of the rivers end in picturesque waterfalls. Others bring the water used to irrigate rice fields. A few provide hydro-electric power.

A long coastline with many natural harbors is a valuable asset. It has helped Japan become an important port of foreign ships.

Because the islands cover such a large latitude, Japan has a variety of climates. The southern part of the country is subtropical. Summers are hot and humid, and winters are mild. The bulk of the population lives in this area. Their housing, clothing, and farming methods are suited to a warm climate.

Hokkaido, Japan's northernmost island, has cold winters. Temperatures fall below freezing for at least four months during the winter, and snowfall is heavy.

Japan receives more than adequate moisture. Seasonal winds, called *monsoons*, bring rain in summer and snow in winter. During September, severe storms, called *typhoons*, bring heavy rains and damaging winds.

Japanese Culture

The exact origin of the Japanese people is uncertain. However, archaeologists believe the first inhabitants came from the arid steppes of northern Asia.

Play It Safe

Becoming lost in an unfamiliar place is not only frightening, it can also be dangerous. This problem can be further complicated if you are unable to communicate with the local people. You should carry the name and address of the place you are staying with you. (When visiting a country that uses a different alphabet, ask someone who knows the language to write it for you.) You can show the address to taxi drivers or others who might be helping you with directions.

Influences on Japanese Culture

The imperial family that later set up the first state is thought to have consolidated scattered clans in Japan. This happened around A.D. 4. The imperial family, headed by an emperor, actively ruled Japan until 1192. Then, a military government took over, and the emperor became a figurehead. Military rule under the shoguns lasted for nearly 700 years.

The first *Occidentals* (Westerners) arrived in the sixteenth century. The Portuguese were the first to arrive. Jesuit missionaries and, later, groups of Spanish, Dutch, and English traders followed the Portuguese. The Japanese ruling class encouraged both trade and Christianity.

In the early seventeenth century, the shoguns began to see Occidental influence as a threat to their power. As a result, they closed Japan's doors to the rest of the world. They banned Christianity, and they allowed only the Dutch to send a few ships each year.

For two centuries, Japan kept its doors closed. During this time, national unity developed, and Japan prospered. As they had done in the past, the Japanese adopted ideas they had learned from other cultures. They discarded the ideas that they did not find useful.

In 1853, a United States naval fleet entered Tokyo Bay. The following year, the Japanese agreed to open two ports to United States trade. A treaty was signed, and trade with other countries soon followed.

Further changes occurred in 1867, when the shogun gave up his power. With the emperor again in control, class distinction ended and feudalism was abolished. Two years later, a constitutional monarchy was established.

Modern Culture in Japan

Japan experienced a tremendous period of expansion toward the end of the nineteenth century. By the end of World War I, Japan was recognized as one of the world's great powers. Japanese military strength continued to grow, and the government became a military dictatorship.

World War II gave the militarists a new opportunity for expansion. Instead of obtaining new territory, however, they suffered a crushing defeat.

Following the war, Japan began to rebuild. In the decades that followed, Japan experienced rapid industrial growth. Today, Japan plays a major role in world affairs.

Japanese Agriculture

Providing enough food has always been a challenge for the Japanese. Japanese farmers are able to raise excellent crops through intensive cultivation and hard work. However, Japan is able to produce only about 70 percent of its food needs.

Rice is Japan's most important crop. Over half the tillable land is used for rice production. In the far south, Japanese farmers can grow two crops each year. Other important crops include sweet potatoes, wheat, and sugar beets.

The Japanese raise tea bushes on terraced hillsides. They grow mandarin oranges and strawberries in the South. They grow peaches, pears, persimmons, cherries, apples, and other hearty fruits in the North. The Japanese also grow beans, large radishes, cucumbers, lettuce, onions, cabbage, turnips, carrots, and spinach. They grow many varieties of peas, squash, and pumpkins, too.

Land always has been scarce, and the teachings of Buddhism forbid the eating of meat. Therefore, the Japanese have traditionally raised little livestock. In recent years, however, livestock production has increased. This is partly due to the abandonment of Buddhist dietary laws. Also, a taste for eggs, milk, meat, and poultry has been developing among the Japanese people.

Seafood provides most of the protein in the Japanese diet. Japan's fishing industry is one of the world's largest. Sardines, salmon, herring, cuttlefish, yellowtail, and other kinds of fish, as well as seaweed, live in coastal waters. The Japanese fish for bonito, mackerel, sardines, shark, tuna, and shellfish in the North Pacific. They freeze or can some of the catch for export.

Chapter 31

Japanese Industry

In less than 100 years, Japan developed from an agricultural country into a manufacturing country. Today, it is one of the world's largest industrial powers. Some of Japan's major exports are machinery, transportation equipment, textiles, processed fish, chemicals, and toys. Other exports include microscopes, telescopes, cameras, and electronic equipment, such as televisions, CD players, and stereo components.

Japanese Lifestyle

Nearly two thirds of Japan's people are city dwellers. Japan is one of the largest countries in terms of population. This explains the crowded conditions of Japanese cities. See 31-10.

City people must learn to live without a great deal of space. However, they do not need to give up their love for nature. City families need only to open their sliding porch screens to see a miniature landscape. Japanese gardens are often complete with a stream, bridge, and flowering bushes. Those who are too poor to have a garden often have small potted trees.

Japanese families are close-knit. Family members deeply respect the elderly. Most Japanese today live in small family units. However, it was once common for grandparents, parents, and children to all live under one roof.

The majority of Japanese people are either Buddhists or Shintos. The Chinese introduced Buddhism, Japan's leading religion. Shinto, which originated in Japan, is based on nature and ancestor worship.

Japanese Cuisine

In a country where tillable land is scarce, food is an important commodity. By necessity, the Japanese diet is simple. Rice, legumes, vegetables, fruits, fish, and seaweed can be easily obtained from the land and sea. These foods are the staple foods in the Japanese diet.

Basic Japanese Ingredients

Ingredients commonly used in Japanese cooking include sesame oil, mild rice vinegar, daikon, mirin, and sake. Kanpyo, gobo, and shirataki are common ingredients, too. *Kanpyo* is strips of dried gourd. *Gobo* is burdock root, and *shirataki* is a mixture made from a yamlike tuber. The Japanese also use salt, pepper, sugar, chives, onions, mustard, scallions, and other familiar seasonings. However,

Japan National Tourist Organization

31-10 The streets of Japanese cities become especially crowded during festival celebrations.

four ingredients are basic to Japanese cookery: rice, soybeans, fish, and seaweed.

Rice

Rice is so important to the Japanese diet that the Japanese word for meal is **gohan,** which means *rice.* Japanese rice is a short grain variety. Cooks usually steam it and serve it plain. Sometimes they cook rice with other ingredients or serve it with a sauce. Two other products, *sake* (Japanese rice wine) and *mirin* (sweet wine), are obtained from rice.

Soybeans

The Chinese introduced the soybean to the Japanese. The **soybean** is a legume with seeds that are rich in protein and oil. The Japanese use soybeans in many different forms.

Miso is a fermented soybean paste. The Japanese use miso in a soup that they serve for breakfast. It may also be an ingredient in a marinade used to prepare fish and vegetables.

Tofu is a custardlike cake made from soybeans. It has a very mild flavor. The Japanese may roll tofu in cornstarch and deep-fry it. They may scramble it with eggs. They may also sauté, boil, or broil it. Sometimes, they add tofu to soups. *Sumashi* (clear broth with tofu and shrimp) is an example. See 31-11.

Shoyu, Japanese soy sauce, contains wheat or barley, salt, water, and malt along with soybeans. Shoyu is an all-purpose seasoning in the Japanese kitchen. (You cannot use the heavier Chinese soy sauce as a substitute.)

Fish

Japan's earliest settlers discovered the bounty of the seas. Tuna, bass, flounder, cod, mackerel, *ayu* (sweet fish), carp, and squid are most popular. The Japanese also eat many varieties of shellfish and more unusual subtropical species. *Katsuo* (dried bonita) is an essential ingredient of *dashi,* a Japanese stock. *Fugu* (blowfish) is a Japanese delicacy. Fugu contains a lethal toxin that can kill a diner unless the fish has been properly cleaned. Licensed fugu chefs perform this function.

Japanese cooks demand that all fish and shellfish must be fresh. Therefore, they do not kill shellfish until minutes before cooking. They keep freshwater varieties that will be eaten raw alive until serving time.

Two of the most popular fish dishes are sashimi and sushi. *Sashimi* are raw fillets of fish eaten alone or with a sauce. (Most Westerners are amazed that Japanese-style raw fish have a mild flavor and do not taste raw or fishy.) *Sushi* are balls of cooked rice flavored with vinegar. They are served with strips of raw or cooked fish, eggs, vegetables, or seaweed. These two dishes are so popular that sashimi and sushi restaurants and snack bars are found throughout Japan.

Seaweed

The Japanese use *seaweed* from the surrounding oceans both fresh and dried. They roll *nori,* a dried variety, around fish or rice. They also use it as a garnish. The Japanese use *konbu* (dried kelp) in dashi. They use other varieties of seaweed as flavorings, garnishes, and vegetables in soups.

Japanese Vegetables and Fruits

Japanese farmers grow many vegetables. Traditional Japanese vegetables include daikon,

Japan National Tourist Organization

31-11 Tofu is one of the components of the Japanese dish called sukiyaki.

negi, wasabi, and bakusai. *Daikon* is a giant white radish. *Negi* is a thin Japanese leek. *Wasabi* is Japanese horseradish, and *bakusai* is Chinese cabbage. Lotus roots and shoots, edible chrysanthemum leaves, burdock, spinach, ginger root, and bamboo shoots are also popular. Many types of peas, beans, ferns, and mushrooms are common, too.

Japanese cooks often mix vegetables together in salads. Japan has two kinds of salads: *aemono* (mixed foods) and *sunomono* (vinegared foods). Aemono salads contain several raw or cooked vegetables in a thick dressing. Sunomono salads contain crisp, raw vegetables and cold, cooked fish or shellfish. They are served with a thin dressing made of rice vinegar, sugar, and soy sauce. *Namusu* (vegetables in a vinegar dressing) is an example.

Japanese fruits are plentiful. Persimmons and many types of oranges grow in Japan. One of the best-known oranges is the *mikan,* or mandarin orange. Apples, pears, cherries, strawberries, plums, and melons also grow well.

Japanese Main Dishes

Meat traditionally was not part of the Japanese diet. Today, however, meat appears on many Japanese tables. Because it is costly, the Japanese usually serve meat in small amounts with other foods.

Although the Japanese eat both pork and beef, their beef is famous. The tenderness of the meat results in part from the treatment the cattle receive. Japanese farmers feed the animals bran, beans, rice, and beer. They massage each steer daily with *shochu* (Japanese gin).

Poultry production in Japan has grown in recent years. Chickens are less costly to raise, so they appear more often in Japanese recipes than meat. Eggs are becoming more popular, too. *Tamago dashimaki* is the Japanese version of an omelet.

Japanese Cooking Methods

Japanese cooks usually cook foods in small pieces. They boil, steam, fry, and broil foods instead of baking or roasting them.

Japanese cooks boil a variety of foods, including meat, poultry, seafood, and vegetables. The cooking liquid may be a strongly flavored stock or a mild broth. Foods cooked in boiling liquid are called *nimono.* Examples of nimono are *kimini* (sake-seasoned shrimp with egg yolk glaze) and *kiriboshi daikon* (chicken simmered with white radish threads).

Steaming is the simplest of all cooking methods. *Mushimono* (steamed foods) retain their fresh flavors, colors, and nutrients. Japanese cooks use two steaming methods. *Mushi* foods are foods cooked on a plate suspended over boiling water. *Chawan mushi* foods are foods steamed in an egg custard. Mushi foods are mild in flavor, so the Japanese usually serve them with a dipping sauce. Chawan mushi foods are richer in flavor and usually are served without a sauce.

The Japanese learned frying from early Portuguese traders. The Japanese modified the Portuguese method by using a lighter batter and a lighter oil. They use this method to prepare *tempura.* Japanese cooks prepare tempura by coating vegetables, meat, poultry, and seafood in a batter. Then they quickly fry the coated pieces in oil. Other Japanese *agemono* (fried foods) are deep-fried in oil. All Japanese agemono are light and delicate. They are never greasy or heavy.

The Japanese usually use broiling for meat, poultry, and fish. One popular *yakimono* (broiled food) is beefsteak. It is dipped in a mixture of soy sauce and mirin and grilled over charcoal. Beef teriyaki and yakitori are two types of yakimono popular in the United States. *Beef teriyaki* is slices of beef glazed with a special sauce. *Yakitori* is chicken, scallions, and chicken livers broiled on a skewer.

Japanese cooks prepare many dishes at the table. They use one or a combination of the above cooking methods. Sukiyaki combines two cooking methods—*nabemono* (dishes cooked at the table) and *nimono* (foods cooked in boiling liquid). **Sukiyaki** is a popular Japanese dish made of thinly sliced meat, bean curd, and vegetables cooked in a sauce. Cooks prepare all the raw ingredients in the kitchen. Then, they cook the beef and vegetables with their accompanying sauce in a skillet at the table. Another method of preparing food at the table uses the hibachi. A *hibachi* is a small grill that can be built into the center of the table or used free standing.

Aesthetic Appearance of Foods

An important element of Japanese cuisine is subtlety of taste. Cooks achieve this subtlety through the careful selection of ingredients and cooking methods. Another important element, aesthetic appearance, demands a trained eye and artistic touch. It is just one more example of the importance nature has played in the development of Japanese culture.

Japanese cooks place great emphasis on the color, shape, and arrangement of food on a serving dish, 31-12. They strive to make each arrangement unique. Many times, an arrangement may suggest a particular season or mood. For instance, a cook might arrange ingredients to represent the

Japan National Tourist Organization

31-12 The color, shape, and arrangement of these foods reflect the importance Japanese cooks place on aesthetic appearance.

mountains, rivers, trees, and flowers of a Japanese spring. Such a dish might be served at the spring fish festival.

Japanese Tea Ceremony

Tea, Japan's national drink, came to Japan from China. In the past, the Japanese used tea only as a medicine or as a special drink for priests and aristocrats. Today, they serve tea with every meal. The Japanese serve green teas (teas made from unfermented tea leaves), which they call **nihon-cha.**

The traditional Japanese tea ceremony developed during the seventeenth century. From this social custom sprang kaiseka. **Kaiseka** is a delicate meal served after the tea ceremony. It represents the highest point of Japanese cuisine.

Today, the Japanese perform the tea ceremony just as their ancestors did hundreds of years ago. Harmony must exist between the host and the guests and between the food and the season. There must also be harmony between the food and its serving containers. Finally, there must be harmony between one food and all the other foods. To ensure this harmony, the host must receive a great deal of training.

Each step of the tea ceremony is done according to established rules. Each movement the host makes is designed to bring pleasure to the guest.

Simple tea ceremonies may last just 40 minutes. Those that include kaiseka may last as long as four hours.

Japanese Eating Customs

Many of the manners and behaviors that are a part of the tea ceremony carry over to everyday life. Freshly bathed and dressed in clean kimonos, many Japanese families sit down together at a low table. Family members engage in polite conversation. Meanwhile, the mother prepares the meal at the table or serves what she prepared in the kitchen.

The Japanese do not use napkins. Instead, a small, soft towel called an *oshibori* is brought to the table on a small platter or basket. The oshibori is warm, damp, and fragrant. The Japanese use it to wipe their face and hands. Then they return it to its basket and remove it from the table. They usually use oshibori at both the beginning and end of the meal.

Bowls used for hot foods are served covered. Diners usually remove the cover of the individual rice bowl first. This indicates that rice is Japan's most honored food. The Japanese must use both hands to place a rice bowl on a tray for refilling. To use one hand is a breach of courtesy.

In Japan, cooks always cut food into small pieces before cooking. This makes the food easy to pick up with chopsticks. (The Japanese use knives only for food preparation. They do not place knives on the table.) The oldest guest always picks up his or her chopsticks first as a token of respect. After use, diners return their chopsticks to the chopstick rest.

The Japanese do not eat rice all at once. Instead, they eat it with the other foods in much the same way people in the United States eat bread.

The Japanese drink soup from a cup rather than spooning it from a bowl. They remove the bowl from the table and hold it in the left hand. Then they hold their chopsticks in the right hand to secure the food.

To show appreciation for the cook's skill, it is quite proper to smack the lips or make sucking sounds. Guests often exchange sake cups with their host as a sign of respect.

Japanese Meals

Japanese meals are made up of many dishes. The dishes are light, and the quantities served are much smaller than those served in the West. Meals are varied, delicious, and nourishing.

In the morning, some Japanese people eat eggs and other breakfast foods popular in the United States. In many parts of Japan, however, people eat more traditional breakfast foods. Such foods include umeboshi and miroshiru. *Umeboshi* is a tiny, red, pickled plum. *Miroshiru* is a hearty soup made of dashi, miso, and rice. Japanese breakfast foods also include rice, which is often sprinkled with *nori* (a type of dried seaweed).

Japanese families may serve a carefully prepared lunch if family members come home at noon or they are expecting guests. Otherwise, Japanese cooks usually prepare simple lunches. The morning rice is reheated and served with leftover vegetables and meat or a simple sauce.

The evening meal is much more elaborate. Because businesses stay open later in Japan than in the United States, the meal usually is served later. The young children eat their meal first. The Japanese prepare children's versions of many popular foods. An example is *kushizashi* (meats, fowl, and vegetables grilled on a skewer). Cooks make kushizashi with hot peppers for adults. However, they use milder scallions when preparing the dish for children.

The Japanese usually serve all the dishes in the main meal together. They usually serve broiled or fried meat, poultry, or fish as a main course. Although the main course can vary, rice, soup, and tsukemono must be served. **Tsukemono** (soaked foods) are lightly pickled pieces of daikon, cucumber, melon, eggplant, and other vegetables. The Japanese eat them with rice near the end of the meal. See 31-13.

The Japanese rarely eat sweet desserts. They reserve sweets for special occasions. Instead, most meals end with fresh fruit.

31-13 All the dishes of the main Japanese meal are served together.

Japanese Menu
Sumashi Wan
(Clear Broth with Tofu and Shrimp)
Sukiyaki
(Beef and Vegetables Cooked in Seasoned
Liquid)
Namasu
(Vegetables in a Vinegar Dressing)
Gohan
(Steamed Rice)
Snow Peas
Mikan
(Mandarin Oranges)
Nihon-Cha
(Green Tea)

Sumashi Wan
(Clear Broth with Tofu and Shrimp)
Serves 6

2 cups water
1 cake tofu (soybean curd), 6 ounces, cut into 6
     equal squares
1 cup water
   salt
7 spinach leaves (or ½ package frozen leaf spinach
     thoroughly defrosted and separated into leaves)
4 cups clam broth
2 cups chicken broth
6 small canned shrimp

1. In small saucepan, bring 2 cups of water to a boil.
2. Add tofu and let water return to a simmer.
3. Remove from heat immediately and cover. Set
   aside until ready to serve soup.
4. In a second saucepan, bring 1 cup lightly salted
   water to a boil.
5. Add spinach and cook just until crisp-tender.
6. Drain immediately and rinse under cold running
   water. Remove excess moisture with paper towels
   and set aside.
7. Wash saucepan. Combine clam broth and chicken
   broth and bring to a boil.
8. Meanwhile, set six soup bowls on a tray. Place a
   spinach leaf, a shrimp, and a cube of tofu in the
   bottom of each.
9. Pour soup into bowls, filling each about ¾ full and
   being careful not to disturb garnish. (Pour soup
   down the sides of the bowls.) Serve immediately.

Per serving: 50 Cal. (41% from fat), 5 g protein, 2 g
carbohydrate, 2 g fat, 7 mg cholesterol, 0.2 g fiber, 169
mg sodium.

Sukiyaki
(Beef and Vegetables Cooked in Seasoned
Liquid)
Serves 4 to 6

2 pounds beef tenderloin or sirloin steak
8 ounces shirataki (long noodlelike threads) or
     vermicelli
2 medium onions, sliced crosswise
5 leeks, split lengthwise and cut in 1½-inch lengths
¾ pound fresh mushrooms, washed and split
     lengthwise in ¼-inch pieces
5 stalks celery, cut diagonally into ¼-inch slices
1 pound fresh spinach, cleaned (or 1 package frozen
     leaf spinach thoroughly defrosted)
½ pound tofu (soybean curd), cut into cubes
½ cup low-sodium soy sauce
2 tablespoons sugar
1½ cups beef broth
6 tablespoons margarine

1. Slice beef crossgrain into paper-thin slices, 1 by 2
   inches. (Slightly frozen meat is easier to slice.)
   Trim fat.
2. Bring one cup of water to a boil.
3. Add shirataki and return to boil.
4. Drain and slice shirataki into thirds.
5. Prepare other vegetables as directed.
6. Arrange meat and vegetables attractively on serving platter and refrigerate, covered with plastic
   wrap.
7. Combine soy sauce, sugar, and beef broth in a
   small bowl. Cover and refrigerate.
8. To cook sukiyaki, heat three tablespoons margarine in wok (over moderately high heat) or electric skillet (425°F).
9. Add half of the beef slices and cook until meat
   loses its pink color. Push meat to the side.

10. Add half of the-onions and leeks and cook until transparent and lightly browned. (Turn meat as needed.) Push vegetables to the side.
11. Add half of the mushrooms and half of the celery in two groups. Stir-fry 2 to 3 minutes.
12. Add half the sauce and simmer about 5 minutes. Turn all foods occasionally.
13. Add half of the spinach and cook 1 minute.
14. Add half of the noodles or vermicelli and bean curd. (These will absorb the broth.) Serve immediately or keep warm in a 225°F oven while you cook the remaining half of the ingredients.

Per serving: 667 Cal. (35% from fat), 43 g protein, 66 g carbohydrate, 26 g fat, 77 mg cholesterol, 6.9 g fiber, 2387 mg sodium.

Namasu
(Vegetables in a Vinegar Dressing)
Serves 6

½ pound daikon or white turnip, peeled and shredded
1 medium carrot, scraped and shredded
1 tablespoon salt
¼ cup preflaked, dried bonito
1 tablespoon white vinegar
2 teaspoons sugar
   monosodium glutamate (MSG), optional

1. In small bowl, combine daikon, carrot, salt, and 1 cup cold water. Stir to mix and let stand 30 minutes.
2. Put dried bonito in a small pan and heat over low heat for 3 to 4 minutes to dry further.
3. Transfer to a blender container and grind to a fine powder.
4. Drain carrot and daikon. Squeeze dry and put in mixing bowl.
5. Add vinegar, sugar, and two pinches of monosodium glutamate. Mix well and add powdered bonito. Serve at room temperature.

Per serving: 38 Cal. (5% from fat), 5 g protein, 4 g carbohydrate, 0 g fat, 8 mg cholesterol, 1.0 g fiber, 451 mg sodium.

Gohan
(Steamed Rice)
Makes 3 cups

1 cup uncooked long grain rice
2 cups cold water

1. Place rice and water in a large, heavy saucepan.
2. Bring water to a boil, reduce heat to medium and cook rice covered for about 5 minutes, or until rice has absorbed all the liquid.

3. Remove from heat. Let the rice rest, undisturbed, 5 minutes.
4. Remove cover, fluff with fork, and serve.

Per serving: 112 Cal. (1% from fat), 2 g protein, 25 g carbohydrate, 0 g fat, 0 mg cholesterol, 0.8 g fiber, 2 mg sodium.

Snow Peas
Serves 6

1½ pounds snow peas (or two 10 ounce packages frozen snow peas)
    water
    salt

1. Snap ends from fresh snow peas and remove center rib. Rinse in cool water.
2. In medium saucepan, bring small amount of salted water to a boil.
3. Add snow peas and return water to a boil. Simmer peas until crisp-tender.
4. Drain and serve immediately.

Per serving: 33 Cal. (4% from fat), 3 g protein, 6 g carbohydrate, 0 g fat, 0 mg cholesterol, 1.3 g fiber, 3 mg sodium.

Japan National Tourist Organization

The tea ceremony is a ritual that has been performed in Japan for hundreds of years.

Summary

Russia, India, China, and Japan have cuisines that differ greatly from the cuisine of the United States. The cuisines of these countries also differ greatly from one another.

Russian cuisine was influenced by the Slavs and Mongols. The czars also made a number of contributions. In the days of the Russian Empire, however, most Russians were peasants. The staple foods of their diet were bread, kasha, and soup. Today, Russian meals often begin with appetizers, called *zakuska*. A hearty soup, such as schi or borscht, and a meat, fish, or poultry main dish would follow. Rye bread, potatoes, and a seasonal vegetable would accompany the main dish. A simple dessert of pureed fruit might round out the meal.

Religious dietary restrictions play a major role in the cuisine of India. In addition, Indian cuisine has some geographic distinctions. Different climates and influences have created some specific differences between the cuisines of Northern and Southern India. Four basic cooking techniques are used to prepare Indian cuisine: tandoori, korma, vindaloo, and chasnidarth. Curry is a dish found throughout India. However, cooks in different regions prepare and season it in different ways.

Chinese foods contain some unique ingredients. A few special utensils, including a wok, are helpful for preparing Chinese foods. Most Chinese foods are prepared by stir-frying, steaming, deep-frying, or simmering. Rice is a staple of the Chinese diet. Vegetables also play an important role. Vegetables and meat or poultry are cut into small pieces to make them easier to eat with chopsticks.

Four ingredients are basic to Japanese cuisine: rice, soybeans, fish, and seaweed. Many Japanese foods feature vegetables with smaller amounts of meat, poultry, or fish. The Japanese often boil, steam, fry, or broil their foods. The aesthetic appearance of foods is an important aspect of Japanese cuisine. The Japanese also follow some specific eating customs. Many of these are observed in the traditional tea ceremony.

Review What You Have Read

Write your answers on a separate sheet of paper.

 1. What are four contributions the Mongols made to Russian cuisine?
 2. Name the three staple foods of Russian peasants during the days of the czars.
 3. Name and describe two Russian desserts.
 4. In general, how does the cuisine of Northern India differ from the cuisine of Southern India?
 5. Many Indian dishes are cooked in a clarified butter called _____.
 6. Which of the following Indian cooking techniques involves braising foods in yogurt?
    A. Chasnidarth.
    B. Korma.
    C. Tandoori.
    D. Vindaloo.
 7. What is China's chief agricultural product?
 8. Choose four important ingredients in Chinese cooking and briefly define each.
 9. What is the most versatile of all Chinese cooking utensils?
10. Why have the Japanese traditionally raised little livestock?
11. Name and describe three food products made from soybeans in Japan.
12. Describe two Japanese eating customs.

Build Your Basic Skills

1. Use library resources to research one of the Russian czars. Prepare an oral report for the class.
2. Investigate the major differences between Hinduism and Buddhism. Summarize your findings in a written report.

Build Your Thinking Skills

1. Prepare ghee. Fry potatoes in lard, vegetable shortening, margarine, and ghee. Evaluate differences in browning and flavor.
2. Design an evaluation form for a tea tasting. Then complete the form as you taste and compare several different varieties of tea popular in China.
3. Work with a small group to research the traditional Japanese tea ceremony. Each member of the group should be responsible for demonstrating one aspect of the ceremony in a presentation to the class.

Chapter 31

Appendix A   *Recommended Dietary Allowances* [a]

Designed for the maintenance of good nutrition of practically all healthy people in the U.S.A.

Category	Age (years) or Condition	Weight[b] (kg)	(lb)	Height[b] (cm)	(in)	Protein (g)	Fat-Soluble Vitamins				Water-Soluble Vitamins							Minerals						
							Vitamin A (µg RE)[c]	Vitamin D (µg)[d]	Vitamin E (mg α-TE)[e]	Vitamin K (µg)	Vitamin C (mg)	Thiamin (mg)	Riboflavin (mg)	Niacin (mg NE)[f]	Vitamin B6 (mg)	Folate (µg)	Vitamin B12 (µg)	Calcium (mg)	Phosphorus (mg)	Magnesium (mg)	Iron (mg)	Zinc (mg)	Iodine (µg)	Selenium (µg)
Infants	0.0–0.5	6	13	60	24	13	375	7.5	3	5	30	0.3	0.4	5	0.3	25	0.3	400	300	40	6	5	40	10
	0.5–1.0	9	20	71	28	14	375	10	4	10	35	0.4	0.5	6	0.6	35	0.5	600	500	60	10	5	50	15
Children	1–3	13	29	90	35	16	400	10	6	15	40	0.7	0.8	9	1.0	50	0.7	800	800	80	10	10	70	20
	4–6	20	44	112	44	24	500	10	7	20	45	0.9	1.1	12	1.1	75	1.0	800	800	120	10	10	90	20
	7–10	28	62	132	52	28	700	10	7	30	45	1.0	1.2	13	1.4	100	1.4	800	800	170	10	10	120	30
Males	11–14	45	99	157	62	45	1000	10	10	45	50	1.3	1.5	17	1.7	150	2.0	1200	1200	270	12	15	150	40
	15–18	66	145	176	69	59	1000	10	10	65	60	1.5	1.8	20	2.0	200	2.0	1200	1200	400	12	15	150	50
	19–24	72	160	177	70	58	1000	10	10	70	60	1.5	1.7	19	2.0	200	2.0	1200	1200	350	10	15	150	70
	25–50	79	174	176	70	63	1000	5	10	80	60	1.5	1.7	19	2.0	200	2.0	800	800	350	10	15	150	70
	51+	77	170	173	68	63	1000	5	10	80	60	1.2	1.4	15	2.0	200	2.0	800	800	350	10	15	150	70
Females	11–14	46	101	157	62	46	800	10	8	45	50	1.1	1.3	15	1.4	150	2.0	1200	1200	280	15	12	150	45
	15–18	55	120	163	64	44	800	10	8	55	60	1.1	1.3	15	1.5	180	2.0	1200	1200	300	15	12	150	50
	19–24	58	128	164	65	46	800	10	8	60	60	1.1	1.3	15	1.6	180	2.0	1200	1200	280	15	12	150	55
	25–50	63	138	163	64	50	800	5	8	65	60	1.1	1.3	15	1.6	180	2.0	800	800	280	15	12	150	55
	51+	65	143	160	63	50	800	5	8	65	60	1.0	1.2	13	1.6	180	2.0	800	800	280	10	12	150	55
Pregnant						60	800	10	10	65	70	1.5	1.6	17	2.2	400	2.2	1200	1200	300	30	15	175	65
Lactating	1st 6 months					65	1300	10	12	65	95	1.6	1.8	20	2.1	280	2.6	1200	1200	355	15	19	200	75
	2nd 6 months					62	1200	10	11	65	90	1.6	1.7	20	2.1	260	2.6	1200	1200	340	15	16	200	75

Food and Nutrition Board, National Academy of Sciences National Research Council, Revised 1989

[a] The allowances, expressed as average daily intakes over time, are intended to provide for individual variations among most normal persons as they live in the United States under usual environmental stresses. Diets should be based on a variety of common foods in order to provide other nutrients for which human requirements have been less well defined.

[b] Weights and heights of Reference Adults are actual medians for the U.S. population of the designated age, as reported by NHANES II. The median weights and heights of those under 19 years of age were taken from Hamill et al. (1979) (see pages 16–17). The use of these figures does not imply that the height-to-weight ratios are ideal.

[c] Retinol equivalents. 1 retinol equivalent = 1µg retinol or 6 µg β-carotene.

[d] As cholecalciferol. 10µg cholecalciferol = 400 IU of vitamin D.

[e] α-Tocopherol equivalents. 1 mg d-α tocopherol = 1 ∝TE.

[f] 1 NE (niacin equivalent) is equal to 1 mg of niacin or 600 mg of dietary tryptophan.

Appendix B

Nutritive Values of Foods

(Tr indicates nutrient present in trace amount.)

(A) Item No. Foods, approximate measures, units, and weight (weight of edible portion only)	(B) Grams	(C) Water Percent	(D) Food energy Calories	(E) Protein Grams	(F) Fat Grams	(G) Cholesterol Milligrams	(H) Carbohydrate Grams	(I) Calcium Milligrams	(J) Phosphorus Milligrams	(K) Iron Milligrams	(L) Potassium Milligrams	(M) Sodium Milligrams	(N) Vitamin A (IU) International units	(O) Vitamin A (RE) Retinol equivalents	(P) Thiamin Milligrams	(Q) Riboflavin Milligrams	(R) Niacin Milligrams	(S) Ascorbic acid Milligrams
Beverages																		
Carbonated:[2]																		
Club soda — 12 fl. oz.	355	100	0	0	0	0	0	18	0	Tr	0	78	0	0	0.00	0.00	0.0	0
Cola type:																		
Regular — 12 fl. oz.	369	89	160	0	0	0	41	11	52	0.2	7	18	0	0	0.00	0.00	0.0	0
Diet, artificially sweetened — 12 fl. oz.	355	100	Tr	0	0	0	Tr	14	39	0.2	7	[3]32	0	0	0.00	0.00	0.0	0
Ginger ale — 12 fl. oz.	366	91	125	0	0	0	32	11	0	0.1	4	29	0	0	0.00	0.00	0.0	0
Grape — 12 fl. oz.	372	88	180	0	0	0	46	15	0	0.4	4	48	0	0	0.00	0.00	0.0	0
Lemon-lime — 12 fl. oz	372	89	155	0	0	0	39	7	0	0.4	4	33	0	0	0.00	0.00	0.0	0
Orange — 12 fl. oz.	372	88	180	0	0	0	46	15	4	0.3	7	52	0	0	0.00	0.00	0.0	0
Pepper type — 12 fl. oz.	369	89	160	0	0	0	41	11	41	0.1	4	37	0	0	0.00	0.00	0.0	0
Root beer — 12 fl. oz.	370	89	165	0	0	0	42	15	0	0.2	4	48	0	0	0.00	0.00	0.0	0
Cocoa and chocolate-flavored beverages. See Dairy Products.																		
Coffee:																		
Brewed — 6 fl. oz.	180	100	Tr	Tr	Tr	0	Tr	4	2	Tr	124	2	0	0	0.00	0.02	0.4	0
Instant, prepared — 6 fl. oz.	182	99	Tr	Tr	Tr	0	1	2	6	0.1	71	Tr	0	0	0.00	0.03	0.6	0
(2 tsp. powder plus 6 fl. oz. water)																		
Fruit drinks, noncarbonated:																		
Canned:																		
Fruit punch drink — 6 fl. oz.	190	88	85	Tr	0	0	22	15	2	0.4	48	15	20	2	0.03	0.04	Tr	461
Grape drink — 6 fl. oz.	187	86	100	Tr	0	0	26	2	2	0.3	9	11	Tr	Tr	0.01	0.01	Tr	464
Pineapple-grapefruit juice drink — 6 fl. oz.	187	87	90	Tr	Tr	0	23	13	7	0.9	97	24	60	6	0.06	0.04	0.5	4110
Frozen:																		
Lemonade concentrate:																		
Undiluted — 6-fl.-oz. can	219	49	425	Tr	Tr	0	112	9	13	0.4	153	4	40	4	0.04	0.07	0.7	66
Diluted with 4 1/3 parts water by volume — 6 fl. oz.	185	89	80	Tr	Tr	0	21	2	2	0.1	30	1	10	1	0.01	0.02	0.2	13
Limeade concentrate:																		
Undiluted — 6-fl.-oz. can	218	50	410	Tr	Tr	0	108	11	13	0.2	129	Tr	Tr	Tr	0.02	0.02	0.2	26
Diluted with 4-1/3 parts water by volume — 6 fl. oz	185	89	75	Tr	Tr	0	20	2	2	Tr	24	Tr	Tr	Tr	Tr	Tr	Tr	4
Fruit juices. See type under Fruits and Fruit Juices.																		
Milk beverages. See Dairy Products.																		
Tea:																		
Brewed — 8 fl. oz.	240	100	Tr	Tr	Tr	0	Tr	0	2	Tr	36	1	0	0	0.00	0.03	Tr	0
Instant, powder, prepared:																		
Unsweetened (1 tsp. powder plus 8 fl. oz. water) — 8 fl. oz.	241	100	Tr	Tr	Tr	0	1	1	4	Tr	61	1	0	0	0.00	0.02	0.1	0
Sweetened (3 tsp. powder plus 8 fl. oz. water) — 8 fl. oz.	262	91	85	Tr	Tr	0	22	1	3	Tr	49	Tr	0	0	0.00	0.04	0.1	0
Dairy Products																		
Butter. See Fats and Oils																		
Cheese:																		
Cheddar:																		
Cut pieces — 1 oz.	28	37	115	7	9	30	Tr	204	145	0.2	28	176	300	86	0.01	0.11	Tr	0
— 1 in.3	17	37	70	4	6	18	Tr	123	87	0.1	17	105	180	52	Tr	0.06	Tr	0
Shredded — 1 cup	113	37	455	28	37	119	1	815	579	0.8	111	731	1,200	342	0.03	0.42	0.1	0
Cottage (curd not pressed down):																		
Creamed (cottage cheese, 4% fat):																		
Large curd — 1 cup	225	79	235	28	10	34	6	135	297	0.3	190	911	370	108	0.05	0.37	0.3	Tr
Small curd — 1 cup	210	79	215	26	9	31	6	126	277	0.3	177	850	340	101	0.04	0.34	0.3	Tr
Lowfat (2%) — 1 cup	226	79	205	31	4	19	8	155	340	0.4	217	918	160	45	0.05	0.42	0.3	Tr

(A)	(B)	(C)	(D)	(E)	(F)	(G)	(H)	(I)	(J)	(K)	(L)	(M)	(N)	(O)	(P)	(Q)	(R)	(S)
Uncreamed (cottage cheese dry curd, less than 1/2% fat)	1 cup / 145	80	125	25	1	10	3	46	151	0.3	47	19	40	12	0.04	0.21	0.2	0
Cream	1 oz. / 28	54	100	2	10	31	1	23	30	0.3	34	84	400	124	Tr	0.06	Tr	0
Mozzarella, made with:																		
Whole milk	1 oz. / 28	54	80	6	6	22	1	147	105	0.1	19	106	220	68	Tr	0.07	Tr	0
Part skim milk (low moisture)	1 oz. / 28	49	80	8	5	15	1	207	149	0.1	27	150	180	54	0.01	0.10	Tr	0
Parmesan, grated:																		
Tablespoon	1 tbsp. / 5	18	25	2	2	4	Tr	69	40	Tr	5	93	40	9	Tr	0.02	Tr	0
Ounce	1 oz. / 28	18	130	12	9	22	1	390	229	0.3	30	528	200	49	0.01	0.11	0.1	0
Swiss	1 oz. / 28	37	105	8	8	26	1	272	171	Tr	31	74	240	72	0.01	0.10	Tr	0
Pasteurized process cheese:																		
American	1 oz. / 28	39	105	6	9	27	Tr	174	211	0.1	46	406	340	82	0.01	0.10	Tr	0
Swiss	1 oz. / 28	42	95	7	7	24	1	219	216	0.2	61	388	230	65	Tr	0.08	Tr	0
Pasteurized process cheese food, American	1 oz. / 28	43	95	6	7	18	2	163	130	0.2	79	337	260	62	0.01	0.13	Tr	0
Pasteurized process cheese spread, American	1 oz. / 28	48	80	5	6	16	2	159	202	0.1	69	381	220	54	0.01	0.12	Tr	0
Cream, sweet:																		
Half-and-half (cream and milk)	1 cup / 242	81	315	7	28	89	10	254	230	0.2	314	98	1,050	259	0.08	0.36	0.2	2
	1 tbsp. / 15	81	20	Tr	2	6	1	16	14	Tr	19	6	70	16	0.01	0.02	Tr	Tr
Light, coffee, or table	1 cup / 240	74	470	6	46	159	9	231	192	0.1	292	95	1,730	437	0.08	0.36	0.1	2
	1 tbsp. / 15	74	30	Tr	3	10	1	14	12	Tr	18	6	110	27	Tr	0.02	Tr	Tr
Whipping, unwhipped (volume about double when whipped):																		
Light	1 cup / 239	64	700	5	74	265	7	166	146	0.1	231	82	2,690	705	0.06	0.30	0.1	1
	1 tbsp. / 15	64	45	Tr	5	17	Tr	10	9	Tr	15	5	170	44	Tr	0.02	Tr	Tr
Heavy	1 cup / 238	58	820	5	88	326	7	154	149	0.1	179	89	3,500	1,002	0.05	0.26	0.1	1
	1 tbsp. / 15	58	50	Tr	6	21	Tr	10	9	Tr	11	6	220	63	Tr	0.02	Tr	Tr
Whipped topping, (pressurized)	1 cup / 60	61	155	2	13	46	7	61	54	Tr	88	78	550	124	0.02	0.04	Tr	0
	1 tbsp. / 3	61	10	Tr	1	2	Tr	3	3	Tr	4	4	30	6	Tr	Tr	Tr	0
Cream, sour	1 cup / 230	71	495	7	48	102	10	268	195	0.1	331	123	1,820	448	0.08	0.34	0.2	2
	1 tbsp. / 12	71	25	Tr	3	5	1	14	10	Tr	17	6	90	23	Tr	0.02	Tr	Tr
Cream products, imitation (made with vegetable fat):																		
Whipped topping:																		
Frozen	1 cup / 75	50	240	1	19	0	17	5	6	0.1	14	19	5650	565	0.00	0.00	0.0	0
	1 tbsp. / 4	50	15	Tr	1	0	1	Tr	Tr	Tr	1	1	530	53	0.00	0.00	0.0	0
Pressurized	1 cup / 70	60	185	1	16	0	11	4	13	Tr	13	43	5330	533	0.00	0.00	0.0	0
	1 tbsp. / 4	60	10	Tr	1	0	1	Tr	1	Tr	1	2	520	52	0.00	0.00	0.0	0
Ice cream. See Milk desserts, frozen.																		
Ice milk. See Milk desserts, frozen.																		
Milk:																		
Fluid:																		
Whole (3.3% fat)	1 cup / 244	88	150	8	8	33	11	291	228	0.1	370	120	310	76	0.09	0.40	0.2	2
Lowfat (2%):																		
No milk solids added	1 cup / 244	89	120	8	5	18	12	297	232	0.1	377	122	500	139	0.10	0.40	0.2	2
Milk solids added, label claim less than 10 g of protein per cup	1 cup / 245	89	125	9	5	18	12	313	245	0.1	397	128	500	140	0.10	0.42	0.2	2
Lowfat (1%):																		
No milk solids added	1 cup / 244	90	100	8	3	10	12	300	235	0.1	381	123	500	144	0.10	0.41	0.2	2
Milk solids added, label claim less than 10 g of protein per cup	1 cup / 245	90	105	9	2	10	12	313	245	0.1	397	128	500	145	0.10	0.42	0.2	2
Nonfat (skim):																		
No milk solids added	1 cup / 245	91	85	8	Tr	4	12	302	247	0.1	406	126	500	149	0.09	0.34	0.2	2
Milk solids added, label claim less than 10 g of protein per cup	1 cup / 245	90	90	9	1	5	12	316	255	0.1	418	130	500	149	0.10	0.43	0.2	2
Buttermilk	1 cup / 245	90	100	8	2	9	12	285	219	0.1	371	257	80	20	0.08	0.38	0.1	2
Canned:																		
Condensed, sweetened	1 cup / 306	27	980	24	27	104	166	868	775	0.6	1,136	389	1,000	248	0.28	1.27	0.6	8
Evaporated:																		
Whole milk	1 cup / 252	74	340	17	19	74	25	657	510	0.5	764	267	610	136	0.12	0.80	0.5	5
Skim milk	1 cup / 255	79	200	19	1	9	29	738	497	0.7	845	293	1,000	298	0.11	0.79	0.4	3
Dried:																		
Nonfat, instantized:																		
Envelope, 3.2 oz., net wt.[6]	1 envelope / 91	4	325	32	1	17	47	1,120	896	0.3	1,552	499	2,160	646	0.38	1.59	0.8	5

Nutritive Values of Foods – Continued
(Tr indicates nutrient present in trace amount.)

Nutrients in Indicated Quantity

Item No. (A)	Foods, approximate measures, units, and weight (weight of edible portion only) (B)		Water (C)	Food energy (D)	Pro-tein (E)	Fat (F)	Cho-lesterol (G)	Carbo-hydrate (H)	Calcium (I)	Phos-phorus (J)	Iron (K)	Potas-sium (L)	Sodium (M)	Vitamin A value (IU) (N)	Retinol equiva-lents (RE) (O)	Thiamin (P)	Ribo-flavin (Q)	Niacin (R)	Ascorbic acid (S)
		Grams	Per-cent	Cal-ories	Grams	Grams	Milli-grams	Grams	Milli-grams	Milli-grams	Milli-grams	Milli-grams	Milli-grams	Inter-national units	Retinol equiva-lents	Milli-grams	Milli-grams	Milli-grams	Milli-grams
Milk beverages:																			
	Chocolate milk (commercial):																		
	Regular	1 cup	250	82	210	8	8	31	26	280	251	0.6	417	149	300	73	0.09	0.41	0.3	2
	Lowfat (2%)	1 cup	250	84	180	8	5	17	26	284	254	0.6	422	151	500	143	0.09	0.41	0.3	2
	Lowfat (1%)	1 cup	250	85	160	8	3	7	26	287	256	0.6	425	152	500	148	0.10	0.42	0.3	2
	Cocoa and chocolate-flavored beverages:																		
	Powder containing nonfat dry milk	1 oz.	28	1	100	3	1	1	22	90	88	0.3	223	139	Tr	Tr	0.03	0.17	0.2	Tr
	Powder without nonfat dry milk	3/4 oz.	21	1	75	1	1	0	19	7	26	0.7	136	56	Tr	Tr	Tr	0.03	0.1	Tr
	Eggnog (commercial)	1 cup	254	74	340	10	19	149	34	330	278	0.5	420	138	890	203	0.09	0.48	0.3	4
	Malted milk:																		
	Chocolate:																		
	Powder	3/4 oz.	21	2	85	1	1	1	18	13	37	0.4	130	49	20	5	0.04	0.04	0.4	0
	Shakes, thick:																		
	Chocolate	10-oz. container	283	72	335	9	8	30	60	374	357	0.9	634	314	240	59	0.13	0.63	0.4	0
	Vanilla	10-oz. container	283	74	315	11	9	33	50	413	326	0.3	517	270	320	79	0.08	0.55	0.4	0
Milk desserts, frozen:																			
	Ice cream, vanilla:																		
	Regular (about 11% fat):																		
	Hardened	1/2 gal.	1,064	61	2,155	38	115	476	254	1,406	1,075	1.0	2,052	929	4,340	1,064	0.42	2.63	1.1	6
		1 cup	133	61	270	5	14	59	32	176	134	0.1	257	116	540	133	0.05	0.33	0.1	1
	Soft serve (frozen custard)	1 cup	173	60	375	7	23	153	38	236	199	0.4	338	153	790	199	0.08	0.45	0.2	1
	Ice milk, vanilla:																		
	Hardened (about 4% fat)	1/2 gal.	1,048	69	1,470	41	45	146	232	1,409	1,035	1.5	2,117	836	1,710	419	0.61	2.78	0.9	6
		1 cup	131	69	185	5	6	18	29	176	129	0.2	265	105	210	52	0.08	0.35	0.1	1
	Soft serve (about 3% fat)	1 cup	175	70	225	8	5	13	38	274	202	0.3	412	163	175	44	0.12	0.54	0.2	1
	Sherbet (about 2% fat)	1/2 gal.	1,542	66	2,160	17	31	113	469	827	594	2.5	1,585	706	1,480	308	0.26	0.71	1.0	31
		1 cup	193	66	270	2	4	14	59	103	74	0.3	198	88	190	39	0.03	0.09	0.1	4
Yogurt:																			
	With added milk solids:																		
	Made with lowfat milk:																		
	Fruit-flavored[8]	8-oz. container	227	74	230	10	2	10	43	345	271	0.2	442	133	100	25	0.08	0.40	0.2	1
	Plain	8-oz. container	227	85	145	12	4	14	16	415	326	0.2	531	159	150	36	0.10	0.49	0.3	2
	Made with nonfat milk	8-oz. container	227	85	125	13	Tr	4	17	452	355	0.2	579	174	20	5	0.11	0.53	0.3	2
Eggs																			
	Eggs, large (24 oz. per dozen):																		
	Raw:																		
	Whole, without shell	1 egg	50	75	80	6	6	274	1	28	90	1.0	65	69	260	78	0.04	0.15	Tr	0
	White	1 white	33	88	15	3	Tr	0	Tr	4	4	Tr	45	50	0	0	Tr	0.09	Tr	0
	Yolk	1 yolk	17	49	65	3	6	272	Tr	26	86	0.9	15	8	310	94	0.04	0.07	Tr	0
	Cooked:																		
	Fried in butter	1 egg	46	68	95	6	7	278	1	29	91	1.1	66	162	320	94	0.04	0.14	Tr	0
	Hard-cooked, shell removed	1 egg	50	75	80	6	6	274	1	28	90	1.0	65	69	260	78	0.04	0.14	Tr	0
	Poached	1 egg	50	74	80	6	6	273	1	28	90	1.0	65	146	260	78	0.03	0.13	Tr	0
	Scrambled (milk added) in butter. Also omelet	1 egg	64	73	110	7	8	282	2	54	109	1.0	97	176	350	102	0.04	0.18	Tr	Tr
Fats and Oils																			
	Butter (4 sticks per lb.):																		
	Tablespoon (1/8 stick)	1 tbsp.	14	16	100	Tr	11	31	Tr	3	3	Tr	4	[9]116	[10]430	[10]106	Tr	Tr	Tr	0
	Pat (1 in. square, 1/3 in. high; 90 per lb.)	1 pat	5	16	35	Tr	4	11	Tr	1	1	Tr	1	[9]41	[10]150	[10]38	Tr	Tr	Tr	0
	Fats, cooking (vegetable shortenings)	1 cup	205	0	1,810	0	205	0	0	0	0	0.0	0	0	0	0	0.00	0.00	0.0	0
		1 tbsp.	13	0	115	0	13	0	0	0	0	0.0	0	0	0	0	0.00	0.00	0.0	0

(A)	(B)	(g)	(C)	(D)	(E)	(F)	(G)	(H)	(I)	(J)	(K)	(L)	(M)	(N)	(O)	(P)	(Q)	(R)	(S)
Margarine:																			
Imitation (about 40% fat), soft	8-oz. container	227	58	785	1	88	0	1	40	31	0.0	57	[11]2,178	[12]7,510	[12]2,254	0.01	0.05	Tr	Tr
	1 tbsp.	14	58	50	Tr	5	0	Tr	2	2	0.0	4	[11]134	[12]460	[12]139	Tr	Tr	Tr	Tr
Regular (about 80% fat):																			
Hard (4 sticks per lb.):																			
Tablespoon (1/8 stick)	1 tbsp.	14	16	100	Tr	11	0	Tr	4	3	Tr	6	[11]132	[12]460	[12]139	Tr	0.01	Tr	Tr
Pat (1 in. square, 1/3 in. high; 90 per lb.)	1 pat	5	16	35	Tr	4	0	Tr	1	1	Tr	2	[11]47	[12]170	[12]50	Tr	Tr	Tr	Tr
Soft	8-oz. container	227	16	1,625	2	183	0	1	60	46	0.0	86	[11]2,449	[12]7,510	[12]2,254	0.02	0.07	Tr	Tr
	1 tbsp.	14	16	100	Tr	11	0	Tr	4	3	0.0	5	[11]151	[12]460	[12]139	Tr	Tr	Tr	Tr
Spread (about 60% fat):																			
Hard (4 sticks per lb.):																			
Tablespoon (1/8 stick)	1 tbsp.	14	37	75	Tr	9	0	0	3	2	0.0	4	[11]139	[12]460	[12]139	Tr	Tr	Tr	Tr
Pat (1 in. square, 1/3 in. high; 90 per lb.)	1 pat	5	37	25	Tr	3	0	0	1	1	0.0	1	[11]50	[12]170	[12]50	Tr	Tr	Tr	Tr
Soft	8-oz. container	227	37	1,225	1	138	0	0	47	37	0.0	68	[11]2,256	[12]7,510	[12]2,254	0.02	0.06	Tr	Tr
	1 tbsp.	14	37	75	Tr	9	0	0	3	2	0.0	4	[11]139	[12]460	[12]139	Tr	Tr	Tr	Tr
Oils, salad or cooking:																			
Corn	1 cup	218	0	1,925	0	218	0	0	0	0	0.0	0	0	0	0	0.00	0.00	0.0	0
	1 tbsp.	14	0	125	0	14	0	0	0	0	0.0	0	0	0	0	0.00	0.00	0.0	0
Safflower	1 cup	218	0	1,925	0	218	0	0	0	0	0.0	0	0	0	0	0.00	0.00	0.0	0
	1 tbsp.	14	0	125	0	14	0	0	0	0	0.0	0	0	0	0	0.00	0.00	0.0	0
Soybean oil, hydrogenated (partially hardened)	1 cup	218	0	1,925	0	218	0	0	0	0	0.0	0	0	0	0	0.00	0.00	0.0	0
	1 tbsp.	14	0	125	0	14	0	0	0	0	0.0	0	0	0	0	0.00	0.00	0.0	0
Sunflower	1 cup	218	0	1,925	0	218	0	0	0	0	0.0	0	0	0	0	0.00	0.00	0.0	0
	1 tbsp.	14	0	125	0	14	0	0	0	0	0.0	0	0	0	0	0.00	0.00	0.0	0
Salad dressings:																			
Commercial:																			
Blue cheese	1 tbsp.	15	32	75	1	8	3	1	12	11	Tr	6	164	30	10	Tr	0.02	Tr	Tr
French:																			
Regular	1 tbsp.	16	35	85	Tr	9	0	1	2	1	Tr	2	188	Tr	Tr	Tr	Tr	Tr	Tr
Low calorie	1 tbsp.	16	75	25	Tr	2	0	2	6	5	Tr	3	306	Tr	Tr	Tr	Tr	Tr	Tr
Italian:																			
Regular	1 tbsp.	15	34	80	Tr	9	0	1	1	1	Tr	5	162	30	3	Tr	Tr	Tr	Tr
Low calorie	1 tbsp.	15	86	5	Tr	Tr	0	2	1	1	Tr	4	136	Tr	Tr	Tr	Tr	Tr	Tr
Mayonnaise:																			
Regular	1 tbsp.	14	15	100	Tr	11	8	Tr	3	4	0.1	5	80	40	12	0.00	0.00	Tr	0
Imitation	1 tbsp.	15	63	35	Tr	3	4	2	Tr	Tr	0.0	2	75	0	0	0.00	0.00	0.0	0
Tartar sauce	1 tbsp.	14	34	75	Tr	8	4	1	3	4	0.1	11	182	30	9	Tr	Tr	0.0	Tr
Thousand island:																			
Regular	1 tbsp.	16	46	60	Tr	6	4	2	2	3	0.1	18	112	50	15	Tr	Tr	Tr	Tr
Low calorie	1 tbsp.	15	69	25	Tr	2	2	2	2	3	0.1	17	150	50	14	Tr	Tr	Tr	Tr
Prepared from home recipe:																			
Cooked type	1 tbsp.	16	69	25	1	2	9	2	13	14	0.1	19	117	70	20	0.01	0.02	Tr	Tr
Vinegar and oil	1 tbsp.	16	47	70	0	8	0	Tr	0	0	0.0	1	Tr	0	0	0.00	0.00	0.0	0

Fish and Shellfish

(A)	(B)	(g)	(C)	(D)	(E)	(F)	(G)	(H)	(I)	(J)	(K)	(L)	(M)	(N)	(O)	(P)	(Q)	(R)	(S)
Clams:																			
Raw, meat only	3 oz.	85	82	65	11	1	43	2	59	138	2.6	154	102	90	26	0.09	0.15	1.1	9
Crabmeat, canned	1 cup	135	77	135	23	3	135	1	61	246	1.1	149	1,350	50	14	0.11	0.11	2.6	
Fish sticks, frozen, reheated, (stick, 4 by 1 by 1/2 in.)	1 fish stick	28	52	70	6	3	26	4	11	58	0.3	94	53	20	5	0.03	0.05	0.6	0
Haddock, breaded, fried[14]	3 oz.	85	61	175	17	9	75	7	34	183	1.0	270	123	70	20	0.06	0.10	2.9	0
Halibut, broiled, with butter and lemon juice	3 oz.	85	67	140	20	6	62	Tr	14	206	0.7	441	103	610	174	0.06	0.07	7.7	1
Salmon:																			
Canned (pink), solids and liquid	3 oz.	85	71	120	17	5	34	0	[15]167	243	0.7	307	443	60	18	0.03	0.15	6.8	0
Sardines, Atlantic, canned in oil, drained solids	3 oz.	85	62	175	20	9	85	0	[15]371	424	2.6	349	425	190	56	0.03	0.17	4.6	0
Scallops, breaded, frozen, reheated	6 scallops	90	59	195	15	10	70	10	39	203	2.0	369	298	70	21	0.11	0.11	1.6	0
Shrimp:																			
Canned, drained solids	3 oz.	85	70	100	21	1	128	1	98	224	1.4	104	1,955	50	15	0.01	0.03	1.5	0
French fried (7 medium)[16]	3 oz.	85	55	200	16	10	168	11	61	154	2.0	189	384	90	26	0.06	0.09	2.8	0
Tuna, canned, drained solids:																			
Oil pack, chunk light	3 oz.	85	61	165	24	7	55	0	7	199	1.6	298	303	70	20	0.04	0.09	10.1	0
Water pack, solid white	3 oz.	85	63	135	30	1	48	0	17	202	0.6	255	468	110	32	0.03	0.10	13.4	0

Nutritive Values of Foods – Continued
(Tr indicates nutrient present in trace amount.)

Nutrients in Indicated Quantity

Item No. / Foods, approximate measures, units, and weight (weight of edible portion only) (A)	(B) Grams	(C) Water Per-cent	(D) Food energy Cal-ories	(E) Pro-tein Grams	(F) Fat Grams	(G) Cho-lesterol Milli-grams	(H) Carbo-hydrate Grams	(I) Calcium Milli-grams	(J) Phos-phorus Milli-grams	(K) Iron Milli-grams	(L) Potas-sium Milli-grams	(M) Sodium Milli-grams	(N) Vitamin A value Inter-national units	(O) Vitamin A value Retinol equiva-lents (RE)	(P) Thiamin Milli-grams	(Q) Ribo-flavin Milli-grams	(R) Niacin Milli-grams	(S) Ascorbic acid Milli-grams
Fruits and Fruit Juices																		
Apples:																		
Raw:																		
Unpeeled, without cores:																		
2-3/4-in. diam. (about 3 per lb. with cores) — 1 apple	138	84	80	Tr	Tr	0	21	10	10	0.2	159	Tr	70	7	0.02	0.02	0.1	8
Peeled, sliced — 1 cup	110	84	65	Tr	Tr	0	16	4	8	0.1	124	Tr	50	5	0.02	0.01	0.1	4
Dried, sulfured — 10 rings	64	32	155	1	Tr	0	42	9	24	0.9	288	[18]56	0	0	0.00	0.10	0.6	2
Apple juice, bottled or canned[19] — 1 cup	248	88	115	Tr	Tr	0	29	17	17	0.9	295	7	Tr	Tr	0.05	0.04	0.2	[20]2
Applesauce, canned:																		
Sweetened — 1 cup	255	80	195	Tr	Tr	0	51	10	18	0.9	156	8	30	3	0.03	0.07	0.5	[20]4
Unsweetened — 1 cup	244	88	105	Tr	Tr	0	28	7	17	0.3	183	5	70	7	0.03	0.06	0.5	[20]3
Apricots:																		
Raw, without pits (about 12 per lb. with pits) — 3 apricots	106	86	50	1	Tr	0	12	15	20	0.6	314	1	2,770	277	0.03	0.04	0.6	11
Canned (fruit and liquid):																		
Heavy syrup pack — 1 cup	258	78	215	1	Tr	0	55	23	31	0.8	361	10	3,170	317	0.05	0.06	1.0	8
Juice pack — 1 cup	248	87	120	2	Tr	0	31	30	50	0.7	409	10	4,190	419	0.04	0.05	0.9	12
Dried:																		
Uncooked (28 large or 37 medium halves per cup) — 1 cup	130	31	310	5	1	0	80	59	152	6.1	1,791	13	9,410	941	0.01	0.20	3.9	3
Apricot nectar, canned — 1 cup	251	85	140	1	Tr	0	36	18	23	1.0	286	8	3,300	330	0.02	0.04	0.7	[20]2
Avocados, raw, whole, without skin and seed:																		
California (about 2 per lb. with skin and seed) — 1 avocado	173	73	305	4	30	0	12	19	73	2.0	1,097	21	1,060	106	0.19	0.21	3.3	14
Bananas, raw, without peel:																		
Whole (about 2-1/2 per lb. with peel) — 1 banana	114	74	105	1	1	0	27	7	23	0.4	451	1	90	9	0.05	0.11	0.6	10
Blackberries, raw — 1 cup	144	86	75	1	1	0	18	46	30	0.8	282	Tr	240	24	0.04	0.06	0.6	30
Blueberries:																		
Raw — 1 cup	145	85	80	1	1	0	20	9	15	0.2	129	9	150	15	0.07	0.07	0.5	19
Frozen, sweetened — 10-oz. container	284	77	230	1	Tr	0	62	17	20	1.1	170	3	120	12	0.06	0.15	0.7	3
Cantaloupe. See Melons																		
Cherries:																		
Sour, red, pitted, canned, water pack — 1 cup	244	90	90	2	Tr	0	22	27	24	3.3	239	17	1,840	184	0.04	0.10	0.4	5
Sweet, raw, without pits and stems — 10 cherries	68	81	50	1	1	0	11	10	13	0.3	152	Tr	150	15	0.03	0.04	0.3	5
Cranberry juice cocktail, bottled, sweetened — 1 cup	253	85	145	Tr	Tr	0	38	8	3	0.4	61	10	10	1	0.01	0.04	0.1	[21]108
Cranberry sauce, sweetened, canned, strained — 1 cup	277	61	420	1	Tr	0	108	11	17	0.6	72	80	60	6	0.04	0.06	0.3	6
Dates:																		
Whole, without pits — 10 dates	83	23	230	2	Tr	0	61	27	33	1.0	541	2	40	4	0.07	0.08	1.8	0
Fruit cocktail, canned, fruit and liquid:																		
Heavy syrup pack — 1 cup	255	80	185	1	Tr	0	48	15	28	0.7	224	15	520	52	0.05	0.05	1.0	5
Juice pack — 1 cup	248	87	115	1	Tr	0	29	20	35	0.5	236	10	760	76	0.03	0.04	1.0	7
Grapefruit:																		
Raw, without peel, membrane and seeds (3-3/4 in. diam., 1 lb. 1 oz., whole, with refuse) — 1/2 grapefruit	120	91	40	1	Tr	0	10	14	10	0.1	167	Tr	[22]10	[22]1	0.04	0.02	0.3	41
Grapefruit juice:																		
Canned:																		
Unsweetened — 1 cup	247	90	95	1	Tr	0	22	17	27	0.5	378	2	20	2	0.10	0.05	0.6	72
Sweetened — 1 cup	250	87	115	1	Tr	0	28	20	28	0.9	405	5	20	2	0.10	0.06	0.8	67
Frozen concentrate, unsweetened:																		
Diluted with 3 parts water by volume — 1 cup	247	89	100	1	Tr	0	24	20	35	0.3	336	2	20	2	0.10	0.05	0.5	83
Grapes, European type (adherent skin), raw:																		
Thompson seedless — 10 grapes	50	81	35	Tr	Tr	0	9	6	7	0.1	93	1	40	4	0.05	0.03	0.2	5
Grape juice:																		
Canned or bottled — 1 cup	253	84	155	1	Tr	0	38	23	28	0.6	334	8	20	2	0.07	0.09	0.7	[20]Tr
Frozen concentrate, sweetened:																		
Diluted with 3 parts water by volume — 1 cup	250	87	125	Tr	Tr	0	32	10	10	0.3	53	5	20	2	0.04	0.07	0.3	[21]60
Lemons, raw, without peel and seeds (about 4 per lb. with peel and seeds) — 1 lemon	58	89	15	1	Tr	0	5	15	9	0.3	80	1	20	2	0.02	0.01	0.1	31

(A)	(B)		(C)	(D)	(E)	(F)	(G)	(H)	(I)	(J)	(K)	(L)	(M)	(N)	(O)	(P)	(Q)	(R)	(S)
Lemon juice:																			
Canned or bottled, unsweetened	1 cup	244	92	50	1	Tr	0	16	27	22	0.3	249	[23]51	40	4	0.10	0.02	0.5	61
Frozen, single-strength, unsweetened	6 fl. oz. can	244	92	55	1	Tr	0	16	20	20	0.3	217	2	30	3	0.14	0.03	0.3	77
Lime juice:																			
Canned, unsweetened	1 cup	246	93	50	1	Tr	0	16	30	25	0.6	185	[23]39	40	4	0.08	0.01	0.4	16
Melons, raw, without rind and cavity contents:																			
Cantaloupe, orange-fleshed (5 in. diam., 2-1/3 lb., whole, with rind and cavity contents)	1/2 melon	267	90	95	2	1	0	22	29	45	0.6	825	24	8,610	861	0.10	0.06	1.5	113
Honeydew (6-1/2 in. diam., 5-1/4 lb., whole, with rind and cavity contents)	1/10 melon	129	90	45	1	Tr	0	12	8	13	0.1	350	13	50	5	0.10	0.02	0.8	32
Nectarines, raw, without pits (about 3 per lb. with pits)1 nectarine	1 nectarine	136	86	65	1	1	0	16	7	22	0.2	288	Tr	1,000	100	0.02	0.06	1.3	7
Oranges, raw:																			
Whole, without peel and seeds (2-5/8 in. diam., about 2-1/2 per lb., with peel and seeds)	1 orange	131	87	60	1	Tr	0	15	52	18	0.1	237	Tr	270	27	0.11	0.05	0.4	70
Orange juice:																			
Raw, all varieties	1 cup	248	88	110	2	Tr	0	26	27	42	0.5	496	2	500	50	0.22	0.07	1.0	124
Canned, unsweetened	1 cup	249	89	105	1	Tr	0	25	20	35	1.1	436	5	440	44	0.15	0.07	0.8	86
Frozen concentrate:																			
Diluted with 3 parts water by volume	1 cup	249	88	110	2	Tr	0	27	22	40	0.2	473	2	190	19	0.20	0.04	0.5	97
Orange and grapefruit juice, canned	1 cup	247	89	105	1	Tr	0	25	20	35	1.1	390	7	290	29	0.14	0.07	0.8	72
Peaches:																			
Raw:																			
Whole, 2-1/2 in. diam., peeled, pitted (about 4 per lb. with peels and pits)	1 peach	87	88	35	1	Tr	0	10	4	10	0.1	171	Tr	470	47	0.01	0.04	0.9	6
Canned, fruit and liquid:																			
Heavy syrup pack	1 cup	256	79	190	1	Tr	0	51	8	28	0.7	236	15	850	85	0.03	0.06	1.6	7
Juice pack	1 cup	248	87	110	2	Tr	0	29	15	42	0.7	317	10	940	94	0.02	0.04	1.4	9
Dried:																			
Uncooked	1 cup	160	32	380	6	1	0	98	45	190	6.5	1,594	11	3,460	346	Tr	0.34	7.0	8
Frozen, sliced, sweetened 10 oz. container	10-oz container	284	75	265	2	Tr	0	68	9	31	1.1	369	17	810	81	0.04	0.10	1.9	[21]268
	1 cup	250	75	235	2	Tr	0	60	8	28	0.9	325	15	710	71	0.03	0.09	1.6	[21]236
Pears:																			
Raw, with skin, cored:																			
Bartlett, 2-1/2 in. diam. (about 2-1/2 per lb. with cores and stems)	1 pear	166	84	100	1	1	0	25	18	18	0.4	208	Tr	30	3	0.03	0.07	0.2	7
Bosc, 2-1/2 in. diam. (about 3 per lb. with cores and stems)	1 pear	141	84	85	1	1	0	21	16	16	0.4	176	Tr	30	3	0.03	0.06	0.1	6
Canned, fruit and liquid:																			
Heavy syrup pack	1 cup	255	80	190	1	Tr	0	49	13	18	0.6	166	13	10	1	0.03	0.06	0.6	3
Juice pack	1 cup	248	86	125	1	Tr	0	32	22	30	0.7	238	10	10	1	0.03	0.03	0.5	4
Pineapple:																			
Raw, diced	1 cup	155	87	75	1	1	0	19	11	11	0.6	175	2	40	4	0.14	0.06	0.7	24
Canned, fruit and liquid:																			
Heavy syrup pack:																			
Crushed, chunks, tidbits	1 cup	255	79	200	1	Tr	0	52	36	18	1.0	265	3	40	4	0.23	0.06	0.7	19
Juice pack:																			
Chunks or tidbits	1 cup	250	84	150	1	Tr	0	39	35	15	0.7	305	3	100	10	0.24	0.05	0.7	24
Pineapple juice, unsweetened, canned	1 cup	250	86	140	1	Tr	0	34	43	20	0.7	335	3	10	1	0.14	0.06	0.6	27
Plums, without pits:																			
Raw:																			
2-1/8 in. diam. (about 6-1/2 per lb. with pits)	1 plum	66	85	35	1	1	0	9	3	7	0.1	114	Tr	210	21	0.03	0.06	0.3	6
Canned, purple, fruit and liquid:																			
Heavy syrup pack	1 cup	258	76	230	1	Tr	0	60	23	34	2.2	235	49	670	67	0.04	0.10	0.8	1
Juice pack	1 cup	252	84	145	1	Tr	0	38	25	38	0.9	388	3	2,540	254	0.06	0.15	1.2	7
Prunes, dried:																			
Uncooked	4 extra large or 5 large prunes	49	32	115	1	1	0	31	25	39	1.2	365	2	970	97	0.04	0.08	1.0	2
Cooked, unsweetened, fruit and liquid	1 cup	212	70	225	2	Tr	0	60	49	74	2.4	708	4	650	65	0.05	0.21	1.5	6
Prune juice, canned or bottled	1 cup	256	81	180	2	Tr	0	45	31	64	3.0	707	10	10	1	0.04	0.18	2.0	10
Raisins, seedless:																			
Cup, not pressed down	1 cup	145	15	435	5	1	0	115	71	141	3.0	1,089	17	10	1	0.23	0.13	1.2	5

Nutritive Values of Foods – Continued
(Tr indicates nutrient present in trace amount.)

Nutrients in Indicated Quantity

Item No. (A)	Foods, approximate measures, units, and weight (weight of edible portion only) (B)	Water (C) Percent	Food energy (D) Calories	Protein (E) Grams	Fat (F) Grams	Cholesterol (G) Milligrams	Carbohydrate (H) Grams	Calcium (I) Milligrams	Phosphorus (J) Milligrams	Iron (K) Milligrams	Potassium (L) Milligrams	Sodium (M) Milligrams	Vitamin A value (IU) (N) International units	Vitamin A value (RE) (O) Retinol equivalents	Thiamin (P) Milligrams	Riboflavin (Q) Milligrams	Niacin (R) Milligrams	Ascorbic acid (S) Milligrams
Raspberries:																		
Raw	1 cup	123	87	60	1	1	0	14	27	15	0.7	187	Tr	160	16	0.04	0.11	1.1	31
Frozen, sweetened	10-oz. container	284	73	295	2	Tr	0	74	43	48	1.8	324	3	170	17	0.05	0.13	0.7	47
Rhubarb, cooked, added sugar	1 cup	240	68	280	1	Tr	0	75	348	19	0.5	230	2	170	17	0.04	0.06	0.5	8
Strawberries:																		
Raw, capped, whole	1 cup	149	92	45	1	1	0	10	21	28	0.6	247	1	40	4	0.03	0.10	0.3	84
Tangerines:																		
Raw, without peel and seeds (2-3/8 in. diam., about 4 per lb., with peel and seeds)	1 tangerine	84	88	35	1	Tr	0	9	12	8	0.1	132	1	770	77	0.09	0.02	0.1	26
Watermelon, raw, without rind and seeds:																		
Piece (4 by 8 in. wedge with rind and seeds; 1/16 of 32-2/3 lb. melon, 10 by 16 in.)	1 piece	482	92	155	3	2	0	35	39	43	0.8	559	10	1,760	176	0.39	0.10	1.0	46
Grain Products																		
Bagels, plain or water, enriched, 3-1/2 in. diam.[24]	1 bagel	68	29	200	7	2	0	38	29	46	1.8	50	245	0	0	0.26	0.20	2.4	0
Biscuits, baking powder, 2 in. diam. (enriched flour, vegetable shortening):																		
From home recipe	1 biscuit	28	28	100	2	5	Tr	13	47	36	0.7	32	195	10	3	0.08	0.08	0.8	Tr
From mix	1 biscuit	28	29	95	2	3	Tr	14	58	128	0.7	56	262	20	4	0.12	0.11	0.8	Tr
From refrigerated dough	1 biscuit	20	30	65	1	2	1	10	4	79	0.5	18	249	0	0	0.08	0.05	0.7	0
Breads:																		
Cracked-wheat bread (3/4 enriched wheat flour, 1/4 cracked wheat flour):[25]																		
Slice (18 per loaf)	1 slice	25	35	65	2	1	0	12	16	32	0.7	34	106	Tr	Tr	0.10	0.09	0.8	Tr
French or Vienna bread, enriched:[25]																		
Slice:																		
French, 5 by 2-1/2 by 1 in.	1 slice	35	34	100	3	1	0	18	39	30	1.1	32	203	Tr	Tr	0.16	0.12	1.4	Tr
Vienna, 4-3/4 by 4 by 1/2 in.	1 slice	25	34	70	2	1	0	13	28	21	0.8	23	145	Tr	Tr	0.12	0.09	1.0	Tr
Italian bread, enriched:																		
Slice, 4-1/2 by 3-1/4 by 3/4 in.	1 slice	30	32	85	3	Tr	0	17	5	23	0.8	22	176	0	0	0.12	0.07	1.0	0
Pita bread, enriched, white, 6-1/2 in. diam.	1 pita	60	31	165	6	1	0	33	49	60	1.4	71	339	0	0	0.27	0.12	2.2	0
Pumpernickel (2/3 rye flour, 1/3 enriched wheat flour):[25]																		
Slice, 5 by 4 by 3/8 in.	1 slice	32	37	80	3	1	0	16	23	71	0.9	141	177	0	0	0.11	0.17	1.1	0
Raisin bread, enriched:[25]																		
Slice (18 per loaf)	1 slice	25	33	65	2	1	0	13	25	22	0.8	59	92	Tr	Tr	0.08	0.15	1.0	Tr
Rye bread, light (2/3 enriched wheat flour, 1/3 rye flour):[25]																		
Slice, 4-3/4 by 3-3/4 by 7/16 in.	1 slice	25	37	65	2	1	0	12	20	36	0.7	51	175	0	0	0.10	0.08	0.8	0
Wheat bread, enriched:[25]																		
Slice (18 per loaf)	1 slice	25	37	65	2	1	0	12	32	47	0.9	35	138	Tr	Tr	0.12	0.08	1.2	Tr
White bread, enriched:[25]																		
Slice (18 per loaf)	1 slice	25	37	65	2	1	0	12	32	27	0.7	28	129	Tr	Tr	0.12	0.08	0.9	Tr
Slice (22 per loaf)	1 slice	20	37	55	2	1	0	10	25	21	0.6	22	101	Tr	Tr	0.09	0.06	0.7	Tr
Cubes	1 cup	30	37	80	2	1	0	15	38	32	0.9	34	154	Tr	Tr	0.14	0.09	1.1	Tr
Crumbs, soft	1 cup	45	37	120	4	2	0	22	57	49	1.3	50	231	Tr	Tr	0.21	0.14	1.7	Tr
Whole-wheat bread:[25]																		
Slice (16 per loaf)	1 slice	28	38	70	3	1	0	13	20	74	1.0	50	180	Tr	Tr	0.10	0.06	1.1	Tr
Bread stuffing (from enriched bread), prepared from mix:																		
Dry type	1 cup	140	33	500	9	31	0	50	92	136	2.2	126	1,254	910	273	0.17	0.20	2.5	0

(A)	(B)	(C)	(D)	(E)	(F)	(G)	(H)	(I)	(J)	(K)	(L)	(M)	(N)	(O)	(P)	(Q)	(R)	(S)
Moist type	1 cup	203	420	9	26	67	40	81	134	2.0	118	1,023	850	256	0.10	0.18	1.6	0
Breakfast cereals:																		
Hot type, cooked:																		
Corn (hominy) grits:																		
Regular and quick, enriched	1 cup	242	145	3	Tr	0	31	0	29	[27]1.5	53	280	[29]0	[29]0	[27]0.24	[27]0.15	[27]2.0	0
Instant, plain	1 pkt.	137	80	2	Tr	0	18	7	16	[27]1.0	29	343	0	0	[27]0.18	[27]0.08	[27]1.3	0
Cream of Wheat®:																		
Regular, quick, instant	1 cup	244	140	4	Tr	0	29	[30]54	[31]43	[30]0.9	46	[31]325	0	0	[30]0.24	[30]0.07	[30]1.5	0
Mix'n Eat, plain	1 pkt.	142	100	3	Tr	0	21	[30]20	[30]20	[30]8.1	38	241	[30]1,250	[30]376	[30]0.43	[30]0.28	[30]5.0	0
Malt-O-Meal®	1 cup	240	120	4	Tr	0	26	5	[30]24	[30]9.6	31	332	0	0	[30]0.48	[30]0.24	[30]5.8	0
Oatmeal or rolled oats:																		
Regular, quick, instant, nonfortified	1 cup	234	145	6	2	0	25	19	178	1.6	131	342	40	4	0.26	0.05	0.3	0
Instant, fortified:																		
Plain	1 pkt.	177	105	4	2	0	18	[27]163	133	[27]6.3	99	[27]285	[27]1,510	[27]453	[27]0.53	[27]0.28	[27]5.5	0
Ready-to-eat:																		
All-Bran® (about 1/3 cup)	1 oz.	28	70	4	1	0	21	23	264	[30]4.5	350	320	[30]1,250	[30]375	[30]0.37	[30]0.43	[30]5.0	[30]15
Cap'n Crunch® (about 3/4 cup)	1 oz.	28	120	1	3	0	23	5	36	[27]7.5	37	213	40	4	[30]0.50	[30]0.55	[30]6.6	[30]15
Cheerios® (about 1-1/4 cup)	1 oz.	28	110	4	2	0	20	48	134	[30]4.5	101	307	[30]1,250	[30]375	[30]0.37	[30]0.43	[30]5.0	[30]15
Corn Flakes (about 1-1/4 cup):																		
Toasties®	1 oz.	28	110	2	Tr	0	24	1	12	[27]0.7	33	297	[30]1,250	[30]375	[30]0.37	[30]0.43	[30]5.0	0
40% Bran Flakes:																		
Kellogg's® (about 3/4 cup)	1 oz.	28	90	4	1	0	22	14	139	[30]8.1	180	264	[30]1,250	[30]375	[30]0.37	[30]0.43	[30]5.0	[30]15
Froot Loops® (about 1 cup)	1 oz.	28	110	2	1	0	25	3	24	[30]4.5	26	145	[30]1,250	[30]375	[30]0.37	[30]0.43	[30]5.0	[30]15
Golden Grahams® (about 3/4 cup)	1 oz.	28	110	2	1	Tr	24	17	41	[30]4.5	63	346	[30]1,250	[30]375	[30]0.37	[30]0.43	[30]5.0	[30]15
Grape-Nuts® (about 1/4 cup)	1 oz.	28	100	3	Tr	0	23	11	71	1.2	95	197	[30]1,250	[30]375	[30]0.37	[30]0.43	[30]5.0	[30]15
Honey Nut Cheerios® (about 3/4 cup)	1 oz.	28	105	3	1	0	23	20	105	[30]4.5	99	257	[30]1,250	[30]375	[30]0.37	[30]0.43	[30]5.0	[30]15
Nature Valley® Granola (about 1/3 cup)	1 oz.	28	125	3	5	0	19	18	89	0.9	98	58	20	2	0.10	0.05	0.2	0
Product 19® (about 3/4 cup)	1 oz.	28	110	3	Tr	0	24	3	40	[30]18.0	44	325	[30]5,000	[30]1,501	[30]1.50	[30]1.70	[30]20.0	[30]60
Raisin Bran:																		
Kellogg's® (about 3/4 cup)	1 oz.	28	90	3	1	0	21	10	105	[30]3.5	147	207	[30]960	[30]288	[30]0.28	[30]0.34	[30]3.9	[30]15
Rice Krispies® (about 1 cup)	1 oz.	28	110	2	Tr	0	25	4	34	[30]1.8	29	340	[30]1,250	[30]375	[30]0.37	[30]0.43	[30]5.0	[30]15
Shredded Wheat (about 2/3 cup)	1 oz.	28	100	3	1	0	23	11	100	1.2	102	3	0	3	0.07	0.08	1.5	0
Special K® (about 1-1/3 cup)	1 oz.	28	110	6	Tr	0	21	8	55	[30]4.5	49	265	[30]1,250	[30]375	[30]0.37	[30]0.43	[30]5.0	[30]15
Frosted Flakes, Kellogg's® (about 3/4 cup)	1 oz.	28	110	1	Tr	0	26	1	21	[30]1.8	18	230	[30]1,250	[30]375	[30]0.37	[30]0.43	[30]5.0	[30]15
Golden Crisps® (about 3/4 cup)	1 oz.	28	105	2	1	0	25	3	31	[30]1.8	42	75	[30]1,250	[30]375	[30]0.37	[30]0.43	[30]5.0	[30]15
Total® (about 1 cup)	1 oz.	28	100	3	1	0	22	48	118	[30]18.0	106	352	[30]5,000	[30]1,501	[30]1.50	[30]1.70	[30]20.0	[30]60
Wheaties® (about 1 cup)	1 oz.	28	100	3	1	0	23	43	98	[30]4.5	106	354	[30]1,250	[30]375	[30]0.37	[30]0.43	[30]5.0	[30]15
Buckwheat flour, light, sifted	1 cup	98	340	6	1	0	78	11	86	1.0	314	2	0	0	0.08	0.04	0.4	0
Cakes prepared from cake mixes with enriched flour:[35]																		
Angel food: Piece, 1/12 of cake	1 piece	53	125	3	Tr	0	29	44	91	0.2	71	269	0	0	0.03	0.11	0.1	0
Coffeecake, crumb: Piece, 1/6 of cake	1 piece	72	230	5	7	47	38	44	125	1.2	78	310	120	32	0.14	0.15	1.3	Tr
Devil's food with chocolate frosting: Piece, 1/16 of cake	1 piece	69	235	3	8	37	40	41	62	1.4	90	181	100	31	0.07	0.10	0.6	Tr
Cupcake, 2-1/2 in. diam.	1 cupcake	35	120	2	4	19	20	21	37	0.7	46	92	50	16	0.04	0.05	0.3	Tr
Gingerbread: Piece, 1/9 of cake	1 piece	63	175	2	4	1	32	57	50	1.2	173	192	0	0	0.09	0.11	0.8	Tr
Yellow with chocolate frosting: Whole, 2-layer cake. Piece, 1/16 of cake	1 piece	69	235	3	8	36	40	63	126	1.0	75	157	100	29	0.08	0.10	0.7	Tr
Cakes prepared from home recipes using enriched flour:																		
Carrot, with cream cheese frosting:[36] Piece, 1/16 of cake	1 piece	96	385	4	21	74	48	44	62	1.3	108	279	140	15	0.11	0.12	0.9	1
Fruitcake, dark:[36] Piece, 1/32 of cake, 2/3 in. arc	1 piece	43	165	2	7	20	25	41	50	1.2	194	67	50	13	0.08	0.08	0.5	16
Plain sheet cake:[37] Without frosting: Piece, 1/9 of cake	1 piece	86	315	4	12	61	48	55	88	1.3	68	258	150	41	0.14	0.15	1.1	Tr
With uncooked white frosting: Piece, 1/9 of cake	1 piece	121	445	4	14	70	77	61	91	1.2	74	275	240	71	0.13	0.16	1.1	Tr

Nutritive Values of Foods – Continued
(Tr indicates nutrient present in trace amount.)

Item No. / Foods, approximate measures, units, and weight (weight of edible portion only) (A)	(B) Grams	(C) Water Percent	(D) Food energy Calories	(E) Protein Grams	(F) Fat Grams	(G) Cholesterol Milligrams	(H) Carbohydrate Grams	(I) Calcium Milligrams	(J) Phosphorus Milligrams	(K) Iron Milligrams	(L) Potassium Milligrams	(M) Sodium Milligrams	(N) Vitamin A value (IU) International units	(O) Vitamin A value (RE) Retinol equivalents	(P) Thiamin Milligrams	(Q) Riboflavin Milligrams	(R) Niacin Milligrams	(S) Ascorbic acid Milligrams
Pound:38																		
Slice, 1/17 of loaf	30	22	120	2	5	32	15	20	28	0.5	28	96	200	60	0.05	0.06	0.5	Tr
Cakes, commercial, made with enriched flour:																		
Pound:																		
Slice, 1/17 of loaf	29	24	110	2	5	64	15	8	30	0.5	26	108	160	41	0.06	0.06	0.5	0
Snack cakes:																		
Devil's food with creme filling (2 small cakes per pkg.)	28	20	105	1	4	15	17	21	26	1.0	34	105	20	4	0.06	0.09	0.7	0
Sponge with creme filling (2 small cakes per pkg.)	42	19	155	1	5	7	27	14	44	0.6	37	155	30	9	0.07	0.06	0.6	0
White with white frosting:																		
Piece, 1/16 of cake	71	24	260	3	9	3	42	33	99	1.0	52	176	40	12	0.20	0.13	1.7	0
Yellow with chocolate frosting:																		
Piece, 1/16 of cake	69	23	245	2	11	38	39	23	117	1.2	123	192	120	30	0.05	0.14	0.6	0
Cheesecake:																		
Piece, 1/12 of cake	92	46	280	5	18	170	26	52	81	0.4	90	204	230	69	0.03	0.12	0.4	5
Cookies made with enriched flour:																		
Brownies with nuts:																		
Commercial, with frosting, 1-1/2 by 1-3/4 by 7/8 in.	25	13	100	1	4	14	16	13	26	0.6	50	59	70	18	0.08	0.07	0.3	Tr
Chocolate chip:																		
Commercial, 2-1/4 in. diam., 3/8 in. thick	42	4	180	2	9	5	28	13	41	0.8	68	140	50	15	0.10	0.23	1.0	Tr
From refrigerated dough, 2-1/4 in. diam., 3/8 in. thick	48	5	225	2	11	22	32	13	34	1.0	62	173	30	8	0.06	0.10	0.9	0
Oatmeal with raisins, 2-5/8 in. diam., 1/4 in. thick	52	4	245	3	10	2	36	18	58	1.1	90	148	40	12	0.09	0.08	1.0	0
Peanut butter cookie, from home recipe, 2-5/8 in. diam.25	48	3	245	4	14	0	28	21	60	1.1	110	142	20	5	0.07	0.07	1.9	0
Sandwich type (chocolate or vanilla), 1-3/4 in. diam., 3/8 in. thick	40	2	195	2	8	0	29	12	40	1.4	66	189	0	0	0.09	0.07	0.8	0
Sugar cookie, from refrigerated dough, 2-1/2 in. diam., 1/4 in. thick	48	4	235	2	12	29	31	50	91	0.9	33	261	40	11	0.09	0.06	1.1	0
Vanilla wafers, 1-3/4 in. diam., 1/4 in. thick	40	4	185	2	7	25	29	16	36	0.8	50	150	50	14	0.07	0.10	1.0	0
Corn chips	28	1	155	2	9	0	16	35	52	0.5	52	233	110	11	0.04	0.05	0.4	1
Cornmeal:																		
Degermed, enriched:																		
Dry form	138	12	500	11	2	0	108	8	137	5.9	166	1	610	61	0.61	0.36	4.8	0
Cooked	240	88	120	3	Tr	0	26	2	34	1.4	38	0	140	14	0.14	0.10	1.2	0
Crackers:39																		
Cheese:																		
Plain, 1 in. square	10	4	50	1	3	6	6	11	17	0.3	17	112	20	5	0.05	0.04	0.4	0
Sandwich type (peanut butter)	8	3	40	1	2	1	5	7	25	0.3	17	90	Tr	Tr	0.04	0.03	0.6	0
Graham, plain, 2-1/2 in. square	14	5	60	1	1	0	11	6	20	0.4	36	86	0	0	0.02	0.03	0.6	0
Saltines40	12	4	50	1	1	4	9	3	12	0.5	17	165	0	0	0.06	0.05	0.6	0
Snack-type, standard	3	3	15	Tr	1	0	2	3	6	0.1	4	30	Tr	Tr	0.01	0.01	0.1	0
Wheat, thin	8	3	35	1	1	0	5	3	15	0.3	17	69	Tr	Tr	0.04	0.03	0.4	0
Croissants, made with enriched flour, 4-1/2 by 4 by 1-3/4 in.	57	22	235	5	12	13	27	20	64	2.1	68	452	50	13	0.17	0.13	1.3	0
Danish pastry, made with enriched flour:																		
Plain without fruit or nuts:																		
Round piece, about 4-1/4 in. diam., 1 in. high	57	27	220	4	12	49	26	60	58	1.1	53	218	60	17	0.16	0.17	1.4	Tr
Fruit, round piece	65	30	235	4	13	56	28	17	80	1.3	57	233	40	11	0.16	0.14	1.4	Tr
Doughnuts, made with enriched flour:																		
Cake type, plain, 3-1/4 in. diam., 1 in. high	50	21	210	3	12	20	24	22	111	1.0	58	192	20	5	0.12	0.12	1.1	Tr
Yeast-leavened, glazed, 3-3/4 in. diam., 1-1/4 in. high	60	27	235	4	13	21	26	17	55	1.4	64	222	Tr	Tr	0.28	0.12	1.8	0

(A)	(B)	(C)	(D)	(E)	(F)	(G)	(H)	(I)	(J)	(K)	(L)	(M)	(N)	(O)	(P)	(Q)	(R)	(S)
English muffins, plain, enriched	1 muffin	57	42	140	5	1	0	27	96	67	1.7	331	378	0	0	0.26	0.19	2.2	0
French toast, from home recipe	1 slice	65	53	155	6	7	112	17	72	85	1.3	86	257	110	32	0.12	0.16	1.0	Tr
Macaroni, enriched, cooked (cut lengths, elbows, shells): Firm stage (hot)	1 cup	130	64	190	7	1	0	39	14	86	2.1	103	1	0	0	0.23	0.13	1.8	0
Muffins made with enriched flour, 2-1/2 in. diam., 1-1/2 in. high: From home recipe: Blueberry[25]	1 muffin	45	37	135	3	5	19	20	54	46	0.9	47	198	40	9	0.10	0.11	0.9	1
Bran[36]	1 muffin	45	35	125	3	6	24	19	60	125	1.4	99	189	230	30	0.11	0.13	1.3	3
From commercial mix (egg and water added): Blueberry	1 muffin	45	33	140	3	5	45	22	15	90	0.9	54	225	50	11	0.10	0.17	1.1	Tr
Bran	1 muffin	45	28	140	3	4	28	24	27	182	1.7	50	385	100	14	0.08	0.12	1.9	0
Corn	1 muffin	45	30	145	3	6	42	22	30	128	1.3	31	291	90	16	0.09	0.09	0.8	Tr
Noodles (egg noodles), enriched, cooked	1 cup	160	70	200	7	2	50	37	16	94	2.6	70	3	110	34	0.22	0.13	1.9	0
Noodles, chow mein, canned	1 cup	45	11	220	6	11	5	26	14	41	0.4	33	450	0	0	0.05	0.03	0.6	0
Pancakes, 4 in. diam.: Buckwheat, from mix (with buckwheat and enriched flours), egg and milk added	1 pancake	27	58	55	2	2	20	6	59	91	0.4	66	125	60	17	0.04	0.05	0.2	Tr
Plain: From mix (with enriched flour), egg, milk, and oil added	1 pancake	27	54	60	2	2	16	8	36	71	0.7	43	160	30	7	0.09	0.12	0.8	Tr
Piecrust, made with enriched flour and vegetable shortening, baked: From home recipe, 9 in. diam.	1 pie shell	180	15	900	11	60	0	79	25	90	4.5	90	1,100	0	0	0.54	0.40	5.0	0
From mix, 9 in. diam.	Piecrust for 2-crust pie	320	19	1,485	20	93	0	141	131	272	9.3	179	2,602	0	0	1.06	0.80	9.9	0
Pies, piecrust made with enriched flour, vegetable shortening, 9 in. diam.: Apple: Piece, 1/6 of pie	1 piece	158	48	405	3	18	0	60	13	35	1.6	126	476	50	5	0.17	0.13	1.6	2
Blueberry: Piece, 1/6 of pie	1 piece	158	51	380	4	17	0	55	17	36	2.1	158	423	140	14	0.17	0.14	1.7	6
Cherry: Piece, 1/6 of pie	1 piece	158	47	410	4	18	0	61	22	40	1.6	166	480	700	70	0.19	0.14	1.6	0
Creme: Piece, 1/6 of pie	1 piece	152	43	455	3	23	8	59	46	154	1.1	133	369	210	65	0.06	0.15	1.1	0
Custard: Piece, 1/6 of pie	1 piece	152	58	330	9	17	169	36	146	172	1.5	208	436	350	96	0.14	0.32	0.9	0
Lemon meringue: Piece, 1/6 of pie	1 piece	140	47	355	5	14	143	53	20	69	1.4	70	395	240	66	0.10	0.14	0.8	4
Peach: Piece, 1/6 of pie	1 piece	158	48	405	4	17	0	60	16	46	1.9	235	423	1,150	115	0.17	0.16	2.4	5
Pecan: Piece, 1/6 of pie	1 piece	138	20	575	7	32	95	71	65	142	4.6	170	305	220	54	0.30	0.17	1.1	0
Pumpkin: Piece, 1/6 of pie	1 piece	152	59	320	6	17	109	37	78	105	1.4	243	325	3,750	416	0.14	0.21	1.2	0
Pies, fried: Apple	1 pie	85	43	255	2	14	14	31	12	34	0.9	42	326	30	3	0.09	0.06	1.0	1
Cherry	1 pie	85	42	250	2	14	13	32	11	41	0.7	61	371	190	19	0.06	0.06	0.6	1
Popcorn, popped: Air-popped, unsalted	1 cup	8	4	30	1	Tr	0	6	1	22	0.2	20	Tr	10	1	0.03	0.01	0.2	0
Popped in vegetable oil, salted	1 cup	11	3	55	1	3	0	6	3	31	0.3	19	86	20	2	0.01	0.02	0.1	0
Sugar syrup coated	1 cup	35	4	135	2	1	0	30	2	47	0.5	90	Tr	30	3	0.13	0.02	0.4	0
Pretzels, made with enriched flour: Twisted, dutch, 2-3/4 by 2-5/8 in.	1 pretzel	16	3	65	2	1	0	13	4	15	0.3	16	258	0	0	0.05	0.04	0.7	0
Twisted, thin, 3-1/4 by 2-1/4 by 1/4 in.	10 pretzels	60	3	240	6	2	0	48	16	55	1.2	61	966	0	0	0.19	0.15	2.6	0
Rice: Brown, cooked, served hot	1 cup	195	70	230	5	1	0	50	23	142	1.0	137	0	0	0	0.18	0.04	2.7	0
White, enriched: Commercial varieties, all types: Cooked, served hot	1 cup	205	73	225	4	Tr	0	50	21	57	1.8	57	0	0	0	0.23	0.02	2.1	0
Instant, ready-to-serve, hot	1 cup	165	73	180	4	0	0	40	5	31	1.3	0	0	0	0	0.21	0.02	1.7	0

Nutritive Values of Foods – Continued
(Tr indicates nutrient present in trace amount.)

Nutrients in Indicated Quantity

Item No. (A) — Foods, approximate measures, units, and weight (B)	Measure	Weight (g)	Water (%) (C)	Food energy (Cal) (D)	Protein (g) (E)	Fat (g) (F)	Cholesterol (mg) (G)	Carbohydrate (g) (H)	Calcium (mg) (I)	Phosphorus (mg) (J)	Iron (mg) (K)	Potassium (mg) (L)	Sodium (mg) (M)	Vitamin A (IU) (N)	Vitamin A (RE) (O)	Thiamin (mg) (P)	Riboflavin (mg) (Q)	Niacin (mg) (R)	Ascorbic acid (mg) (S)
Rolls, enriched:																			
Commercial:																			
Dinner, 2-1/2 in. diam., 2 in. high	1 roll	28	32	85	2	2	Tr	14	33	44	0.8	36	155	Tr	Tr	0.14	0.09	1.1	Tr
Frankfurter and hamburger (8 per 11-1/2 oz. pkg.)	1 roll	40	34	115	3	2	Tr	20	54	44	1.2	56	241	Tr	Tr	0.20	0.13	1.6	Tr
Hard, 3-3/4 in. diam., 2 in. high	1 roll	50	25	155	5	2	Tr	30	24	46	1.4	49	313	0	0	0.20	0.12	1.7	0
Hoagie or submarine, 11-1/2 by 3 by 2-1/2 in.	1 roll	135	31	400	11	8	Tr	72	100	115	3.8	128	683	0	0	0.54	0.33	4.5	0
Spaghetti, enriched, cooked:																			
Firm stage, "al dente," served hot	1 cup	130	64	190	7	1	0	39	14	85	2.0	103	1	0	0	0.23	0.13	1.8	0
Toaster pastries	1 pastry	54	13	210	2	6	0	38	104	104	2.2	91	248	520	52	0.17	0.18	2.3	4
Tortillas, corn	1 tortilla	30	45	65	2	1	0	13	42	55	0.6	43	1	80	8	0.05	0.03	0.4	0
Waffles, made with enriched flour, 7 in. diam.:																			
From mix, egg and milk added	1 waffle	75	42	205	7	8	59	27	179	257	1.2	146	515	170	49	0.14	0.23	0.9	Tr
Wheat flours:																			
All-purpose or family flour, enriched:																			
Sifted, spooned	1 cup	115	12	420	12	1	0	88	18	100	5.1	109	2	0	0	0.73	0.46	6.1	0
Cake or pastry flour, enriched, sifted, spooned	1 cup	96	12	350	7	1	0	76	16	70	4.2	91	2	0	0	0.58	0.38	5.1	0
Self-rising, enriched, unsifted, spooned	1 cup	125	12	440	12	1	0	93	331	583	5.5	113	1,349	0	0	0.80	0.50	6.6	0
Whole-wheat, from hard wheats, stirred	1 cup	120	12	400	16	2	0	85	49	446	5.2	444	4	0	0	0.66	0.14	5.2	0
Legumes, Nuts, and Seeds		0																	
Almonds, shelled:																			
Slivered, packed	1 cup	135	4	795	27	70	0	28	359	702	4.9	988	15	0	0	0.28	1.05	4.5	1
Beans, dry:																			
Cooked, drained:																			
Lima	1 cup	190	64	260	16	1	0	49	55	293	5.9	1,163	4	0	0	0.25	0.11	1.3	0
Canned, solids and liquid:																			
White with:																			
Pork and tomato sauce	1 cup	255	71	310	16	7	10	48	138	235	4.6	536	1,181	330	33	0.20	0.08	1.5	5
Red kidney	1 cup	255	76	230	15	1	0	42	74	278	4.6	673	968	10	1	0.13	0.10	1.5	0
Black-eyed peas, dry, cooked (with residual cooking liquid)	1 cup	250	80	190	13	1	0	35	43	238	3.3	573	20	30	3	0.40	0.10	1.0	0
Brazil nuts, shelled	1 oz.	28	3	185	4	19	0	4	50	170	1.0	170	1	Tr	Tr	0.28	0.03	0.5	Tr
Carob flour	1 cup	140	3	255	6	Tr	0	126	390	102	5.7	1,275	24	Tr	Tr	0.07	0.07	2.2	Tr
Cashew nuts, salted:																			
Dry roasted	1 cup	137	2	785	21	63	0	45	62	671	8.2	774	[41]877	0	0	0.27	0.27	1.9	0
Roasted in oil	1 cup	130	4	750	21	63	0	37	53	554	5.3	689	[42]814	0	0	0.55	0.23	2.3	0
Chestnuts, European (Italian), roasted, shelled	1 cup	143	40	350	5	3	0	76	41	153	1.3	847	3	30	3	0.35	0.25	1.9	37
Chick-peas, cooked, drained	1 cup	163	60	270	15	4	0	45	80	273	4.9	475	11	Tr	Tr	0.18	0.09	0.9	0
Coconut:																			
Dried, sweetened, shredded	1 cup	93	13	470	3	33	0	44	14	99	1.8	313	244	0	0	0.03	0.02	0.4	1
Filberts (hazelnuts), chopped	1 cup	115	5	725	15	72	0	18	216	359	3.8	512	3	80	8	0.58	0.13	1.3	1
	1 oz.	28	5	180	4	18	0	4	53	88	0.9	126	1	20	2	0.14	0.03	0.3	1
Lentils, dry, cooked	1 cup	200	72	215	16	1	0	38	50	238	4.2	498	26	40	4	0.14	0.12	1.2	0
Macadamia nuts, roasted in oil, salted	1 cup	134	2	960	10	103	0	17	60	268	2.4	441	[43]348	10	1	0.29	0.15	2.7	0
Mixed nuts, with peanuts, salted:																			
Dry roasted	1 oz.	28	2	170	5	15	0	7	20	123	1.0	169	[44]190	Tr	Tr	0.06	0.06	1.3	0
Roasted in oil	1 oz.	28	2	175	5	16	0	6	31	131	0.9	165	[44]185	10	1	0.14	0.06	1.4	0
Peanuts, roasted in oil, salted	1 cup	145	2	840	39	71	0	27	125	734	2.8	1,019	[45]626	0	0	0.42	0.15	21.5	0
Peanut butter	1 tbsp.	16	1	95	5	8	0	3	5	60	0.3	110	75	0	0	0.02	0.02	2.2	0
Peas, split, dry, cooked	1 cup	200	70	230	16	1	0	42	22	178	3.4	592	26	80	8	0.30	0.18	1.8	0
Pecans, halves	1 cup	108	5	720	8	73	0	20	39	314	2.3	423	1	140	14	0.92	0.14	1.0	2
Pistachio nuts, dried, shelled	1 oz.	28	4	165	6	14	0	7	38	143	1.9	310	2	70	7	0.23	0.05	0.3	Tr

(A)	(B)	(C)	(D)	(E)	(F)	(G)	(H)	(I)	(J)	(K)	(L)	(M)	(N)	(O)	(P)	(Q)	(R)	(S)
Refried beans, canned	1 cup / 290	72	295	18	3	0	51	141	245	5.1	1,141	1,228	0	0	0.14	0.16	1.4	17
Sesame seeds, dry, hulled	1 tbsp. / 8	5	45	2	4	0	1	11	62	0.6	33	3	10	1	0.06	0.01	0.4	0
Soy products:																		
Tofu, piece 2-3/4 by 2-3/4 by 1 in.	1 piece / 120	85	85	9	5	0	3	108	151	2.3	50	8	0	0	0.07	0.04	0.1	0
Sunflower seeds, dry, hulled	1 oz. / 28	5	160	6	14	0	5	33	200	1.9	195	1	10	1	0.65	0.07	1.3	Tr
Walnuts:																		
Black, chopped	1 cup / 125	4	760	30	71	0	15	73	580	3.8	655	1	370	37	0.27	0.14	0.9	Tr
English or Persian, pieces or chips	1 cup / 120	4	770	17	74	0	22	113	380	2.9	602	12	150	15	0.46	0.18	1.3	4
Meat and Meat Products																		
Beef, cooked:[46]																		
Cuts braised, simmered, or pot roasted:																		
Relatively fat such as chuck blade:																		
Lean and fat, piece, 2-1/2 by 2-1/2 by 3/4 in.	3 oz. / 85	43	325	22	26	87	0	11	163	2.5	163	53	Tr	Tr	0.06	0.19	2.0	0
Relatively lean, such as bottom round:																		
Lean and fat, piece, 4-1/8 by 2-1/4 by 1/2 in.	3 oz. / 85	54	220	25	13	81	0	5	217	2.8	248	43	Tr	Tr	0.06	0.21	3.3	0
Ground beef, broiled, patty, 3 by 5/8 in.:																		
Lean	3 oz. / 85	56	230	21	16	74	0	9	134	1.8	256	65	Tr	Tr	0.04	0.18	4.4	0
Regular	3 oz. / 85	54	245	20	18	76	0	9	144	2.1	248	70	Tr	Tr	0.03	0.16	4.9	0
Liver, fried, slice, 6-1/2 by 2-3/8 by 3/8 in.[47]	3 oz. / 85	56	185	23	7	410	7	9	392	5.3	309	90	[48]30,690	[48]9,120	0.18	3.52	12.3	23
Roast, oven cooked, no liquid added:																		
Relatively fat, such as rib:																		
Lean and fat, 2 pieces, 4-1/8 by 2-1/4 by 1/4 in.	3 oz. / 85	46	315	19	26	72	0	8	145	2.0	246	54	Tr	Tr	0.06	0.16	3.1	0
Relatively lean, such as eye of round:																		
Lean and fat, 2 pieces, 2-1/2 by 2-1/2 by 3/8 in.	3 oz. / 85	57	205	23	12	62	0	5	177	1.6	308	50	Tr	Tr	0.07	0.14	3.0	0
Steak:																		
Sirloin, broiled:																		
Lean and fat, piece, 2-1/2 by 2-1/2 by 3/4 in.	3 oz. / 85	53	240	23	15	77	0	9	186	2.6	306	53	Tr	Tr	0.10	0.23	3.3	0
Beef, canned, corned	3 oz. / 85	59	185	22	10	80	0	17	90	3.7	51	802	Tr	Tr	0.02	0.20	2.9	0
Beef, dried, chipped	2.5 oz. / 72	48	145	24	4	46	0	14	287	2.3	142	3,053	Tr	Tr	0.05	0.23	2.7	0
Lamb, cooked:																		
Chops, (3 per lb. with bone):																		
Lean and fat	2.2 oz. / 63	44	220	20	15	77	0	16	132	1.5	195	46	Tr	Tr	0.04	0.16	4.4	0
Leg, roasted:																		
Lean and fat, 2 pieces, 4-1/8 by 2-1/4 by 1/4 in.	3 oz. / 85	59	205	22	13	78	0	8	162	1.7	273	57	Tr	Tr	0.09	0.24	5.5	0
Rib, roasted:																		
Lean and fat, 3 pieces, 2-1/2 by 2-1/2 by 1/4 in.	3 oz. / 85	47	315	18	26	77	0	19	139	1.4	224	60	Tr	Tr	0.08	0.18	5.5	0
Pork, cured, cooked:																		
Bacon:																		
Regular	3 medium slices / 19	13	110	6	9	16	Tr	2	64	0.3	92	303	0	0	0.13	0.05	1.4	6
Canadian-style	2 slices / 46	62	85	11	4	27	1	5	136	0.4	179	711	0	0	0.38	0.09	3.2	10
Ham, light cure, roasted:																		
Lean and fat, piece, 4-1/8 by 2-1/4 by 1/4 in.	3 oz. / 85	58	205	18	14	53	0	6	182	0.7	243	1,009	0	0	0.51	0.19	3.8	0
Ham, canned, roasted, 2 pieces, 4-1/8 by 2-1/4 by 1/4 in.	3 oz. / 85	67	140	18	7	35	Tr	6	188	0.9	298	908	0	0	0.82	0.21	4.3	[49]19
Luncheon meat:																		
Canned, spiced or unspiced, slice, 3 by 2 by 1/2 in.	2 slices / 42	52	140	5	13	26	1	3	34	0.3	90	541	0	0	0.15	0.08	1.3	Tr
Cooked ham (8 slices per 8 oz. pkg.):																		
Regular	2 slices / 57	65	105	10	6	32	2	4	141	0.6	189	751	0	0	0.49	0.14	3.0	[49]16
Extra lean	2 slices / 57	71	75	11	3	27	1	4	124	0.4	200	815	0	0	0.53	0.13	2.8	[49]15
Pork, fresh, cooked:																		
Chop, loin (cut 3 per lb. with bone):																		
Broiled:																		
Lean and fat	3.1 oz. / 87	50	275	24	19	84	0	3	184	0.7	312	61	10	3	0.87	0.24	4.3	Tr
Ham (leg), roasted:																		
Lean and fat, piece, 2-1/2 by 2-1/2 by 3/4 in.	3 oz / 85	53	250	21	18	79	0	5	210	0.9	280	50	10	2	0.54	0.27	3.9	Tr
Rib, roasted:																		
Lean and fat, piece, 2-1/2 by 2-1/2 by 3/4 in.	3 oz. / 85	51	270	21	20	69	0	9	190	0.8	313	37	10	3	0.50	0.24	4.2	Tr
Shoulder cut, braised:																		
Lean and fat, 3 pieces, 2-1/2 by 2-1/2 by 1/4 in.	3 oz. / 85	47	295	23	22	93	0	6	162	1.4	286	75	10	3	0.46	0.26	4.4	Tr
Sausages:																		
Bologna, slice (8 per 8 oz. pkg.)	2 slices / 57	54	180	7	16	31	2	7	52	0.9	103	581	0	0	0.10	0.08	1.5	[49]12
Braunschweiger, slice (6 per 6 oz. pkg.)	2 slices / 57	48	205	8	18	89	2	5	96	5.3	113	652	8,010	2,405	0.14	0.87	4.8	[49]6

Nutritive Values of Foods – Continued
(Tr indicates nutrient present in trace amount.)

Item No. (A)	Foods, approximate measures, units, and weight (weight of edible portion only) (B)	Grams	Water Per-cent (C)	Food energy Cal-ories (D)	Pro-tein Grams (E)	Fat Grams (F)	Cho-lesterol Milli-grams (G)	Carbo-hydrate Grams (H)	Calcium Milli-grams (I)	Phos-phorus Milli-grams (J)	Iron Milli-grams (K)	Potas-sium Milli-grams (L)	Sodium Milli-grams (M)	Vitamin A value Inter-national units (N)	Vitamin A value Retinol equiva-lents (RE) (O)	Thiamin Milli-grams (P)	Ribo-flavin Milli-grams (Q)	Niacin Milli-grams (R)	Ascorbic acid Milli-grams (S)
Brown and serve (10-11 per 8 oz. pkg.), browned	1 link	13	45	50	2	5	9	Tr	1	14	0.1	25	105	0	0	0.05	0.02	0.4	0
Frankfurter (10 per 1 lb. pkg.), cooked (reheated)	1 frankfurter	45	54	145	5	13	23	1	5	39	0.5	75	504	0	0	0.09	0.05	1.2	49[12]
Salami:																			
Dry type, slice (12 per 4 oz. pkg.)	2 slices	20	35	85	5	7	16	1	2	28	0.3	76	372	0	0	0.12	0.06	1.0	4[95]
Sandwich spread (pork, beef)	1 tbsp.	15	60	35	1	3	6	2	2	9	0.1	17	152	10	1	0.03	0.02	0.3	0
Veal, medium fat, cooked, bone removed:																			
Cutlet, 4-1/8 by 2-1/4 by 1/2 in., braised or broiled	3 oz.	85	60	185	23	9	109	0	9	196	0.8	258	56	Tr	Tr	0.06	0.21	4.6	0
Rib, 2 pieces, 4-1/8 by 2-1/4 by 1/4 in., roasted	3 oz.	85	55	230	23	14	109	0	10	211	0.7	259	57	Tr	Tr	0.11	0.26	6.6	0

Mixed Dishes and Fast Foods

Item No. (A)	Foods, approximate measures, units, and weight (B)	Grams	Water % (C)	Cal (D)	Protein (E)	Fat (F)	Chol (G)	Carb (H)	Calcium (I)	Phos (J)	Iron (K)	Potas. (L)	Sodium (M)	Vit A IU (N)	Vit A RE (O)	Thiamin (P)	Ribo. (Q)	Niacin (R)	Ascorbic (S)
Mixed dishes:																			
Beef and vegetable stew, from home recipe	1 cup	245	82	220	16	11	71	15	29	184	2.9	613	292	5,690	568	0.15	0.17	4.7	17
Beef potpie, from home recipe, baked, piece, 1/3 of 9 in. diam. pie[51]	1 piece	210	55	515	21	30	42	39	29	149	3.8	334	596	4,220	517	0.29	0.29	4.8	6
Chicken a la king, cooked, from home recipe	1 cup	245	68	470	27	34	221	12	127	358	2.5	404	760	1,130	272	0.10	0.42	5.4	12
Chicken chow mein:																			
Canned	1 cup	250	89	95	7	Tr	8	18	45	85	1.3	418	725	150	28	0.05	0.10	1.0	13
From home recipe	1 cup	255	72	340	19	16	28	31	82	321	4.3	594	1,354	150	15	0.08	0.18	3.3	8
Chop suey with beef and pork, from home recipe	1 cup	250	75	300	26	17	68	13	60	248	4.8	425	1,053	600	60	0.28	0.38	5.0	33
Macaroni (enriched) and cheese:																			
Canned[52]	1 cup	240	80	230	9	10	24	26	199	182	1.0	139	730	260	72	0.12	0.24	1.0	Tr
From home recipe[38]	1 cup	200	58	430	17	22	44	40	362	322	1.8	240	1,086	860	232	0.20	0.40	1.8	1
Spaghetti (enriched) in tomato sauce with cheese:																			
Canned	1 cup	250	80	190	6	2	3	39	40	88	2.8	303	955	930	120	0.35	0.28	4.5	10
From home recipe	1 cup	250	77	260	9	9	8	37	80	135	2.3	408	955	1,080	140	0.25	0.18	2.3	13
Spaghetti (enriched) with meatballs and tomato sauce:																			
Canned	1 cup	250	78	260	12	10	23	29	53	113	3.3	245	1,220	1,000	100	0.15	0.18	2.3	5
From home recipe	1 cup	248	70	330	19	12	89	39	124	236	3.7	665	1,009	1,590	159	0.25	0.30	4.0	22
Fast food entrees:																			
Cheeseburger:																			
Regular	1 sandwich	112	46	300	15	15	44	28	135	174	2.3	219	672	340	65	0.26	0.24	3.7	1
4 oz. patty	1 sandwich	194	46	525	30	31	104	40	236	320	4.5	407	1,224	670	128	0.33	0.48	7.4	3
Chicken, fried. See Poultry and Poultry Products.																			
Enchilada	1 enchilada	230	72	235	20	16	19	24	322	662	11.0	2,180	4,451	2,720	352	0.18	0.26	Tr	Tr
English muffin, egg, cheese, and bacon	1 sandwich	138	49	360	18	18	213	31	197	290	3.1	201	832	650	160	0.46	0.50	3.7	1
Fish sandwich:																			
Regular, with cheese	1 sandwich	140	43	420	16	23	56	39	132	223	1.8	274	667	160	25	0.32	0.26	3.3	2
Large, without cheese	1 sandwich	170	48	470	18	27	91	41	61	246	2.2	375	621	110	15	0.35	0.23	3.5	1
Hamburger:																			
Regular	1 sandwich	98	46	245	12	11	32	28	56	107	2.2	202	463	80	14	0.23	0.24	3.8	1
4 oz. patty	1 sandwich	174	50	445	25	21	71	38	75	225	4.8	404	763	160	28	0.38	0.38	7.8	1
Pizza, cheese, 1/8 of 15 in. diam. pizza[51]	1 slice	120	46	290	15	9	56	39	220	216	1.6	230	699	750	106	0.34	0.29	4.2	2
Taco	1 taco	81	55	195	9	11	21	15	109	134	1.2	263	456	420	57	0.09	0.07	1.4	1

Poultry and Poultry Products

Item No. (A)	Foods, approximate measures, units, and weight (B)	Grams	Water % (C)	Cal (D)	Protein (E)	Fat (F)	Chol (G)	Carb (H)	Calcium (I)	Phos (J)	Iron (K)	Potas. (L)	Sodium (M)	Vit A IU (N)	Vit A RE (O)	Thiamin (P)	Ribo. (Q)	Niacin (R)	Ascorbic (S)
Chicken:																			
Fried, flesh, with skin:[53]																			
Batter dipped:																			
Breast, 1/2 breast (5.6 oz. with bones)	4.9 oz.	140	52	365	35	18	119	13	28	259	1.8	281	385	90	28	0.16	0.20	14.7	0

(A)	(B)	(C)	(D)	(E)	(F)	(G)	(H)	(I)	(J)	(K)	(L)	(M)	(N)	(O)	(P)	(Q)	(R)	(S)
Drumstick (3.4 oz. with bones)	2.5 oz.	53	195	16	11	62	6	12	106	1.0	134	194	60	19	0.08	0.15	3.7	0
Roasted, flesh only:																		
Breast, 1/2 breast (4.2 oz. with bones and skin)	3.0 oz.	65	140	27	3	73	0	13	196	0.9	220	64	20	5	0.06	0.10	11.8	0
Drumstick, (2.9 oz. with bones and skin)	1.6 oz.	67	75	12	2	41	0	5	81	0.6	108	42	30	8	0.03	0.10	2.7	0
Chicken liver, cooked	1 liver	68	30	5	1	126	Tr	3	62	1.7	28	10	3,270	983	0.03	0.35	0.9	3
Duck, roasted, flesh only	1/2 duck	64	445	52	25	197	0	27	449	6.0	557	144	170	51	0.57	1.04	11.3	0
Turkey, roasted, flesh only:																		
Dark meat, piece, 2-1/2 by 1-5/8 by 1/4 in.	4 pieces	63	160	24	6	72	0	27	173	2.0	246	67	0	0	0.05	0.21	3.1	0
Light meat, piece, 4 by 2 by 1/4 in.	2 pieces	66	135	25	3	59	0	16	186	1.1	259	54	0	0	0.05	0.11	5.8	0
Poultry food products:																		
Chicken:																		
Canned, boneless	5 oz.	69	235	31	11	88	0	20	158	2.2	196	714	170	48	0.02	0.18	9.0	3
Frankfurter (10 per 1-lb. pkg.)	1 frankfurter	58	115	6	9	45	3	43	48	0.9	38	616	60	17	0.03	0.05	1.4	0
Roll, light (6 slices per 6 oz. pkg.)	2 slices	69	90	11	4	28	1	24	89	0.6	129	331	50	14	0.04	0.07	3.0	0
Turkey:																		
Gravy and turkey, frozen	5 oz. package	85	95	8	4	26	7	20	115	1.3	87	787	60	18	0.03	0.18	2.6	0
Loaf, breast meat (8 slices per 6 oz. pkg.)	2 slices	72	45	10	1	17	0	3	97	0.2	118	608	0	0	0.02	0.05	3.5	540
Patties, breaded, battered, fried (2.25 oz.)	1 patty	50	180	9	12	40	10	9	173	1.4	176	512	20	7	0.06	0.12	1.5	0
Roast, boneless, frozen, seasoned, light and dark meat, cooked	3 oz.	68	130	18	5	45	3	4	207	1.4	253	578	0	0	0.04	0.14	5.3	0

Soups, Sauces, and Gravies

(A)	(B)	(C)	(D)	(E)	(F)	(G)	(H)	(I)	(J)	(K)	(L)	(M)	(N)	(O)	(P)	(Q)	(R)	(S)
Soups:																		
Canned, condensed:																		
Prepared with equal volume of milk:																		
Clam chowder, New England	1 cup	85	165	9	7	22	17	186	156	1.5	300	992	160	40	0.07	0.24	1.0	3
Cream of chicken	1 cup	85	190	7	11	27	15	181	151	0.7	273	1,047	710	94	0.07	0.26	0.9	1
Cream of mushroom	1 cup	85	205	6	14	20	15	179	156	0.6	270	1,076	150	37	0.08	0.28	0.9	2
Tomato	1 cup	85	160	6	6	17	22	159	149	1.8	449	932	850	109	0.13	0.25	1.5	68
Prepared with equal volume of water:																		
Bean with bacon	1 cup	84	170	8	6	3	23	81	132	2.0	402	951	890	89	0.09	0.03	0.6	2
Beef broth, bouillon, consommé	1 cup	98	15	3	1	Tr	Tr	14	31	0.4	130	782	0	0	Tr	0.05	1.9	0
Beef noodle	1 cup	92	85	5	3	5	9	15	46	1.1	100	952	630	63	0.07	0.06	1.1	Tr
Chicken noodle	1 cup	94	60	4	2	7	9	17	36	0.8	55	1,106	710	71	0.05	0.06	1.4	Tr
Chicken rice	1 cup	94	60	4	2	7	7	17	22	0.7	101	815	660	66	0.02	0.02	1.1	Tr
Clam chowder, Manhattan	1 cup	90	80	4	2	2	12	34	59	1.9	261	1,808	920	92	0.06	0.05	1.3	3
Pea, green	1 cup	83	165	9	3	0	27	28	125	2.0	190	988	200	20	0.11	0.07	1.2	2
Vegetable beef	1 cup	92	80	6	2	5	10	17	41	1.1	173	956	1,890	189	0.04	0.05	1.0	2
Vegetarian	1 cup	92	70	2	2	0	12	22	34	1.1	210	822	3,010	301	0.05	0.05	0.9	1
Dehydrated:																		
Prepared with water:																		
Chicken noodle	1 pkt. (6 fl. oz.)	94	40	2	1	2	6	24	24	0.4	23	957	50	5	0.05	0.04	0.7	Tr
Tomato vegetable	1 pkt. (6 fl. oz.)	94	40	1	1	0	8	6	23	0.5	78	856	140	14	0.04	0.03	0.6	5
Sauces:																		
From dry mix:																		
Cheese, prepared with milk	1 cup	77	305	16	17	53	23	569	438	0.3	552	1,565	390	117	0.15	0.56	0.3	2
From home recipe:																		
White sauce, medium[55]	1 cup	73	395	10	30	32	24	292	238	0.9	381	888	1,190	340	0.15	0.43	0.8	2
Ready to serve:																		
Barbecue	1 tbsp.	81	10	Tr	Tr	0	2	3	3	0.1	28	130	140	14	Tr	Tr	0.1	1
Soy	1 tbsp.	68	10	2	0	0	2	3	38	0.5	64	1,029	0	0	0.01	0.02	0.6	0
Gravies:																		
Canned:																		
Beef	1 cup	87	125	9	5	7	11	14	70	1.6	189	117	0	0	0.07	0.08	1.5	0
Chicken	1 cup	85	190	5	14	5	13	48	69	1.1	259	1,373	880	264	0.04	0.10	1.1	0
Mushroom	1 cup	89	120	3	6	0	13	17	36	1.6	252	1,357	0	0	0.08	0.15	1.6	0
From dry mix:																		
Brown	1 cup	91	80	3	2	2	14	66	47	0.2	61	1,147	Tr	Tr	0.04	0.09	0.9	0
Chicken	1 cup	91	85	3	2	3	14	39	47	0.3	62	1,134	0	0	0.05	0.15	0.8	3

Sugars and Sweets

(A)	(B)	(C)	(D)	(E)	(F)	(G)	(H)	(I)	(J)	(K)	(L)	(M)	(N)	(O)	(P)	(Q)	(R)	(S)
Candy:																		
Caramels, plain or chocolate	1 oz.	8	115	1	3	1	22	42	35	0.4	54	64	Tr	Tr	0.01	0.05	0.1	Tr

Nutritive Values of Foods – Continued
(Tr indicates nutrient present in trace amount.)

Item No. (A)	Foods, approximate measures, units, and weight (weight of edible portion only) (B)	Grams	Water Percent (C)	Food energy Calories (D)	Protein Grams (E)	Fat Grams (F)	Cholesterol Milligrams (G)	Carbohydrate Grams (H)	Calcium Milligrams (I)	Phosphorus Milligrams (J)	Iron Milligrams (K)	Potassium Milligrams (L)	Sodium Milligrams (M)	Vitamin A value International units (N)	Vitamin A value Retinol equivalents (RE) (O)	Thiamin Milligrams (P)	Riboflavin Milligrams (Q)	Niacin Milligrams (R)	Ascorbic acid Milligrams (S)
Chocolate:																			
	Milk, plain	1 oz.	28	1	145	2	9	6	16	50	61	0.4	96	23	30	10	0.02	0.10	0.1	Tr
	Milk, with almonds	1 oz.	28	2	150	3	10	5	15	65	77	0.5	125	23	30	8	0.02	0.12	0.2	Tr
	Milk, with peanuts	1 oz.	28	1	155	4	11	5	13	49	83	0.4	138	19	30	8	0.07	0.07	1.4	Tr
	Milk, with rice cereal	1 oz.	28	2	140	2	7	6	18	48	57	0.2	100	46	30	8	0.01	0.08	0.1	Tr
	Semisweet, small pieces (60 per oz.)	1 cup or 6 oz.	170	1	860	7	61	0	97	51	178	5.8	593	24	30	3	0.10	0.14	0.9	Tr
	Sweet (dark)	1 oz.	28	1	150	1	10	0	16	7	41	0.6	86	5	10	1	0.01	0.04	0.1	Tr
	Fudge, chocolate, plain	1 oz.	28	8	115	Tr	3	1	21	22	24	0.3	42	54	Tr	Tr	0.01	0.03	Tr	Tr
	Gum drops	1 oz.	28	12	100	Tr	Tr	0	25	2	Tr	0.1	1	10	0	0	0.00	Tr	Tr	0
	Hard	1 oz.	28	1	110	0	Tr	0	28	Tr	2	0.1	1	7	0	0	0.00	0.00	0.0	0
	Jelly beans	1 oz.	28	6	105	Tr	Tr	0	26	1	1	0.3	11	7	0	0	0.00	Tr	Tr	0
	Marshmallows	1 oz.	28	17	90	1	0	0	23	1	2	0.5	2	25	0	0	0.00	Tr	Tr	0
Custard, baked	1 cup	265	77	305	14	15	278	29	297	310	1.1	387	209	530	146	0.11	0.50	0.3	1
Gelatin dessert prepared with gelatin dessert powder and water	1/2 cup	120	84	70	2	0	0	17	2	23	Tr	Tr	55	0	0	0.00	0.00	0.0	0
Honey, strained or extracted	1 cup	339	17	1,030	1	0	0	279	17	20	1.7	173	17	0	0	0.02	0.14	1.0	3
Jams and preserves	1 tbsp.	21	17	65	Tr	Tr	0	17	4	2	0.1	11	1	Tr	Tr	Tr	0.01	0.1	Tr
Jellies	1 tbsp.	20	29	55	Tr	Tr	0	14	2	1	0.2	18	2	Tr	Tr	Tr	0.01	Tr	1
Popsicle, 3 fl. oz. size	1 popsicle	95	80	70	0	0	0	18	0	0	Tr	4	11	0	0	0.00	0.00	0.0	0
Puddings:																			
Canned:																			
	Chocolate	5 oz. can	142	68	205	3	11	1	30	74	117	1.2	254	285	100	31	0.04	0.17	0.6	Tr
	Vanilla	5 oz. can	142	69	220	2	10	1	33	79	94	0.2	155	305	Tr	Tr	0.03	0.12	0.6	Tr
Dry mix, prepared with whole milk:																			
Chocolate:																			
	Instant	1/2 cup	130	71	155	4	4	14	27	130	329	0.3	176	440	130	33	0.04	0.18	0.1	1
	Rice	1/2 cup	132	73	155	4	4	15	27	133	110	0.5	165	140	140	33	0.10	0.18	0.6	1
Vanilla:																			
	Instant	1/2 cup	130	73	150	4	4	15	27	129	273	0.1	164	375	140	33	0.04	0.17	0.1	1
Sugars:																			
	Brown, pressed down	1 cup	220	2	820	0	0	0	212	3	Tr	0.1	7	5	0	0	0.00	0.00	0.0	0
White:																			
	Granulated	1 cup	200	1	770	0	0	0	199	Tr	Tr	Tr	Tr	Tr	0	0	0.00	0.00	0.0	0
	Granulated	1 tbsp.	12	1	45	0	0	0	12	Tr	Tr	Tr	Tr	Tr	0	0	0.00	0.00	0.0	0
	Powdered, sifted, spooned into cup	1 cup	100	1	385	0	0	0	99	6	49	0.8	85	36	Tr	Tr	Tr	0.02	0.1	0
Syrups:																			
Chocolate-flavored syrup or topping:																			
	Thin type	2 tbsp.	38	37	85	1	Tr	0	21	38	60	0.5	82	42	40	13	0.02	0.08	0.1	0
	Fudge type	2 tbsp.	38	25	125	2	5	0	22	274	34	10.1	1,171	38	0	0	0.04	0.08	0.8	0
Table syrup (corn and maple)	2 tbsp.	42	25	122	0	0	0	212	187	56	4.8	757	97	0	0	0.02	0.07	0.2	0
Vegetables and Vegetable Products																			
Alfalfa seeds, sprouted, raw	1 cup	33	91	10	1	Tr	0	1	11	23	0.3	26	2	50	5	0.03	0.04	0.2	3
Asparagus, green:																			
Cooked, drained:																			
From raw:																			
	Cuts and tips	1 cup	180	92	45	5	1	0	8	43	110	1.2	558	7	1,490	149	0.18	0.22	1.9	49
From frozen:																			
	Cuts and tips	1 cup	180	91	50	5	1	0	9	41	99	1.2	392	7	1,470	147	0.12	0.19	1.9	44
Bamboo shoots, canned, drained	1 cup	131	94	25	2	1	0	4	10	33	0.4	105	9	10	1	0.03	0.03	0.2	1

(A)	(B)	(C)	(D)	(E)	(F)	(G)	(H)	(I)	(J)	(K)	(L)	(M)	(N)	(O)	(P)	(Q)	(R)	(S)
Beans:																		
Lima, immature seeds, frozen, cooked, drained:																		
Thick-seeded types (Ford-hooks)	1 cup	74	170	10	1	0	32	37	107	2.3	694	90	320	32	0.13	0.10	1.8	22
Snap:																		
Cooked, drained:																		
From raw (cut and French style)	1 cup	89	45	2	Tr	0	10	58	49	1.6	374	4	57,830	57⁸³	0.09	0.12	0.8	12
From frozen (cut)	1 cup	92	35	2	Tr	0	8	61	32	1.1	151	18	58,710	5871	0.06	0.10	0.6	11
Canned, drained solids (cut)	1 cup	93	25	2	Tr	0	6	35	26	1.2	147	59339	60,470	6047	0.02	0.08	0.3	6
Beets:																		
Canned, drained solids, diced or sliced	1 cup	91	55	2	Tr	0	12	26	29	3.1	252	61466	20	2	0.02	0.07	0.3	7
Beet greens, leaves and stems, cooked, drained	1 cup	89	40	4	Tr	0	8	164	59	2.7	1,309	347	7,340	734	0.17	0.42	0.7	36
Broccoli:																		
Cooked, drained:																		
From raw:																		
Spears, cut into 1/2 in. pieces	1 cup	90	45	5	Tr	0	9	177	74	1.8	253	17	2,180	218	0.13	0.32	1.2	97
From frozen:																		
Chopped	1 cup	91	50	6	Tr	0	10	94	102	1.1	333	44	3,500	350	0.10	0.15	0.8	74
Brussels sprouts, cooked, drained:																		
From frozen	1 cup	87	65	6	1	0	13	37	84	1.1	504	36	910	91	0.16	0.18	0.8	71
Cabbage, common varieties:																		
Raw, coarsely shredded or sliced	1 cup	93	15	1	Tr	0	4	33	16	0.4	172	13	90	9	0.04	0.02	0.2	33
Cooked, drained	1 cup	94	30	1	Tr	0	7	50	38	0.6	308	29	130	13	0.09	0.08	0.3	36
Cabbage, red, raw, coarsely shredded or sliced	1 cup	92	20	1	Tr	0	4	36	29	0.3	144	8	30	3	0.04	0.02	0.2	40
Carrots:																		
Raw, without crowns and tips, scraped:																		
Whole, 7-1/2 by 1-1/8 in., or strips, 2-1/2 to 3 in. long	1 carrot or 18 strips	88	30	1	Tr	0	7	19	32	0.4	233	25	20,250	2,025	0.07	0.04	0.7	7
Cooked, sliced, drained:																		
From frozen	1 cup	90	55	2	Tr	0	12	41	38	0.7	231	86	25,850	2,585	0.04	0.05	0.6	4
Cauliflower:																		
Raw, (flowerets)	1 cup	92	25	2	Tr	0	5	29	46	0.6	355	15	20	2	0.08	0.06	0.6	72
Cooked, drained:																		
From frozen (flowerets)	1 cup	94	35	3	Tr	0	7	31	43	0.7	250	32	40	4	0.07	0.10	0.6	56
Celery, pascal type, raw:																		
Stalk, large outer, 8 by 1-1/2 in. (at root end)	1 stalk	95	5	Tr	Tr	0	1	14	10	0.2	114	35	50	5	0.01	0.01	0.1	3
Collards, cooked, drained:																		
From frozen (chopped)	1 cup	88	60	5	1	0	12	357	46	1.9	427	85	10,170	1,017	0.08	0.20	1.1	45
Corn, sweet:																		
Cooked, drained:																		
From raw, ear 5 by 1-3/4 in.	1 ear	70	85	3	1	0	19	2	79	0.5	192	13	63,170	63¹⁷	0.17	0.06	1.2	5
From frozen:																		
Ear, trimmed to about 3-1/2 in. long	1 ear	73	60	2	Tr	0	14	2	47	0.4	158	3	63,130	63¹³	0.11	0.04	1.0	3
Kernels	1 cup	76	135	5	Tr	0	34	3	78	0.5	229	8	63,410	63⁴¹	0.11	0.12	2.1	4
Canned:																		
Cream style	1 cup	79	185	4	1	0	46	8	131	1.0	343	64730	63,250	63²⁵	0.06	0.14	2.5	12
Whole kernel, vacuum pack	1 cup	77	165	5	1	0	41	11	134	0.9	391	65571	63,510	63⁵¹	0.09	0.15	2.5	17
Cucumber, with peel, slices, 1/8 in. thick (large, 2-1/8 in. diam.; small, 1-3/4 in. diam.)	6 large or 8 small slices	96	5	Tr	Tr	0	1	4	5	0.1	42	1	10	1	0.01	0.01	0.1	1
Eggplant, cooked, steamed	1 cup	92	25	1	Tr	0	6	6	21	0.3	238	3	60	6	0.07	0.02	0.6	1
Kale, cooked, steamed	1 cup	91	40	4	1	0	7	179	36	1.2	417	20	8,260	826	0.06	0.15	0.9	33
Lettuce, raw:																		
Butterhead, as Boston types:																		
Head, 5 in. diam.	1 head	96	20	2	Tr	0	4	52	38	0.5	419	8	1,580	158	0.10	0.10	0.5	13
Crisphead, as iceberg:																		
Head, 6 in. diam.	1 head	96	70	5	1	0	11	102	108	2.7	852	49	1,780	178	0.25	0.16	1.0	21
Wedge, 1/4 of head	1 wedge	96	20	1	Tr	0	3	26	27	0.7	213	12	450	45	0.06	0.04	0.3	5
Pieces, chopped or shredded	1 cup	96	5	1	Tr	0	1	10	11	0.3	87	5	180	18	0.03	0.02	0.1	2
Mushrooms:																		
Raw, sliced or chopped	1 cup	92	20	1	Tr	0	3	4	73	0.9	259	3	0	0	0.07	0.31	2.9	2
Canned, drained solids	1 cup	91	35	3	Tr	0	8	17	103	1.2	201	663	0	0	0.13	0.03	2.5	0

Nutritive Values of Foods – Continued
(Tr indicates nutrient present in trace amount.)

Nutrients in Indicated Quantity

Item No. (A)	Foods, approximate measures, units, and weight (weight of edible portion only) (B)	Grams	Water (C) Percent	Food energy (D) Calories	Protein (E) Grams	Fat (F) Grams	Cholesterol (G) Milligrams	Carbohydrate (H) Grams	Calcium (I) Milligrams	Phosphorus (J) Milligrams	Iron (K) Milligrams	Potassium (L) Milligrams	Sodium (M) Milligrams	Vitamin A value (IU) (N) International units	Vitamin A value (RE) (O) Retinol equivalents	Thiamin (P) Milligrams	Riboflavin (Q) Milligrams	Niacin (R) Milligrams	Ascorbic acid (S) Milligrams
	Onions:																		
	Raw:																		
	Chopped	1 cup	160	91	55	2	Tr	0	12	40	46	0.6	248	3	0	0	0.10	0.02	0.2	13
	Cooked (whole or sliced), drained	1 cup	210	92	60	2	Tr	0	13	57	48	0.4	319	17	0	0	0.09	0.02	0.2	12
	Onion rings, breaded, par-fried, frozen, prepared	2 rings	20	29	80	1	5	0	8	6	16	0.3	26	75	50	5	0.06	0.03	0.7	Tr
	Parsley:																		
	Freeze-dried	1 tbsp.	0.4	2	Tr	Tr	Tr	0	Tr	1	2	0.2	25	2	250	25	Tr	0.01	Tr	1
	Peas, edible pod, cooked, drained	1 cup	160	89	65	5	Tr	0	11	67	88	3.2	384	6	210	21	0.20	0.12	0.09	77
	Peas, green:																		
	Canned, drained solids	1 cup	170	82	115	8	1	0	21	34	114	1.6	294	66372	1,310	131	0.21	0.13	1.2	16
	Frozen, cooked, drained	1 cup	160	80	125	8	Tr	0	23	38	144	2.5	269	139	1,070	107	0.45	0.16	2.4	16
	Peppers:																		
	Hot chili, raw	1 pepper	45	88	20	1	Tr	0	4	8	21	0.5	153	3	674,840	67484	0.04	0.04	0.4	109
	Sweet (about 5 per lb., whole), stem and seeds removed:																		
	Raw	1 pepper	74	93	20	1	Tr	0	4	4	16	0.9	144	2	68390	6839	0.06	0.04	0.4	6995
	Potatoes, cooked:																		
	Baked (about 2 per lb., raw):																		
	With skin	1 potato	202	71	220	5	Tr	0	51	20	115	2.7	844	16	0	0	0.22	0.07	3.3	26
	Flesh only	1 potato	156	75	145	3	Tr	0	34	8	78	0.5	610	8	0	0	0.16	0.03	2.2	20
	Boiled (about 3 per lb., raw):																		
	Peeled after boiling	1 potato	136	77	120	3	Tr	0	27	7	60	0.4	515	5	0	0	0.14	0.03	2.0	18
	French fried, strip, 2 to 3-1/2 in. long, frozen:																		
	Oven heated	10 strips	50	53	110	2	4	0	17	5	43	0.7	229	16	0	0	0.06	0.02	1.2	5
	Fried in vegetable oil	10 strips	50	38	160	2	8	0	20	10	47	0.4	366	108	0	0	0.09	0.01	1.6	5
	Potato products, prepared:																		
	Au gratin:																		
	From dry mix	1 cup	245	79	230	6	10	12	31	203	233	0.8	537	1,076	520	76	0.05	0.20	2.3	8
	Hashed brown, from frozen	1 cup	156	56	340	5	18	0	44	23	112	2.4	680	53	0	0	0.17	0.03	3.8	10
	Mashed:																		
	From home recipe:																		
	Milk and margarine added	1 cup	210	76	225	4	9	4	35	55	97	0.5	607	620	360	42	0.18	0.08	2.3	13
	Potato chips	10 chips	20	3	105	1	7	0	10	5	31	0.2	260	94	0	0	0.03	Tr	0.8	8
	Pumpkin:																		
	Canned	1 cup	245	90	85	2	1	0	20	64	86	3.4	505	12	54,040	5,404	0.06	0.13	0.9	10
	Radishes, raw, stem ends, rootlets cut off	4 radishes	18	95	5	Tr	Tr	0	1	4	3	0.1	42	4	Tr	Tr	Tr	0.01	0.1	4
	Spinach:																		
	Raw, chopped	1 cup	55	92	10	2	Tr	0	2	54	27	1.5	307	43	3,690	369	0.04	0.10	0.4	15
	Cooked, drained:																		
	From frozen (leaf)	1 cup	190	90	55	6	Tr	0	10	277	91	2.9	566	163	14,790	1,479	0.11	0.32	0.8	23
	Canned, drained solids	1 cup	214	92	50	6	1	0	7	272	94	4.9	740	72683	18,780	1,878	0.03	0.30	0.8	31
	Squash, cooked:																		
	Summer (all varieties), sliced, drained	1 cup	180	94	35	2	1	0	8	49	70	0.6	346	2	520	52	0.08	0.07	0.9	10
	Winter (all varieties), baked, cubes	1 cup	205	89	80	2	1	0	18	29	41	0.7	896	2	7,290	729	0.17	0.05	1.4	20
	Sweet potatoes:																		
	Cooked (raw, 5 by 2 in.; about 2-1/2 per lb.):																		
	Baked in skin, peeled	1 potato	114	73	115	2	Tr	0	28	32	63	0.5	397	11	24,880	2,488	0.08	0.14	0.7	28
	Candied, 2-1/2 by 2 in. piece	1 piece	105	67	145	1	3	8	29	27	27	1.2	198	74	4,400	440	0.02	0.04	0.4	7
	Canned:																		
	Vacuum pack, piece 2-3/4 by 1 in.	1 piece	40	76	35	1	Tr	0	8	9	20	0.4	125	21	3,190	319	0.01	0.02	0.3	11
	Tomatoes:																		
	Raw, 2-3/5 in. diam. (3 per 12 oz. pkg.)	1 tomato	123	94	25	1	Tr	0	5	9	28	0.6	255	10	1,390	139	0.07	0.06	0.7	22
	Canned, solids and liquid	1 cup	240	94	50	2	1	0	10	62	46	1.5	530	73391	1,450	145	0.11	0.07	1.8	36

(A)	(B)	(C)	(D)	(E)	(F)	(G)	(H)	(I)	(J)	(K)	(L)	(M)	(N)	(O)	(P)	(Q)	(R)	(S)
Tomato juice, canned	1 cup	244	94	40	2	Tr	0	10	22	46	1.4	537	881[74]	1,360	136	0.11	0.08	1.6	45
Tomato products, canned:																		
Paste	1 cup	262	74	220	10	2	0	49	92	207	7.8	2,442	170[75]	6,470	647	0.41	0.50	8.4	111
Puree	1 cup	250	87	105	4	Tr	0	25	38	100	2.3	1,050	50[76]	3,400	340	0.18	0.14	4.3	88
Sauce	1 cup	245	89	75	3	Tr	0	18	34	78	1.9	909	1,482[77]	2,400	240	0.16	0.14	2.8	32
Turnip greens, cooked, drained:																		
From frozen (chopped)	1 cup	164	90	50	5	1	0	8	249	56	3.2	367	25	13,080	1,308	0.09	0.12	0.8	36
Vegetable juice cocktail, canned	1 cup	242	94	45	2	Tr	0	11	27	41	1.0	467	883	2,830	283	0.10	0.07	1.8	67
Vegetables, mixed:																		
Canned, drained solids	1 cup	163	87	75	4	Tr	0	15	44	68	1.7	474	243	18,990	1,899	0.08	0.08	0.9	8
Frozen, cooked, drained	1 cup	182	83	105	5	Tr	0	24	46	93	1.5	308	64	7,780	778	0.13	0.22	1.5	6
Water chestnuts, canned	1 cup	140	86	70	1	Tr	0	17	6	27	1.2	165	11	10	1	0.02	0.03	0.5	2

1 Value not determined.
2 Mineral content varies depending on water source.
3 Blend of aspartame and saccharin; if only sodium saccharin is used, sodium is 75 mg; if only aspartame is used, sodium is 23 mg.
4 With added ascorbic acid.
5 Vitamin A value is largely from beta-carotene used for coloring.
6 Yields 1 qt. of fluid milk when reconstituted according to package directions.
7 With added vitamin A.
8 Carbohydrate content varies widely because of amount of sugar added and amount and solids content of added flavoring. Consult the label if more precise values for carbohydrate and calories are needed.
9 For salted butter, unsalted butter contains 12 mg sodium per stick, 2 mg per tbsp., or 1 mg per pat.
10 Values for vitamin A are year-round average.
11 For salted margarine.
12 Based on average vitamin A content of fortified margarine. Federal specifications for fortified margarine require a minimum of 15,000 IU per pound.
14 Dipped in egg, milk, and breadcrumbs; fried in vegetable shortening.
15 If bones are discarded, value for calcium will be greatly reduced.
16 Dipped in egg, breadcrumbs, and flour; fried in vegetable shortening.
18 Sodium bisulfite used to preserve color; unsulfited product would contain less sodium.
19 Also applies to pasteurized apple cider.
20 Without added ascorbic acid. For value with added ascorbic acid, refer to label.
21 With added ascorbic acid.
22 For white grapefruit; pink grapefruit have about 310 IU or 31 RE.
23 Sodium benzoate and sodium bisulfite added as preservatives.
24 Egg bagels have 44 mg cholesterol and 22 IU or 7 RE vitamin A per bagel.
25 Made with vegetable shortening.
27 Nutrient added.
28 Cooked without salt. If salt is added according to label recommendations, sodium content is 540 mg.
29 For white corn grits. Cooked yellow corn grits contain 145 IU or 14 RE.
30 Value based on label declaration for added nutrients.
31 For regular and instant cereal. For quick cereal, phosphorus is 102 mg and sodium is 142 mg.
32 Cooked without salt. If salt is added according to label recommendations, sodium content is 390 mg.
33 Cooked without salt. If salt is added according to label recommendations, sodium content is 324 mg.
34 Cooked without salt. If salt is added according to label recommendations, sodium content is 374 mg.
35 Excepting angel food cake, cakes were made from mixes containing vegetable shortening and frostings were made with margarine.
36 Made with vegetable oil.
37 Cake made with vegetable shortening; frosting with margarine.
38 Made with margarine.
39 Crackers made with enriched flour except for rye wafers and whole-wheat wafers.
40 Made with lard.
41 Cashews without salt contain 21 mg sodium per cup or 4 mg per oz.
42 Cashews without salt contain 22 mg sodium per cup or 5 mg per oz.
43 Macadamia nuts without salt contain 9 mg sodium per cup or 2 mg per oz.
44 Mixed nuts without salt contain 3 mg sodium per oz.
45 Peanuts without salt contain 22 mg sodium per cup or 4 mg per oz.
46 Outer layer of fat was removed to within approximately 1/2 inch of the lean. Deposits of fat within the cut were removed.
47 Fried in vegetable shortening.
48 Value varies widely.
49 Contains added sodium ascorbate. If sodium ascorbate is not added, ascorbic acid content is negligible.
51 Crust made with vegetable shortening and enriched flour.
52 Made with corn oil.
53 Fried in vegetable shortening.
54 If sodium ascorbate is added, product contains 11 mg ascorbic acid.
55 Made with enriched flour, margarine, and whole milk.
57 For green varieties; yellow varieties contain 101 IU or 10 RE.
59 For regular pack; special dietary pack contains 3 mg sodium.
60 For green varieties; yellow varieties contain 142 IU or 14 RE.
61 For regular pack; special dietary pack contains 78 mg sodium.
63 For yellow varieties; white varieties contain only a trace of vitamin A.
64 For regular pack; special dietary pack contains 8 mg sodium.
65 For regular pack; special dietary pack contains 6 mg sodium.
66 For regular pack; special dietary pack contains 3 mg sodium.
67 For red peppers; green peppers contain 350 IU or 35 RE.
68 For green peppers; red peppers contain 4,220 IU or 422 RE.
69 For green peppers; red peppers contain 141 mg ascorbic acid.
72 With added salt; if none is added, sodium content is 58 mg.
73 For regular pack; special dietary pack contains 31 mg sodium.
74 With added salt; if none is added, sodium content is 24 mg.
75 With no added salt; if salt is added, sodium content is 2,070 mg.
76 With no added salt; if salt is added, sodium content is 998 mg.
77 With salt added.

Glossary

A

a la carte. Type of menu in which each menu item is individually priced. (24)

additives. Substances that are added to food for a specific purpose, such as a means of preservation. (11)

ají. The Peruvian and Chilean term for chilies. (27)

al dente. Italian term describing the way pasta is cooked so that its texture is slightly resistant to the bite. (29)

American (family) service. Style of meal service in which diners pass serving dishes from hand to hand around the table and serve themselves. (7)

amino acid. A chemical compound that serves as a building block of proteins. (2)

anorexia nervosa. An eating disorder characterized by self-starvation. (4)

anthocyanin. A redish-blue pigment found in vegetables. (19)

antipasto. An Italian appetizer course. (29)

appetizer. Light food or beverage that begins a meal and is designed to stimulate the appetite. (24)

arcing. Sparking that occurs in a microwave oven when metal comes in contact with the oven walls. (12)

arepa. A corn pancake similar to a tortilla that is a traditional Venezuelan bread. (27)

artificial light. Light that most often comes from electrical fixtures. (7)

ascorbic acid. A food additive that prevents color and flavor loss and adds nutritive value; another name for vitamin C. (25)

aseptic packaging. A commercial method of packaging food in which a food and its packaging material are sterilized separately and then the food is packed in the container in a sterile chamber. (25)

avgolemono. A popular Greek sauce made from a mixture of egg yolks and lemon juice. (29)

Aztecs. The original inhabitants of Mexico. (27)

B

bacteria. Single-celled microorganisms that live in soil, water, organic matter, and the bodies of plants and animals. They are important because they can produce chemical reactions in living organisms and cause disease. (25)

baking powder. Mixture of a dry acid (or acid salt), baking soda, and starch (or flour) that will form carbon dioxide when mixed with liquid and/or heated; leavening agent used in food preparation. (22)

baking soda. Term for sodium bicarbonate, an alkali, which, when added to a flour mixture and heated, releases carbon dioxide; leavening agent used in food preparation. (22)

basal metabolism. The amount of heat a person gives off when the body is at physical, digestive, and emotional rest; the amount of energy the human body needs just to stay alive and carry on vital life processes. (2)

batter. Flour-liquid mixture with a consistency ranging from a thin liquid to a stiff liquid depending on the proportion of dry to liquid ingredients. (22)

beading. Golden droplets of moisture that sometimes appear on the surface of a meringue. (16)

beef stroganov. A popular Russian meat dish made with tender strips of beef, mushrooms, and a seasoned sour cream sauce. (31)

beef. Meat obtained from mature cattle over 12 months of age. (13)

berries. Classification of fruits, including strawberries, raspberries, and grapes, that are small and juicy and have thin skins. (18)

beverageware. Glasses of many shapes and sizes used for a variety of purposes. (7)

bisque. A rich, thickened cream soup. (17)

blanch. To scald or parboil in water or steam. (25)

blend. Combination of spices and herbs (20); several varieties of coffee beans mixed together to produce a particular flavor and aroma. (24)

blue plate service. Type of meal service in which the plates are filled in the kitchen, carried to the dining room, and served. (7)

borscht. Russian beet soup. (31)

botulism. Food-borne illness caused by eating foods containing the spore-forming bacteria clostridium botulinum. (25)

bouillon. Clear broth made from strained, clarified stock. (20)

bouquet garni. Small group of herbs tied together in a cheesecloth bag and added to a food during cooking for flavor. Parsley, thyme, and bay leaf usually are used. (20)

braising. Cooking in a small amount of liquid in a tightly covered pan over low heat. (13)

Note: Numbers in parentheses refer to the chapter in which each term is defined.

bran. The outer protective covering of a kernel of grain. (21)

braten. German term for *roast,* which is Germany's national dish. (28)

budget. A plan for managing income and expenses. (10)

buffet service. Style of meal service in which a large table or buffet holds the serving dishes and utensils, dinnerware, flatware, and napkins and from which guests serve themselves. (7)

bulgur. Grain product made from whole wheat that has been cooked, dried, partly debranned, and cracked. (30)

bulimia nervosa. An eating disorder characterized by repeated eating binges followed by purging via vomiting or taking laxatives or diuretics. (4)

C

cacao. A plant that produces beans that are ground into cocoa or made into chocolate. (30)

caffeine. A compound found in products like coffee, tea, chocolate, and cola beverages that acts as a stimulant. (24)

Cajun cuisine. Hearty fare of rural Southern Louisiana that reflects the foods and cooking methods of the Acadians, French, Native Americans, Africans, and Spanish. (26)

calorie. A unit used to measure the energy value of food when it is burned in the body. (2)

candling. Process by which eggs are quality-graded. (16)

caramelize. To heat sugar until it changes into a brown, bitter substance called *caramel.* (17)

carbohydrate. Chemical compounds that are the body's chief source of energy; major nutrient needed by the body. (2)

career ladder. Method of advancement in a particular career by obtaining experience and/or more education. (6)

carotene. Chemical substance found in dark green and yellow fruits and vegetables that can be converted into vitamin A by the body; chemical substance that gives yellow vegetables and fruits their yellow-orange color. (19)

cassava. A starchy root plant eaten as a side dish and used in flour form in cooking and baking in South America. (27)

casserole. A baking dish with high sides (9); combination of foods baked in a single dish. (20)

caste system. A social system that has had a great influence on the development of Indian culture. (31)

catering. Business in which food and beverages are prepared for small and large parties, banquets, weddings, and other large gatherings. (6)

caviar. The processed, salted roe (eggs) of large fish, most often sturgeon. (31)

cereal. Starchy grain that is suitable to use as food. (21)

ceviche. A marinated raw fish dish served throughout South America. (27)

chapatis. A flat bread that is common in India. (31)

chasnidarth. A major cooking technique in Indian cuisine that resembles Chinese sweet and sour. (31)

chelo kebab. Iran's national dish, which consists of thin slices of marinated, charcoal-broiled lamb served with plain rice accompanied by a pat of butter, a raw egg, and a bowl of sumac. (30)

chiffon cake. Cake that is a combination of a shortened and unshortened cake; cake that contains fat and beaten egg whites. (23)

chilies. Term used in Mexico for hot peppers. (27)

chlorophyll. Green pigment found in green plants (including vegetables) that can be adversely affected by heat. (19)

cholesterol. A fatlike substance that occurs naturally in the body and is found in every cell, but occurs only in foods of animal origin. (2)

chopsticks. Chinese eating utensils. (31)

chorizo. A dark sausage with a spicy, smoky flavor. (29)

chowder. Cream soup that contains pieces of seafood, vegetables, poultry, or meat and is made from unthickened milk. (17)

citrus fruits. Classification of fruits, including oranges, lemons, and grapefruit, that have a thick outer rind and thin membranes separating the flesh into segments. (18)

clan. A group of families who are related to each other and live in the same area. (28)

clarify. To make a substance clear or pure. Butter and stock sometimes are clarified. (20)

coagulation. Act of thickening or forming a congealed mass. (Proteins are coagulated by heat and can cause a mixture to thicken.) (13)

coagulum. Thickened or congealed mass. (16)

cockles. A type of mussel common along the coast of Wales. (28)

colander. A perforated bowl used to drain fruits, vegetables, and pasta. (9)

colcannon. An Irish dish made with mashed potatoes mixed with chopped scallions, shredded cooked cabbage, and melted butter. (28)

collagen. Protein constituent of connective tissue in meat. Collagen is tough and elastic but can be softened by cooking. (13)

comida. The main meal of the day in Mexico and Spain. (27)

comparison shopping. Evaluating different brands, sizes, and forms of a product before making a purchase decision. (11)

complete protein. Protein that contains all nine essential amino acids in sufficient amounts to promote growth and normal maintenance of body tissues. (2)

complex carbohydrate. Sugars including polysaccharides. (2)

compromise service. Style of meal service in which part of the food is served from the kitchen and part is served at the table. (7)

congee. A thick porridge made from rice or barley often served for breakfast in China. (31)

conquistador. Spanish conqueror who invaded Mexico during the early 1500s. (27)

conserve. Jam made from a mixture of fruits, usually including citrus fruits and sometimes raisins and nuts. (25)

consommé. Clear, rich-flavored soup made from strained and clarified stock. (20)

convection cooking. Method of cooking in which foods are baked or roasted in a stream of heated air. (8)

convenience food. Food product that has had some amount of service added to it. (10)

conventional method. Mixing method used for shortened cakes in which the fat and sugar are creamed together, the eggs are added, and the sifted dry ingredients are added alternately with the liquid ingredients. (23)

cooking losses. Fat, water, and other volatile substances that are retained in pan drippings or cooking liquid when meats are cooked. (13)

cover. The amount of space needed by each person at a dining table; area on a table that contains the linen, dinnerware, flatware, and glassware needed by one person. (7)

crayfish. A crustacean related to the lobster. (28)

Creole cuisine. Food that combines cooking techniques of the French with ingredients of the Africans, Caribbeans, Spanish, and Native Americans. (26)

crêpe. A thin, delicate pancake that is usually rolled around a filling. (28)

crisp-tender. Term used to describe vegetables that have been cooked to the proper degree of doneness. (19)

croissant. A flaky, buttery yeast roll shaped into a crescent. (28)

crustacean. Shellfish with a segmented body that is covered by a crustlike shell. (15)

crystalline candy. Type of candy with very small and fine sugar crystals, which give it a smooth and creamy texture. (23)

culture. The customs and beliefs of a racial, religious, or social group. (1)

curd. Solid portion of coagulated milk. (17)

curdling. Formation of curds (coagulated proteins) that can happen when milk is overheated or an acid food, such as tomato juice, is added to milk incorrectly. (17)

curry. A type of Indian stew. (31)

custard. Mixture of milk (or cream), eggs, sugar, and a flavoring that is cooked until thickened. (16)

D

Daily Value. A dietary reference that appears on food labels. (11)

decaffeinated. Term describing a product, such as coffee or tea, made by removing most of the caffeine. (24)

dehydration. The process of drying; the removal of water from foods or other items. (12)

del pueblo. Term meaning *food of the people,* which is used to describe Spanish cuisine. (29)

dendé oil. Palm oil that gives Brazilian dishes a bright yellow-orange color. (27)

diet. All the food and drink a person regularly consumes. (4)

Dietary Guidelines for Americans. A set of seven guidelines developed by the U.S. departments of Agriculture and Health and Human Services to encourage healthy people over age two to form certain healthful diet habits. (3)

dietitian. Member of the health care team who has knowledge and training in food and nutrition, the health sciences, and institution management. (6)

dinnerware. Plates, cups, saucers, and bowls. (7)

double boiler. Small pan that fits into a larger pan. Food is put in the smaller pan, and water is placed in the larger pan. The food cooks by steam heat. (9)

dough. Flour-liquid mixture that is stiff enough to be shaped by hand. (22)

dovetail. To overlap tasks to use time more efficiently. (12)

downdraft ventilation. A ventilation system used in some ranges in which a fan is mounted under the cooktop. It draws cooking fumes away from food before they have a chance to rise through the room. (8)

drawn fish. Fish that has the entrails (insides) removed. (15)

dressed fish. Fish that has the entrails (insides), head, fins, and scales removed. (15)

drupes. Fruits, such as cherries, peaches, and plums, that have an outer skin covering a soft flesh that surrounds a single, hard pit. (18)

E

eggplant. A fleshy, oval-shaped vegetable with a deep purple skin frequently used in Mediterranean dishes. (29)

elastin. Protein constituent of connective tissue in meat that is tough and elastic and cannot be softened by cooking. (13)

electro-magnetic energy. Energy that is generated when a magnetic attraction is formed by an electric current; heat that is generated in cookware when a magnetic attraction exists between it and an electric coil in an induction cooktop. (8)

elevating. Lifting a food off the floor of a microwave oven to allow microwaves to penetrate foods from the bottom as well as the top and sides. (12)

empanada. An Argentine appetizer. (27)

emulsion. Mixture that forms when oil and liquid are combined. (16)

endosperm. The largest part of a kernel of grain containing most of the starch and the protein of the kernel but few minerals and little fiber. (21)

English service. Style of meal service in which the plates are served by the host and/or hostess and passed around the table until each guest has been served. (7)

enriched. Having added nutrients to replace those lost through processing. (21)

entrepreneur. A person who sets up and runs his or her own business. (6)

enzymatic browning. Darkening process some fruits undergo when exposed to the air. (18)

enzyme. Complex proteins produced by living cells that cause specific chemical reactions. (25)

escargot. A snail eaten as food. (28)

etiquette. Rules set by society to guide social behavior. (24)

extension agent. Family and consumer science professional employed by the Cooperative Extension Service who works with adults and young people involved in 4-H programs, offers classes, and/or writes educational materials that are published by the Department of Agriculture. (6)

F

fasting. Denying oneself food. (1)

fat fish. Fish having flesh that is fattier than that of lean fish. (15)

fat. Chemical compound belonging to a larger group of compounds known as lipids; major nutrient needed by the body. (2)

fatty acid. Organic acid containing carbon, oxygen, and hydrogen, which combine with glycerol to form fat. (2)

feijoada completa. Brazil's national dish, which is made with meat and black beans. (27)

felafel. A mixture of ground chick-peas, bulgur, and spices that is formed into balls and deep-fried. (30)

fermentation. Process that takes place when yeast cells act upon sugars to produce carbon dioxide and alcohol; enzymatically controlled process in which a compound is broken down, such as a carbohydrate into carbon dioxide and ethyl alcohol. (22)

fiber. Complex carbohydrate found in plants not digested by human beings. It provides bulk in the diet by stimulating the action of the muscles in the digestive tract. (2)

filé. Flavoring and thickening agent made from the leaves of the sassafras tree, which have been dried and ground into a powder. (26)

fines herbes. A mixture of fresh chives, parsley, tarragon, and chervil used to flavor many French soups and stews. (28)

finfish. Fish that have fins and backbones. (15)

finished food. Convenience food that is ready for eating either immediately or after heating or thawing. (10)

fish and chips. Battered, deep-fried fish fillets served in England with a British version of French fries. (28)

fish fillet. The side of a fish cut lengthwise away from the backbone. (15)

fish steak. Cross-sectional slice taken from a dressed fish. (15)

fitness. The body's ability to meet physical demands. (4)

fixed expense. A regularly recurring cost in a set amount, such as rent, mortgage, or installment loan payments. (10)

flat-sour. Type of spoilage caused by bacteria in which canned food becomes sour, but gas is not created. (25)

flatware. Forks, knives, spoons, serving utensils, and specialty utensils used to serve and eat food. (7)

flavones. Pigments that make white vegetables, such as cauliflower, white. (19)

fleishig foods. Meat foods as described by Jewish dietary laws. (30)

flexible expense. A regularly recurring cost that varies in amount, such as food, clothing, or utility bills. (10)

folding. A blending process in which a wire whisk or rubber spatula is used to cut down into a mixture, across the bottom, up the opposite side, and across the top. (16)

food-borne illness. A disease transmitted by food.

Food Guide Pyramid. A visual representation of an eating plan designed to help people choose a well-balanced diet. This plan groups foods of similar nutritive values into categories and gives a recommended number of daily servings for each category. (3)

fortified. Describes a food product to which nutrients have been added in amounts greater than what would naturally occur in the food. (17)

freeze-drying. A method of commercial food preservation in which water vapor is removed from frozen food items. (25)

freezer burn. Dry, tough areas on food that occur where the dry air from the freezer has come in contact with food surfaces, causing dehydration. (25)

French knife. A versatile kitchen knife that is most often used to cut, chop, and dice fruits and vegetables. (9)

frijoles refritos. Refried beans, a popular Mexican dish. (27)

fritters. Fruits, vegetables, or meats that are dipped into a batter and fried in hot fat. (18)

fruit leather. A pliable sheet of dried fruit puree. (25)

G

garnish. Attractive and complementary foodstuffs added to decorate a food or serving dish. (10)

gaucho. Nomadic herders of the Pampas in South America during the eighteenth and nineteenth centuries. (27)

gazpacho. A Spanish soup made with coarsely pureed tomatoes, onions, garlic, and green peppers; olive oil; and vinegar. (29)

gelatin. Gummy substance made from the bones and some connective tissues of animals. It may be flavored or unflavored for use as a food product. (17)

gelatin cream. Milk-based dessert thickened with unflavored gelatin. (17)

gelatinization. Swelling and subsequent thickening of starch granules when heated in water. (21)

generic product. A plain-labeled, no-brand grocery. (11)

germ. The reproductive part of a kernel of grain. It is rich in vitamins, protein, and fat. (21)

ghee. Indian clarified butter. (31)

giblets. The edible internal organs of poultry. (14)

glass-ceramic. Material originally developed for use in the aerospace industry that is now used to make dinnerware. It is strong and durable and can be subjected to a wide range of temperatures without being damaged. (9)

gluten. Protein substance that gives strength and elasticity to batters and doughs. Formed when wheat flour is moistened and thoroughly mixed. (22)

gohan. The Japanese word for meal, which means *rice.* (31)

gourmet. A person who enjoys being able to distinguish the complex combinations of flavors that make up foods. (20)

GRAS (Generally Recognized As Safe) list. List of food additives accepted as safe by the Food and Drug Administration (FDA). (11)

gratuity. Sum of money given to a waiter in a restaurant for service rendered. (24)

grazing. Sampling small portions of a variety of appetizer-type foods. (1)

grind. Material obtained after pulverization to a particular degree of fineness. Coffee is sold in three grinds—fine, medium (or drip), and coarse (or regular). (24)

grounding. Use of a large conducting body, such as the earth, as a common return for an electric circuit. Appliances are grounded to prevent the deliverance of a severe or fatal shock if a wire should be damaged. (7)

growth spurt. A period of rapid growth. (4)

guacamole. A spread made from mashed avocado, tomato, and onion that is popular in Mexico. (27)

gumbo. A Creole specialty that is a thick, souplike mixture containing a variety of seafood, poultry, meats, vegetables, and rice. (26)

H

haggis. A Scottish dish made from a sheep's stomach stuffed with a pudding made from oatmeal and the sheep's organs. (28)

haute cuisine. A style of French cooking characterized by elaborate preparations, fancy garnishes, and rich sauces. (28)

headspace. Space between the food and the closure of a food storage container. (25)

Heimlich maneuver. A procedure used to save choking victims. (5)

herb. A leaf of a plant usually grown in a temperate climate and used to season food. (20)

holloware. Tableware, such as bowls, tureens, and pitchers, used to serve food and liquids. (7)

homogenization. Mechanical process by which milk-fat globules are broken into tiny particles and spread throughout milk or cream. (17)

hors d'oeuvres. Small dishes designed to stimulate the appetite. (28)

hot pack. Process of packing vegetables or fruits that have been preheated in water or steam into canning jars and covering them with cooking liquid or boiling water. (25)

house brand. A brand sold only by a store or chain of stores. (11)

husmankost. The traditional, everyday style of cooking enjoyed in Swedish homes. (28)

hydrate. To cause a substance to absorb water. (17)

hydrogenation. Process by which hydrogen is chemically added to an unsaturated compound, especially to an unsaturated fat or fatty acid. (2)

I

immature fruit. Fruit that is small and has poor color, flavor, and texture. These characteristics will not improve with time. (18)

impulse buying. Making an unplanned purchase without much thought. (11)

imu. A pit lined with hot rocks used to roast a whole, young pig at a Hawaiian luau. (26)

Inca. A group of Native South Americans who built a large empire in the Andes mountains prior to the Spanish conquest. (27)

income. Money received. (10)

incomplete protein. Protein that is lacking in one or more essential amino acids. Incomplete proteins will neither support growth nor normal maintenance. (2)

induction cooking. Method of cooking in which foods are cooked with electro-magnetic energy. (8)

injera. Ethiopia's main dish, which is a large, sour-doughlike pancake made from teff. (30)

interview. A meeting between an employer and a job applicant held to discuss the applicant's qualifications for a job opening. (6)

irradiation. A commercial food preservation method that exposes food to low level doses of gamma rays, electron beams, or X rays. (25)

J

jam. Jellied food product made from crushed fruit. It is cooked to a fairly even consistency and is less firm than jelly. (25)

jambalaya. A Creole specialty that is a mixture of rice; seasonings; and shellfish, poultry, and/or sausage. (26)

jelly. Jellied food product made from fruit juice, acid, sugar, and pectin. (25)

K

kaiseka. A delicate meal served after the Japanese tea ceremony. (31)

kartoffelpuffer. The famous potato pancakes enjoyed throughout Germany. (28)

kasha. A Russian staple food made of buckwheat or other grains that are fried and then simmered until tender. (31)

kashrut. Jewish dietary laws. (30)

kernel. A whole seed of a cereal. (21)

kibbutzim. Cooperative farm villages in Israel. (30)

knead. To work a dough by pressing it with the heels of the hand, folding it, turning it, and repeating each motion until the dough is smooth and elastic. (22)

korma. A major Indian cooking technique in which foods are braised, usually in yogurt. (31)

kosher. Foods prepared according to Jewish dietary laws. (30)

kulich. A tall, cylindrical Russian yeast cake filled with fruits and nuts. (31)

Kwanzaa. A family-centered observance of cultural unity among African people throught the world celebrated during the week between Christmas and New Year's Day. (30)

L

lamb. The meat of sheep less than one year old. (13)

Latin America. The land mass that stretches southward from the Rio Grande to the tip of South America. (27)

lead glass. Material made by combining lead with silica (in the form of sand) and other materials used in the production of glassware; finest and most expensive type of glass. (7)

leader. A person who commands authority and takes a principal role in a group. (6)

lean fish. Fish that have very little fat in their flesh. (15)

lime glass. Material used in the production of glassware, which is made by combining the mineral lime with silica (in the form of sand) and soda or potash; least costly type of glass. (7)

lingonberry. A tart, red berry used in Swedish desserts. (28)

luau. Elaborate outdoor feast popular in the Hawaiian Islands in which a whole pig is dressed, stuffed, and cooked in a pit lined with hot rocks. (26)

lutefisk. Dried cod that have been soaked in a lye solution before cooking, which is a traditional Norwegian fish dish. (28)

M

malnutrition. Poor nutrition, usually over an extended period of time, which can be caused by an inadequate diet or the body's inability to use the nutrients taken in. (2)

manioc. A starchy root plant eaten as a side dish and used in flour form in cooking and baking in South America. (27)

manners. Social behaviors. (24)

marbling. Flecks of fat found throughout the lean muscles of meat. (13)

marinate. To soak meat in a solution containing an acid, such as vinegar or tomato juice, that helps tenderize the connective tissue. (13)

marmalade. Tender jelly containing small pieces of fruit, often citrus fruits. (25)

masala. A mixture of spices used to make Indian curry. (31)

matzo meal. Meal made from unleavened bread called *matzos* used in Jewish cooking. (30)

mazza. Arabian appetizers. (30)

meal manager. Someone who uses resources to reach goals related to preparing and serving food. (10)

meal pattern. Basic meal format based on the kinds of foods usually served at a meal; used in meal planning. (10)

meat. The edible portion of mammals. (13)

medical diet. An eating plan prescribed by a physician to address special needs of a person with a specific health problem. (4)

melons. Classification of fruits, including cantaloupe, honeydew, and watermelon, that are in the gourd family and are large and juicy and have thick skins and many seeds. (18)

meringue. Fluffy white mixture of beaten egg whites and sugar, which may be soft or hard. (16)

metabolism. The chemical processes that take place in the cells after nutrients have been absorbed by the body. (2)

mezedhes. Greek appetizers. (29)

microorganism. A microscopic living substance, such as bacteria or yeast. (25)

microwave. High frequency energy wave used in microwave ovens to cook foods quickly. (8)

milchig foods. Dairy foods as described by Jewish dietary laws. (30)

milk solids. Nonfat portion of milk, which contains most of the vitamins, minerals, proteins, and sugar found in milk. (17)

milkfat. Fat portion of milk. (17)

mineral. Inorganic substance known to be needed by the body for good health. (2)

minestrone. A popular Italian vegetable soup thick with pasta. (29)

mold. Growth produced on damp or decaying organic matter or on living organisms. (25)

mole. A complex sauce used in Mexican cuisine. (27)

mollusk. Shellfish that has a soft body fully or partially covered by a hard shell. (15)

monounsaturated fatty acid. Fatty acid that is missing one hydrogen atom. (2)

N

national brand. A brand that is advertised and sold throughout the country. (11)

natural light. Light that comes from the sun. (7)

new potatoes. Potatoes that are harvested and sent directly to market. (19)

nihon-cha. Japanese term for green teas. (31)

noncrystalline candy. Type of candy in which the sugar syrup is not allowed to form crystals; candy may be chewy or brittle. (23)

nonstick finish. Coating with nonstick properties used on some cookware and bakeware. (9)

nouvelle cuisine. A style of French cooking that emphasizes lightness and natural taste in foods. (28)

nutrient. A chemical substance in food that helps maintain the body. (2)

nutrition. The study of how the body uses the foods taken in; the sum of the processes by which a human being or animal takes in and utilizes food substances. (2)

nutritionist. Registered dietitian who works directly in nutrition education. (6)

O

obesity. A condition whereby a person exceeds the healthy weight for his or her height and body composition by 20 percent or more. (4)

okra. Pod-shaped vegetable brought to the United States from Africa and popular in the Deep South. (26)

omelet. A beaten egg mixture that is cooked without stirring and served folded in half. (16)

open dating. A system of putting dates on perishable and semiperishable foods to help consumers obtain products that are fresh and wholesome. (11)

organic foods. Foods that have been grown in soil enriched with organic (rather than chemical) fertilizers and without the use of pesticides. (11)

organically processed foods. Organically grown foods that have not been treated with preservatives, hormones, antibiotics, or synthetic additives. (11)

oven spring. Sudden dramatic rise of a yeast dough that takes place during the first few minutes of baking. (22)

overweight. A condition whereby a person exceeds the healthy weight for his or her height and body composition by 10 percent. (4)

P

paella. A variable Spanish rice dish often containing chicken, shrimp, mussels, whitefish, peas, and rice and flavored with saffron, salt, pepper, and pimiento. (29)

pareve foods. Foods that contain neither meat nor milk as described by Jewish dietary laws. (30)

paskha. A rich cheese cake that is a popular Russian dessert. (31)

pasta. A nutritious, shaped dough that may or may not be dried. Macaroni, noodles, and spaghetti are pastas. (21)

pasteurization. Process by which milk and milk products are heated to destroy harmful bacteria. (17)

pastry. Tender, flaky baked product containing flour, fat, water, and salt, which is used as the base for pies, tarts, and other desserts. (23)

pectin. Carbohydrate found naturally in fruits that makes fruit juices jell. (25)

Pennsylvania Dutch. Group of German immigrants who settled in the southeast section of Pennsylvania. (26)

peristalsis. Wavelike movement produced by the longitudinal and circular fibers of the digestive tract. (2)

permanent emulsion. Type of emulsion that will not separate upon standing; type of emulsion that is formed when an emulsifying agent is added to an oil and liquid mixture. (20)

petcock. Vent in the lid of a steam-pressure canner that allows air to be exhausted and steam to be released as needed. (25)

phyllo. A paper-thin pastry made with flour and water used to make many Greek desserts. (29)

pigtail. Small wire that is part of a two-prong adapter. The pigtail is attached to the screw on the electrical outlet plate, thereby grounding the appliance. (7)

pilotless ignition. Energy-saving feature used on gas ranges that eliminates the need for a pilot light. (8)

pita bread. A flat, round, hollow bread common to the cuisines of Africa and the Middle East. (30)

pitting. Tiny indentations that mark the surface of some aluminum cookware due to a reaction with some foods and minerals. (9)

plantain. A green, starchy fruit that has a bland flavor and looks much like a large banana. (27)

polyunsaturated fatty acid. Fatty acid that contains the fewest number of hydrogen atoms. (2)

pomes. Classification of fruits, including apples and pears, that have a central, seed-containing core surrounded by a thick layer of flesh. (18)

porcelain enamel. Glasslike surface fused to a base metal at very high temperatures. (9)

pork. The meat of swine. (13)

pot. A two-handled cooking utensil. (9)

potluck. A shared meal to which each person or family brings food for the whole group to eat. (26)

poultry. Any domesticated bird. (14)

preserves. Jellied fruit product consisting of whole fruits or large pieces of fruit in a thick syrup. (25)

pressure saucepan. Saucepan that cooks foods more quickly than a conventional pan because as pressure is increased, temperature also increases. (9)

process cheese. One of several types of products, including pasteurized process cheese, pasteurized process cheese food, pasteurized process cheese spread, coldpack cheese, and coldpack cheese food, made from various cheeses. (17)

processed food. A food that has undergone some preparation procedure, such as canning, freezing, drying, cooking, or fortification. (3)

processing time. The amount of time canned goods remain under heat (or under heat and pressure) in a canner. (25)

protein. A chemical compound composed of amino acids that is found in every body cell. A major nutrient needed by the human body. (2)

provincial cuisine. The style of French cooking practiced by most French families using locally grown foods and simple cooking methods. (28)

pudding basin. A deep, thick-rimmed bowl used to steam British puddings. (28)

puree. To push foods through a fine sieve or a food mill to form a thick and smooth liquid. (17)

Q

quiche. A custard tart served in many variations as an appetizer and a main dish. (28)

quick mix method. Mixing method used for shortened cakes in which the dry ingredients are placed in the mixing bowl, then the fat and part of the liquid are added followed by the remaining liquid and unbeaten eggs. (23)

quick-freezing. Process of subjecting foods to extremely low temperatures for a short time and then maintaining them at a normal freezing temperature. (25)

R

raw pack. Process of packing cold, raw vegetables in canning jars and covering them with boiling water or syrup. (25)

recipe. Instructions for preparing a particular food. (12)

Recommended Dietary Allowances (RDA). Dietary standard that is a summary of nutrient requirements stated quantitatively. (3)

reference. A person that an employer can call to ask about a job applicant's capabilities as a worker. (6)

refined. Term used to refer to cereal products made from grain that has had the bran and germ removed during processing and contains only the endosperm. (21)

refrigerant. A cooling agent. (8)

reservation. An arrangement made with a restaurant to hold a table for a guest on a given date at a given time. (24)

retail cut. A smaller cut of meat taken from a larger wholesale cut and sold to consumers in retail stores. (13)

retort packaging. A commerical method of packaging food in which food is sealed in a foil pouch and then sterilized in a steam-pressure vessel known as a *retort*. (25)

ripened cheese. Cheese in which controlled amounts of bacteria, mold, yeast, or enzymes were added and that was stored for a certain period of time at controlled temperatures. (17)

risotto. An Italian rice dish made with butter, chopped onion, stock or wine, and Parmesan cheese. Meats or seafood and vegetables may also be added. (29)

rotating. Turning food in a microwave oven one-quarter to one-half turn at one or more intervals in the cooking period to allow microwaves to hit it in a more even pattern. (12)

roux. Cooked fat and flour mixture used as the thickening agent in many sauces and gravies. (17)

R.S.V.P. Letters often included on an invitation that stand for the French, "Repondez s'il vous plait," which means *please respond*. (24)

Russian (continental) service. Style of meal service that requires the help of servants. No food is placed on the table; servants do all of the serving and clearing. (7)

S

salad. Combination of raw and/or cooked ingredients, usually served cold with a dressing. (20)

sangria. A Spanish punch made with red wine, fruit juice, and sparkling water. (29)

saturated fatty acid. Fatty acid that has as many hydrogen atoms as it can hold. (2)

saucepan. A one-handled cooking utensil. (9)

sauerkraut. Fermented or pickled cabbage. (28)

sauna. A steam bath in which water is poured on hot stones to create steam. (28)

sauté. To cook food in a small amount of hot fat. (18)

schi. Cabbage soup, which is one of the most popular Russian soups. (31)

scorching. Burning that results in a color change. (17)

scum. Solid layer made up of milk solids and some fat that often forms on the surface of milk during heating. (17)

semiprepared food. Convenience food that still needs to have some service performed. (10)

serrated blade. A sawtooth edge on a knife. (9)

service contract. An insurance policy for a major appliance that can be purchased from an appliance dealer to cover the cost of repairs for a period of time after the warranty on the appliance has expired. (8)

shellfish. Fish that have shells instead of backbones. (15)

shielding. Using small pieces of aluminum foil to cover areas of a food, such as the corners of a square pan or the wing tips on a chicken, to prevent them from overcooking in a microwave oven. (12)

shohet. A licensed slaughterer who butchers animals and fowl following methods described in Jewish dietary laws. (30)

shortened cake. Cake made with fat. Most shortened cakes are leavened by baking powder or by baking soda and sour milk. (23)

siesta. A rest period that usually follows the midday meal in Mexico. (27)

silver plate. A type of flatware that is made by coating a base metal with silver. (7)

simple carbohydrate. Sugars including monosaccharides and disaccharides. (2)

smörgåsbord. A Swedish buffet that includes a wide variety of hot and cold dishes. (28)

smørrebrød. Danish open-faced sandwiches usually made with thin, sour rye bread spread thickly with butter. (28)

soufflé. Fluffy baked preparation made with a starch-thickened sauce into which stiffly beaten egg whites are folded. (16)

soul food. A cuisine developed in the South that combines food customs of African slaves with food customs of Native Americans and European sharecroppers. (26)

sourdough. A dough containing active yeast plants that is used as a leavening agent. (26)

soybean. A legume with seeds that are rich in protein and oil, which is used in many different forms in Japanese and Chinese cooking. (31)

spätzle. Small dumplings made from wheat flour, which are a popular German side dish. (28)

spice. A dried root, stem, or seed of a plant grown mainly in the tropics and used to season food. (20)

sponge. Mixture of liquid, sugar, yeast, and flour used in the preparation of yeast breads. (22)

springform pan. A round pan with a removable bottom that is held together by means of a spring or latch on the side of the pan. (9)

stainless steel. A solid alloy composed of steel, nickel, and chromium used in the manufacture of flatware. (7)

standing time. The time during which foods finish cooking by internal heat after being removed from a microwave oven. (12)

starch. Complex carbohydrates stored in plants. (21)

stemware. Glassware with three distinct parts: a bowl, a stem, and a base. (7)

sterling silver. Material that contains 92.5 percent silver used in the manufacture of flatware. (7)

stir-frying. A cooking method in which foods are cooked over high heat in a small amount of fat. (31)

stock soup. Soup made with a rich-flavored liquid in which meat, poultry, or fish; vegetables; and seasonings have been cooked. (20)

stockinette. A cloth cover for a rolling pin used to keep dough from sticking to the rolling pin. (9)

strain. To separate solid from liquid materials. (20)

strudel. A German dessert made with paper-thin layers of pastry filled with fruit. (28)

succulents. Vegetables, such as cucumbers and peppers, that have a high moisture content. (19)

sugar syrup. Sugar and water solution. (23)

sukiyaki. A popular Japanese dish made of thinly sliced meat, bean curd, and vegetables cooked in a sauce. (31)

sulfuring. Antidarkening treatment used on some fruits before they are dried. (25)

syneresis. Leakage of liquid from a gel. (21)

T

table d'hôte. Type of menu in which one price is given for an entire meal. (24)

table linens. Table coverings and napkins. (7)

tandoori. A simple Indian cooking technique, which requires a clay oven called a *tandoor.* (31)

tang. Prong that attaches a knife blade to the handle. (9)

tapas. Spanish appetizers. (29)

taverna. A Greek café that serves as a public meeting place in small communities. (29)

tea. Leaves of a tropical evergreen or bush used to make a beverage, which is also called *tea* (24); the evening meal in rural areas or an afternoon snack in cities throughout the British Isles. (28)

teff. A milletlike grain grown only in Africa and the Middle East. (30)

temporary emulsion. Type of emulsion that forms when two mixtures are agitated but breaks when the agitation stops. (20)

time-work schedule. Organized schedule that lists what tasks need to be performed, an estimate of the time it will take to perform each task, and the order in which the tasks should be performed. (12)

tip. Sum of money given to a waiter in a restaurant for service rendered. (24)

tofu. A mild-flavored, custardlike cake made from soybeans. (31)

tortilla. A flat, unleavened bread made from cornmeal and water used to make many Mexican dishes. (27)

toxin. Substances produced by living organisms that can be poisonous. (5)

trace element (micromineral). A mineral, such as iron, iodine, manganese, copper, zinc, or fluorine, that is found in a very small quantity in the body. (2)

tropical fruits. Classification of fruits, including avocados, bananas, and pineapples, that are grown in warm climates and are considered to be somewhat exotic. (18)

truffles. A rare type of fungi that grow underground near oak trees and are used in many French recipes. (28)

trussing. Preparing fowl for cooking by binding the wings and legs. (14)

tsukemono. Soaked foods, or lightly pickled pieces of daikon, cucumber, melon, eggplant, and other vegetables, which are a standard part of the main course at Japanese meals. (31)

tumbler. A piece of glassware without a stem. (7)

tunnel. One of many narrow, open areas that form inside overmixed muffins. (22)

U

UHT processed milk. Milk that is heated to a temperature higher than that of regular pasteurization and, when packaged in pre-sterilized containers, can be stored refrigerated for up to three months. (17)

underripe fruit. Fruit that has reached full size but has yet to ripen. (18)

underweight. A condition whereby a person weighs 10 percent less than the healthy weight for his or her height and body composition. (4)

unit pricing. System of listing a cost per standard unit, weight, or measure of a product in addition to the selling price. (11)

universal product code (UPC). Series of lines, bars, and numbers that appears on packages of food and nonfood items. This code is used by a computer scanner to identify a product, its manufacturer, and its size and form. (11)

unripened cheese. Cheese that is prepared for marketing as soon as the whey has been removed without being allowed to ripen or age. (17)

unsaturated fatty acids. Fatty acids that have fewer hydrogen atoms than they can hold.

unshortened cake. Cake made without fat. (23)

V

variety meats. Edible parts of animals other than muscle, such as liver, heart, and tongue. (13)

veal. The meat of cattle less than three months of age. (13)

vegetarian diet. A diet that is built partially or completely on fruits, vegetables, and other plant foods. (4)

venting. Leaving an opening in the covering of food to be cooked in a microwave oven through which steam can escape. (12)

vindaloo. A major Indian cooking technique in which foods have a hot, slightly sour flavor created by combining vinegar with spices. (31)

vitamin. Complex organic substance needed by the human body in very small amounts for normal growth, maintenance, and reproduction. (2)

W

warranty. A seller's promise that a product will perform as specified or will be free from defects. (8)

wat. A spicy sauce or stew that is part of Ethiopian cuisine. (30)

watt. A unit of power; the cooking power of microwave ovens is measured and expressed in watts. (12)

weeping. Layer of moisture that sometimes forms between a meringue and a filling. (16)

weight management. Using resources like food choices and exercise to reach and/or maintain a healthy weight. (4)

whey. Liquid part of coagulated milk. (17)

whisk. A mixing tool made of loops of wire attached to a handle used to incorporate air into foods and to keep sauces from lumping. (9)

white sauce. Thickened milk product made by combining milk, fat, flour, and seasonings. It is used as a base for other sauces and as a component in many recipes. (17)

whole grain. Term used to refer to cereal products made from grain that contains all three parts of the kernel. (21)

wholesale cut. Large cut of meat shipped to a retail grocery store or meat market. (13)

wok. A versatile Chinese cooking utensil that looks like a metal bowl that is wider at the top than at the bottom and has sloping sides. (31)

work center. Section in a kitchen that has been designed around a specific activity or activities. (7)

work simplification. Act of performing tasks in the simplest way possible in order to conserve both time and energy. (10)

work triangle. Imaginary triangle formed by the focal points of the three major work centers found in a kitchen. (7)

Y

yam. Dark orange tuber with moist flesh often confused with a sweet potato. (26)

yeast. Microscopic, single-celled plant that produces the leavening gas carbon dioxide through the process of fermentation (22); type of fungus that can cause fermentation in preserved foods resulting in spoilage. (25)

yield. The average amount or number of servings a given recipe will produce. (12)

Z

zakuska. Russian appetizers. (31)

Index

Recipe Index

Appetizers

Antipasto, 541
Ch'un-chuan, 604, 605
Empanadas, 477
Empanadillas, 520
Nachos, 448
Pirozhki, 584
Samosas, 592, 593
Sill med kremsaus, 518
Welsh rabbit, 491

Beverages

Sangria falsa, 531, 532
Sweet lelani, 458

Cakes

Honey cake, 569
Pflaumenkuchen, 510
Shortened cake, 374

Candies

Micro brittle, 385

Cookies

Brasileiras, 479
Cenci, 543
Chocolate chip nuggets, 217
Fattigmand, 520
Hsing-jen-ping, 605
Kourambiedes, 551
Kringla, 520
Makroud el louse, 574, 575
Polverones, 470

Desserts

Baked custard, 282
Baklava, 562
Blackberry buckle, 453
Chocolate Spanish cream, 299
English trifle, 492

Flan, 532
Ground nut ice cream, 574
Halva, 594
Lowfat vanilla ice cream, 300
Mousse au chocolat, 502
Paskha, 586
Sopapillas, 449

Dressings and sauces

Mayonnaise, 330

Fish

Gefilte fish, 567
Salmon steaks with dill sauce, 452

Fruits

Chatni, 593, 594
Fruit whip, 282
Plàtanos tumulto, 479

Main dishes

Boiled dinner, 432
Carbonada criolla, 477, 478
Cheese enchiladas, 302
Couscous, 574
Enchiladas verdes, 468
Hero sandwich, 229
Moussaka, 549, 550
Paella, 531
Tacos, 469

Meats

Badami gosht korma, 593
Barbecued beef short ribs, 448
Brik bil lahm, 573
Broiled steak, 444
Corned beef and cabbage, 491
Frikadeller, 519
Sauerbraten, 508

Shish kebabs, 561
Sukiyaki, 613, 614
Tahitian pork, 456, 457
T'ien-suan-ku-lao-jou, 604

Pies

Apple, 445
Macadamia nut chiffon, 458
Pastry, 383
Pecan, 442
Pumpkin, 433
Shoofly, 437

Poultry

Kotlety po-kyivskomu, 585
Pollo alla cacciatore, 541, 542
Poulet au citron, 500
Roasted chicken, 567
Southern fried chicken, 441
Stewed chicken and dumplings, 436

Quick breads

Aloha loaf, 457
Biscuits, 358
Blueberry muffins, 433
Brown bread, 433
Buttermilk biscuits, 442
Chapatis, 594
Mexican cornbread, 449
Scones, 492
Tortillas, 468, 469
Tortillas de maiz, 478

Rice and pasta dishes

Fettuccine verde al burro, 542
Fried rice, 457
Gohan, 614
Noodle kugel, 568
Pai-fan, 605
Pilav, 561